SAP PRESS e-books

Print or e-book, Kindle or iPad, workplace or airplane: Choose where and how to read your SAP PRESS books! You can now get all our titles as e-books, too:

- By download and online access
- For all popular devices
- And, of course, DRM-free

Convinced? Then go to www.sap-press.com and get your e-book today.

Implementing SAP® Manufacturing Execution

SAP PRESS

SAP PRESS is a joint initiative of SAP and Rheinwerk Publishing. The know-how offered by SAP specialists combined with the expertise of Rheinwerk Publishing offers the reader expert books in the field. SAP PRESS features first-hand information and expert advice, and provides useful skills for professional decision-making.

SAP PRESS offers a variety of books on technical and business-related topics for the SAP user. For further information, please visit our website: *www.sap-press.com*.

Abesh Bhattacharjee, Dipankar Saha
Implementing and Configuring SAP MII
2009, 468 pages, hardcover and e-book
www.sap-press.com/1990

Jochen Balla, Frank Layer
Production Planning with SAP APO (3rd Edition)
2016, 431 pages, hardcover and e-book
www.sap-press.com/3927

Jawad Akhtar
Production Planning and Control with SAP ERP
2013, 1033 pages, hardcover and e-book
www.sap-press.com/3358

Chandan Jash, Dipankar Saha

Implementing SAP® Manufacturing Execution

Editor Meagan White
Acquisitions Editor Emily Nicholls
Copyeditor Melinda Rankin
Cover Design Graham Geary
Photo Credit Shutterstock.com/174807428/© 06photo
Layout Design Vera Brauner
Production Graham Geary
Typesetting III-satz, Husby (Germany)
Printed and bound in the United States of America, on paper from sustainable sources

ISBN 978-1-4932-1239-2

© 2016 by Rheinwerk Publishing, Inc., Boston (MA)
1st edition 2016

Library of Congress Cataloging-in-Publication Data
Names: Jash, Chandan. | Saha, Dipankar.
Title: Implementing SAP manufacturing execution / Chandan Jash, Dipankar Saha.
Description: 1st edition. | Bonn ; Boston : Rheinwerk Publishing, 2015. | Includes index.
Identifiers: LCCN 2015034360| ISBN 9781493212392 (print : alk. paper) | ISBN 1493212397 (print : alk. paper) | ISBN 9781493212408 (ebook) | ISBN 9781493212415 (print and ebook : alk. paper)
Subjects: LCSH: Production management--Data processing. | SAP ERP.
Classification: LCC TS155.6 .J375 2015 | DDC 658.50285--dc23 LC record available at http://lccn.loc.gov/2015034360

All rights reserved. Neither this publication nor any part of it may be copied or reproduced in any form or by any means or translated into another language, without the prior consent of Rheinwerk Publishing, 2 Heritage Drive, Suite 305, Quincy, MA 02171.

Rheinwerk Publishing makes no warranties or representations with respect to the content hereof and specifically disclaims any implied warranties of merchantability or fitness for any particular purpose. Rheinwerk Publishing assumes no responsibility for any errors that may appear in this publication.

"Rheinwerk Publishing" and the Rheinwerk Publishing logo are registered trademarks of Rheinwerk Verlag GmbH, Bonn, Germany. SAP PRESS is an imprint of Rheinwerk Verlag GmbH and Rheinwerk Publishing, Inc.

All of the screenshots and graphics reproduced in this book are subject to copyright © SAP SE, Dietmar-Hopp-Allee 16, 69190 Walldorf, Germany.

SAP, the SAP logo, ABAP, BAPI, Duet, mySAP.com, mySAP, SAP ArchiveLink, SAP EarlyWatch, SAP NetWeaver, SAP Business ByDesign, SAP BusinessObjects, SAP BusinessObjects Rapid Mart, SAP BusinessObjects Desktop Intelligence, SAP BusinessObjects Explorer, SAP Rapid Marts, SAP BusinessObjects Watchlist Security, SAP BusinessObjects Web Intelligence, SAP Crystal Reports, SAP GoingLive, SAP HANA, SAP MaxAttention, SAP MaxDB, SAP PartnerEdge, SAP R/2, SAP R/3, SAP R/3 Enterprise, SAP Strategic Enterprise Management (SAP SEM), SAP StreamWork, SAP Sybase Adaptive Server Enterprise (SAP Sybase ASE), SAP Sybase IQ, SAP xApps, SAPPHIRE NOW, and Xcelsius are registered or unregistered trademarks of SAP SE, Walldorf, Germany.

All other products mentioned in this book are registered or unregistered trademarks of their respective companies.

Contents at a Glance

PART I Administration and Configuration
1 Configuring and Monitoring SAPMEINT 31
2 Configuring SAP ME 67
3 Master Data Management 99

PART II Features and Functionality
4   Routing Design 137
5   Shop Order Management 171
6   Shop Floor Control Management 187
7   Data Collection 211
8   Nonconformance and Quality Control 233
9   Product Genealogy and Tracking 275
10 Production Operator Dashboards 307
11 Message Board Service 347
12 Labor Tracking 365
13 Packing Service 383

PART III Advanced Enhancement
14 Custom Enhancements Using Public API Web Services ... 397
15 Shop Floor Systems Integration Using SAP MII and
    Plant Connectivity 411
16 Advanced Reporting in SAP ME 423
17 Enhancing SAP ME with SDKs 431

Dear Reader,

A manufacturing execution system is part of a healthy manufacturing ecosystem, bringing together shop floor data with organization-wide ERP systems. With it, you have better access to real-time data to track compliance, manage product quality, and flag defective products before they even leave the shop floor—ensuring a healthy habitat for your product in its earliest stages.

Between these pages you will find all the information you need to connect SAP ME to your ERP system, configure it, use it, and enhance it. Vetted by the SAP ME team, and the result of months of work by expert authors Chandan Jash and Dipankar Saha, this guide is your go-to resource. Looking for information on tracking product genealogy? Try Chapter 9. Need to set shift length for laborers? Chapter 12 has you covered! Just want to get a handle on the configuration activities? Chapter 2 and Chapter 3 will set you straight. Want to master SAP ME from end-to-end? Well, for that you need to read the whole book.

As always, your comments and suggestions are the most useful tools to help us make our books the best they can be. Let us know what you thought about *Implementing SAP Manufacturing Execution*! Please feel free to contact me and share any praise or criticism you may have.

Thank you for purchasing a book from SAP PRESS!

Meagan White
Editor, SAP PRESS

Rheinwerk Publishing
Boston, MA

meaganw@rheinwerk-publishing.com
www.sap-press.com

Contents

Foreword 15
Preface 17
Introduction to SAP ME 21

PART I Administration and Configuration

1 Configuring and Monitoring SAPMEINT 31

1.1 Configuring SAP MII for SAP ME 31
    1.1.1 SAP ERP and ME Integration 32
    1.1.2 SAPMEINT CTC Configuration Wizard 34
    1.1.3 SAPMEINT Configuration 40
    1.1.4 Available Message Types in SAPMEINT 48
    1.1.5 Message Type Lifecycle Configuration 50
    1.1.6 SAPMEINT Enhancement Use Cases and Best Practices 55
1.2 Monitoring 61
    1.2.1 Queue Monitor 61
    1.2.2 Transaction Manager 63
    1.2.3 Log Viewer 64
    1.2.4 Configuration Diagnostics Tool 64
1.3 Summary 65

2 Configuring SAP ME 67

2.1 Site and User Configurations 67
    2.1.1 SAP ME Site Creation 68
    2.1.2 User Administration and SAP ME Role Assignment 72
    2.1.3 User Group Maintenance 74
    2.1.4 User Maintenance 75
    2.1.5 Certification Type Maintenance 77
    2.1.6 Certification Maintenance 77
    2.1.7 User Certificate Assignment Maintenance 78
    2.1.8 User Certifications Report 79
2.2 System Configuration Management 79
    2.2.1 Activity Maintenance 80
    2.2.2 Activity Group Maintenance 82
    2.2.3 Activity Code Maintenance 83
    2.2.4 Background Processing 84

		2.2.5	Collaboration Directive Maintenance	85
		2.2.6	Collaboration Link Maintenance	86
		2.2.7	System Rule Maintenance	87
		2.2.8	System Setup Maintenance and Audit Log Configuration	89
		2.2.9	Document Maintenance	90
		2.2.10	Printer Maintenance	92
		2.2.11	ODS Rule Maintenance	93
	2.3	Process Configuration Management		93
		2.3.1	SAP ERP Field Maintenance	94
		2.3.2	Next Number Maintenance	95
		2.3.3	Reason Code Maintenance	96
		2.3.4	Time Granularity Maintenance	97
		2.3.5	Time Granularity Assignment Maintenance	97
	2.4	Summary		98

3 Master Data Management ... 99

	3.1	Managing Master Data		99
		3.1.1	Material	100
		3.1.2	Bill of Materials	109
		3.1.3	Resource	113
		3.1.4	Work Center	118
		3.1.5	Tool Group Maintenance	120
		3.1.6	Tool Number Maintenance	122
		3.1.7	Work Instruction Maintenance	123
	3.2	Data Enhancement in SAP ME		126
		3.2.1	Custom Data Maintenance	127
		3.2.2	Data Field Definition Maintenance	127
		3.2.3	Data Field Assignment Maintenance	128
		3.2.4	Standard Value Key Maintenance	130
		3.2.5	Scheduling Standard Maintenance	130
	3.3	Summary		133

PART II Features and Functionality

4 Routing Design ... 137

	4.1	Operation Maintenance		137
		4.1.1	Operation Type	139
		4.1.2	Assigning Resource Type and Default Resource in Operation	140
		4.1.3	Additional Parameters	140

4.2	Designing Routings		143
	4.2.1	Routing Types	144
	4.2.2	Routing Status	146
	4.2.3	Return Steps Options	147
	4.2.4	Any Order Group	148
	4.2.5	Simultaneous Group	149
	4.2.6	Making Decisions for Routing Next Operation	149
	4.2.7	Routing Design Scenario	151
4.3	Enhancing Routings		158
4.4	Maintaining the Control Key		164
4.5	Synchronizing Routings from SAP ME to SAP ERP		165
4.6	Routing Flow Control with Custom Scripting		168
4.7	Summary		169

5 Shop Order Management 171

5.1	Shop Order in SAP ME		171
5.2	Creating Shop Orders from SAP ERP Orders		179
	5.2.1	Transfer of Production Orders	179
	5.2.2	Transfer of Planned Orders	181
	5.2.3	Transfer of RMA Service Orders	181
5.3	Releasing Shop Orders		181
5.4	Reports for Shop Order		183
	5.4.1	Shop Order by Step Report	183
	5.4.2	Shop Order Schedule Report	184
	5.4.3	Shop Order Report	185
	5.4.4	Shop Order Cycle Time Report	185
5.5	Summary		186

6 Shop Floor Control Management 187

6.1	Overview of SFCs and Generating SFCs on Order Release		187
	6.1.1	Generating SFCs through Shop Order Releases	188
	6.1.2	Create and Release SFCs	189
	6.1.3	Create Trackable SFCs	190
	6.1.4	Return Material Authorization SFC Receipt	192
	6.1.5	SFC Group	193
	6.1.6	SFC Status	194
6.2	Performing SFC Activities		195
	6.2.1	SFC Merge	195
	6.2.2	SFC Split	196
	6.2.3	SFC Place Hold	197

Contents

		6.2.4	SFC Release Hold	198
		6.2.5	SFC Quantity Adjustment	199
		6.2.6	SFC Scrap/Delete	200
		6.2.7	SFC Unscrap/Undelete	201
		6.2.8	Change Production	202
	6.3	Reporting on SFC Activities		204
		6.3.1	Activity Log Report	204
		6.3.2	Hold Report	205
		6.3.3	SFC Report	206
		6.3.4	SFC Average Cycle Time by Operation Report	208
		6.3.5	SFC Average Cycle Time by Shop Order Report	209
		6.3.6	SFC Cycle Time Report	210
	6.4	Summary		210

7 Data Collection 211

	7.1	Maintaining Data Collection		211
		7.1.1	Creating a DC Group	212
		7.1.2	Creating DC Parameters	215
	7.2	Assigning Data Collection Groups to Process Objects		220
		7.2.1	Activity Hooks for Data Collection Check	221
	7.3	Data Collection Activities		222
		7.3.1	Data Collection Edit	222
		7.3.2	Data Collection Standalone	223
		7.3.3	Data Collection Definition Report	224
		7.3.4	Data Collection Results Report	226
	7.4	Data Collection Scenario in Assembly Manufacturing		227
	7.5	Summary		232

8 Nonconformance and Quality Control 233

	8.1	Maintaining NC Codes		234
	8.2	Maintaining NC Groups		240
	8.3	Maintaining Disposition Groups		243
	8.4	Maintaining NC Clients		244
	8.5	Maintaining a Sample Plan		248
	8.6	Quality Inspection Process		253
		8.6.1	Transferring Inspection Lots as DC Groups from SAP ERP	253
		8.6.2	Transferring Data Collection as Quality Inspection Results to SAP ERP	256

		8.6.3	Transferring Nonconformances as Quality Notifications to SAP ERP 258
	8.7	Quality Reports 260
		8.7.1	NC Log Report 260
		8.7.2	NC Summary by Material Report 260
		8.7.3	NC Summary by NC Code Report 261
		8.7.4	Open NC Summary Report 262
		8.7.5	Repair Loop Report 262
		8.7.6	DPMO Report 263
	8.8	SPC Analysis and Reporting 264
		8.8.1	Configuring SPC Charts 265
		8.8.2	Displaying SPC Charts 272
	8.9	Summary 273

9   Product Genealogy and Tracking 275

	9.1	Setting Up Discrete and Time-Based Genealogy Processes 276
	9.2	Managing Floor Stock 280
		9.2.1	Floor Stock Receipt 280
		9.2.2	Rule Settings for Floor Stock Receipt 282
		9.2.3	Maintain Floor Stock 282
		9.2.4	SAP ERP Integration for Floor Stock Maintenance 285
	9.3	Storage Location Maintenance 287
	9.4	Slot Configuration Maintenance 288
	9.5	Resource Slot Configuration Setup 290
	9.6	Resource Setup 293
	9.7	As-Built Configuration 294
	9.8	Genealogy Reports 300
		9.8.1	As-Built Summary Report 300
		9.8.2	BOM Report 301
		9.8.3	Device History Report 302
		9.8.4	Floor Stock Report 303
		9.8.5	Resource Setup Report 304
	9.9	Summary 305

10   Production Operator Dashboards 307

	10.1	Types of Available POD 308
		10.1.1	Operation POD 308
		10.1.2	Work Center POD 309
		10.1.3	Mobile POD 313
		10.1.4	Message Board 314

	10.1.5	Visual Test and Repair POD	314
10.2		List Maintenance	317
10.3		Designing PODs	318
	10.3.1	Main Tab	319
	10.3.2	Buttons Tab	320
	10.3.3	Layout Tab	323
	10.3.4	List Options Tab	326
	10.3.5	POD Selection Tab	328
	10.3.6	Printer Tab	329
	10.3.7	Custom Tab	330
10.4		Assigning PODs to User Groups	330
10.5		Executing SFCs in the POD	333
	10.5.1	Starting and Completing the SFC	334
	10.5.2	Displaying Work Instructions	336
	10.5.3	Performing Data Collection	337
	10.5.4	Performing Nonconformance Logging	337
	10.5.5	Equipment Status Change	339
10.6		Production Reports	340
	10.6.1	Production Report	340
	10.6.2	Operation Yield Report	341
	10.6.3	Operation Yield by Material Report	342
	10.6.4	Material Yield Report	342
10.7		WIP Reports	343
	10.7.1	WIP by Material Report	343
	10.7.2	WIP by Operation Report	345
	10.7.3	WIP by Work Center Report	345
10.8		Summary	346

11 Message Board Service — 347

11.1	Message Board Features	348
11.2	Message Type Maintenance	351
11.3	Maintaining Process Workflow	353
11.4	Use of Different Message Types	357
11.5	Creating Message	359
11.6	Real-Time Message Display	362
11.7	Summary	364

12 Labor Tracking — 365

12.1	Maintaining Production Shifts and Calendar	366
12.2	Maintaining Cost Centers	368

Contents

12.3	Maintaining Labor Charge Codes	369
12.4	Maintaining Labor Rules	370
	12.4.1 Attendance Rules	370
	12.4.2 LCC Rules	372
	12.4.3 Rollup Processing Rules	372
12.5	Maintaining User Shifts	374
12.6	Labor Clock In/Clock Out	376
12.7	Supervisor Clock In/Out	380
12.8	Supervisor Time Edit and Approval	380
	12.8.1 Supervisor Mode	381
	12.8.2 User Mode	381
12.9	Summary	382

13 Packing Service ... 383

13.1	Container Maintenance	383
13.2	Pack and Unpack Activity	387
13.3	Packing Report	392
13.4	Maintaining Activity Rules for Container Maintenance	392
13.5	Summary	394

PART III Advanced Enhancement

14 Custom Enhancements Using Public API Web Services ... 397

14.1	Finding Required Public API Services	397
14.2	Configuring and Accessing Public API Web Services	398
14.3	Executing PAPI Services from SAP MII Action Blocks	403
14.4	Examples of Enhancements Using PAPI Services	404
	14.4.1 Assigning External SFC Numbers	404
	14.4.2 Developing Custom PODs	406
14.5	OData Services for SAP ME	408
14.6	Summary	409

15 Shop Floor Systems Integration Using SAP MII and Plant Connectivity ... 411

15.1	End-to-End Integration Scenarios Using SAP PCo, SAP MII, and SAP ME	413
15.2	Maintaining Equipment Status through SAP PCo Notification Agent	413

	15.3	Automating Data Collection in SAP ME	419
	15.4	Summary	421

16 Advanced Reporting in SAP ME ... 423

	16.1	Reporting Databases and Options in SAP ME	423
	16.2	Executive Dashboards in SAP ME	424
	16.3	SAP ME Standard Reports in SAP MII	427
	16.4	Developing Custom Reports in MII	427
	16.5	Summary	429

17 Enhancing SAP ME with SDKs ... 431

	17.1	Overview of SAP ME SDK		432
	17.2	Development Environment for SAP ME SDK		433
		17.2.1	Configuration of SAP NWDI and SLD	434
		17.2.2	Creating Software Components	435
		17.2.3	Creating Development Configurations	437
		17.2.4	Name Reservation in SLD	439
		17.2.5	Configuration of SAP NWDS in Client System	439
		17.2.6	Configuring Name Servers in SAP NWDS	441
		17.2.7	Configuring SAP NetWeaver Application Server Java in SAP NWDS	441
	17.3	Enhancement Options Using SAP ME SDK		442
		17.3.1	Activity Hook	442
		17.3.2	Service Extension	448
		17.3.3	POD Plugin	451
		17.3.4	Developing Custom Web Services	454
		17.3.5	Developing Custom PAPI Services	457
		17.3.6	Print Plugins	459
	17.4	SDK APIs and Libraries		462
	17.5	Summary		463

Conclusion	465
The Authors	471
Index	473

Foreword

The evolution of manufacturing has been completely transformed over the last couple of decades with the introduction and integration of IT systems, none of which has been more impactful to the shop floor then the manufacturing execution system (MES), which has transformed the way manufacturing processes are tracked, recorded, and controlled. It has ultimately provided the manufacturer with more transparency into their own production, while also enabling them to be more responsive to their customers.

SAP Manufacturing Execution (SAP ME) is the leading MES focused on discrete manufacturing, targeted at industries such as automotive, aerospace and defense, industrial machinery and components, high-tech, and life sciences. It's an integrated solution that is highly flexible, extendable, and feature-rich, providing customers a powerful and robust solution to meet the needs of their manufacturing. SAP ME enables a manufacturer to have complete control over manufacturing operations; decrease costs and time to market with lower process downtime; meet highly specific and time-sensitive customer demands through more agile, flexible production operations; and reduce compliance costs and risks with powerful traceability.

What truly sets SAP ME apart is that it's a comprehensive end-to-end MES solution offering an extensive out-of-the-box integration to SAP ERP. Customers can fully leverage the investment they have made into SAP ERP, providing them with a closed loop integration between the top floor and shop floor that enables the decision makers to make decisions more quickly and adapt to real time events.

This book, written by leading experts who have in-depth knowledge of SAP ME and manufacturing technologies, as well as experience in collaborating with customers across many industries, will familiarize you with everything you need to know to connect and manage your production processes from the shop floor to supply chain. In particular, you will learn how SAP ME can be applied to your manufacturing operations, as the authors have provided you with the detailed know-how necessary to ensure a successful implementation. This book includes detailed overviews, examples, screen shots, tips, etc. to give you a broad understanding of SAP ME from a single source.

Like a tutorial, it's written in a clear and easy-to-read style, covering every major area of SAP ME—and it's the only available book of its kind. I hope you find it a useful and enjoyable read.

Michael Cressman
Chief Product Owner SAP ME
SAP SE

Preface

SAP Manufacturing Execution (SAP ME) is a manufacturing execution system solution from SAP used for managing processes and data in discrete and assembly manufacturing. This book is intended to provide a thorough guide to customizing and using SAP ME. It is the product of many months of effort to bring together our knowledge and expertise in this topic with the lessons we have learned through several SAP ME implementations. We sincerely hope that, as the first book on the topic, this will be a useful resource for all those who intend to use and implement SAP ME.

Target Audience

This book is intended for consultants, developers, and users implementing and using SAP ME.

Structure of this Book

This book is organized into three part, with seventeen total chapters. Part I will provide an overview of SAP ME, along with information on the administration and basic configurations of SAP ME. Part II will detail the different features and functionality of SAP ME, and Part III will explain the more advanced topics and customization options within SAP ME.

The introduction explains the need for an MES in discrete manufacturing, the positioning of SAP ME, and SAP ME's components and architecture.

Part I explains the administration and configuration of SAP ME through the following chapters:

- **Chapter 1** explains the integration mechanism between SAP ERP and SAP ME and the configurations required for the SAPMENINT component in SAP MII. It details how to configure SAPMEINT for different message types and describes the functionality of different monitoring activities.

- **Chapter 2** explains the basic system configurations to get your SAP ME system ready to use. The basic system configuration must be completed before defining the shop floor master data and setting up certain features for production usage.
- **Chapter 3** describes how to manage master data, such as material, BOM, and work center/resource, among others, in SAP ME and walks through how to enhance master data downloaded from SAP ERP to SAP ME.

Part II explains the features and functionality of SAP ME through the following chapters:

- **Chapter 4** explains the details of operations and routing design in SAP ME and how to synchronize and enhance routings downloaded from SAP ERP.
- **Chapter 5** covers shop order management functionality in SAP ME. This chapter explains how to create a shop order in SAP ME from an SAP ERP production order or planned order, how to create one independently in SAP ME, and how to release a shop order in SAP ME.
- **Chapter 6** describes functionality related to shop floor control (SFC), such as external SFC number assignment; SFC merge, split, hold, and release; quantity adjustment; and SFC scrap/delete and unscrap/undelete and related reporting functions.
- **Chapter 7** explains the data collection mechanism in SAP ME. It walks through the data collection (DC) group, DC parameters, assignment of DC in operation through the Data Collection Management activity, DC edit, and standalone data collection in SAP ME. It also provides a data collection result report in SAP ME and an example of data collection in a discrete industry.
- **Chapter 8** provides the details of quality control mechanisms in SAP ME and how SAP ME quality data is integrated with SAP ERP. This chapter also covers nonconformance-related activities, such as nonconformance client maintenance, NC code maintenance, and NC group maintenance, and provides real-life examples for logging and closing NC.
- **Chapter 9** explains how to setup genealogy tracking of products by time-based or discrete processes. It explains the various data collection points and mechanisms available in SAP ME for materials, which help track components and their use in finished products.
- **Chapter 10** provides steps for designing SAP ME PODs based on business requirements and assignment of PODs to user groups. The chapter also con-

tains layout configurations for PODs, multiple button assignment, and SFC execution through SAP ME.

- **Chapter 11** explains the shop floor, real-time messaging mechanism in SAP ME using the Message Board Service activity. A shop floor operator can create, view, and process messages related to the manufacturing process. This chapter also teaches you how to use the message board as a standalone service or within the standard SAP ME POD.
- **Chapter 12** explains the functionality of labor tracking on the shop floor using SAP ME. It will describe how to track time for employee labor and time spent finishing a product on the shop floor. This chapter covers related activities, such as labor charge codes (LCCs), cost centers, defining of shifts, clocking in and clocking out, and labor rules. It also includes a real-world example for labor tracking from the shop floor.
- **Chapter 13** provides an overview of the packing service in SAP ME to track packing of finished products into containers and also unpacking features.

Part III explains the advanced enhancements possible in SAP ME through the following chapters:

- **Chapter 14** provides an overview of available public API web services for SAP ME. It teaches you how and where to find public web services APIs, how to test them, and how to consume them from the SAP MII workbench through action blocks.
- **Chapter 15** provides an end-to-end integration scenario for shop floor equipment and SAP ME using SAP MII and SAP PCo. It also covers SAP PCo configuration for integration with both OPC and SAP MII, SAP ME PAPI service integration with SAP PCo, SAP ME equipment status control through SAP PCo notification, and automated shop floor equipment data collection in SAP ME.
- **Chapter 16** explains how to develop custom reports in SAP MII using SAP ME PAPI services and SQL queries and how to use the reports delivered in SAP MII.
- **Chapter 17** explains how to enhance a standard SAP ME implementation using SDKs and covers available APIs and the library for SAP ME SDKs.

Acknowledgments

Writing a book is not an easy task and behind the scene there are always many who contribute selflessly to make the book a success. We'd like to take this opportunity to thank all those without whose help this book would not have seen the light of the day.

First of all we would like to thank Meagan White and Emily Nicholls, our editors for this book. Rather than being just editors, they acted as our guide and mentors and immensely helped to make the content perfect, so that you, our readers, get a product of high quality.

We like to thank our families without whose help and constant support this endeavor would have been just a dream. They tolerated us and provided constant support when we burnt many midnight oil on writing the book.

We are grateful to Michael Cressman, Product Owner of SAP ME and his SAP ME product development team at SAP Labs, namely Sara Mani, Bakhtiyar Mirkhidoyatov, Charlie Cutler, Mike Houston, Camille Keglovitz, Dmitry Chizhikov, Ilias Skordilis, Peggy Enriquez, Steve Stubbs and Sundar Chakravarthy who helped us all through reviewing the book content despite their busy schedule and providing help and support whenever required.

We like to thank Kalpati Srinivas, Srikanta Satapathy, Niraj Sharma, Anirban Banerjee, Soumen Mondal, Amit Khandelwal, Swapna Mukherjee, Moumita De, Mahalakshmi Syamsunder, Sushabhan Banerjee, Laboni Bhowmik and Animesh Mondal of IBM, who have enriched the content at every step. Being our friends and colleagues, they did not for a moment hesitate to constructively criticize the content when required also helped us with facts, figures and other technical suggestions which ensure a much more fulfilling experience to you, the reader.

We also like to thank G Venkatraghavan, Somnath Dey, Subhabrata Ganguly, Anup K Ghosh, Sauti Sen and Asidhara Lahiri of IBM leadership team without whose encouragement and support the process of writing this book would not have been as smooth as it was.

Last but not the least, the SAP Community Network, without which we would not been able to collaborate and learn so much and always find the help whenever required from the community of developers, users and experts. We owe you.

Dipankar Saha
Chandan Jash
Kolkata, India—November 2015

This chapter provides an overview of SAP ME from both a functional and an architectural perspective, as well as discussing its role as the manufacturing execution system for discrete industries.

Introduction to SAP ME

This chapter introduces the concept of the manufacturing execution system (MES) and discusses SAP ME's suitability as an MES for discrete manufacturing. It also details the application architecture of SAP ME.

Manufacturing Execution and the Need for an MES

For any manufacturing company, execution processes at the manufacturing plant are of utmost importance and require close control to ensure quality, timely delivery, and cost efficiency. Although the enterprise planning and logistics processes are typically managed by an enterprise resource planning (ERP) system, the execution control and reporting processes at the manufacturing plants are usually handled elsewhere. From an IT perspective, the challenges faced by manufacturing companies at the manufacturing shop floor production processes are as follows:

- **Design and control of process steps**
  Manufacturing execution processes, especially those related to assembly manufacturing in discrete industry, require more granular design of their execution steps, which are not usually maintained in an ERP system in production routing data. To cover all assembly scenarios, it is important for a shop floor execution system to manage execution steps or production routing design at a detailed level.

- **Traceability**
  It is important to trace all levels of execution at the manufacturing shop floor so that, the work in progress (WIP) product state can be determined at any time

during production execution and to be able to trace back process details in case issues arise later.

- **Non conformance management/quality control**
  It is of the utmost important for a manufacturer to track and minimize defects in products and to take proper actions to rework or quarantine products in case of defects. It is also of paramount importance that a manufacturer be able to close out these defects by taking corrective actions.

- **Capturing process data in real time from machines**
  In some manufacturing operation steps (e.g., in high-speed and high-volume discrete manufacturing), real-time machine data should be captured before moving to the next operation step in order to determine a product's quality.

- **Real-time reporting**
  Because product traceability is important, real-time reporting for processes and products is required throughout the execution process.

- **Production line control**
  Production operators are often required to control the speed of production line and need to be able to start and stop the production line as required, assigning appropriate reason codes for downtimes.

- **End-to-end integration with SAP Enterprise Planning System**
  Different shop-floor systems used in a manufacturing process need to be integrated with SAP ERP for seamless, bidirectional master data, planning, and actuals data transfer.

- **Failover Support**
  Shop floor manufacturing processes must be able to be carried out at any point in time from the local execution system, even when SAP ERP connectivity, which may rely on a global data center, is temporarily down.

As you can see, manufacturing processes at the shop floor need a manufacturing execution system. In a discrete industry, in which most of the execution processes are manual assemblies on different machines or semi-automated with different shop-floor control systems, an MES must address the previously listed challenges and provide a single-window system for managing and tracking the end-to-end manufacturing execution process.

In the next section, you'll discover how SAP Manufacturing Execution (ME) can be used as an MES for discrete industry.

Overview of SAP ME as an MES for Discrete Manufacturing

Although SAP produces one of the leading products for enterprise planning and logistics execution—SAP ERP—manufacturing execution control, specifically for discrete industry, is not fully addressed by that product. Manufacturing plants need a local system that is simple for shop-floor users and that addresses the challenges mentioned earlier.

SAP acquired Visiprise in 2008 for its Visiprise Manufacturing Execution product, now renamed to SAP Manufacturing Execution. SAP ME is positioned as the MES for discrete manufacturing, augmenting SAP ERP. Over the years, SAP ME has undergone changes and become more seamlessly integrated with SAP ERP and the SAP NetWeaver platform and has established itself as a useful MES for SAP customers in discrete industries.

The key features available in SAP ME are as follows:

- Integrates the shop floor with an SAP ERP system in real-time ("Shop Floor to Top Floor Integration")
- Integrates with SAP ERP to synchronize master data, shop floor control information, inventory management, quality management, and plant maintenance
- Enhances production routing defined in SAP ERP with granular steps for shop-floor execution
- Handles make-to-stock (MTS), make-to-order (MTO), and repetitive manufacturing production processes
- Provides functionality for tracking WIP, defect/nonconformance logging, data collection (manual/automated), user-specific access control/certification, traceability of components at each step, and so on
- Includes visual test and repair (integration with SAP Visual Enterprise to provide a graphical display of an assembly with relevant data and action)
- Provides a disposition function in routing management to handle products with defects
- Allows for connectivity to plant equipment through SAP Manufacturing Integration and Intelligence (MII) and SAP Plant Connectivity (PCo)
- Provides statistical process control (SPC) features through SAP MII

Introduction to SAP ME

- Allows for a customizable user interface through the production operator dashboard (POD)
- Provides access to a number of reporting functions that enable real-time analysis of production data and processes

SAP ME runs on SAP NetWeaver Java Application Server (AS) as a web application and provides real-time integration with SAP ERP through SAP MII, the manufacturing integration platform provided by SAP to exchange master and transactional data for manufacturing execution. It provides functions to manage and enhance master data, such as material, equipment, work center, and routing data, and transactional data such as shop order (from SAP ERP production or planned orders), inventory, and other data, either locally or synchronized with SAP ERP.

SAP ME provides customizable production operator dashboards that users at manufacturing plants can use to view their tasks and to record actual data from the production process, such as nonconformance due to quality defects, process data collected during production, inventory consumption, and so on. One of SAP ME's key features is its ability to track WIP products throughout their lifecycles in order to ensure quality compliance and adherence to various production rules for manufacturing assembly processes.

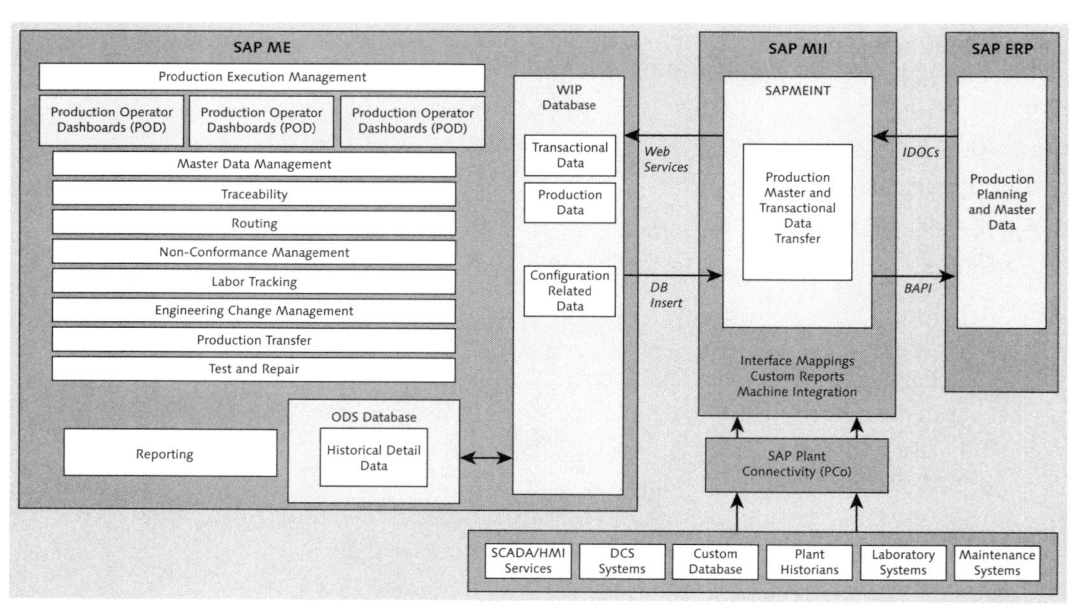

Figure 1 Solution Overview of SAP ME

SAP ME also provides options for real-time reporting and analysis of production data and processes to enhance understanding of the status of manufacturing operations, which prompts quick business decisions and helps avoid deviations.

The solution overview of SAP ME is shown in Figure 1.

In the next section, you will learn about the architecture and different components of SAP ME.

Application Architecture for SAP ME

The SAP ME solution consists of the SAP MII and SAP Manufacturing Execution components deployed in the same SAP NetWeaver Java AS. SAP MII acts as the integration platform between SAP ME and SAP ERP to exchange transactional and master data. A component called SAPMEINT is provided in SAP MII as part of SAP ME to manage message workflows between SAP ERP and SAP ME.

SAP ME uses a separate application database, the WIP database, to store all system data. All master, transactional, and configuration data used in SAP ME are stored in this database. Whenever any data is sent from SAP ERP to SAP ME or created in SAP ME, it is stored in the WIP database. The SAP NetWeaver AS database cannot be used to host this database due to different settings, so you must install the database on a separate host. SAP ME also uses the operational data store (ODS) database, which can be installed on a separate host or on the same database server where the WIP database is installed. The ODS database is used to store historical data for long-term reporting purposes, which is summarized from the WIP database and is populated from the WIP database data only by archiving, performed by certain predefined database scripts. It is also possible to have a global ODS (GODS) database to accumulate data from the ODS database of each site in order to provide cross-plant analytics.

Finally, SAP ME also uses a database called SAPMEINT, which should be installed on a separate host or in the same database server as the other two databases. SAPMEINT is used to store messages exchanged between SAP ERP and SAP ME through SAP MII and related configurations.

All three databases only can be installed on either MS SQL Server or Oracle databases.

Two of the most important functionalities provided by SAP ME are the operator dashboards and reports, which are used by the users at the manufacturing plants for operational data recording and analysis.

SAP ME also provides customizable PODs, which can be modified as required, or new dashboards can be configured for certain tasks.

Using SAP MII and SAP PCo, SAP ME can be integrated with machines and real-time, shop-floor automation control systems, such as SCADA, DCS, and a plant data historian, to get real-time information for machines and processes. Custom reports can be developed in SAP MII for SPC analysis and other analysis and monitoring based on the ME data.

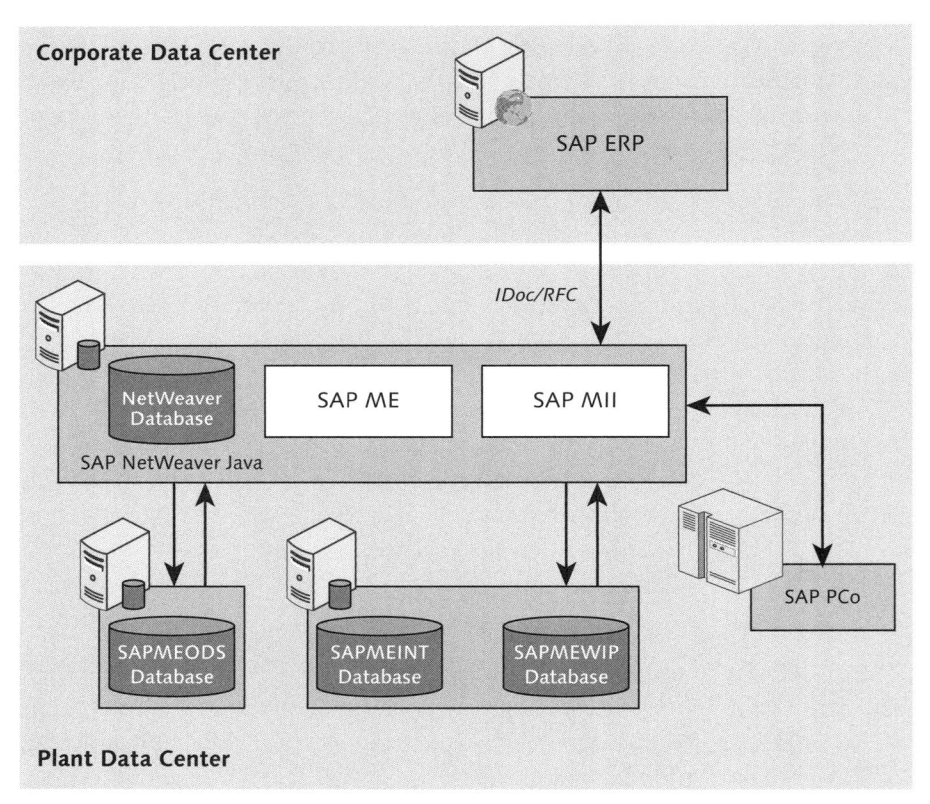

Figure 2 SAP ME Architeture Overview

Most SAP ME functionalities are exposed as public API (PAPI) services, available as JAVA API and SOAP Web Services, which can be executed from SAP MII and other external applications. SAP ME also provides a Java-based SDK, through which the standard functionality of SAP ME can be extended as required. SAP MII can be also used to extend the SAP ME functionality and to develop custom reports on SAP ME data.

Figure 2 illustrates the component architecture of SAP ME. This book is based on SAP ME 15.0, the latest version available as of the time of writing.

SAP ME is typically installed at each manufacturing plant location for easy integration with local legacy systems and to provide a local execution system for each site.

> **Note**
>
> Although it is possible to configure multiple sites (plants) in a single SAP ME instance, we recommend that you use a single ME instance per site for large plants for the reasons discussed previously. In some scenarios where the number of plant users and amount of data is lower, multiple plants can be supported by single SAP ME instance.

SAPMEINT, the integration component between SAP ERP and SAP ME provided by SAP MII, provides a guaranteed delivery and retry mechanism to buffer and retry sending messages in case of connection issues.

Summary

In this chapter, you learned about the solution overview of SAP ME and its architecture. In the next chapter, you will learn about the integration between SAP ERP and SAP ME through the SAPMEINT component and how you can customize the SAPMEINT workflows for specific business requirements.

PART I
Administration and Configuration

This chapter explains the integration mechanism between SAP ERP and SAP ME and the configurations required in the SAPMENINT component in SAP MII for integration. It explains how to configure SAPMEINT and describes the functionality of different monitoring activities.

1 Configuring and Monitoring SAPMEINT

Because SAP ME is an MES solution, you need to integrate it with SAP ERP and other external applications to exchange master and transactional data bi-directionally. The integration with SAP ERP is most important, because most of the master data such as material, work center, routing as well as transactional data such as production orders, and inventory are maintained in SAP ERP and need to be sent to SAP ME for its operations. In addition, SAP ME needs to send different information such as shop order confirmations, nonconformances, and equipment breakdown information to SAP ERP for recording actuals.

Because SAP MII is an SAP product for manufacturing systems integration, it is a natural platform of choice for integrating SAP ERP with SAP ME. SAP delivers the integration content for most of the standard master and transactional interfaces to exchange data bi-directionally between SAP ERP and SAP ME. SAP ME/SAP ERP integration, or SAPMEINT, is a component of SAP ME on SAP MII that contains all required interfaces for communication between SAP ERP and SAP ME. In this chapter, we'll explain the SAPMEINT configuration details and features and also go over your monitoring options.

1.1 Configuring SAP MII for SAP ME

SAP MII is an integration and composition platform which is used along with SAP ME for integrating with SAP ERP and other systems. In the following sections you will learn how to configure SAP MII and the SAPMEINT framework for integrating SAP ERP with SAP ME.

1 | Configuring and Monitoring SAPMEINT

1.1.1 SAP ERP and ME Integration

The SAPMEINT component of SAP MII provides a framework through which message workflows can be defined to integrate SAP ERP and other external systems with SAP ME using different interfaces. The SAPMEINT workflow framework is designed to provide a mechanism through which any interface mapping can be easily incorporated between SAP ERP and SAP ME and changed as needed through simple configurations. SAP provides integration content in the SAPMEINT component as message workflows for the interfaces listed in Table 1.1 and Table 1.2. These message workflows provide the mapping, error-handling, and transfer mechanisms between SAP ERP and SAP ME.

SAP ERP Interface	SAP ME Interface
Material	Material
Material with classification	Material with custom data
BOM	BOM
Work center	Resource or work center
Work center with individual capacities	Work center with resources
Routing (standard and rate)	Routing with operations
Routing with document info record	Routing with work instruction
Personnel with qualification	User with certification

Table 1.1 Master Data Interfaces Provided by SAPMEINT

SAP ERP Interface	SAP ME Interface
Production order	Production shop order
Production order with serial numbers	Production shop order with SFC numbers
Production order with document info record	Production shop order with work instruction
Production order with quality inspetion lot	Production shop order with quality inspection lot
Production order with BOM and routing	Production shop order with BOM
Production order with scheduling information	Production shop order with quantity splits associated with resources and scheduling information

Table 1.2 Transactional Data Interfaces Provided by SAPMEINT

Configuring SAP MII for SAP ME | 1.1

SAP ERP Interface	SAP ME Interface
Planned order	Repetitive shop order
Planned order with BOM and routing	Repetitive shop order with BOM and routing
Service order	RMA shop order
Inventory	Floor stock (inventory ID)
Quality notification	Nonconformance
Equipment (PM), technical resource, and tool	Resource and tool number and usage with information and downtimes
Production/planned order confirmation	Shop order completion
Production/planned order scrap	Shop order scrap
Activity confirmation for production order	Approved direct labor records (only collected work time)
Quality inspection results	Data collection for quality inspection

Table 1.2 Transactional Data Interfaces Provided by SAPMEINT (Cont.)

SAPMEINT uses the message service available in SAP MII for receiving messages from SAP ERP. All messages from SAP ERP for SAP ME are sent as IDoc messages. From SAP ERP 6.0 Enhancement Pack 5 onwards, a new component is available in SAP ERP called the Data Replication Framework (DRF), which can be used to automatically send IDoc messages on specific events, such as release of production orders, goods movement, and so on. The message listener in SAP MII provides a listener for IDoc messages and receives IDoc messages sent from SAP ERP, buffers them in the message service, and executes a category-based message-processing rule, after which a predefined scheduled job enqueues the messages and executes the specific workflow defined for the message. Messages received by SAP MII and processed by the SAPMEINT framework are buffered in the SAPMEINT application database, for which a monitoring framework is also provided. The SAPMEINT framework is developed using Java and deployed in SAP MII as a custom action.

Figure 1.1 shows the architecture overview of the SAPMEINT component.

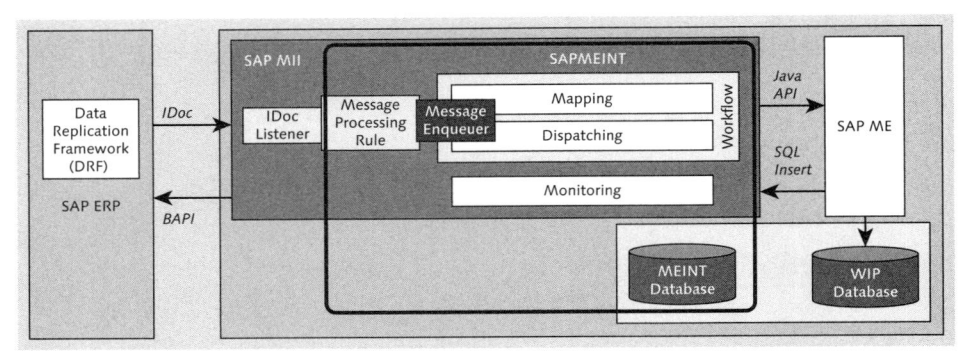

Figure 1.1 Integration Architecture Overview of SAPMEINT

In the following sections, you will learn how to set up and configure the standard SAPMEINT interfaces, how to enhance them, and how to create new ones.

1.1.2 SAPMEINT CTC Configuration Wizard

To configure the standard interface workflows and the relevant configurations in SAP MII for SAPMEINT, a configuration wizard is provided in SAP NetWeaver Administrator of the Java WebAS that creates all the required configurations in SAP MII. To open the CTC Wizard, open SAP NetWeaver Administrator via *http://<host>:<port>/nwa* in the browser for the server on which SAP ME and SAP MII are installed. Then, navigate to CONFIGURATION • SCENARIOS • CONFIGURATION WIZARD. Enter "SAPMEINT" in the FIND field, click on GO, select the SAPMEINT Standard Interfaces CTC template displayed in the results, and click on the EXECUTE button, as shown in Figure 1.2.

The wizard will ask for specific information about the configurations that needs to be specified to create the configurations in background automatically. In the first step, it will ask for the site (plant) information which is used in SAP ME based on an existing plant in SAP ERP, the data for which will be replicated in SAP ME, as shown in Figure 1.3. You also need to specify the password for the SITE_ADMIN user (the master user to create sites in SAP ME), the time zones of the site in SAP ERP and SAP ME, and the language maintained for the site in SAP ERP. If the SAP ERP version is EHP 5 or higher, that information also needs to be specified to enable data replication by DRF, which uses different message types in some cases.

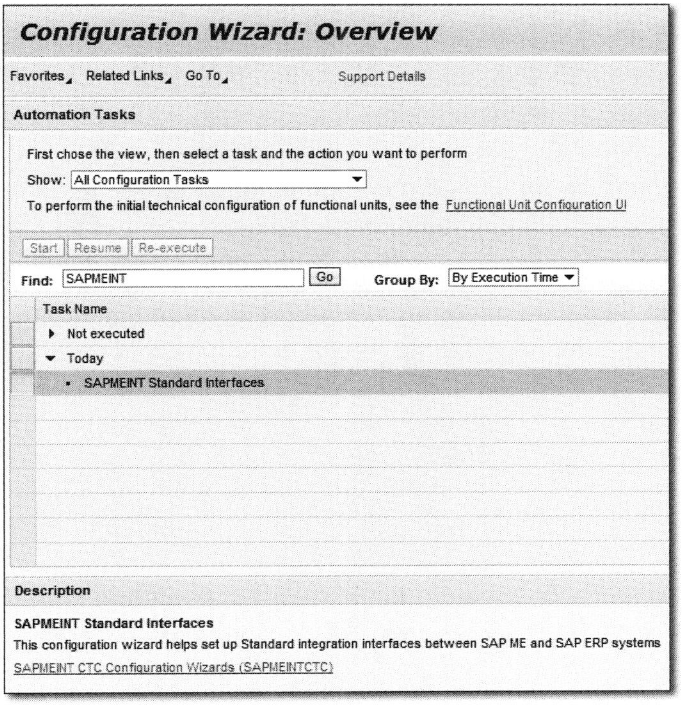

Figure 1.2 SAPMEINT CTC Wizard

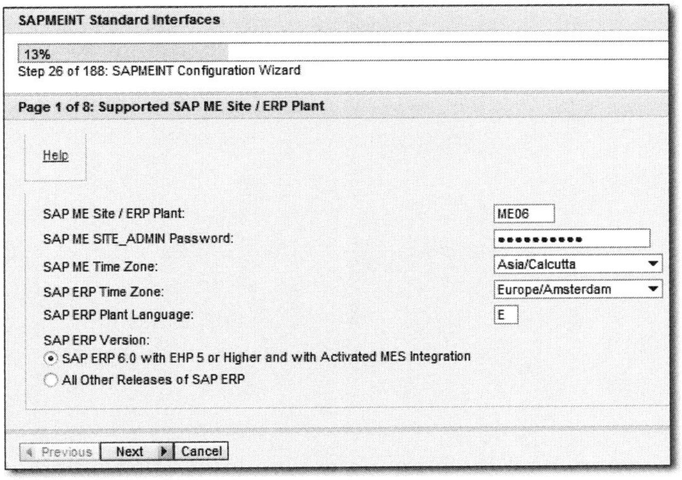

Figure 1.3 Site Configuration in SAPMEINT CTC Wizard

In the next step, the wizard will ask for technical information for the SAP ME server and for the IDoc listener, which needs to be configured in SAP NetWeaver and in SAP MII to receive the IDoc messages from SAP ERP as shown in Figure 1.4. Select the IDoc listener and specify the program ID and SAP ERP system connection details and credentials. Configure an RFC destination in SAP ERP of the TCP/IP type and the corresponding ALE configuration (partner profile, partner port, logical system, and distribution model) pointing to the SAP MII server. The program ID specified here must be same as in the RFC destination configured in SAP ERP to send the IDoc messages. Also ensure that the user details for the SAP ERP system specified here have the required authorization to execute RFC.

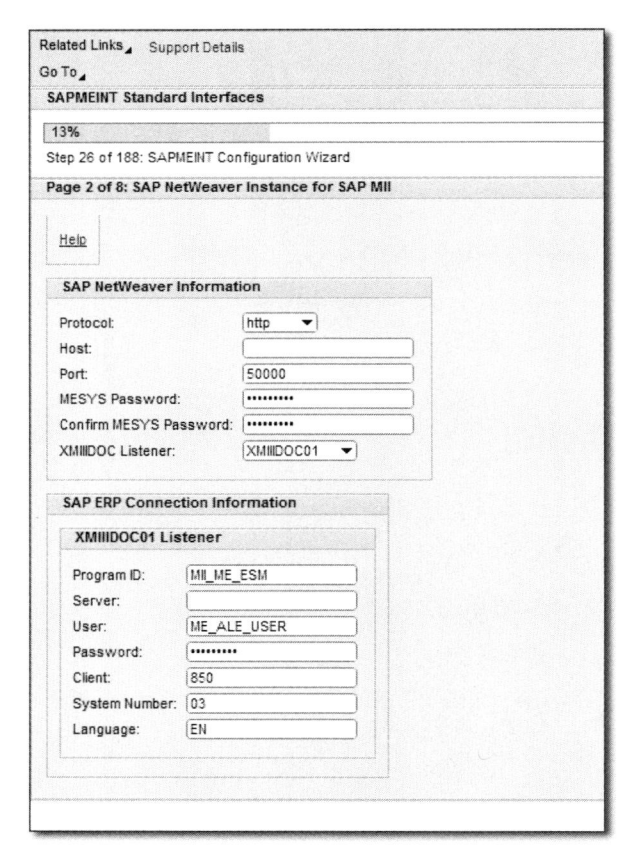

Figure 1.4 Message Listener Configuration in SAPMEINT CTC Wizard

In the next step, specify the SAP NetWeaver instance details corresponding to where SAP ME and the SAP MII servers are installed as shown in Figure 1.5. The USED FOR REPORTING IN SAP MII checkbox is used to specify that the same host is used for the SAPMEINT dashboards available as activities in SAPMEINT menu.

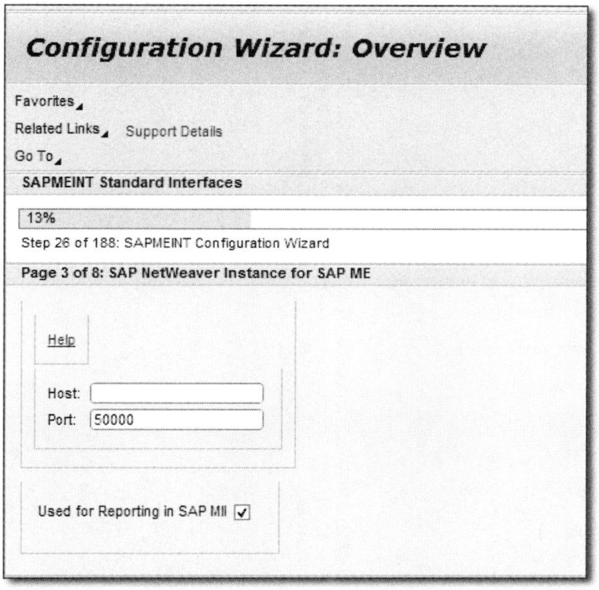

Figure 1.5 SAP NetWeaver Instance Details in SAPMEINT CTC Wizard

In the next step, specify the application-specific parameters to be used in SAP ERP to create quality notifications based on nonconformance (NC) logging in SAP ME, as shown in Figure 1.6. Ensure the notification type, catalog, code, and code group specified here are configured and available in SAP ERP for quality notifications.

In the next step, specify the SAP JCo connection alias that should be created in SAP MII to send messages back from SAP ME to SAP ERP by executing BAPI interfaces, as shown in Figure 1.7. Use the SAP ERP credentials specified earlier, which can be changed later manually from the SAP MII configuration if required (see Section 1.1.3 for more information).

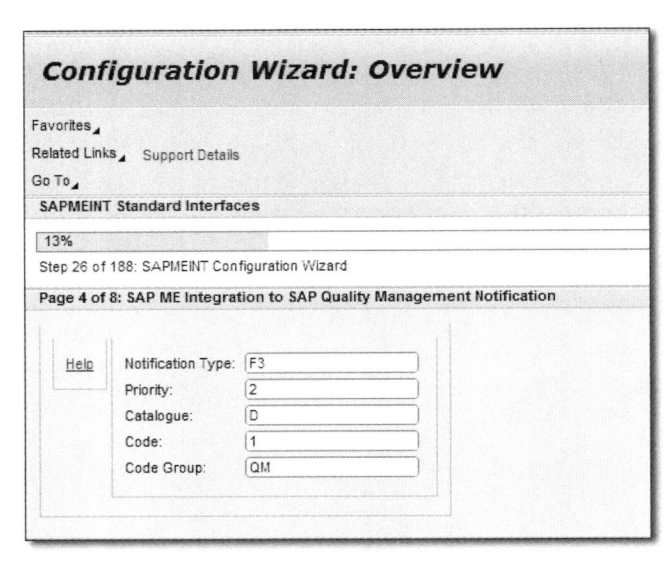

Figure 1.6 SAP ME Application Parameters Configuration in SAPMEINT CTC Wizard

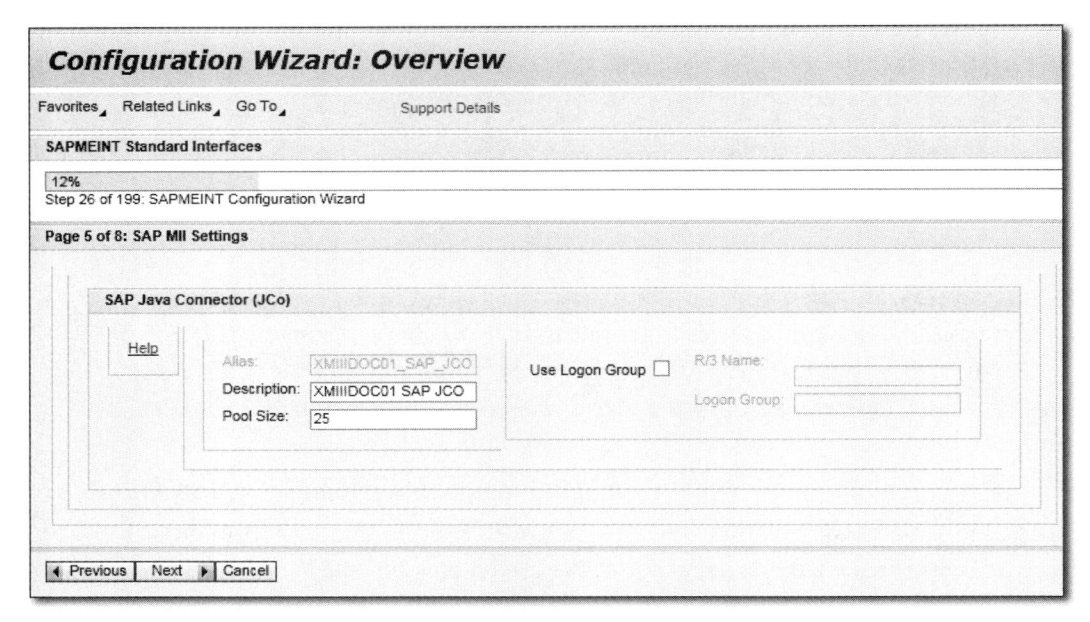

Figure 1.7 SAP JCo Alias Configuration for SAP MII in SAPMEINT CTC Wizard

In the next step, specify the number of messages to be processed by each scheduled job in SAP MII for the inbound and outbound messages, along with the execution pattern, as shown in Figure 1.8.

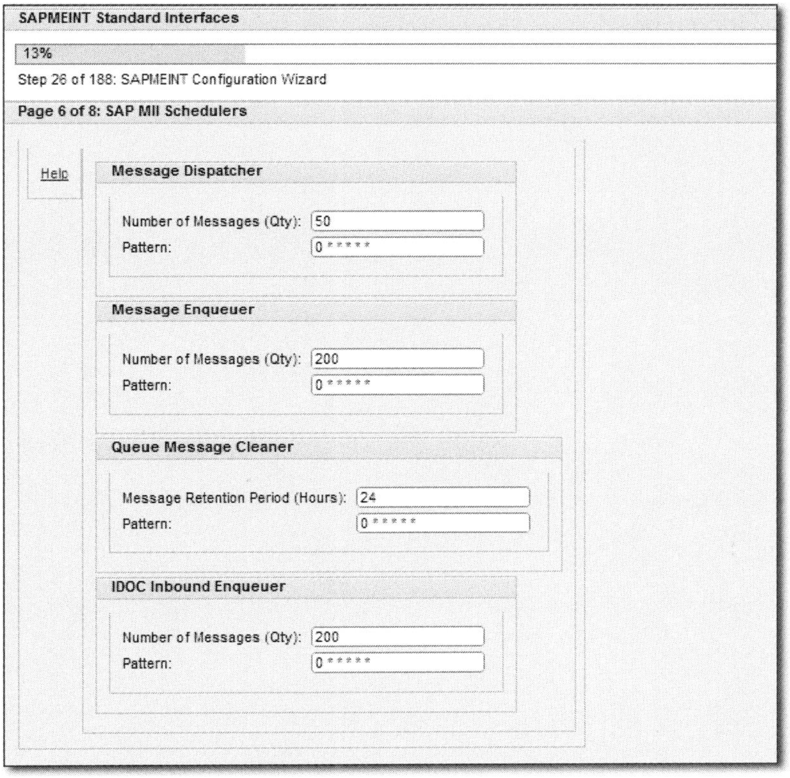

Figure 1.8 Scheduler Parameter Configuration in SAPMEINT CTC Wizard

In the final step, specify the connection details of the SAPMEINT and WIP databases that were installed with the SAP ME application, as shown in Figure 1.9. In most cases, both the MEINT and WIP databases should be installed on the same database server.

Once you execute the CTC Wizard after specifying these details, it will create the configurations specified. All the workflows, the message listeners, processing rules, data sources, and scheduled jobs in SAP MII are created.

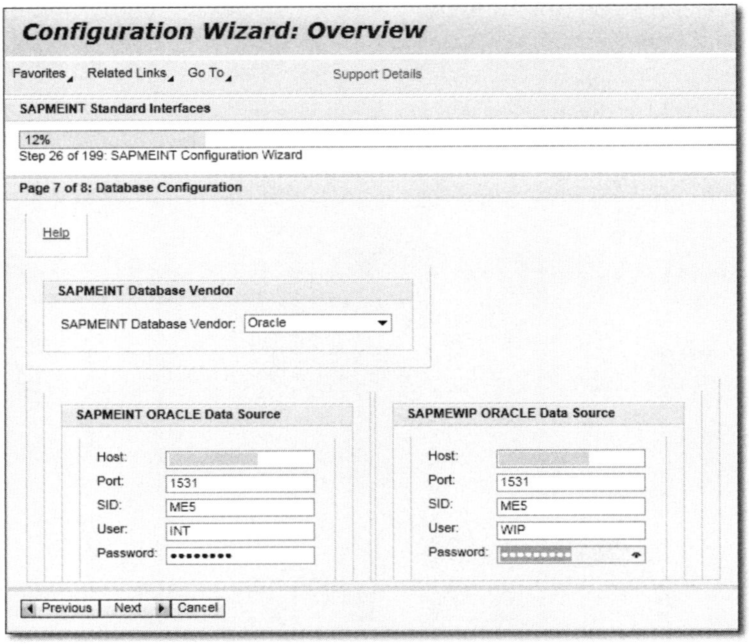

Figure 1.9 SAP ME Database Configuration in SAPMEINT CTC Wizard

You need to execute the SAP ME Standard Interface CTC wizard for each site created in SAP ME

1.1.3 SAPMEINT Configuration

The configurations created by the CTC wizard spread across different areas in SAP MII, NWA, and SAPMEINT, as we will discuss in the next sections.

You can view the SAPMEINT configurations in SAP MII from the portal navigation. Open *http://<host>:<port>/XMII* and click on the SAP ERP INTEGRATION portal navigation link displayed on the left pane. Ensure that the user with which you are logging in has ROLE_SAPMEINT assigned.

Global Configuration

Global configurations are used in SAPMEINT for integrating with SAP ME. They are available from the SAPMEINT menu SAPMEINT CONFIGURATION • GLOBAL CONFIGURATION, as shown in Figure 1.10.

1.1 Configuring SAP MII for SAP ME

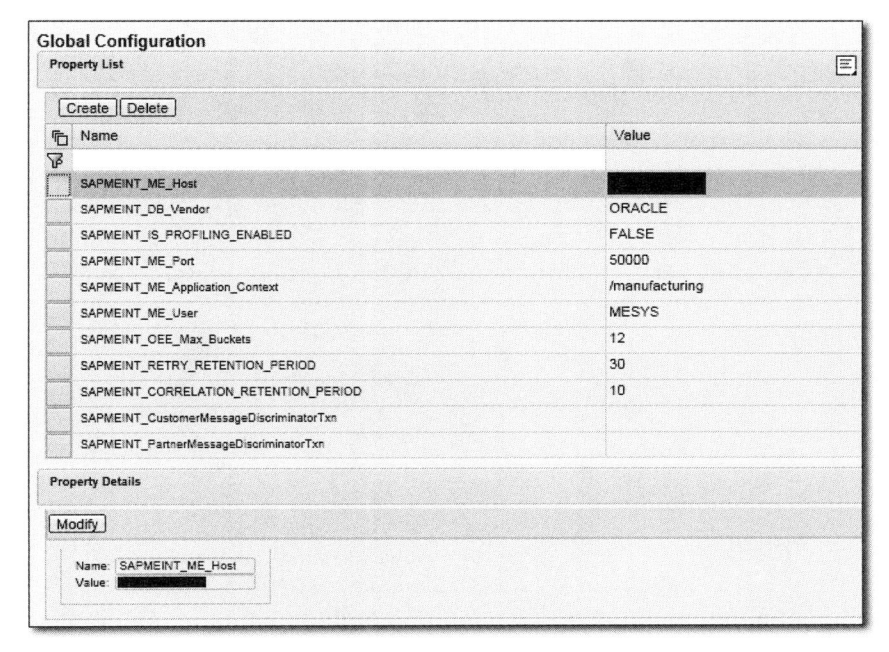

Figure 1.10 Global Configurations of SAPMEINT

Some of the configuration property values, such as `SAPMEINT_ME_Host`, `SAPMEINT_ME_Port`, `SAPMEINT_ME_Application_Context`, and `SAPMEINT_DB_Vendor`, should not be changed. All these configuration property values are set by the CTC Wizard itself. You can change the parameters listed in Table 1.3 if required.

Property Name	Description
SAPMEINT_IS_PROFILING_ENABLED	Specifies whether profiling is enabled for SAPMEINT messages for analyzing performance and processing details from the Queue Monitor. You can also specify a step ID number to enable profiling only for a specific step instead of the whole workflow. Refer to SAP ME help documentation for more information.
SAPMEINT_ME_User	SAP ME user used by SAPMEINT or by any custom enhancement developed on SAP MII for executing the APIs.

Table 1.3 Global Properties of SAPMEINT

Property Name	Description
SAPMEINT_OEE_Max_Buckets	Specifies the number of buckets or data points displayed in the OEE report available in SAPMEINT.
SAPMEINT_RETRY_RETENTION_PERIOD	Specifies the time in minutes for which a message in SAPMEINT will be retried after a system error.
SAPMEINT_CORRELATION_RETENTION_PERIOD	Specifies the time in minutes for which a message in SAPMEINT will wait for next processing in case the correlation condition is not met.
SAPMEINT_CustomerMessageDiscriminatorTxn SAPMEINT_PartnerMessageDiscriminatorTxn	Discriminator transactions are used in SAPMEINT to determine the message type or workflow type of a message flowing through SAPMEINT. SAPMEINT provides a standard logic to determine the identifier, but if that needs to be overridden, the customer or partner discriminator transaction can be specified here. If used, the output parameter type of the transaction should be used as the identifier. The customer discriminator transaction has higher precedence than the partner transaction while executing.

Table 1.3 Global Properties of SAPMEINT (Cont.)

Supported SAP ME Plants Configuration

In the supported ME Plants configuration, the plants or sites that are defined in SAP ME and integrated with SAP ERP need to be specified. This configuration is created by the SAPMEINT CTC Wizard. The plant code is specified along with the language and the SAP JCo connection alias for the SAP ERP server. The SAP JCo connection alias is created in SAP MII (DATA SERVICES • CONNECTIONS menu). It is used to execute an RFC from the Business Logic Service (BLS) transaction in SAP MII to update the messages from SAP ME to SAP ERP using the message workflow that we will explore in the next section. The SAP JCo alias also is created by the SAPMEINT CTC Wizard, with the connection details of the SAP ERP system. The connection property values can be changed if required later from the SAP MII connection configuration of SAP JCo.

The SAP ME host URL, language, and the time zone of the plant in SAP ERP and SAP ME are also specified here. The language and time zone options are available in case the SAP ERP and SAP ME servers use different languages and are in different time zones.

Data Server Configuration

Data servers are connection aliases created in SAP MII for connecting to external databases and other systems. In SAPMEINT, three data server connections are created in SAP MII using a data source connector to connect to the databases for SAPMEINT, WIP and ODS, which are used by SAPMEINT and SAP ME as application databases. Follow the DATA SERVICES • DATA SERVER menu path in SAP MII to access the data server configurations. SAPMEINT, SAPMEWIP, and SAPMEODS are the three data server configurations automatically created by the CTC Wizard while configuring SAPMEINT. These data servers point to the application databases for SAPMEINT, WIP, and ODS respectively via the data source connection created in SAP NetWeaver Administrator. Though MEINT and WIP may be in the same database, separate data server connections are configured for each to ensure sufficient connection handles are available for each database.

SAP ERP Connection Configuration

Connections for SAP ERP with SAP ME are created by the CTC Wizard for both inbound and outbound connections. To receive messages sent from SAP ERP as IDoc messages, the IDoc listener is configured in SAP MII. The IDoc listener is configured in SAP NetWeaver Administrator from the CONFIGURATION • INFRASTRUCTURE • APPLICATION RESOURCES menu. Filter by JCA resources to display the JRA resource configuration for IDoc listener, e.g., XMIIIDoc01. Once the JCA resource is configured in SAP NetWeaver Administrator, you need to update the message listener configuration in the MESSAGE SERVICES • MESSAGE LISTENER menu in SAP MII.

For executing RFCs in SAP ERP for outbound messages from SAP ME, a JCo connection alias is created in the DATA SERVICES • CONNECTIONS menu in MII as XMIIIDOC01_SAP_JCO pointing to the SAP ERP server.

Message Listener Configuration

The IDoc listener in SAP MII is used to receive IDoc messages from SAP ERP and is configured by the CTC Wizard, as explained in the previous section.

> **Note**
> ONCE the CTC Wizard configures the IDoc listener in SAP NetWeaver Administrator, you need to navigate to the SAP MII menu MESSAGE SERVICES • MESSAGE LISTENER, select the configured IDoc listener and click on the UPDATE button to update the listener configuration.

Message Processing Rule Configuration

Message processing rules are configured by the CTC wizard to enable SAP MII to process messages received from SAP ERP and transfer those to SAPMEINT. A category-based processing rule is configured in the MESSAGE SERVICES • MESSAGE PROCESSING RULE menu in SAP MII to specify SAPMEINT_INBOUND_QUEUE as the category of the IDoc messages received in SAP MII for SAP ME from SAP ERP. The IDoc messages categorized in the SAP MII message service are processed by scheduled jobs to move them into the SAPMEINT queue and subsequently process them.

Scheduler Configuration

In SAP MII, the scheduler is used to execute logic services known as BLS transactions in certain periodic time intervals as configured by the user. The scheduled jobs in SAP MII are configured from the menu path SYSTEM MANAGEMENT • SCHEDULER.

SAPMEINT provides four predefined scheduled jobs to execute BLS transactions, as shown in Table 1.4. These jobs are created by the SAPMEINT CTC Wizard.

Scheduled Job	BLS Transaction
InboundMessageEnqueuer	Visiprise/ERPShopFloorIntegration/ InboundEnqueuer/InboundEnqueuer
MessageEnqueuer	Visiprise/ERPShopFloorIntegration/ SAPMEMessageEnqueuer/ SAPMEMessageEnqueuingDispatcher
MessageDispatcher	Visiprise/ERPShopFloorIntegration/ frame/dispatchers/simpleDispatcher/ SimpleMessageDispatcher
QueueMessageCleaner	Visiprise/ERPShopFloorIntegration/ MessagePurging/MessageCleaner

Table 1.4 Scheduled Transactions for SAPMEINT

Let's go over each scheduler option:

- The `InboundMessageEnqueuer` scheduler queries and processes and IDoc messages received from SAP ERP—that is, the inbound messages to SAP ME—which are categorized in MII message service queue, adds them as `SAPMEINT_INBOUND_QUEUE` in the integration processing queue in the SAPMEINT database. You can specify the number of messages to be queried and processed at each run.

- The `MessageEnqueuer` scheduler queries and processes outbound messages—that is, the messages sent out of SAP ME for SAP ERP from a database table in WIP database—and includes them in the integration processing queue.

- The `MessageDispatcher` scheduler queries the messages from the SAPMEINT integration processing queue and triggers the message workflow for the corresponding message type as defined in SAPMEINT for both inbound and outbound messages, as defined in the SAPMEINT workflow configuration for the message type.

- The `QueueMessageCleaner` scheduler deletes the processed messages in the SAPMEINT integration processing queue.

> **Note**
>
> All content in SAP MII for SAPMEINT is available in a predefined SAP MII project delivered by SAP called *Visiprise*. The Visiprise project in the SAP MII workbench contains all the BLS transactions, data queries, and web objects, such as XSLT files and the reports in SAP MII. You can access the project content from the SAP MII workbench, which is read-only.

Security Configuration

Two credential aliases used to execute SAP ERP and SAP ME interfaces are created in SAP MII for SAPMEINT by the CTC Wizard. You can find the credential aliases under the SAP MII menu SECURITY SERVICES • CREDENTIAL STORE. The credential alias stores the username and password pair for system authentication details. The aliases are used in the workflow execution in SAPMEINT to execute the target system interface instead of specifying username and password inside the code so that the username and password can be changed at any point in time if required.

`SAPMEINT_ALE` is the credential alias created for SAP ERP. `SAPMEINT_ME_AUTH` is the credential alias for SAP ME, but it is not used from SAP ME 6.1 onwards for SAP ME interfaces, because SAPMEINT now calls the Java API for SAP ME, and both systems are installed on the same server. It was used earlier (until SAP ME 6.0) to execute SAP ME web services, back when SAP MII and SAP ME were installed on separate servers. It can be used for a web service call to SAP ME from custom or legacy components, if required.

> **Note**
>
> `Role_MEINT` is used to access the SAPMEINT application and the portal navigation in SAP MII. `SAP_ME_INTEGRATOR` is used to execute any SAP ME web service and also should be assigned to the corresponding user who wants to execute those functions.

Workflow Configuration

Workflow configuration is available in SAPMEINT to manage the message workflow and routing from SAP ERP to SAP ME and vice versa. SAP provides a set of workflows for the standard messages supported by SAP ME for integrating with SAP ERP.

The workflow framework is provided in SAP MII, where the logic to validate the message content, enrich it, and map the message to the target message format can be provided. Although the standard validation, enrichment, and mapping logic are provided along with the standard SAPMEINT messages, it is possible to override the standard logic by specifying custom logic developed on SAP MII. For SAPMEINT, a database called SAPMEINT stores all the incoming messages to SAP MII from both SAP ERP and SAP ME along with the corresponding statuses. The messages sent from SAP ERP are received in the IDoc listener of SAP MII and are queued by the processing rule and added to the SAPMEINT queue. The messages received from SAP ME are directly added to the SAPMEINT queue in table `SAPMEINT_ME_MESSAGES` in the SAPMEINT database and processed from there. The processing of the messages and movement from one queue to another is handled by the schedulers, as explained in the Scheduler Configuration section. The messages in the integration queue are stored in table `SAPMEINT_MESSAGE_QUEUE` in the SAPMEINT database. The following three types of workflows are supported by SAPMEINT:

- **Standard**

    Used to transfer a message from SAP ERP to SAP ME and vice versa with the corresponding transformation, validation, and enrichment of the message as required.

- **Correlation**
  Used to merge two or more different message based on certain conditions. For example, this workflow can be used to collect multiple confirmation messages from SAP ME to send as a single message to SAP ERP.
- **Split**
  The opposite of the correlation workflow, this workflow splits a single message into multiple messages. For example, a material master message sent from SAP ERP in a single IDoc message for different plants can be split into separate messages for each plant.

> **Note**
>
> We'll explain the configuration for each of these types of workflows in Section 1.1.5.

You can specify the logic for message mapping, validation, enrichment, and message dispatching in the workflow configuration. The logic for the workflow handler, key determination, validation, split, merge, error handler, and pass handler can be provided either by a Java program or by a Business Logic Service (BLS) transaction developed on SAP MII. The mapping or transformation between the message structures can be achieved via XML Style Language Transformation (XSLT). The logic and mapping for the standard messages delivered in SAPMEINT are provided as well and can be enhanced if required.

To configure a workflow, specify a message type and the workflow type. The workflow handler is automatically selected based on the workflow type selected. Specify workflow handler parameters with the XPath of the values in the input XML message, or fixed values that will be passed to the workflow program. The typical parameters are plant and identifier. Plant is specified by the XPath of the plant element specified in the message, and the identifier is usually constructed by concatenating multiple identifiers, such as plant and the order number for a LOIPRO (production order) message.

You need to specify the logic services and XSLT mappings as required in the message lifecycle methods, as explained in Section 1.1.5. You can also specify the automatic retry limit for the message in case it encounters a system error during workflow processing. Figure 1.11 shows an example of a standard workflow in SAPMEINT for a LOIPRO01 message.

1 | Configuring and Monitoring SAPMEINT

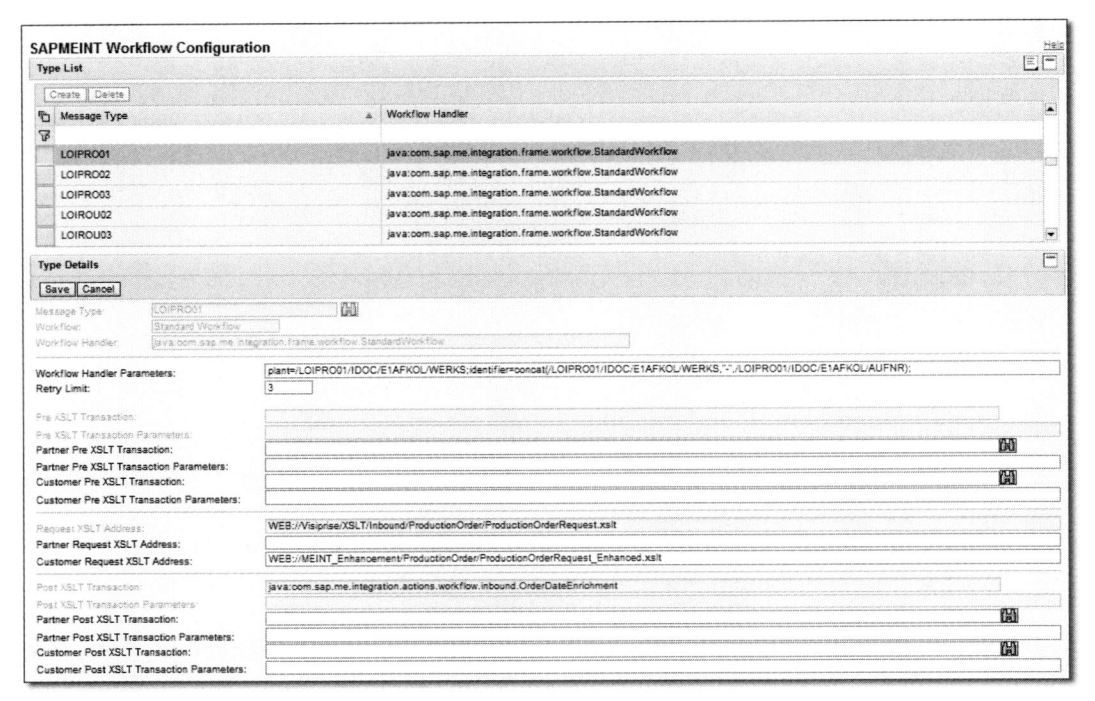

Figure 1.11 SAPMEINT Message Workflow Configuration

1.1.4 Available Message Types in SAPMEINT

Most of the master and transactional data required by SAP ME are replicated from SAP ERP and updated back into SAP ERP from SAP ME. SAP delivers the message workflows in SAPMEINT for all the standard messages, as shown in Table 1.5, Table 1.6, and Table 1.7, with interface names and corresponding SAP ERP message types.

Interface Name	SAP ERP Message Type
Material	MATMAS03/MATMAS05
Workcenter	LOIWCS02/LOIWCS03
Routing	LOIROU02/LOIROU03
BOM	BOMMAT03
Material classification	CLFMAS02

Table 1.5 Master Data Messages Replication from SAP ERP to SAP ME

Interface Name	SAP ERP Message Type
Personnel (HR) data with qualification to user certification	HRMD_A06
Classification	CLFMAS02

Table 1.5 Master Data Messages Replication from SAP ERP to SAP ME (Cont.)

Interface Name	SAP ERP Message Type
Production order	LOIPRO01/LOIPRO02/LOIPRO03/LOIPRO04
Planned order	LOIPLO01/LOIPLO02
Inventory	INVCON02
Maintenance order	IORDER01
Change equipment status	IORDER01_CHG_EQ_STATUS

Table 1.6 Transactional Data Messages Replication From SAP ERP to SAP ME

Interface Name	SAP ERP Message Type
Direct labor record (work center activity)	BAPI (BAPI_PRODORDCONF_CREATE_TT)
Quality inspection result	BAPI (BAPI_INSPOPER_RECORDRESULTS)
Material batch character posting	BAPI (BAPI_OBJCL_CHANGE)
Change inventory at shopfloor	BAPI (BAPI_GOODSMVT_CREATE)
Planned order complete	BAPI (BAPI_PLANNEDORDER_DELETE)
Production order complete	BAPI (BAPI_PRODORDCONF_CREATE_TT)
Quality notification create/change	BAPI (BAPI_QUALNOT_CREATE/ BAPI_QUALNOT_ADD_DATA)
Read quality inspection result	BAPI (BAPI_INSPOPER_GETDETAIL)
RMA order complete	BAPI (BAPI_ALM_ORDER_MAINTAIN)
Scrap backflushing for REM order	BAPI (BAPI_REPMANCONF1_CREATE_MTS)
Scrap confirmation for production order	BAPI (CO_MES_PRODORDCONF_CREATE_TT)
Goods movement from storage locatioon	BAPI (BAPI_GOODSMVT_CREATE)
Yield backflushing for REM order	BAPI (BAPI_REPMANCONF1_CREATE_MTS)
Yield backflushing for prod order	BAPI (CO_MES_PRODORDCONF_CREATE_TT)

Table 1.7 Transactional Data Messages Replication from SAP ME to SAP ERP

Interface Name	SAP ERP Message Type
Equipment status change (start production)	BAPI (BAPI_ALM_ORDER_MAINTAIN)
Equipment status change (start downtime)	BAPI (BAPI_ALM_NOTIF_CREATE)
Equipment usage (measurement doc)	BAPI (MEASUREM_DOCUM_RFC_SINGLE__001)

Table 1.7 Transactional Data Messages Replication from SAP ME to SAP ERP (Cont.)

Each interface has a corresponding message workflow defined in SAPMEINT. There are a few more workflows available for correlation of yield confirmations, production order confirmation, labor confirmation, splitting material classification, material master, equipment usage, and so on.

1.1.5 Message Type Lifecycle Configuration

The workflow of the message consists of different steps depending on the workflow type. Typically, there is a workflow handler logic, and depending on the workflow type, merge, split, pre-XSLT, mapping, and dispatch and error handler logic are specified in the workflow. We will explore the different lifecycle methods of the messages for different types of workflows in the following subsections.

Standard Workflow

In standard workflows, the message is passed from SAP ERP (or any external system) to SAP ME or vice versa by validation, enrichment, and transformation. Typically, SAP ERP sends messages as IDocs to SAP MII, and they are transformed to the SAP ME interface format and updated in SAP ME by executing the APIs available for the interfaces. Similarly, SAP ME sends messages in XML format through the SAPMEINT database, and they are transformed to a BAPI interface format and then updated in SAP ERP by executing the corresponding BAPI. The standard workflow consists of the different sequential steps or lifecycle methods in the workflow as in the following order:

1. **Pre-XSLT transaction**

   A service implemented in a SAP MII BLS transaction or in Java, can be specified to validate or enhance the input structure of the message by adding additional elements. For example, serial numbers of finished products can be added to the production order message sent by a LOIPRO IDoc message type by executing an RFC. A BLS transaction developed in SAP MII or a Java program developed by implementing a specific interface can be provided. Some of the pre-XSLT transactions are provided in SAPMEINT for some messages or workflows. This is an optional configuration.

2. **Request XSLT address**
An XSLT needs to be specified to transform the source structure of the message to the target structure—for example, to transform an LOIPRO IDoc message structure to the SAP ME shop order interface structure. All XSLT files for the standard workflows provided in SAPMEINT are available by default. This configuration can be changed if required.

3. **Post-XSLT transaction**
A service can be specified to perform any validation or enrichment of the target message after the mapping in the previous step. This option can be used to add additional elements in the target structure without changing the mapping XSLT. A BLS transaction developed in SAP MII or a Java program implementing a specific interface can be specified here. This is an optional configuration.

4. **Service transaction**
A service transaction is used to send a message to the target system, e.g. SAP ERP or SAP ME, by executing a BAPI or Java API respectively. This configuration is provided for all workflows in SAPMEINT by default as a generic program that executes the specific BAPI in SAP ERP or the Java API in SAP ME based on the input message. A BLS transaction developed in SAP MII or a Java program implementing a specific interface can be specified here.

5. **Response XSLT address**
An XSLT file can be specified to transform the response message from the target system to a specific XML message which is understood by SAP ME, which is then received while executing the service transaction, if required.

6. **Pass handler transaction**
A BLS transaction or a Java program implementing a specific interface can be specified to perform some action when the mapping and dispatching of the message is successful—for example, to update a custom database table or trigger another process.

7. **Fail handler transaction**
A BLS transaction or a Java program implementing a specific interface can be specified to perform some action when the mapping and dispatching of the

1 | Configuring and Monitoring SAPMEINT

message fails—for example, send an alert or email notification, update a custom database table, or trigger another process.

Figure 1.12 shows the workflow configuration of a message in SAPMEINT using the standard workflow.

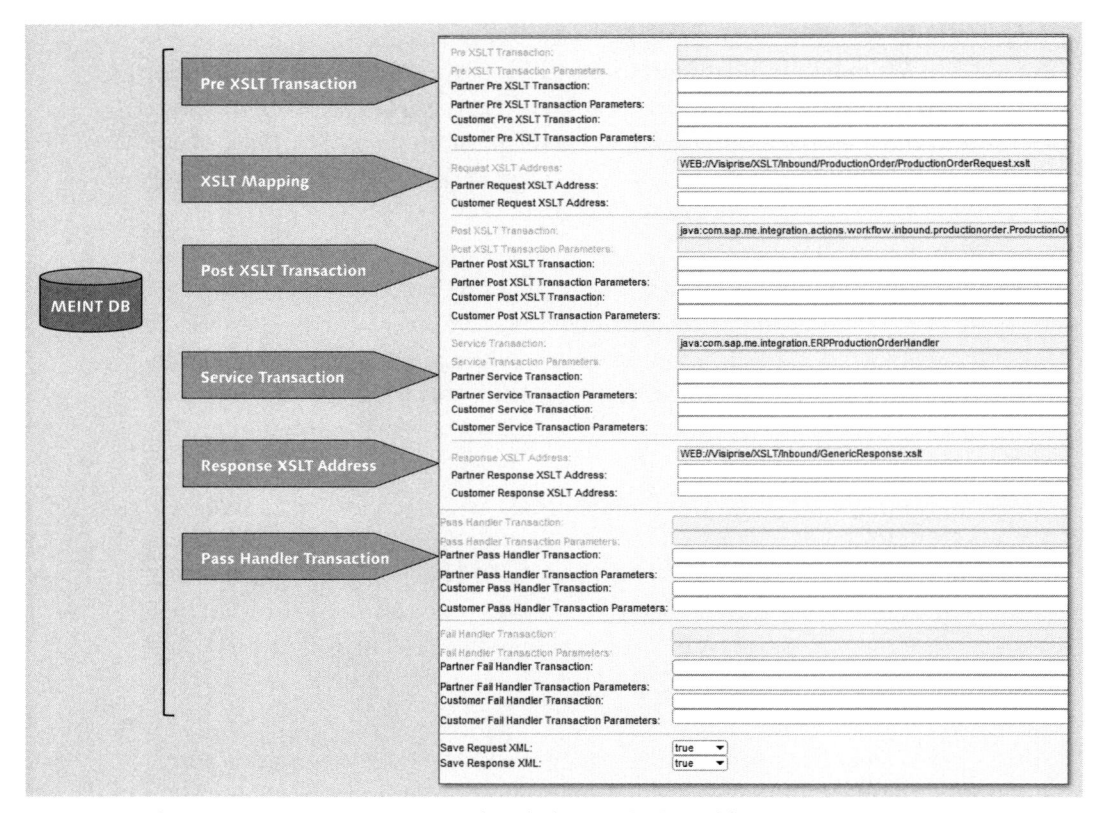

Figure 1.12 SAPMEINT Message Lifecycle for Standard Workflow

When the message is received in SAP MII from SAP ERP or SAP ME, it is enqueued in the SAPMEINT queue from the message service category (IDoc messages from SAP ERP) or from the WIP database (outbound messages from SAP ME). Then, depending on the workflow type configured for the message type, the lifecycle methods are executed sequentially by the workflow framework.

Split Workflow

The split workflow consists of pre-XSLT and pass and fail handler lifecycle methods like the standard workflow, but no post-XSLT, service transaction, request XSLT, or response XSLT. It only has a split XSLT address lifecycle method after pre-XSLT, which is used to split the message into multiple messages. This is because the split workflow does not send the message to a target system; it only splits it. There has to be a standard workflow defined to process and send the split messages. After splitting one message into multiple messages in the split workflow, the workflow enqueues each of the new messages in the SAPMEINT queue. If any one of the messages fails to generate or be enqueued, then all the generated messages are dequeued, and the parent message status is marked as failed and retried depending on the retry limit. The sequence of lifecycle methods for the split workflow is as follows:

1. Pre-XSLT transaction
2. Split-XSLT address
3. Pass handler transaction
4. Fail handler transaction

Correlation Workflow

The correlation workflow merges multiple messages based on message type and content. This workflow is used in different scenarios to group and optimize the target system calls for similar messages; for example, yield confirmation requests from SAP ME are usually grouped together by operation and order for each product piece individually confirmed and by declared yield for a shop order in SAP ME, but updated in SAP ERP for each operation only once.

The correlation workflow has the following lifecycle methods:

- **Get Correlation Key Transaction**
  This service is used to process a message based on the correlation key defined for the message type and to group the messages with the same key in the SAPMEINT database. It generates the correlation key from the message content, such as combination of site, order number, and operation number, and checks if any message for the same key exists in the SAPMEINT database. If exists, it just updates certain values that need to be grouped in the existing message, such as confirmation quantity, by taking the values from the current message and adding up the

value in the existing messages. If no message for the same key is available earlier, then it stores the message in the SAPMEINT database with the correlation key as the first message for the key and merges the message with messages coming later with the same key. The key and grouping information will vary for different message types or for identical message type received at different times. SAP provides BLS transactions in the *Visiprise* project in SAP MII, where it is used in any standard workflows.

- **Merge Validation Transaction**
  This service is used to validate whether the correlated message will be completed and put in the SAPMEINT queue for further processing. There is a standard BLS transaction provided for the merge validation named `Visiprise/ERPShopFloorIntegration/frame/workflow/CorrelationWorkflow/StdMergeValidationHandler`, where you can specify the merge conditions based on a number of documents or a time period to merge messages matching the same identifier or correleation key, in the parameters of the lifecycle method in the workflow. Depending on the values specified in the workflow, the framework will wait for either the number of messages or the time, whichever is attained earlier. For example, the parameters are specified as `numberOfDocuments=2;waitTimeInSec=90`, which indicates that if two or more documents with the same correlation key are waiting in the queue with the status IN_CORRELATION or if they are in the queue for more than 90 seconds, they will be taken by up by the framework to merge together. Note that the `numberofDOcuments` and `waitTimeInSec` parameters are available in the standard merge validation transaction only and not in the custom partner or customer transactions.

- **Merge Transaction**
  This service is used to merge the messages received with the same correlation key and stored in the SAPMEINT database. This service is executed only when the *Merge Validation Transaction* determines that the specified condition for waiting time or the maximum documents to merge has been achieved. It creates a single XML document from the individual messages with the correlation key with the grouped information, such as sum of yield quantity and list of all serial numbers in the individual messages. The new document root node is specified in the lifecycle method parameter `newDocType` in the workflow configuration. There is a standard merge transaction provided, called `Visiprise/ERPShopFloorIntegration/frame/workflow/CorrelationWorkflow/StdMergeHandler`, where you need to pass the `newDocType` parameter to specify the new

XML document root node to be created. Note that the `newDocType` parameter is available in the standard merge transaction only and not in the custom partner or customer transactions, if created.

After the previously listed lifecycle methods, the standard pass handler and fail handler methods are also available, which can be configured to handle success logging or error handling or notification.

There has to be a standard workflow for messages generated by correlation workflow as well, because the correlation workflow does not send a message to any system; it only merges multiple messages and generates one single message. The standard workflow is used to process the merged message, transform it, and send it to the target system.

1.1.6 SAPMEINT Enhancement Use Cases and Best Practices

You may need to enhance SAPMEINT workflows for different scenarios. See Table 1.8 for some common use cases.

Scenario/Use Case	Enhanced Workflow (Message Type)	Lifecycle Method for Enhancement
YieldConfirmationRequest: To stop the multiple confirmation from a single operation when a product is cycling multiple times between a standard operation and rework	yieldConfirmationRequest	Pre-XSLT Enhancement
Equipment Number download: To download the equipment number with resource download from SAP ERP to SAP ME	LOIWCS02	Post-XSLT Enhancement
Production Version for Production Order: To download the production version for production order from SAP ERP to SAP ME	LOIPRO02	XSLT Mapping Enhancement
Storage Location in Material: To download the storage location and material group from SAP ERP to SAP ME	MATMAS03	XSLT Mapping Enhancement

Table 1.8 Enhancement User Cases for SAPMEINT Workflow

Scenario/Use Case	Enhanced Workflow (Message Type)	Lifecycle Method for Enhancement
Routing Description and Operation Description: To send the routing description and operation description with the routing master data download from SAP ERP to SAP ME	LOIROU02	XSLT Mapping Enhancement

Table 1.8 Enhancement User Cases for SAPMEINT Workflow (Cont.)

In the examples in Table 1.8, you can define a pre-XSLT service using a BLS transaction in SAP MII to check if the confirmation for the same product occurred earlier; if found, you can stop the current confirmation message for the `yieldConfirmationRequest` message.

Similarly, for enhancing the resource interface with the equipment number, you can add a BLS transaction as post-XSLT to get the corresponding equipment numbers from SAP ERP by executing an RFC from a BLS transaction and adding the equipment numbers in the transformed XML message for the resource interface in SAP ME where a field for SAP ERP equipment number is present.

To add elements that are already present in the source message, such as storage location, the material group in the material master IDoc, or the operation description in the routing IDoc, enhance the XSLT mapping by adding the required field mapping. Copy the standard XSLT file from the Visiprise project to a custom project in the SAP MII workbench, enhance it there, and specify a partner or customer extension in the XSLT mapping.

You cannot change or delete the SAP-provided lifecycle service or mapping in the workflow, but you can override it. If you want to specify a BLS transaction for any service of the message lifecycle, you need to have the same transaction available in the SAP MII workbench. This is true for XSLT files as well, which should be stored in the web catalog of the SAP MII workbench. Instead of writing a BLS transaction, you can also write a custom Java program to be used with the lifecycle methods of the workflow. This program needs to be deployed on the SAP NetWeaver server where SAP MII runs, as a SAP MII custom action package or dependency to existing custom actions from the SAP MII CONFIGURATIONS • CUSTOM ACTIONS menu in SAPMEINT. For each service, you can also specify some input parameters if required in the workflow configuration. You can specify the custom service logic or XSLT mapping in the partner or customer extensions specified with each lifecycle method in the workflow configuration. Customer extensions, if specified, will have a higher preference than the original and partner extension, which means that if only the original service is specified with the partner extension, only the partner extension will be executed, but if the customer extension is also specified, then it will be executed alone instead of the other two.

Create a BLS transaction to use in the SAPMEINT standard workflow lifecycle services via a specific interface in the SAP MII workbench, as shown in Figure 1.13. The input parameters used in the BLS transaction are as follows:

- `inputXML` is the inbound message XML.
- `params` represents the BLS parameters of the service specified in the workflow.
- The value for `plant` is retrieved from the queued message XML using the XML path of the `plant` parameter of the WORKFLOW HANDLER PARAMETERS field.
- `recordId` is a GUID of the message in the SAPMEINT integration queue.
- `typeId` is the message type.

You can use a template BLS transaction by copying one of the BLS transaction available for SAPMEINT standard lifecycle method into the Visiprise project in the SAP MII workbench. You would then remove the logic inside it in order to add new custom logic for your enhancement.

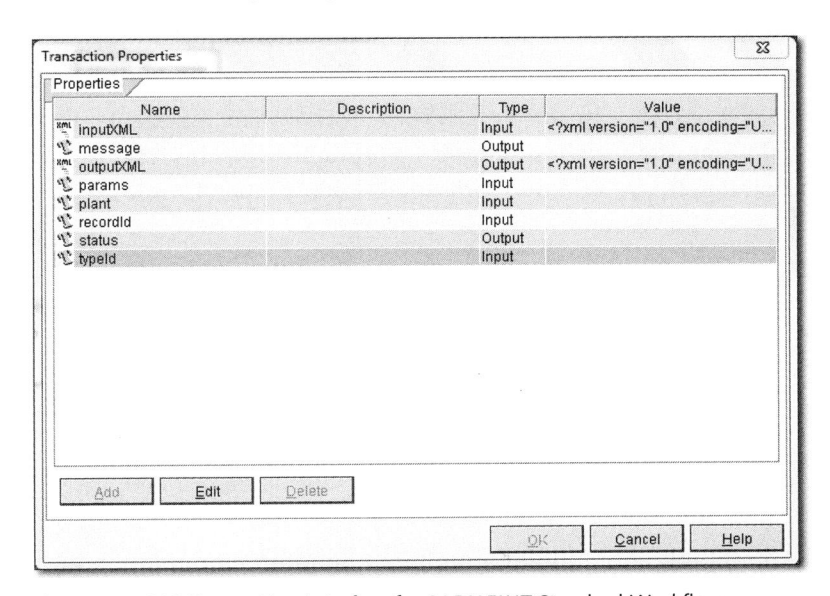

Figure 1.13 BLS Transaction Interface for SAPMEINT Standard Workflow

All parameter values are passed by the workflow while executing the service during the message processing. The `plant` and `recordId` parameters are specified in the workflow handler parameters, `typeid` is the message type, and the `inputXML` is the message XML document. You can specify the `params` as multiple parameters with corresponding values in the workflow configuration for the corresponding lifecycle method in the TRANSACTION PARAMETER field separated by semicolons (;). You can specify the values of the parameters as fixed values or the XPath of the input XML message to get the actual values dynamically inside the transaction.

Depending on the lifecycle method for which you are specifying the transaction, you need to develop the logic inside the BLS transaction to incorporate that logic and process the XML message. For example, in a post-XSLT transaction to add serial numbers to a shop order (production order) message, you can execute an RFC from SAP ERP to get the corresponding material classification details for the material of the corresponding order and add the same in the output XML document with the shop order information already present. Apart from the standard action blocks available in SAP MII BLS transactions, there are some custom actions available for SAPMEINT that can be used depending on the requirements. See Chapter 14 for information on some of the actions required for executing PAPI services.

You can also use a Java program to develop the services for the lifecycle methods instead of using BLS transactions. To develop the Java class, you need to implement a Java interface called `PluginInterface`, which is available in SAPMEINT. The interface definition is as shown in Listing 1.1. Note that the `processMessage` method is important; there, you need to include the logic for the lifecycle method to process the `inputXML` XML document and return a `WorkflowResponse` object.

```
package com.sap.me.integration.frame.workflow;

import org.w3c.dom.Document;

/**
 * Interface class for executing user exit plugin classes in SAPMEINT.
 * <p>Title: PluginInterface </p>
 * <p>Description: Interface class for executing user exit plugin
 classes in SAPMEINT.<p>
 */
public interface PluginInterface {
```

```
    /**
     * This method handles user exit plugin processing.
     * @param plant The name of the plant.
     * @param workflowContext The <code>WorkflowContext</code> object.
     * @param inputXml The input XML.
     * @return <code>WorkflowResponse</code> object.
     */
    public WorkflowResponse processMessage(String plant,
WorkflowContext workflowContext, Document inputXml);
}
```
Listing 1.1 Interface Definition of PluginInterface

Listing 1.2 shows one example of a post-XSLT service developed by a Java class. This service changes the dates in the production order message to GMT format, which is used by SAP ME.

```
package com.sap.me.integration.actions.workflow.inbound;

import java.util.logging.Logger;
import org.w3c.dom.Document;
import org.w3c.dom.NodeList;
import com.sap.me.integration.frame.workflow.PluginInterface;
import com.sap.me.integration.frame.workflow.ResponseStatus;
import com.sap.me.integration.frame.workflow.WorkflowContext;
import com.sap.me.integration.frame.workflow.WorkflowInterface;
import com.sap.me.integration.frame.workflow.WorkflowResponse;
import com.sap.me.integration.util.DateUtils;
import com.sap.me.integration.util.XMLHandler;

/**
* ProductionOrderDateEnrichment accepts the result of Production,
Planned and Service Order XSLT as an input and converts predefined
date fields from ERP server time zone to GMT. */

public class OrderDateEnrichment implements PluginInterface
{
        private static final Logger log =
 Logger.getLogger(OrderDateEnrichment.class.getName());
        //List of date field tags to convert
        private static final String[] tagNameArray = {
"PlannedStartDate", "PlannedCompleteDate", "startDate", "endDate" };

        public WorkflowResponse processMessage(String plant,
WorkflowContext workflowContext, Document inputXml)
        {
                WorkflowResponse workflowResponse = null;
```

```
                String erpServerTZ = workflowContext.
getSupportedPlant(plant).getErp_server_tz();

                try
                {
                        convertDateTimeToGMT(inputXml,tagNameArray,
erpServerTZ);
                        workflowResponse =
 new WorkflowResponse(ResponseStatus.PASSED, XMLHandler.xmlToString
(inputXml), plant, "");
                }
                catch(Exception ex)
                {
                        log.severe("ProductionOrderDateEnrichment():
Error in running the plugin" + ex);
                        return new WorkflowResponse(ResponseStatus.APP_
ERROR, "ProductionOrderDateEnrichment(): Error in running the plugin" +
ex, null, WorkflowInterface.STD_POST_XSLT);
                }
                return workflowResponse;
        }

        private void convertDateTimeToGMT(Document inputXml, String[]
tagNameArray, String erpServerTZ) {
                for (String tagName : tagNameArray) {
                        NodeList nodeList =
 inputXml.getElementsByTagNameNS("http://sap.com/xi/ME", tagName);
                        for (int i = 0; i < nodeList.getLength(); i++) {
                                nodeList.item(i).setTextContent
(DateUtils.convertDateTimeZone(erpServerTZ, nodeList.item(i).
getTextContent(), "yyyy-MM-dd\'T\'HH:mm:ss", "yyyy-MM-dd\'T\
'HH:mm:ss", "GMT"));
                        }
                }
        }
}
```

Listing 1.2 Sample Post-XSLT Service Developed by Java

Once the Java class is developed, you need to compile and create the JAR file and upload and deploy it as the dependency of the SAPMEINT custom actions in SAP MII via the SYSTEM RESOURCES • CUSTOM ACTIONS menu option.

To add a Java class as the lifecycle method in the workflow configuration, prefix it with java: in the workflow configuration—for example:

java:com.sap.me.integration.actions.workflow.inbound.OrderDateEnrichment

1.2 Monitoring

Because SAPMEINT is an integration solution between SAP ERP and SAP ME provided in SAP MII, it must be monitored to ensure the interfaces are working properly. In case of errors or server performance issues, you also must debug it and find the root cause by checking the errors and log. There are different tools available as part of SAPMEINT and SAP MII that you can use to monitor and analyze the messages, performance, and logs of the server. In this section, we will explore the Queue Monitor in SAPMEINT, the Transaction Manager of SAP MII, and the Log Viewer of SAP NetWeaver, all of which are used to monitor the SAPMEINT application and the workflows.

1.2.1 Queue Monitor

The Queue Monitor is a user interface provided as part of SAPMEINT on SAP MII to monitor the messages managed by the SAPMEINT workflows. From the Queue Monitor, you can monitor both the inbound and outbound messages from SAP ME to SAP ERP, and vice versa, which are managed by the SAPMEINT workflow, as shown in Figure 1.14.

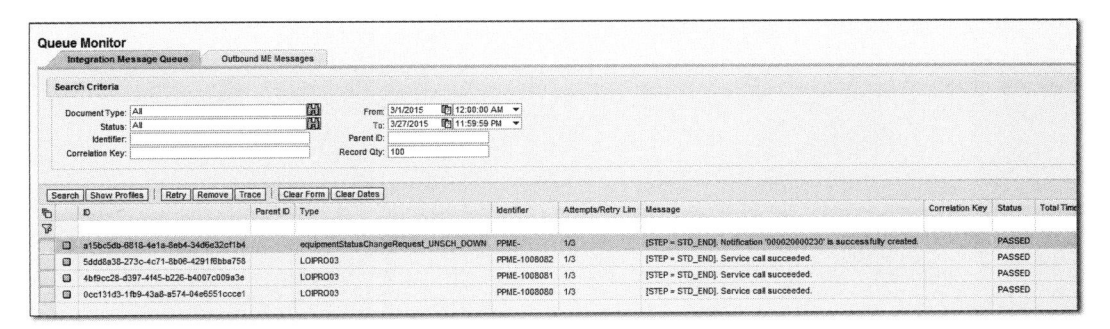

Figure 1.14 SAPMEINT Queue Monitor

The ID displayed for each message in the monitor is a unique identifier generated by the SAPMEINT workflow when the message is queued in SAPMEINT. PARENT-ID is only available for messages generated by a split or correlation workflow—that is, by another message. TYPE refers to the message type as specified in the workflow configuration, and the ATTEMPTS/RETRY LIM refers to the number of retries completed versus the total retry limit as specified in the workflow. You can see the success message or an error message in the MESSAGE column depending on the STATUS column, which specifies the current status of the message. The STATUS value can be QUEUED, PASSED, FAILED, RETRY, SPLIT_DONE, IN_CORRELATION, or CORRELATED depending on the workflow type and message processing status in SAPMEINT. You can also see the total time for the processing of the message and click on its value to analyze the time taken for each step of the workflow, as shown in Figure 1.15.

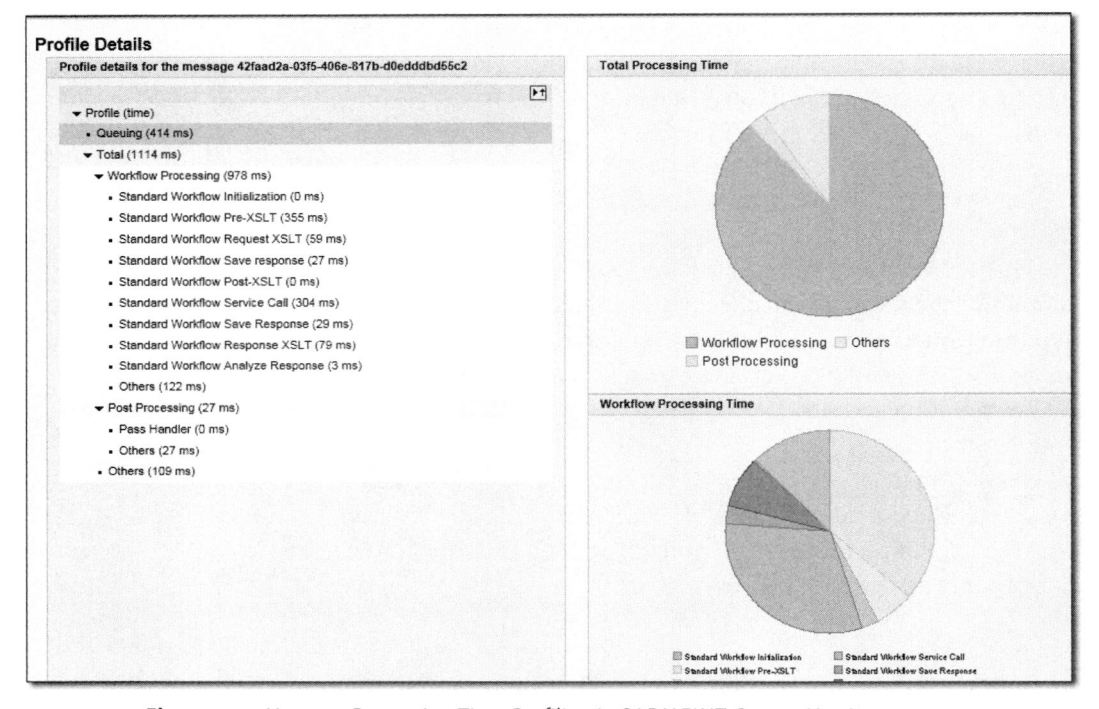

Figure 1.15 Message Processing Time Profiling in SAPMEINT Queue Monitor

There are two Message Queue tabs: INTEGRATION MESSAGE QUEUE and OUTBOUND ME MESSAGES. In INTEGRATION MESSAGE QUEUE, you can see all the messages that are processed by the SAPMEINT workflows flowing in both directions. In OUTBOUND ME MESSAGES, you can see the messages generated by SAP ME before they move to the SAPMEINT integration queue.

When you select a message from the Queue Monitor, you can click on the TRACE button to see the input and output XML documents for the workflow—that is, the inbound IDoc or SAP ME message and the transformed BAPI request and ME interface message—as well as the response received after the interface call, as shown in Figure 1.16. It is useful to view the error message in case of any error. You can also manually trigger the workflow by retrying a message, in case of error; to do so, select it and click on the RETRY button.

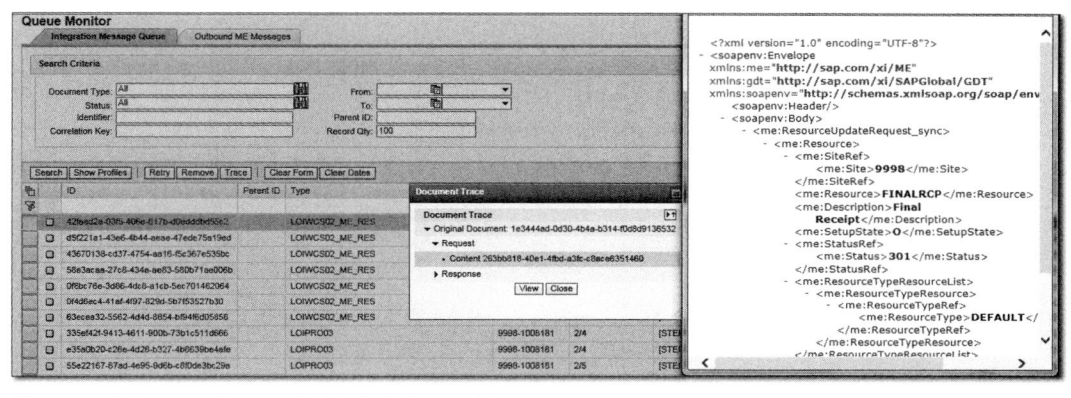

Figure 1.16 Message Trace in SAPMENT Queue Monitor

The SHOW PROFILES button allows you to analyze the performance profile of the message processing for each of the workflow steps for multiple messages. The profiling is enabled for the message processing only if the `SAPMEINT_IS_PROFIL-ING_ENABLED` parameter is set to `true` in the Global Configuration. Profile analysis makes it easier to understand which step of the message processing is taking a longer time across multiple messages.

> **Note**
>
> You can enable profiles for specific steps of the workflow by specifying the step ID. Please note that enabling profiling will slow down the processing of the SAPMEINT workflow. As such, we only recommended enabling profiling for specific steps and for short times, and only for the purpose of analysis.

1.2.2 Transaction Manager

The Transaction Manager in SAP MII is used to monitor the execution status of BLS transactions. The BLS transactions are used in the lifecycle methods of the SAPMEINT workflows. You can monitor the transaction path, its execution status, transaction ID, time, or run and the user who has executed it from the SAP MII menu SYSTEM MANAGEMENT • TRANSACTION MANAGER, and you can also filter

1 | Configuring and Monitoring SAPMEINT

by any of those parameters. Select a transaction to view the transaction log and output, as shown in Figure 1.17.

> **Note**
>
> You only can view the transaction execution status for all BLS transactions in Transaction Manager if the PERSIST TRANSACTION option is set to ALWAYS in the scheduler configuration of the SAPMEINT schedulers. If you specify something else, such as ONERROR, then you can only view the transactions that encountered errors during processing. Unless the transactions are persisted, the transaction log is not maintained in SAP MII for that transaction.

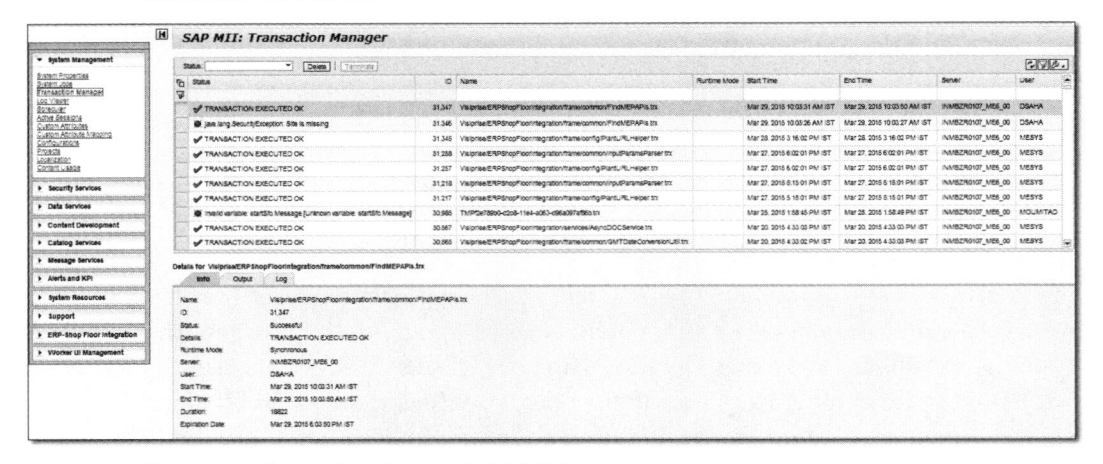

Figure 1.17 Transaction Manager in SAP MII

1.2.3 Log Viewer

SAP MII logs are system logging information in the SAP NetWeaver log or default trace, which you can view to see all the logs in the server. You can access the SAP NetWeaver Log Viewer from the SAP MII menu SYSTEM MANAGEMENT • LOG VIEWER. If required, filtering by time range or specific terms to see specific log entries. You can view both SAPMEINT and SAP ME application and security logs here.

1.2.4 Configuration Diagnostics Tool

Using the Configuration Diagnostics Tool available under the MONITORING menu in SAPMEINT, you can verify the configurations in SAPMEINT for both system-wide and specific plants defined in SAP ME. Once you select the SYSTEM LEVEL or specific plant code from the left navigation pane in the tool, you can see configuration status on the right side. Using this tool, you can quickly check SAPMEINT configurations and navigate to any individual configuration you need to change from here.

> **Note**
>
> Refer to the following SAP OSS Notes for performance optimization of SAPMEINT:
> - 2000811 — Support for Multiple Queues in SAPMEINT
> - 2003366 — Setting up correlation workflow for `yieldConfirmation` with components
> - 1855705 — Setting up parallel processing for SAPMEINT workflows in SAP ME 6.0

1.3 Summary

In this chapter, you learned about the SAPMEINT configurations in SAP MII for SAP ERP to SAP ME integration and about the global configurations, supported plant configurations, and SAP MII–specific configurations, such as message listener and processing rule, all of which are created by executing the SAPMEINT CTC Wizard.

We also covered workflow configurations in SAPMEINT and how to enhance them by custom development using SAP MII or Java and the different methods of monitoring the message processing in SAP MII.

In the next chapter, we will explore the various configurations you need to set up in SAP ME for the application and system before you can send any data from SAP ERP to SAP ME and start working with that data.

This chapter provides the basic system configurations to start getting your SAP ME system ready. The basic system configurations must be completed before defining the shop floor master data and using the manufacturing execution management application.

2   Configuring SAP ME

In the last chapter, you learned how the integration between SAP ERP and SAP ME works. You learned how to use the SAPMEINT component, which SAP MII uses to exchange master and transactional data bi-directionally. Building on that information, in this chapter we will explore the basic configurations required to start using SAP ME.

Along with SAP MII, the SAP ME component is deployed and runs on the SAP NetWeaver AS and provides data management, execution control, and reporting functionality. Before you can download the master and transactional data from SAP ERP to SAP ME, you need to set up a few configurations in SAP ME to make it ready to receive the data from SAP ERP. In this chapter, we will cover user and site configurations, SAP ME role assignment, certification maintenance, system configuration management, activity codes, ODS rule maintenance, and process configuration maintenance, including next number maintenance and reason code maintenance.

2.1   Site and User Configurations

The first configurations you should perform after installing SAP ME will set up sites and users. These are basic and mandatory configurations that will make the system ready and able to receive messages from SAP ERP. In this section you will learn how to create a site in SAP ME and the configurations related to user management.

2.1.1 SAP ME Site Creation

Sites in SAP ME are created based on plant codes in SAP ERP or locally in SAP ME only. SAP ME usually is deployed for each plant site, but each site sometimes may have multiple plant codes, or the same SAP ME instance sometimes may be used for multiple sites or plants. You can define one or more sites in SAP ME as required. You must create a site in SAP ME with the same plant code as defined in SAP ERP before data can be transferred from SAP ERP to SAP ME.

During installation, SAP ME creates two default users: SITE_ADMIN and MESYS. To configure a site in SAP ME, log in to SAP ME as SITE_ADMIN by using the URL *http://<host>:<port>/manufacturing*. Open the Site Maintenance activity from the left navigation pane.

> **Note**
> The menu options in SAP ME displayed on the left navigation pane are called *activities*. You can configure new activities and provide access to existing activities for specific users or user group. You will learn about activity configurations in Section 2.2.1 in this chapter.

The system creates a global site * automatically during installation. When you log in as SITE_ADMIN, by default the * site is selected, as you can see in the upper-right pane for the site selection.

> **Note**
> You also need to execute the following CTC Wizards as part of the installation to set up the basic configurations for SAP ME before you start using the system:
> - SAP ME Database Setup for Installation
> - SAP ME NetWeaver Engine Configuration
> - SAP ME Configuration for Installation
>
> These configurations create the basic SAP NetWeaver configurations and the global site (denoted as *) in SAP ME.

To create a new site, specify the site code and the site type, as shown in Figure 2.1, and click on SAVE. There are two site types available in SAP ME:

- **Production**
  Where you will carry out production activities.

▶ **Transfer**
Where you can export product-related information and from where users at one or more destination sites can import information. A transfer site is a template for a site you can maintain to export and import product and configuration data from one production site to another.

When specifying the site type, select SITE IS LOCAL if the site is maintained in the same database as the current SAP ME instance; deselect it if the site information is maintained in a remote database or SAP ME instance. For a remote site, the COLLABORATION configuration tab is required to specify the SAP ME server details for where the information for the site will be transferred. Usually sites in SAP ME are created as local sites, unless you need to setup a remote site for site-to-site transfer.

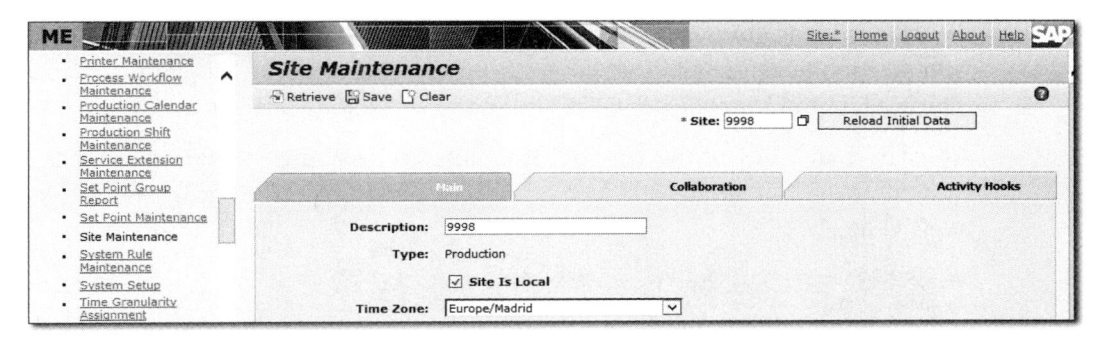

Figure 2.1 Site Maintenance in SAP ME

> **Note**
>
> In SAP ME, you can select key values in any activity using the lookup. Click on RETRIEVE to display details, or specify the key value (identifier) and its details below the retrieve button and click on SAVE to create or update the data in any activity.

When you create a new site, you need to click on RELOAD INITIAL DATA to initialize the data for the site. This is also required if you have performed any customization for the site at any time using the SAP ME SDK, which you will learn about in Chapter 17.

The next step in site creation is configuring the activity hooks, which are the activities you configure for different events defined at the site level.

Activities are logic or user interface component units in SAP ME that perform specific tasks. You'll learn more about SAP ME activities in Section 2.2.1.

Hook points are predefined events in SAP ME that can trigger certain activities as background logic execution when they occur. There are hook points available in the following configurations in SAP ME:

- Site maintenance
- Operation maintenance
- Routing maintenance
- Resource maintenance
- NC code maintenance

Activity hooks are custom or standard SAP ME activities that can be assigned to a hook point, and there are typically pre and post activity hooks that determine whether the hook activity will be executed before or after the triggering event. The hook points that you set up in SITE MAINTENANCE are specific for that site.

You can change any of the activities if required to customize the behavior of the system on specific events. Table 2.1 provides a list of activity hooks available at the site level.

Hook Point	Triggering Point
POST_ORDER_RELEASE	After the system releases a shop order to the shop floor through the Shop Order Release activity.
POST_PROD_CHANGE	After the user clicks SAVE in CHANGE PRODUCTION; hook point passes old and new values for the material, routing, BOM, or shop order to the activity
PRE_MERGE	After the user clicks MERGE in SFC MERGE, before the system merges SFCs
POST_MERGE	After the user clicks MERGE in SFC MERGE, after the system merges SFCs
POST_SERIALIZE	After the user clicks OK in SERIALIZE, after the SFC is serialized
POST_SPLIT	After the user clicks OK in SFC SPLIT, after the SFC is split
PRE_RMA_SFC_RECEIPT	After the user clicks DONE in RMA SFC RECEIPT, before the system adds the SFCs to the RMA shop order

Table 2.1 Hook Points for Site Maintenance

Hook Point	Triggering Point
PRE_SERIALIZE	After the user clicks OK in SERIALIZE, before the SFC is serialized
PRE_SPLIT	After the user clicks OK in SFC SPLIT, before the SFC is split
POST_RMA_SFC_RECEIPT	After a user clicks DONE in RMA SFC RECEIPT, after the system adds the SFCs to the RMA shop order
POST_CONTAINER_SAVE	After the user clicks SAVE or CLOSE CONTAINER in PACK/UNPACK
POST_CONTAINER_CLOSE	After the user clicks CLOSE CONTAINER in PACK/UNPACK
PRE_PACKING_SFC	After the user clicks ADD in PACK/UNPACK, before the system adds the SFC to the container
PACKING_VALIDATION	After the user clicks ADD in PACK/UNPACK, before the system adds the SFC to the container
REOPEN_CONTAINER	After the user clicks UNPACK in PACK/UNPACK
CALC_DIMENSIONS	After the user clicks CLOSE CONTAINER in PACK/UNPACK
ADD_COMPONENT	After the user clicks ADD on the ADD COMPONENT window of AS-BUILT CONFIGURATION
REMOVE_COMPONENT	After the user clicks SCRAP, RETURN, or SEND TO ROUTING on the REMOVE COMPONENT window of AS-BUILT CONFIGURATION
POST_ORDER_CLOSE	After the system closes a shop order and the status of the shop order changes to DONE
POST_PL_REMOVE	After an SFC is removed from a process lot in the Process Lot activity (PR560)
POST_PL_ADD	After an SFC is added to a process lot in the Process Lot activity
POST_INV_RECEIPT	After an Inventory ID is received and added to the floor stock
PARSE_COMPONENT	On assembly point to specify component identifier
PARSE_SLOT_COMPONENT	On resource slot configuration to specify slot identifier

Table 2.1 Hook Points for Site Maintenance (Cont.)

Each hook point has a sequence number and activity to trigger as shown in Figure 2.2. If multiple activities need to be triggered for the same hook point, we recommend using different sequential numbers for each activity so that activities are executed in a specific sequence, not randomly.

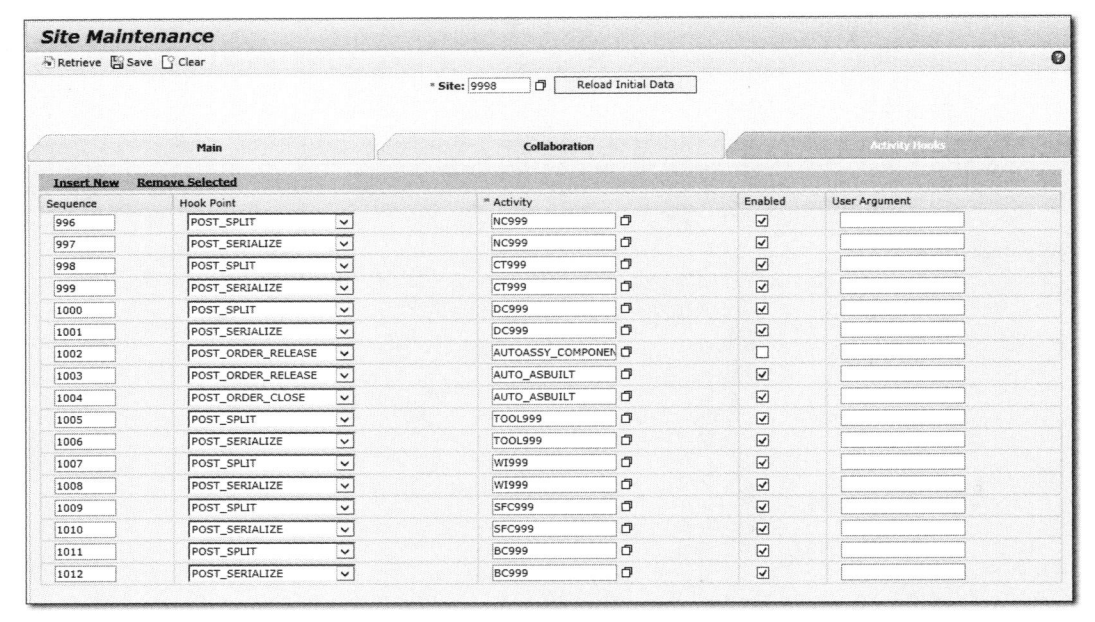

Figure 2.2 Activity Hook Configuration for Site

You can change the site once it's available by clicking on the SITE link on the top-right corner of the toolbar pane, which displays the list of sites you are assigned to and from which you can select any one site to become the current site for the user. The selected site will be used for the all subsequent activities for the user. You need to assign the user to the site so that they may access and execute any activity for the site as explained in the next section.

> **Note**
>
> Once the site is created in SAP ME manually, you also need to create the relevant configurations for the site in SAPMEINT by executing the MEINT Standard Interfaces CTC wizard, as explained in Chapter 1.

2.1.2 User Administration and SAP ME Role Assignment

User management for SAP ME is performed within the SAP User Management Engine (UME), available as part of the SAP NetWeaver AS on which SAP ME is installed. All users who will access SAP ME should be first configured in SAP UME. You can access SAP UME via *http://<host>:<port>/useradmin*, where *host* and *port* are the hostname and the port of the SAP NetWeaver server on which SAP ME is installed.

Table 2.2 identifies SAP UME roles available in SAP ME and the corresponding users to which they need to be assigned.

SAP UME Role Name	Description
Role_SAPMEINT	User role to access the SAP ME ERP Integration (MEINT) portal navigation, SAPMEINT, and SAPMEWIP data servers. All users configuring SAPMEINT should have this role assigned.
SAP_ME_ADMINISTRATOR	Administrator role for SAP ME configurations. All users performing system configuration in SAP ME should have this role assigned.
SAP_ME_INTEGRATOR	User role to access the PAPI Web Services and site-to-site data transfer.
SAP_ME_READONLY	Read-only user role to view all data and configurations in SAP ME
SAP_ME_USER	User role for all end users accessing SAP ME through the web interface.

Table 2.2 SAP UME Roles for SAP ME

There are a few standard users available in SAP ME, such as SITE_ADMIN, which is used to manage the SAP ME sites, as explained earlier. MESYS is a default user created during installation, used for system-to-system communication between SAP-MEINT and SAP ME Core. ADSUser is a standard user in SAP NetWeaver used for printing via Adobe Document Services from SAP ME.

There are two SAP UME permission actions available that need to be assigned to specific user roles in order to manage and execute routing scripts (explained further in Chapter 4) in SAP ME: ME.Service.ManageScript and ME.Service.ExecuteScript.

You can also specify a default site for all users of SAP ME in SAP UME while configuring users. This will ensure that a user will be automatically logged in to a specified default site when logging in to SAP ME. To do so, click on the CONFIGURATIONS button in SAP UME Identity Management. Open the USER ADMINISTRATOR UI configuration tab, and click on MODIFY CONFIGURATIONS. In the ADMINISTRATOR-MANAGED CUSTOM ATTRIBUTES field under CUSTOM ATTRIBUTES OF THE USER PROFILE, specify "SAPME:DEFAULT SITE" (Figure 2.3). Save the configuration.

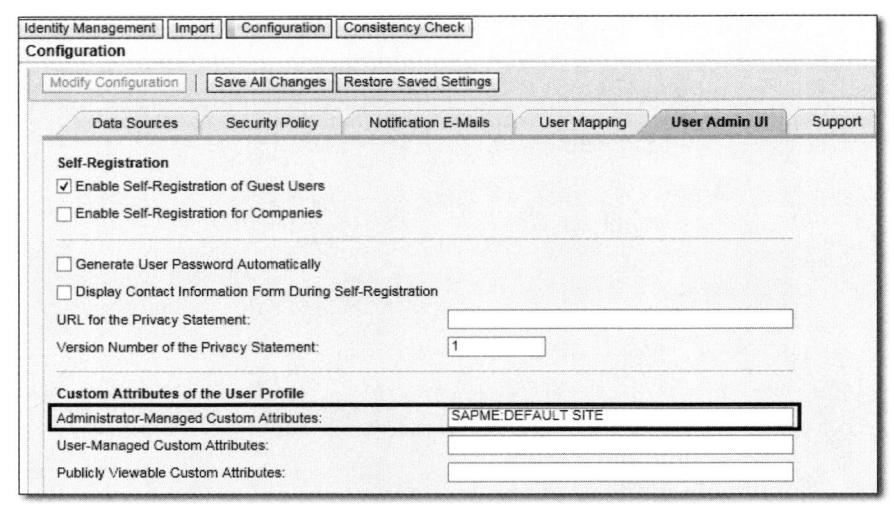

Figure 2.3 Custom Attribute Configuration in SAP UME Configuration

Now you can see the default site in the CUSTOMIZED INFORMATION tab in IDENTITY MANAGEMENT when creating or configuring any user, as shown in Figure 2.4.

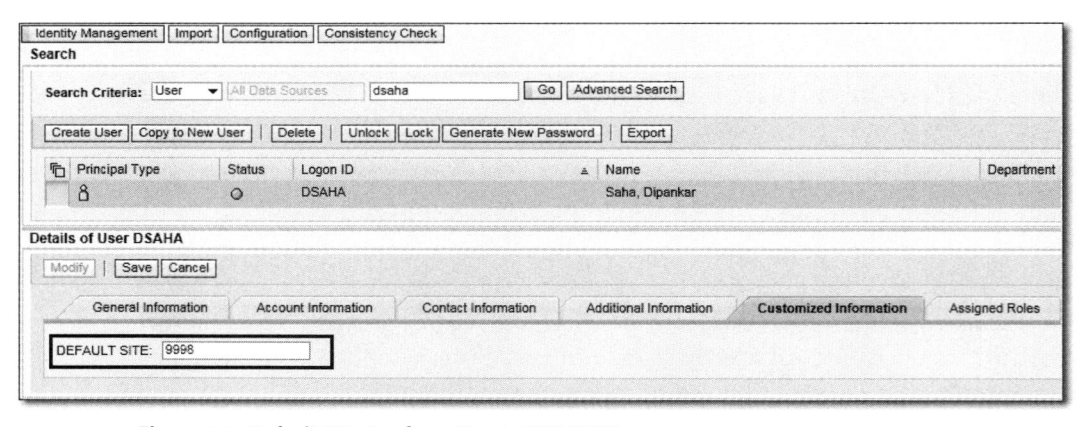

Figure 2.4 Default Site Configuration in SAP UME

2.1.3 User Group Maintenance

User groups are created in SAP ME to group users for different functionality access. To configure a user group in SAP ME, log in to SAP ME as an administrator, and open the User Group Maintenance activity from the left navigation pane.

You can create a new user group here by specifying the group name in the USER GROUP field and clicking on SAVE or by selecting an existing group from the lookup and clicking on RETRIEVE to change or display the group, as shown in Figure 2.5.

Figure 2.5 User Group Maintenance in SAP ME

You can specify a description for the group and select a default POD (an optional task) for the user group. Then, you can assign users to the group from the USERS configuration tab: Select available users from the list on the left to assign them as part of the list on the right.

You can also select the activities the user group can access from the PERMISSIONS configuration tab and can specify custom data field values if available. You will learn about custom data in the next chapter.

2.1.4 User Maintenance

You can manage SAP ME users, including assigning users to sites, from the User Maintenance activity which you can access from the SAP ME activity list on the left navigation pane. Before you can use User Maintenance in SAP ME for a user, the user must be created and available in SAP UME. Then, you can open the User Maintenance activity in SAP ME, select the user from the lookup, and click on RETRIEVE to display the user details, as shown in Figure 2.6.

If you save the user configuration, the user will be assigned to the currently selected site. This activity is mandatory to assign a user to a site in SAP ME. On the User Maintenance page, you can also specify the user groups to which the user will be assigned, as well as the work centers under the WORK CENTERS tab. The work center specified in User Maintenance will be available in the selection list when the user opens a POD.

2 | Configuring SAP ME

Figure 2.6 User Maintenance in SAP ME

> **Note**
>
> PODs are configurable user interfaces that serve as dashboards for production operators to perform all their activities in SAP ME (see Chapter 10 for more details).

You can also enter settings on the following tabs:

- On the LABOR TRACKING configuration tab, you can assign a user to specific shifts and cost centers for specific date ranges.
- On the SUPERVISOR configuration tab, you can specify a supervisor's cost centers for a user for specific date ranges.
- On the LABOR RULES configuration tab, you can specify the rules for clocking labor time for a user, as explained in Table 2.3.

Labor Rule	Description
AUTOMATIC CLOCK OUT AT SHIFT END	If selected as true, the system automatically clocks the user out at the end of the shift and signs off the timesheet.
ALLOW CLOCK IN ON NONPRODUCTION DAY	If selected as true, the user will be allowed to clock in on a nonproduction day, as specified in the user shift maintenance for the user. Note that a supervisor can clock in a user on any day regardless.
CLOCK IN/OUT RANGE CONTROL	Controls when the user can clock in or out (i.e., within a specific interval for clock in/out, within a shift only, or anytime).
CLOCK IN CONTROL	Controls how the clock in will start (i.e., automatically at logon, or forcefully before logon or anytime).

Table 2.3 Labor Rules Configuration for Users

76

You can also maintain some system rule overrides for users, which you will learn about in Section 2.2.7 in this chapter. Custom data is explained in Chapter 3.

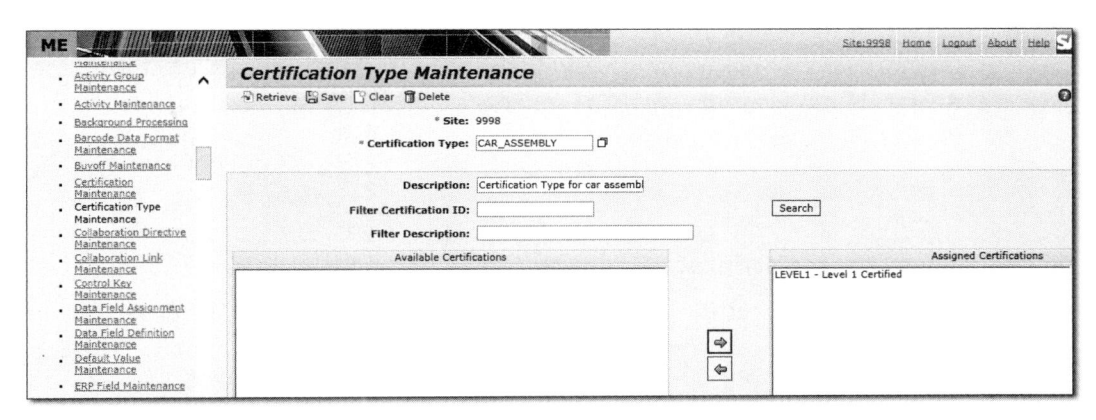

2.1.5 Certification Type Maintenance

To work on certain operations, materials, or resources, an operator may need some certifications to ensure he or she has the right skills to work on the task at hand. SAP ME provides features to manage certifications and assign them to users based on their actual certifications held, to ensure that only operators with required certifications can actually execute certain operations or resources. You can specify the certification(s) required to execute an operation, and a user who does not have that specific certification will not be able to execute it.

In the Certification Type Maintenance activity, you can define types of certifications in order to group certifications together, as shown in Figure 2.7. You can specify a new certification type and save or retrieve an existing certification type from the lookup and then assign different certifications to it. The FILTER CERTIFICATION ID and FILTER DESCRIPTION fields (Figure 2.7) are available to search for certifications from a large list of certifications.

Figure 2.7 Certification Type Maintenance

2.1.6 Certification Maintenance

You can specify a new certificate name and save or retrieve an existing certificate from the Certification Maintenance activity lookup, as shown in Figure 2.8.

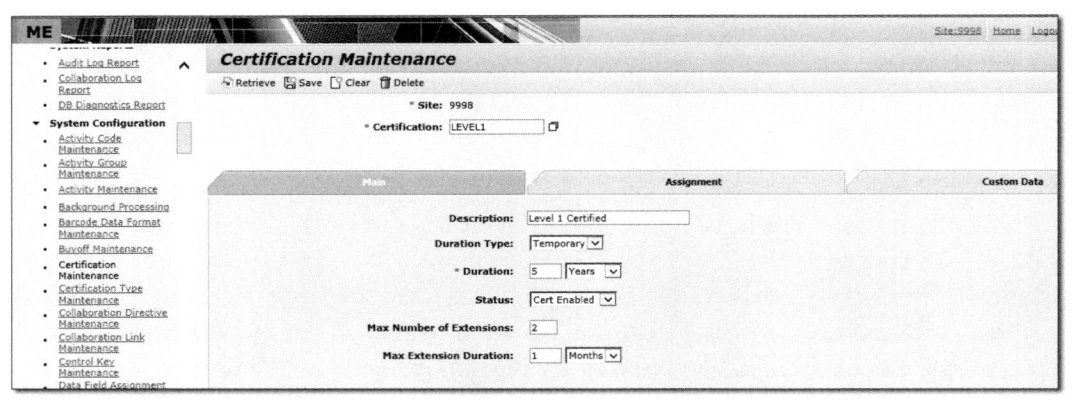

Figure 2.8 Certification Maintenance

You can specify the DURATION TYPE as TEMPORARY or PERMANENT; for temporary, you need to specify a duration for which the certification will remain valid. You can also specify whether certification extension is allowed, for how many times, and for what duration. For permanent duration, the certification will never expire. You can also specify the current status of the certificate as ENABLED, HOLD, or OBSOLETE.

From the ASSIGNMENT configuration tab, you can assign user groups to the certificate. If you want to assign an individual user to a certificate, you need to use the *User Certificate Assignment Maintenance* activity, as explained in the next section.

2.1.7 User Certificate Assignment Maintenance

You can assign a certificate to an individual user via the User Certificate Assignment Maintenance activity to enable the user to execute operations which requires that specific certification. Select an existing user already configured in SAP ME from the lookup, and retrieve that user's data, as shown in Figure 2.9. To add a new certificate for the user, click on INSERT NEW, search for the required certification, and click on APPLY from the lookup dialog to add it. While adding the certificate for the user, you can specify the validity period for the certification for that user and can specify the status of the certification for the user as ENABLED, HOLD, or REVOKED.

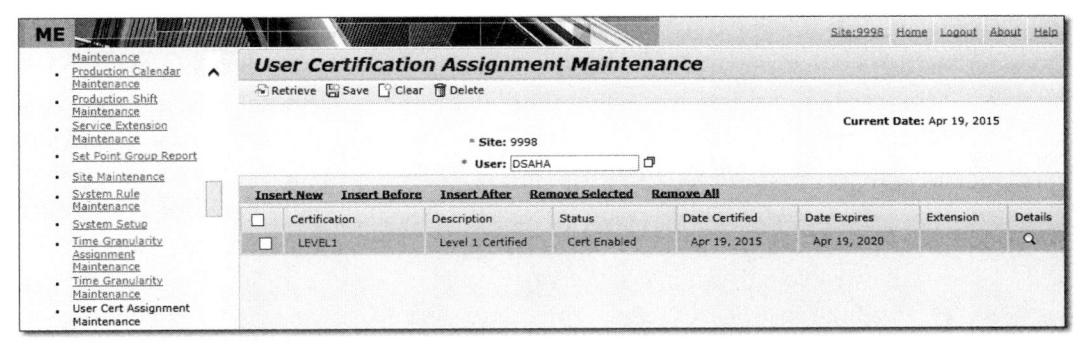

Figure 2.9 User Certificate Assignment Maintenance

2.1.8 User Certifications Report

You can use the User Certification Report to view the users which are assigned to one or any certificate and the validity status of the certificate as shown in Figure 2.10. You can view the status of the certification and the expiration date of the certification for each user.

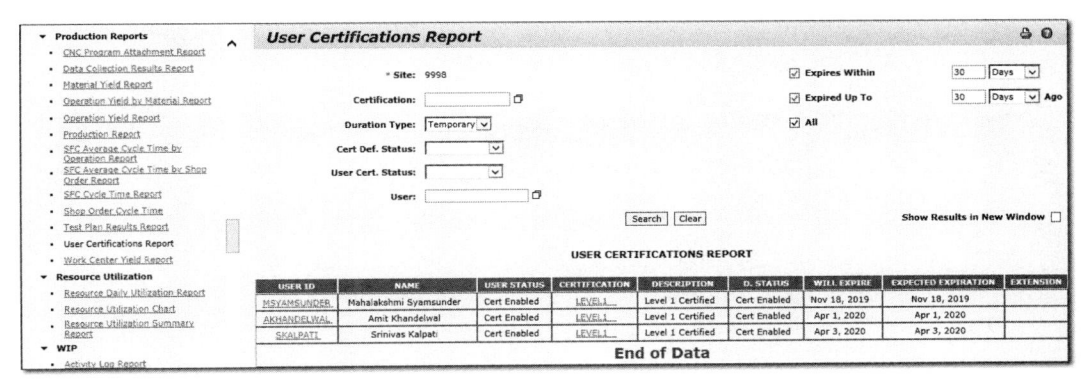

Figure 2.10 User Certification Report

2.2 System Configuration Management

Once you set up the site and user configuration in SAP ME, you may need to configure some additional system features such as activities, background jobs, collaboration directives, system and ODS rules, and document and printer maintenance as explained in the following sections.

2.2.1 Activity Maintenance

Activities are system functionalities in SAP ME that are used to provide UI components, visual components within dashboards, or background logic components. All the standard SAP ME functionalities, including the transactional UIs and reports, are available as SAP ME activities. SAP ME activities can be in the form of either background logic or UIs. Background logic is usually developed using Java classes or Enterprise Java Beans (EJBs) implementing a specific interface. UIs are usually developed using Java Server Pages (JSP) or Light Speed Faces (LSF; an extension of Java Server Faces). You can create an SAP ME activity as a hook-point activity or as an activity that is visible in the Activity Manager. Hook-point activities can be automatically triggered by the system during certain events called *hook-points*, as explained in Section 2.1.1, whereas activities visible in the activity manager are invoked by the user from the SAP ME activity navigation.

Open Activity Maintenance, specify an activity name or select one from the lookup, and click on RETRIEVE to view an existing activity, as shown in Figure 2.11. You can find all the SAP ME activities already configured. If you want to create a new activity, first deploy the program for the activity, e.g. Java class, in the SAP ME server. In the activity configuration, specify the activity name, description, and the class/program and the type of the activity.

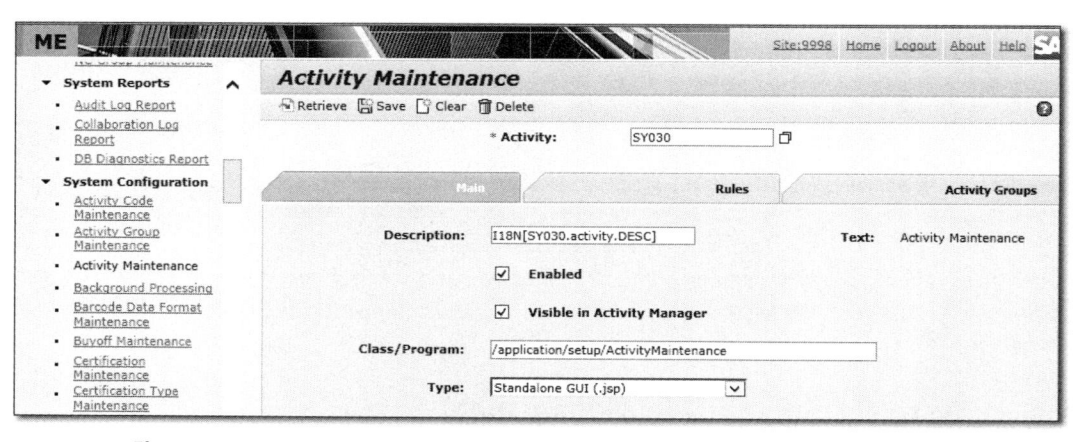

Figure 2.11 Activity Maintenance

You can create an SAP ME activity using the SAP ME SDK (see Chapter 17). The different types of SAP ME activities are explained in Table 2.4. Depending on the activity type, the class/program will change, which refers to a JSP or Java class. You need to check the ENABLE checkbox to enable the activity to be used in SAP ME. If the activity is of type JSP or URL, which should be displayed as a menu link in the SAP ME activity manager, you need to check the VISIBLE IN ACTIVITY MANAGER checkbox. If the activity is not configured in Activity Maintenance, it is not accessible by users. All activities are global. You cannot define an activity that is specific for a site only.

Activity Type	Description
EJB	Enterprise Java bean implementing Hookable Interface, which has an `execute()` method, which is executed for a hook point. This is for background processing only.
Java Class	Java class implementing Hookable Interface which has an `execute()` method, which is executed for a hook point. This is for background processing only.
Standalone GUI (JSP)	Any JSP web user interface that is visible in the activity manager for the UIs available in SAP ME.
Button/Plug-in GUI (JSP)	A JSP web UI opened when a button is clicked on the dashboard. The activity name is linked with the button click event in the POD.
Native Executable	Activity to execute native EXE, BAT, or a script file in the OS, as a background task.
Collaboration Data Acquisition Plug-In	A Java class that acquires data in addition to the standard data that a triggering action provides. Used for collaboration activities, such as sending outbound messages from SAP ME to SAP ERP using the collaboration directives.
Collaboration Format Plug-In	A Java class that formats the standard and additional data for the collaboration directive used for outbound messages from SAP ME.
Collaboration Transport Plug-In	A Java class that sends the data using a specific transport mechanism for the outbound messages using the collaboration directives.
Collaboration Callback Plug-In	A Java class used to parse and process the response from a remote system, triggered after the transport plug-in, if specified using the collaboration directives.
Process Workflow Manual Activity	Activities performed by the user in the message board.

Table 2.4 Activity Types

Activity Type	Description
Process Workflow Automatic Activity	Activities processed by the system in the message board.
Service	A Java class which executes a SAP ME PAPI service or a service extension.
WPMF Plug-In	A Java class used as the POD plugin.
POD Selection	An activity used for POD selection area plug-in.
External URL	Activities to open an external web page when the user clicks a button in the POD.
Mobile View	Activities used to launch a mobile application from mobile POD on button click.

Table 2.4 Activity Types (Cont.)

You can define activity rules for activities on the RULES configuration tab to control the behavior of the activities. There are certain specific activity rules available in SAP ME for each activity which you can specify along with some parameters to enable a rule for an activity from the RULES configuration tab. You can find the rules for specific activities all through the book while explaining the activity. You can assign an activity to one or more activity groups from the ACTIVITY GROUPS configuration tab.

2.2.2 Activity Group Maintenance

You can define activity groups for grouping activities or other activity groups, as shown in Figure 2.12. There are multiple activity groups already defined in SAP ME, e.g. Product Configuration, Product Genealogy, Quality Management, Labor Tracking, etc., through which SAP ME activities are grouped in the standard navigation.

If you want to add activity subgroups under an activity group, assign them to the ASSIGNED ACTIVITY GROUPS list box on the right side. You can also assign activities under the group from the ACTIVITIES configuration tab. Activities are displayed under their corresponding groups in the SAP ME activity manager (navigation) and in the User Maintenance activity, where you can assign the activity group and the activities to the user.

System Configuration Management | 2.2

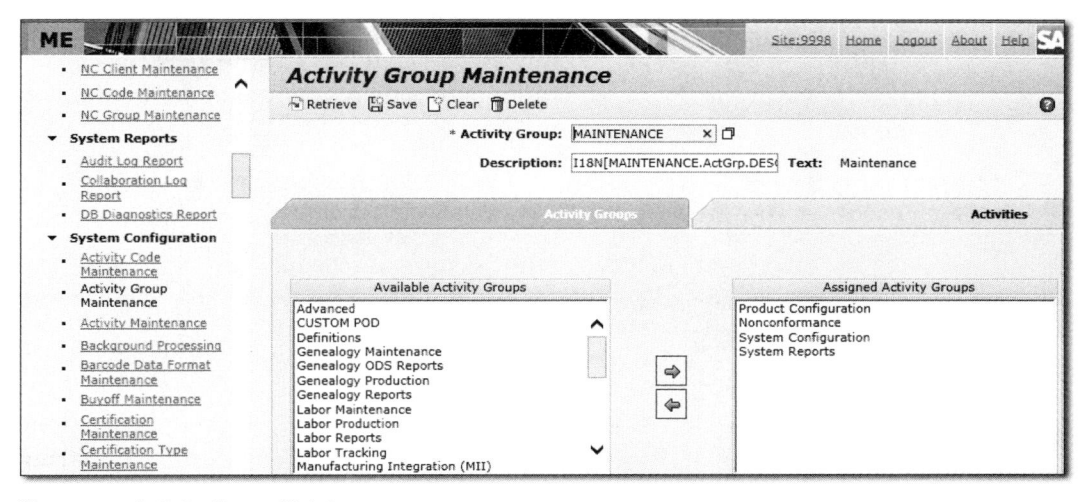

Figure 2.12 Activity Group Maintenance

2.2.3 Activity Code Maintenance

Using Activity Code Maintenance, you can change the name of the activity code for activities used with disposition groups, which are functions used in nonconformance management as explained in Chapter 8, as shown in Figure 2.13.

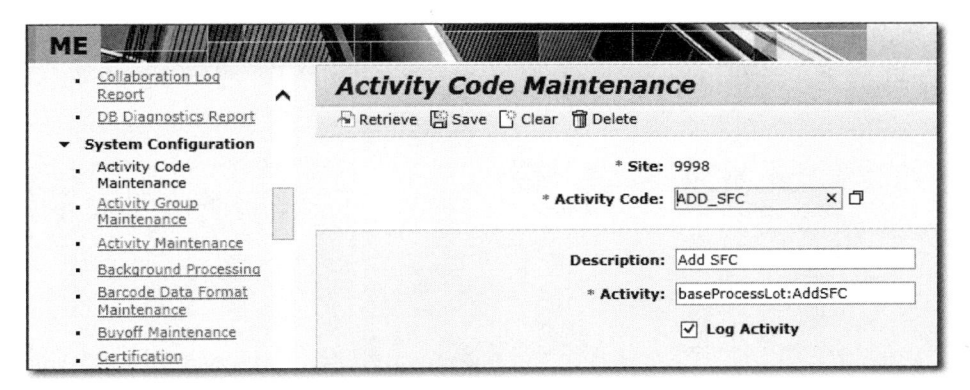

Figure 2.13 Activity Code Maintenance

The standard activity codes used in SAP ME are already defined. You can change the activity code and description, but do not change the activity value, which is an internal name used by SAP ME. Select the LOG ACTIVITY checkbox if you want the activity code to be recorded in the activity log when a user performs the corresponding action e.g. Start SFC. This is useful when you want to view the *Activity Log Report*, which will display the customized activity code names for easy understanding.

2.2.4 Background Processing

Using the Background Processing activity, you can schedule four types of system tasks, as shown in Figure 2.14. You can configure the following types of tasks in BACKGROUND PROCESSING:

- ARCHIVING
  You can configure this task to move the data of completed products from the transactional WIP database to an archive database (ODS), which you can configure in the System Setup activity.

- AUTO CLOSE MESSAGE BY THE SYSTEM
  Automatically changes the status of messages in the message board to CLOSE as defined in MESSAGE TYPE MAINTENANCE.

- AUTO DELETE OLD XSRF TOKENS
  Automatically deletes old tokens that were generated to prevent cross-site request forgery attacks.

- CERTIFICATION EXPIRATION CHECK
  Checks the certification validity and changes the status of the certificates accordingly, if required.

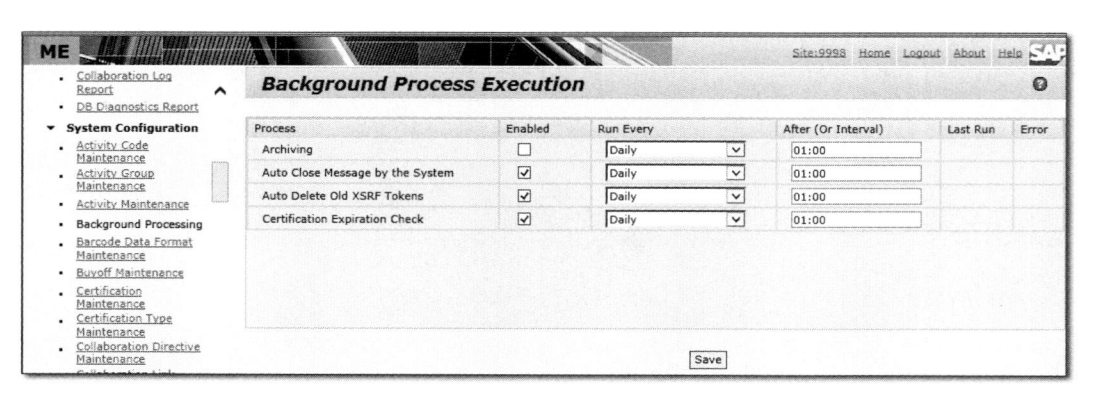

Figure 2.14 Background Processing Configuration

You can enable the tasks you need to execute periodically by checking the corresponding ENABLED checkbox and specifying the periodicity (execute it EVERY *x* MINUTE, HOURLY, DAILY, or WEEKLY) and the time period between the runs. If you select EVERY *x* MINUTE, you need to specify the time interval between the runs in minutes. For other periodicities, you need to specify the time of the execution.

2.2.5 Collaboration Directive Maintenance

Collaboration directives are used to trigger an outbound interface from SAP ME on certain events. You can use the Collaborative Directive Maintenance activity to define the outbound data transfer from SAP ME to external systems such as SAP ERP via SAPMEINT, as shown in Figure 2.15. SAP ME already provides the standard collaboration directives for all the standard outbound messages from SAP ME to transfer to SAP ERP through SAPMEINT, as well as site-to-site for exporting data from one SAP ME site to another.

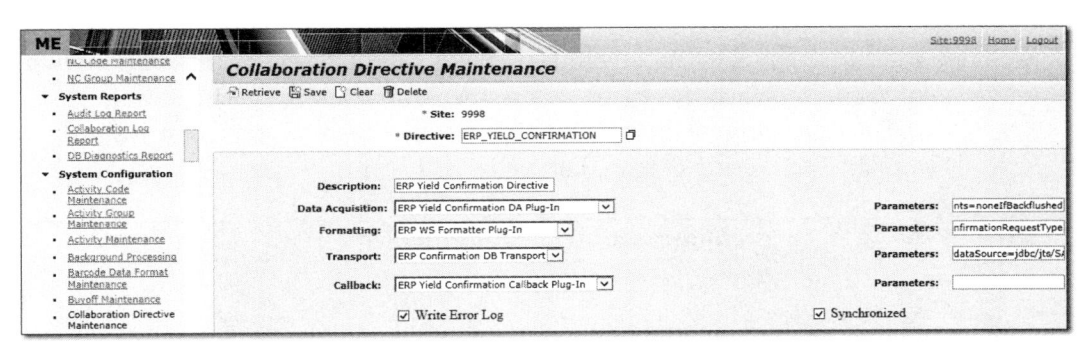

Figure 2.15 Collaborative Directive Maintenance

The DATA ACQUISITION field contains a plug-in that is an activity deployed in SAP ME for gathering required data for the outbound message. The FORMATTING field holds the plug-in activity that formats the data as required by the destination. The TRANSPORT field specifies the transport mechanism, specified as ERP CONFIRMATION DB TRANSPORT for transporting the SAPMEINT outbound messages to the SAPMEINT database or SITE-TO-SITE TRANSPORT for site transfer messages. ERP CONFIRMATION TRANSPORT is also available as a transport option for legacy support, which is no longer used. You can also optionally select a callback plug-in in the CALLBACK field, which will execute after the outbound link is triggered.

Some parameters are specified for each of the preceding options to pass additional data. For transport parameters the SAPMEINT data source is specified as `dataSource=jdbc/jts/SAPMEINTXA` if the WIP and SAPMEINT databases are installed in different databases; otherwise, it is specified as `dataSource=jdbc/jts/SAPMEINT`. If SYNCHRONIZED is checked, then the directive is executed synchronously; else, asynchronously. You can specify WRITE ERROR LOG to write errors in the collaboration log, which you can view using the COLLABORATION LOG REPORT.

2.2.6 Collaboration Link Maintenance

Using Collaborative Link Maintenance, you can link the collaborative directive with a triggering action in SAP ME to send outbound messages. There are different trigger actions available in SAP ME that are executed on specific events, such as yield or scrap confirmations, operation complete, and so on. Using the collaborative directive, the data is read from the triggering event via the *Data Acquisition Plug-In* specified there and sent to the destination as specified in the directive. You can configure the collaboration directive for a trigger action as shown in Figure 2.16 to execute that on that predefined event.

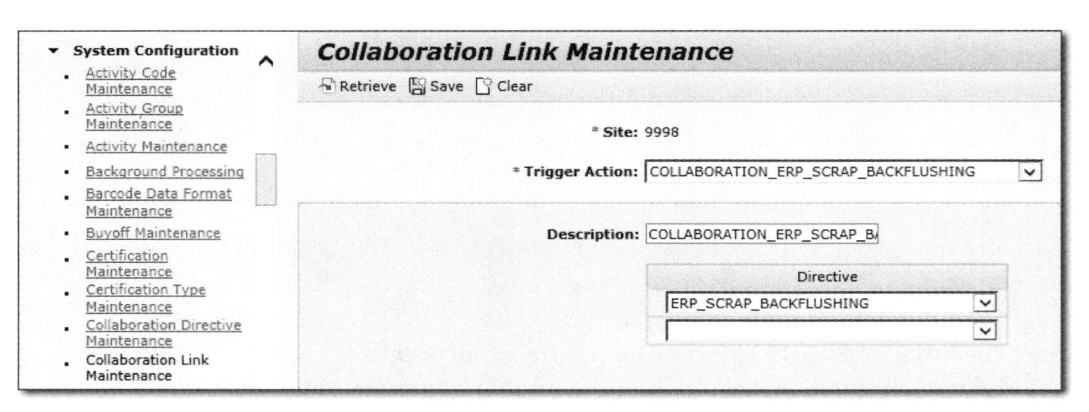

Figure 2.16 Collaborative Link Maintenance

The standard collaborative directives and the links are provided by default to trigger the SAPMEINT interfaces, as listed in Table 2.5.

Link	Trigger Action	Directive
ERP Scrap Backflushing	COLLABORATION_ERP_SCRAP_BACKFLUSHING	ERP_SCRAP_BACKFLUSHING
ERP Scrap Confirmation	COLLABORATION_ERP_SCRAP_CONFIRMATION	ERP_SCRAP_CONFIRMATION
ERP Yield Backflushing	COLLABORATION_ERP_YIELD_BACKFLUSHING	ERP_YIELD_BACKFLUSHING
ERP Yield Confirmation	COLLABORATION_ERP_YIELD_CONFIRMATION	ERP_YIELD_CONFIRMATION
ERP Clear Floor Stock Reservation	COLLABORATION_ERP_INV_CLEAR_RESERVATION	ERP_INV_CLEAR_RESERVATION
ERP Equipment Status Change	COLLABORATION_EQUIPMENT_STATUS_CHANGE	ERP_EQUIPMENT_STATUS_CHANGE
ERP Equipment Usage	COLLABORATION_ERP_EQUIPMENT_USAGE	ERP_EQUIPMENT_USAGE
ERP Shop Order Complete	COLLABORATION_SHOPORDER_COMPLETE	ERP_SO_COMPLETE
ERP Nonconformance Logged	COLLABORATION_NC_LOG	ERP_QUALITY_NOTIFICATION
ERP Storage Location Move	COLLABORATION_STORAGE_LOC_MOVE	ERP_STORAGE_LOC_MOVE
ERP Direct Labor Confirmation	COLLABORATION_ERP_DIRCT_LABOR_CNFRM	ERP_DIRECT_LABOR_CONFIRMATION
ERP Routing Export	COLLABORATION_ERP_ROUTING_EXPORT	ERP_ROUTING_EXPORT

Table 2.5 Standard Collaboration Directive and Links

2.2.7 System Rule Maintenance

Using the System Rule Maintenance activity, you can configure the system behavior by maintaining the rules as shown in Figure 2.17. There are several system rules available for system setup, component traceability, SAP ERP integration, nonconformance management, and so on, which you can specify either at a global level or at a site level—and some at the object level. The object level rule value gets the highest precedence, which if not present, the site level value gets precedence over global rule value. To maintain the system rules at a global level, you need to log in to SAP ME using the global site (*) and specify each rule as True or False as applicable. Then, you can log in to each individual site defined in SAP ME and specify each rule to follow the global rule or an alternative, where applicable. If you want to restrict a rule to be changed at subsequent levels, you should uncheck the Overridable checkbox. If Overridable is checked, you will be able to change a rule at site level or an object level as required; otherwise, the rule set at the global level or site level will be used in the next level. By default, rules are provided a value at a global level, which you can change as required.

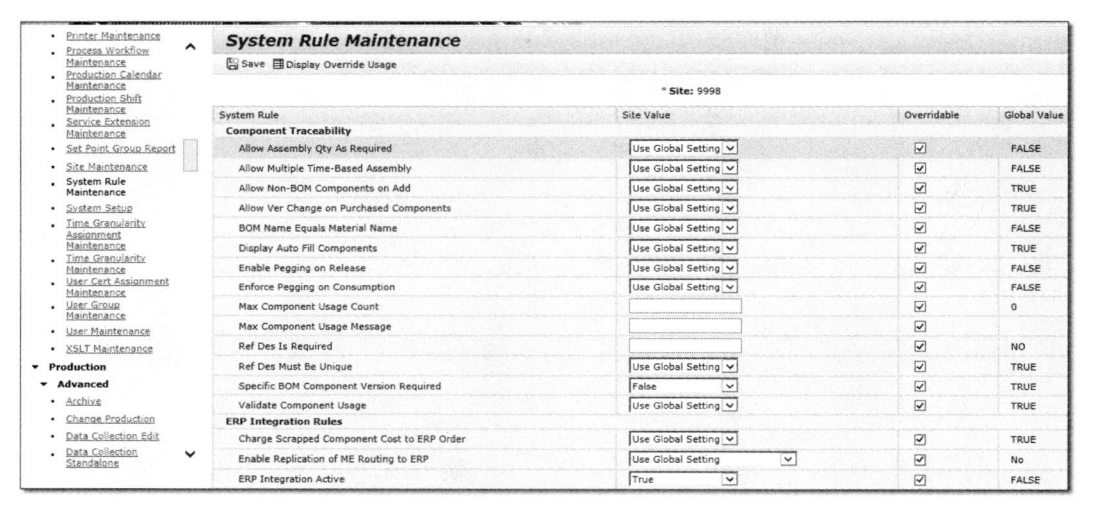

Figure 2.17 System Rule Maintenance

To override a rule at the object level, you need to work with the corresponding object configuration, such as operation maintenance, material maintenance and so on. You can view the rule override details by selecting a rule from the list and clicking on Display Override Usage, which displays the overridden value of the rule if available as shown in Figure 2.18. In the rule override details, *Context Type* specifies at which object level the rule is overridden, such as OperationBO, MaterialBO, and the Content Value specifies the specific object value for which the rule is overridden, such as OperationBO:9998, PAINTING,A, which signifies the rule is modified for operation PAINTING, version A, at site 9998. The rule value specifies the value of the rule setting at that object level.

System Configuration Management | 2.2

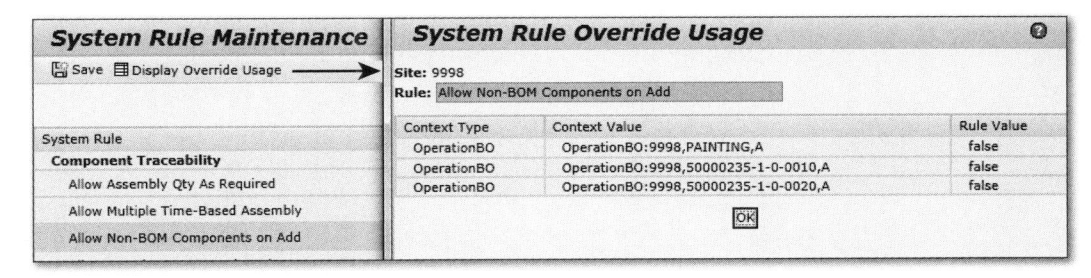

Figure 2.18 System Rule Override Usage

2.2.8 System Setup Maintenance and Audit Log Configuration

Using the *System Setup Maintenance* activity, you can specify various system settings, such as session timeouts for various activities, look and feel settings, and so on. Select PROPERTY from the TYPE dropdown and click on RETRIEVE to display the properties, as shown in Figure 2.19. If required, you can change the values of any properties and click on SAVE. The properties configured here are global in nature and are valid for all sites configured in the same SAP ME server.

Figure 2.19 System Setup Maintenance

You can also maintain the AUDIT LOG configuration as shown in Figure 2.20, to specify which objects in SAP ME will receive audit logging (i.e., change tracking) when any configuration or value is changed. You can specify ALL, which means all

89

change history will be logged, CURRENT, which means only the last change will be logged, or OFF, which means no audit logging will be used.

You can view the audit log report to view the audit log details as shown in Figure 2.21.

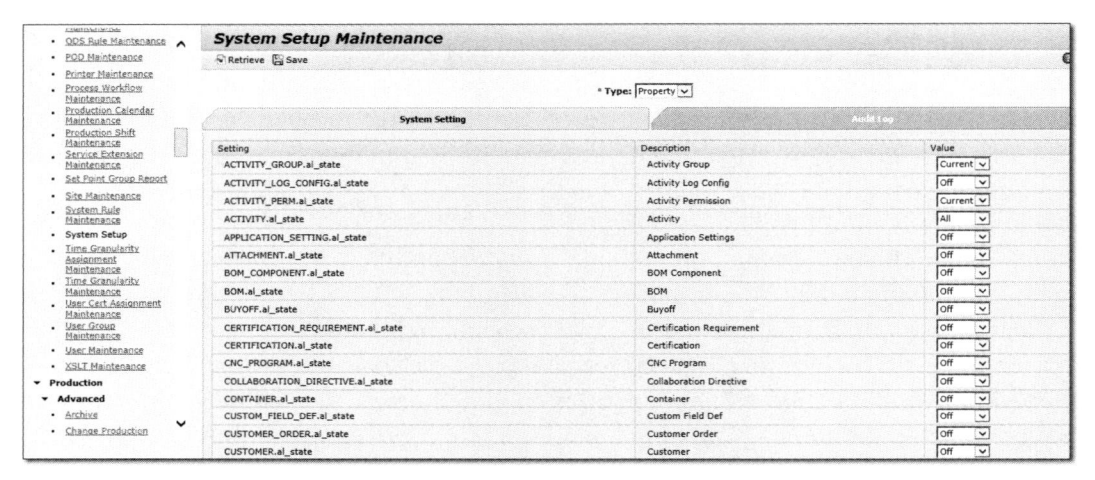

Figure 2.20 Audit Log Configuration

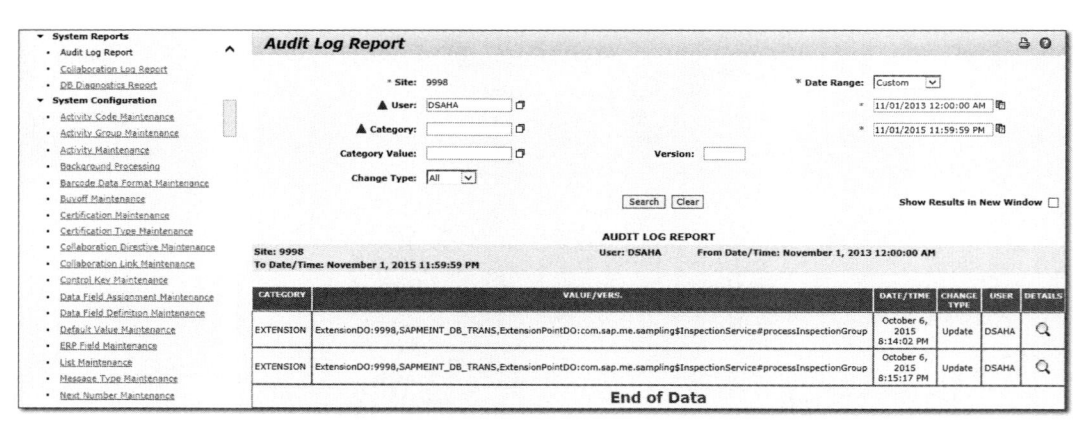

Figure 2.21 Audit Log Report

2.2.9 Document Maintenance

The Document Maintenance activity is used to manage different types of documents in SAP ME, such as product labels, shop orders, or SFC documents for printing purposes, as shown in Figure 2.22. The printed documents are generated dynamically based on the templates maintained here, by standard or custom plug-ins deployed in SAP ME and can be printed either as PDFs or in other specific formats.

On the MAIN configuration tab, specify the document template as an XDP file, which is used for Adobe Document Services (ADS) printing and available in SAP NetWeaver as a PDF document. The template file needs to be stored in the template folder as specified in the system rule *ADS—Document Printing Template Directory* in the *System Rule Maintenance* activity. You need to specify DOCUMENT TYPE to specify the type of document printed as a document, label, or traveler; PRINT BY to specify which document to print; and PRINT METHOD to specify whether to print it automatically at certain hook points or manually.

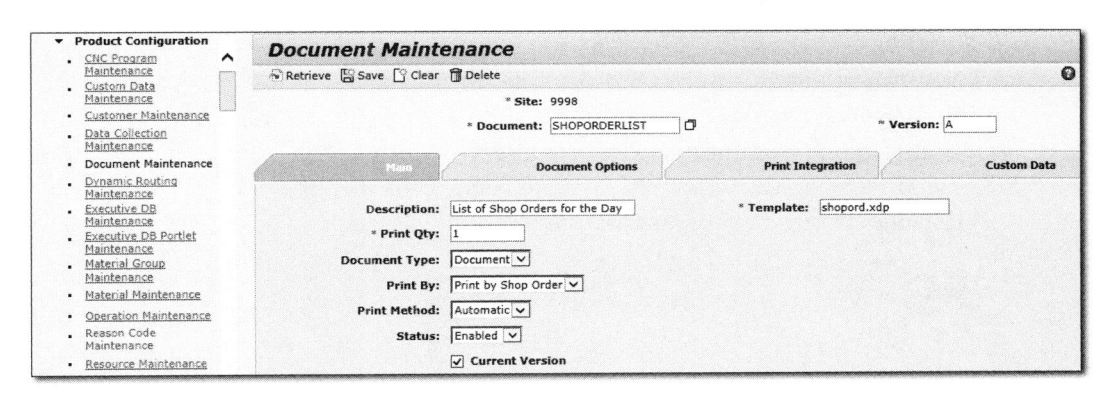

Figure 2.22 Document Maintenance

On the DOCUMENT OPTIONS configuration tab, specify the document information, such as SHOP ORDER HEADER DATA, SHOP ORDER CUSTOM DATA, SFC HEADER, and so on, that needs to be included in the document.

On the PRINT INTEGRATION configuration tab, you need to specify the plug-ins for data acquisition, formatting, and transport to the printer. The following standard plug-ins are provided in SAP ME for ADS printing:

- **Data Acquisition**
  This plug-in is used to acquire the data for the document from one or more source objects. The standard plug-in for ADS is com.sap.me.document$PrintingDataAcquisitionService.

▶ **Formatting**
This plug-in is used to format the data for the document for a specific format. The standard plug-in for ADS is com.sap.me.document$PrintingFormatAdsService.

▶ **Transport**
This plug-in is used to transport the formatted data to the print package. The standard plug-in provided is com.sap.me.document$PrintingTransportAdsService for ADS.

You can also specify some user arguments for formatting to specify the format of the document (e.g., PRINT_FORMAT=PCL) and transport parameters to include shop order or SFC number on the document name.

2.2.10 Printer Maintenance

You can maintain printers for printing documents from SAP ME by using the Printer Maintenance activity, as shown in Figure 2.23. Here, you can specify a printer name and the types of documents it prints. You can select the printer name in POD MAINTENANCE or DOCUMENT (RE)PRINT activities to print certain documents manually or automatically.

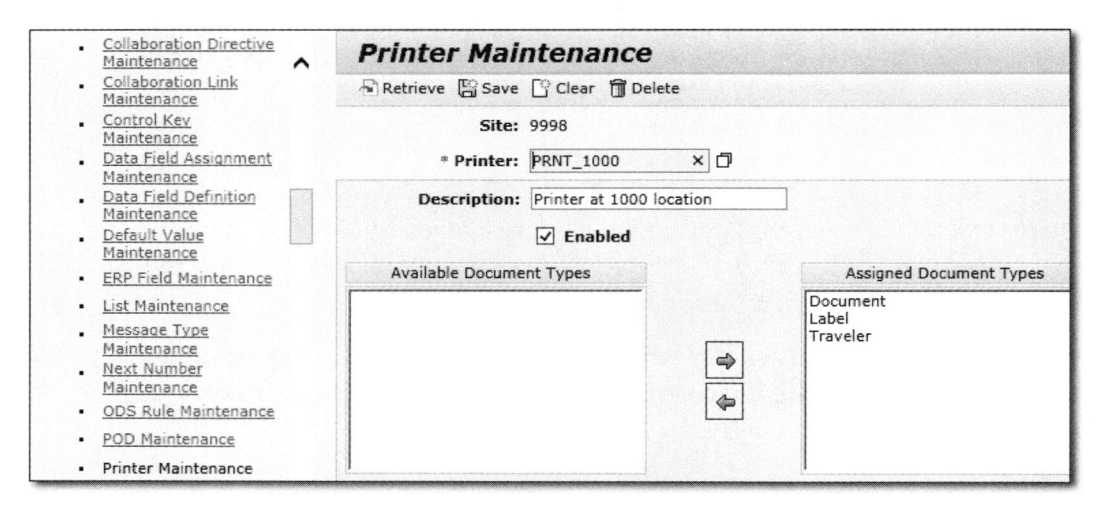

Figure 2.23 Printer Maintenance

2.2.11 ODS Rule Maintenance

The ODS Rule Maintenance activity is used to define how the data is managed in the ODS database used for reporting in SAP ME. You can specify the rules globally by logging in to site * and then either use the same rules in other site or override for specific sites same way as System Rule Maintenance, as shown in Figure 2.24.

The ODS rules are used to define aggregation methods, periods of extraction, and retention of various types of data such as work centers and resources, production and shop order data, defects and non-conformance, and so on in ODS.

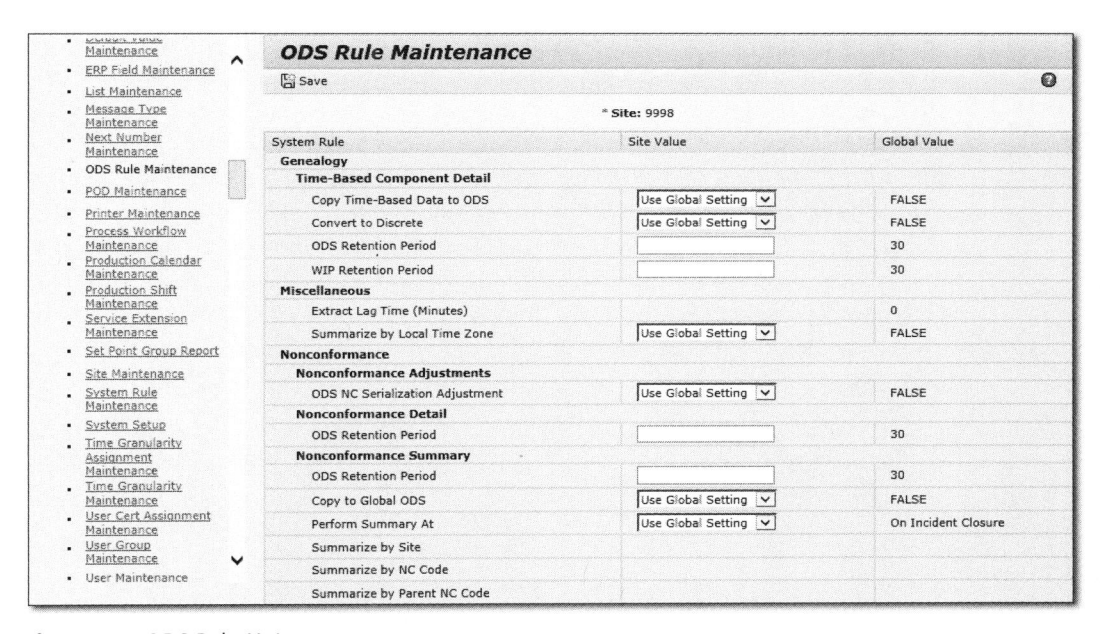

Figure 2.24 ODS Rule Maintenance

2.3 Process Configuration Management

In SAP ME, you need to configure some settings related to the manufacturing execution process and data used in activities and process management. The configurations related to the processes such as ERP Field Maintenance, Next Number Maintenance, Reason Code Maintenance and Time Granularity Maintenance are explained in the following sections.

2.3.1 SAP ERP Field Maintenance

When a master data element present both in SAP ERP and SAP ME is changed in SAP ERP, it is usually sent down to SAP ME for replication. However, for certain elements of a data object, you may want to create a new version of the data in SAP ME, change it in the existing version, or even restrict the change by rejecting the changed data message from SAP ERP. You can configure this behavior in the ERP Field Maintenance activity, as shown in Figure 2.25. You only can make this configuration for the elements present in both SAP ERP and SAP ME for a data object. The fields of the data object that are present in SAP ME only cannot be used in this configuration.

You can select one of the data objects from the CATEGORY drop-down list, which are replicated from SAP ERP, such as BOM, routing, work center, resource, shop order, and so on. Once you've made your selection, click on RETRIEVE to display the configured SAP ERP fields for that object. You can also add other fields supported for that object from the FIELD NAME lookup and specify UPDATE INDICATOR as UPDATE, UPVERSION, or RESTRICTED as applicable. If UPDATE is selected, then the current data will be updated with the new field value without creating a new version, whereas UPVERSION will create a new version of the data object in SAP ME. If RESTRICTED is selected, then the change will be rejected in SAP ME. In this way, you can implement change management of the data in SAP ME when replicated from SAP ERP.

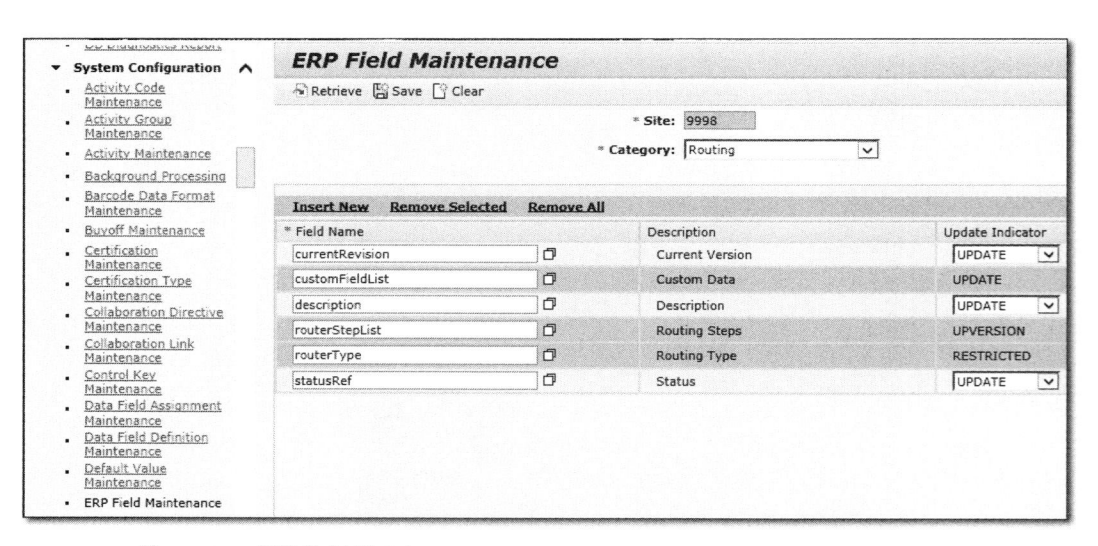

Figure 2.25 ERP Field Maintenance

2.3.2 Next Number Maintenance

You can define a numbering pattern for objects that need an auto-generated number or ID in SAP ME in the Next Number Maintenance activity. Define this configuration for SFC number, SFC serial number, shop order, process lot, batch number, inventory, and so on, as shown in Figure 2.26.

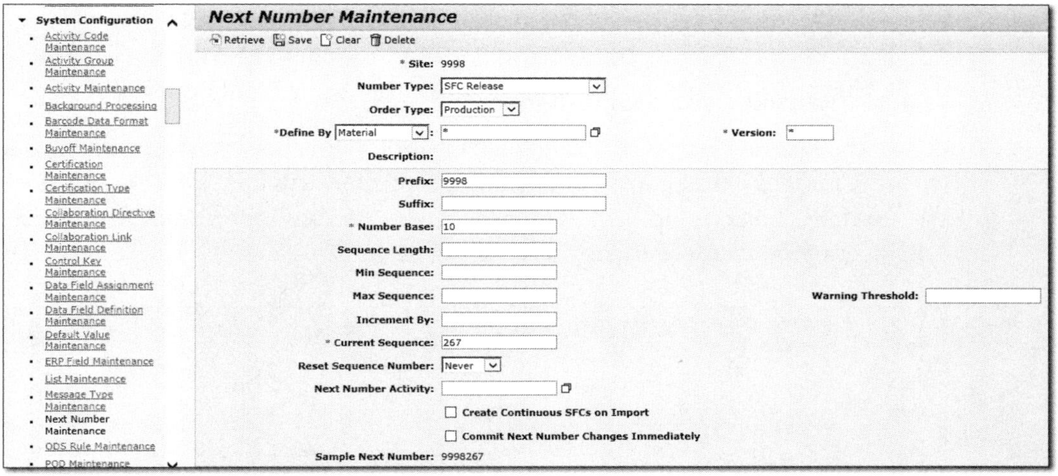

Figure 2.26 Next Number Maintenance

Begin by selecting the object in NUMBER TYPE dropdown, then click on RETRIEVE to display the next number configuration for the key value. Depending on the type of object selected, you may have to specify whether the number is generated based on material or material group, which is required mostly for SFC, inventory (floor stock receipt), and so on. To specify the same configuration for all materials or all material groups, you can enter "*" in the corresponding field or select a specific value for the same. You can specify a prefix (in PREFIX field) and suffix (in SUFFIX field) for the number by using replaceable parameters supported in SAP ME. Specify the NUMBER BASE for the sequence portion of the number, which can range from two to thirty-six (e.g., ten for number and sixteen for hexadecimal). Higher number bases (ten to thirty-six) use letters to represent digits higher than nine. You can also specify SEQUENCE LENGTH to always get a number with a fixed length if required with leading zeros and also to specify the limits of the sequence, incremental value, and when to reset the number and provide warning. You can specify the limits in MIN. SEQUENCE and MAX. SEQUENCE, with zero

(0) signifying the highest integer number allowed (i.e., 2,147,483,647). You can also specify an activity in NEXT NUMBER ACTIVITY to execute when the next number is generated to add custom replaceable parameters for the number. If you select the checkbox CREATE CONTINUOUS SFCS ON IMPORT SFC numbers will be generated for each shop order with sequential numbers only. Leave the COMMIT NEXT NUMBER CHANGES IMMEDIATELY option unchecked to lock the process until all numbers required for an object (e.g., a shop order release) are generated.

2.3.3 Reason Code Maintenance

Using the Reason Code Maintenance activity, you can define the reason codes that identify reasons or categories for different production activities, such as floor stock receipt, SFC hold, equipment status change, corrective action (message board), engineering change request, as shown in Figure 2.27.

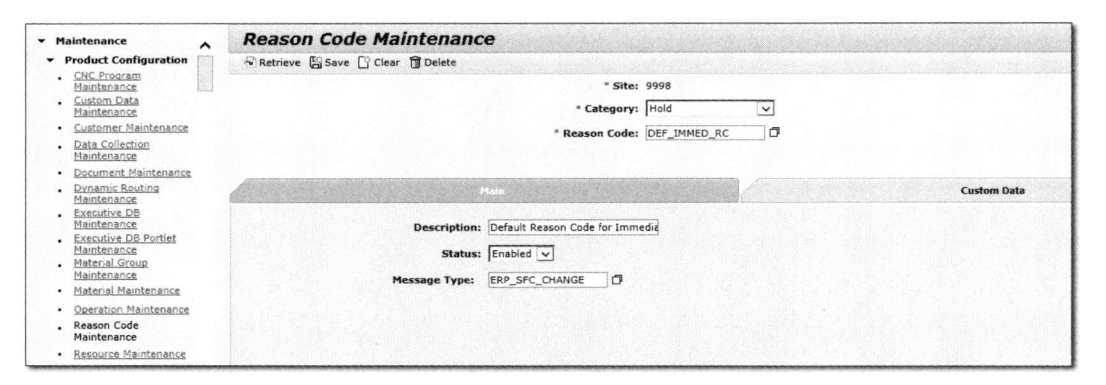

Figure 2.27 Reason Code Maintenance

Once you select the reason code category, you can select the corresponding reason code from the lookup or specify a new one. On the MAIN tab, you can specify a DESCRIPTION text for the reason code, and choose ENABLED under STATUS to use the code for the transactions it's defined for. Optionally, you can also specify a MESSAGE TYPE that may be triggered when the reason code is assigned. Message type maintenance is explained in detail in Chapter 11. On the CUSTOM DATA tab, you can also enter a value for custom data defined through the CUSTOM DATA MAINTENANCE activity in SAP ME.

2.3.4 Time Granularity Maintenance

You can use the Time Granularity Maintenance activity to define the time-brackets such as year, fiscal year, quarter, etc., that the ODS data is partitioned into for ODS reporting in SAP ME. For example, you may want to summarize non-conformances into daily and quarterly brackets of time. This configuration allows to create new bracket sizes and use them for the summarization. You need to define the granularities with a start and end time as show in Figure 2.28. They will typically have the RECURRING YEARLY checkbox checked, so that the time-frame can be re-used every year after the specified one. For example, a QUARTER1 will start at 1/1/2015 and end on 3/31/2015 and recur each year after that.

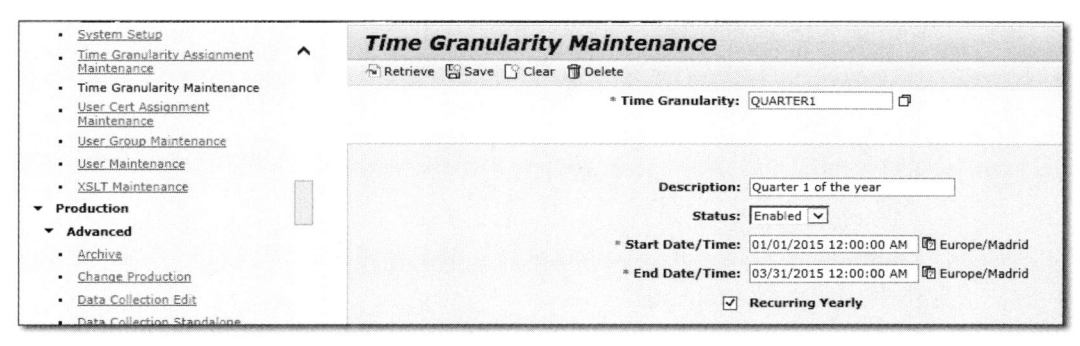

Figure 2.28 Time Granularity Maintenance

2.3.5 Time Granularity Assignment Maintenance

Using the Time Granularity Assignment Maintenance activity you can assign the granularities to summary objects such as Nonconformance, Defect Transfer Table (DPMO), Production Operation, Work Center Production, Production Cycle Time or Resource Utilization, which are used for ODS reporting. There are three system-defined granularities (Hour, Day, Shift). These are pre-defined and use the current hour, day, shift to define when a new time bracket is created for the summarization. You can't see these in Time Granularity Maintenance activity, but you can assign them in Time Granularity Assignment Maintenance. For a specific summarization (e.g. Nonconformance), you can define specific summarization time brackets (e.g. hourly, daily, quarterly for the user-defined bracket described earlier). For the example QUARTER1, you would choose the WORK CENTER UTILIZATION summary from the drop-down at the top and the check the SELECT checkbox for the granularity you want to use for the Nonconformance summaries. Pressing SAVE will save it.

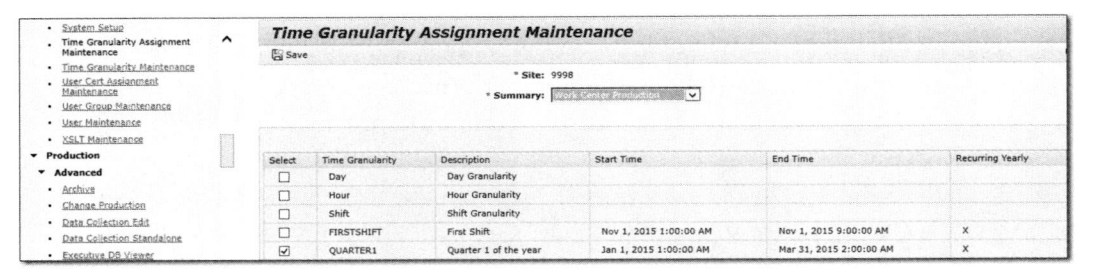

Figure 2.29 Time Granularity Assignment Maintenance

2.4 Summary

In this chapter, you learned about the site and user configurations in SAP ME that are mandatory prerequisites to use the SAP ME system, along with various other system and process configurations that are required to perform different activities in SAP ME. You will learn more about the use of these configurations in subsequent chapters. In the next chapter, you will explore master data setup, configurations, and the data extension mechanisms available in SAP ME.

This chapter describes how to manage master data, such as material data, BOMs, work centers/resources, work instructions, tools, and so on, in SAP ME. It also explains how to enhance master data and define custom data objects.

3 Master Data Management

In any MES, master data provides important information about materials, assets, and processes that informs shop floor execution and actuals reporting.

In SAP ME, various master data—material data, bills of material (BOMs) for shop orders, resources, work centers, operations, routings, customer data, tools data, work instructions, etc.—are maintained and used in the shop floor execution process. Most master data is defined in SAP ERP and synchronized to SAP ME via SAPMEINT, but a few are defined in SAP ME only with no placeholder in SAP ERP. It is also possible to define all master data directly in SAP ME and in some cases, such as routing, update them in SAP ERP. Once downloaded from SAP ERP to SAP ME, you can also enhance the master data in SAP ME to add manufacturing-execution-specific information that is not required or not maintained in SAP ERP. In this chapter, you will learn how to configure and enhance most master data in SAP ME. Operations and routings are covered in the next chapter.

3.1 Managing Master Data

Some of the very common master data types used in SAP ME are material, BOM, resources, workcenter, tool group, tool number, and work instructions. In the subsequent sections you will learn how to manage these master data types in SAP ME.

3 | Master Data Management

3.1.1 Material

Material data is one of the most important master data types in SAP ME and is required in many activities, such as shop orders, routings, process lots, and so on. This data represents a material that is either purchased or manufactured in house by a shop order or consumed in a production process.

You can maintain the material master data using the Material Maintenance activity, as shown in Figure 3.1.

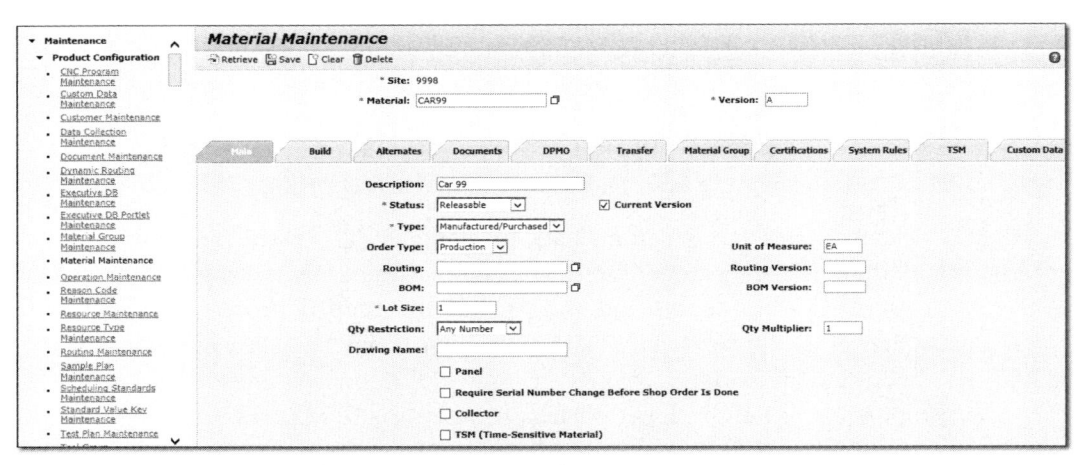

Figure 3.1 Material Maintenance Main Configuration

You need to have material master data defined for each material used in a BOM or shop order. Usually, materials are defined in SAP ERP and transferred to SAP ME through the SAPMEINT interface using the MATMAS IDoc from SAP ERP. After the transfer you can view and change the material data in SAP ME in this activity. The material number is the key value mapped to the material number defined for material master data in SAP ERP, and it can be mapped to a material external number for long material number when transferred via the MATMAS05 IDoc type. A version of the material is automatically assigned based on the system rule to differentiate configuration changes of the material, when no specific version is specified. Select the CURRENT VERSION checkbox to make the version the current one that will be used for all activities.

Material Status

When transferred from SAP ERP, STATUS is set to RELEASABLE, which signifies that the material can be used for production. You can change the status to HOLD to restrict the usage of the material temporarily in shop orders. NEW restricts release of any shop order using the material, and FROZEN restricts change of the material record in Material Maintenance activity, but still allows the material to be used in shop orders. OBSOLETE indicates the material record is no longer used. Any materials that were released in a shop order and then the status changed to hold, frozen, obsolete, or new will not be prevented from being processed, because they were released in a shop order when their status was releasable.

BOM and Routing

You can specify a BOM and routing for the material if the material is a finished product produced by a manufacturing process. You will learn more about BOMs and routing in the next section and the next chapter, respectively.

Lot Management

Lot size is an important attribute of a material that defines how many pieces of a material are stored or processed together. This attribute is used for inventory management and for production while generating the trackable units for production, which you will learn about in Chapter 6.

The quantity multiplier specifies the planned number of pieces that will be produced for the material. It is useful for semiconductor manufacturing, in which multiple pieces are produced on a wafer and it is used to calculate the new lot size by multiplying by the number of SFCs generated which is used as an adjustment factor to calculate the pieces produced. You can also specify a quantity restriction of the material quantity produced in a shop order by specifying in the QTY. RESTRICTION field whether any whole number or just one piece will be produced at a time.

> **Note**
>
> When produced in SAP ME and/or tracked, a material is defined by a shop floor control (SFC) number, which is an identification number for a batch of material pieces. The quantity of material in an SFC is defined by the material's lot size. Lot size 1 is used for serial-managed material whereas lot sizes greater than 1 are used for batch-managed material. For a material with lot size 1, the SFC number can be used as the serial number.

Drawing File

You can specify a drawing file name (which should be of type CAD) for the material, if required, which is used in Visual Test and Repair by the SAP Visual Enterprise component.

Collector

You can use the COLLECTOR indicator to specify whether the material is a collector for installation-type shop orders, which are used to perform the tasks to build the material. Typically, collector materials have components that are manufactured while manufacturing the parent material and generate installation orders for components when a shop order for the collector material is created.

Specify REQUIRE SERIAL NUMBER CHANGE BEFORE SHOP ORDER IS DONE to indicate that the tracking/lot number of the collector shop order must be changed using the Serialization activity before the shop order status is changed to DONE.

Panel

When you are defining materials that can consist of a panel with multiple pieces of the same material within it (e.g., semiconductor wafers), select the PANEL checkbox with LOT SIZE specifying the number of pieces present in the panel and QUANTITY RESTRICTION set to WHOLE NUMBER. You can specify the location and component description of the pieces in the panel in the BUILD configuration tab, as shown in Figure 3.2. The panel is modeled as a single lot, which is later split up into individual, trackable units for the pieces using the Serialize activity. This helps operators scrap individual pieces of the panel due to nonconformance.

Data Collection

You can specify the data collection requirements while using the material at various stages, such as assembly, removal, and floor stock receipt, in the BUILD configuration tab (see Figure 3.2). Based on what you specify there, fields for external serial number, inventory ID, and so on will appear in the production operator dashboard (POD) during those specific events when working with the material. If no specific data collection is required, you can leave the field value as NONE. The data types available in the lookups for data collection are defined by the data field definition of the assembly type, which you will learn more about in Section 3.2.2 in this chapter.

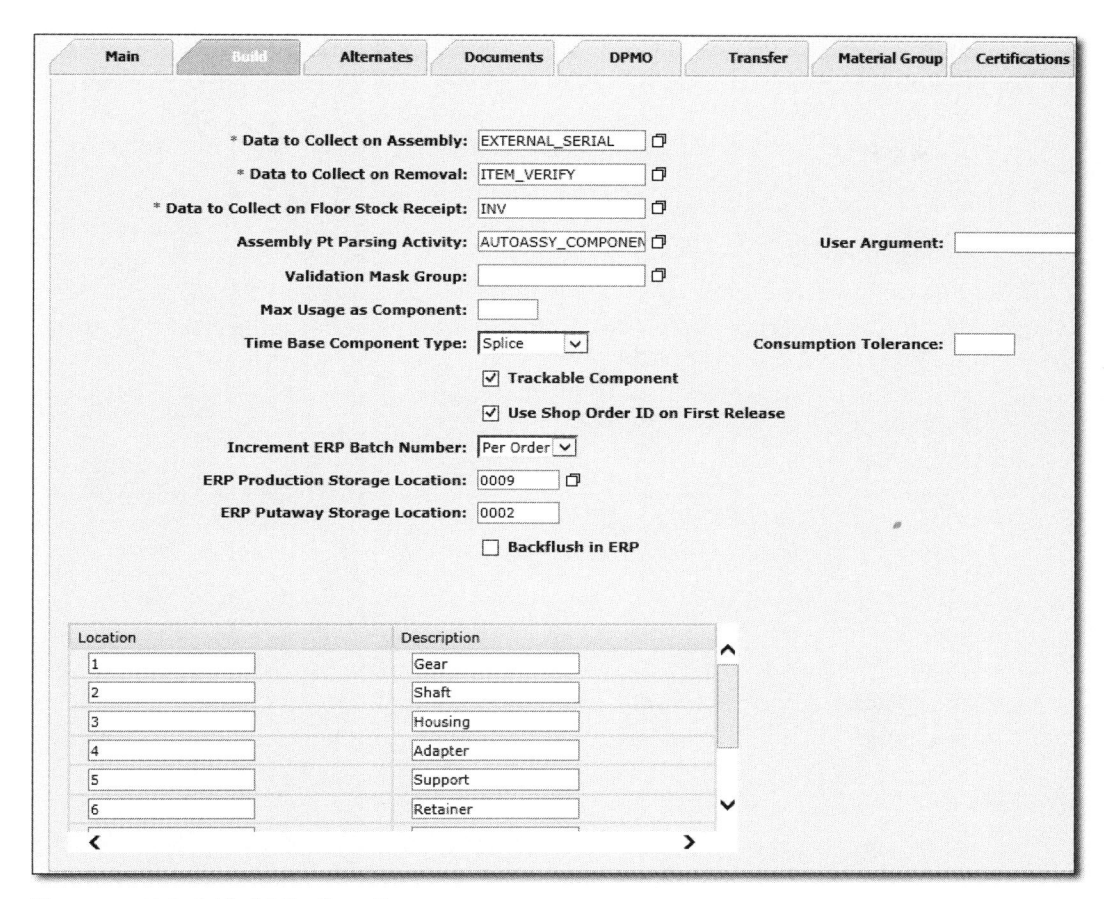

Figure 3.2 Material Build Configuration

Time-Sensitive Material

You can specify details for time-sensitive materials in the TSM tab. Time-sensitive materials have a specific shelf life and floor life and can be only kept outside of a controlled environment for a specific period of time. You can use this functionality only for *manufactured/purchased* or *purchased* material types. Once the TSM indicator is checked on the MAIN configuration tab page, you can specify the maximum shelf life and maximum floor life for the material in the TSM configuration tab as shown in Figure 3.3. Optionally, you can specify a note to be displayed when using the material. The MAX. SHELF LIFE and MAX. FLOOR LIFE fields indicate the maximum period for which the material can be stored on a shelf (warehouse) and on the shop floor, respectively. Beyond these times, the system will not allow consumption of the material in any operation. You can also edit the shelf life for the material during inventory receipt if the activity rule `ALLOW_UPDATE_FLOOR_LIFE` is set to YES in the Floor Stock Maintenance activity (using Activity Maintenance for the `MAINT_INV` activity).

Figure 3.3 Material TSM Configuration

SAP ME provides the standard activity `TSM_CHECK_IN_OUT` to check in and check out a material for shop floor use. This activity is available as a dashboard plug-in for the operator to record when the material is taken from the storage and kept in. You can use the `CHECK_TSM_COMPONENT` activity in `PRE_START` hook point of an operation, where the component is used to check if the material is valid for use. You can stop the time-sensitivity clock for a material lot by using the `STOP_TIME_SENS_CLOCK` activity in the `PRE_COMPLETE` or `POST_COMPLETE` hook point of the operation, which is used to install the material lot to the assembly, after which no time-sensitivity check is required.

Trackable Component

Component traceability enables data collection at the material's assembly point to record which specific components are used in manufacturing the material, using which machine, and by which operator. You can specify TRACKABLE COMPONENT in the BUILD configuration tab to allow creating trackable units (i.e., trackable SFCs for a material at assembly points). For a trackable component, trackable SFCs can be created without a shop order to test or collect data for the unit of material for a purchased material.

The TIME-BASED COMPONENT TYPE field specifies the different types of time-based tracking component: NORMAL, SPLICE, or CONTINUOUS. *Normal* specifies that only one assembly data record is loaded into a resource slot at a time. *Splice* allows multiple assembly data records of a component to be loaded on a resource slot during runtime, and when the current assembly data record reaches zero or threshold value, the next assembly data record is consumed. *Continuous* allows multiple assembly records to be loaded in the resource slot together and consumed together.

SAP ERP Integration

You can specify INCREMENT ERP BATCH NUMBER in the BUILD configuration tab to specify how the batch number will be generated for the material while sending the goods receipt to SAP ERP from SAP ME on production completion for a shop order as shown in Figure 3.2. If you select NONE, then no batch number is used. PER DAY, PER SHIFT, and PER ORDER create new material batch numbers accordingly while sending the goods receipts to SAP ERP if the SAP ERP integration rule (i.e., SAPMEINT) is active.

ERP PRODUCTION STORAGE LOCATION specifies the storage location of the material defined in SAP ERP and populated by the MATMAS interface transferred through SAPMEINT. The ERP PUTAWAY STORAGE LOCATION field indicates the storage location used while sending the yield confirmation to SAP ERP, which is also populated automatically for materials with an in-house production procurement type in SAP ERP.

You can specify BACKFLUSH IN ERP to enable backflush (i.e., not sending goods issue or receipt information from SAP ME to SAP ERP when the material is consumed in a BOM in an assembly operation). The goods movement occurs automatically in SAP ERP by backflushing based on the planned component quantities specified in the production order.

Alternate Components

You can specify alternate components for a material, which can be substituted for the material during production, in the ALTERNATES configuration tab, as shown in Figure 3.4. Specify the alternate material name and version along with the validity period. You also need to specify the valid assembly, version, and material group for which the alternate component will be valid during production. If both the VALID ASSEMBLY and MATERIAL GROUP fields are blank, then the alternate components are applicable for all assemblies. You can specify multiple assemblies

3 | Master Data Management

by specifying a wildcard using an ampersand (&) with the material assembly (e.g., "CAR&", meaning any assembly name that starts with "CAR").

Figure 3.4 Material Alternates Configuration

Material Group

Material groups are a way to classify materials of different types. You can also assign a single material into different groups. When you define next number maintenance for a material or perform a site-to-site transfer export or import of materials, you can configure the same information via material groups, instead of via the material number. Define the details using the MATERIAL GROUP MAINTENANCE activity, as shown in Figure 3.5. On the MAIN configuration tab, specify the group name and a description for the group and a validation mask for materials to be assigned to the group. You can define validation masks in the VALIDATION MASK MAINTENANCE activity.

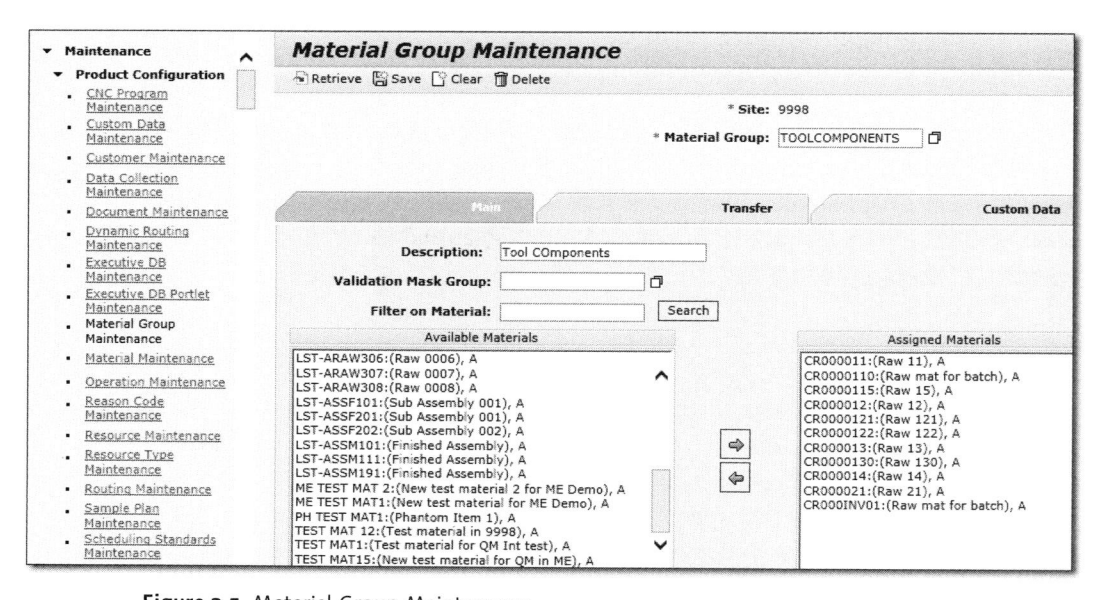

Figure 3.5 Material Group Maintenance

Managing Master Data | **3.1**

In the Material Maintenance activity, you can specify the material groups to which the material is assigned.

Documents and Certifications

You can assign certification and documents to a material in the CERTIFICATIONS and DOCUMENTS configuration tabs. If you assign a certification to a material, only users who are assigned to the same certification can only work with that material in their PODs.

The documents assigned to the material can be retrieved for printing based on the material selection (e.g., material info sheet or specification document) while working with the material in the POD.

Defects per Million Opportunities

You can specify defects per million opportunities (DPMO) settings for a material to calculate defects occurring while producing the material for certain categories, which is a standard methodology for defect tracking and analysis. You will learn more about DPMO in Chapter 8.

In the DPMO configuration tab of MATERIAL MAINTENANCE, specify the category of the DPMO as ASSEMBLY, COMPONENT, PLACEMENT, or TERMINATION to capture the defects occurring at those specific activities or categories. Also specify the specific operations where the defect can occur, or just any operations by specifying ALL and the number of defect points, as shown in Figure 3.6. When the defects are logged using the DPMO codes, the DPMO calculated statistics will be calculated and can be viewed in the DPMO report.

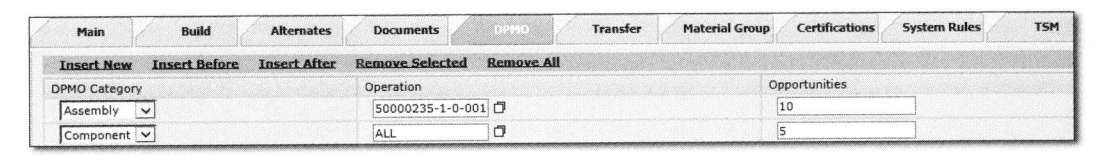

Main	Build	Alternates	Documents	DPMO	Transfer	Material Group	Certifications	System Rules	TSM
Insert New	**Insert Before**	**Insert After**	**Remove Selected**	**Remove All**					
DPMO Category			Operation				Opportunities		
Assembly			50000235-1-0-001				10		
Component			ALL				5		

Figure 3.6 Material DPMO Confiuration

> **Note**
>
> DPMO codes and categories are predefined values to categorize defect types and are installed during SAP ME installation if APPLICATION SERVER NC CODES FOR DPMO is set to YES in the installer.

Material Transfer

You can define the configurations for site-to-site transfer of a material in the TRANSFER configuration tab, as shown in Figure 3.7. This is required when you want to transfer trackable lots (SFC) of a material from one site to another during or after the production via the site-to-site transfer functionality in SAP ME, as explained in Chapter 2.

You can configure the transfer and receiving functionality of materials here. To enable transfer of WIP material lots, you need to specify the material group to which the material will be transferred or received. You also need to specify the transfer type for the destination site as SFC_SPAN, which signifies that the materials being processed in the source site are transferred and will have additional processing at the destination site. SFC_CONSUME signifies the production for the material is finished processing at the source site will be transferred to the destination site for consuming in top-level assembly. If you specify NO_TRANSFER, you signify that the current material will not be transferred. You can define only a specific transfer type for a specific destination site. If you select the RECEIVE checkbox, you signify that you need to receive the transferred material in the destination site using the SFC NUMBER RECEIPT activity. If this checkbox is not selected, then the material is received automatically in the destination site. In the DESTINATION SITE field, you need to specify where the SFC data will be transferred, and specify a template configured in the EXPORT TEMPLATE MAINTENANCE activity in the EXPORT TEMPLATE field. The message type specified is generated after the SFC data is transferred, which is visible in the message board.

Figure 3.7 Material Transfer Configuration

System Rules

You can maintain the material-specific system rules in the SYSTEM RULES configuration tab to customize the system behavior for material maintenance. You can override the system rules maintained in the System Rules Maintenance activity as explained in Chapter 2 at the material object level, as shown in Figure 3.8. The site or global value is displayed here, which you can override by making a selection in CURRENT OBJECT VALUE.

Managing Master Data | **3.1**

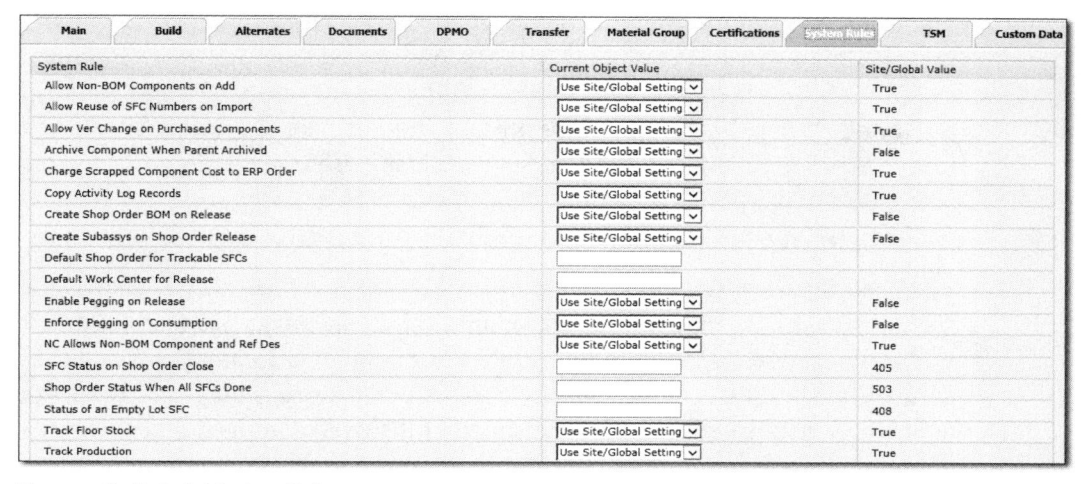

Figure 3.8 Material System Rules

3.1.2 Bill of Materials

When a finished material is manufactured, it is produced by multiple different materials through the production process. The list of materials and the corresponding quantities that make up a finished good or assembly is called a *bill of materials* (BOM). The BOM is used in shop orders in SAP ME to specify the components and their quantities. The BOM master data is defined in SAP ERP and transferred to SAP ME through the BOMMAT interface by SAPMEINT. You can maintain BOMs in SAP ME or view and edit the ones transferred from SAP ERP in the BOM Maintenance activity, as shown in Figure 3.9.

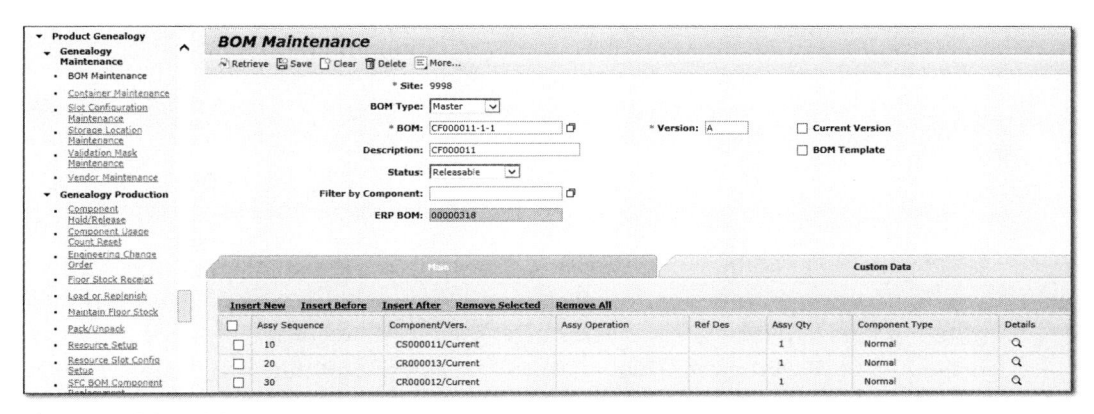

Figure 3.9 BOM Maintenance

109

You can specify BOM TYPE as MASTER BOM, SHOP ORDER BOM, or SFC BOM. *Master BOM* is the BOM master data that is transferred from SAP ERP or defined in SAP ME, which can be used while creating a shop order. If a specific shop order, which may be generated from production or planned orders transferred from SAP ERP, contains a different set of BOMs, a shop order BOM is created automatically. If an SFC, which is generated from a shop order or generated independently, contains different BOMs, an SFC BOM is created.

You need to specify a specific version identifier for the BOM and mark it as the current version, which will be used for all shop orders which use that BOM. For BOMs transferred from SAP ERP, the *ERP BOM* number is automatically added as defined in SAP ERP. You can specify a BOM template to signify that the BOM defined is a template that can be used in other BOMs to add the group of components directly.

On the MAIN configuration tab, the components of the BOM are displayed with fields for the ASSEMBLY SEQUENCE, COMPONENT NAME, and ASSEMBLY QUANTITY. ASSEMBLY OPERATION and REFERENCE DESIGNATORS can be specified optionally. For each component, you can specify more details while adding it initially or later on. Clicking on the DETAILS icon for an existing component or clicking on INSERT NEW link opens the COMPONENT DETAILS view, as shown in Figure 3.10.

For COMPONENT TYPE, choose NORMAL, TEST, PHANTOM, BY-PRODUCT, or CO-PRODUCT. Components used normally are *normal*, whereas components produced in the process of manufacturing, consumed in subsequent operations of the process, and not stored are called *phantom* components. *Test components* are temporary components that will be removed from final assembly—for example, a casing holder required during manufacturing. You need to specify a disassembly operation for these components. A *coproduct component* is a possible variation of the final product. The most optimum material should be specified as the final product, and all other possible variations, if required, should be specified as coproduct components, which are not consumed but received at the end of the process. *Byproduct components* are additional materials that are produced along with the final product.

For phantom components, specify the phantom material in PHANTOM COMPONENT/VERSION and specify the PHANTOM COMPONENT ASSEMBLY SEQUENCE to indicate when the phantom component will be added in the assembly. You can set up the assembly sequence increment rule using the system rule `ASSY_SEQ_INCREMENT` in the ACTIVITY MAINTENANCE section of BOM Maintenance (PD050).

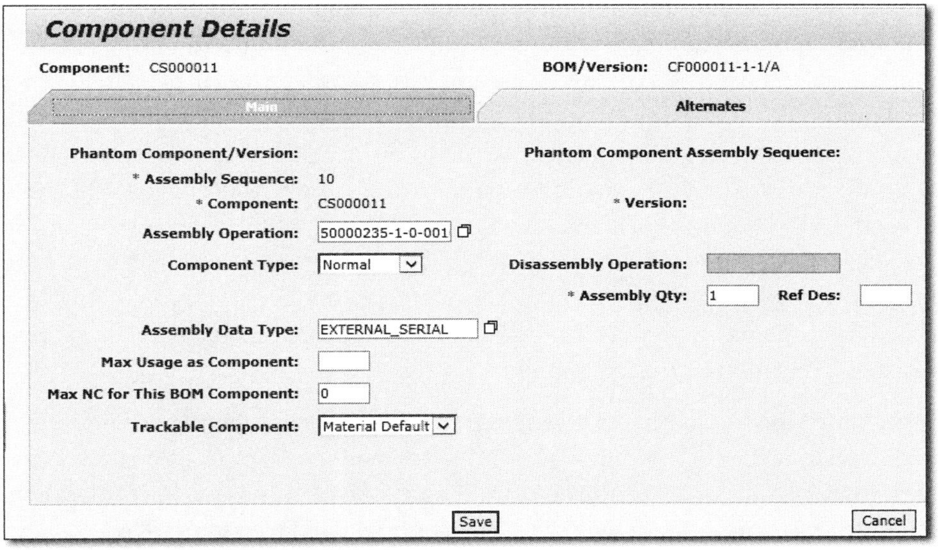

Figure 3.10 BOM Component Details Configuration

> **Note**
>
> When BOM master data is transferred from SAP ERP, the BOM status is set to *releasable* and the current version, and the first version number set as *A*, with subsequent versions suffixed with an incremental number: *A-01*, *A-02*, and so on. A new version is created when the components or their quantities or header quantities or BOM statuses are changed in SAP ERP and transferred to SAP ME.
>
> Phantom, coproduct, and byproduct types of BOM components are transferred from SAP ERP only by production order or planned order interfaces through SAPMEINT.

The *reference designator* (REF DES) is the physical location of the component in the assembly (e.g., in a printed circuit board). This information can be transferred from SAP ERP to SAP ME via SAPMEINT if the installation point of the component is defined in the BOM master and configured as a BOM sub-item in SAP ERP.

Specify ASSEMBLY SEQUENCE to signify when the component will be added and the assembly operation in which the BOM can be used. You can specify ASSEMBLY OPERATION to indicate in which operation the component will be assembled or leave it blank to use the component for multiple operations. You can also specify the data type for data collection during assembly, such as external serial number, ERP batch number, and so on, which is explained in more detail in Chapter 7. If the system rule ALLOW ASSEMBLY QUANTITY AS REQUIRED is set to TRUE, then a checkbox called ASSEMBLY QUANTITY AS REQUIRED appears, which you can select to allow using an assembly quantity of fewer or more than the ASSEMBLY QUANTITY value that specifies the required component quantity. MAX NC FOR THIS BOM COMPONENT specifies the maximum number of nonconformances that can be logged for this component. Set TRACKABLE COMPONENT to MATERIAL DEFAULT to use the configuration from material maintenance, set it to TRUE to create trackable SFC numbers for this component in the ASSEMBLY POINT activity, or set it to FALSE to prevent trackable component.

Specify alternate components if required in the ALTERNATES configuration tab for each component, as shown in Figure 3.11. To enable using the alternate component for a BOM, you need to select the ENABLE BOM ALTERNATE USE checkbox. Then, the specified component can be substituted with the alternate component if required while creating a shop order.

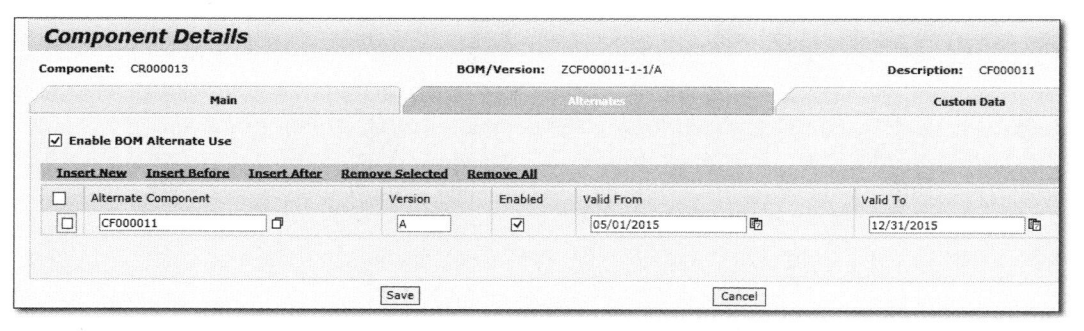

Figure 3.11 Alternate Component Configuration for BOM

> **Note**
>
> If you have changed the BOM master data transferred from SAP ERP in SAP ME, you should set the system rule IGNORE BOM UPDATE to TRUE so that if the BOM master data is again sent from SAP ERP, it will not overwrite the changed BOM in SAP ME. In addition, production orders with the specified BOM transferred from SAP ERP will then use the BOM defined in SAP ME and not the one from SAP ERP.

3.1.3 Resource

A resource is a machine, a piece of equipment, or a specific production area defined in SAP ME. Resources are used to execute an operation while producing or processing a product. When transferring the data from SAP ERP, work centers defined in SAP ERP as part of category 9100 are created as resources in SAP ME through the LOIWCS interface by SAPMEINT. Each individual capacity of a work center in SAP ERP corresponds to a resource in SAP ME, so when a work center with individual capacities defined in SAP ERP is transferred to SAP ME, a work center with nested resources is created in SAP ME.

Using the Resource Maintenance activity, you can define and view the resources in SAP ME as shown in Figure 3.12. The resource is identified by a resource name and optional description, and STATUS specifies the current state of the resource to track its performance. When used to execute an operation, for example, the resource status changes to *productive*, which signifies that resource is being utilized and is logged as utilized machine time for the resource. Similarly, during a breakdown, fault, or repair, the resource status is changed to *unscheduled down* or *scheduled down* to signify the time loss for the resource.

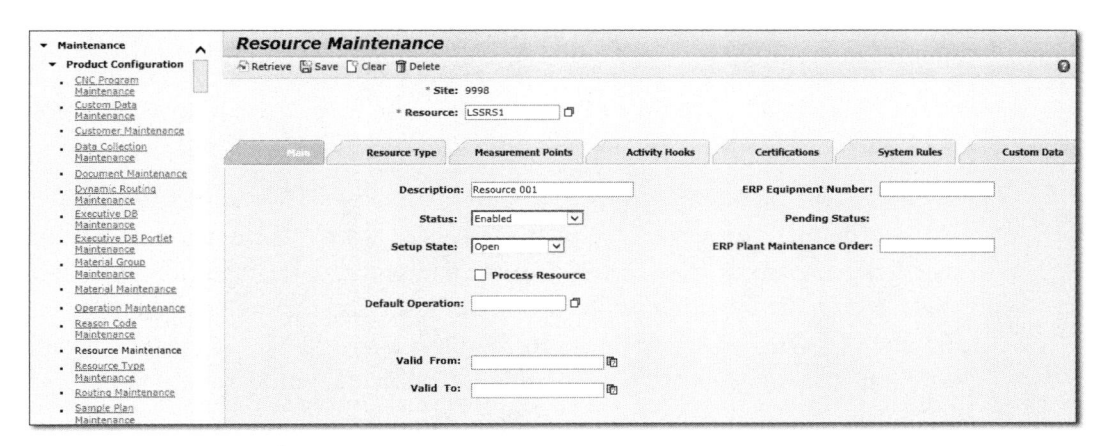

Figure 3.12 Resource Configuration

A resource can be used a process manufacturing resource; that is, an operation started in the resource by one operator can be completed by another operator. Otherwise, the resource is treated as a discrete manufacturing resource: An operation started on the resource by an operator has to be completed by the same operator. Set PROCESS RESOURCE to specify the resource as a process resource. PENDING STATUS indicates the status of the resource being set through the CHANGE EQUIPMENT STATUS activity or through an update from SAP ERP via SAPMEINT, but it cannot be changed immediately if there are active SFCs being processed in that resource. The status change will automatically take place when all active SFCs in that resource are processed. To use a resource for production, you may need to do some setup activities, such as cleaning, heating, and so on. SETUP STATE specifies the current state of the resource for production setup—for example, NOT SETUP, SETTING UP, and SETUP. The OPEN setup state signifies that the resource does not need any additional setup for production, and BREAKING DOWN signifies that the resource is down for production.

You can also specify a DEFAULT OPERATION for a resource, which will appear while selecting the resource in a POD. You need to assign the resource to the specific resource type specified for the operation.

ERP EQUIPMENT NUMBER is specified for the resource if the corresponding work center is assigned to a piece of equipment in SAP ERP and transferred to SAP ME. ERP PLANT MAINTENANCE ORDER will appear if a plant maintenance work order is created in SAP ERP for the equipment assigned to the resource based on the plant maintenance notification sent from SAP ME.

To set a validity period for the resource usage, specify the VALID FROM and VALID TO dates.

A *resource type* is used to categorize resources used for similar purposes together. You can define a resource type in the Resource Type Maintenance activity by specifying a name and description and can add the resource types for a resource in RESOURCE TYPE configuration tab of the Resource Maintenance activity, as shown in Figure 3.13. Operations can be linked resource type so that the default selection of resources can be provided when an operation is selected in the POD.

For resources assigned to equipment in SAP ERP, you may want to collect some running values of different parameters associated with the resource via the *measurement document* functionality available in SAP ERP in the Plant Maintenance module. If you have defined measurement points for the equipment related to the resource in SAP ERP, you can specify the same measurement points in the MEASUREMENT POINTS configuration tab for Resource Maintenance, as shown in

Figure 3.14. When you start an SFC on that resource in the POD and are working on an *ERP reporting step* — that is, the operation for which the confirmation is sent to SAP ERP — you need to specify the measurement point values defined for the resource. The equipment usage data will be updated to SAP ERP through SAP-MEINT by triggering the collaboration action `COLLABORATION_ERP_EQUIPMENT_USAGE` to update the corresponding measuring point in SAP ERP.

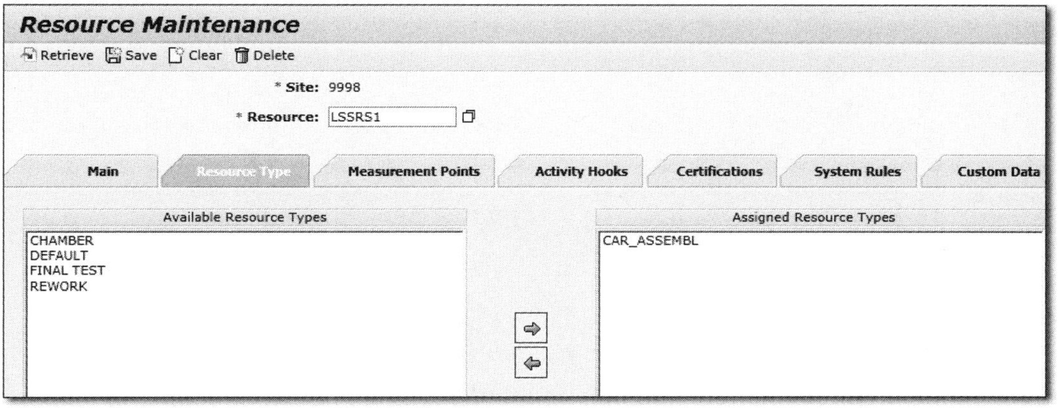

Figure 3.13 Resource Type Configuration

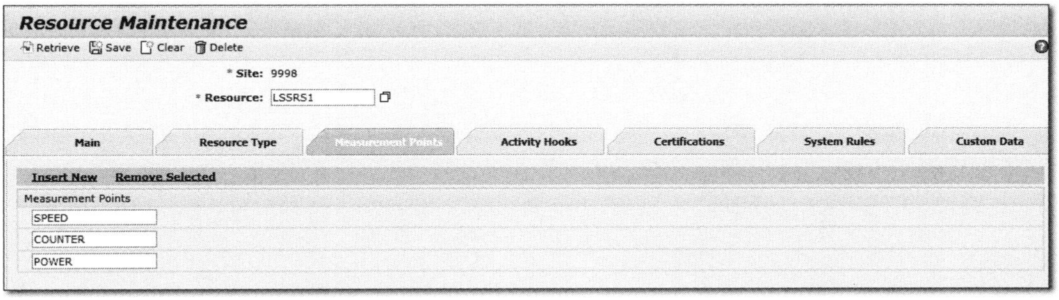

Figure 3.14 Measurement Points Configuration

You can configure activity hooks for the resource in the ACTIVITY HOOK configuration, as shown in Figure 3.15. *Activity hooks* are background activities or services invoked at specific events, as explained in Chapter 2. You can specify standard or custom-developed activities in the hook points as required, such as creating a SFC number when an operation is started on the resource to validate the SFC number input.

3 | Master Data Management

Figure 3.15 Resource Activity Hook Configuration

The hook points listed in Table 3.1 are available for resources for which you can specify activities to be executed as required.

Hook Point	Description
PRE_VALIDATE_START	Before execution of the PRE_START hook point
PRE_START	Before starting an operation
POST_START	After starting an operation
PRE_COMPLETE	Before completing an operation
POST_COMPLETE	After completing an operation
PRE_BATCH_START	After the operator chooses START, before the system executes the start
POST_BATCH_START	After the operator chooses START, after the system executes the start
PRE_BATCH_COMPLETE	After the operator chooses COMPLETE, before the system executes the completion
POST_BATCH_COMPLETE	After the operator chooses COMPLETE, after the system executes the completion

Table 3.1 Resource Hook Points

Specify the certifications if required for operators to work with a resource in the CERTIFICATION configuration tab, as shown in Figure 3.16. If you specify a certification in the resource—for example, because a skill is required to work on that resource—an operator who will work on the resource must have the certification assigned in the user profile to be allowed to process any SFC in the resource.

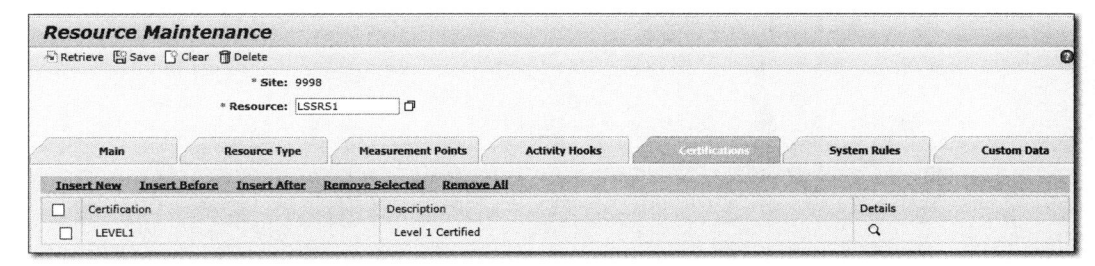

![Figure 3.16 Resource Certification Maintenance]

Figure 3.16 Resource Certification Maintenance

You can specify the system rules specific for a resource in the SYSTEM RULES configuration tab, as shown in Figure 3.17 As explained in Chapter 2, you can specify the object-level system rules for a resource if required, to override the global or site-specific rules.

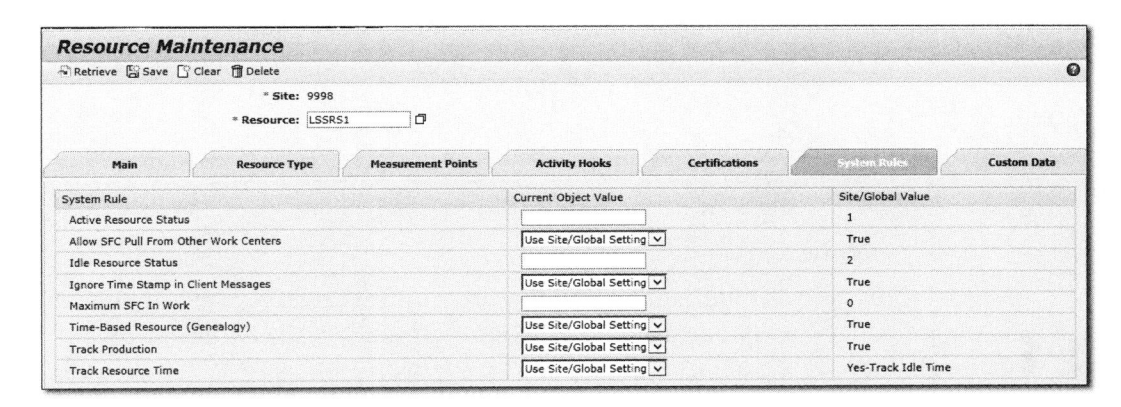

![Figure 3.17 Resource System Rule Maintenance]

Figure 3.17 Resource System Rule Maintenance

You can modify the system rules for the resources as listed in Table 3.2.

Rule Name	Description
Active Resource Status	Status code of the resource, logged when in active/productive state. Default value is 1.
Allow SFC Pull From Other Work Centers	Allow transfer of SFC from another resource for processing.

Table 3.2 Resource System Rules

Rule Name	Description
Idle Resource Status	Status code of the resource, logged when it is in idle/unproductive state. Default value is 2, which corresponds to the *standby* status.
Ignore Time Stamp in Client Messages	Ignores time stamps from the client during validations for starts, completes, nonconformances, and parametric data collection if set to True.
Maximum SFC In Work	Maximum number of SFCs which can be processed together in the resource.
Time-Based Resource (Genealogy)	Enable time-based genealogy tracking for the resource.
Track Production	If set to True, the system logs production time and quantities to the production log, which tracks yield, completed production, rework time/quantity, and cycle time. For the OEE report, this rule must be set to True.
Track Resource Time	Specifies whether to log the resource time (productive and idle) and retain details. Enabling time tracking for the resource is performance intensive.

Table 3.2 Resource System Rules (Cont.)

3.1.4 Work Center

A *work center* in SAP ME is a group of resources or work centers maintained in the shop floor and used to manage production, such as a production line. Work centers in SAP ERP created as category 9000 are transferred to SAP ME as work centers through the LOIWCS interface by SAPMEINT. However, if a work center has split capacity, then it can be of any category, and when transferred to SAP ME, a parent work center will be created for it and its capacities will be created as individual resources. You can also maintain and view the work centers in SAP ME using the Work Center Maintenance activity, as shown in Figure 3.18. Work centers created in SAP ERP with individual capacities of other work center types create work centers with nested resources in SAP ME.

> **Note**
>
> You can add multiple resources or work centers under a single work center, but this cannot be done recursively. Thus, a work center cannot have itself as its child.

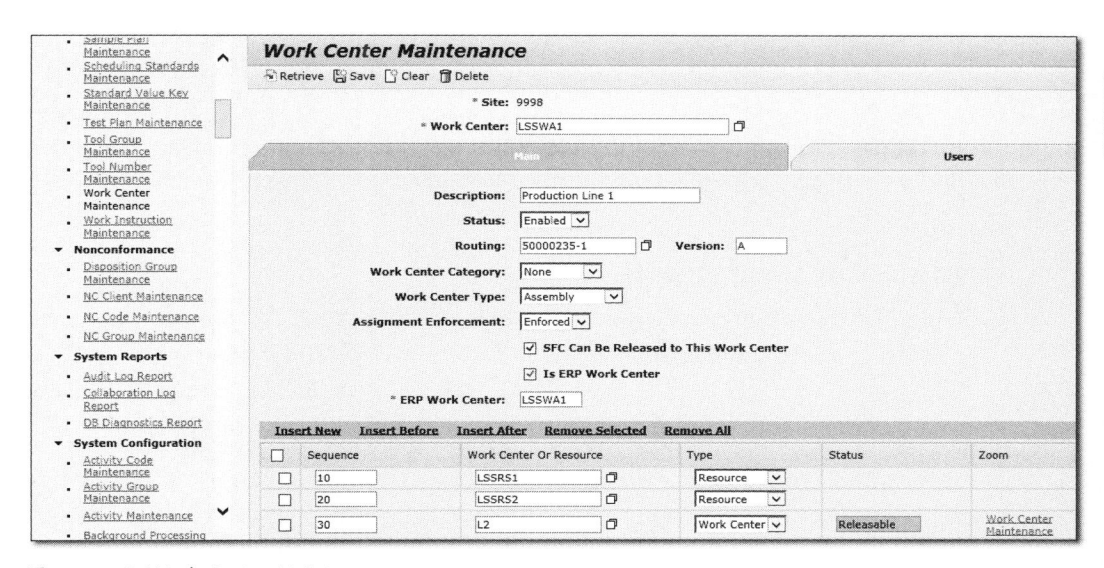

Figure 3.18 Work Center Maintenance

The work center status can be set to ENABLED or DISABLED to signify whether it can be used or not. You can specify a default routing for the work center if required and a category set to NONE, CELL, CELL GROUP, LINE, LINE GROUP, or BUILDING to classify it. You can also specify the work center type to signify the type of work performed in it as FABRICATION, ASSEMBLY, DISPATCH, SHIPPING, CUSTOMER, PROD CONTROL, RECORD CONTROL, or DIVERSION.

You can specify the ASSIGNMENT ENFORCEMENT for the work center to restrict users performing any transaction on it. You can assign individual users to the work center from the USERS configuration tab and to a specific operation and SFC using the Supervisor Work Assignment activity. If ASSIGNMENT ENFORCEMENT is set to NONE, any user, even if not assigned to the work center, can perform any transaction (e.g., labor clocking) on the work center. If specified as WARNING or ENFORCED, the system displays a warning message or error message when the user tries to perform an operation on the SFC for an operation to which he or she is not assigned.

If the work center data is transferred from SAP ERP through the SAPMEINT interface, IS ERP WORK CENTER is checked and the ERP WORK CENTER identifier is populated with the SAP ERP work center ID. If you specify SFC CAN BE RELEASED TO THIS WORK CENTER, then SFC can be released to the work center from a shop order or the CREATE SFC activity.

You can add nested or child resources or work centers to the parent work center by clicking on INSERT NEW or can delete an existing one by selecting it and clicking on REMOVE SELECTED. In this way, you can define a production line for the shop floor through combination of resources and work centers and can set multiple capacities (as resources) for one work center.

3.1.5 Tool Group Maintenance

You can define equipment types as tool groups using the Tool Group Maintenance activity, as shown in Figure 3.19. Tools can be used by the operators in the production process, who record use through the POD and it defines the tool requirement for objects such as material, attachment point in operations in SAP ME.

Specify the STATUS field for the tool group as ENABLED or DISABLED to signify whether it can be used or not. Specify TRACKING CONTROL as NONE, LOT, or SERIALIZED to indicate whether the tool is managed as a lot with a quantity specified or is serialized—that is, with a specific serial number (quantity is always 1). NONE specifies that the tool is not managed as a lot or serialized. TIME-BASED specifies that the tool is tracked based on time and used in the RESOURCE SETUP activity to specify the resource on which it is loaded at a point of time. Time-based configuration is enabled only if the tool tracking is of the serialized type. ERP GROUP specifies that the tool is maintained in SAP ERP, and an additional confirmation message is sent to SAP ERP for the tool in operations in which it is used.

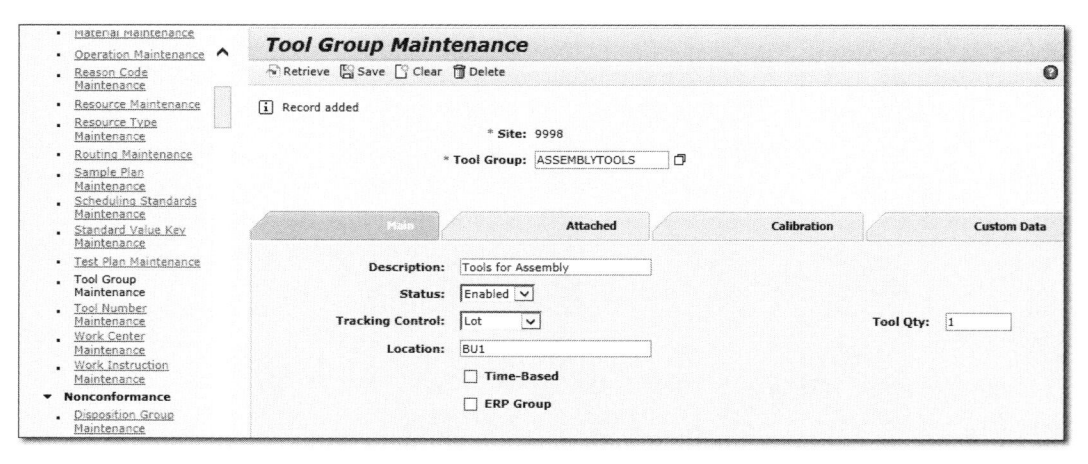

Figure 3.19 Tool Group Maintenance

You can assign the tool group with a material, routing, operation, resource, resource type, and so on in the ATTACHED configuration tab to indicate that the tool group is required for that object in the assembly process. Tools assigned to the tool group will be required and assigned to the object to which it is assigned and is displayed (through the TOOL GROUP LIST activity) to the operator in the PODs when working on the specific resource, work center, operation, and so on. Click on INSERT NEW on the ATTACHED configuration tab to open the Attachment Point Details page, where you can specify the associated object for the tool as shown in Figure 3.20. You can specify the sequence number for each attachment within the tool group to the attached point and the quantity of the tool required for the tool group.

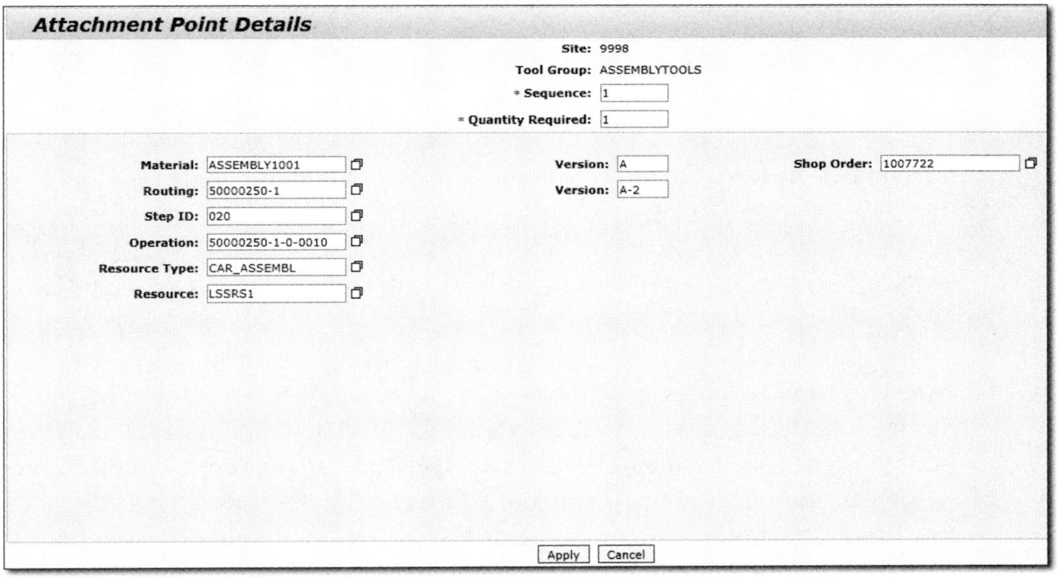

Figure 3.20 Tool Group Attached Configuration

You can specify the calibration period for tool, which you may need to do to ensure the precision of the tool, in the CALIBRATION configuration tab (see Figure 3.21) only if the tool is locally maintained in SAP ME (i.e., ERP GROUP is not specified for the tool). You can specify the time period—months, days, years, or a fixed date—for the calibration of the tool.

121

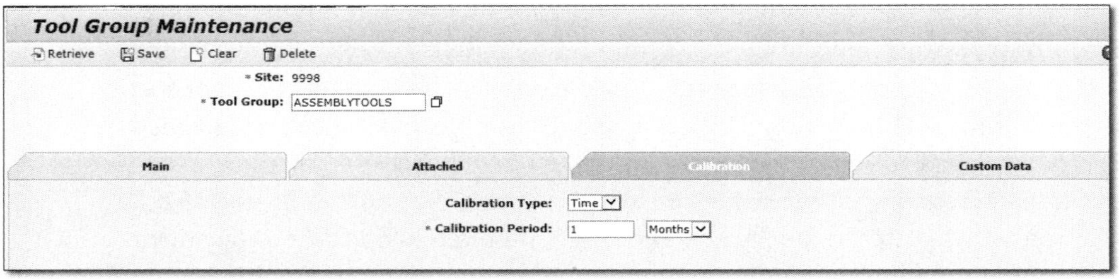

3 | Master Data Management

Figure 3.21 Tool Group Calibration Configuration

3.1.6 Tool Number Maintenance

You can maintain equipment or production tools in SAP ME using the Tool Number Maintenance activity, as shown in Figure 3.22. You can link a tool number in SAP ME with equipment in SAP ERP for plant maintenance activities and can use them in the production activities in the PODs in SAP ME. The STATUS values of the tool are same as those of the resource and can be changed based on the production or maintenance or production state.

> **Note**
>
> The STATUS field options UNKNOWN, HOLD, HOLD SPC WARN, HOLD CONSEC NC, HOLD YIELD RATE, and HOLD SPC VIOL. should not be used; they are not relevant for tools.

The tool number is a specific instance of a tool group. You can assign a tool group to the tool, based on which other properties from the tool group are automatically assigned to the tool. The quantity specified for the tool is automatically assigned from the corresponding tool group and cannot exceed the value specified there. For tool numbers assigned to serialized tool groups, the quantity is always 1. You can specify ERP EQUIPMENT NUMBER and ERP PLANT MAINTENANCE ORDER in the tool when it is related to equipment in SAP ERP. In the LOCATION field, you can optionally specify the location of the tool if used or present in a fixed location only.

The calibration settings are copied from the corresponding tool group for the specific tool number, which you configure in the CALIBRATION configuration tab, as shown in Figure 3.23. Based on the calibration settings, the EXPIRATION DATE is displayed if CALIBRATION TYPE is specified as TIME, meaning the tool needs to be calibrated and reset.

Managing Master Data | **3.1**

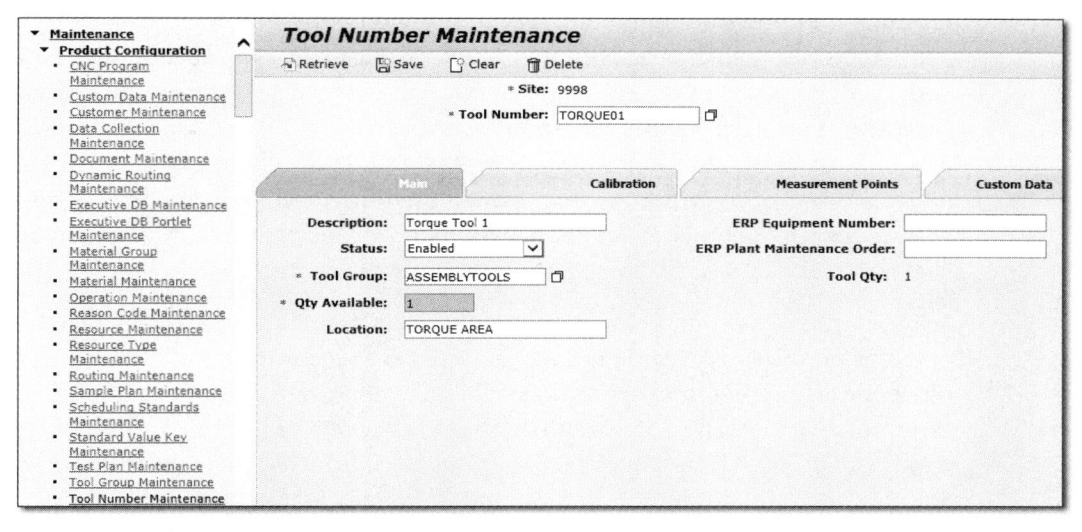

Figure 3.22 Tool Number Maintenance

Figure 3.23 Tool Calibration Configurations

You can configure measurement points for tools like resources, which can be linked to measurement point in SAP ERP to update the measurement values for different parameters of a tool in SAP ERP.

3.1.7 Work Instruction Maintenance

Work instructions provide diagrammatic or textual information that can be displayed to operators in PODs while executing certain tasks for assembly. Work instructions are typically assembly instructions or additional information such as standard operating procedures (SOPs) that operators need to follow while executing an operation. You can define work instructions in SAP ME using the Work Instruction Maintenance activity, as shown in Figure 3.24. You can specify a name and description and version for the work instruction. The CURRENT VERSION checkbox specifies the work instruction as the current one to be used. The status of the work instruction can be set as RELEASABLE, FROZEN, OBSOLETE, or HOLD. *Releasable* and *frozen* work instructions are used in PODs, whereas *obsolete* and *hold* status work instructions cannot be used. Frozen work instructions cannot be changed, whereas *hold* is a temporary frozen status that can change later.

Select REQUIRED to automatically open the work instruction in the POD when the operator performs the relevant tasks. Select LOG VIEWING to log the viewing of the work instruction in order to track whether the operator has viewed it while executing the operation. Select CHANGE ALERT to display icons for the work instruction in the POD. You can transfer the work instructions from SAP ERP to SAP ME through the routing interface. If the work instructions are replicated from SAP ERP, then the ERP WI checkbox will be selected.

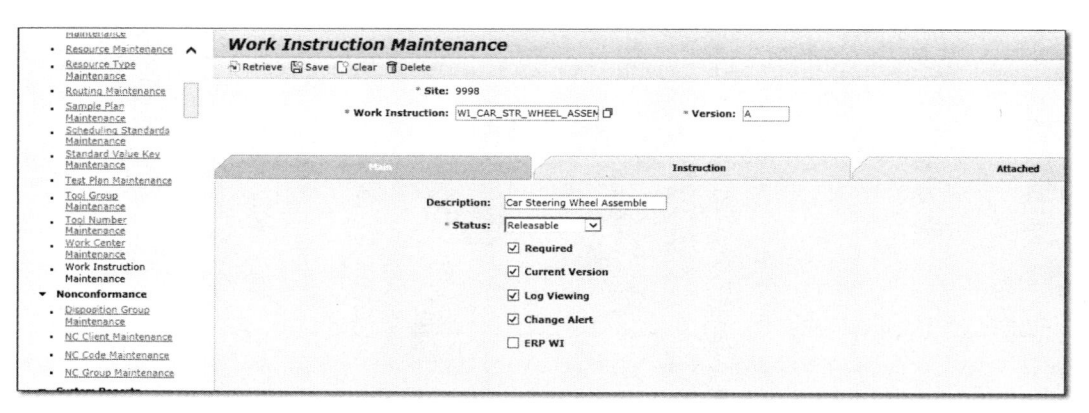

Figure 3.24 Work Instruction Maintenance

You can specify the work instruction content in the INSTRUCTION configuration tab, as shown in Figure 3.25. If the work instruction is sent from SAP ERP, then you can find the values for the instruction content already populated. Usually, work instruction files in SAP ERP are maintained in SAP Document Management System (DMS), which is specified under ERP FILENAME and is sent along with the routing interface to SAP ME, if assigned to operations. Otherwise, you can specify an URL if the work instruction is hosted on a web server as web content, or you can maintain textual content.

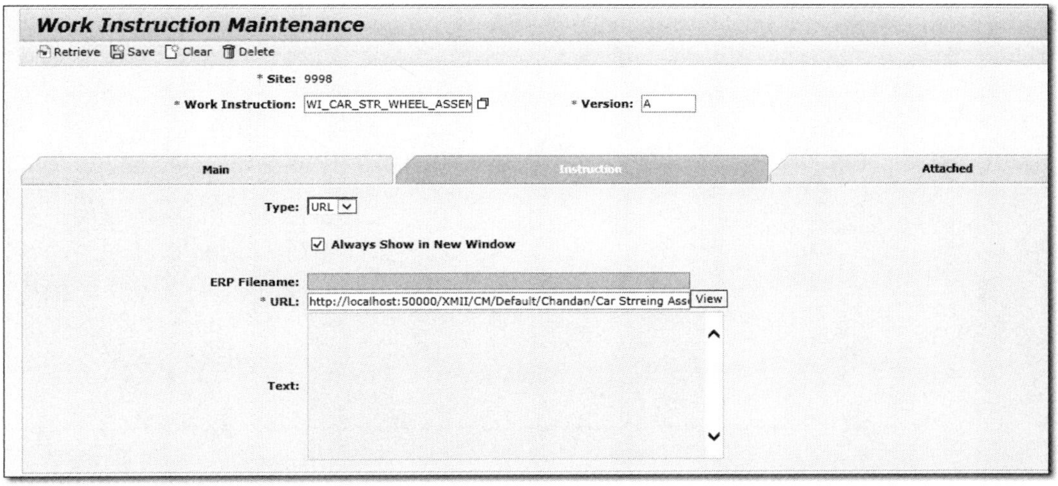

Figure 3.25 Work Instruction Configuration

> **Note**
>
> Work instruction can be any electronic content, such as MS Word, MS PowerPoint, or PDF files, video files, or 3-D models, the latter of which can be created using SAP Visual Enterprise, generating an RH file.

You can create an attachment for the work instruction in the ATTACHED configuration tab to assign it with specific objects displayed when used in the POD. Click on INSERT NEW to add a new attachment; you can specify different objects such as a material, operation, resource, work center, routing, and so on to assign with the work instruction, as shown in Figure 3.26. You can specify the sequence number of the attachment point and choose to apply the attachment for the current version of the work instruction so that the assignment remains even if the work instruction changes.

Once you specify the assigned objects and click on APPLY, the work instruction attachment is displayed in the ATTACHED configuration tab, as shown in Figure 3.27.

Figure 3.26 Work Instruction Assignment

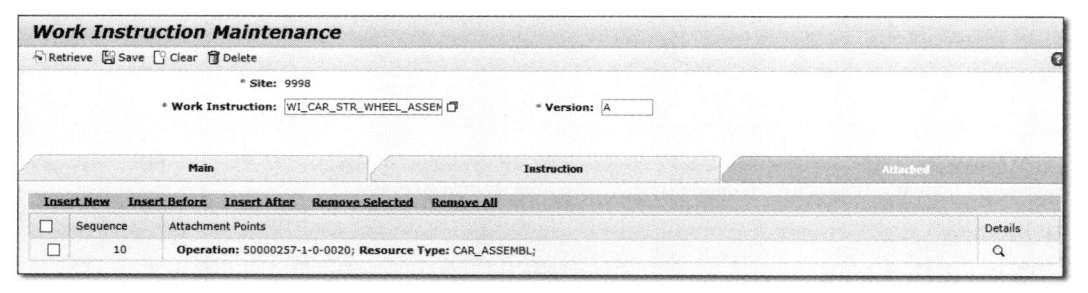

Figure 3.27 Work Instruction Attachment

If the work instructions are transferred from SAP ERP, the attachment points are created when the production orders are sent from SAP ERP referring to the work instructions.

3.2 Data Enhancement in SAP ME

As you learned earlier, master data in SAP ME comes with a set of standard data models, data for which is either transferred from SAP ERP or created locally in SAP ME. In addition to using the standard data elements that are available for any master data object, you may want to add new data elements. You may also want to define custom data fields to be used for various purposes, such as collecting data during the assembly process.

SAP ME provides easy configuration options for defining custom data fields that you can use for master and transactional data, which are explained in the next sections.

3.2.1 Custom Data Maintenance

You can assign custom data fields for master data objects to capture additional data elements that are not present in the standard data model in SAP ME but are required for any reporting or manufacturing process, e.g. Material Class Type for a material or Equipment Serial Number for a resource, etc. You can define the custom data using the Custom Data Maintenance activity as shown in Figure 3.28.

Figure 3.28 Custom Data Maintenance

You can select the master data object under CATEGORY and add custom data fields as required or select them from the existing list. You can select REQUIRED for the data field if the value needs to be provided mandatorily when maintaining the corresponding master data. The data fields defined for the object will appear in the CUSTOM DATA configuration tab, which is present in all the master data maintenance activity. You can manually specify the custom data values or transfer from SAP ERP through SAPMEINT by enhancing the XSLT mapping.

3.2.2 Data Field Definition Maintenance

You can define custom data fields to add additional data elements for data objects, such as Assembly, NC, Packaging Container, Packing SFC, RMA SFC, RMA shop order, and SFC. Define data fields using the Data Field Definition Maintenance activity, as shown in Figure 3.29. Define a data field with a name and description, and specify the data field TYPE as LIST, NUMBER, CHECKBOX, DATE, TEXTAREA, or

TEXT. For list types, you can maintain a list of allowed values for the field in the LIST configuration tab. Depending on the type selected, the custom data will appear in the related data object maintenance accordingly. You can specify the FIELD LABEL to be displayed in the data object and can specify MASK GROUP only for text and number types with a validation mask (defined in the Validation Mask Maintenance activity) to define the validation pattern for the input value. BROWSER ICON is enabled only for the list type and displays a lookup icon for the data field to select its allowed values. You can optionally specify a PRE-SAVE ACTIVITY that will be executed while saving the value for the data field in the assigned category. You can specify either a standard or custom SAP ME activity to validate the input or trigger certain actions if required by the presave activity.

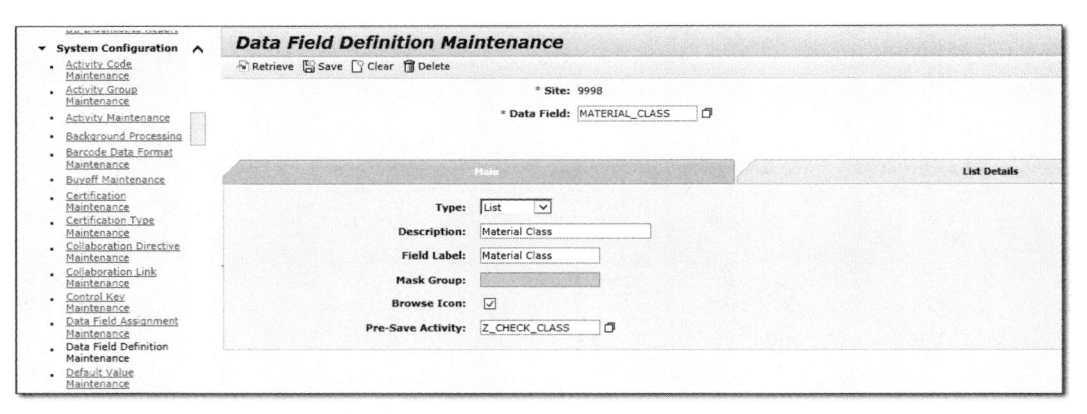

Figure 3.29 Data Field Definition Maintenance

3.2.3 Data Field Assignment Maintenance

Once you define the data fields, you can assign them to different categories so that data fields can be used by operators to collect specific data. You can assign a data field to categories using the Data Field Assignment Maintenance activity, as shown in Figure 3.30.

You can select any of the following options for CATEGORY:

- ASSEMBLY
  Displays data fields for material or BOM when the operator creates the assembly by adding or removing components, or updates floor stock inventory, configures or changes resources slots, or places a component on hold.

- NC
  Displays data fields assigned in NC code maintenance when the operator logs a nonconformance for quality issues.
- PACKING CONTAINER
  Displays data fields for container when the operator during packing operation.
- PACKING SFC
  Displays data fields for SFC number when packing the SFC into a container for data types defined for containers.
- RMA SFC
  Displays fields for RMA SFC for the data types assigned in an RMA shop order.
- RMA SHOP ORDER
  Displays fields for an RMA shop order receipt for data types assigned to an RMA shop order.
- SFC
  Displays fields for SFC number in SFC data entry.

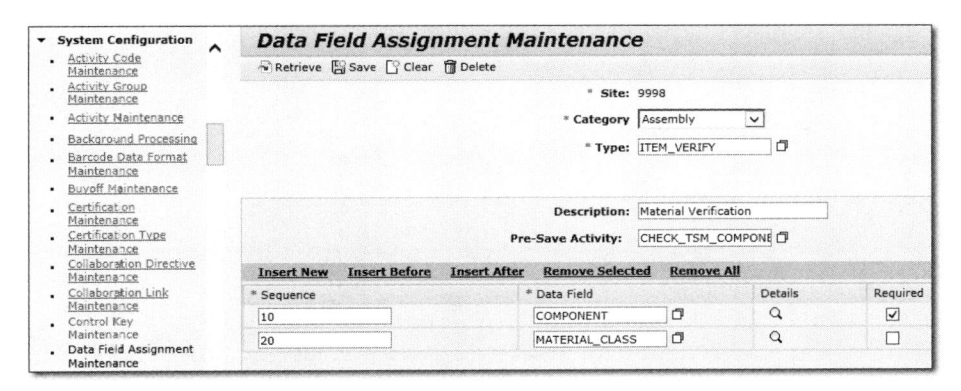

Figure 3.30 Data Field Assignment Maintenance

You can specify a type for the data fields defined for the selected category. For SFC, TYPE is automatically set to DEFAULT and cannot be changed.

Optionally, you can specify a custom activity as a presave activity that will be executed before saving the data for the data fields.

You need to add the data fields by clicking on INSERT NEW and specifying SEQUENCE NUMBER and DATA FIELD. You can specify whether the value for the data field is mandatory by selecting the REQUIRED checkbox.

3 Master Data Management

The data fields defined for the category and type will be displayed to the user when performing operations in SAP ME to collect data for the field identifiers.

3.2.4 Standard Value Key Maintenance

Standard values refer to the activities performed while executing an operation of a shop order or working with a resource or work center. You can use the standard values to collect the time for various activities in production process, such as labor time. You can define the standard value key using the Standard Value Key Maintenance activity, as shown in Figure 3.31.

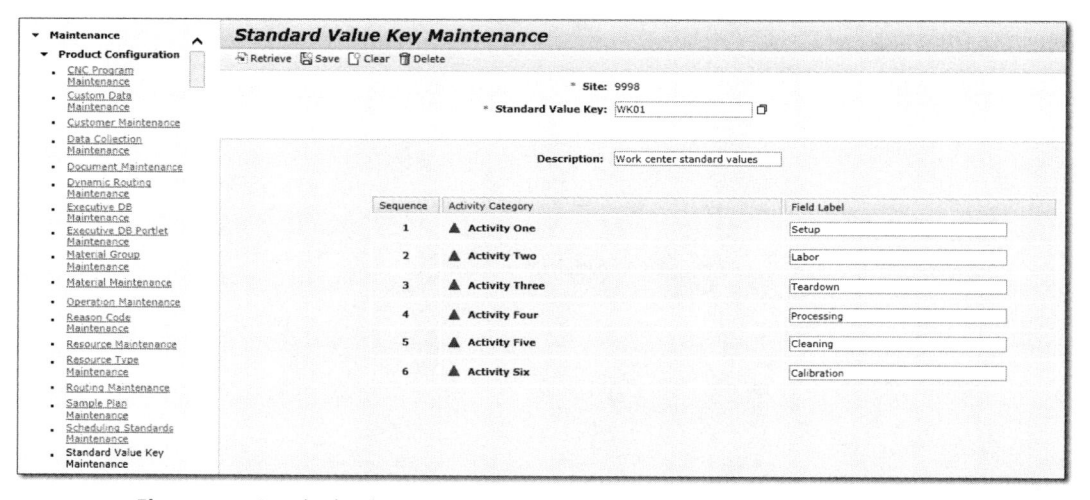

Figure 3.31 Standard Value Key Maintenance

SAP ME supports six activities for a standard value key, just like SAP ERP. You can define any standard value key and specify the activity names and maintain it, as in SAP ERP. Then, you can assign the standard value key to a routing step through the Scheduling Standards Maintenance activity, based on which the activity values need to be specified by the user while executing the operation. The standard value key activities can be used for labor clocking.

3.2.5 Scheduling Standard Maintenance

For production reporting and planning, you may want to maintain the standard values of the metrics of production activities so that you can analyze and compare

Data Enhancement in SAP ME | **3.2**

how much the actuals are deviating, if at all. You can maintain standard values for production processes using the Scheduling Standards Maintenance activity as shown in Figure 3.32. You can define the planned production values for production rates, yields, machine setup time, machine wait time, and standard cycle time.

Operation	Step ID	Production Rate	Planned Yield (%)	Setup Time	Wait Time	Standard Cycle Time
50001320-1-0-0010	10	20 per 2 Hour	98	1 Hour	1 Hour	1.1 Hour
50001320-1-0-0020	20	25 per 2 Hour	98	1.5 Hour	1 Hour	1 Hour

Cum Cycle Time: 2.1000 Hour   Cum Yield: 96%

Figure 3.32 Scheduling Standards Maintenance

> **Note**
>
> You can assign the production standards at any of the following levels, which you need to select under STANDARD SOURCES:
>
> - OPERATIONS: Applies to all routings using the operation
> - ROUTING: Applies to only operation in a specific routing
> - MATERIAL: Applies to only specific material when used in a routing for each SFC created for that material
> - MATERIAL-ROUTING: Applies to specific routings using the specific material for each operation or routing step
> - MATERIAL-OPERATIONS: Applies to specific operation of a routing using specific material

The CUM. CYCLE TIME field specifies the total cycle time for all operations, and CUM. YIELD specifies the total yield percentage. These are not valid for the operation and material levels.

Once you specify the STANDARDS SOURCE, the corresponding items are populated in the list displayed below the standard source field. For ROUTING, for example, once you specify a routing, the corresponding operations are populated. You can click on the DETAILS icon to specify the standard values, as shown in Figure 3.33.

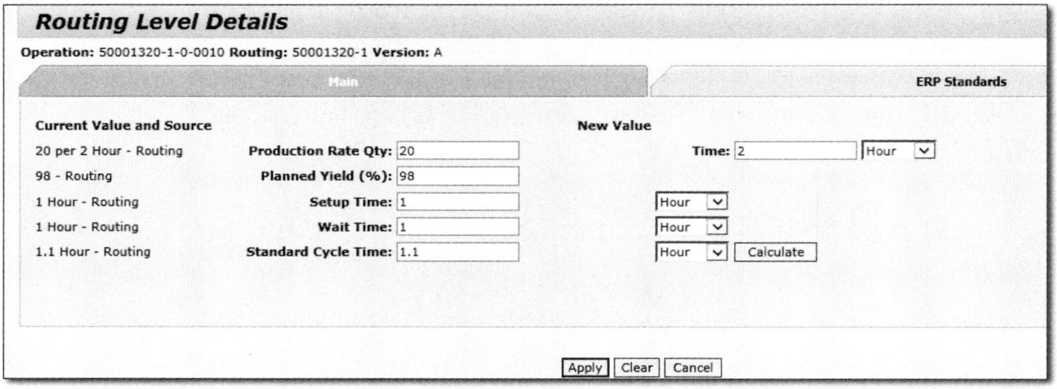

3 | Master Data Management

Figure 3.33 Standard Value Definitions

Once you specify PRODUCTION RATE QUANTITY, TIME, PLANNED YIELD, SETUP TIME, and WAIT TIME, you can calculate STANDARD CYCLE TIME automatically by clicking the CALCULATE button.

You need to specify PRODUCTION RATE QUANTITY, and the time unit indicates the quantity produced at the specified time in the operation. Specify the planned yield for the percentage of the yield in that operation and the setup time and wait time required.

You can also specify the standard values as defined in SAP ERP by assigning the STANDARD VALUE KEY in the ERP STANDARDS configuration tab, as shown in Figure 3.34. The activities defined in the selected standard value key are populated, and you can specify the planned time for each activity.

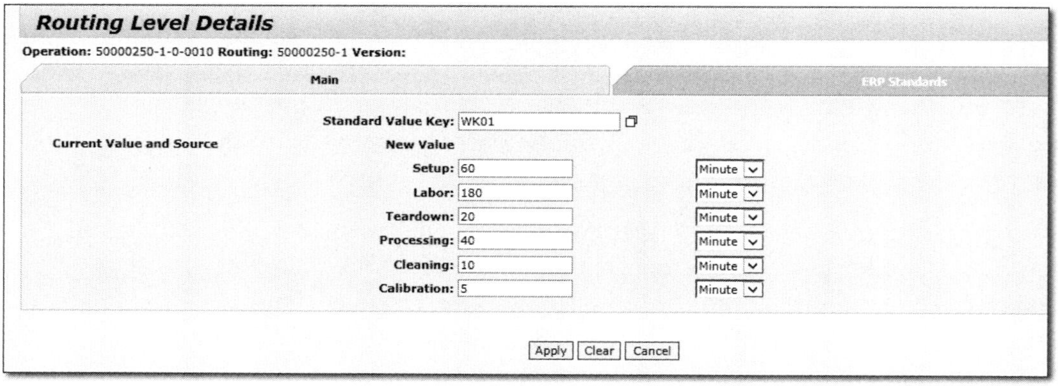

Figure 3.34 ERP Standard Values for Scheduling Standards

3.3 Summary

In this chapter, you learned about various master data and how to configure them in SAP ME. You also discovered how to enhance master data and define custom data objects to set up planned data for various production processes.

In the next chapter, you will learn how to configure operations and routings in SAP ME and also how to enhance routings downloaded from SAP ERP and synchronize those enhancements.

PART II
Features and Functionality

This chapter explains routing design and enhancement in SAP ME and the different types of routings, control keys, operation details, and routing transfers from SAP ME to SAP ERP.

4 Routing Design

In the shop floor production process, execution steps are defined through routings. Routings contain sets of process steps that specify the flow of the production process. In SAP ME, each routing step is defined by an operation. Before designing routings, you need to know the details of operation maintenance. Figure 4.1 shows an example of a routing that contains three sequential steps.

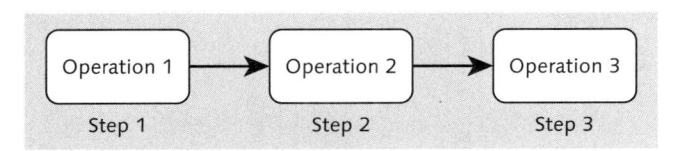

Figure 4.1 Routing Example

In this chapter, we will discuss routing design and enhancement in SAP ME for required activities. We will also focus on details of operation maintenance, different types of routings, control key maintenance, routing design decisions based on different scenarios, and routing transfers from SAP ME to SAP ERP. We will cover routing design in SAP ME, using a shop floor car assembly process as an example.

4.1 Operation Maintenance

Each operation is an individual execution step of a routing, and an operation is executed by an operator manually or by machines automatically with a product at a resource. For example, in a car assembly process, painting body inspection, visual inspection, and quality inspection are each individual operations.

In SAP ME, operations are downloaded from SAP ERP with routing master data. You can retrieve and manage each operation in SAP ME through the Operation

4 | Routing Design

Maintenance activity. You can also create new operations in SAP ME by specifying mandatory parameters and assigning an operation to a routing step. When you create an operation, you must specify its type.

> **Note**
>
> A unit of a product is referred to as a *shop floor control* (SFC), a trackable unit of a material produced in a specific quantity as defined by the material's lot size. For example, in a car assembly process, each car is identified by an SFC number with a quantity of 1 in SAP ME. Refer to Chapter 6 for more details about SFC management.

Figure 4.2 shows an example of operation maintenance in SAP ME using the Operation Maintenance activity.

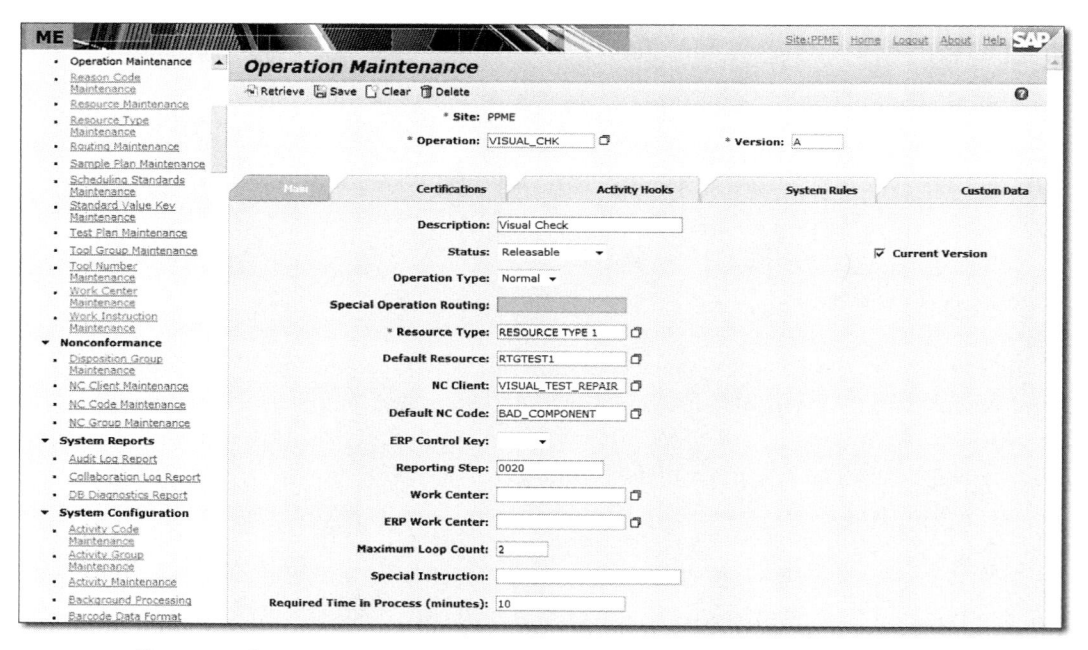

Figure 4.2 Operation Maintenance

In the following sections we will discuss configurations of operations using multiple parameters such as operation type, resource type, and default resource assignment and assigning NC, ERP control keys, reporting steps, work centers, maximum loop counts, special instructions, activity hooks, required processing times, and certifications.

138

4.1.1 Operation Type

In Operation Maintenance, specify the type of operation you are defining in the OPERATION TYPE field. In SAP ME, there are three types of operations available: Normal, Special, and Test. The details of each type are as follows:

- **Normal operation**
  The standard manufacturing operation. In manufacturing processes, most operations are of type normal.

- **Special operation**
  Using special operations, an operator can pull a unit of WIP product from another routing for processing—for example, for rework processing of a defective unit. When you create a special operation, the system can create a special routing with the same name as the operation name. In that special routing, the special operation is the first step. For example, say you create an operation called REWORK and the operation type is special. When you save the operation in SAP ME, the system will create a special routing named REWORK, and the operation you created will be its entry step. Figure 4.3 illustrates creating a special operation.

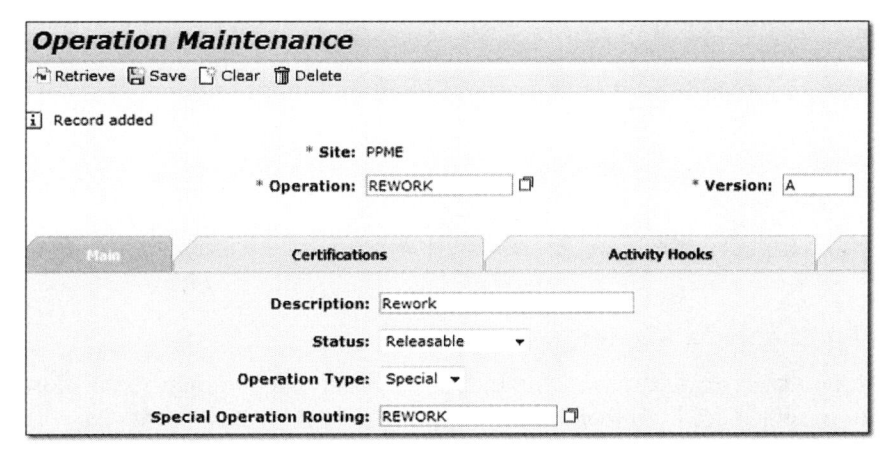

Figure 4.3 Special Operation Creation

- **Test operation**
  Test operations are used for quality testing purposes. In a test operation, a product is tested to determine its quality.

4.1.2 Assigning Resource Type and Default Resource in Operation

When an operator works on a Production Operator Dashboard, he or she selects an operation from the available operation list and may expect that the corresponding resource will appear automatically in resource field (otherwise, he or she needs to enter the resource name manually). To enable automatically getting the resource for an operation, you need to assign the resource type and resource name in operation maintenance. RESOURCE TYPE is a mandatory parameter in operation maintenance. If you assign only a resource type in operation maintenance, the operator can select any resource in the dashboard that belongs to the same resource type. For example, in SAP ME you have defined a resource type called RT that contains four resources: RS-1, RS-2, RS-3, and RS-4. If you assign only resource type RT for an operation, an operator can choose from RS-1, RS-2, RS-3, or RS-4 to execute the operation, as shown in Figure 4.4.

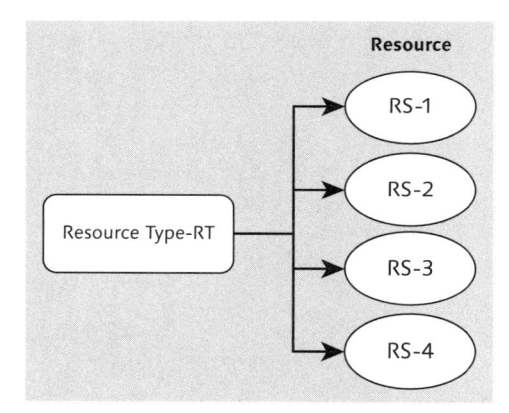

Figure 4.4 Resource Type includes Resources

4.1.3 Additional Parameters

There are a number of additional parameters for operation maintenance, the most important of which are as follows:

- **Assigning NC client and default NC code in operation**

  In shop floor execution process, operations can be used for quality inspection or testing purposes. In an operation, if any defect is found, the operator can record the defect through *nonconformance* (NC). Details of NC client and NC code maintenance are described in Chapter 8. Here, you need to assign the NC client for operation, and based on NC client assignment the nonconformance process and behavior in the Production Operator Dashboard will be different. You can also assign a default NC code for an operation. These two fields are optional for operation maintenance.

- **ERP control key**
  The control key defines the SAP ERP reporting step and also specifies the behavior of operation in production. Details are explained in Section 4.4.

- **Reporting step**
  The reporting step in an operation is a required indicator for SAP ERP integration. If an operation is local to SAP ME and not an executing step or operation in an SAP ERP routing, then you don't need to enter any value for the reporting step. No yield confirmation will be updated in SAP ERP, because the operation is local to SAP ME and contains no SAP ERP reporting step. On the other hand, all operations defined in SAP ERP should have the SAP ERP reporting step defined automatically when downloaded to SAP ME.

- **Work center**
  In operation maintenance, you can assign a work center that is either downloaded from SAP ERP or maintained locally in SAP ME only through the Work Center Maintenance activity. In SAP ME, you can define a production line as a work center in a site.

- **ERP work center**
  A routing contains a sequence of operations along with a work center in which the operations are performed. To get an SAP ERP work center into SAP ME, you need to download it. This field is required when you export routings from SAP ME to SAP ERP and you need to assign an SAP ERP work center to operations.

- **Maximum loop count**
  The maximum loop count is how many times an SFC can be executed in an operation. For example, say that Operator 1 is working in the QUALITY_CHECK operation and has logged NC for defect. Per the routing flow, the SFC has moved to the REWORK operation. Operator 2 is working in the REWORK operation and has closed the NC. Again, per the routing flow, the SFC has moved to the QUALITY_CHECK operation. Now, Operator 1 finds another defect and logs NC in the QUALITY_CHECK operation for the same SFC. The SFC moves to the REWORK operation again. This forms a cycle between the QUALITY_CHECK and REWORK operations. By defining the maximum loop count, you can specify the maximum number of times an SFC can be executed in an operation.

4 | Routing Design

- **Special instructions**
  Through a special instruction, you can specify some instruction (text) for a routing step. The same instruction will be available in the dashboard when the operator works on the routing operation. The special instruction is used as a default value for routing step and visible in routing step property which is taken from the operation and used in the routing step.

- **Activity hook**
  In operation maintenance, you can assign multiple activities to be triggered by the operation during different events in execution process. In addition to standard activities, you can also assign custom activities based on requirements. SAP ME provides a list of hook points such as PRE_START, POST_START, PRE_COMPLETE, POST_COMPLETE, PRE_SIGNOFF, POST_SIGNOFF, and so on for operations. Per your requirements, you can select a hook point from the available list and assign activities as shown in Figure 4.5. For example, in an assembly process, the requirement is to complete assembly of components automatically in an operation in which goods issue will occur. Now, you can retrieve that operation and assign the AUTOASSY_COMPONENT activity to the PRE_COMPLETE hook point. Make sure that you have checked the ENABLED checkbox and saved the operation.

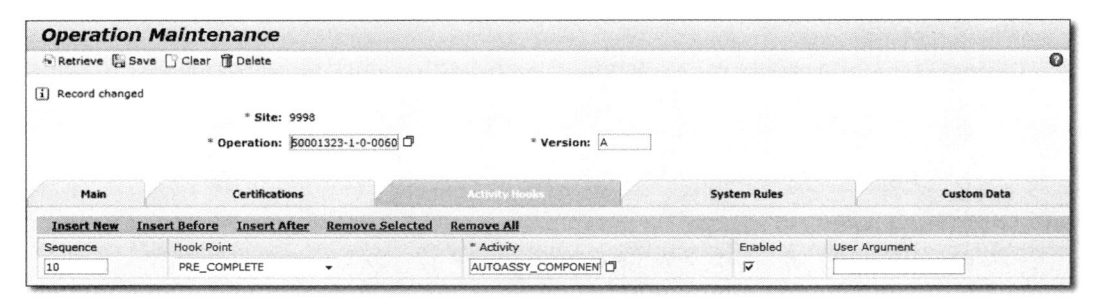

Figure 4.5 Maintaining Activity Hooks in Operation

- **Required time in process (minutes)**
  This setting specifies the time required to execute an operation. An operator who is working on an operation will not be able to complete the operation before the specified time. To enable this functionality, you need to assign the ELAPSED_TIME_CHECK hook activity with the PRE_COMPLETE hook point in operation. Figure 4.6 shows how to do so in the ACTIVITY HOOKS tab of an operation.

Figure 4.6 ELAPSED_TIME_CHECK as Activity Hook

▶ **Certification assignment in operation**
You can assign a certification to an operation so that only operators who have that certification maintained in their user profiles can execute the operation, as shown in Figure 4.7. Before assigning a certificate to an operation, you need to create and assign a certificate to a user group, which is done through the Certification Maintenance activity (explained in Chapter 2). The certification assigned to the user group will only be enforced but not to other user groups.

Figure 4.7 Certification Assignment in Operation

Now that you understand key parameters for operation maintenance, you can create an operation in SAP ME based on production requirements.

4.2 Designing Routings

For routing design, you first need to understand the different types of routings available in SAP ME and their purposes.

> **Note: Routing Design Workbench**
>
> The Routing Design Workbench is a Java Swing applet-based application that opens in a web browser window through the Routing Maintenance activity in SAP ME. You can design routing in the Routing Design Workbench either through the *tabular mode* or the *graphical mode*. In tabular mode, you can design routing by inserting or deleting records in a table in which operations are displayed in sequence. In graphical mode, all operations appear in the left panel, and you can drag and drop the operations in the drawing board and create links. You can also set scripts for each link by editing the link properties.

Other than routing type we will also discuss related parameters and functions required for designing the routing through routing design workbench such as routing status, return steps options, any order group, simultaneous group and routing next operation decision. You will also find the details of routing design scenario based on a car assembly process.

4.2.1 Routing Types

Routing in SAP ME is categorized by routing types, which we explain in the following subsections.

Production Routing

The production routing type is used for shop floor production purposes. Production routings are downloaded from SAP ERP to SAP ME or it can be created in SAP ME and transported to SAP ERP. You can release and execute orders only for production routings.

NC Disposition Routing

Before exploring NC disposition routings, you need to understand disposition functions and available types of NC-based dispositions. In the shop floor execution process, disposition functions provide a list of functions in which an SFC can be conditionally moved to another step based on the operator's choice, which is explained in Chapter 8. In SAP ME, two types of NC-based disposition are available:

- Function-based dispositions
- Routing-based dispositions

4.2 Designing Routings

In function-based dispositions, you can assign a disposition group to an NC code when you are maintaining the NC code through the NC CODE MAINTENANCE activity. In the shop floor execution process, when an operator logs a defect using that NC code, the system provides a list of disposition functions available for that group.

In routing-based dispositions, you can assign a special or NC type of routing to the NC code. When an operator logs a defect using that NC code, the system sends the SFC to the assigned routing. Figure 4.8 shows the available special routings in SAP ME that can be used for routing-based dispositions: INSPECTION_REJECTED, PMR, and REWORK. You can also create disposition routings with special or NC routing types.

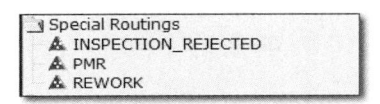

Figure 4.8 Available Special Routings in System

Figure 4.9 provides an example of a disposition routing scenario in which the preliminary material review (PMR) step is assigned as a disposition for an NC code. In the execution process, an SFC can be moved to disposition routing PMR if the NC code is logged by an operator in Operation 2.

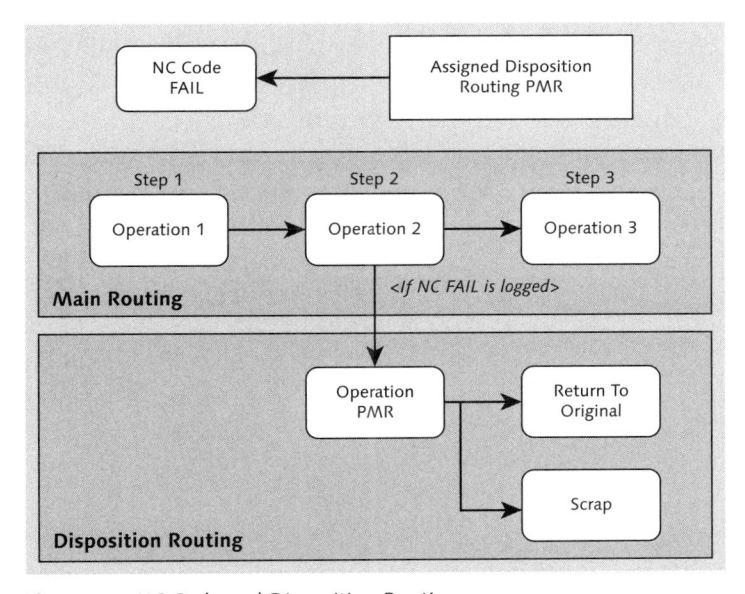

Figure 4.9 NC Code and Disposition Routing

Disposition Function Routing

This routing type is used by SAP ME to denote disposition functions. In the previous section, you learned about disposition functions and function-based disposition. In routing maintenance, you can find a list of available disposition functions (shown in Figure 4.10), which are used by SAP ME.

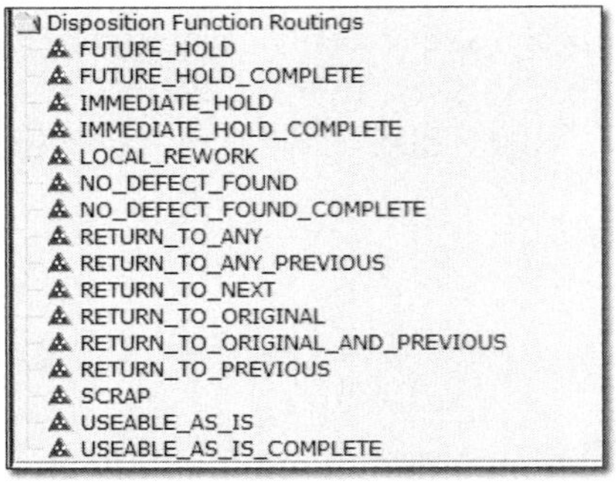

```
Disposition Function Routings
    FUTURE_HOLD
    FUTURE_HOLD_COMPLETE
    IMMEDIATE_HOLD
    IMMEDIATE_HOLD_COMPLETE
    LOCAL_REWORK
    NO_DEFECT_FOUND
    NO_DEFECT_FOUND_COMPLETE
    RETURN_TO_ANY
    RETURN_TO_ANY_PREVIOUS
    RETURN_TO_NEXT
    RETURN_TO_ORIGINAL
    RETURN_TO_ORIGINAL_AND_PREVIOUS
    RETURN_TO_PREVIOUS
    SCRAP
    USEABLE_AS_IS
    USEABLE_AS_IS_COMPLETE
```

Figure 4.10 Available Disposition Function Routings

Sample Routing

Sample routing is used when you create sampling plans in SAP ME via the SAMPLE PLAN MAINTENANCE activity. The selected sampling product can be executed through sample routing operations. You can find the usage of sample routing in Chapter 8 for sampling process.

> **Note: Relaxed Routing Flow**
>
> If the RELAXED ROUTING FLOW checkbox is checked then SAP ME will allow a non-serialized SFC to be in work at more than one operation on a single routing at the same time and the quantity will flow down the routing in the standard way that physical product flows down in production line. The released quantity will be added to the same SFC until the SFC quantity equals the lot size of the material. The relaxed routing flow is not selected when the routing is downloaded from SAP ERP. You need to either select the RELAXED ROUTING FLOW checkbox manually or customize the SAPMEINT interface to set the RELAXED ROUTING FLOW checkbox automatically on routing download from SAP ERP.

4.2.2 Routing Status

In routing maintenance, you can set the routing status, which is available on the MAIN tab as RELEASABLE, which allows you to release an SFC to the routing;

OBSOLETE, which will stop you from releasing an SFC to the routing and the routing is no longer used; HOLD, which will also stop you from releasing an SFC to the routing but is temporary and can be changed after resolving the issue; or FROZEN, which will allow you to release SFC to the routing, but you will not be able to change the routing record.

4.2.3 Return Steps Options

In routing maintenance, a few available in-built return steps and operations are particularly useful for routing design. A *return step* is the step to which the SFC will be returned to the previous routing after completion of nonconformance. The functionality of the steps are described in Table 4.1.

Step	Functionality
Hold	A hold step can be used in two ways: ▶ An immediate hold will set the SFC on hold as soon as the SFC is queued in the hold step. ▶ A future hold needs a future hold operation assigned. Whenever the SFC moves to that operation, the SFC will be in a hold status.
Scrapped	Scrap the SFC. For example, an SFC has come to a REWORK operation through the NC log. The defect is not closed in the REWORK operation, and the operator wants to scrap the SFC. Here, you need to design routing such a way that if the NC is not closed in the REWORK operation, then it will be scrapped.
Return (original)	Returns the SFC to original step.
Return (any)	Returns the SFC to any step on the original routing. Here, the operator can select any step of the original routing.
Return (previous)	Returns the SFC to the previous step of original routing.
Return (any previous)	Returns the SFC to any step of the original routing. The operator needs to select the step.
Return (next)	Returns the SFC to the next step of original routing.
Return to original and previous	Returns the SFC to the original step or previous step. The operator needs to select the step.
Done	Sets the SFC status to DONE.

Table 4.1 Available Steps

4.2.4 Any Order Group

SAP ME provides the feature to execute a group of steps in any order through the Any Order Group step (available under the operation list in the Routing Maintenance window). For Any Order Group, SAP ME puts the SFC in the queue state for all the operations available in Any Order Group. The operator can execute each operation only one at a time for the SFC. You cannot execute the product in another operation when an operator is executing one operation of Any Order Group. In routing design, to work with the Any Order Group operation you need to drag ANY ORDER GROUP onto the design area in the Routing Workbench. Then, you can drag the operations inside the Any Order Group operation. In Figure 4.11, Operation 2, Operation 3, and Operation 4 are inside the Any Order Group operation. When an SFC is completed in Operation 1, it is placed in the queue state of Operation 2, Operation 3, and Operation 4. When an operator starts the SFC in Operation 2, SAP ME takes the SFC from Operation 3 and Operation 4. After completion of the SFC in Operation 2, SAP ME puts the SFC back in the queue of Operation 3 and Operation 4. In the same way, the operator can complete Operation 3 and Operation 4 only one at a time. When all three operations of Any Order Group are completed, the SFC is queued at Operation 5.

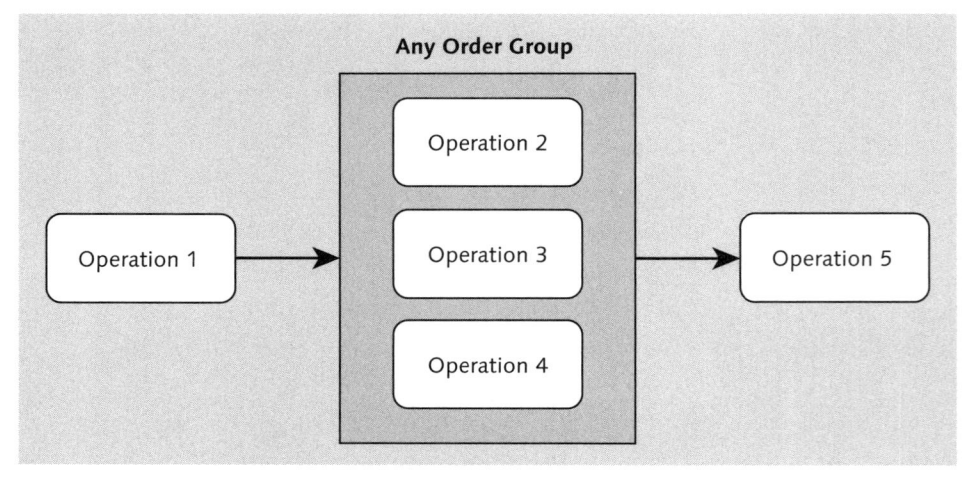

Figure 4.11 Any Order Group Step Example

4.2.5 Simultaneous Group

SAP ME provides the functionality to execute multiple operations at the same time through the Simultaneous Group step (available under the operation list of the Routing Maintenance window). For Simultaneous Group, SAP ME puts the SFC in the queued state for all the operations available in the group. Operators can execute the operations in Simultaneous Group in parallel for the SFC, which will not be moved out of Simultaneous Group operations until all operations of the Simultaneous Group are completed. For example, in a car assembly production line, operators work on both sides of the production line for multiple torque operations. They use torque tools independently to complete each operation for the same car. Here, an operator working on one side of the production line will not wait for other side to complete. In this situation, you can design routing using Simultaneous Group for torque operations. In Figure 4.12, you can see that the SFC will be moved to Operation 5 when all four torque operations are completed.

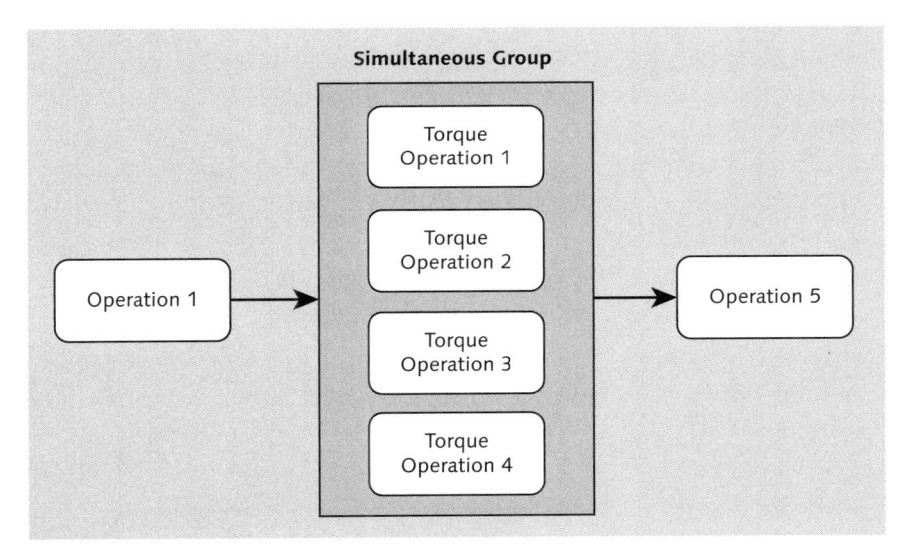

Figure 4.12 Simultaneous Group with Torque Operations

4.2.6 Making Decisions for Routing Next Operation

Consider a production scenario in which an operator is working on a QUALITY_CHK operation and an SFC is in a queue state for that operation. After completion of the SFC in the QUALITY_CHK operation, it can go either to the REPAIR operation or the VISUAL_CHK operation (shown in Figure 4.13).

4 | Routing Design

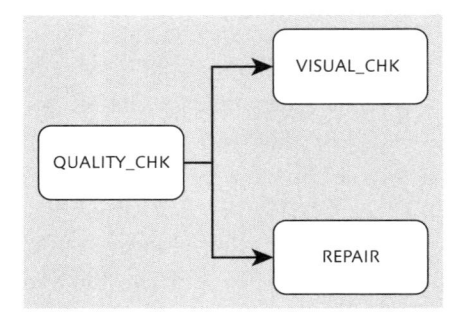

Figure 4.13 Next Operation Decision

Here, the next operation flow decision can be made manually by the operator or automatically through a script. For manual selection, you don't need to specify anything in routing design, but for automatic flow you need to specify a script in a link. Suppose that based on the open NC logged in QUALITY_CHK operation, the SFC will move to the REAPIR operation. You need to maintain a script for open NC for the link between the QUALITY_CHK and REPAIR operations. To maintain the script, double-click on the link between QUALITY_CHK and REPAIR. Each script is associated with the paths between routing steps. The scripting language is basically normal JavaScript but there are some differences. All variables must be defined before using them. The `exit()` method is used to return a value to the next step logic. The LINK PROPERTIES popup will appear. Here, you can select OPEN NONCONFORMANCES from the dropdown. Check the syntax and click on OK. Figure 4.14 shows how to maintain an open nonconformance script for link.

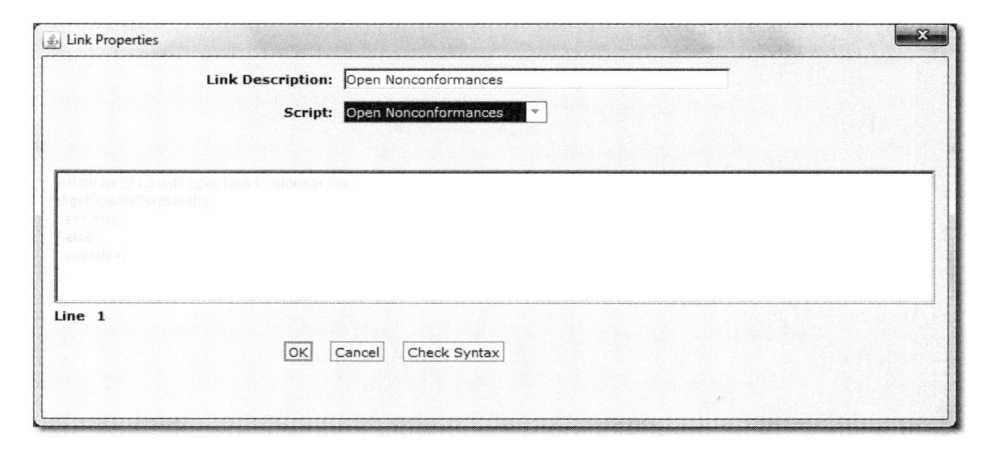

Figure 4.14 Maintaining Open Nonconformances Script

4.2.7 Routing Design Scenario

Now you should understand all the required components for designing routing in SAP ME. To design routing, first open the Routing Maintenance activity from the activity list in SAP ME; to do so, you must install the Oracle Java Runtime Environment (JRE) in your local system, because it is a Java Swing applet-based application. Routing Maintenance appears in a new window. You can create and maintain routing either through the graphical mode or tabular mode. Graphical mode is very user-friendly for designing routing through drag-and-drop functionality, as shown later in Figure 4.15.

To design a routing, let's consider a business scenario in which there are multiple steps and substeps for the assembly. In a car assembly process on shop floor, say you have fourteen steps for the normal assembly process. You also need to consider the repair and quarantine steps. Refer to Table 4.2 for the car assembly step sequence, operations, resources, and related SAP ERP work centers.

Step Id	Operation	Description	Resource	ERP Work Center
10	UPLOAD_CAR_BODY	Upload Car Body on Line	BODASM	WC01
20	FRNT_RIGHT_DR_ASSEMBL	Front Right Door Assembly	DRASFR	WC02
30	FRNT_LEFT_DR_ASSEMBL	Front Left Door Assembly	DRASFL	WC03
40	REAR_RIGHT_DR_ASSEMBL	Rear Right Door Assembly	DRASRR	WC04
50	REAR_LEFT_DR_ASSEMBL	Rear Left Door Assembly	DRASRL	WC05
60	WIRING_HARNESS	Wiring Harness	WIRING	WC06
70	INTER_ASSEMBL	Interior Assembly	INTERAS	WC07
80	WIND_SHLD_ASSEMBL	Front and Back Wind Shield Installation	WINSHLD	WC08
90	VISUAL_INSP	Visual Inspection	VISINSP	WC09

Table 4.2 Step ID, Operation, Resource, and SAP ERP Work Center Relations for Car Assembly Scenario

Step Id	Operation	Description	Resource	ERP Work Center
100	PAINTING	Painting	PAINTING	WC10
110	PAINT_INSP	Paint Inspection	PAINTINS	WC11
120	MATE	Mate	MATE	WC12
130	QLTY_INSP	Quality Inspection	QUALINSP	WC13
140	FINAL_CHK	Final Check	FINALCHK	WC14
150	REPAIR_1	Repair 1	REPR1	Not required; local operation for SAP ME, and should not be updated in SAP ERP
160	QUARTN_1	Quarantine 1	QUART1	Not required; local operation for SAP ME, and should not be updated in SAP ERP
170	REPAIR_2	Repair 2	REPR2	Not required; local operation for SAP ME, and should not be updated in SAP ERP
180	QUARTN_2	Quarantine 2	QUART2	Not required; local operation for SAP ME, and should not be updated in SAP ERP
190	REP_PAINT_BODY	Repair Paint Body	REPR_PNT_BDY	Not required; local operation for SAP ME, and should not be updated in SAP ERP

Table 4.2 Step ID, Operation, Resource, and SAP ERP Work Center Relations for Car Assembly Scenario (Cont.)

In addition to the steps in Table 4.2, you also need to use two scrapped steps (built-in steps in SAP ME, described in Table 4.1), for which you can set step IDs 200 and 210. You need to create the operations described in Table 4.2 in SAP ME or download them from SAP ERP. Let's consider a scenario in which we create the routing in SAP ME and then upload it to SAP ERP. From the SAP ME activity list, open the activity Operation Maintenance and create all the previously noted operations (except REPAIR_1, REPAIR_2, QUARTN_1, QUARTN_2, and REP_PAINT_BODY) as normal operations. You also need to assign resource type, default resource, ERP control key, and ERP work center.

Before assigning a resource type to an operation, you have to create a resource type called CAR_ASSEMBL through the Resource Type Maintenance activity. Here, we assume that you have downloaded all required resources (except

Designing Routings | **4.2**

REPR1, REPR2, QUART1, QUART2 and REPR_PNT_BDY, which will be created in SAP ME) and work centers from SAP ERP. You need to assign all resources to the CAR_ASSEMBL resource type. Use operation type special for the REPAIR_1, REPAIR_2, QUARTN_1, QUARTN_2, and REP_PAINT_BODY operations, and don't assign an ERP control key or ERP work center for these five operations. These five operations are local to SAP ME and should not be updated in SAP ERP.

After you have opened the Routing Maintenance workbench using the Routing Maintenance activity, create a new routing and specify the routing number (CAR_ASSEMBL_0001), version (A), and description (Car Assembly Routing). You need to select the production routing type and also the new status on the MAIN tab. Now, switch to the ROUTING tab. On the left side panel, you will see all the operations that you have created through operation maintenance. Drag UPLOAD_CAR_BODY onto the routing drawing board and double-click it to open the routing step properties. There, enter the step ID (10) and reporting step (0010). The remaining fields are automatically populated using data from the operation, and step 10 is marked as the entry step because it is the first step of CAR_ASSEMBL_0001 routing. Figure 4.15 shows the routing step configuration for the first step.

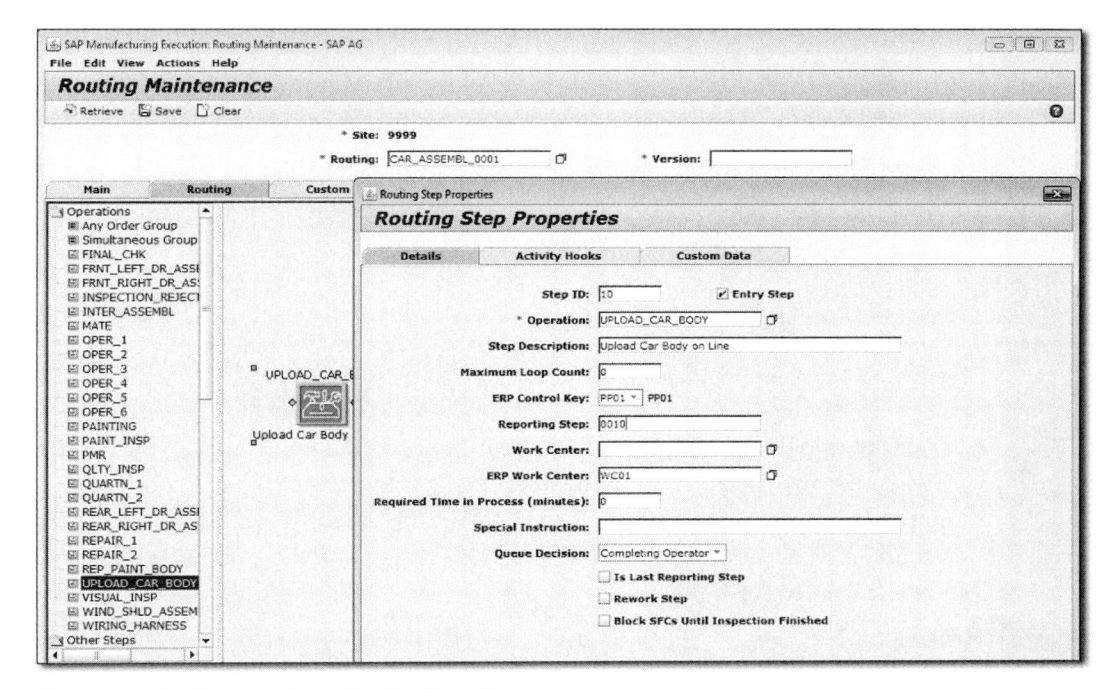

Figure 4.15 Routing Step Properties Configuration

153

4 | Routing Design

Click on OK button to set the step properties, and click on SAVE to save the routing. Next, drag the SIMULTANEOUS GROUP operation onto the drawing board. Now, drag FRNT_RIGHT_DR_ASSEMBL, FRNT_LEFT_DR_ASSEMBL, REAR_RIGHT_DR_ASSEMBL, and REAR_LEFT_DR_ASSEMBL operations inside the SIMULTANEOUS GROUP operation. Those four operations can be executed in parallel for assembly process. You can open the step property for the simultaneous group and enter the step group ID (11). For each operation, open the DETAILS window to enter the step ID and reporting step like in the first operation (UPLOAD_CAR_BODY). Then, make a link from UPLOAD_CAR_BODY step to SIMULTANEOUS GROUP and save the routing. Figure 4.16 shows how to configure the simultaneous group in routing design.

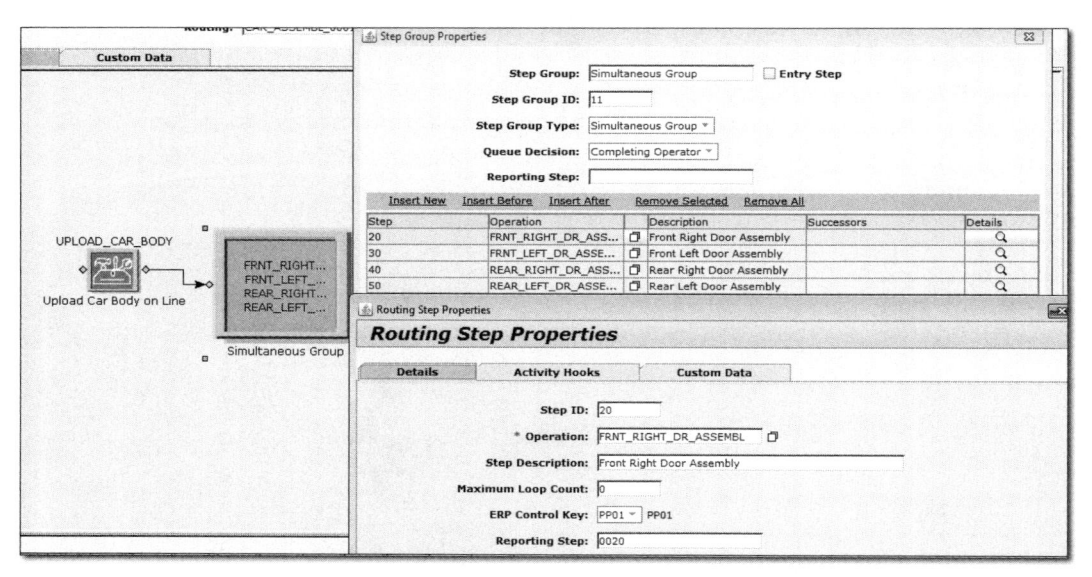

Figure 4.16 Simultaneous Group Configuration

As per the step IDs from Table 4.2, drag the operations one by one and make links between the two steps. You also need to configure the step ID and reporting step number for each step. When you save the routing, the last step (FINAL_CHK) will be marked as IS LAST REPORTING STEP. The routing will now look like the one shown in Figure 4.17.

Designing Routings | **4.2**

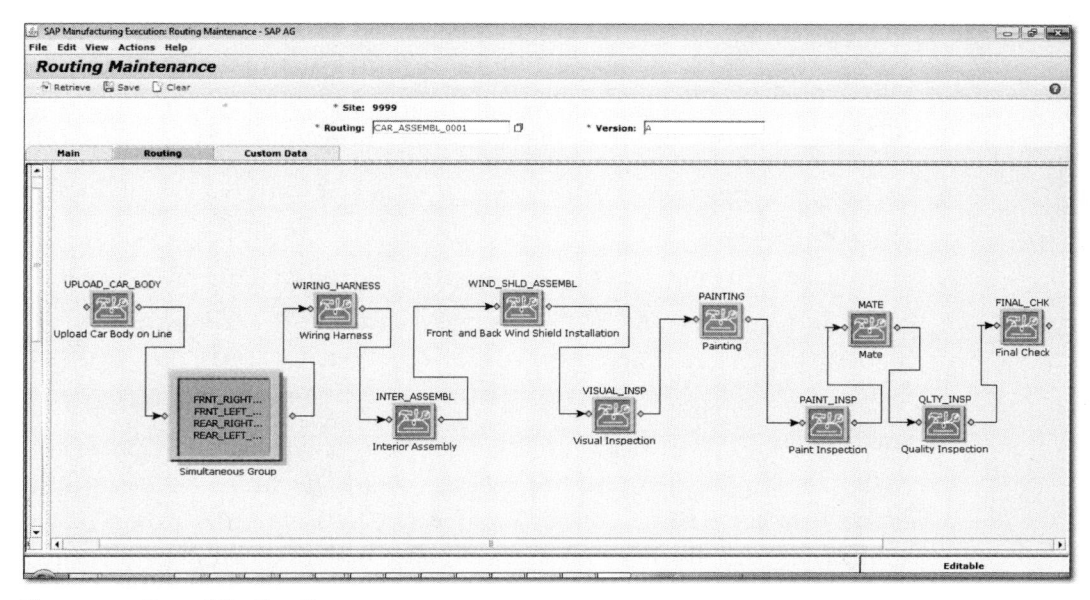

Figure 4.17 Flow of Routing Steps

Now, we need to work with the nonconformance recording part of the car assembly process. Work through the following steps:

1. Drag REPAIR_1 onto the drawing board and place it below VISUAL_INSP. You need to set the step ID (150) for REPAIR_1; the reporting step number is not required because this is a local step in SAP ME.

2. Add a right anchor by right-clicking on VISUAL_INSP, and make a link from VISUAL_INSP to REPAIR_1.

3. Double-click on the link between VISUAL_INSP and REPAIR_1. In the LINK PROPERTIES popup, select OPEN NONCONFORMANCES for the script and click on OK.

> **Note**
> After completion of the VISUAL_INSP operation, the system will send the SFC to the REPAIR_1 operation for any open NC; otherwise, the SFC will move to the PAINTING operation.

4. Next, add a left anchor to VISUAL_INSP and make a link from the right anchor of REPAIR_1 to VISUAL_INSP.

4 | Routing Design

5. Drag QUARTN_1 onto the Routing Design workbench, place it to the right of REPAIR_1, and set the step ID (170) for QUARTN_1.

6. Next, add a right anchor to REPAIR_1 and make a link from REPAIR_1 to QUARTN_1.

7. Set the OPEN NONCONFORMANCES script in the link property between REPAIR_1 and QUARTN_1.

8. Drag SCRAPPED from the OTHER STEPS group to the right side of QUARTN_1.

9. Make a link from QUARTN_1 to SCRAPPED, and set the OPEN NONCONFORMANCES script in the link property. If the defect is not closed in the QUARTN_1 step, then the SFC will be scrapped after completion of QUARTN_1 step.

10. Add another left anchor to VISUAL_INSP and a right anchor to QUARTN_1.

11. Make a link from QUARTN_1 to VISUAL_INSP and add the NO OPEN NONCONFORMANCES script in the link property. If the defect is closed in the QUARTN_1 step, then the SFC will be moved to the VISUAL_INSP step after completion of QUARTN_1. Now, the nonconformance part of the routing design will look like Figure 4.18.

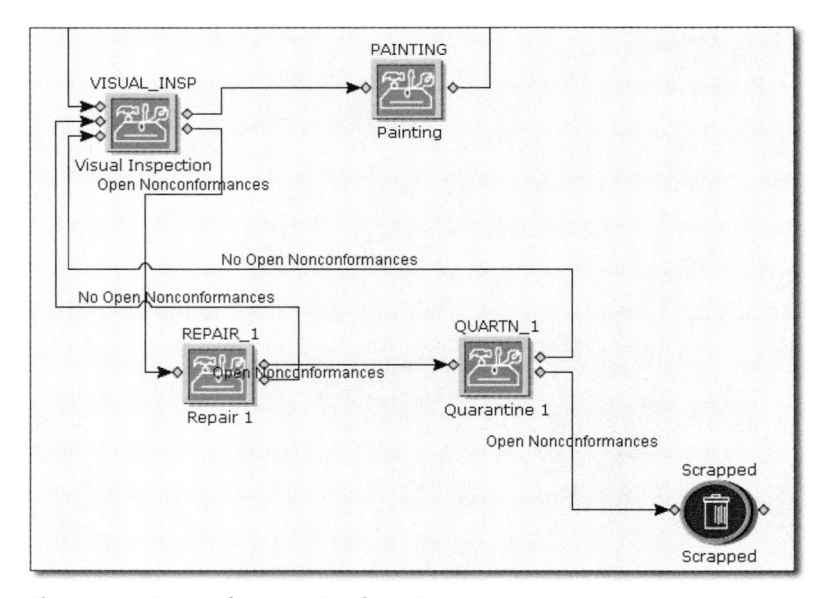

Figure 4.18 Nonconformance Configuration in Routing Design

Next, configure another nonconformance for the QLTY_INSP operation. After completion of the QLTY_INSP operation, the system will send the SFC (in this case, a car) to the REPAIR_2 operation for any open NC; otherwise, the system will send the SFC to the FINAL_CHK operation if NC is closed (NO OPEN NONCONFORMANCES). If open NC is closed in REPAIR_2, then the SFC will come back to the QLTY_INSP step; otherwise, it will move to the QUARTN_2 step for open NC. If open NC is not closed in QUARTN_2, then the system will scrap the SFC after completion of the QUARTN_2 operation; otherwise, the SFC will be moved to FINAL_CHK for closed NC. After configuring the flow for such a requirement, the nonconformance of the routing design will look like Figure 4.19.

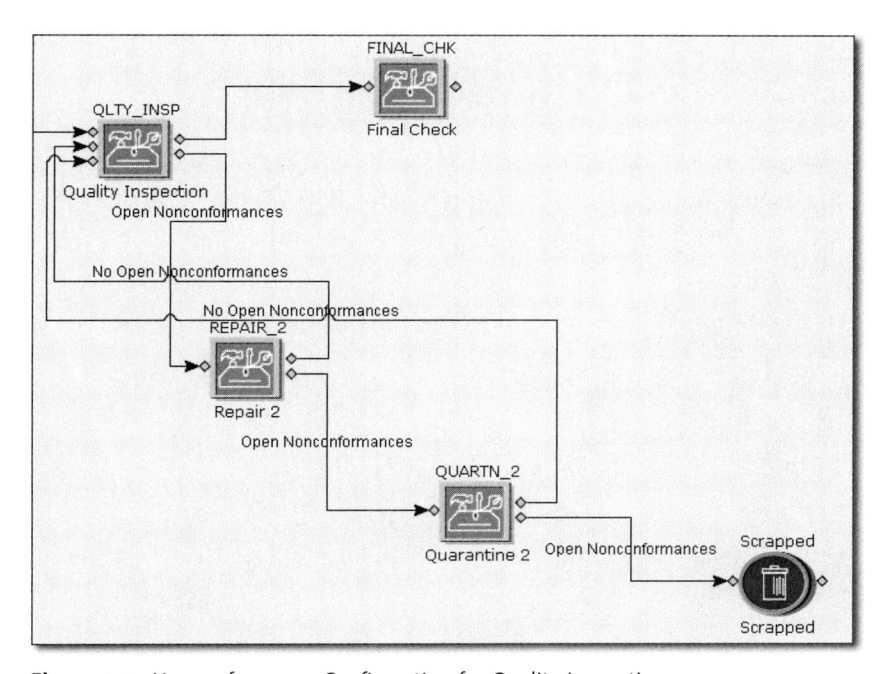

Figure 4.19 Nonconformance Configuration for Quality Inspection

Another operation, REP_PAINT_BODY, will be used to repair body painting. Drag the operation onto the drawing board and place it below PAINT_INSP. For any defect in PAINT_INSP, the system will send the SFC to the REP_PAINT_BODY step. The defect must be closed (assume no defects after the REP_PAINT_BODY operation) in the REP_PAINT_BODY step, and the SFC will come back to the PAINT_INSP step (see Figure 4.20).

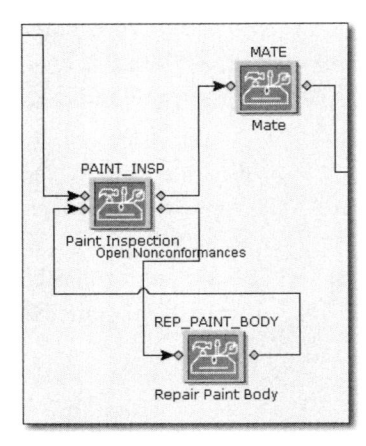

Figure 4.20 Nonconformance Configuration for Paint Inspection

Now, save the routing and switch to the Main tab. Change the routing status to Releasable and select the Current Version checkbox. The routing design is complete; click on Save. Figure 4.21 shows the final routing for car the assembly process in SAP ME.

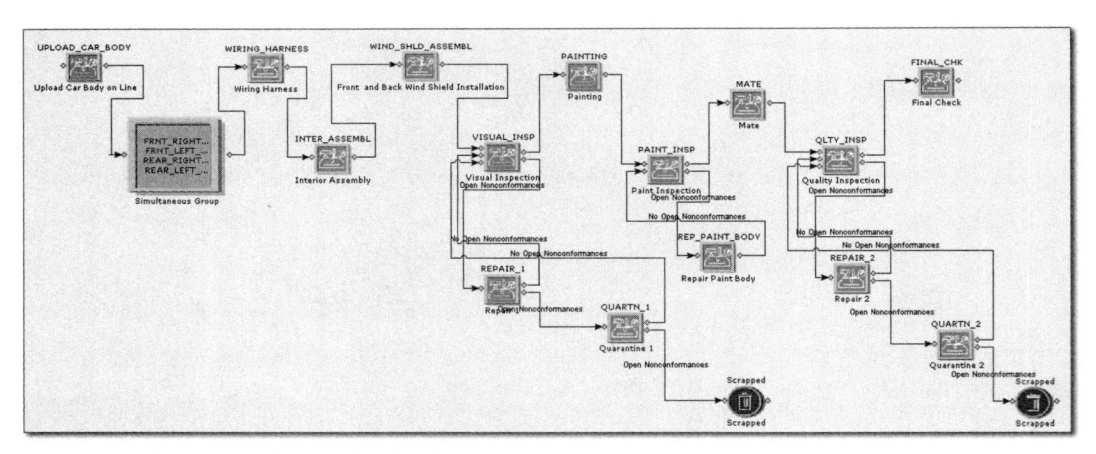

Figure 4.21 Final Routing for Car Assembly

4.3 Enhancing Routings

Usually, routings are created in SAP ERP and downloaded into SAP ME as master data through SAPMEINT. Routing enhancement is required in SAP ME when you need to modify a routing based on the shop floor execution process. For example, you can add extra steps, update the routing flow, add NC-based branching, or perform other changes to a routing. We will work again with the fourteen-step car assembly routing downloaded from SAP ERP (see Figure 4.22).

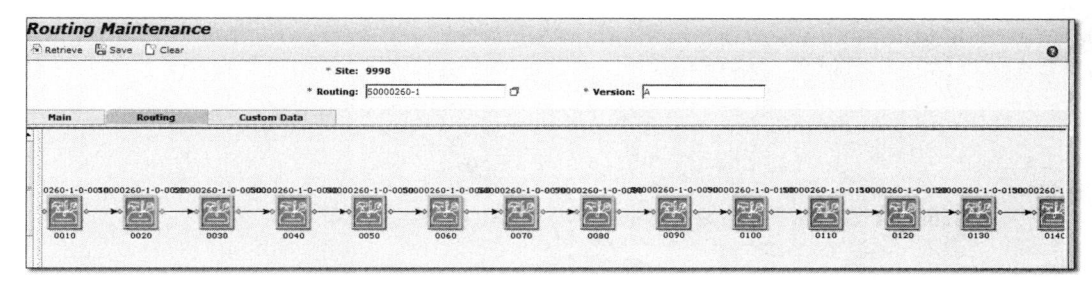

Figure 4.22 Routing Downloaded from SAP ERP

Through the Operation Maintenance activity, you can assign a resource type and default resource to each operation. Table 4.3 lists operation-specific default resources.

Step ID	Operation	Resource Type	Default Resource
10	50000260-1-0-0010	CAR_ASSEMBL	BODASM
20	50000260-1-0-0020	CAR_ASSEMBL	DRASFR
30	50000260-1-0-0030	CAR_ASSEMBL	DRASFL
40	50000260-1-0-0040	CAR_ASSEMBL	DRASRR
50	50000260-1-0-0050	CAR_ASSEMBL	DRASRL
60	50000260-1-0-0060	CAR_ASSEMBL	WIRING
70	50000260-1-0-0070	CAR_ASSEMBL	INTERAS
80	50000260-1-0-0080	CAR_ASSEMBL	WINSHLD
90	50000260-1-0-0090	CAR_ASSEMBL	VISINSP
100	50000260-1-0-0100	CAR_ASSEMBL	PAINTING
110	50000260-1-0-0110	CAR_ASSEMBL	PAINTING
120	50000260-1-0-0120	CAR_ASSEMBL	MATE
130	50000260-1-0-0130	CAR_ASSEMBL	QUALINSP
140	50000260-1-0-0140	CAR_ASSEMBL	FINALCHK

Table 4.3 Operation-Specific Default Resource Assignment

Now, create five special operations using the data in Table 4.4. These special operations will be used to handle a nonconformance scenario.

Step Id	Operation	Description	Resource Type	Default Resource
150	REPAIR_1	Repair 1	CAR_ASSEMBL	REPR1
160	QUARTN_1	Quarantine 1	CAR_ASSEMBL	QUART1
170	REPAIR_2	Repair 2	CAR_ASSEMBL	REPR2
180	QUARTN_2	Quarantine 2	CAR_ASSEMBL	QUART2
190	REP_PAINT_BODY	Repair Paint Body	CAR_ASSEMBL	REPR_PNT_BDY

Table 4.4 Default Resource Assignment for Special Operations

To enhance a routing, follow these steps:

1. Open the Routing Maintenance activity.
2. Retrieve the routing (e.g., 50000260-1), which is downloaded from SAP ERP.
3. Per your business requirements, door assembly can be performed in parallel. Therefore, place the 50000260-1-0-0020, 50000260-1-0-0030, 50000260-1-0-0040, and 50000260-1-0-0050 operations within SIMULTANEOUS GROUP.
4. After retrieving the routing (50000260-1), switch to the ROUTING tab and remove 50000260-1-0-0020, 50000260-1-0-0030, 50000260-1-0-0040, and 50000260-1-0-0050 from the drawing board.
5. Drag SIMULTANEOUS GROUP from the left panel onto the drawing board. Drag the four operations listed previously into SIMULTANEOUS GROUP.
6. To open the step properties, double-click on SIMULTANEOUS GROUP and enter the step ID and reporting step number for the four operations by clicking on the DETAILS icon.
7. Make a link from 50000260-1-0-0010 to SIMULTANEOUS GROUP and another link from SIMULTANEOUS GROUP to 50000260-1-0-0060 (as shown in Figure 4.23).

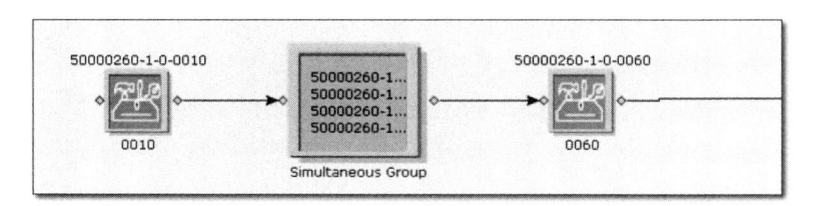

Figure 4.23 Routing Enhancement with Simultaneous Group

Now, you can enhance the routing with nonconformance parts. Operation 50000260-1-0-0090 is used for visual inspection of the car assembly process. If any defect is found, then NC will be logged. After completing the 50000260-1-0-0090 operation, the system will send the SFC to another operation, called REPAIR_1. To implement this process:

1. Drag REPAIR_1 onto the drawing board and place it below 50000260-1-0-0090.
2. Set the step ID (150) for REPAIR_1; the reporting step number is not required, because it is a local step in SAP ME.
3. Add one right anchor and two left anchors to 50000260-1-0-0090.
4. Make a link from the 50000260-1-0-0090 right anchor to the REPAIR_1 left anchor.
5. To add an open NC script, double-click on the link and choose the OPEN NONCONFORMANCES script.
6. Add a right anchor to REPAIR_1, and make a link from the REPAIR_1 right anchor to the 50000260-1-0-0090 left anchor.
7. Double-click on the link and add the NO OPEN NONCONFORMANCES script. Doing so means that if an open NC is closed, the SFC will move to the 50000260-1-0-0090 step. Per the business requirements, if the NC is not closed in the REPAIR_1 step, then system will send the SFC to next operation, QUARTN_1.
8. To fulfill the requirements, drag QUARTN_1 onto the drawing board and place it below REPAIR_1.
9. Set the step ID (160) for QUARTN_1, and add a right anchor to the QUARTN_1 step. Make a link from the REPAIR_1 right anchor to the QUARTN_1 left anchor.
10. To add an open NC script, double-click on the link and choose the OPEN NONCONFORMANCES script. If an open NC is closed in the QUARTN_1 step, then the SFC will move to the 50000260-1-0-0090 step; otherwise, the system will scrap the product for open NC.
11. To meet the requirement, make a link from the QUARTN_1 right anchor to the 50000260-1-0-0090 left anchor and add a NO OPEN NONCONFORMANCES script on the line property.

4 | Routing Design

12. Drag SCRAPPED from OTHER STEPS to the right of QUARTN_1 (set the step ID as 200 for the Scrapped step).
13. Make a link from QUARTN_1 to SCRAPPED and also set the OPEN NONCONFORMANCES script in the link property. The enhanced part of the routing for nonconformance will look like Figure 4.24.

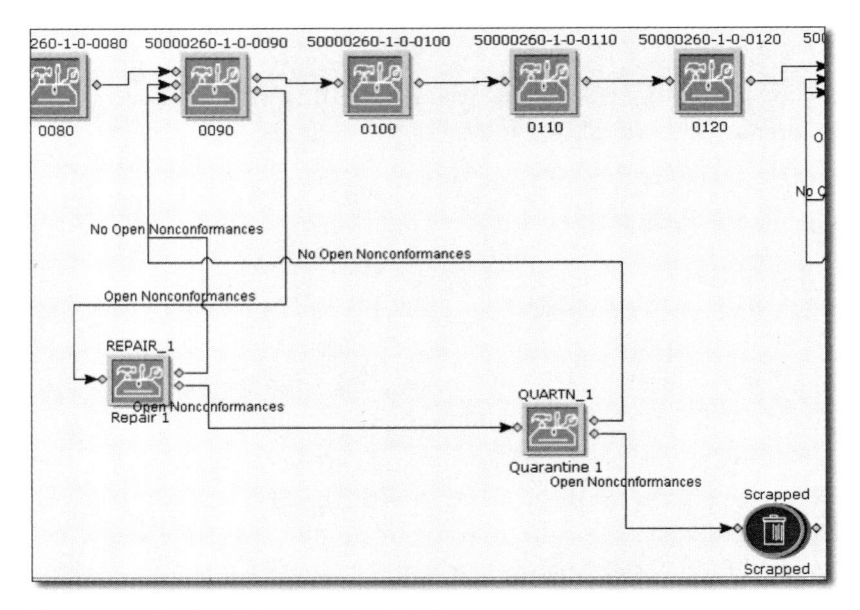

Figure 4.24 Routing Enhancement with NC

Operation 50000260-1-0-0130 is defined for quality inspection. In quality inspection, if any defect is found, the operator will log NC for it, and after completion of the 50000260-1-0-0130 operation, the system will send the SFC to another operation, REPAIR_2, to repair and close the NC. If an open NC is not closed in the REPAIR_2 operation, then the system will send the SFC to the QUARTN_2 operation; otherwise, the SFC will move to the 50000260-1-0-0130 operation. For an open NC in the QUARTN_2 operation, the system will send the SFC for scrapping after completion of the QUARTN_2 operation; otherwise, the SFC will move to the 50000260-1-0-0130 operation. You can enhance the routing for this requirement with the help of the preceding enhancement scenario; the enhanced part will look like Figure 4.25.

Enhancing Routings | **4.3**

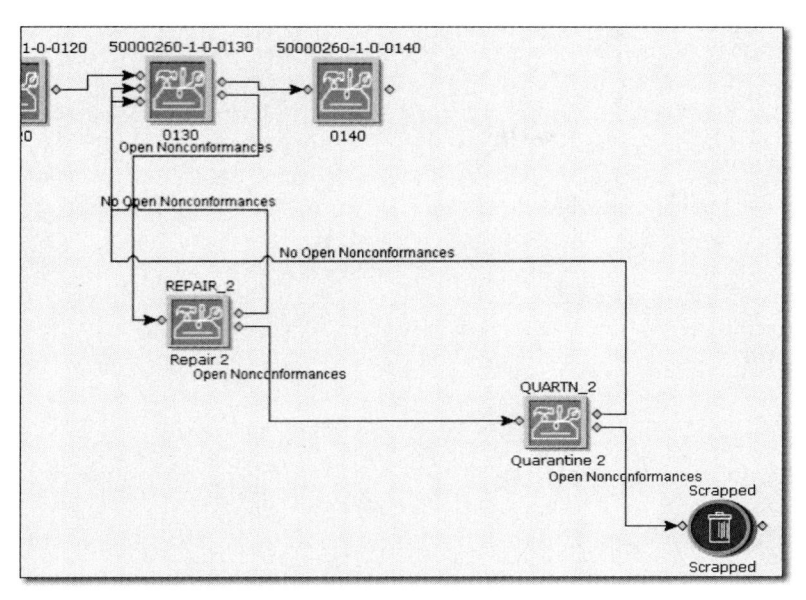

Figure 4.25 Quality Inspection Enhancement with NC

Another enhancement is required here for the REP_PAINT_BODY operation, used for repairing body painting. For any defect in the 50000260-1-0-0110 step, the system will send the SFC to the REP_PAINT_BODY step. After closing the defect in the REP_PAINT_BODY operation, the SFC will come back to the 50000260-1-0-0110 operation. Drag the REP_PAINT_BODY operation onto the drawing board and place it below 50000260-1-0-0110. Make the enhancement using the OPEN NONCONFORMANCE script and save the enhanced routing. The final enhanced routing will look like Figure 4.26.

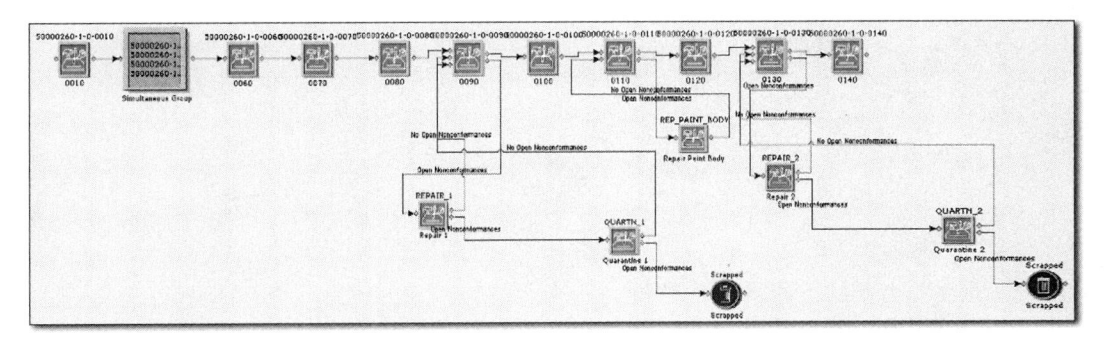

Figure 4.26 Enhanced Routing in SAP ME

163

> **Note: Routing Custom Data**
>
> Define custom data for routing using the activity called Custom Data Maintenance, in which you need to select ROUTING for CATEGORY and insert a new data field with a data field label. The same custom data will appear in the ROUTING MAINTENANCE CUSTOM DATA tab as DATA FIELD. In the Routing Maintenance activity, the CUSTOM DATA tab contains the data Field and corresponding data attribute. The custom fields can be used as the key to integrate with SAP ERP. For example, say that you download a routing from SAP ERP to SAP ME and want to pass some custom filed value to it. You can do so by defining custom data with the routing category, and you can enhance the XSLT in SAP-MEINT for the LOIROU02 message type to map the custom data field with a specific value.

4.4 Maintaining the Control Key

In SAP ME, a control key is required to define the SAP ERP reporting step in routing. It also specifies the behavior of operations in production. You can define a control key for an operation in SAP ME that is used in a routing if the operation is an SAP ERP routing step. In SAP ME, you can maintain the control key that exists in SAP ERP. For an SAP ME local operation, you don't need to maintain a control key. In routing maintenance, you can retrieve the routing and open the any step. Then, you can also assign a control key related to the operation for that particular step.

To maintain a control key in SAP ME you need to open the Control Key Maintenance activity (Figure 4.27). Specify the control key itself and its description, then click on SAVE to save the data in SAP ME. You can also retrieve or delete a control key by clicking on RETRIEVE or DELETE.

Figure 4.27 Control Key Maintenance Activity

4.5 Synchronizing Routings from SAP ME to SAP ERP

Routings can be created in SAP ERP, and you can download them from SAP ERP to SAP ME as master data. Alternately, you can create the routing in SAP ME and export it to SAP ERP. In this section, you will learn how to synchronize a routing from SAP ME to SAP ERP. Earlier, you designed the CAR_ASSEMBL_0001 routing in SAP ME for the car assembly process, and now we will export it to SAP ERP. Before starting the export process you need to do some configurations in SAP ME. First, open the System Rule Maintenance activity from the activity list. Table 4.5 lists three system rules you must update with the specified values; the results are shown in Figure 4.28.

Rule Name	Value
Enable Replication of ME Routing to ERP	Yes or Yes with Change Management
ERP Integration Active	True
Ignore Routing Update	True

Table 4.5 Rule Update in System Rule Maintenance for Routing Export from SAP ME to SAP ERP

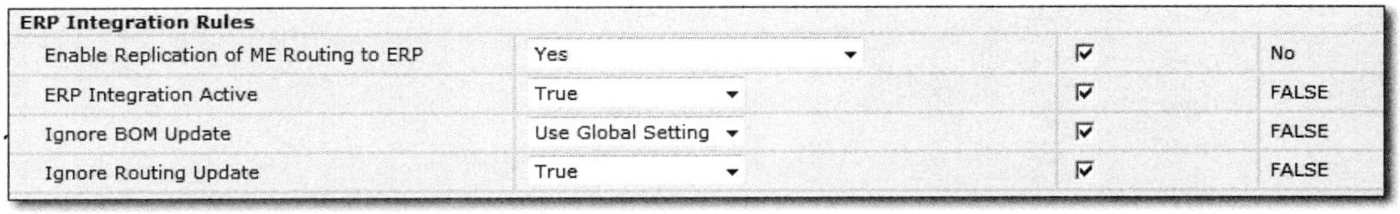

Figure 4.28 System Rule Setup for Exporting Routing from SAP ME to SAP ERP

> **Note**
>
> The *Enable Replication of ME Routing to ERP* rule allows you to export routing from SAP ME to SAP ERP; the *ERP Integration Active* rule is used to integrate SAP ME with SAP ERP; and the *Ignore Routing Update* rule prevents updates to the same routing from SAP ERP to SAP ME when the value is TRUE.

Now, open the Material Maintenance activity from the SAP ME activity list. Select or specify the finished product material number in the MATERIAL field and click on RETRIEVE. Material details will be displayed on the Material Maintenance page.

4 | Routing Design

> **Note**
>
> Before selecting the finished product material, you need to download the same material from SAP ERP to SAP ME. Then, only the same material will be available in SAP ME for selection. In this example, we used CAR98, which is already downloaded from SAP ERP to SAP ME.

In the ROUTING field, select CAR_ASSEMBL_0001 as shown in Figure 4.29 and click on SAVE. The material record will be updated with a routing number, and the ROUTING SENT TO ERP checkbox will be selected automatically.

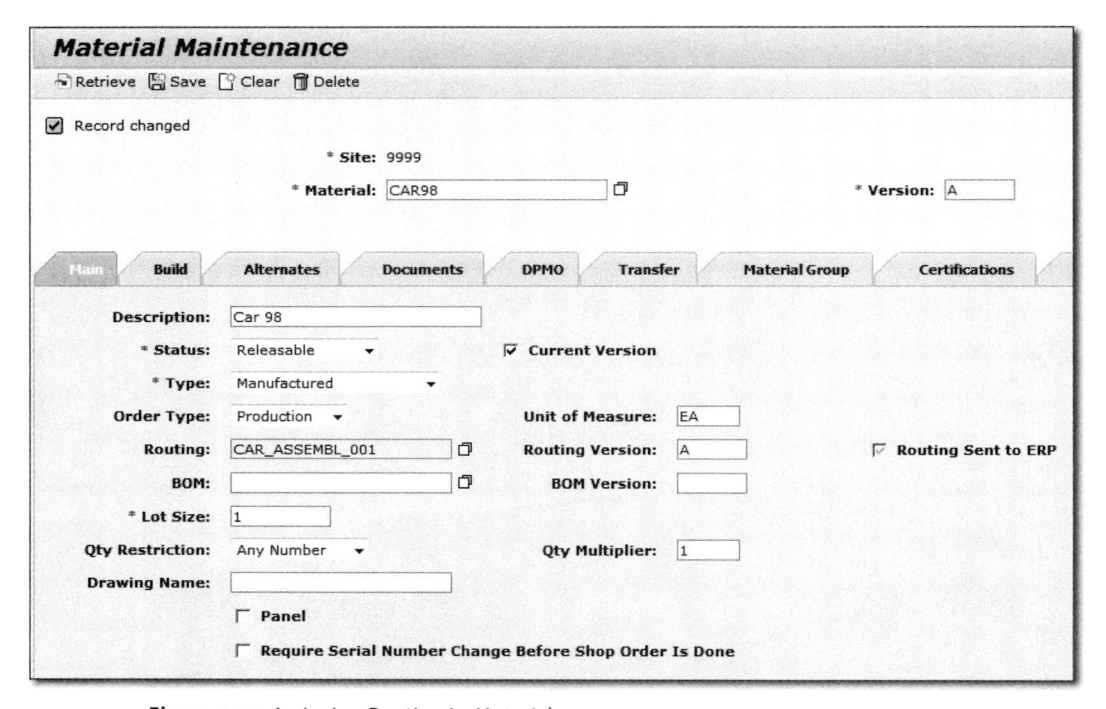

Figure 4.29 Assigning Routing in Material

Now, open the SAPMEINT Queue Monitor as described in Chapter 1. You can find an entry in the queue monitor table with the message type `routingExportRequest which is triggered from SAP ME for SAVE event of Material Maintenance activity`. That message will be picked and executed by the predefined SAPMEINT workflow automatically, which will update the routing details for SAP

4.5 Synchronizing Routings from SAP ME to SAP ERP

ERP. After successful posting to SAP ERP, the message status will be green. As shown in Figure 4.30, you can select the message and check the response structure (click on TRACE • RESPONSE • CONTENT • VIEW) to get the routing number that is created in SAP ERP. In the response structure, you will find message in which the CAR_ASSEMBL_0001 routing will be converted into an SAP ERP routing number.

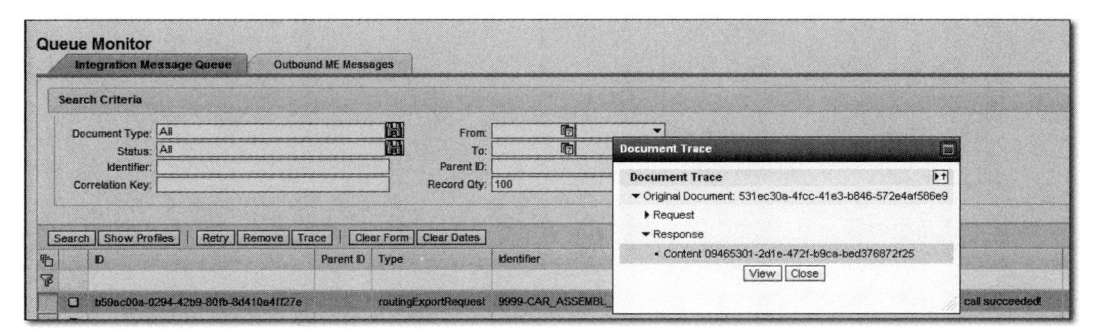

Figure 4.30 Response Message of routingExportRequest

To check the routing in SAP ERP, log in to SAP ERP and open Transaction CA03. Specify the routing number in the GROUP field and click on ROUTINGS to open DISPLAY ROUTING OVERVIEW. Click on OPERATIONS to see the operation overview with all operations, as shown in Figure 4.31.

Figure 4.31 Operation Overview of Exported Routing in SAP ERP

4.6 Routing Flow Control with Custom Scripting

You have seen the Next Step Flow in routing, which can be controlled through standard script assignment in link properties. You can also specify a custom script in link properties to meet your business requirements. For example, say that in a car assembly process if the SFC arrives more than or equal to three times in the REPAIR_1 operation, then it will be scrapped after completion of REPAIR_1 operation if the NC is not closed. If the SFC arrival count is less than three and the NC is not closed, then it will move to the QUARTN_1 operation after completion of the REPAIR_1 operation. If the NC is closed in the REPAIR_1 operation, then the SFC will move to the Visual Inspection operation (50000260-1-0-0090). Here, you need to consider three branches from REPAIR_1:

- **Branch 1**
  The link from REPAIR_1 to 50000260-1-0-0090 where NO OPEN NC is present. You can assign the standard NO OPEN NONCONFORMANCES script in link properties.

- **Branch 2**
  The link from REPAIR_1 to QUARTN_1 where the NC is not closed and LOOP_COUNT is less than 3. Here, you need to assign a custom script (see Listing 4.1).

  ```
  if(getOpenNCs()!=null && LOOP_COUNT < 3) {
    exit (true);
  }else{
  exit(false);
  }
  ```

  Listing 4.1 Custom Script where NC is not Closed and is less than 3

- **Branch 3**
  The link from REPAIR_1 to SCRAPPED where the NC is not closed and LOOP_COUNT is greater than or equal to 3. The custom script is shown in Listing 4.2.

  ```
  if(NC_CODE!=null && LOOP_COUNT>=3) {
    exit (true);
  }
  ```

  Listing 4.2 Custom Script where NC is not Closed and is Greater than or Equal to 3

Figure 4.32 illustrates how to configure custom scripts in link properties. In Figure 4.32 you can find one standard and two custom scripts are configured for three link proprieties. The standard NO OPEN NONCONFORMANCES script is used to link from REPAIR_1 to 50000260-1-0-0090, a custom script is used to link from REPAIR_1 to QUARTN_1 when the NC is not closed and the LOOP_COUNT is less than 3, and another custom script is used to link from REPAIR_1 to SCRAPPED when the NC is not closed and the LOOP_COUNT is greater than or equal to 3.

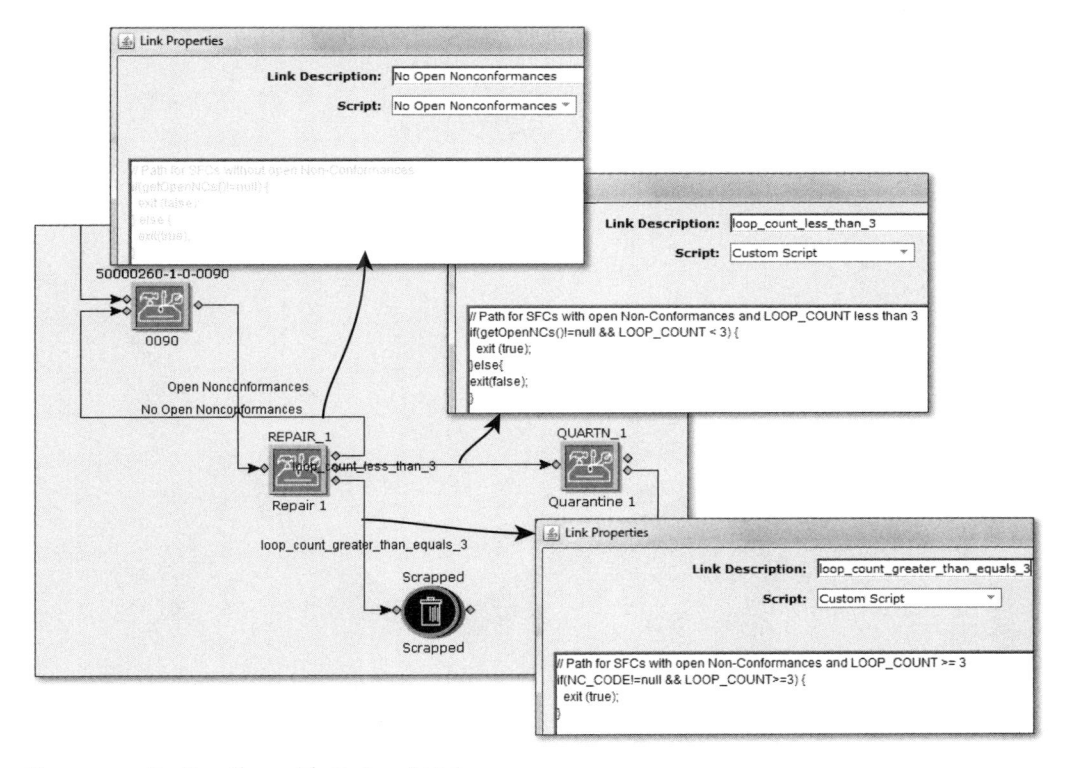

Figure 4.32 Routing Flow with Custom Script

4.7 Summary

In this chapter, you learned about routing maintenance with different types of operations and the required operation maintenance in SAP ME. For operation maintenance, you discovered the different properties and assignment of those properties' values and how they appear in routing maintenance within each step. Different routing scenarios with branching and nonconformances were described with examples. You also learned the steps for routing design and transferring routing from SAP ME to SAP ERP.

Standard routing enhancement and control key maintenance were also covered, with examples to aid understanding. We also discussed certification assignment, hook point assignment in operations, and the use of custom scripts in routing flow maintenance.

The next chapter explains shop order management in SAP ME.

This chapter explains the shop order management functionality in SAP ME, including how to create a shop order from an SAP ERP production order or planned order, RMA service order and how to configure and release a shop order in SAP ME, and the available shop order reports.

5 Shop Order Management

In the last chapter, you learned how operations and routings are used in SAP ME to define the production process for specific materials. To create a production plan for a specific quantity of a specific material within a specific time, create a shop order in SAP ME. You can create a shop order in SAP ME itself (when SAP ERP is not available and you need to continue the shop floor manufacturing process with a new shop order), or an order can be downloaded from SAP ERP through a LOIPRO IDoc. The shop order specifies a complete plan for how to manufacture a material of specific quantity, with routings and BOMs to be used and scheduled start and end times. It also specifies other details for the manufacturing process, such as the transfer plan of the semi-finished or finished material to other sites if required, the quality inspection plan, and the serial numbers of the material produced. Once the shop order is generated in SAP ME, the operator works with it in the POD to view the details and confirm the actual quantity against the planned quantity. The SAP ME shop order is the most important object to plan and track the production process and is the gateway for SAP ME shop floor production execution processes.

In this chapter, you will learn how to configure and manage shop orders in SAP ME for different scenarios and how to transfer production orders, planned orders and RMA service orders from SAP ERP into SAP ME as shop orders. Finally, we will discuss the various reports available in SAP ME related to shop orders.

5.1 Shop Order in SAP ME

A shop order in SAP ME consists of detailed information to manufacture a product (material) through an assembly process. For example, a company that assembles cars from its components has different production lines (work centers) in the factory and assembles multiple cars each day. Shop orders are generated for the car assembly process, one for each or for multiple cars, with specific routings, BOMs, and planned start and finish dates and times for the production process.

Shop orders are maintained in SAP ME using the Shop Order Maintenance activity, as shown in Figure 5.1.

SAP ME includes the following types of shop orders:

- **PRODUCTION**
  Shop order for specific quantity of material
- **REPETITIVE**
  Shop order with no build quantity limits (planned orders)
- **RMA**
  Shop order type for returned material authorization (service order)
- **REWORK**
  Order for product that is reworked after first build
- **ENGINEERING**
  Shop order for developing new product or experiments
- **TOOLING**
  Shop order used for building tools that are used for manufacturing
- **SPARE**
  Shop order used for producing spare materials
- **INSPECTION**
  Order to inspect incoming purchased materials
- **INSTALLATION**
  Order to build a collector material

The shop order STATUS field can be set to RELEASABLE, HOLD, DONE, or CLOSED. When a shop order is created and ready for release, it is releasable and can be put on HOLD temporarily, and can be changed to DONE automatically after the execution is completed or to closed if manually closed by the user.

The ERP ORDER checkbox is selected if the shop order is created and transferred from SAP ERP.

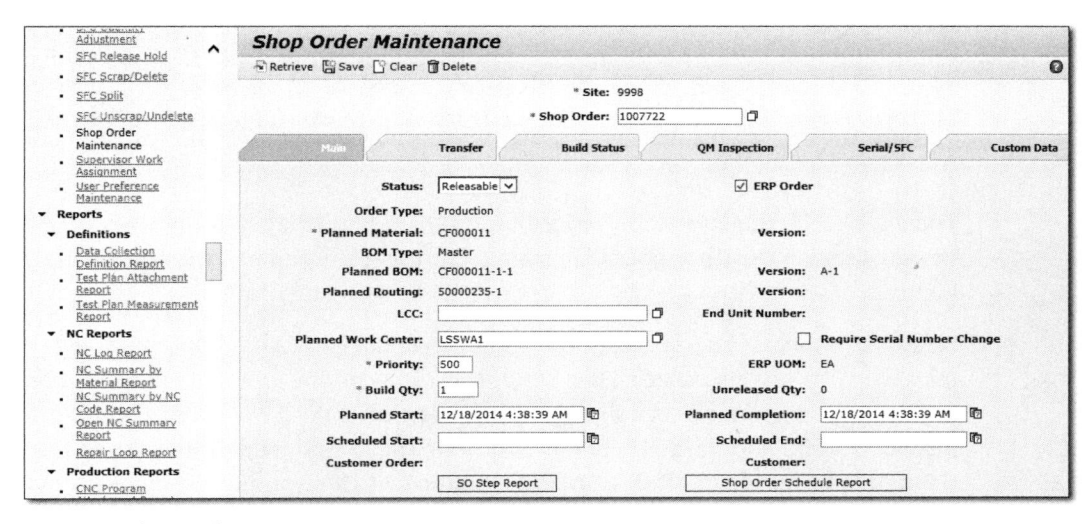

Figure 5.1 Shop Order in SAP ME

> **Note**
>
> Shop orders can be created in SAP ME locally or replicated from SAP ERP. When created locally in SAP ME, you need to specify the shop order number manually when creating it through the *Shop Order Maintenance* activity. When the shop order is generated automatically in SAP ME e.g. while creating SFCs in ad-hoc basis, then the corresponding shop order number is generated based on the *Next Number Maintenance* for shop order. When the production order, planned order, or RMA service orders are transferred from SAP ERP to SAP ME, the same order number in SAP ERP is used as the shop order number in SAP ME.

The material to be produced is specified in the PLANNED MATERIAL field with its VERSION. The BOM used for the shop order is specified in the PLANNED BOM with its VERSION, and the BOM TYPE can be MASTER, SHOP ORDER, or SFC. BOM type *master* is used if it is defined in the BOM master and used in the shop order; if created for the shop order and not present as a BOM master, it becomes a *shop order* BOM. If the BOM used in the SFCs generated from the shop order is different from that in the parent the shop order, it becomes an *SFC* BOM. The routing used for the shop order is specified in PLANNED ROUTING along with its VERSION. Specify the corresponding type of routing depending on the shop order type.

> **Note**
>
> If the PLANNED BOM and PLANNED ROUTING fields are left blank, then the system uses the BOM and routing specified for the PLANNED MATERIAL in MATERIAL MAINTENANCE for production shop orders.

You can specify the *labor charge code* in the LCC field if labor tracking is set up for the site to track the labor hours for manufacturing (see Chapter 12 for more information).

PLANNED WORK CENTER specifies the work center to which the shop order will be released. You can also specify the PRIORITY field to define a priority for the shop order, with a higher number signifying higher priority (SAP ME uses a default priority of 500 for shop orders). BUILD QUANTITY specifies the quantity of the material to be produced, and ERP UoM is the unit of measure of the material quantity transferred from SAP ERP. UNRELEASED QUANTITY specifies the quantity of the material in the shop order that is not released for production yet.

PLANNED START and PLANNED COMPLETION specify the date and time for the planned start and completion of the order. SCHEDULED START and SCHEDULED END fields usually remain blank, but are specified if any external scheduling application is used to schedule the order. You can use the Shop Floor Dispatching and Monitoring (SFDM) tool or SAP ERP to schedule the orders and map the fields for the LOIPRO interface workflow in SAPMEINT to populate these fields automatically from SAP ERP orders.

You can optionally use the CUSTOMER ORDER field to link the customer order (sales order) based on which the shop order is created and the corresponding CUSTOMER.

> **Note**
>
> You can set the system rule *Shop Order Requires Customer Order* in the System Rule Maintenance activity to mandate associating every shop order with a customer order.

Some fields appear for different types of orders, such as the following:

- The PRODUCTION VERSION field appears only for *Repetitive* shop orders and specifies the production version of the SAP ERP planned order if the order is created and transferred from SAP ERP to SAP ME.
- The RMA NUMBER field appears only for *RMA* (return material authorization) shop orders. The value for this field is read-only if the RMA (service order) is

transferred from SAP ERP and is same as the service order number used; otherwise, the value is generated automatically by the number pattern configured for the RMA shop order number in Next Number Maintenance.

- You can specify the RMA SHOP ORDER DATA TYPE and RMA SFC DATA TYPE for an RMA shop order based on the data types you have assigned in the RMA shop order category and RMA SFC category in the Data Field Assignment Maintenance activity (see Chapter 2). These data types are used in the SERIAL/SFC & RMA configuration tab.

To manufacture a collector type of material for complex assembly, when the components of the finished products are also manufactured along with it, installation shop orders are generated automatically for each component of the BOM (the type is set as INSTALLATION in the Material Maintenance activity) and automatically pegged to the parent order if the system rule *Create Subassys on Shop Order Release* is set to TRUE in the System Rule Maintenance activity.

The following fields are displayed only if the system rule Display End Unit Number is set to TRUE in the System Rule Maintenance activity:

- The END UNIT NUMBER field is mainly used for production and installation shop orders and only for the component orders to tag them to the parent finished product order. You can specify the serial number/SFC number used in the parent order as the end unit number.

- The COLLECT PARENT SERIAL NUMBER checkbox appears only for installation shop orders. When checked, it indicates that the parent serial number needs to be collected for the order before the shop order status is changed to DONE, which links the components with the end unit.

- For production shop orders, the REQUIRE SERIAL NUMBER CHANGE checkbox appears. It indicates that the material of the order needs a change made to the serial number before the shop order status is changed to DONE. This is required when the final serial number of the product is generated at the end of the process.

> **Note**
>
> The rule *COPY_ERPORDER_VALUE* when set to true, for the Shop Order Maintenance activity (DM010), indicates that any shop order copied from an SAP ERP shop order (a shop order generated from a production/planned/service order transferred from SAP ERP) also gets saved as an SAP ERP order when the ERP ORDER checkbox is checked and disabled (i.e. unable to be changed).

If the product manufactured by a shop order needs to be transferred from or to another site during its processing, you can configure that in the TRANSFER configuration tab as shown in Figure 5.2. This feature is useful when you manufacture different assemblies or components of a product at different sites with specific activities at each site. You can specify the TRANSFER TYPE as SFC_SPAN, SFC_CONSUME, or NO_TRANSFER:

- SFC_SPAN signifies that the product or the SFC numbers generated from the shop order can begin manufacturing in one site and then move to another site for further processing.

- SFC_CONSUME signifies that the SFC numbers for the shop order after completion at one site are consumed in a shop order at another site as a subassembly in a higher-level assembly of a product.

- NO_TRANSFER signifies that the SFC numbers for the shop order cannot be transferred to another site.

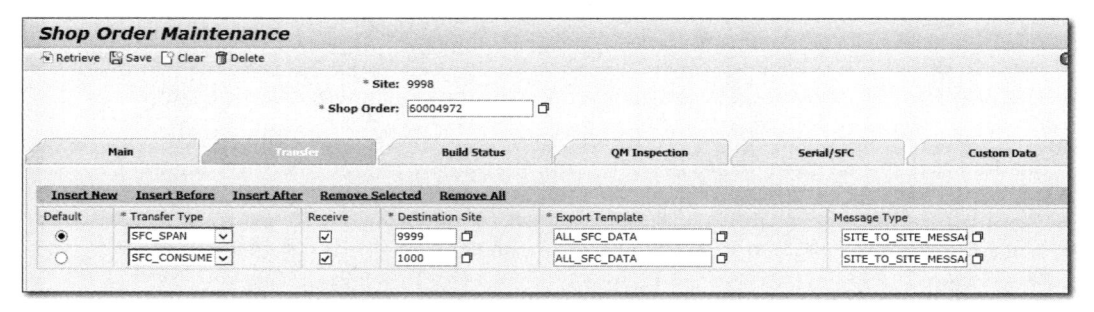

Figure 5.2 Site Transfer Configuration for Shop Order

You can add multiple transfer types and have to select one as the default, which cannot be the NO_TRANSFER type. If you check the RECEIVE checkbox, then you need to receive the SFC manually at the destination site using the SFC RECEIPT activity; otherwise, the SFCs are transferred automatically to the destination site. You also need to specify the DESTINATION SITE to which the SFCs will be transferred and the EXPORT TEMPLATE to specify the data to be transferred (maintained in the Export Template Maintenance activity). MESSAGE TYPE specifies the message to be displayed in the message board of the destination site once the SFC transfer is completed. For the NO_TRANSFER type, you cannot specify any of this information. The transfer happens automatically based on the default transfer type specified in the shop order when the SFC status is set to DONE in the source site.

You can view the actuals information for the shop order execution in the BUILD STATUS tab, as shown in Figure 5.3. You can view the released, done, and scrap quantities of the shop order as the order is executed and the yield quantities are confirmed. You can also specify ORDERED QUANTITY as the total quantity ordered by the customer while creating the shop order; if left blank, it takes the BUILD QUANTITY value specified in the MAIN configuration tab. For orders transferred from SAP ERP, BATCH NUMBER, ERP PUTAWAY STORAGE LOCATION are displayed as specified in the SAP ERP order. The actual start and end dates are also displayed once the order is started execution.

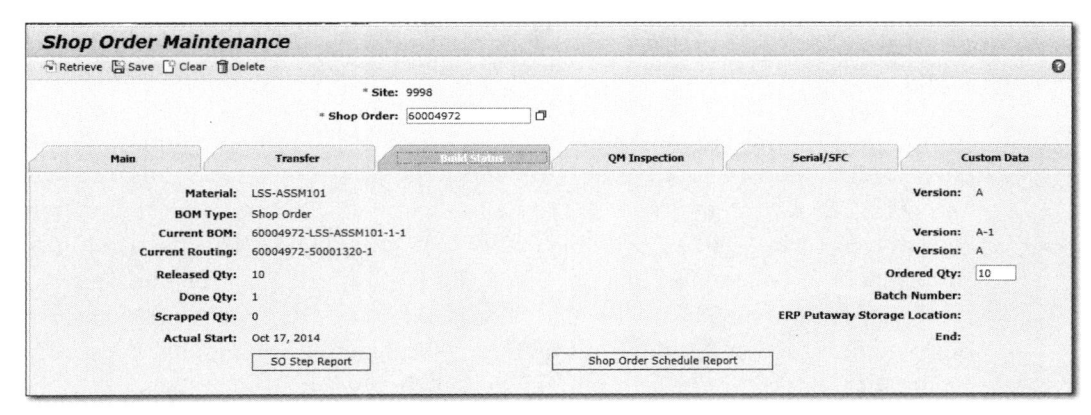

Figure 5.3 Build Configuration for Shop Order

During the manufacturing/assembling process, you may need to perform quality inspections on the material being assembled to ensure it conforms to quality standards. In a shop order, the quality inspection information is specified in the QM INSPECTION configuration tab, as shown in Figure 5.4. The quality inspection details are only available in the shop order if the order is an SAP ERP order and the inspection details are maintained in the corresponding routing used for the production order in SAP ERP. INSPECTION LOT—that is, the lot number for the inspection—is displayed along with SFC GROUP SIZE, which signifies the total quantity of the pieces of the material in the sampling group for inspection. There can be multiple operations for which inspections need to be performed, which is specified in the OPERATION/ROUTING STEP section and the INSPECTION SAMPLE SIZE section as the quantity of the pieces of the material in the SFC group to be inspected.

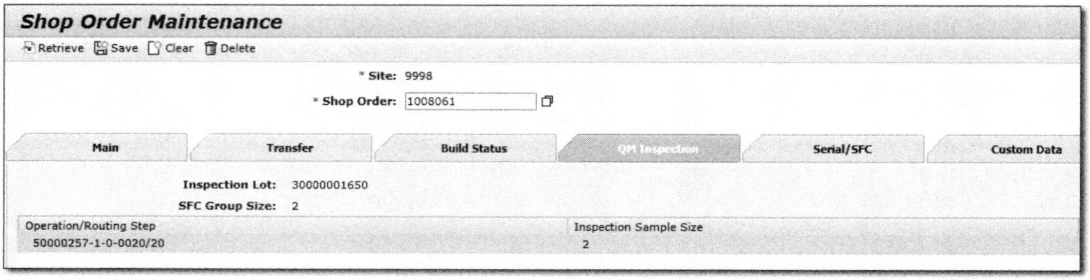

Figure 5.4 QM Inspection Configurations for Shop Order

In a discrete assembly process, each piece of the product being manufactured usually is designated with a unique serial number to track and identify individual pieces. SAP ME also generates SFC numbers for each lot of the product in a shop order for WIP tracking and processing. In the SERIAL/SFC configuration tab of the shop order, you can specify and view the serial numbers and SFC information generated for the shop order, as shown in Figure 5.5. If the serial numbers are transferred from SAP ERP with an order, then they are displayed as read-only numbers in the SERIAL/SFC tab. For non-SAP ERP shop orders, serial numbers can be edited only if no SFC numbers are released for the orders. The SFC numbers are generated once the order is released or you can define them in the shop-order maintenance, if not to be released, as you will discover in Section 5.3.

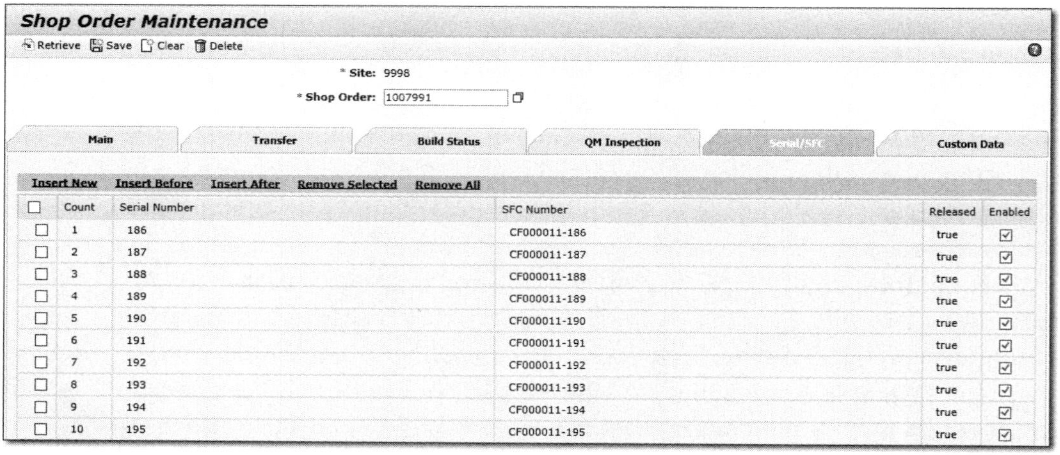

Figure 5.5 Serial/SFC Configuration for Shop Order

For an RMA shop order, another column called ORIGINAL SFC NUMBER is displayed for the original SFC numbers created in the parent shop order, which were produced on the same site before. It also shows the details of the RMA SFC.

5.2 Creating Shop Orders from SAP ERP Orders

Shop orders in SAP ME can be generated from production orders, planned orders, or service orders created in SAP ERP, which are transferred to SAP ME via SAPMEINT. In this section, we will detail the transfer of each type of order.

5.2.1 Transfer of Production Orders

Production orders are created in SAP ERP for discrete manufacturing to manufacture a specific material of specific quantity in a specific time. They consist of the material and its quantity, components (maintained in BOM), and the operations and work centers (maintained in routing) required for manufacturing. Once the order is created, configure the Data Replication Framework (DRF) in SAP ERP to send the order automatically to the logical system configured for SAP MII (in the SAP ME instance) or by using Transaction DRFOUT, or send it by using Transaction POIT in SAP ERP 6.0–6.4. This transaction, when executed, generates an LOIPRO IDoc message, which is transferred to SAPMEINT and creates a corresponding production shop order in SAP ME. Before transferring a production order, you have to transfer the required master data in SAP ME, as explained in Chapter 3. Unlike production orders in SAP ERP, shop orders in SAP ME just refer to the routing and BOM and do not contain the details themselves.

SAP ME supports both *make-to-stock* and *make-to-order* manufacturing (with variant configurations). Make-to-stock manufacturing is used to manufacture the same material in large quantities to build the stock and deliver when a sales order is available. The *KDAUF* element is not present or is blank, and the *KDPOS* element value is zero in the *E1AFKOL* segment in the LOIPRO IDoc for make-to-stock orders. While transferring the production order for make-to-stocks order through SAPMEINT, the system checks if the BOM and routing used in the production order is present in the system. If exactly the same data are present in the BOM and routing already, they are referred to in the shop order, and if not, then updated version for the BOM and routing are created in SAP ME and are referred to in the shop order. You can configure this behavior in the System Rule Maintenance activity, as explained in Chapter 3.

For make-to-order manufacturing, the KDAUF and KDPOS elements contain the sales order number and the item number in the LOIPRO IDoc, and shop order–specific BOMs and routings are created in SAP ME to be used for the shop order.

You can use the Shop Floor Dispatching and Monitoring tool to schedule shop orders by adding quantity splits to allocate order quantity to individual capacities for operations before sending to SAP ME from SAP ERP, when SAP ERP work centers with multiple capacities are used in the production order operation. As a prerequisite before sending the production orders from SAP ERP, you need to send the material master, work centers with individual capacities, and optionally BOMs, and routings used in the production orders. You also need to set ERP INTEGRATION ACTIVE as TRUE in the System Rule Maintenance activity. If a production order is sent again to SAP ME from SAP ERP after the corresponding shop order is created, the order information is updated if changed in SAP ERP; if it is already released in SAP ME, then the BOM and routing cannot be changed. If DRF is activated in SAP ERP (by activating the `LOG_PP_MES_INT_02` business function), then any changes to the BOM and routing in the production order is prevented once the order is sent to SAPMEINT.

You can send the work instructions in the shop order by attaching document info records in a production order in SAP ERP. You can create document info record of type *PRT* to attach in the production order operations or of type *non-PRT* to attach in the production order headers in SAP ERP. When transferred to SAP ME, production shop orders are generated with attachment points and work instructions. Attachment points are used to link the work instruction with the shop-order.

For transferring production orders with a quality inspection lot, in the customization for quality inspection in SAP ERP select BASIC SETTINGS and execute MAINTAIN SETTING AT PLANT LEVEL by clicking on its icon. Select the plant to configure and open the DETAILS configuration. On the RESULT RECORDING tab, deselect SUMM. RECORDING FOR N=1. Also, assign and activate INSPECTION TYPE 03 for the material in the Material Master configuration in the Quality Management view in SAP ERP. Assign the inspection characteristics to the relevant operations in the routing and transfer the production order to SAPMEINT.

> **Note**
>
> The following restrictions exist for shop orders created in SAP ME from production orders in SAP ERP:
>
> - Milestone operations, if present in the production order, are not supported in SAP ME. Refer to SAP Note 0001502536 for more details. You can customize the mapping for production order in SAPEMINT to filter only the milestone operations in the production order to send to SAP ME.
> - All operations in the production order must have the same base unit of measure of the output material.

5.2.2 Transfer of Planned Orders

Planned orders are used for repetitive manufacturing—that is, to manufacture bulk quantities of a material within a larger time frame. Usually, planned orders are created in SAP ERP by running Materials Requirements Planning (MRP) periodically based on demands and stock availability. You can transfer planned orders automatically to SAPMEINT by activating DRF or through Transaction POIT or DRFOUT. Repetitive shop orders are created in SAP ME. You cannot transfer capacity consumption data, such as operation dates with planned orders, from SAP ERP to SAP ME. Planned orders are transferred to SAP ME via the LOIPLO IDoc.

5.2.3 Transfer of RMA Service Orders

Service or repair orders are created in SAP ERP for repairing a product defect detected after the production is complete or the product already sold to the customer. The repair order is transferred to SAPMEINT by the IORD IDoc message and creates an RMA shop order in SAP ME for executing the repair activities on the material returned with defects. In the SERIAL/SFC & RMA configuration tab, you can specify the serial numbers or SFC numbers of the product if required for tracking purposes.

5.3 Releasing Shop Orders

To start the manufacturing/assembly process at the production line to build the material for a shop order, release the shop-order to be available in the POD and start the production. You can release the full or partial quantity of the shop order while releasing the shop order. To release a shop order, open the SHOP ORDER RELEASE activity, specify the shop order number, and click on the RETRIEVE button, as shown in Figure 5.6. You will see the shop order details and can specify QTY TO RELEASE to release either all the build quantity or less than all. Click on RELEASE to release the specified release quantity only.

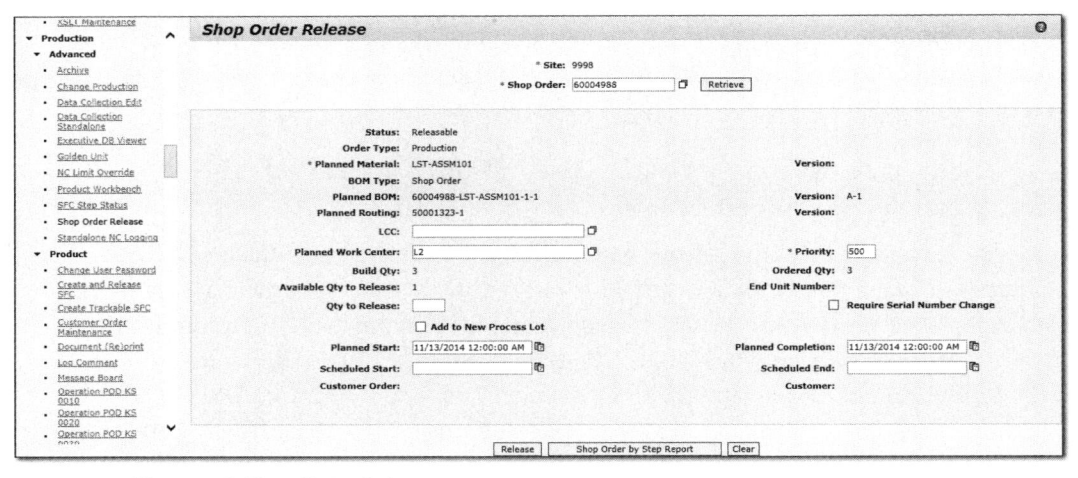

Figure 5.6 Shop Order Release

You can also change any values in the shop order before the first release, except for the following fields:

- STATUS
- ORDER TYPE
- BUILD QUANTITY
- ORDERED QUANTITY
- AVAILABLE QUANTITY TO RELEASE
- RMA NUMBER

On release of the shop order, SFCs are generated automatically based on the released quantity and lot size of the material. You will learn more about SFC management in the next chapter.

There are some rules available for the Shop Order Release activity (activity ID: DM510) in the Activity Maintenance activity, which you can configure to allow modifications of the fields of the shop order upon release. By default, all these system rules are set to YES, which allows modifications to the fields during release of the shop order. The following rules are available for Shop Order Release activity:

- CUSTOMER_MODIFY
- CUSTOMER_ORDER_MODIFY
- LCC_MODIFY
- PLANNED_BOM_MODIFY
- PLANNED_END_MODIFY
- PLANNED_ITEM_MODIFY
- PLANNED_ROUTER_MODIFY
- PLANNED_START_MODIFY
- PLANNED_WORK_CENTER_MODIFY
- PRIORITY_MODIFY
- RELEASE_QTY_REQUIRED
- RMA_SFC_RELABLE
- SCHEDULED_END_MODIFY
- SCHEDULED_START_MODIFY

5.4 Reports for Shop Order

There are several reports available in SAP ME you can use to view the shop order execution details. In this section we will discuss reports for Shop Order by Step, Shop Order by Schedule, Shop Order Report, and Cycle Time.

5.4.1 Shop Order by Step Report

You can use the Shop Order by Step Report to view the execution details for a shop order. You can open the report from the activity available or from the Shop Order Maintenance activity, as shown in Figure 5.7. You need to specify a released shop order number to view the report. The report displays the step and operation numbers along with the routing for each operation. It also displays the quantity of the build product which are queued, in work, and complete for each operation. This report shows the progress of SFCs in routing steps and does not count the scrapped or deleted SFC quantity in the queue from any step of the routing.

5 | Shop Order Management

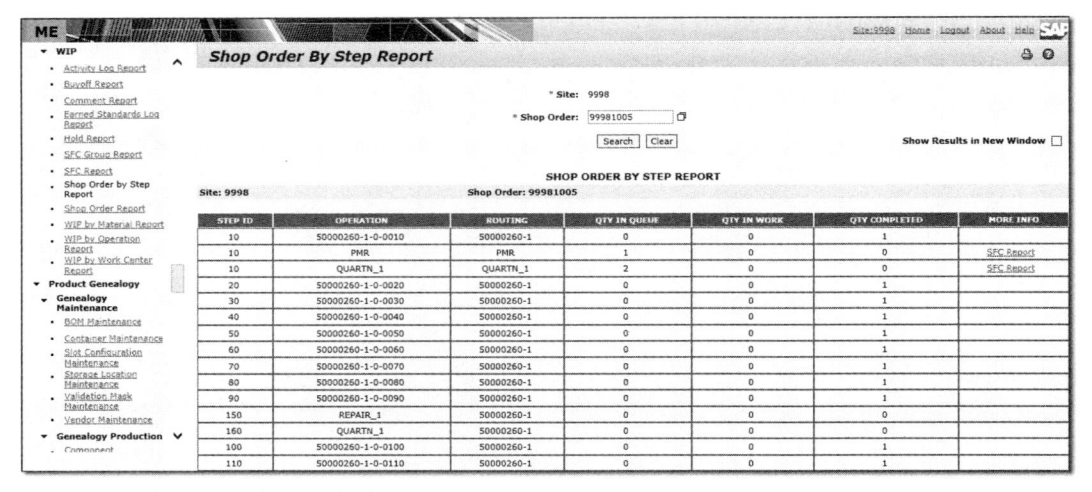

Figure 5.7 Shop Order by Step Report

5.4.2 Shop Order Schedule Report

Production orders with work centers with multiple capacities defined in SAP ERP have operations executed at multiple resources in shop orders in SAP ME within a scheduled period of time, because multiple resources are created for work centers with multiple capacities in SAP ME. As a prerequisite, the SAP ERP production order with multiple-capacity work centers should be transferred to SAP ME with scheduling information, and the Shop Floor Dispatching and Monitoring Tool can be used for production scheduling purposes. Using the Shop Order Schedule Report (Figure 5.8), which you can open from the Shop Order Maintenance activity, you can view the quantity split and times of execution of the same operations at different resources when there is a quantity split due to multiple resources under a work center being assigned to an operation.

Figure 5.8 Shop Order Schedule Report

5.4.3 Shop Order Report

Use the Shop Order Report to view all details of the shop order and different reports related to it. You can search by shop order number, work center, date range, or end unit number, as shown in Figure 5.9. You can view the quantities of the order planned, released, in queue, done, or scrapped for the shop order, along with the work center and the RMA number, end unit number, or customer, if available. The report also provides the hyperlink to other reports, such as Details, Shop Order Step, Shop Order Schedule and SFC Reports, which you can use to view details.

You can set the SHOP_ORDER_HYPERLINK rule for the Shop Order Report activity (DM730) in Activity Maintenance as set to YES to display a hyperlink for the order number that opens the Shop Order Maintenance activity.

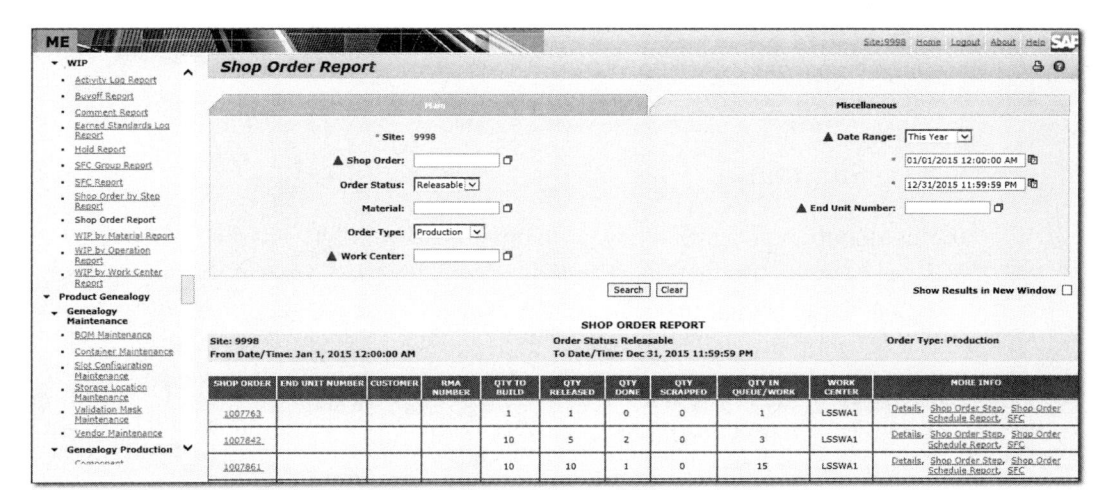

Figure 5.9 Shop Order Report

5.4.4 Shop Order Cycle Time Report

Use the Shop Order Cycle Time Report to view the time taken for execution (from start to finish) for shop orders, as shown in Figure 5.10. You can search by a material, shop order number, RMA number, or date range to display cycle time for each shop order, either in tabular or graphical format. Click on each bar of the chart or the shop order number displayed to view the SFC Cycle Time Report for the shop order.

5 | Shop Order Management

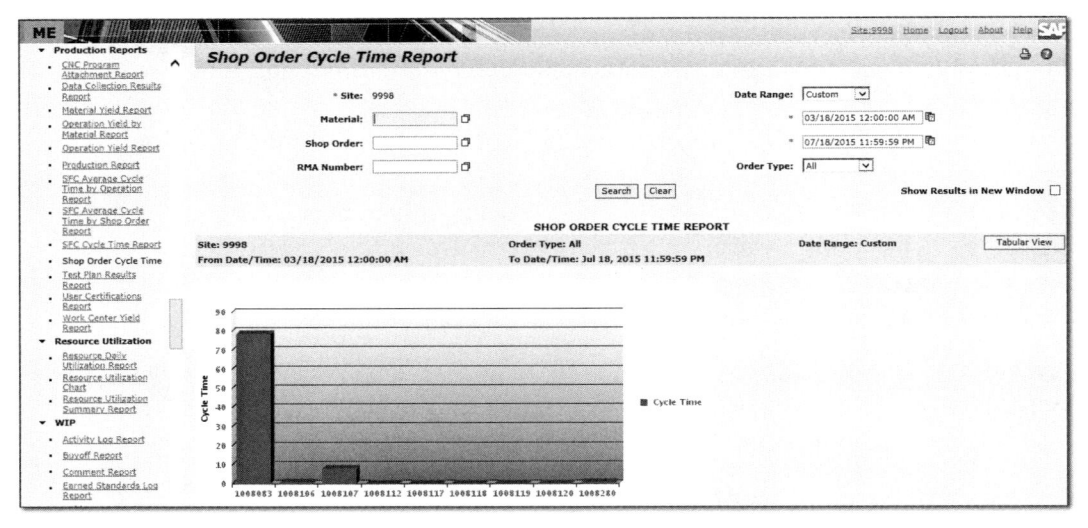

Figure 5.10 Shop Order Cycle Time Report

5.5 Summary

In this chapter, you learned how to maintain different types of shop orders in SAP ME and how the production, planned, or service orders are transferred from SAP ERP to generate shop orders in SAP ME. You also learned about the release mechanism for shop orders in SAP ME and the reports related to shop orders.

In the next chapter, you'll learn about the SFCs generated while releasing a shop order to execute the assembly process.

This chapter explains SFC generation and the use of SFCs in SAP ME. It also addresses SFC-related activities in the shop floor, such as SFC number assignment, SFC merge, split, hold, release, quantity adjustment, scrap/delete, and unscrap/undelete. SFC reporting activities are also described here.

6   Shop Floor Control Management

In the last chapter, you learned about shop orders in SAP ME and their use in the shop floor execution process. When a shop order is released, one or more quantities of the shop order material is produced by the manufacturing execution process. To track the materials being assembled and produced, specific quantities of the material, as defined by the material's lot size, are tracked individually throughout the execution/assembly process.

In SAP ME, SFC stands for *shop floor control* and is the key element for shop floor execution. Each unit of manufactured or processed product in SAP ME is identified by an SFC that contains a unique number generated for each SFC. On the shop floor, each operation's execution is performed on an SFC, and a product can be tracked at any time on the shop floor through its SFC number. Multiple reports are available in SAP ME for tracking products from different viewpoints.

6.1   Overview of SFCs and Generating SFCs on Order Release

In SAP ME, an SFC number is a unique number that refers to a batch of a material for which work is in progress. An SFC contains the single or multiple quantity of the material, and SFC quantity depends on the lot size of material produced (specified in the Material Maintenance activity). When an operator executes an operation on the shop floor, he or she needs to select one or more SFCs to start and complete the operation. After starting and completing the SFC at an operation

6 | Shop Floor Control Management

based on the routing flow, the SFC will move to next operation and will be in the INQUEUE state in next operation. In the following sections, we will discuss generating SFCs through shop order releases, creating and releasing SFCs, creating trackable SFCs, return material authorization SFC receipts, SFC groups, and SFC statuses.

6.1.1 Generating SFCs through Shop Order Releases

In regular practice, an SFC is generated by the release of a shop order (through the Shop Order Release activity), and the number of SFCs generated depends on the lot size configuration (available in the Material Maintenance activity) of the material. For example, in a plant, one shop order contains fifty units of a material MAT56 used in a shop order for production. A lot size of ten is configured in material MAT56. If the shop order is released, the system will generate five SFCs from that shop order, and each SFC will contain a quantity of ten, as shown in Figure 6.1.

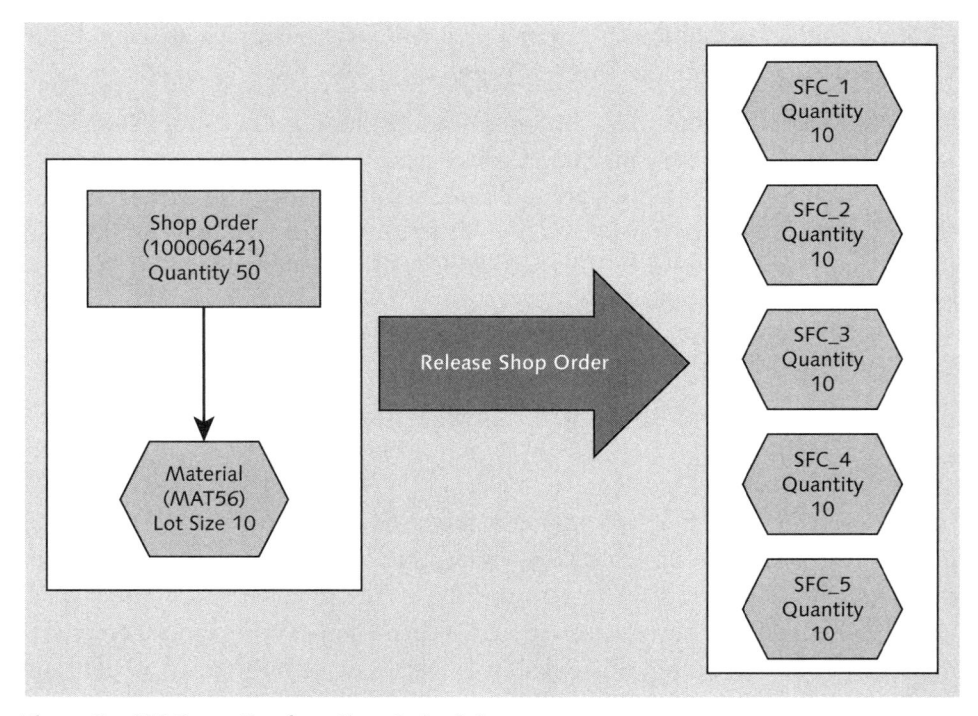

Figure 6.1 SFC Generation from Shop Order Release

SFCs can contain a quantity of one or more, depending on the lot size. For example, in a car assembly process, each car can be identified as an SFC with a quantity of one. Each SFC number can be used as a vehicle identification number (VIN) for the individual car or a serial number of the material when the SFC quantity is defined by the lot size as one. An SFC that contains a quantity greater than one is a non-serialized SFC and represents the lot size of the material.

In the next sections, you will learn how SFC numbers are generated in SAP ME. SAP ME provides an activity called Next Number Maintenance (explained in Chapter 2), which is used to configure the number generation pattern for SFC. In this activity, you can define the pattern for SFC numbers. When a shop order is released, SAP ME checks the last generated number from the WIP database, and based on the last number it generates the next unique number for an SFC. SFCs can also be generated when a shop order is downloaded from SAP ERP to SAP ME through SAPMEINT. However, enhancement in SAPMEINT is required in that scenario, to execute the SFC creation service available in SAP ME.

6.1.2 Create and Release SFCs

In addition to being generated while releasing a shop order, SFCs can also be created through the Create and Release SFC activity in SAP ME. Through this activity, the shop order creation and SFC release for a material can be performed together. You need to enter a material number for which the SFC will be generated and the corresponding quantity of the SFC. You can also enter SHOP ORDER number, LCC (labor charge code), and the WORK CENTER to be used. You cannot use same shop order number for repeated SFC releases. Select ADD TO NEW PROCESS LOT to group the SFC numbers to a process lot. The material for the SFC must have a routing assigned in the Material Maintenance activity before the SFCs can be released. Released SFCs are placed in the queue at the first routing operation, as assigned in the material. By clicking on CREATE, you can create and release SFCs that will be displayed in a new screen with the SFC number and other details (Figure 6.2). This activity also creates the shop order (based on next number configuration for shop order) which is local to SAP ME and the shop order is not linked with SAP ERP.

> **Note**
>
> The CUSTOMER ORDER field is used to specify the customer order (sales order) optionally, if linked with the shop order specified.

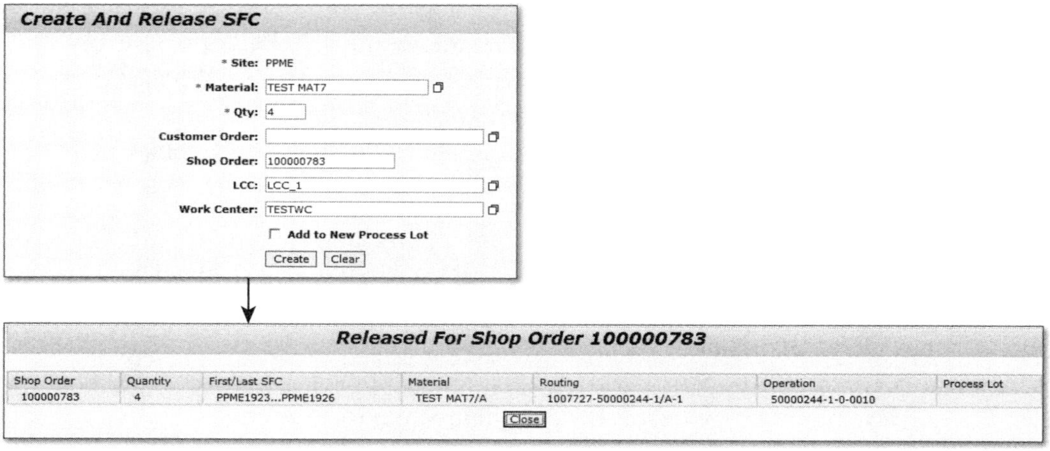

Figure 6.2 Create and Release SFCs

6.1.3 Create Trackable SFCs

If you want to create an SFC number for a material that will be tracked for quality checking in your system, use the Create Trackable SFC activity. For example, say you want to check the quality of a manufactured or purchased material through a separate routing; a trackable SFC will help you to do that. When an SFC is released, the system places it in the queue of the specified routing. Make sure that material type is set to either PURCHASED or PURCHASED/MANUFACTURED and that the TRACKABLE COMPONENT checkbox is selected in the BUILD configuration tab of the Material Maintenance activity. In the BOM Maintenance activity, retrieve the header material (the actual product) and select the component for which quality check will be done. On the component details page, for ASSEMBLY DATA TYPE, select SFC (see Figure 6.3). In the assembly operation of shop floor execution, the operator must provide a trackable SFC number for assembly data.

The SHOP ORDER field value depends on the rule settings in the Create Trackable SFC activity. For the CREATE TRACKABLE SFC (activity id: PR300) activity in Activity Maintenance, set the REQUIRE_SHOP_ORDER rule to either TRUE or FALSE. For FALSE, you don't need to specify a shop order number for creating a trackable SFC.

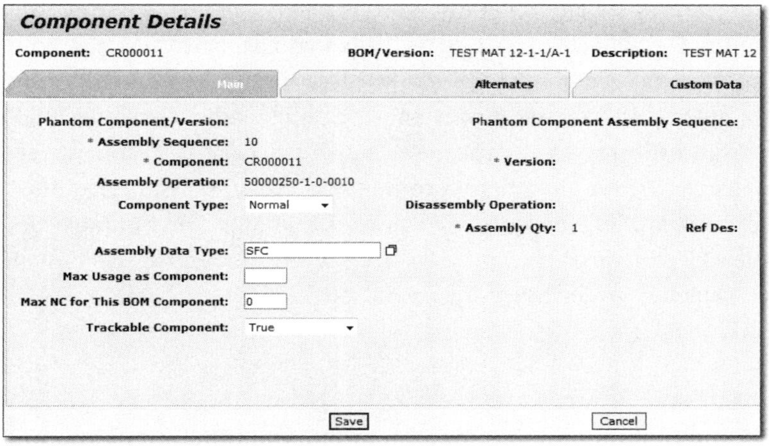

Figure 6.3 Selecting Component Assembly Data Type

In the Create Trackable SFC activity, enter the SFC number, quantity, and material. After specifying all field values (including values for LCC and WORK CENTER if required), click on CREATE to generate the trackable SFC. If MARK SFC AS DONE is checked, then the SFC will have the Done status after creation (see Table 6.1 for SFC statuses). SAP ME will not allow you to select MARK SFC AS DONE for special or NC routings; the option is only applicable for production routings. Figure 6.4 shows how to create a trackable SFC using production routing, and the MARK SFC AS DONE checkbox is unchecked. After creating the trackable SFC, it will be placed in queue at the first operation of the specified routing.

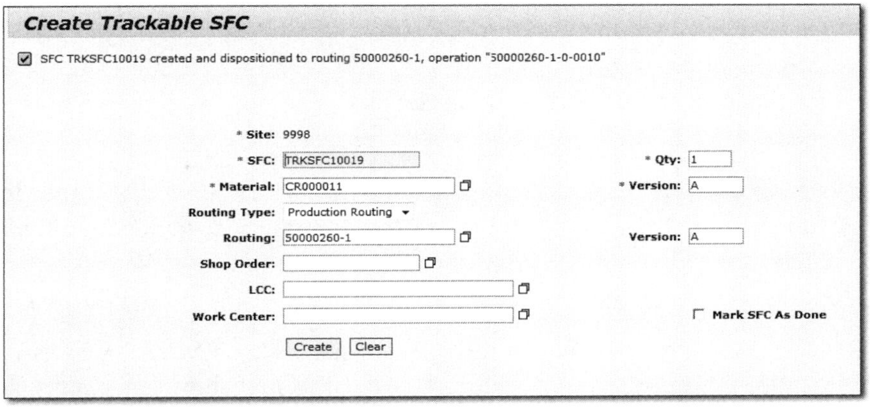

Figure 6.4 Creating Trackable SFC

An operator needs to execute all operations of routing for the trackable SFC, and then the status of the SFC will change to DONE. When you execute the actual routing for a finished material using a production operator dashboard, in the assembly operation you need to select the component (the same material used for trackable SFC creation) and specify the trackable SFC number to add it. You may need to create the trackable SFC for a purchased component which is assembled into a finished product with other components. Figure 6.5 shows the trackable SFC assignment in the assembly process. Trackable SFCs with Done status will only be available for SFC selection in the assembly operation.

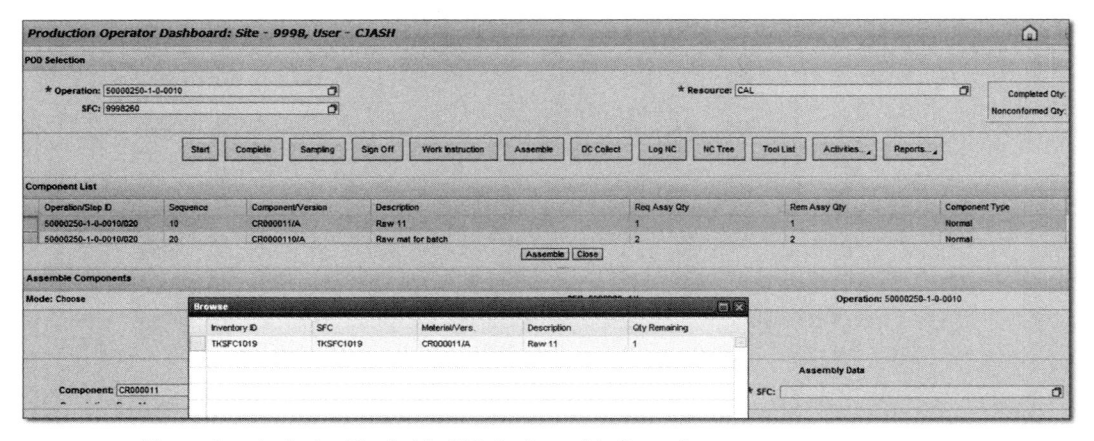

Figure 6.5 Assigning Trackable SFCs in Assembly Operations

6.1.4 Return Material Authorization SFC Receipt

RMAs are used when a product is returned to the shop floor for any defect repair, after it has been shipped to the customer. For example, if an assembled car is returned for repair of any defect (from the customer or from the dealer company itself), it needs to go through a separate routing process.

Before working with RMA SFC receipt, you need to have an RMA shop order in SAP ME. In the Shop Order Maintenance activity you can find the RMA number associated with the shop order. Now, start working in the RMA SFC Receipt activity in SAP ME.

In the RMA SFC RECEIPT activity, you can select or specify the RMA NUMBER associated with RMA shop order and retrieve it. An associated shop order number will be populated automatically in the SHOP ORDER field and in the SFC field, create a new SFC (first configure the RMA SFC number in the Next Number Maintenance activity) by clicking on CREATE, or use the same SFC that was used to create the product (for example, for a damaged car, use the same SFC number used as the car VIN). Also enter the quantity, comment, and return date in the QTY, COMMENTS, and RETURN DATE fields, and provide the customer part number. Then, click on the ADD button. The SFC will be added in the SFCs RECEIVED list, as shown in Figure 6.6. Click on DONE.

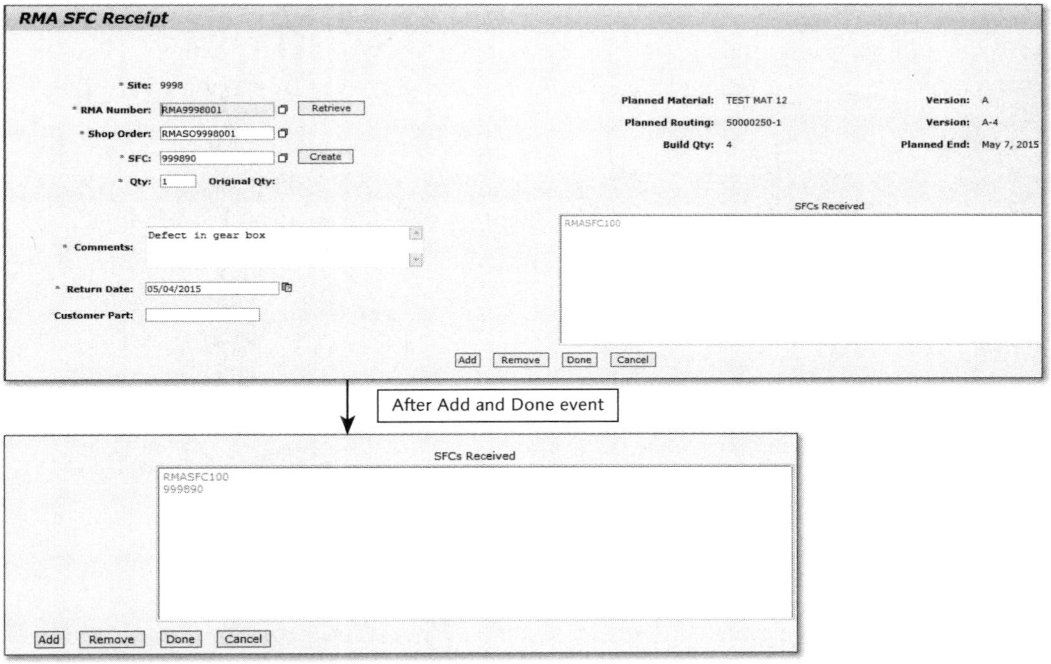

Figure 6.6 Working with RMA SFC Receipt

Now, the SFC will be in queue at the first operation of the routing used in the RMA shop order. The SFC will be inspected through all the operations of the routing.

6.1.5 SFC Group

In SAP ME, an SFC group is the collection of SFCs which is used for a sampling plan (explained in Chapter 8) for quality inspection. For inspection purposes, system selects the SFC from the SFC group. When you maintain a sample plan in SAP ME, you also need to provide the SFC GROUP SIZE, a mandatory field in the Sam-

6 | Shop Floor Control Management

ple Plan Maintenance activity. By providing the SFC group size, you indicate how many SFCs will be selected to create this group. For example, if the SFC group size is four and each SFC contains a quantity of one, then SAP ME needs a minimum of four SFCs to perform sampling. If the SFC quantity is two, then SAP ME needs a minimum of two SFCs to perform sampling. When an operator triggers sampling activity from the POD, SAP ME generates an SFC group number automatically, and that group number includes the SFCs that are used for sampling. Whenever an operator selects an SFC and triggers sampling activity, the selected SFC status changes to Complete Pending. Sample SFCs from the SFC group are used in sample routing assigned in the Sample Plan Maintenance activity. Figure 6.7 shows the SFC Group created in the sampling process from shop floor execution through the Production Operator Dashboard.

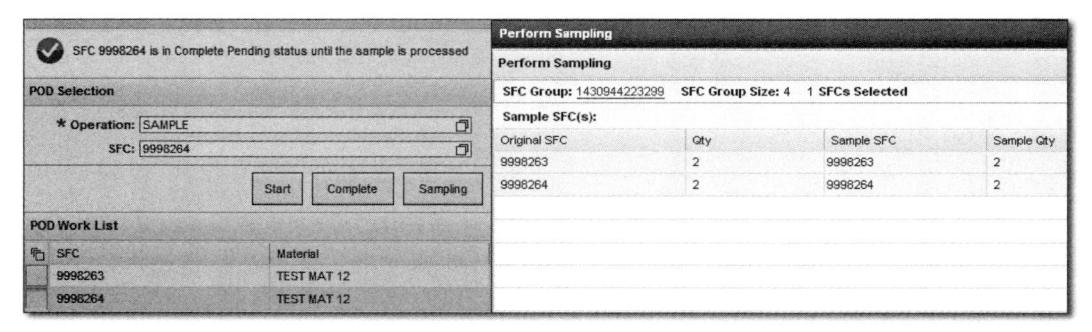

Figure 6.7 SFC Group Creation in Sampling

6.1.6 SFC Status

In shop floor production processes, an SFC moves from one operation to another (based on routing steps design) until production is finished using that SFC. During the execution process, the SFC can have multiple statuses in different operations. Table 6.1 provides the details of SFC status codes (used by SAP ME to store the SFC status in WIP or ODS databases), status description, and details of each status.

Status Code	Status Description	Details
401	New	SFC is generated from shop order release and not yet used in any operation.
402	InQueue	SFC is in queue at any operation and SFC can be used for starting the operation.

Table 6.1 SFC Status

Status Code	Status Description	Details
403	Active	Operation is started using the SFC but not yet completed.
404	Hold	SFC is placed on hold at any operation.
405	Done	SFC is completed through the routing.
406	Done (Hold)	SFC is completed in last step of routing and placed on hold.
407	Scrapped	SFC is scrapped for any defect in shop-floor execution process.
408	Invalid	SFC is merged with another SFC and original SFC will become invalid.
409	Deleted	SFC is deleted through SFC Scrap/Delete activity. SAP ME removes the SFC from production by marking the status as DELETED.
410	Returned	SFC becomes RETURNED status when SFC is returned from destination site to source. In site-to-site transfer you can transfer SFC with DONE status at source site.
411	Golden Unit	SFC becomes Golden Unit when it is used for equipment testing purpose. But before making the SFC in Golden Unit status, SFC should have DONE status. After finishing the equipment testing you can again change the SFC status back to DONE. You can use SAP ME activity GOLDEN UNIT to change the SFC status from DONE to Golden Unit and again from Golden Unit to DONE.

Table 6.1 SFC Status (Cont.)

6.2 Performing SFC Activities

In this section you will learn the list of activities which can be performed on SFC during the shop floor manufacturing process. Depending on your situation you may need to merge multiple SFCs into a single SFC or split one SFC into multiple SFCs using the SFC Merge or SFC Split activities. You will also learn the purpose of the SFC Place Hold, SFC Release Hold, SFC Quantity Adjustment, SFC Scrap/Delete, SFC Unscrap/Undelete, and Change Production activities.

6.2.1 SFC Merge

Through the SFC Merge activity, you can merge multiple SFC numbers into a single SFC number: a *parent SFC number*. The parent SFC contains the sum of all child SFCs' quantities. SAP ME allows you to merge SFC numbers across routings, operations, or shop orders, but keep in mind that SFC numbers should have the IN_QUEUE status to perform the merge activity. Before merging, if you perform data collection for child SFCs, the parent SFC will contain all the collected data of child SFCs after the merge. The quantity restriction configured in the material maintenance is also enforced to the merged SFC.

> **Note**
>
> To perform SFC merge across routings, operations, or shop orders, set the activity rule for SFC Merge (PR580) in Activity Maintenance for MERGE_ACROSS_ROUTERS, MERGE_ACROSS_OPERATIONS and MERGE_ACROSS_SHOPORDERS to TRUE.

Figure 6.8 shows three child SFCs (SFC 1, SFC 2, and SFC 3) residing in three different operations being merged into a single parent SFC (SFC 4) in a new operation. The quantity of the parent SFC equals the sum of the quantity of all three child SFCs.

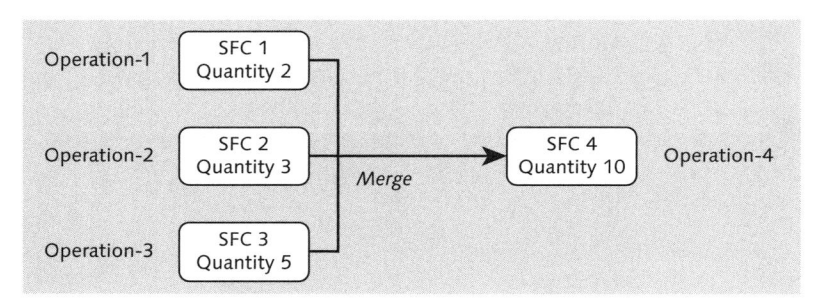

Figure 6.8 Merging Child SFCs into Parent SFC

6.2.2 SFC Split

A single SFC can be split into multiple new SFCs using the SFC SPLIT activity in SAP ME. You can split the quantity of a SFC number into multiple SFC numbers. SFC split can be performed manually through the SFC Split activity, in which you need to specify QUANTITY TO SPLIT and NEW SFC NUMBER.

> **Note**
>
> An SFC with ACTIVE status in an operation can be split if the activity (activity ID: PR570) rule for ALLOW_ACTIVE_SFC_SPLIT is set to TRUE. If AUTOMATIC_ID_GENERATION activity rule is set to TRUE, the system automatically generates new SFC numbers in Next Number Maintenance for the SFC Release pattern.

It is also possible to split SFCs automatically during the shop floor execution process. Non-serialized SFCs can be automatically split from the POD when Relaxed Flow Routing is used for the shop floor execution process. A shop floor user can complete a partial quantity of a non-serialized SFC at any step on the Relaxed Routing Flow. To perform the partial quantity completion at any operation, a shop floor user needs to enter the quantity in the QUANTITY field of the POD (see Chapter 10 for more information about the POD). In a relaxed flow routing, when a shop floor user logs an NC code against the partial quantity of an SFC and disposition the entered quantity to another routing, SAP ME automatically splits the quantity into a new SFC number. To achieve this functionality, maintain the AUTO_SPLIT option as ALWAYS or ASK in the activity rules of the NC_DATA_ENTRY activity through Activity Maintenance. Shop floor users can continue execution of the original SFC through production routing. When the split SFC (executed through disposition routing) comes back to the production routing, SAP ME can merge the split quantity with the original SFC (executed through production routing) on the production routing, and the split SFC becomes invalid. To achieve the auto-merge functionality, set the AUTO_MERGE option to ALWAYS or ASK in the activity rules of SFC COMPLETE (Activity Id: PR510) activity using the Activity Maintenance page.

6.2.3 SFC Place Hold

In shop floor execution, you may need to put an SFC on hold due to an issue. For example, in a car assembly process, say you find a defect on a car during the visual inspection operation. You want to put it on hold immediately and send it for repair. In SAP ME, the hold feature can be achieved through the SFC Place Hold activity. The hold type can be *immediate* or *future*:

- *Immediate* holds allows you to put the SFC on hold status immediately in the current operation.
- *Future* holds put the SFC on hold when it is in queue in the next operation.

You can also set multiple SFCs on hold at a time, but to do so you need to search through shop orders or process lots, which will return multiple SFCs for the same shop orders or process lots.

This activity also provides the option to put the material, routing, and shop order associated with the SFC on hold by selecting the checkbox options as shown in Figure 6.9.

6 | Shop Floor Control Management

If a future hold is selected, you can provide the future hold operation number in the FUTURE HOLD OPERATION input field. For an immediate hold, this field is disabled.

You can also provide REASON CODE, EXPECTED RELEASE DATE/TIME, and COMMENTS when putting an SFC on hold (see Figure 6.9).

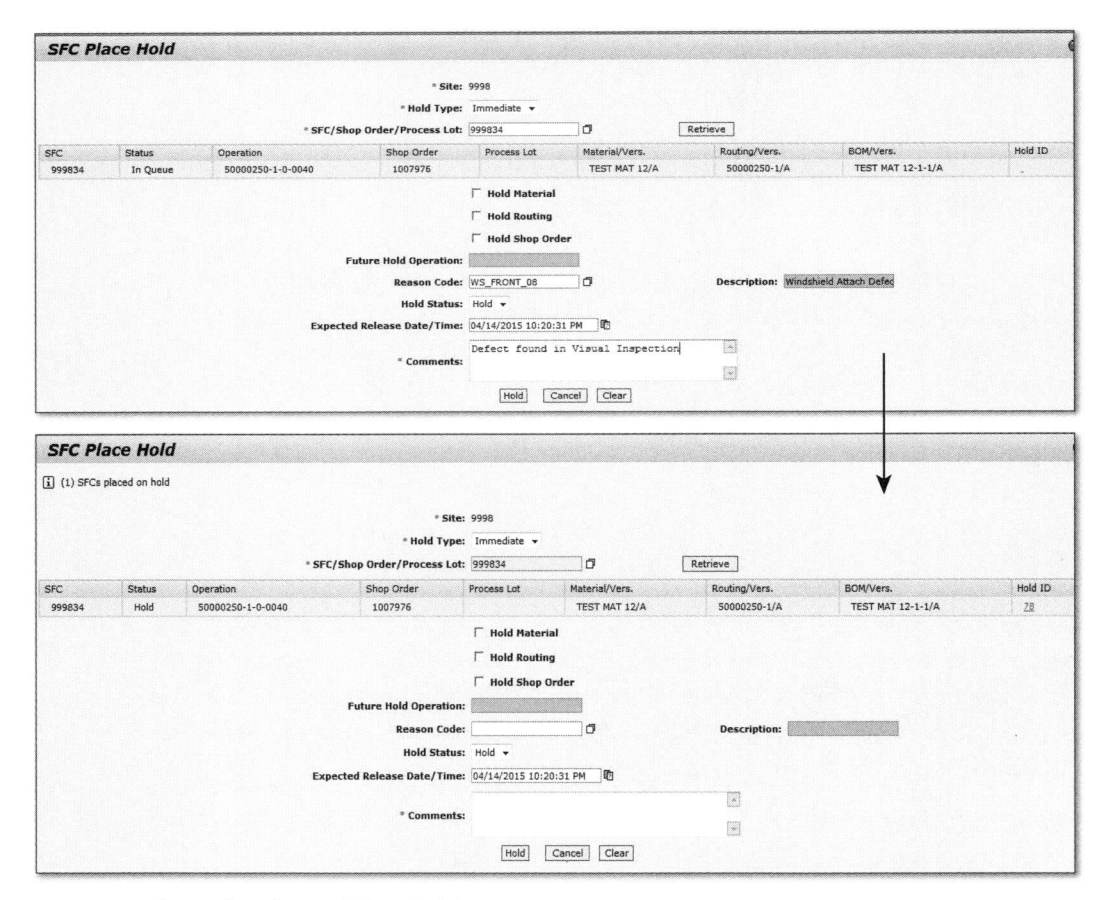

Figure 6.9 Placing SFC on Hold

6.2.4 SFC Release Hold

An SFC on hold cannot be used for any shop floor manufacturing activity until it is released. You can release the SFC hold via the SFC Release Hold activity in SAP ME. Materials, routings, and shop orders, will also be released with this activity if they were placed on hold earlier through the SFC Place Hold activity.

Figure 6.10 illustrates performing the SFC Release Hold activity. In the RELEASE BY field, choose either SFC/SHOP ORDER/PROCESS LOT or HOLD ID (the ID assigned by the system when the SFC is placed on hold). Based on your RELEASE BY field value selection, enter the corresponding value in RELEASE BY input field to retrieve the details. You can also enter RELEASE COMMENTS before releasing the SFC.

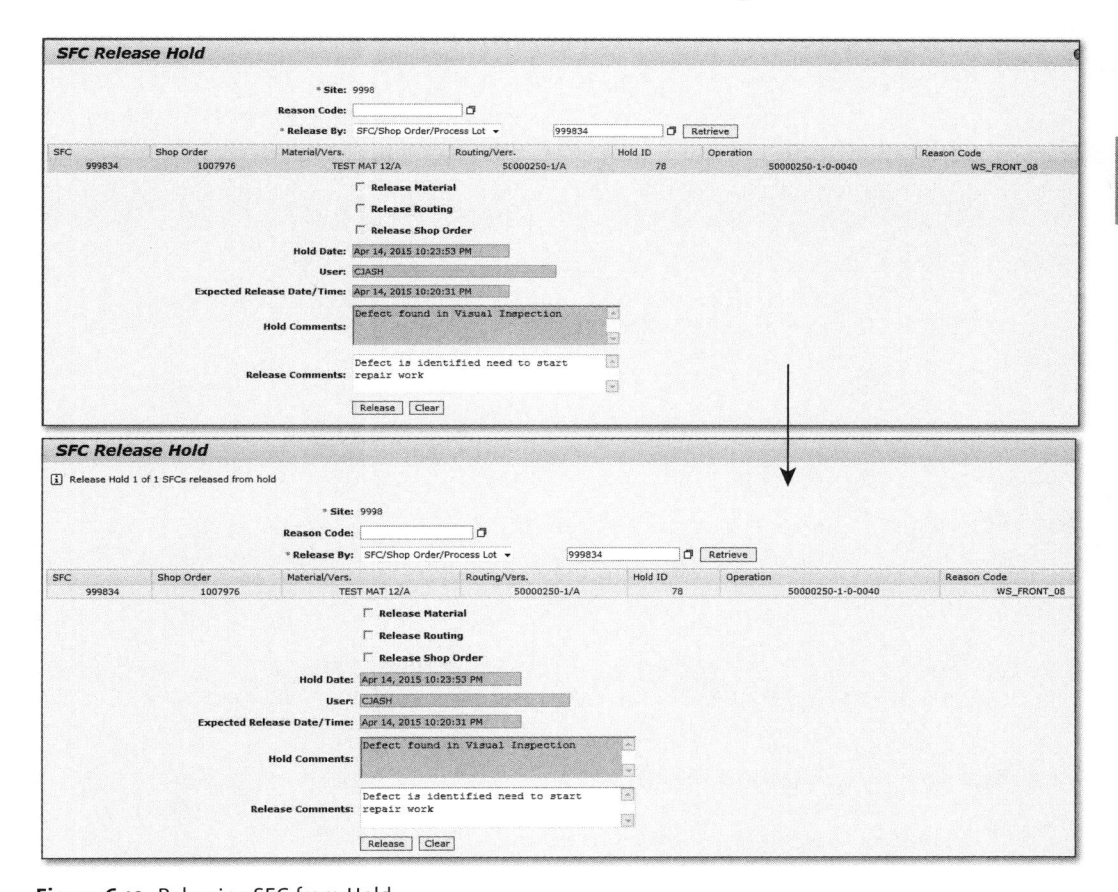

Figure 6.10 Releasing SFC from Hold

6.2.5 SFC Quantity Adjustment

If you want to increase or reduce the quantity of an SFC, use the SFC Quantity Adjustment activity in SAP ME. However, keep in mind that the SFC status should be either New or In Queue. Along with SFC quantity adjustment, the associated shop order quantity will also be adjusted automatically.

6 | Shop Floor Control Management

6.2.6 SFC Scrap/Delete

Use the SFC Scrap/Delete activity when you want to remove an SFC from the shop floor production process for any issue with that SFC. For example, in the car assembly process, if a defect is not closed for a car in the QUARANTINE operation of the designed routing, then you want to scrap it using SFC Scrap/Delete activity. The adjustment through SFC Scrap/Delete activity is not sent to SAP ERP.

In this activity, select SCRAP or DELETE for ACTIVITY. Based on your selection, the SCRAP or DELETE button will appear, as shown in Figure 6.11. SAP ME allows you to scrap multiple SFCs at a time; to do so, you can retrieve the SFC list by shop order number or process lot.

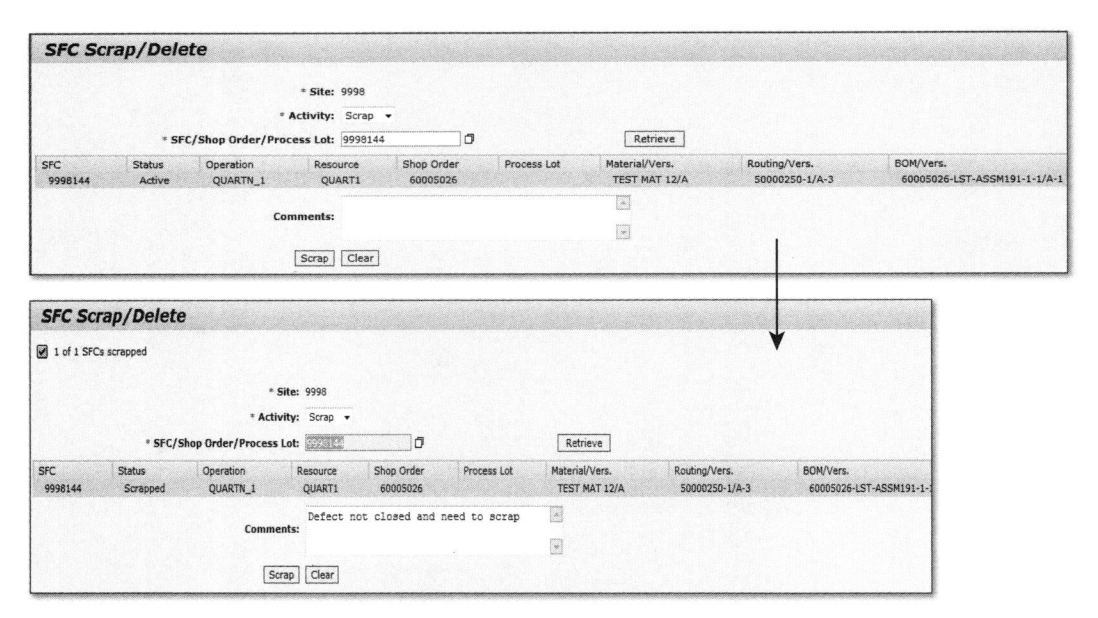

Figure 6.11 Scrapping SFCs in Routing Operation

Based on the activity rule setting in the SFC Scrap/Delete activity (activity ID: SU580), the system takes the appropriate action. Figure 6.12 shows the default rule settings in activity SU580.

The rule settings for the SFC Scrap/Delete activity are as follows:

- **SCRAP_COMPONENT_OPTION**
  The default value for SCRAP_COMPONENT_OPTION is SCRAP_AND_RETURN_

COMP. This default value SCRAP_AND_RETURN_COMP is used to scrap the parent SFC and return components to floor stock.

- **SCRAP_DEL_ACTIVE_SFC**
  The default value for SCRAP_DEL_ACTIVE_SFC is Yes. If the value is Yes, then system will allow you to delete or scrap an SFC with Active status. For No, the system will not allow you to delete or scrap an SFC with Active status.

- **SCRAP_DEL_DONE_SFC**
  The default value for SCRAP_DEL_ACTIVE_SFC is Yes. If the value is Yes then the system will allow you to delete or scrap an SFC with Done status. For No, the system will not allow you to delete or scrap an SFC with Done status.

- **SCRAP_OR_DELETE**
  This rule is used to display the Scrap or Delete options in SFC Scrap/Delete activity page within the ACTIVITY dropdown field. The default value for SCRAP_OR_DELETE is BOTH, which means Scrap and Delete will both be displayed in the ACTIVITY dropdown field of SFC Scrap/Delete activity page. If you specify SCRAP in the SCRAP_OR_DELETE rule, then only the Scrap value will be displayed. If you specify DELETE in the SCRAP_OR_DELETE rule, then only the Delete value will be displayed.

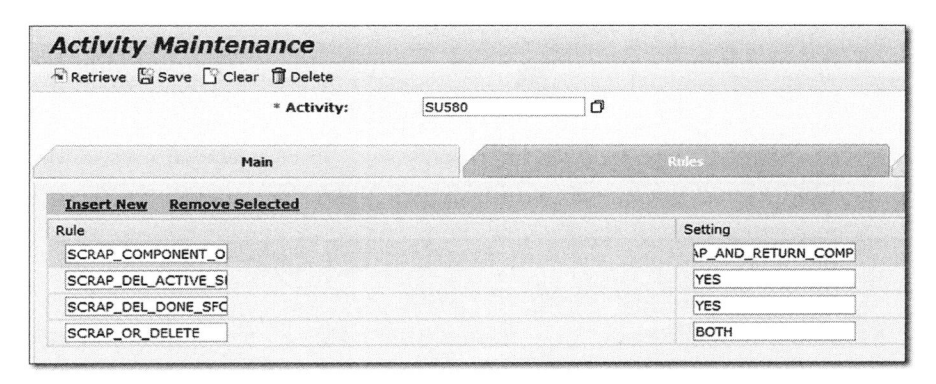

Figure 6.12 Default Rule Settings for SFC Scrap/Delete Activity (SU580)

6.2.7 SFC Unscrap/Undelete

If you want to bring the SFC back from scrapped or deleted status to its previous status, use the SFC Unscrap/Undelete activity in SAP ME. For example, the SFC number 9998144 was in Active status in the QUARTN_1 operation of routing 50000250 (as shown in Figure 6.13), and SFC was scrapped from there. To unscrap the same SFC, return it to In Queue status in the QUARTN_1 operation of routing 50000250.

Figure 6.13 shows an example of unscrapping an SFC using the SFC Unscrap/Undelete activity. Choose one ACTIVITY from the dropdown, either UNSCRAP or UNDELETE; based on your selection, the respective button will appear. SAP ME allows you to unscrap/undelete multiple SFCs at a time; to do so, retrieve the SFC list through SHOP ORDER or PROCESS LOT. You can also enter comments before unscrapping or undeleting.

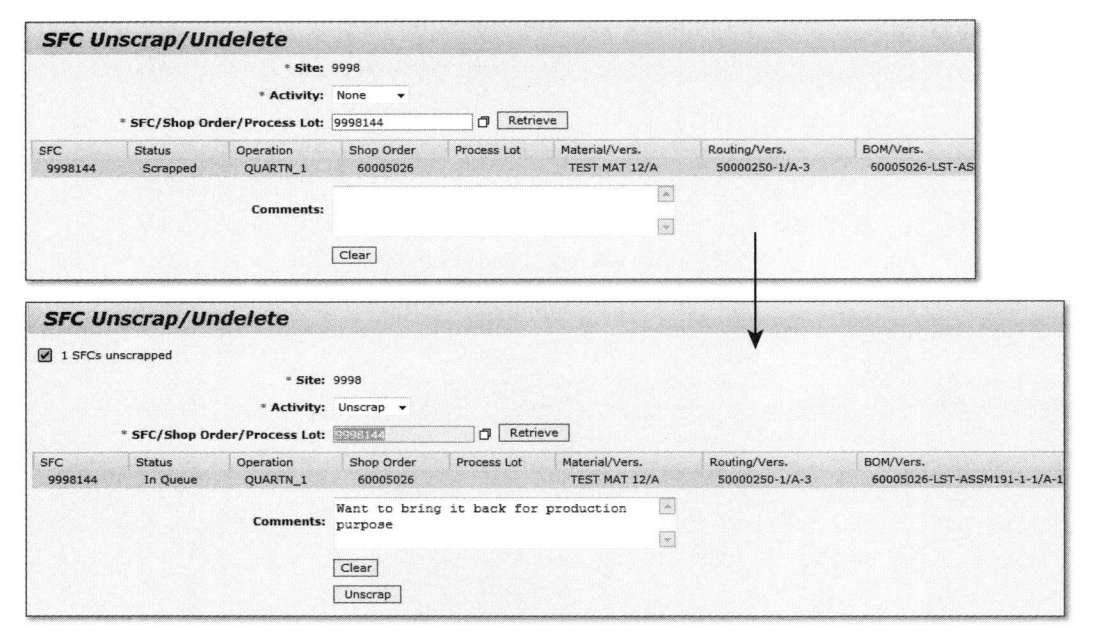

Figure 6.13 Unscrapping SFC to Use it Again in Production

6.2.8 Change Production

In SAP ME, the Change Production activity allows you to change the material, routing, BOM, and shop order for one or multiple SFCs in the shop floor manufacturing process. For example, in the car assembly process, a car can be assembled using two production lines on the shop floor. In middle of the assembly process, if a breakdown happens in line 1, the remaining cars (SFCs) can be assembled using production line 2 (assuming that production line 2 is not occupied with another production) to meet the order quantity within the required time. Here also, we assume that different routings are used for each production line. In SAP ME, using the Change Production activity, you can change the routing of remaining SFCs with routing used in production line 2 and continue the assembly process.

In this activity you can specify an SFC number to retrieve details of a single SFC or providing a shop order number or process lot to retrieve multiple SFCs to change from one routing to another. The Change Production screen provides options to enter NEW MATERIAL and/or NEW ROUTING and/or NEW BOM and/or NEW SHOP ORDER numbers, as shown in Figure 6.14. On the Change Production screen, select the ADJUST ORIGINAL ORDER BUILD QTY DOWN checkbox to reduce the original shop order's build quantity by the total SFC quantity that will be moved to new shop order. You can also specify the engineering change order (ECO) number and COMMENTS.

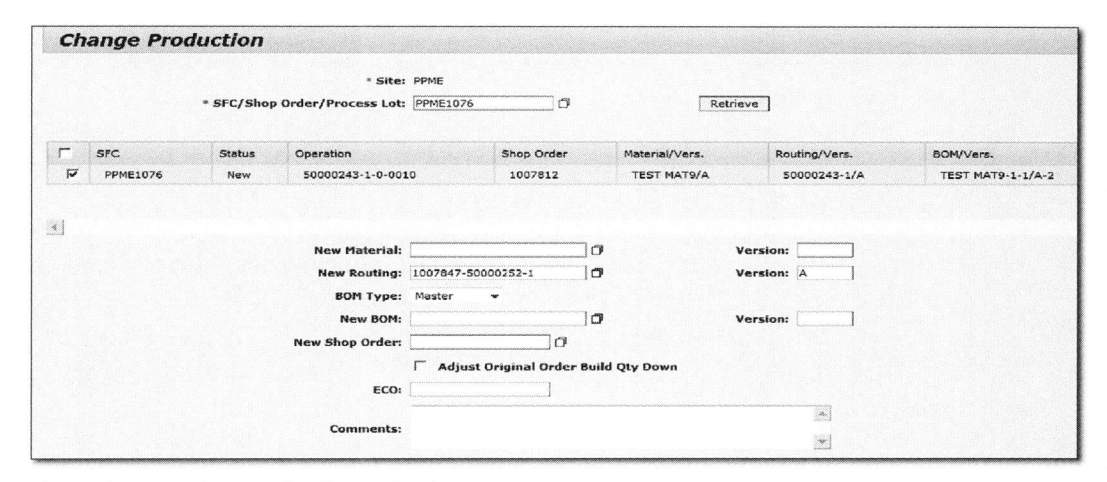

Figure 6.14 Initial Screen for Change Production

Click on CONTINUE to move to the next screen, where you can choose routing operation placement for the SFC. SAP ME provides four options for routing operation placement, as seen in Figure 6.15:

- PLACE IN QUEUE AT OPERATION (specify one operation from routing)
- PLACE IN QUEUE AT FIRST OPERATION
- PLACE IN QUEUE AT FIRST UNCOMPLETED OPERATION
- PLACE IN QUEUE AT CURRENT OPERATION

Click CHANGE PRODUCTION to change the production for the SFC.

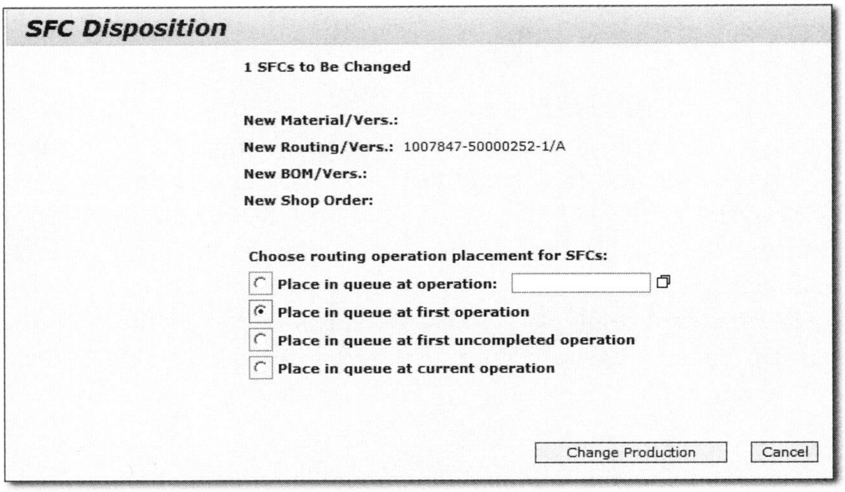

Figure 6.15 SFC Disposition for Change Production

6.3 Reporting on SFC Activities

In this section we will discuss multiple standard reporting activities available in SAP ME such as the Activity Log Report, Hold Report, SFC Report, SFC Average Cycle Time by Operation Report, SFC Average Cycle Time by Shop Order Report, and the SFC Cycle Time Report. These reports are very useful on the shop floor to track the SFCs during the production process and after.

6.3.1 Activity Log Report

In SAP ME, the Activity Log Report provides information about activities performed by the operator on the shop floor during the production process. For example, say that an operator has started an SFC in an operation or put an SFC on hold status and then released it; all those activities will be visible within the Activity Log Report. The report includes activities performed on SFCs, dates and times, activity codes, material numbers related to SFCs with versions, shop order numbers related to SFCs, and details of SFCs, as shown in Figure 6.16. You can search the report by providing at least one input parameter, such as date range, material, SFC, or activity code. You can also search by operation, resource, process lot, work center, or shop order (in the MAIN tab of the report); or RMA number, order type, customer order, work center category, or user (in the MISCELLANEOUS tab of the report) to optimize the search result.

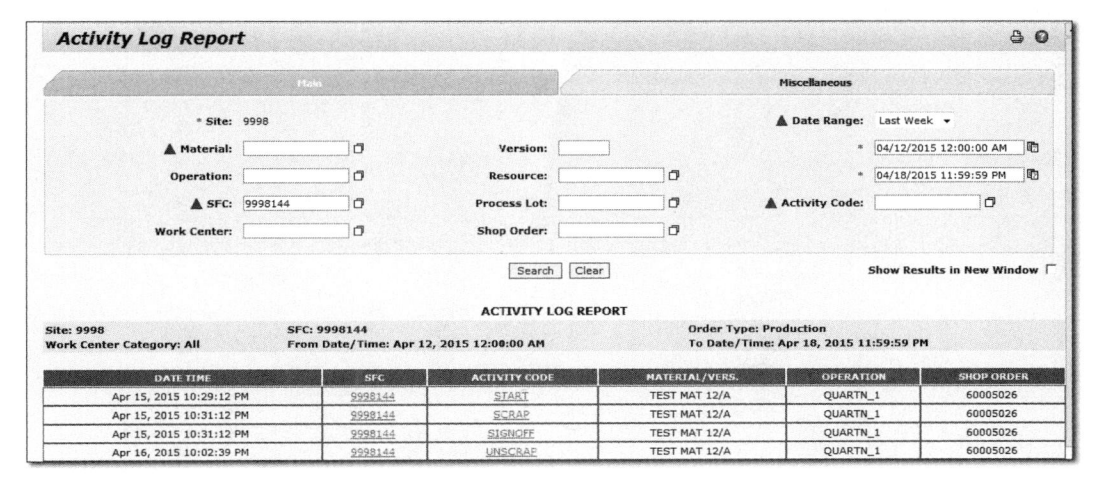

Figure 6.16 Activity Log Report

You can also search activities that are not related to an SFC, such as shop order release, shop order close, resource status change, and so on. To get a search result for those activities, set the shop order type as ALL in the MISCELLANEOUS tab and specify the DATE RANGE value in the MAIN tab. Use the PRINT icon at the top-right to print the report. Click the ACTIVITY CODE link to access the SFC Details Report.

6.3.2 Hold Report

The *Hold Report* provides information about SFCs on hold. For example, say that an operator found a defect in an SFC during an operation and placed the SFC on hold through the SFC Place Hold activity. Search for that SFC using the Hold Report activity to find out the details. For a single SFC, provide an SFC number in the SEARCH BY field, or provide a shop order or process lot to find the report for multiple SFCs if the shop order contains multiple SFCs. The Hold Report provides shop orders, materials, routings, operations, activity codes, hold IDs, and reason codes along with hold details associated with an SFC. Click the HOLD DETAILS icon to access the Hold Details Report, which contains SFC details, hold details, and hold comment sections. Each section describes information for multiple parameters. Figure 6.17 shows a Hold Report and Hold Details Report.

6 | Shop Floor Control Management

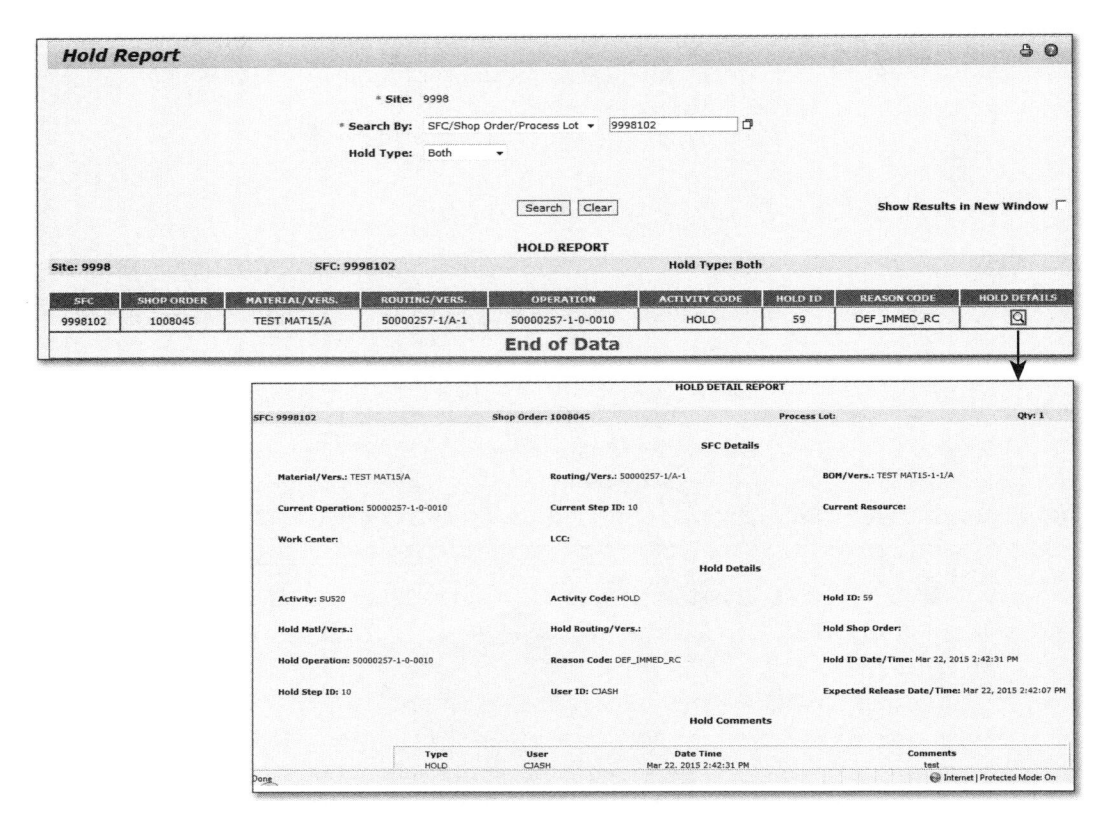

Figure 6.17 Hold Report

6.3.3 SFC Report

The *SFC Report* provides the current status of an SFC in the shop floor production process. For example, say that an operator is working on an SFC and you want to find out the current status of that SFC and for which operation it is in queue or active. You may also want to know how many SFCs are completed for the current shop order or how many SFCs are scrapped. All that information is available through the SFC Report. To find the status for a single SFC, search by SFC number only, and to get the report for all SFCs of a shop order, search by shop order number. In the search input, you can also provide values for material, operation, resource, SFC status, and process lot. In a miscellaneous search, you can provide routing, order type, customer, customer order number, reporting center, work center category, RMA number, and work center.

Search results will provide you with the SFC status, shop order number associated with the SFC, material, operations with current SFC statuses, quantity of the SFC, SFC STEP DETAILS link, AS-BUILT link, and NC LOG link. Through each link you can find the details information.

SFC step details will provide you the status of the SFC in each operation of the routing, and you can find the current position of the SFC in the routing operation with quantity.

The AS-BUILT link will show the details of used BOM components with required quantity, assembled quantity, operation in which it is used, component type, performed user with date and time, and actual component.

The NC LOG link can provide details of nonconformance logged against an SFC with operation, resource, work center, NC code, NC code description, NC state, NC category, incident number, activity date/time, logged user ID, activity close date/time, closed user ID, and so on. This report also shows the parent and child NCs. Figure 6.18 shows an SFC Report with SFC step details, as-built, and NC log details.

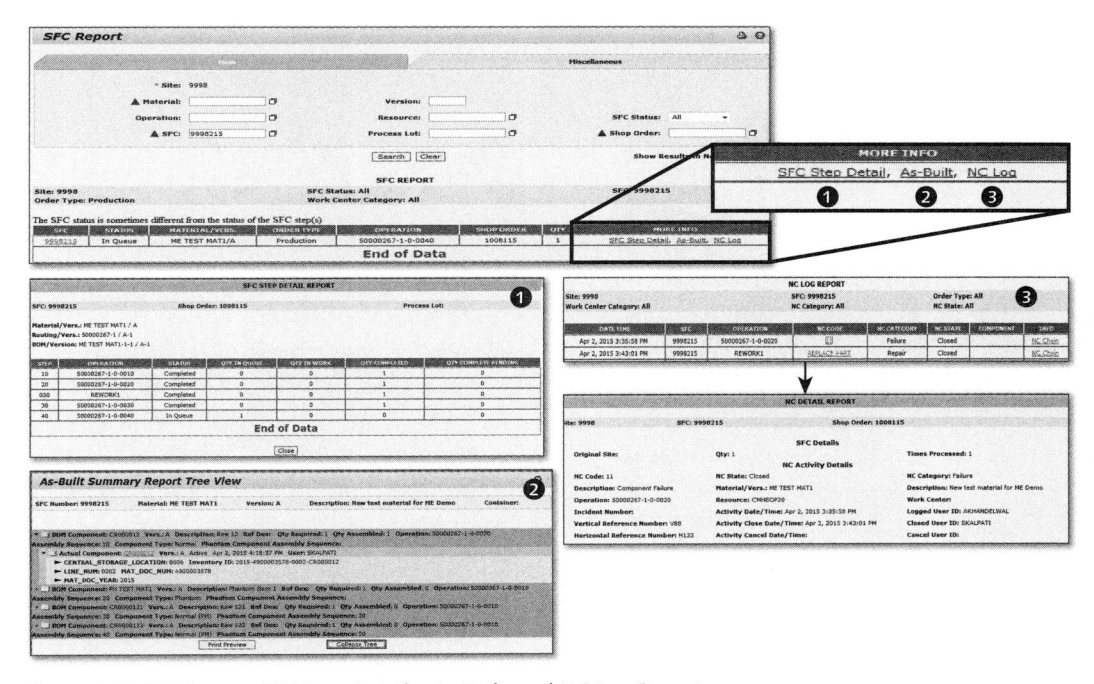

Figure 6.18 SFC Report, SFC Step Details, As-Built, and NC Log Report

6 | Shop Floor Control Management

6.3.4 SFC Average Cycle Time by Operation Report

The *SFC Average Cycle Time by Operation Report* provides the cycle time information of an SFC within an operation. For example, in the car assembly process, you might look for the cycle time spent for a car assembly in each operation of a routing, and you can find out which operation has taken the maximum time and which operation has taken the minimum time for assembling the same car. The SFC Average Cycle Time by Operation Report provides the information in two sections, QUEUE TIME and ELAPSED TIME:

- QUEUE TIME provides the minimum, maximum, and average time of an SFC spent for each operation along with the shop order number.
- ELAPSED TIME provides the waiting time of the SFC in each operation.

You can view the search results in a graphical or tabular view, as shown in Figure 6.19.

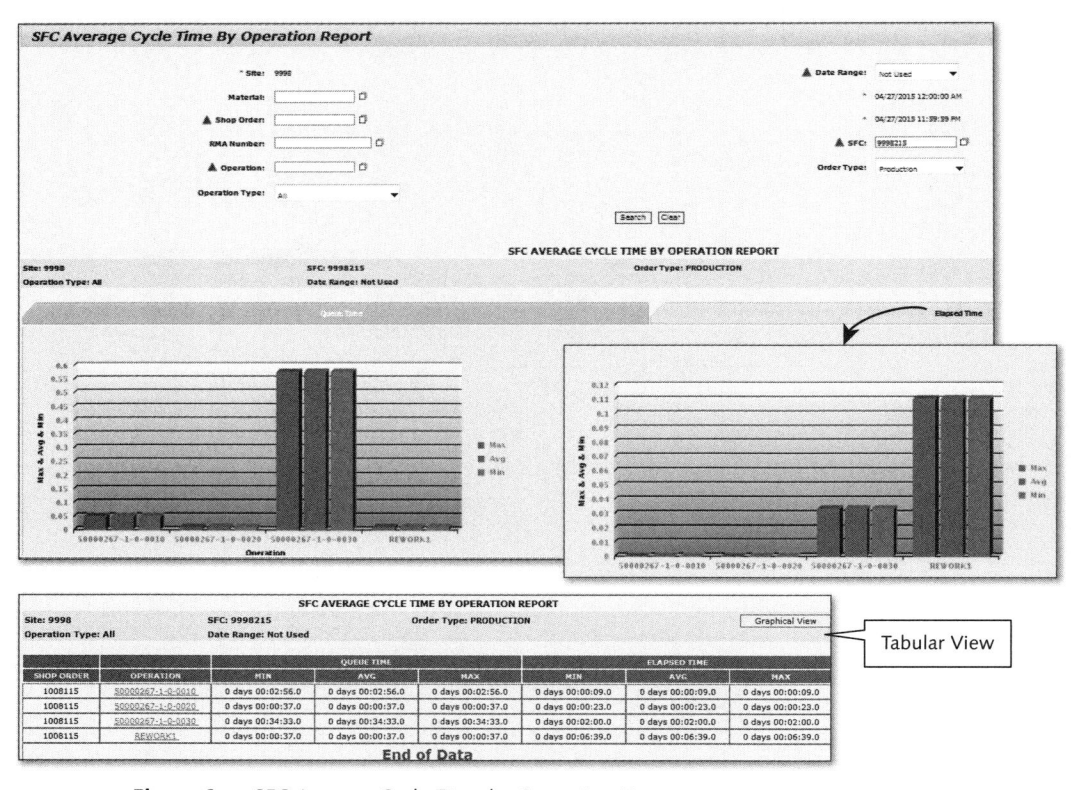

Figure 6.19 SFC Average Cycle Time by Operation Report

6.3.5 SFC Average Cycle Time by Shop Order Report

The *SFC Average Cycle Time by Shop Order Report* provides the total cycle time taken in an operation in a shop floor execution process. For example, in a car assembly process, you might look for the total time taken in each operation to process the shop order, which you can find with this report. You need to keep in mind that this report shows only the total time for SFCs of a shop order with status Done, Done (Hold), or Scrapped.

This report also provides graphical and tabular views of search results. In search results, initially you will see a graphical view of the report with shop order number and cycle time (average, minimum, and maximum). Click on the graphical bar to see the queue time and elapsed time for each operation. In search parameters, you can search by shop order number to see the cycle time for a shop order. Figure 6.20 shows the report.

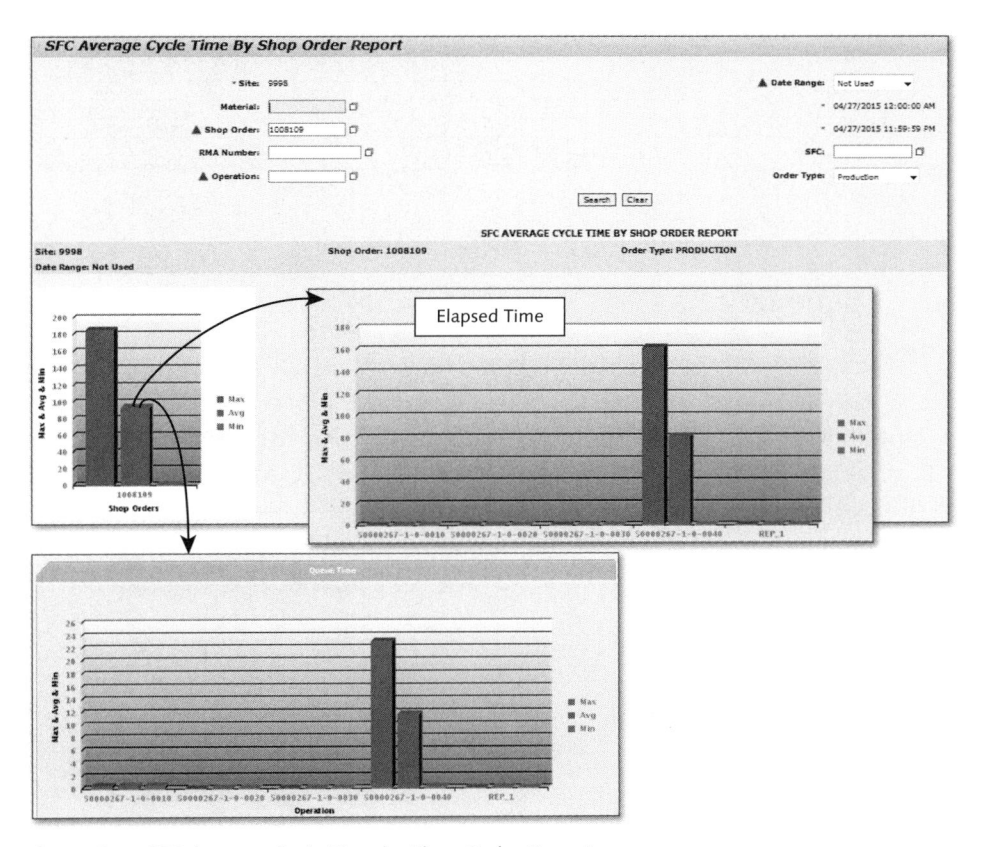

Figure 6.20 SFC Average Cycle Time by Shop Order Report

6.3.6 SFC Cycle Time Report

If you are looking for the cycle time of a particular SFC, use the *SFC Cycle Time Report*. This report provides the queue time and elapsed time of an SFC in each operation where the SFC is executed on the shop floor. When you look for the cycle time for an SFC, SFC is a mandatory input parameter in the search criteria. Figure 6.21 shows an SFC Cycle Time Report.

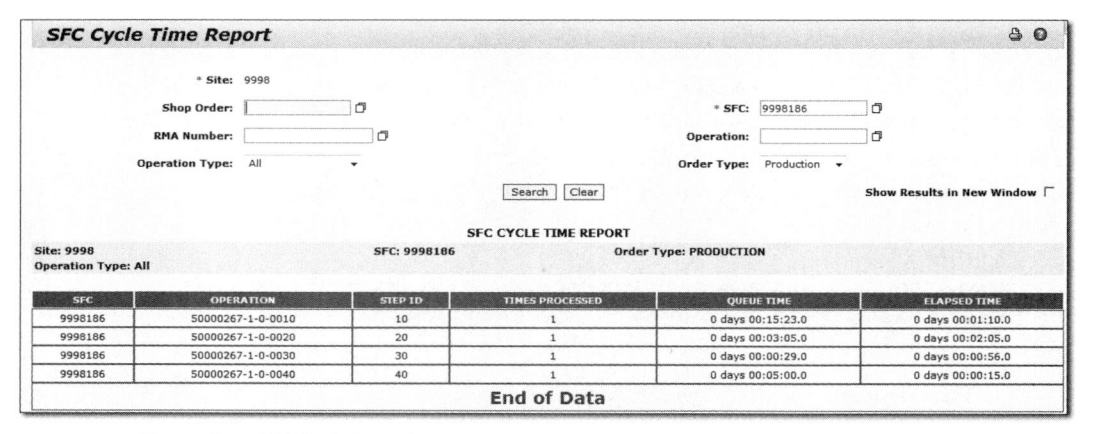

SFC Cycle Time Report

SFC	OPERATION	STEP ID	TIMES PROCESSED	QUEUE TIME	ELAPSED TIME
9998186	50000267-1-0-0010	10	1	0 days 00:15:23.0	0 days 00:01:10.0
9998186	50000267-1-0-0020	20	1	0 days 00:03:05.0	0 days 00:02:05.0
9998186	50000267-1-0-0030	30	1	0 days 00:00:29.0	0 days 00:00:56.0
9998186	50000267-1-0-0040	40	1	0 days 00:05:00.0	0 days 00:00:15.0

End of Data

Figure 6.21 SFC Cycle Time Report

6.4 Summary

In this chapter, you learned about SFCs and how to generate and work with them in SAP ME. You also discovered the purpose of creating trackable SFCs, RMA SFC receipts, SFC groups, and multiple SFC statuses. We also discussed the list of SAP ME activities that can be performed on SFCs, such as SFC Merge, SFC Split, SFC Place Hold, SFC Release Hold, SFC Quantity Adjustment, SFC Scrap/Delete, SFC Unscrap/Undelete, and Change Production. At the end of this chapter, we introduced the SFC-based standard reports in SAP ME and the required setup data to find report results.

The next chapter explains data collection in SAP ME.

This chapter explains data collection functionality and its use in SAP ME. It discusses DC groups, DC parameters, and assignment of a DC group to a process object, DC edits, and standalone DC. The DC Result Report is also covered.

7   Data Collection

In the last chapter, you learned about SFCs and how to work with them for production execution activities in SAP ME. While working with SFCs, you may need to collect information about various parameters of them per production steps.

The main purpose of *data collection* (DC) is to record parameter values during the shop floor manufacturing process so that the same data can be used for analysis and making decisions regarding a product. In SAP ME, DC functionality provides the ability to record data for SFCs, resources, and work centers. DC is based on DC groups and parameters defined within DC groups. The collected data is stored in the WIP database and can also be transferred automatically in the ODS database for analysis based on the system rule setup in SAP ME. Collected data can be edited in the *Data Collection Edit* activity in SAP ME. In the shop floor execution process, operations in which data is collected depend on the configuration within the *Data Collection Maintenance* activity. In SAP ME, data can be collected manually by an operator during the execution process or automatically via public API (PAPI) services and SAP Plant Connectivity to collect directly from external systems. Collected data can also be used in statistical process control (SPC) for analysis purposes. In this chapter, you will learn about the available functionalities for DC in SAP ME.

7.1   Maintaining Data Collection

SAP ME provides the Data Collection Maintenance activity to configure DC features. The Data Collection Maintenance user interface consists of three configuration tabs: MAIN, ATTACHED, and CUSTOM DATA. Before collecting data in the shop floor manufacturing process, configure the DC by defining a DC group and creating DC parameters. You do not need to define DC Group and parameters if the data is coming directly from a resource and is not manually entered by an operator. SAP ME stores the data from the PAPI in the same table where manual data collection is stored.

7.1.1 Creating a DC Group

For Data Collection Maintenance, you need to first define a *DC group*, where the data collection parameters can be defined against which the data values will be collected. A DC group contains a list of related parameters whose values are collected at the same time in a manufacturing operation. Define a DC group to collect data for an SFC or resource or work center by selecting the value in the COLLECTION TYPE field. During manufacturing execution, data can be collected at the start of the operation, completion of the operation, start and completion of the operation, or at any time. In the COLLECTED DATA AT field, select the value to specify at during which stage the DC can occur e.g. *Start, Start/Complete, Complete, Anytime*. Also configure the data collection method by setting the COLLECTION METHOD field to either MANUAL-SINGLE or MANUAL-MULTIPLE. MANUAL-SINGLE indicates that the user enters data individually for each SFC number and MANUAL-MULTIPLE indicates that the user enters data once for a group of SFCs and the data parameter values are copied to each SFC. In Data Collection Maintenance, configure user authentication for DC by selecting the USER AUTHENTICATION REQUIRED checkbox. If the checkbox is checked, the user needs to identify himself/herself through a user ID and password during DC for that particular DC group. If you configure CERTIFICATION for a DC group, the user who has that certification can only perform the DC for that DC group. In the Data Collection Maintenance page, the CERTIFICATION field is enabled only when you select the USER AUTHENTICATION REQUIRED checkbox. Figure 7.1 shows the Data Collection Maintenance activity in SAP ME.

Please note the following points regarding some of the available options under Data Collection Maintenance:

- **Pass/Fail Group**
  If the PASS/FAIL GROUP checkbox is selected, the system automatically sets TRUE (by selecting and disabling the checkbox) for the OVERRIDE MIN/MAx checkbox on the MAIN tab of the PARAMETER DETAIL screen.

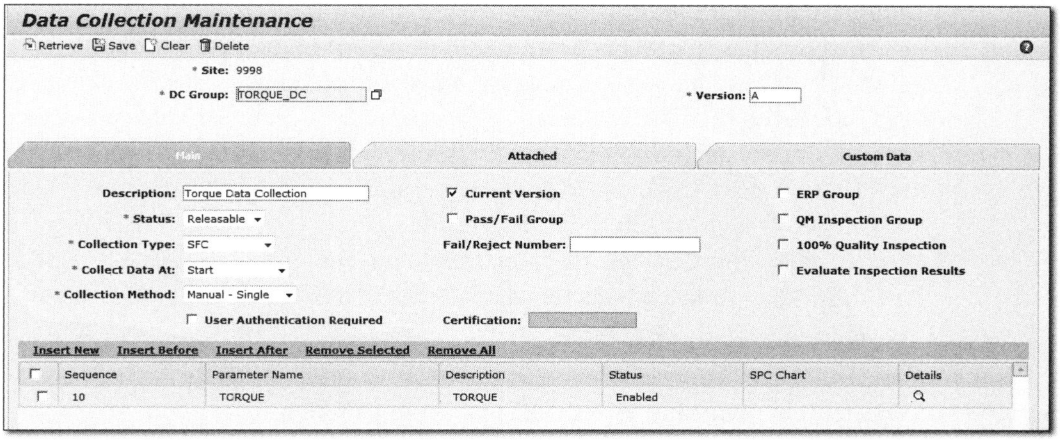

Maintaining Data Collection | **7.1**

Figure 7.1 Maintaining DC in SAP ME

> **Note: Significance of Pass/Fail Group**
>
> If the Pass/Fail setting for the DC group is not checked, then at DC the entered data value is checked against the MIN VALUE and MAX VALUE settings for the numeric or formula DC parameter. A PASS/FAIL GROUP is checked when the data collected is evaluated and the non-conformance plugin is opened automatically in the POD after the data values are saved. If the box is checked it enables the corresponding workflow. In addition, the Fail/Reject Number specifies the number of parameters that must fail before this process is started. If the field is empty it means all parameter values must fail.

- **Fail/Reject Number**
  In the FAIL/REJECT NUMBER field, specify the required number of parameters whose value must be outside of min or max limits to fail the DC group. If you do not specify any number, then all parameters of the DC must be failed (the value for each parameter will be outside of min or max limits) to fail the DC group.

- **ERP Group**
  The ERP GROUP checkbox indicates that the DC group is for SAP ERP, and parameter values are sent to SAP ERP. The collection of these pertain only to batch characteristics and no other data parameters.

- **QM Inspection Group**
  When a production order is sent from SAP ERP with inspection lot and characteristics, the QM INSPECTION GROUP checkbox is checked and becomes read-only for both 100% and less than 100% inspection characteristics from SAP ERP.

7 | Data Collection

- **100% Quality Inspection**
  When a production order is downloaded from SAP ERP with inspection type of 100% in SAP ERP, the 100% QUALITY INSPECTION checkbox is checked automatically and is read-only when the required number of SFCs for each data parameter in a DC Group equals the build quantity of the Shop Order. When the parameters in a DC Group are less than 100%, the data parameter and data values are sent to SAP ERP through qualityInspectionResultRecordingRequest. SAPMEINT then sends the readErpQualityInspectionResultRequest message to SAP ERP QM to get the evaluated data parameter values to disposition the SFCs in SAP ME.

- **Evaluate Inspection Results**
  For 100% quality inspection, the EVALUATE INSPECTION RESULTS checkbox is selected automatically in SAP ME, as shown in Figure 7.2. If it is selected, then SAP ME evaluates all 100% quality inspection items for DC groups. The results determined by SAP ME are sent to SAP ERP QM through *qualityInspectionMEEvalResultRecordingRequest* message.

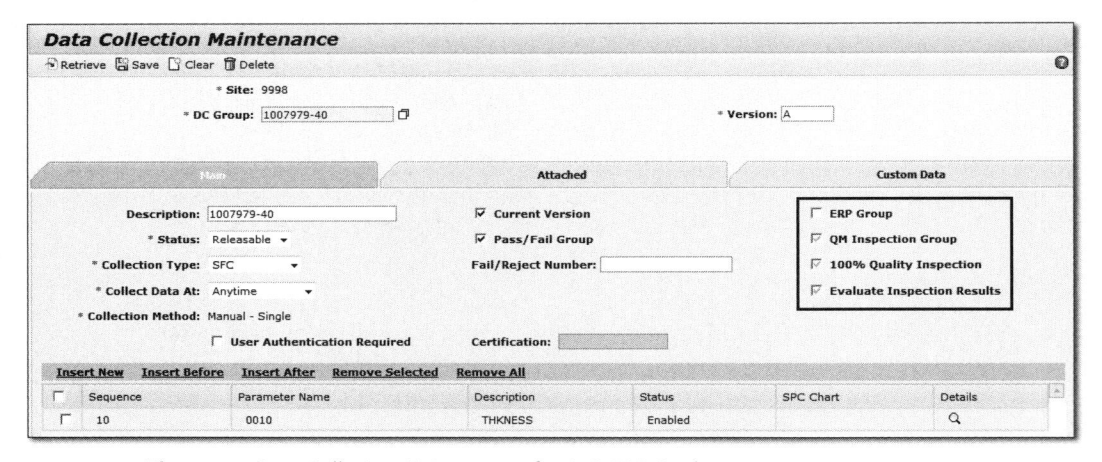

Figure 7.2 Data Collecion Maintenance for SAP ERP Quality Inspection

> **Note**
>
> To make the ERP GROUP, QM INSPECTION GROUP, 100% QUALITY INSPECTION, and EVALUATE INSPECTION RESULT checkboxes visible, set ERP INTEGRATION ACTIVE to TRUE in *System Rule Maintenance* activity. In the System Rule Maintenance activity, you need to check the setup for the following DC rules:

> ▸ **Allow Multiple Data Collection**
> If you want to collect data more than once for the same SFC number, DC group, and operation, set to TRUE; otherwise, FALSE.
> ▸ **Store Data Collection Results in ODS**
> If you want to store the data collection result in the ODS database as well, set the rule to TRUE. Otherwise, data will be stored only in WIP database. Data collected for a work center or resource is not archived, since it is not associated with an SFC. In order to ensure that this data is saved in the ODS database, set this rule to TRUE.
> ▸ **ERP Integration Active**
> Set the rule to TRUE for integration with SAP ERP for data collection to create DC groups for quality inspection characteristics.

7.1.2 Creating DC Parameters

You can define single or multiple parameters for a DC group, and the same parameters can be used for multiple DC groups. To define parameters with DC groups, click on the INSERT NEW link in the MAIN tab page of Data Collection Maintenance to open a page called PARAMETER DETAIL, as shown in Figure 7.3. This page contains four tabs: MAIN, USER OPTIONS, USER-DEFINED FIELDS, and SPC. Let's examine the configuration options for each tab.

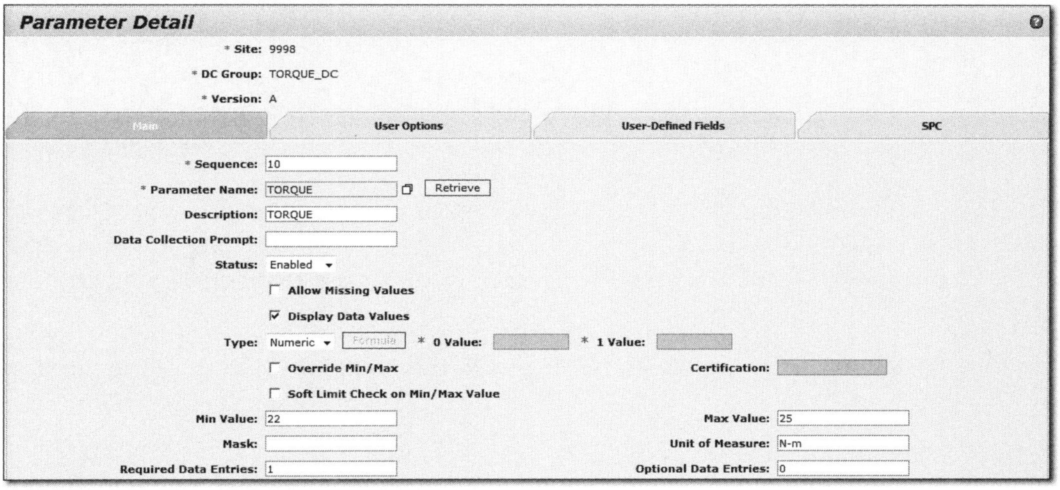

Figure 7.3 Creating DC Parameters in SAP ME

Main

In the MAIN tab, specify the sequence number and parameter name in the SEQUENCE and PARAMETER NAME fields. You can also provide a parameter description and a data collection prompt, which will be prompted at the time of data collection in the Data Collection Data Entry plugin in the POD. You need to select ENABLED for the active parameter status and DISABLED for the inactive parameter status.

The QM CRITICAL field appears when the DC Group is identified as a Quality Inspection Group and if the data parameter is critical and fails and it will cause the entire DC Group to fail whether other parameters.

If the ALLOW MISSING VALUES checkbox is checked, then it will allow the shop floor operator to save the data by entering a special character. Through the Data Collection Edit activity, the operator can change the value.

When the DISPLAY DATA VALUES checkbox is checked then it enables the min and max value to be displayed in the Data Collection Data Entry plugin in the POD.

The parameter TYPE can be set to NUMERIC, BOOLEAN, FORMULA, or TEXT. The numeric type is used for numeric value collection, and the Boolean type is used for Boolean value collection. When BOOLEAN is selected, the 0 VALUE and 1 VALUE fields become active. You can specify text for both fields.

> **Note: Boolean Type Selection for DC Parameter**
>
> If you select the Boolean type for DC parameter, then the OVERRIDE MIN/MAX, CERTIFICATION, SOFT LIMIT CHECK ON MIN/MAX VALUE, MIN VALUE, MAX VALUE, and MASK fields will be disabled.

The formula type allows you to enter custom formulas through scripts. The FORMULA button becomes active when you select FORMULA for TYPE. Click the FORMULA button to open the formula script window, and enter the custom script as shown in Figure 7.4.

Following are the optional parameters in the MAIN tab which you may need to configure:

- OVERRIDE MIN/MAX
  If you select the OVERRIDE MIN/MAX checkbox, then it will allow to save parameter values that are out of minimum and maximum value range, and the CERTIFICATION field will be activated. Assigning a certification makes the assigned certificate mandatory to perform the DC Override Min/Max.

Maintaining Data Collection | **7.1**

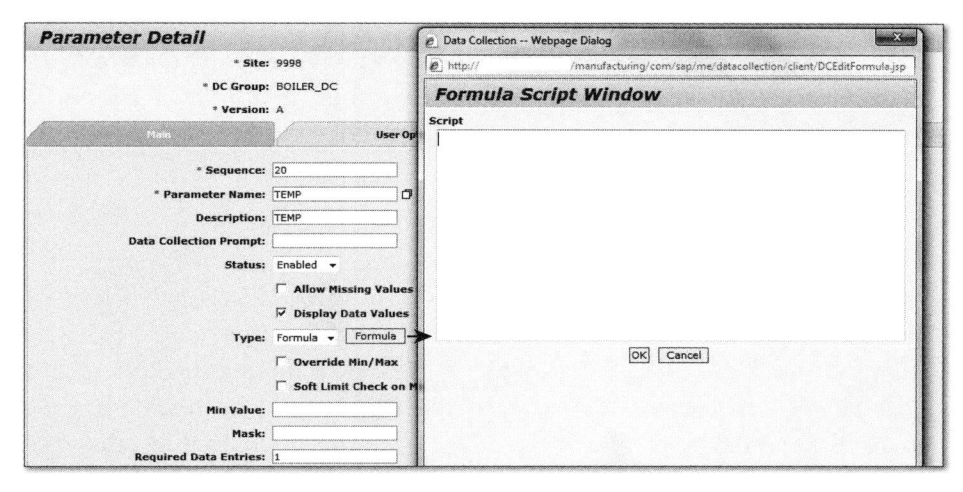

Figure 7.4 Formula Script Window

- SOFT LIMIT CHECK ON MIN/MAX VALUE
  The SOFT LIMIT CHECK ON MIN/MAX VALUE checkbox is selected automatically for quality inspection characteristics parameters downloaded from SAP ERP through a production order with inspection characteristics, as shown in Figure 7.5. If the checkbox is selected, then it allows you to save parameter values that are out of minimum and maximum value range.

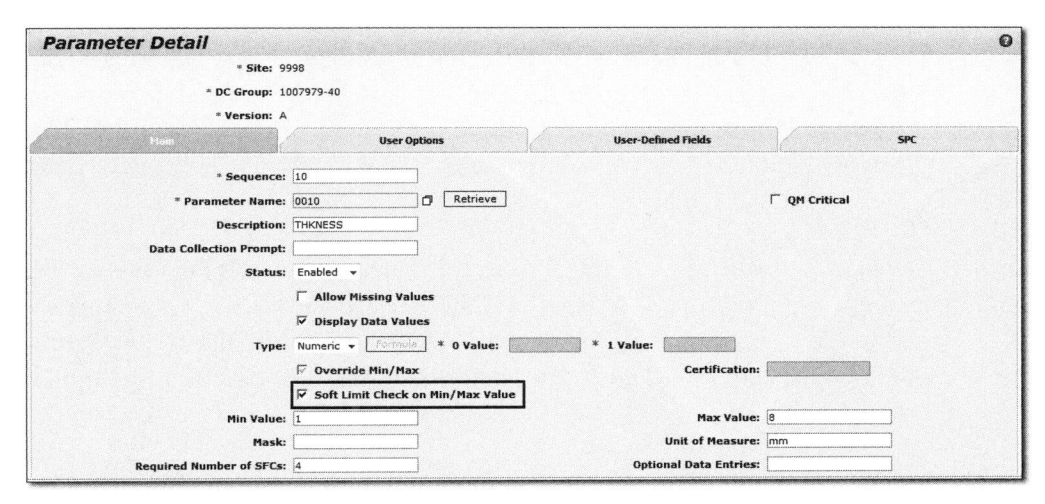

Figure 7.5 Soft Limit Check on Min/Max Value in SAP ME for SAP ERP Quality Inspection Characteristics Parameter

217

- **Min Value**

  In the Min Value field, specify the lower limit value allowed for the parameter at data collection. This value is not mandatory for DC in SAP ME.

- **Max Value**

  In MAX Value field, specify the highest limit value allowed for the DC parameter at data collection. This value also is not mandatory for DC in SAP ME.

- **Mask**

  In the Mask field, specify the mask characters string for collecting data for a DC parameter. SAP ME performs immediate validation on the entered value for numeric, formula, and text DC parameter types. Each entered character is compared to the defined mask for that character position. If all entered characters match the defined mask, then the system accepts the entered value; otherwise, the system does not accept the entered value.

- **Unit of Measure**

  In the Unit of Measure field, specify the measuring unit e.g. the ISO standard of UoM which is defined in SAP ERP for the DC parameter.

- **Required Data Entries**

  In the Required Data Entries field, specify how many data entries are required for the DC parameter. The field label changes if the DC group is a Quality Inspection group and the label becomes Required Number of SFCs.

- **Optional Data Entries**

  In the Optional Data Entries field, specify the number of optional data entries that can be collected for the DC parameter. For a Quality Inspection group this field value is always zero (0).

User Options

If you want to define any additional data and values for the data for a specific DC parameter, go to the User Options tab. There, click on Insert New to create a new row. Next, enter the data in Option Name field and the value in the Option Value field, as shown in Figure 7.6. In the SAP ME WIP database, the option name and value are stored in table `DC_USER_OPTIONS`.

Maintaining Data Collection | 7.1

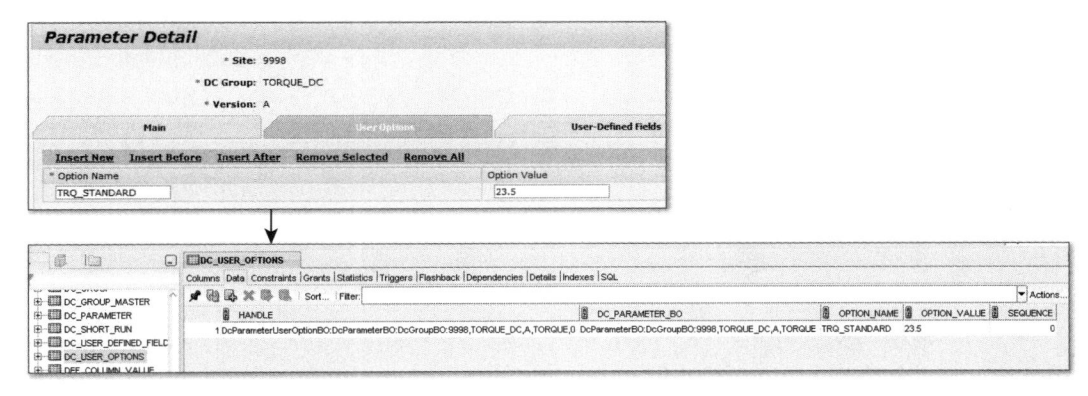

Figure 7.6 Entering User Options Record

User-Defined Fields

User-defined fields allow you to validate and provide a prompt to a shop floor operator for numeric- or text-type DC. To use user-defined fields functionality, click on INSERT NEW in the USER-DEFINED FIELDS tab to create a new row. Now, add text in the PROMPT field; this text will appear to the operator during data collection. Select the either NUMERIC or TEXT for DATA TYPE. If you select the REQUIRED checkbox, then the shop floor operator needs to enter numeric or text data for the data parameter during DC. Figure 7.7 shows the USER-DEFINED FIELDS tab in the data parameter configuration.

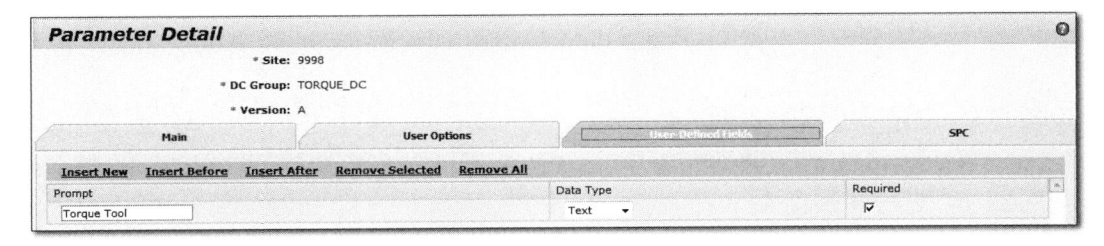

Figure 7.7 Configuring User-Defined Fields in Data Parameter

SPC

On the SPC tab, if the PERFORM SPC ANALYSIS checkbox is checked for the DC parameter, then the SAP MII SPC engine is used to generate an SPC chart. You also need to select an SPC CHART from the available list. To make the SPC chart list available, configure the SPC chart using the SPC Chart Maintenance activity.

219

If the SHORT RUN checkbox is selected, then you need to enter the material and target value for the corresponding material for which data will be collected in the SPC chart. SAP ME provides three options for DISPLAY CHART: NEVER (SPC chart never appears at DC), ALWAYS (SPC chart always appears at DC) and ONLY ALARM (SPC chart appears only when a violation occurs). Figure 7.8 shows the SPC configuration for DC parameter.

> **Note: Short Run Analysis**
>
> In a manufacturing process, a *short run* is used to perform a single analysis on data that comes from several runs of a product. SAP ME supports short run analysis and provides different chart types for it, such as Individuals, Individuals and MR, Moving Range, and X-Bar and R. You will learn more about SPC analysis in Chapter 8.

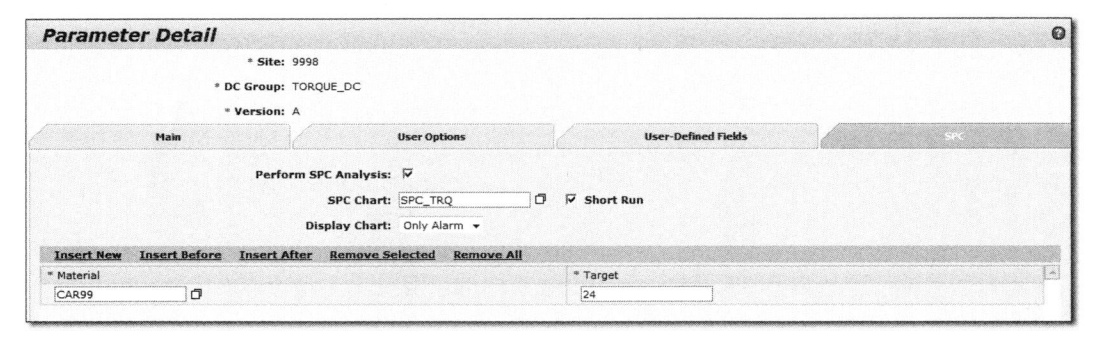

Figure 7.8 Configuring SPC for DC Parameter

7.2 Assigning Data Collection Groups to Process Objects

In the shop floor manufacturing process, you know in which operation DC will be performed by the operator. For example, in a car assembly process, say you have designed the routing in SAP ME and you have an operation called QUALITY_INSPECTION in which you want multiple points to be checked by the operator. The actual data should be collected for those points to complete the quality inspection and recorded in SAP ME.

For this process, create a DC group with DC parameters and attach the QUALITY_INSPECTION operation to it. On the Data Collection Maintenance page, go to the ATTACHED tab, where you can attach the operation by clicking on the INSERT NEW link, which will open a new page called ATTACHMENT POINT DETAILS. Here, enter the SEQUENCE for the attachment, and select the checkbox APPLY THIS ATTACHMENT TO CURRENT VERSION (#) OF THIS DC GROUP, which will apply the attachment for the current DC group version. Next, enter or select the operation in which you want to perform DC. SAP ME provides multiple attachment options: MATERIAL GROUP, MATERIAL, ROUTING, ROUTING STEP, OPERATION, WORK CENTER, RESOURCE TYPE, RESOURCE, CUSTOMER ORDER, SHOP ORDER, and SFC. You can attach multiple points for the same DC group as needed. Finally, click on the APPLY button to complete the attachment. Figure 7.9 shows the ATTACHMENT POINT DETAILS screen.

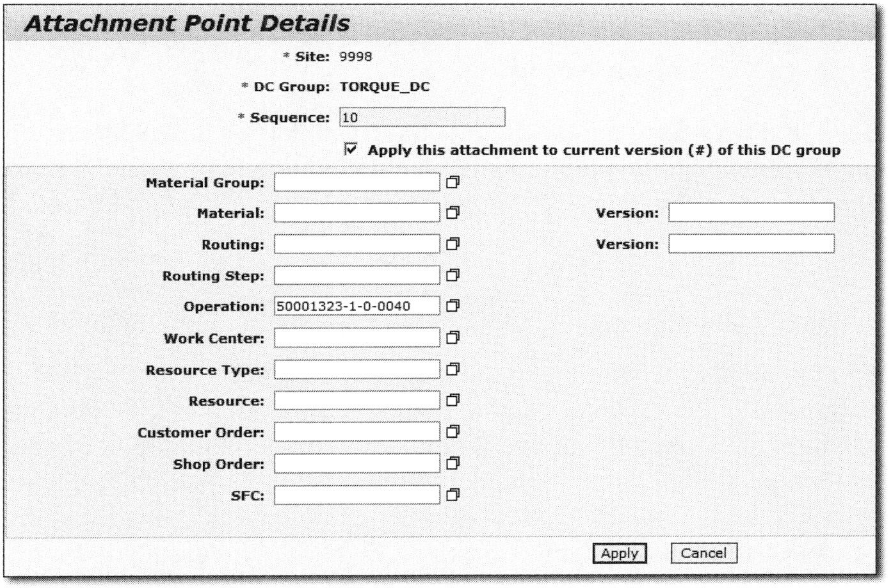

Figure 7.9 Attaching Operation to DC Group

7.2.1 Activity Hooks for Data Collection Check

As explained in Chapter 2, activity hooks are logic services which you can assign to different events e.g. PRE_COMPLETE, POST_COMPLETE, PRE_START, etc. for different process objects to do any validation or activity which is required at that point of time. You can assign the following activity hooks to operation or production routing for data collection related validations.

- **Data Collection Limits Check (DC521)**
  You can attach activity DC521 as a PRE_COMPLETE hook activity in an operation of production routing. The DC521 hook point activity will check data collection limits (the min/max limits for the data parameter) for all operations on the production routing, including the current operation.

- **Open Data Collections Check (DC520)**
  You can attach activity DC520 as a PRE_COMPLETE hook activity in an operation of production routing to make sure that the required data parameters for all associated DC groups have been collected for the current SFC number in all operations, including the current operation of production routing.

7.3 Data Collection Activities

The user needs to perform certain activities for data collection in SAP ME. In this section, we will explore the following data collection activities: Data Collection Edit, Data Collection Standalone, Data Collection Definition Report, and Data Collection Result Report.

7.3.1 Data Collection Edit

SAP ME provides the functionality to edit the previously collected data parameter values through the *Data Collection Edit* activity. You can open the Data Collection Edit activity and search by DC group. SAP ME also provides more search options, such as user, parameter, and SFC/shop order/process lot. The search results are displayed in a list, from which you can click on the DETAILS icon to open the DATA COLLECTION EDIT DETAIL page for a data parameter, as shown Figure 7.10. On this page, you can find the previously collected value for the data parameter. If you want to provide a new value for the data parameter, enter the value in NEW VALUE field and a comment in the COMMENTS field. To save the updated value, click on SAVE. After saving the record, you can find the updated value in the VALUE column of that particular data parameter. You can again click on the DETAILS icon to find the DC edit history, with the previous value, new value, date/time and user (who performed the changes) for that data parameter. SAP ME stores all record history except comments and user-defined fields values.

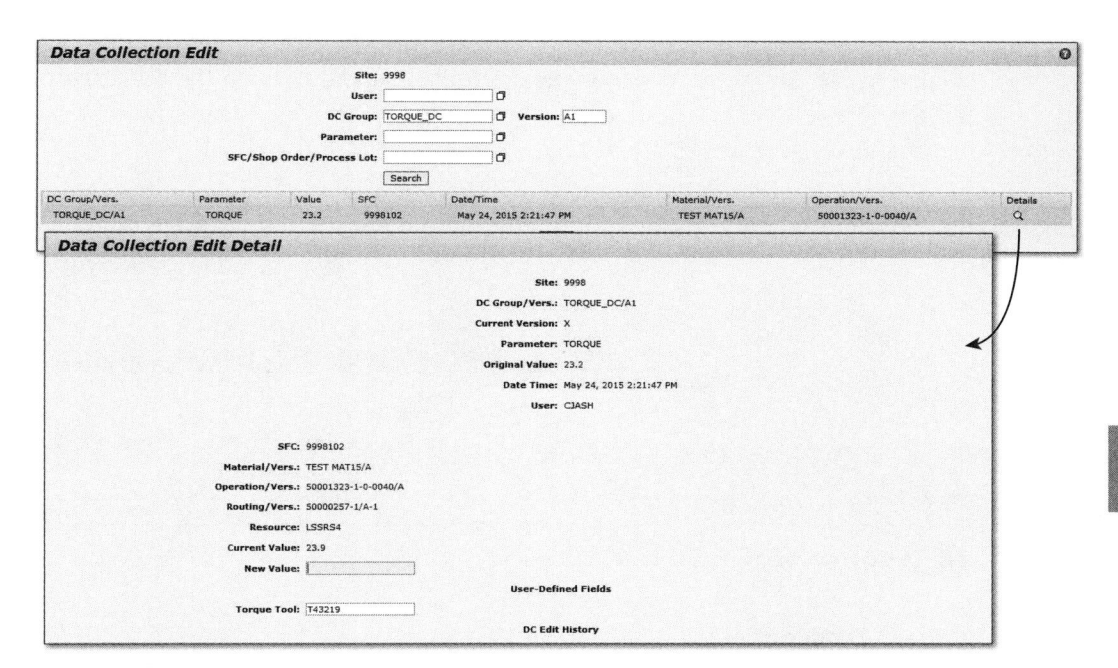

Figure 7.10 Performing Data Collection Edit Activity

7.3.2 Data Collection Standalone

You can collect the value of a data parameter for a DC group defined for a resource or work center. To do so, use the Data Collection Standalone activity in SAP ME. This standalone activity can be opened from the activity list by clicking the link, or you can use it in the Production Operator Dashboard as a plugin. Before performing standalone DC, define the DC group (using the Data Collection Maintenance activity) with a resource or work center collection type, and on the ATTACHMENT tab, attach the operation and work center, or operation, resource type, and resource for which DC will be performed.

On the Standalone Data Collection page, select the operation you attached to the DC group. Then, select RESOURCE or WORK CENTER (whichever you attached in the DC group) from the COLLECT DATA FOR dropdown. Next, enter or select the resource or work center (whichever you attached in the DC group) for which you want to collect data, and click on the RETRIEVE button. The system will display all the data parameter lists that you defined for the DC group in Data Collection Maintenance. Select a data parameter from the list, and click on the DC COLLECT button to open a DATA COLLECTION ENTRY window in which you can enter the value and save the record, as shown in Figure 7.11.

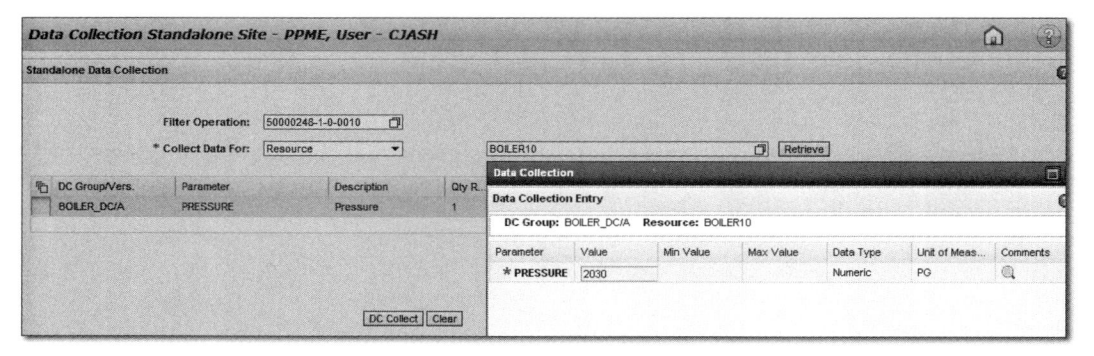

Figure 7.11 Standalone Data Collection for Resource

7.3.3 Data Collection Definition Report

In SAP ME, use the Data Collection Definition Report to view all of the information used to define the DC group and its data parameters. On the DATA COLLECTION DEFINITION REPORT page, search by DC group or by other available options. The system will display a result report from which you can click on the DETAILS icon to open the Data Collection Group Definition Detail Report. Click on the DETAILS icon for each data parameter to view the Data Collection Parameter Definition Detail Report, where you will find the detailed configuration of each data parameter you defined in Data Collection Maintenance. SAP ME provides a print option for the Data Collection Definition Report. Figure 7.12 shows the report.

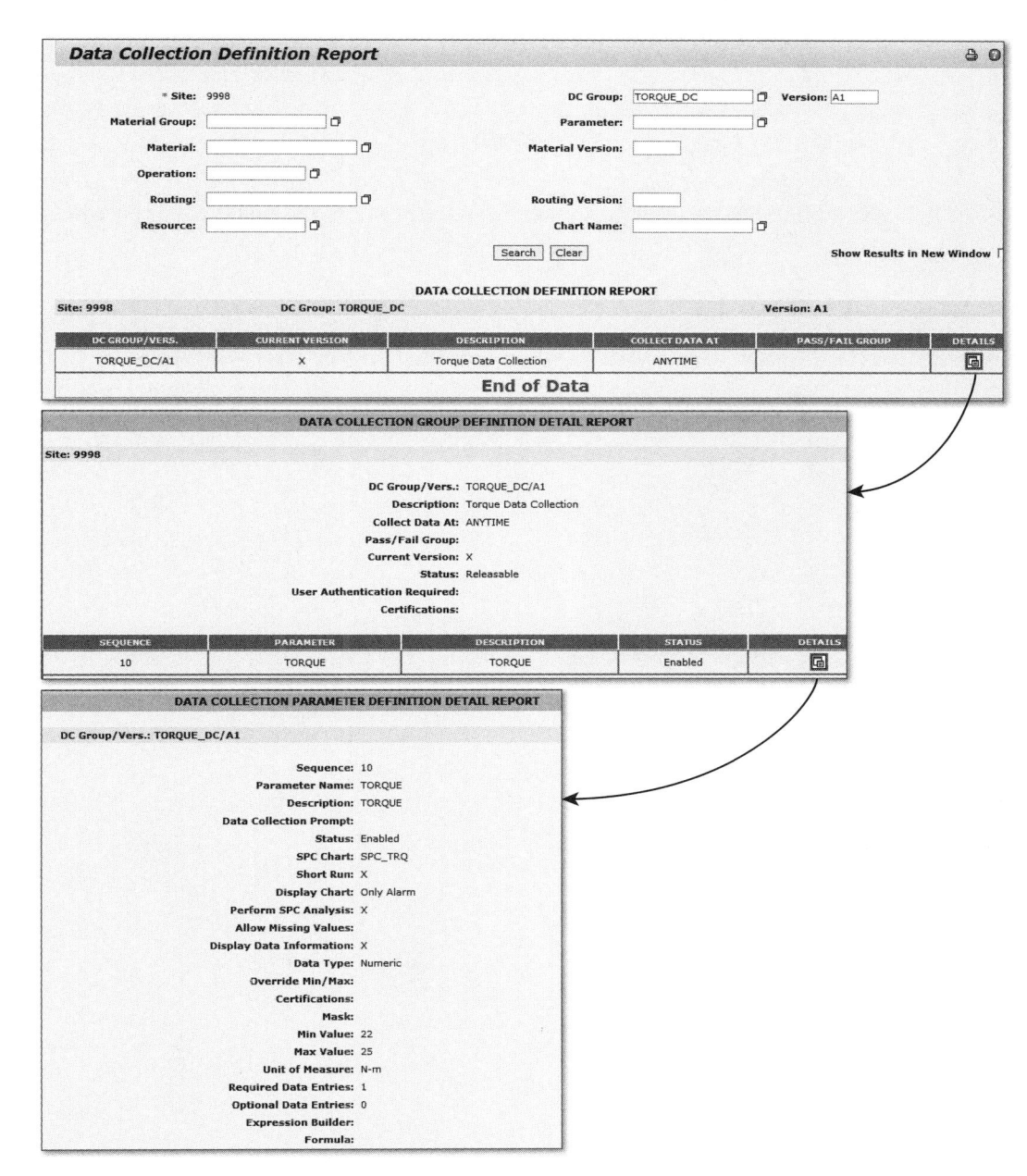

Figure 7.12 Data Collection Definition Report

7.3.4 Data Collection Results Report

You defined the DC group and data parameter for the DC group through the Data Collection Maintenance activity in SAP ME. Now, in the shop floor manufacturing process, the data are collected. You want to check the report for the collected data and print the records. To do so, use the *Data Collection Result Report* activity in SAP ME. SAP ME stores the collected records in the WIP database or ODS database based on the configurations in System Rule Maintenance.

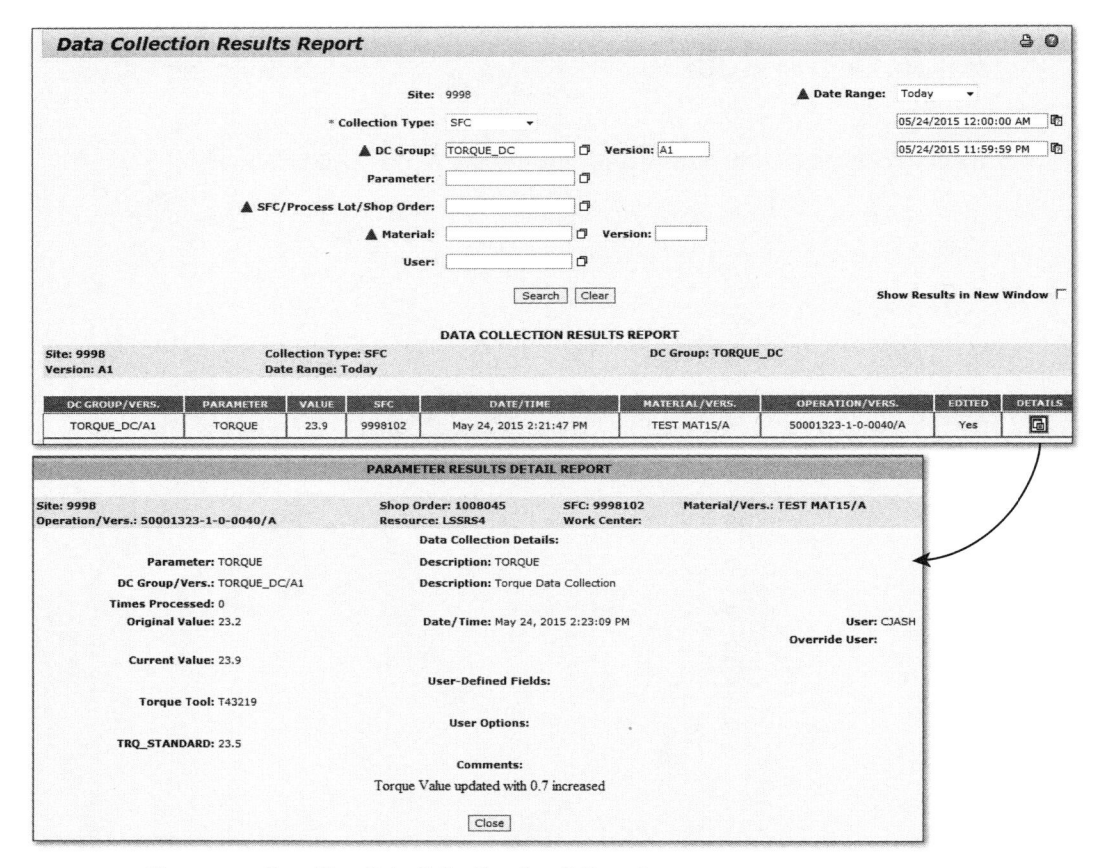

Figure 7.13 Searching Data Collection Result Report

To search the DC results, select the collection type that you want to search for. Select SFC, RESOURCE, or WORK CENTER from the dropdown list. Based on your selection, SAP ME will display other input search parameters. Next, enter or select the DC group with its version. The system also provides other input parameters, such as parameter, SFC/process lot/shop order (available only when you select SFC as the collection type), material with version, user, work center (available only when you select resource or work center for collection type), resource (available only when you select resource or work center for collection type), and date range. Based on your search requirements, you can specify the value for input search parameters. You can also select the date range for the search report in the DATE RANGE dropdown field (for custom values, specify the FROM and TO date/time range). The search results will be displayed in a tabular format; click on the DETAILS icon for each row to see the detailed report for each record, as shown in Figure 7.13.

7.4 Data Collection Scenario in Assembly Manufacturing

We have now covered the details of data collection features and available reports for data collection in SAP ME. Next, let's discuss the data collection scenario for a car assembly process. Here, we assume that in the car assembly process the quality inspection is performed in the `QLTY_INSP` operation of the designed routing and that required data are collected by the shop floor operator in the same operation. See Table 7.1 for the required DC groups and the data collection parameter list for each DC group.

DC Group	Parameter	Data Type	UOM	MIN	MAX
BREAK_SYSTEM_DC	BREAK_SYSTEM_LEAKING	Boolean			
	BRK_SYSTEM_SECURELY_MOUNTAINED	Boolean			
	BRK_PADEL_HARD_WHEN_PRES	Boolean			
	ABS_FAILURE_INDICATOR_LIGHT_ON	Boolean			
	MISSING_BROKEN_BREAK_PADEL	Boolean			
	PARKING_BRK_NOT_HOLD_ON_SLOPE	Boolean			

Table 7.1 DC Group and Parameter List for Each DC Group

DC Group	Parameter	Data Type	UOM	MIN	MAX
	DIFF_BETWEEN_FRONT_WHEEL_BREAK	Numeric	Percent	30	49
	PARKING_BREAK_CABLE_CONDITION	Text			
STEERING_AND_SUSPENSION_DC	ABSENT_OR_LOOSE_U-BOLTS	Boolean			
	INSECURELY_FIXED_STEERING_BOX	Boolean			
	WEAK_SHOCK_ABSORBER	Boolean			
	AIR_SUSPENSION_WRKING_PROPERLY	Boolean			
WHEEL_CHECK_DC	FRONT_LEFT_WHEEL_CONDITION	Text			
	FRONT_RIGHT_WHEEL_CONDITION	Text			
	REAR_LEFT_WHEEL_CONDITION	Text			
	REAR_RIGHT_WHEEL_CONDITION	Text			
	TYRE_TREAD_DEPTH	Number			

Table 7.1 DC Group and Parameter List for Each DC Group (Cont.)

Create the DC groups per Table 7.1 and insert the parameter list for each DC group through the Data Collection Maintenance activity in SAP ME. To begin:

1. On the Data Collection Maintenance page, enter BREAK_SYSTEM_DC as the DC group name in the DC GROUP field, and specify "A" as the version of the DC group in the VERSION field.
2. On the MAIN tab, enter the of DC group description.
3. Specify STATUS as RELEASABLE, COLLECTION TYPE as SFC, COLLECT DATA AT as ANYTIME, and COLLECTION METHOD as MANUAL-SINGLE.
4. Click on the INSERT NEW link to open the PARAMETER DETAIL page.

7.4 Data Collection Scenario in Assembly Manufacturing

5. On the PARAMETER DETAIL page, enter BREAK_SYSTEM_LEAKING as the parameter name in the PARAMETER NAME field, and enter the same value in the DESCRIPTION field.
6. Select BOOLEAN as the type of parameter in the TYPE field.
7. In the 0 VALUE field, enter NO, and in the 1 VALUE field, enter YES.
8. Leave the other fields as is and click on the APPLY button to add the BREAK_SYSTEM_LEAKING in BREAK_SYSTEM_DC group, as shown in Figure 7.14.

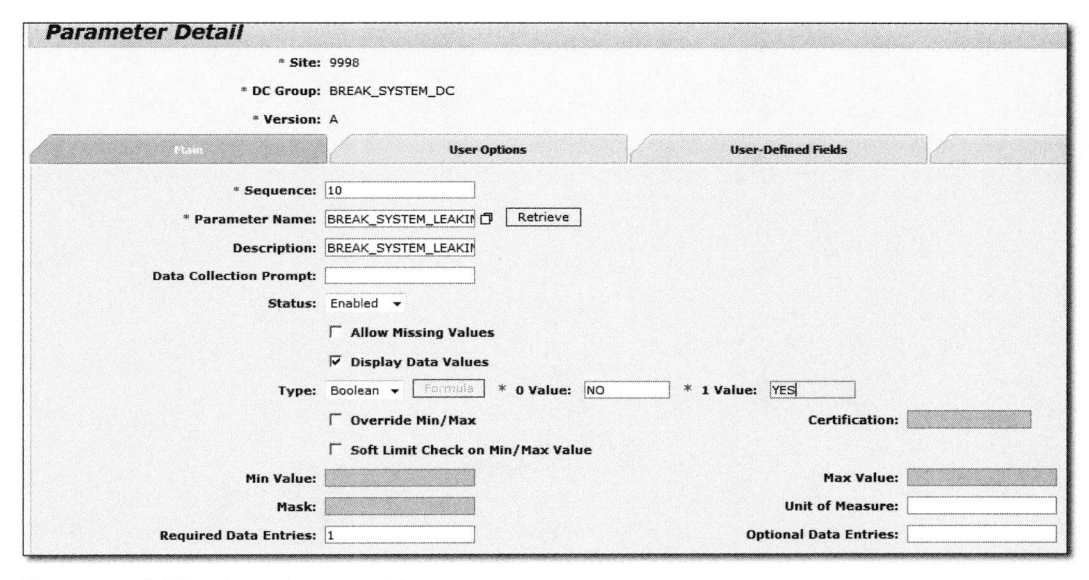

Figure 7.14 Adding Parameters to DC Group

9. In the same way, you can add other Boolean-type parameters in BREAK_SYSTEM_DC per Table 7.1, such as the following:
   - BRK_SYSTEM_SECURELY_MOUNTAINED
   - BRK_PADEL_HARD_WHEN_PRES
   - ABS_FAILURE_INDICATOR_LIGHT_ON
   - MISSING_BROKEN_BREAK_PADEL
   - PARKING_BRK_NOT_HOLD_ON_SLOPE

10. Add the numeric-type parameter DIFF_BETWEEN_FRONT_WHEEL_BREAK in the same DC group.
11. Click on the INSERT NEW link and enter DIFF_BETWEEN_FRONT_WHEEL_BREAK in PARAMETER field and in the DESCRIPTION field.
12. Select NUMERIC for the TYPE field value, and enter "Percent" in the UNIT OF MEASURE field.
13. Specify "30" for MIN VALUE and "49" for MAX VALUE, as shown in Figure 7.15.
14. Click on APPLY to add the parameter in the DC group.

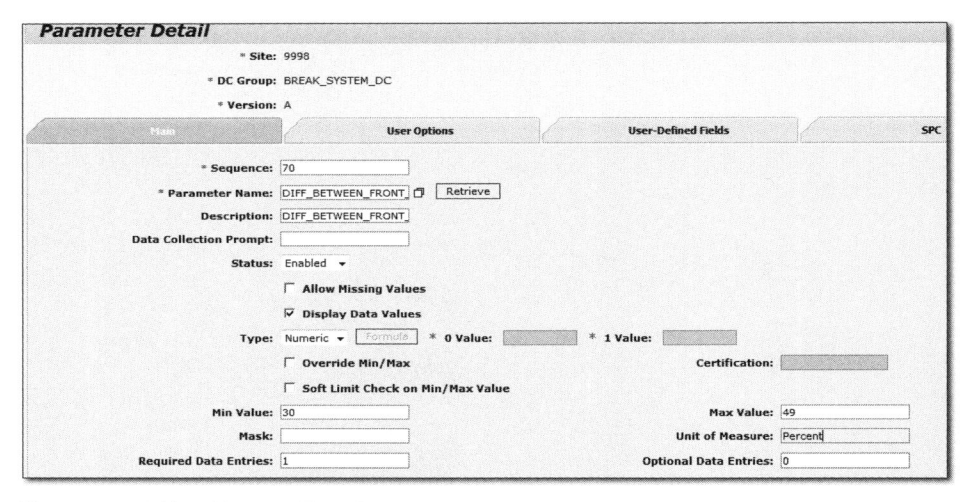

Figure 7.15 Adding Numeric-Type Parameters

15. To add the text-type parameter PARKING_BREAK_CABLE_CONDITION, specify PARKING_BREAK_CABLE_CONDITION in the PARAMETER NAME field and in the DESCRIPTION field.
16. Select TEXT in the TYPE field for PARKING_BREAK_CABLE_CONDITION and click on APPLY to add the parameter in the DC group.
17. Finally, the parameter list will appear in the DC group BREAK_SYSTEM_DC, as shown in Figure 7.16.
18. Now, switch to the ATTACHED tab of DC group BREAK_SYSTEM_DC and attach the QLTY_INSP operation (already created in SAP ME), as shown in Figure 7.17.
19. Next, save the DC group by clicking on SAVE.

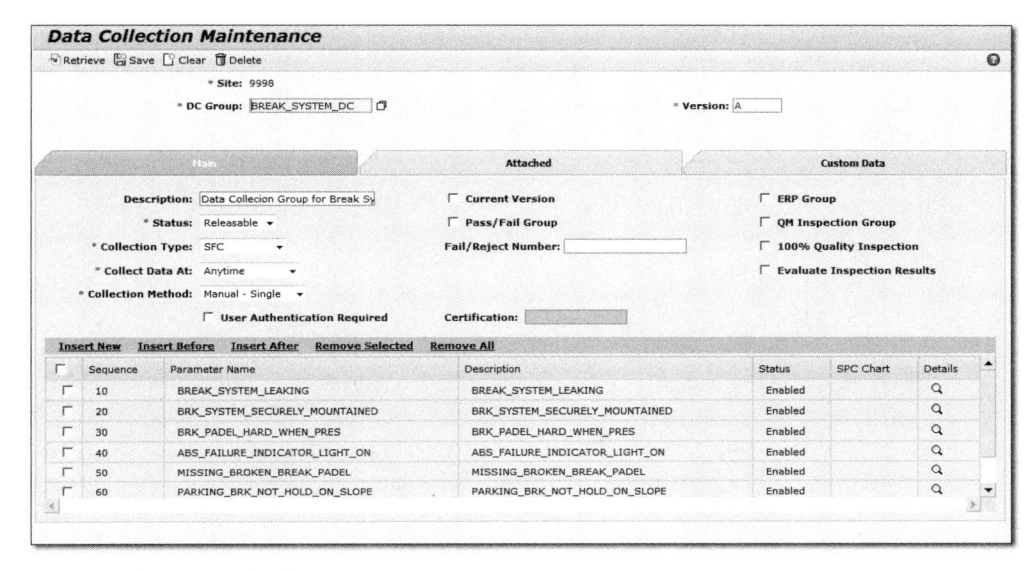

7.4 Data Collection Scenario in Assembly Manufacturing

Figure 7.16 Parameter List in DC Group

Figure 7.17 Attaching an Operation to DC Group

As you did for the BREAK_SYSTEM_DC DC group, create the remaining two DC groups with parameter lists per the details available in Table 7.1, and attach the QULTY_INSP operation to them. The shop floor operator can collect the data for those DC groups and for data parameters when the QULTY_INSP operation will be executed on the shop floor through the POD (see Chapter 10 for more information about DC through the POD).

7.5 Summary

In this chapter, you learned about DC features and how to create and configure DC groups and data parameters using multiple configurations in SAP ME. We covered the SPC configuration for the DC parameter, DC group assignment to process objects, Data Collection Edit functionality, and Data Collection Standalone for resources and work centers. This chapter also covered the available standard reports in SAP ME for DC.

We concluded with a discussion of the DC scenario for discrete manufacturing in a car assembly process.

The next chapter covers nonconformance and quality control in SAP ME.

This chapter explains the quality control process in SAP ME and how the quality inspection data from SAP ERP integrates with SAP ME. This chapter also covers nonconformance-related activities such as NC Client Maintenance, NC Code Maintenance, NC Group Maintenance, Sample Plan Maintenance, quality reports, and SPC analysis.

8 Nonconformance and Quality Control

In any manufacturing process, checking and ensuring the quality of the products being manufactured is an important activity. Because quality issues in products cause rework and profit losses and affect brand value, any manufacturer tries to minimize quality-related defects as much as possible. However, some quality defects may occur during the manufacturing process due to machine, material, or human errors, which need to be identified as soon as possible and eliminated, either through scrapping or rework. As you learned in Chapters 6 and 7, in SFC management and data collection processes some of the production parameter data collected during the execution process provides important information about product quality, which can be checked with the given specification range to determine the quality issue.

To manage defects during the manufacturing and assembly process, SAP ME provides nonconformance (NC) management features that you can use to record defects for specific product instances and to take corrective actions by reworking or scrapping a product, ensuring that the defect does not appear in the finished product shipped to customers. You can also send the nonconformances logged in SAP ME to SAP ERP as quality notifications via SAPMEINT. Finally, you can view the NC reports and perform *statistical process control* (SPC) analysis to make usage decisions and determine process maturity. In this chapter you will learn about NC code and NC group maintenance along with Disposition Groups, NC client and sample plan maintenance in SAP ME. You will also understand about the quality data integration with SAP ERP and the various quality management related reports available in SAP ME.

8.1 Maintaining NC Codes

Quality inspections are usually performed while assembling a product to identify defects and to ensure the product is conforming to specifications. The inspection requirements are planned in routing steps and are available in the shop order as the inspection lot information. Inspections are performed during specific operations as specified by the inspection lot and routing steps. When a defect is encountered during the inspection operation or anywhere during the manufacturing process, an operator needs to log the defect as a nonconformance. Based on the nonconformance code logged, the next step is to decide dynamically, based on the disposition group, which of the following takes place:

- The SFC moves automatically to a new routing for rework, called disposition routing.
- The SFC remains at the current operation.
- The operator chooses to select the next step.

The next step can be another routing or operation, or scrapping the product because it does not meet the product standards. The NC process in SAP ME is illustrated in Figure 8.1.

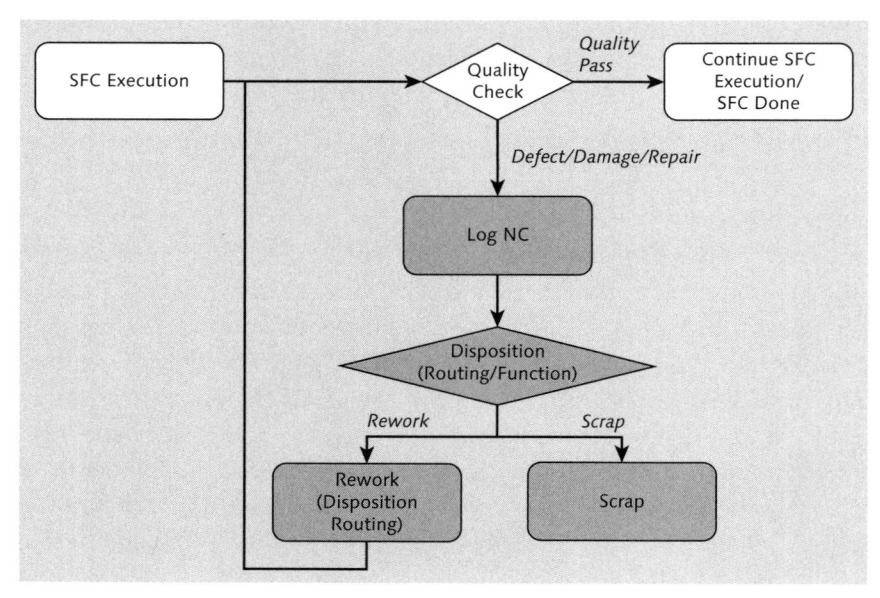

Figure 8.1 NC Logging in SAP ME

As explained in Chapter 4, quality inspection operations are defined in a routing; the operator checks the product based on certain criteria (inspection characteristics), and if he or she finds a defect, he or she logs an NC, based on which the process moves to a different operation defined for nonconformance handling, such as repair or quarantine.

In SAP ME, use the NC Code Maintenance activity to configure codes that you can use for NC logging while processing an SFC, as shown in Figure 8.2. You need to specify a NC code, which will be visible to the user. You can set the status to ENABLED or DISABLED to control whether a user can use the NC code for NC logging. Specify ASSIGN NC TO COMPONENT as STAY to log the NC for the specific SFC for which it is used or as COPY, which is raised against the component of the SFC. If you select MOVE, then the nonconformance information is added to an SFC of the components of the parent SFC. Set NC CATEGORY as FAILURE when the NC code is used to record a nonconformance that does not comply with a standard or requirement, DEFECT when the product is having a defect, and REPAIR for a nonconformance which requires repair work.

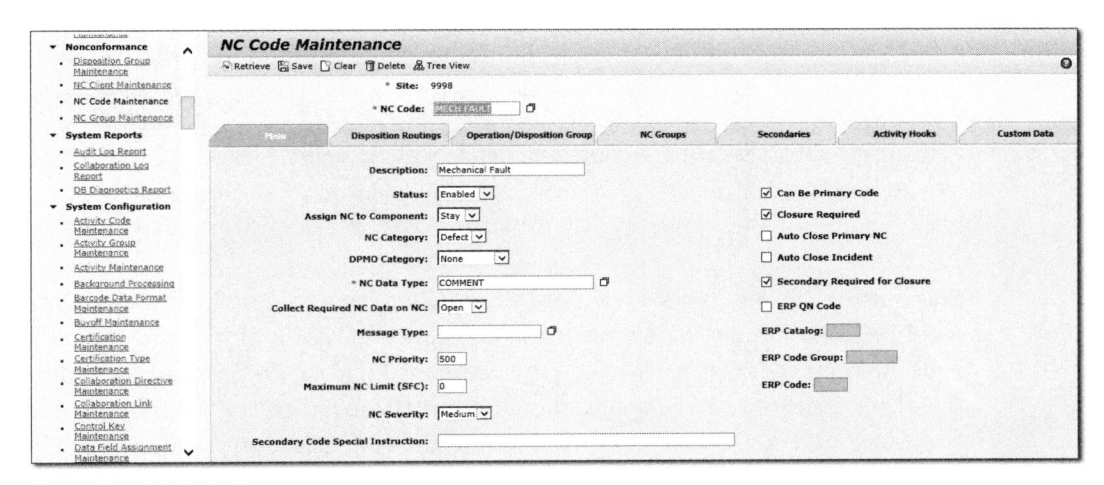

Figure 8.2 NC Code Maintenance

"DPMO" in DPMO CATEGORY stands for "defects per million opportunities," which is a quality measurement system to quantify defect levels that helps reduce the defects. DPMO is based on the IPC-9261 standard and is used mainly for defect management in electronic assembly manufacturing.

> **Note**
> Select Yes on the Application Server NC codes for DPMO screen while installing SAP ME to install the DPMO codes and categories.

The different DPMO categories are as follows:

- Assembly (number of assembly defects/number of assembly opportunities) × 1000000
- Component (number of component defects/number of component opportunities) × 1000000
- Placement (number of placement defects/number of placement opportunities) × 1000000
- Termination (number of termination defects/number of termination opportunities) × 1000000

You should choose the DPMO type based on the type of defects you want to log using the NC code. The DPMO category assigned to the NC code determines how the system calculates DPMO for the nonconformance logged.

> **Note: DPMO Configuration**
> The DPMO category can be only used for defect-type NC codes.
> To use DPMO calculation for a material while logging the defect, you also need to configure DPMO for the material in Material Maintenance, as explained in Chapter 3.

You can use the NC Data Type field to specify a data field defined in the Data Field Definition Maintenance activity and assigned to NC Category using the Data Field Assignment Maintenance activity (explained in Chapter 3) to capture additional information while logging the NC. You also need to specify the Collect Required NC Data on NC value as Open, if the data collection is required while logging the NC, Closed if the data collection is required to edit or close the NC, or Both if the data collection is required both for logging and closing the NC.

> **Note**
> To use DPMO for nonconformance management, create an NC data type in Data Field Assignment Maintenance (see Chapter 3) named Root-Cause Operation. It can be either optional or required. Specify the same in the NC Data Type field as explained previously.

> The operator should specify the root cause operation in that field while logging the NC using a DPMO NC code to indicate the root cause of the problem.
>
> You can analyze DPMO using the DPMO Report available in SAP ME.

You can specify a MESSAGE TYPE, if a message needs to be triggered when a NC is logged using the NC code, which is displayed in the message board (see in Chapter 11 for more information).

You can specify NC PRIORITY for different NC codes; higher priority determines the disposition function precedence. That is, when multiple NCs are logged for an SFC, the NC with a higher priority determines the disposition action. If multiple NCs are logged with same priority, then you can select the disposition function from the NCs with highest priority.

Set MAXIMUM NC LIMIT (SFC) to determine the maximum number of times the same NC code can be used to log a nonconformance for an SFC. You can override the maximum count of the NC code usage for a specific SFC by the *NC Limit Override* activity.

Set SEVERITY to LOW, MEDIUM, HIGH, or NONE; this setting affects the sampling plan result and determines the SFC accept or reject decision when assigned with the NC code. NONE corresponds to 0, and the NC code is not considered when determining sampling result. LOW indicates minor defects, and corresponds to 2 in the total NC severity calculation for sample SFC; MEDIUM corresponds to 3 (medium defect); and HIGH corresponds to 5 and indicates a severe defect. You will learn more about Sample Plan Maintenance in Section 8.5.

An NC code can be a primary or a secondary NC code. A secondary NC code is optional, and you can use it if you want to log additional reasons for a quality issue. Select CAN BE PRIMARY CODE to specify that the code can be used as both a primary and a secondary code. Otherwise, the NC code can be used only as secondary code. You can specify optional text in SECONDARY CODE SPECIAL INSTRUCTION, which is displayed when the operator logs the NC code as a secondary NC. Select AUTO CLOSE PRIMARY NC if the NC code is used as a secondary NC code and you want to close the primary NC logged for an SFC automatically when closing the secondary NC. If you select SECONDARY REQUIRED FOR CLOSURE, then the operator has to assign a secondary NC code (if the current NC code is used as a primary code) before closing the primary NC.

If you select AUTO CLOSE INCIDENT, then the NC is closed automatically when the operator logs the NC data for the SFC. Select CLOSURE REQUIRED to specify that the operator has to manually close the NC; otherwise, the operator can keep it open.

If you select ERP QN CODE, then the system automatically triggers a quality notification in SAP ERP when an NC is logged in SAP ME. You must specify ERP CATALOG, ERP CODE GROUP, and ERP CODE if you want to trigger SAP ERP quality notifications, which are explained in detail in Section 8.6.

When an NC is logged for an SFC, you can specify how to handle the disposition for the SFC for repair or quarantine tasks to rectify the defect or scrap the SFC. Specify disposition by a routing—that is, specifying a process step to rectify the defect—or specify a disposition group to provide a list of choices for the operator for the SFC disposition. Set disposition routing for the NC code in the DISPOSITION ROUTINGS configuration tab to specify a special or NC routing (explained in Chapter 4) that is invoked when the NC code is used to log a nonconformance. All the special and NC routings defined in the system are displayed in the column on the left (AVAILABLE ROUTINGS), from which you can select one or more disposition routings to add to the VALID ROUTINGS list, as shown in Figure 8.3.

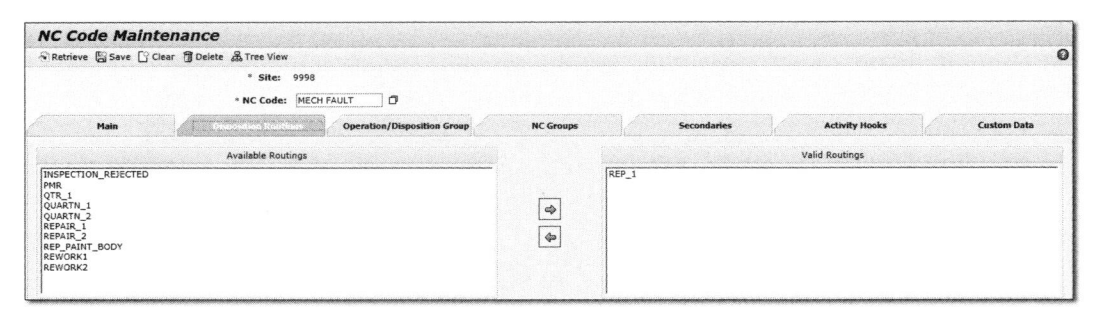

Figure 8.3 Disposition Routing Configuration for NC Code

You can also set one or more disposition groups for a specific operation or any general operation in the OPERATION/DISPOSITION GROUP configuration tab, as shown in Figure 8.4. If you want to assign the disposition group to be used for NC logged in any operation, select *, or specify an operation, select a disposition group, and mark it as ENABLED. You can create the disposition group in the Disposition Group Maintenance activity, which is explained in Section 8.3.

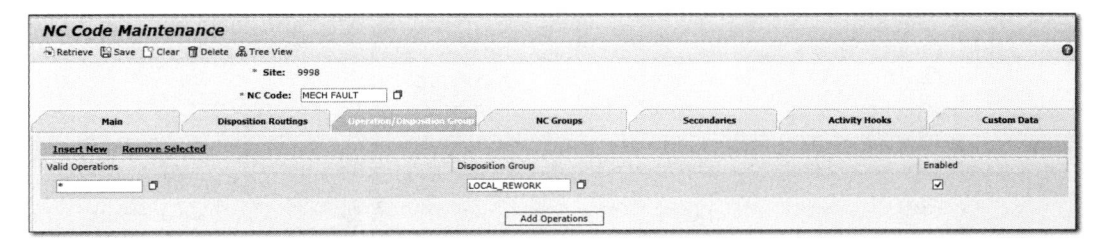

Figure 8.4 Disposition Group Configuration for NC Code

Assign the NC code to one or more NC groups, as shown in Figure 8.5. NC group configuration is explained in Section 8.2.

Figure 8.5 Assigning NC Group to NC Code

In the SECONDARIES configuration tab, you can assign secondary NC Codes for the NC code if it is configured as primary on the MAIN tab, as shown in Figure 8.6. The operator will see the NC codes specified here as secondary NC codes only when logging an NC with a parent NC code selection.

Figure 8.6 Secondary NC Code Assignment to Primary NC Code

8 | Nonconformance and Quality Control

> **Note**
>
> You can create a hierarchy of NC codes by defining a primary NC code of type FAILURE and then secondary NC codes of type DEFECT or REPAIR under it. For example, the primary NC code might be ENGINEFAILURE, under which there can be secondary NC codes defined as PISTONDEFECT.
>
> The operator can view the hierarchy of NC codes from the Visual Test & Repair (VTR) POD using the NC Tree POD Plugin or an NC client. The operator can select the primary NC code to log the nonconformance and then use a secondary code for additional reasons. You can also view the hierarchy of NC codes from the TREE VIEW link on the NC Code Maintenance activity toolbar.

You can specify an activity hook for the NC code for a standard or custom activity in SAP ME, which will be invoked when the NC is dispositioned. You can specify multiple activity hooks (e.g., for document print, SFC split for partial quantity of the SFC as defective, etc.) per your business requirements by entering a number in the SEQUENCE field to indicate the execution sequence. There are only two hook points (see Chapter 2 for more information on hook points) available for NC codes: PRE_DISP and POST_DISP, which specify whether the activity is invoked before the disposition execution or after it, respectively.

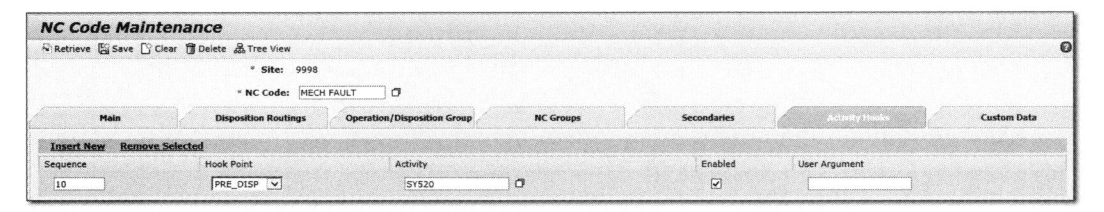

Figure 8.7 Activity Hook Configuration for NC Code

On the CUSTOM DATA configuration tab, you can view any custom data configured for the NC code in Custom Data Maintenance (explained in Chapter 3).

8.2 Maintaining NC Groups

You can define NC groups to group different NC codes, define operations for which the NC groups are available, and override the system rules at the NC group level. You can configure the NC groups using the NC Group Maintenance activity, as shown in Figure 8.8. The NC Groups are displayed to the operator in POD in the NC Selection POD Plugin. The following DPMO-specific NC groups are created along with the corresponding NC codes automatically during installation of SAP ME if DPMO is activated:

- Assembly
- Component
- Placement
- Termination

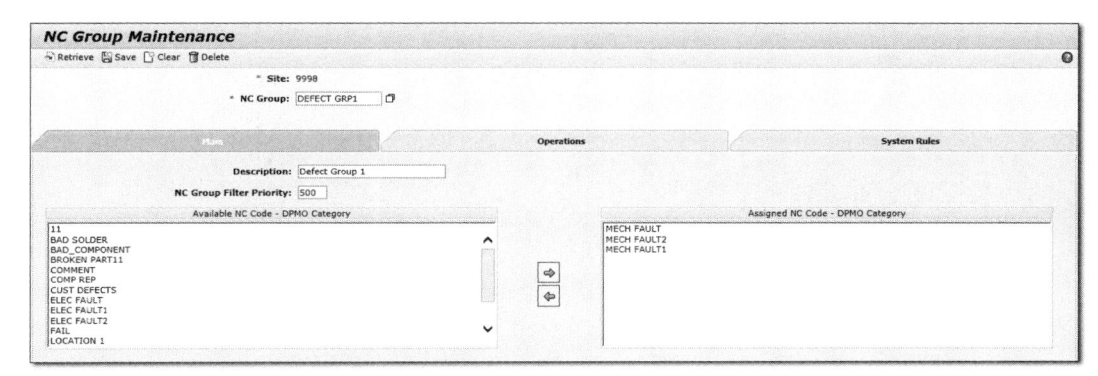

Figure 8.8 NC Group Maintenance

Specify a priority value in NC GROUP FILTER PRIORITY; this value is checked by the activity hook *Check SFCs for Open NCs* for nonconformed SFCs and compared with the `NC_PRIORITY_FILTER` value set for the hook activity. This priority is used to determine if an NC is severe enough to stop processing on the SFC. If any of the NCs logged for the SFC belong to an NC group for which the filter priority is higher than or equal to `NC_PRIORITY_FILTER`, then the SFC cannot be processed until the NC is closed.

Move available NC codes from the left list, AVAILABLE NC CODE—DPMO CATEGORY, to the right list, ASSIGNED NC CODE—DPMO CATEGORY, to assign them to the NC group.

Configure the operations for which the NC group is available in the OPERATIONS tab of NC Group Maintenance, as shown in Figure 8.9. Select VALID FOR ALL OPERATIONS to enable the NC group for all operations, or select specific operations for which the NC group should be available from the AVAILABLE OPERATIONS list and assign them to the ASSIGNED OPERATIONS list.

8 Nonconformance and Quality Control

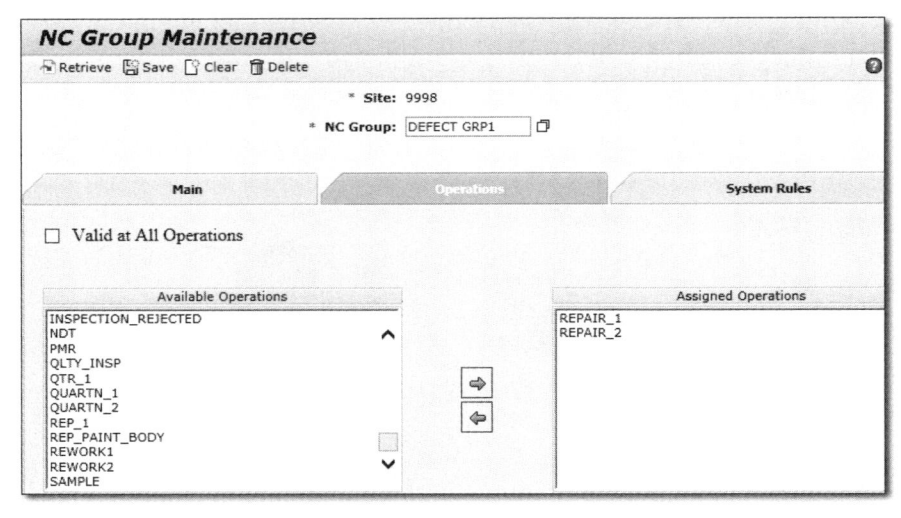

Figure 8.9 Operations Assignment for NC Group

Specify the NC ALLOWS NON-BOM COMPONENT AND REF DES system rule for the NC group to override at the site level, in the SYSTEM RULES tab of NC Group Maintenance, as shown in Figure 8.10. Setting the value for this rule to TRUE lets you log NCs for components and reference designators of SFCs that are not present in the SFC BOM.

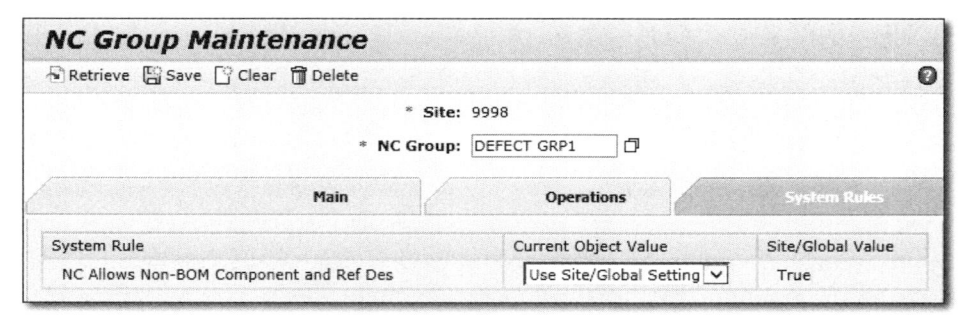

Figure 8.10 System Rules Configuration for NC Group

You can also configure the following system rules for NCs in the System Rule Maintenance activity:

- BYPASS PREVIOUS NC ROUTINGS ON RETURN
  If set to TRUE, the nonconformance disposition with a return step returns the

SFC for which the NC is logged to the last production routing step originally used for the SFC.

- **GENERATE AND LOOKUP VERTICAL REF NUMBERS**
  Automatically generates a vertical reference number when an NC is logged if set to TRUE.
- **GENERATE HORIZONTAL REF NUMBERS**
  Automatically generates a horizontal reference number when an NC is logged if set to TRUE.
- **MAXIMUM LOOP COUNT**
  Maximum number of times an SFC can be processed through an operation after logging an NC.
- **NC ALLOWS UNDEFINED COMPONENT**
  If set to TRUE, then it allows an operator to log an NC against components not defined as materials in SAP ME.
- **NC CLOSURE REQUIRED DEFAULT**
  If set to TRUE, then the NCs logged must be closed by the operator manually if not closed by the system automatically. Setting this option to FALSE allows an operator to keep the NCs open.
- **NC UNASSEMBLED BOM COMPONENTS**
  If set to TRUE, then it allows operators to log NCs against unassembled components.
- **USE NC GROUPS FOR PRODUCTION CLIENTS**
  If set to TRUE, then the NC group is used in NC clients.

8.3 Maintaining Disposition Groups

When an NC is logged for an SFC, you can specify a *disposition function* or a *disposition routing* to control the flow of the SFC for holding, repairing, scraping, and so on. You can define a disposition group to include multiple disposition functions and disposition routings, which you can assign to the NC code as explained in Section 8.1. You can maintain the disposition group via the Disposition Group Maintenance activity, as shown in Figure 8.11. Specify a sequence number in the SEQUENCE field, and select a DISPOSITION FUNCTION and the corresponding ACTIVITY CODE. There are lists of standard disposition functions available in SAP ME, which you can select from the DISPOSITION FUNCTION lookup. If a single disposition function is specified, then options are not shown to an operator; the SFC automatically moves to the disposition function. If multiple disposition functions are specified, then the operator can select a disposition function from the list provided in order to transfer the SFC when an NC is logged. The DISPOSITION ROUTING field is needed only when SPECIAL_OPERATION or STANDARD_NC_ROUTER is selected for DISPOSITION FUNCTION. Select an NC routing configured in the system, or leave the field blank to enable the operator choose any special operation or NC routing available in the system after logging the NC.

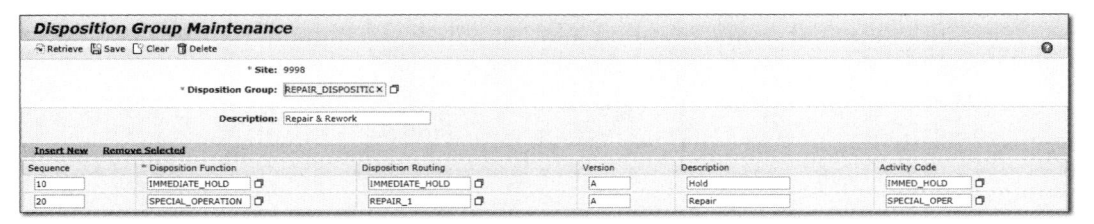

Figure 8.11 Disposition Group Maintenance

8.4 Maintaining NC Clients

You can create an NC client to configure the NC logging options in the POD, through which the operator manages NCs for an SFC while working on the assembly process—that is, SFC execution. Some NC clients are available by default in SAP ME, and you can configure them or can create new clients if required from the NC Client Maintenance activity, as shown in Figure 8.12. See Chapter 10 for more information about using an NC client in the POD.

You have to specify an identifier and a description of the NC client, and can select NONE, MANUAL, or AUTOMATIC in the INCIDENT NUMBER field, which is used to specify how the incident number for the NC logging activity for the particular SFC for which it is logged, will be generated. If you select NONE, then the INCIDENT NUMBER field is disabled in the POD. MANUAL allows the operator to manually specify an incident number. For AUTOMATIC, the system generates an incident number automatically based on the Next Number pattern, which the operator can change if required.

You can set PRELOAD NC FIELDS to NONE, BOTH, REF DES, or FAILURE ID to signify the fields to be preloaded from the primary NC while logging a secondary NC. In the COMPONENT DISPOSITION ROUTING field, specify the routing to which the removed component will be sent. You can only specify the routing of an NC type or a special type.

In the VTR MODEL LOCATION field, you can specify the location of a 3-D model (a Visual Enterprise RH file), which will be displayed while using the NC client.

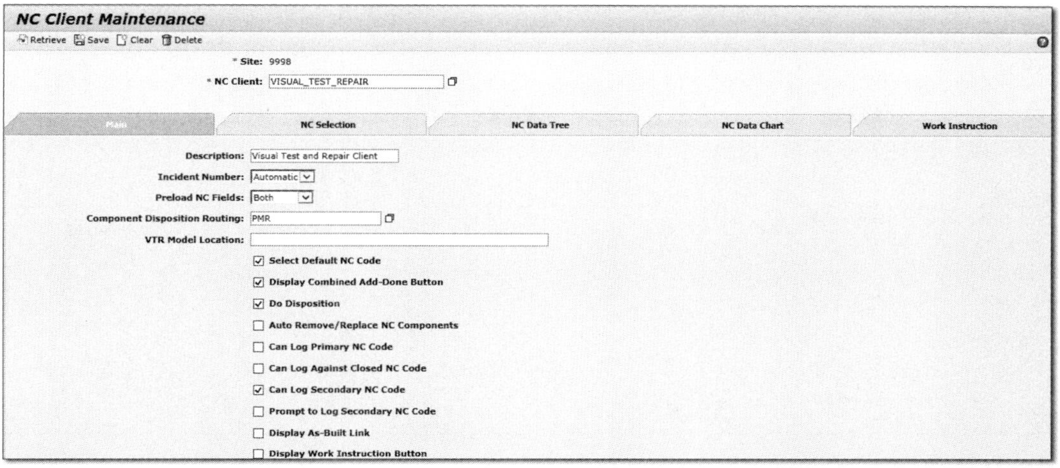

Figure 8.12 NC Client Maintenance

Select the SELECT DEFAULT NC CODE checkbox to have the default NC code selected automatically from the AVAILABLE NC CODES list while using the NC client. If the DISPLAY COMBINED ADD-DONE BUTTON checkbox is selected, the POD will show a single button for NC add and SFC complete, the ADD-DONE button. If the DO DISPOSITION checkbox is selected, the system automatically dispositions the nonconformed SFC based on the NC code configuration. To log a primary NC code, select the CAN LOG PRIMARY NC CODE checkbox and the CAN LOG SECONDARY NC CODE checkbox to log secondary NC. If you select the PROMPT TO LOG SECONDARY NC CODE checkbox, then the user will be prompted to log a secondary NC code when the DONE button is pressed. If you want to log an additional NC against a closed NC, then select the CAN LOG AGAINST CLOSED NC CODE checkbox.

The AS-BUILT CONFIGURATION link appears in the NC DATA ENTRY section of the POD if you select the DISPLAY AS-BUILT LINK checkbox, and a WORK INSTRUCTION button appears to display the work instruction relevant for the inspection operation if you select the DISPLAY WORK INSTRUCTION BUTTON checkbox. In that case you need to specify the work instruction in the work instruction configuration tab.

On the NC SELECTION tab, specify how the list of NC codes will be displayed in the log NC client, as shown in Figure 8.13. You can choose to display the NC codes sort by NC CODE, NC code DESCRIPTION, or PRIORITY by selecting the appropriate option from the NC CODE DISPLAY CRITERIA dropdown. Select the NC CODE DESCRIPTION IN LIST checkbox to display the descriptions of the NC codes in the dropdown for available NCs. You can also specify the NC GROUP COLUMN HEADING and NC CODE COLUMN HEADING to set the column descriptions in the log NC client.

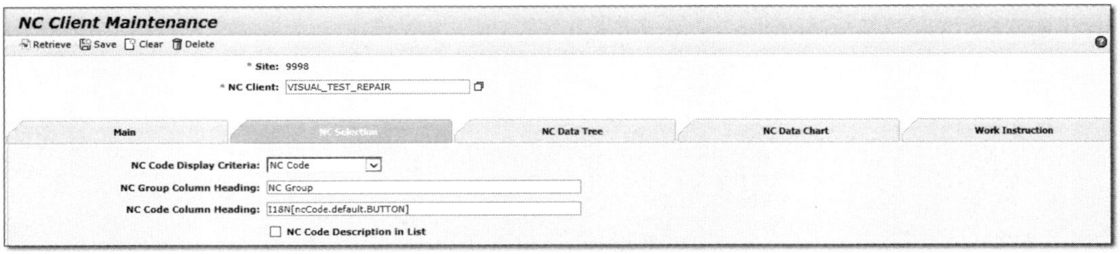

Figure 8.13 NC Client Maintenance: NC Selection

On the NC DATA TREE tab, specify the NC table columns' display order in the NC Tree plug-in in the NC client. Specify a list of the NC_TREE type, which is configured using the List Maintenance activity in the NC DATA TREE LIST selection, as shown in Figure 8.14. You can also select the EXPAND NC DATA TREE, DISPLAY CLOSE ALL OPEN NCS BUTTON, and ALLOW EDIT checkboxes per your requirements.

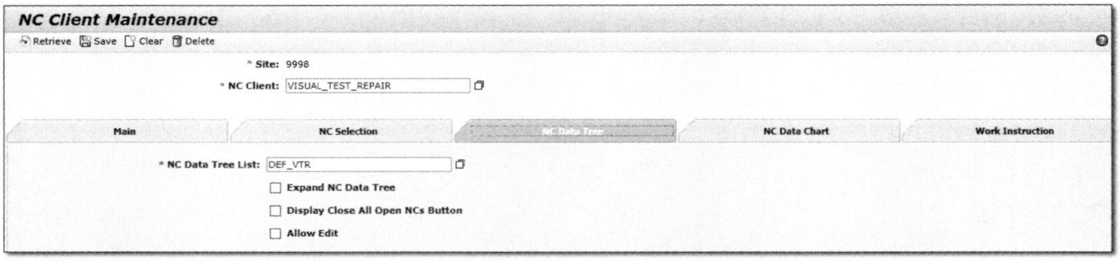

Figure 8.14 NC Client Maintenance: NC Data Tree

In the NC DATA CHART tab, use the NUMBER OF VERIFIED DEFECT BARS field (Figure 8.15) to set the number of bars for verified defects to be displayed in the NC chart, part of the Verified Defect Pareto chart in NC client in the POD.

Selecting DISPLAY COMPONENT/DESCRIPTION ON CHART displays the description of the component for which the NC is logged.

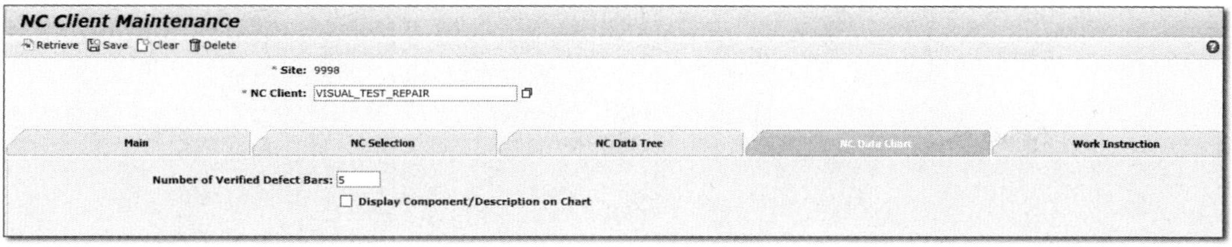

Figure 8.15 NC Client Maintenance: NC Data Chart

In the WORK INSTRUCTION tab (Figure 8.16), specify the work instructions to be displayed in the NC client, which is relevant for NC logging.

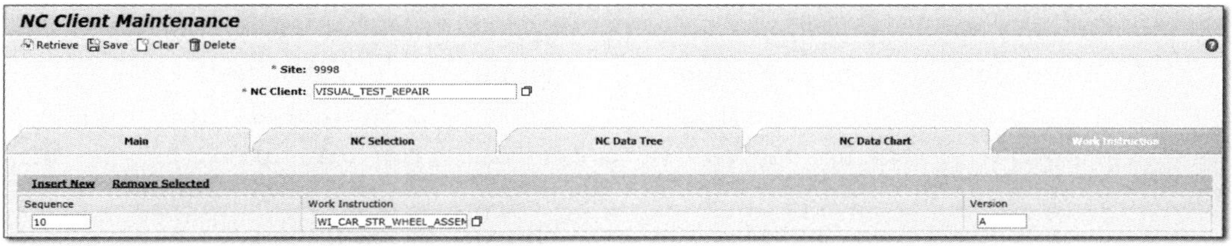

Figure 8.16 NC Client Maintenance: Work Instructions

Once the NC client is configured, you need to assign it to the POD using the POD Maintenance activity in SAP ME, or use the standalone NC client from the Standalone NC Logging activity as shown in Figure 8.17 to log an NC for an SFC.

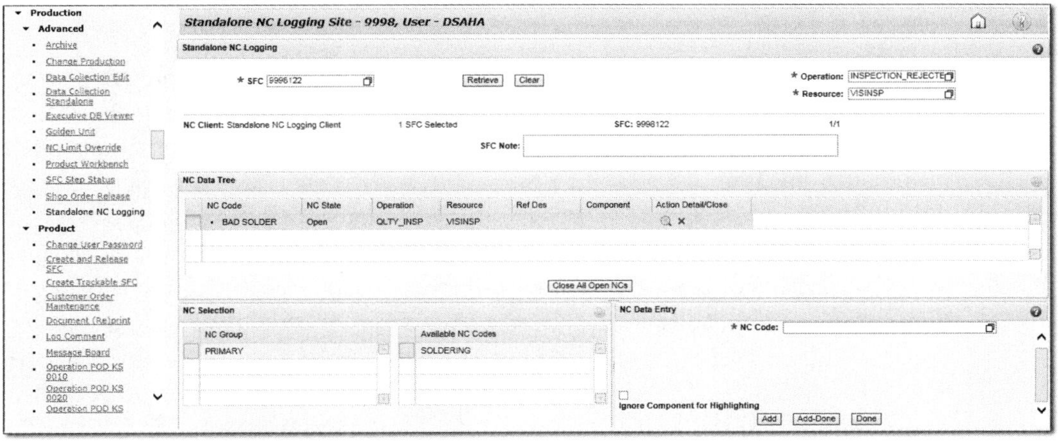

Figure 8.17 NC Logging from Standalone NC Client

> **Note**
>
> To specify the NC client for the Standalone NC Logging activity, open the Standalone NC Logging activity (activity code: NC540) in Activity Maintenance, and on the RULES tab, specify the NC client name, configured in NC Client Maintenance, for the NC_CLIENT rule.

8.5 Maintaining a Sample Plan

During the manufacturing execution process, you may need to take samples from semifinished or finished products to check for quality, based on which you can determine the overall quality of the product. This is useful when you cannot run quality checks individually on each SFC and when you use a repetitive process for manufacturing. Use the Sample Plan Maintenance activity to create a sample plan to which you can attach a material, operation (operation is mandatory), or a resource, as shown in Figure 8.18. You can take a sample for an SFC group, which is planned in its routing, material, operation, or resource. Based on the quality inspections and NCs logged, you can estimate the overall quality of the SFC or SFC group, and therefore whether to use or reject it. In Sample Plan Maintenance, specify the sampling TYPE field as ANSI or CUSTOM, where ANSI follows the standard sampling process defined by ANSI. You also need to specify the SAMPLE PLAN ID and DESCRIPTION fields, respectively. Set the STATUS of the sample plan as RELEASABLE, FROZEN, OBSOLETE, HOLD, or NEW. You can only use a Releasable sample plan to create new samples from an SFC. Select the CURRENT VERSION checkbox to specify the sampling plan version as the current one.

To perform sampling during a production process, configure a sampling-type routing and specify that routing in the SAMPLE ROUTING field in the Sample Plan Maintenance activity to execute the sampling process. You can specify the sample reject message using a message type in SAMPLE REJECT MESSAGE TYPE. The reject message is generated when the sample is rejected due to nonconformances logged. You can specify the NC SEVERITY THRESHOLD for the threshold limit of the all the NCs logged for the sample which is calculated by summing all the severities of the NCs logged for it. The threshold is used to determine whether the sample is accepted or rejected. If you select the ALLOW MIXED MATERIAL checkbox, then different materials can be added to the SFC group for which the sampling is performed. If you select the CREATE DISTINCT SFC GROUP FOR RMA SFC(S) checkbox, then the SFCs in the RMA order type are added to a distinct SFC group. Otherwise, for all other order types, the SFC numbers are added to the same SFC group for sampling. When the

ONLY SFC(S) FIRST TIME THROUGH STEP checkbox is selected, the system only includes the production SFCs that are in queue or in the operation for the first time; RMA SFCs are excluded. If unchecked, then all SFCs, irrespective of how many times they have been processed, are included in the SFC group.

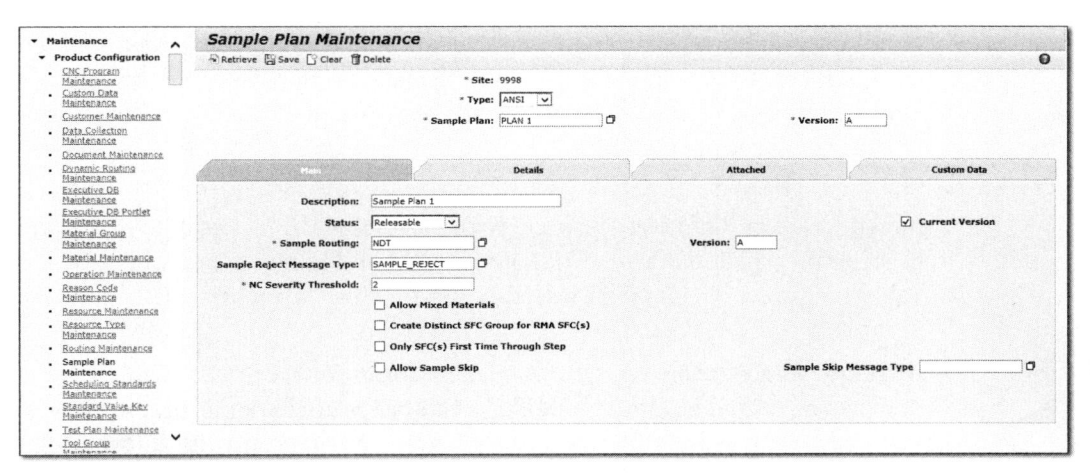

Figure 8.18 Sample Plan Maintenance

> **Note**
>
> Note that you can specify either ONLY SFC(S) FIRST TIME THROUGH STEP or CREATE DISTINCT SFC GROUP FOR RMA SFC(S), but not both.

If you select the ALLOW SAMPLE SKIP checkbox, then the user can skip the sampling process; otherwise, it will be mandatory to move to the next step, if defined in the operation. In the SAMPLE SKIP MESSAGE TYPE field, specify the message type to be generated in the message board when the sampling is skipped.

On the DETAILS configuration tab, you can specify some additional information for the sampling process, as shown in Figure 8.19. Enter a number in the SFC GROUP SIZE field to specify the total quantity of SFCs to be included in the sample group. For serialized SFCs, SFC Group Size is the same as the SFC quantity. The actual sample size will be calculated for an ANSI-type sample plan based on the SFC group size. This group size includes the sampled and non-sampled SFCs.

Some configurations are only applicable for ANSI-type sampling plans. The following fields are disabled for custom sampling plans:

- Set the INSPECTION LEVEL to specify the relationship between sample size and SFC group size. Use GENERAL with Level I, Level II, and Level III, or SPECIAL with S-1, S-2, S-3, and S-4. The inspection level is selected based on various factors, including type of product, probability of defects, previous history of defects, and so on. For general-type sampling, Level II is usually used, but Level I allows for minimal sampling and inspections, and Level III allows for a high level. Special-type sampling is used when small sample sizes are necessary and larger sampling risks can be tolerated. S-1 uses the smallest sample size, whereas S-4 uses the highest.
- The CODE LETTER is an ANSI standard characteristic that is automatically determined based on the INSPECTION LEVEL selected. The values are between A and R, as defined in Table 1 for ANSI standard sampling plans. You can refer the Table 1 from the ANSI standard sampling plan which is publicly available in the internet.
- INSPECTION PROCEDURE can be NORMAL, REDUCED, or TIGHTENED and indicates the level of stringency of the sampling and quality inspection procedures. Normal is the standard sampling procedure, whereas reduced is used for smaller sample sizes and higher acceptance criteria, typically when quality is good and fewer inspections are needed. A tightened sampling procedure is used for larger sample sizes and stringent acceptance criteria, typically when quality is bad and more inspections are needed.
- Specify the message type to be generated in the message board when the inspection procedure value is changed in the INSPECTION PROCEDURE MESSAGE TYPE field.

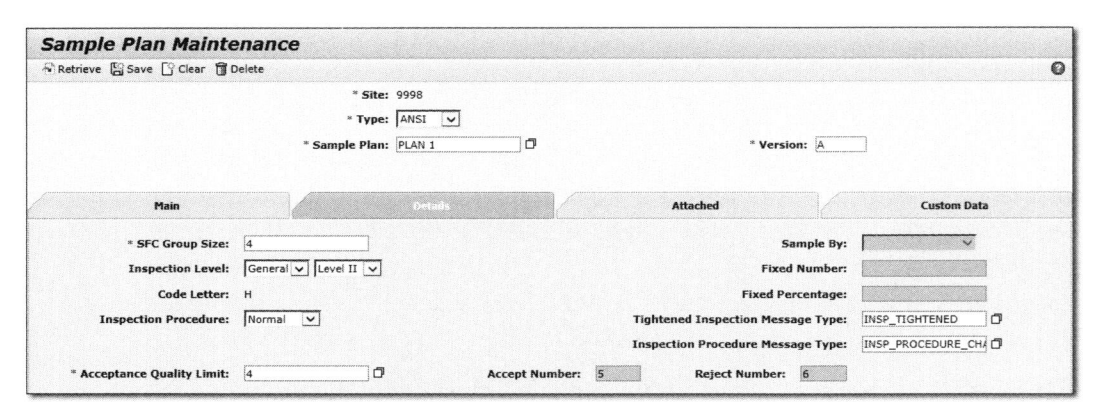

Figure 8.19 Sample Plan Maintenance: Details Configurations

- You can also specify the message type in the TIGHTENED INSPECTION MESSAGE TYPE field, which applies specifically when the inspection procedure is changed to tightened in a sample plan.
- The ACCEPTANCE QUALITY LIMIT field specifies the quality limit of satisfactory process average, which is a key indicator for the sample quality. It automatically calculates the ACCEPT NUMBER and REJECT NUMBER.

The following fields are enabled only for custom sample plans:

- Specify the ACCEPT NUMBER as the largest number of failed sample pieces permitted for the sample to be accepted and the REJECT NUMBER as the smallest number of failed sample pieces for the sample to be rejected during the inspection process.
- Set SAMPLE BY as a FIXED NUMBER or FIXED PERCENTAGE of the SFC group size to define the sample size.
- Depending on your selections, the FIXED NUMBER or FIXED PERCENTAGE fields will be enabled, and the sample size will be determined for custom sample types based on those fields.

You can specify operations and other objects to which the sample plan can be attached in the ATTACHED configuration tab, as shown in Figure 8.20. Click on the INSERT NEW link to create a new attachment, and specify a material group, material, or a resource along with the operation for which the sample plan will be used. You need to specify either MATERIAL or MATERIAL GROUP, and the operation is mandatory.

> **Note**
> You cannot attach sample plans to operations that are used in Simultaneous Group or Any Order Group in a routing (see Chapter 4). Also, you cannot attach a sample plan to an operation with a buy-off configuration (see Chapter 11).

To summarize, the sampling process is configured by creating an operation that is part of the production routing, such as a sampling operation or nondestructive testing of an SFC. The sample plan created needs to be assigned to the same operation, with specific materials and resources if required included from the attachment point. Also, a sample routing needs to be created and attached to the sample plan. When the SFC is executed in the sampling operation, the sample routing will be automatically triggered to perform the sampling process—that is, testing and subsequently scrap or proceed. The process is illustrated in Figure 8.21.

8 | Nonconformance and Quality Control

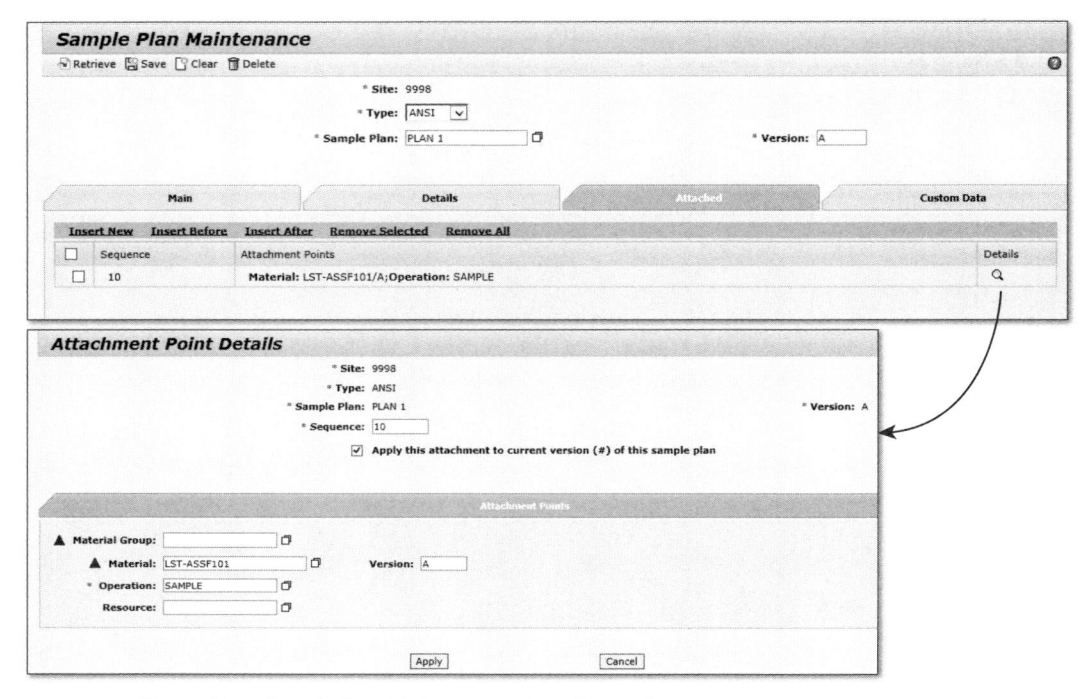

Figure 8.20 Sample Plan Maintenance: Attachment Points

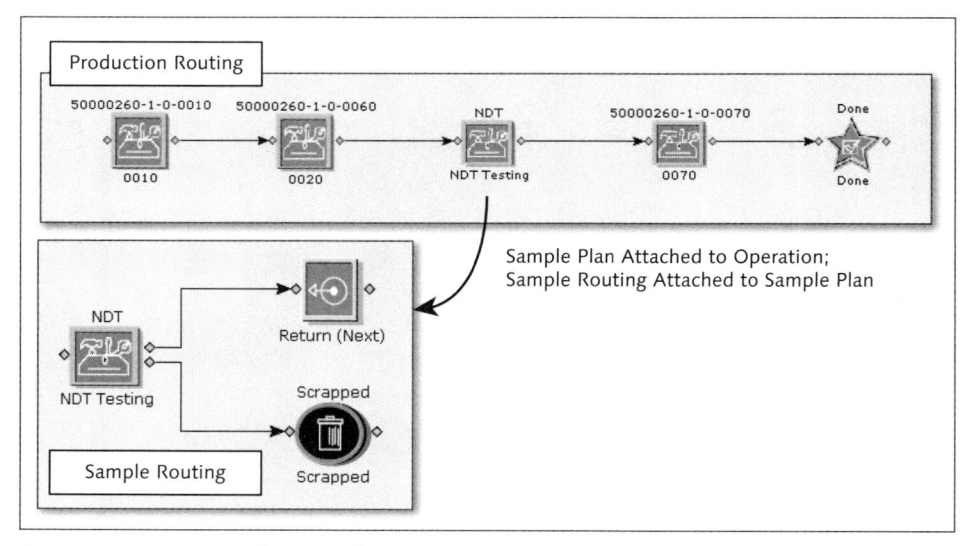

Figure 8.21 Routing Configuration for Sampling Process

8.6 Quality Inspection Process

The quality inspection process during manufacturing execution is typically defined in SAP ERP as part of the production routing. It also can be defined in SAP ME by extending the routing downloaded from SAP ERP, as explained in Chapter 4. When the quality inspection is configured in SAP ERP, the inspection lot is transferred with the production orders, which are created in SAP ME as DC groups associated with shop orders. The DC group is assigned to the SFC groups for a sample size while releasing the shop order in SAP ME. While executing the SFC, the operator needs to execute the inspection operation where the data collection needs to occur, and the data is then transferred to SAP ERP as a quality inspection result. If there is are any quality issues, the operator can log an NC, based on which the quality notification is created in SAP ERP if configured. You can use NC process in SAP ME with or without integrating with the QM module in SAP ERP, per the business requirements.

In the next sections, you will learn about the inspection process in SAP ME based on the SAP ERP inspection planning and how data is synchronized with SAP ERP. Let's work through an example of a car assembly process in which you need to perform a couple of in-process inspections of the assembly and raise nonconformances for scrap or repair if there are any issues. Figure 8.22 shows the production routing, including the inspection operations that determine whether the SFCs will be scrapped, repaired, or assembled.

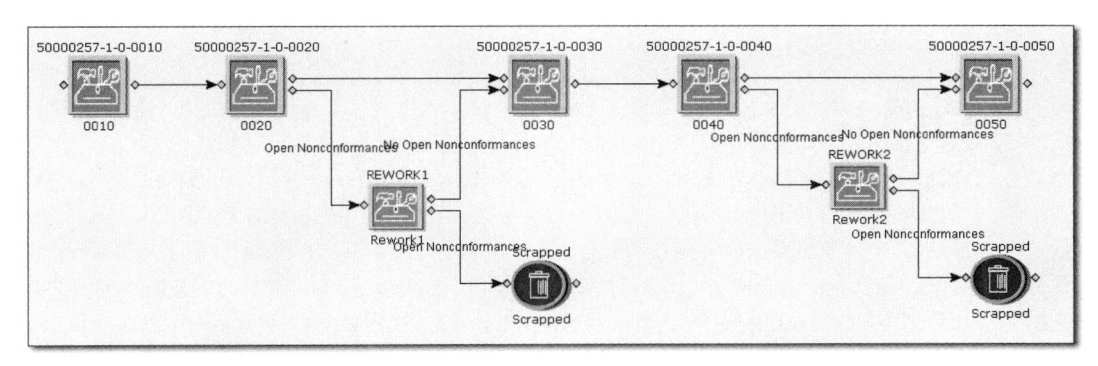

Figure 8.22 Production Routing with In-Process Inspection Operations

8.6.1 Transferring Inspection Lots as DC Groups from SAP ERP

When a production order is transferred to SAP ME from SAP ERP using the LOIPRO IDoc interface through SAPMEINT, the shop order is created in SAP ME.

8 | Nonconformance and Quality Control

Based on the inspection lot in the production order, DC groups are generated in SAP ME. The inspection operations are determined based on the operations to which inspection characteristics are assigned in SAP ERP, and displayed in the QM INSPECTION configuration tab in the Shop Order Maintenance activity, as explained in Chapter 5. The sample size is determined by the sample size specified in the inspection lot in SAP ERP. A sample shop order with an inspection lot and inspection operations is shown in Figure 8.23.

			* Site:	9998	
			* Shop Order:	1008043	
Main		Transfer	Build Status		QM Inspection
	Inspection Lot:	30000001600			
	SFC Group Size:	3			
Operation/Routing Step					Inspection Sample Size
50000257-1-0-0020/20					3
50000257-1-0-0040/40					3
50000257-1-0-0050/50					3

Figure 8.23 Inspection Lot in Shop Order

DC groups are created in SAP ME when the IDoc for production order is sent from SAP ERP to SAP ME, based on the inspection lot and inspection characteristics defined for each inspection operation, as shown in Figure 8.24.

1008043-20	A	1008043-20	Releasable	True
1008043-40	A	1008043-40	Releasable	True
1008043-50	A	1008043-50	Releasable	True

Figure 8.24 DC Group for Inspection Lot

Each DC group created represents the inspection points and is automatically marked as QM INSPECTION GROUP and is read-only, as used for quality inspection for SAP ERP QM inspection group, as shown in Figure 8.25. If you set SAMPLING PROCEDURE to 100% or ALLITEMS in the inspection characteristics in SAP ERP, then the 100% QUALITY INSPECTION checkbox will be checked in the DC group. 100% QUALITY INSPECTION signifies the SFC quantity for the sampling is equal to the build quantity of the shop-order and the quality inspection result evaluation will take place in SAP ME, in that case, which is then sent to SAP ERP. For <100% Quality Inspection scenario, the checkbox is not checked and the quality inspection result are sent to SAP ERP, evaluation of the result happens in SAP

ERP, and the SAP ME reads the evaluation results from SAP ERP to update the status of the SFC.

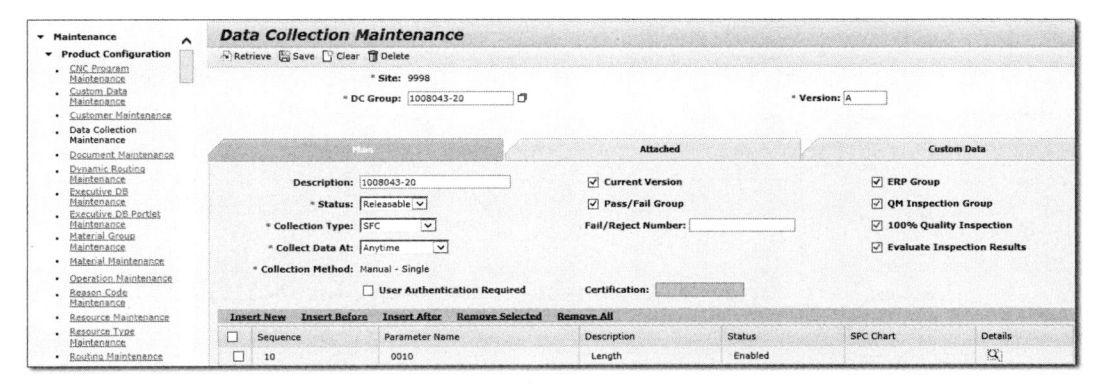

Figure 8.25 DC Group Details

Inspection characteristics which are as coming from SAP ERP to SAP ME with the production order IDoc, are created as DC group parameters, the details of which are shown in Figure 8.26.

Figure 8.26 Parameter Details for Inspection in DC Group

The DC group also is automatically attached to the routing step for the quality inspection, as shown in Figure 8.27.

8 | Nonconformance and Quality Control

Figure 8.27 DC Group Attachment to Routing Step

8.6.2 Transferring Data Collection as Quality Inspection Results to SAP ERP

When the operator starts the SFC using the START button in the POD (see Chapter 10 for more about the POD) for the inspection operation and clicks on the COMPLETE button, the SFC group for sampling is generated, as shown in Figure 8.28.

Figure 8.28 Sample SFC Group

Quality inspection in SAP ME is supported by data collection in DC groups to capture inspection results. Once the sampling SFC group is selected in the POD, the INFO column displays the DATA COLLECTION icon, as defined in the inspection lot for the shop order as shown in Figure 8.29.

Figure 8.29 Sampling SFC for Data Collection (Quality Inspection)

Select the SFC and click on DC COLLECT to record the parameter values, as shown in Figure 8.30. The details for the parameter or inspection characteristics are also displayed, such the acceptable value range, data type, and UoM, and you can add comments as well while recording the result.

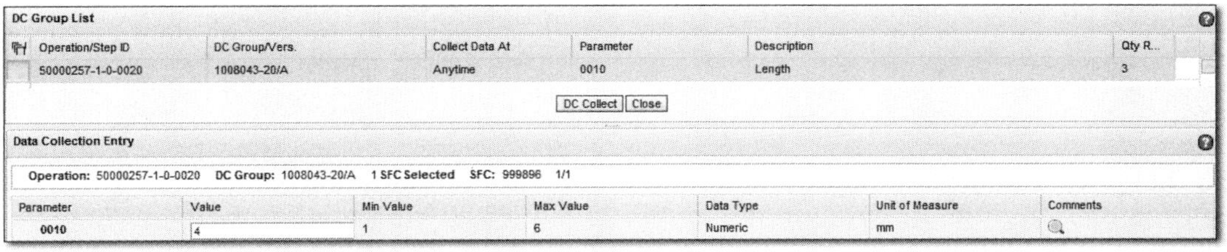

Figure 8.30 Data Collection (Inspection Result Recording) for Sample SFC

Once the data collection is complete and the SFC is completed at the operation in the POD, an outbound message for `qualityInspectionMeEvalResultRecordingRequest` is triggered from SAP ME through SAPMEINT to update the inspection result in SAP ERP for 100% Quality Inspection scenario (see Figure 8.31).

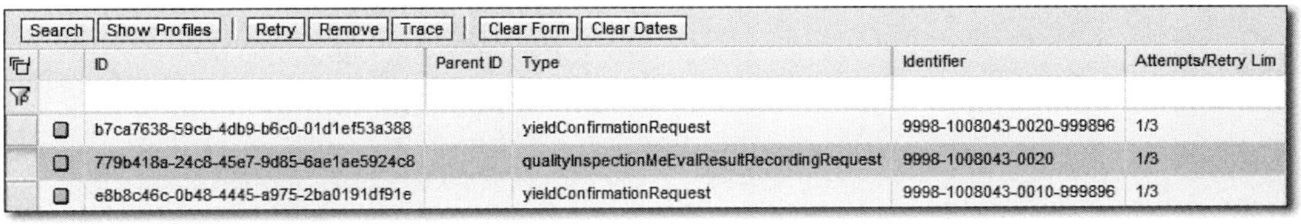

Figure 8.31 SAPMEINT Message for Quality Inspection Result Recording Update to SAP ERP

For <100% Quality Inspection scenario, the data parameter and data values are sent to SAP ERP QM through `qualityInspectionResultRecordingRequest`. SAPMEINT then sends the `readErpQualityInspectionResultRequest` message to SAP ERP QM to read the evaluated data parameter values to disposition the SFCs in SAP ME.

> **Note**
>
> The inspection result is sent to SAP ERP from SAP ME through SAPMEINT by the service extension `InspectionService`. Service extensions in SAP ME are explained in Chapter 17.

Once the interface is executed, view the results in SAP ERP through Transaction QE51N (Record Results—Characteristics Overview), as shown in Figure 8.32.

257

8 | Nonconformance and Quality Control

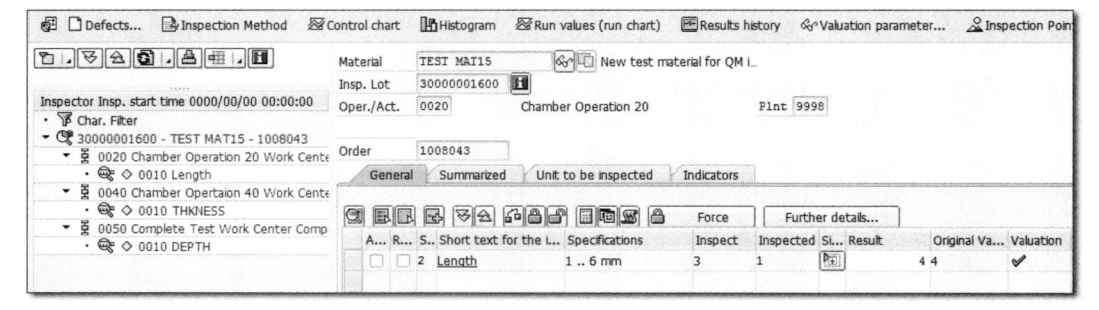

Figure 8.32 Inspection Results in SAP ERP

8.6.3 Transferring Nonconformances as Quality Notifications to SAP ERP

When a nonconformance is logged in SAP ME, if the NC code is marked as an ERP QN CODE in the NC Code Maintenance activity and the NC is logged for an SFC generated from an SAP ERP production order, then the nonconformance information is updated in SAP ERP as a quality notification. You also need to specify the ERP CATALOG, ERP CODE GROUP, and ERP CODE values for the NC code, and they should match those maintained in SAP ERP QM module, as shown in Figure 8.33.

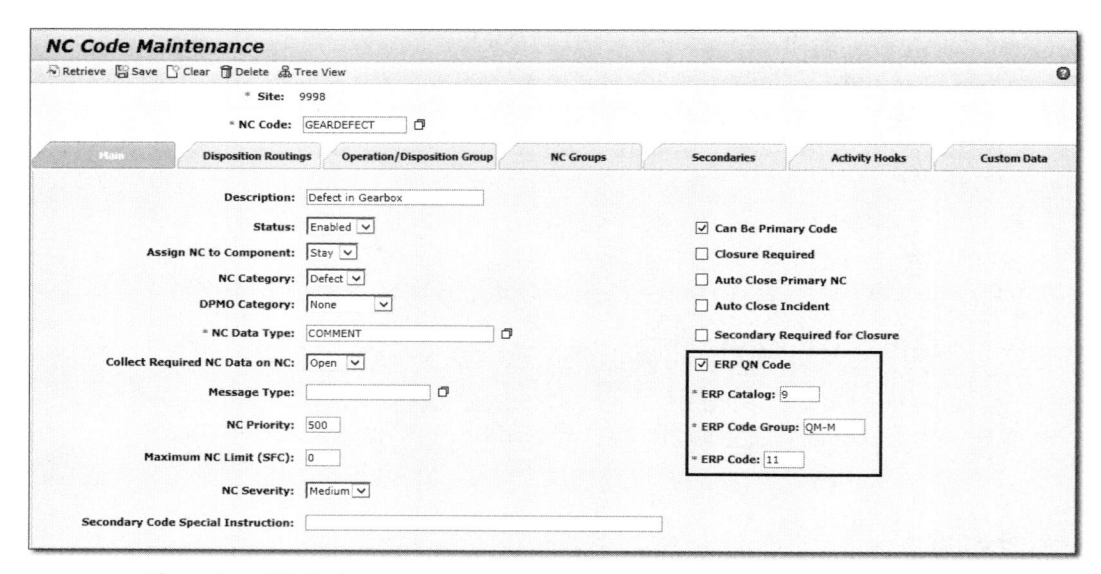

Figure 8.33 NC Code Mapping to SAP ERP QM

You also need to specify a corresponding ERP USER in the User Maintenance activity for the user who will be logging the NC and whose user ID will be used to create the quality notifications in SAP ERP, as shown in Figure 8.34.

Figure 8.34 ERP User in User Maintenance

Once the operator logs an NC code from the POD or from the Standalone NC Client, if the SAP ERP integration system rule is active, then a `qualityNotification-Request` message is generated and sent to SAP ERP through SAPMEINT to create a quality notification (see Figure 8.35).

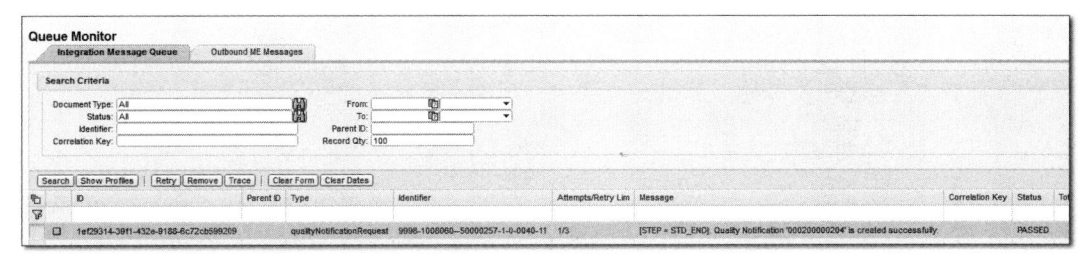

Figure 8.35 Quality Notification Request Message in SAPMEINT for NC Logging

> **Note**
>
> To trigger the quality notification request in SAP ERP through SAPMEINT, ensure the collaboration link ERP NONCONFORMANCE LOGGED is maintained for the trigger action `COLLABORATION_NC_LOG` as `ERP_QUALITY_NOTIFICATION` in the Collaboration Link Maintenance activity, as explained in Chapter 2.

8 | Nonconformance and Quality Control

8.7 Quality Reports

In SAP ME, there are several standard reports available for quality and nonconformance analysis that you can use to view the NC logging information, defect tracking, and statistical process control analysis. We'll discuss the quality-related reports available in SAP ME in the following sections.

8.7.1 NC Log Report

You can use the NC Log Report to view the NC logged. In this report, you can search by material, SFC, or date range, as shown in Figure 8.36. You also can filter the search results by several other parameters, such as operation, resource, work center, process lot, shop order, NC code, RMA number, and so on. On the NC and MISCELLANEOUS tabs, you can set the search parameters.

The results display the NCs logged that match the search criteria. Here, you can view additional details by selecting an NC code.

Figure 8.36 NC Log Report

8.7.2 NC Summary by Material Report

You can use the NC Summary by Material Report to view the NCs logged based on material numbers, as shown in Figure 8.37. The report shows a bar graph with the first-pass quantity and retest quantity for each material. Click on any of the bars for a material to display the NC Summary by NC Code Report for that material, as explained in the next section.

Quality Reports | **8.7**

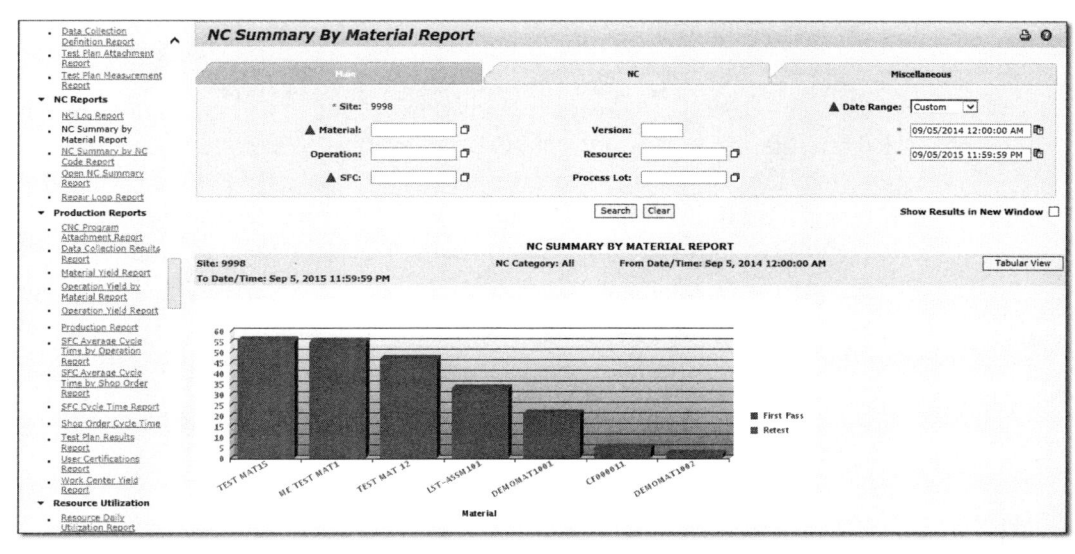

Figure 8.37 NC Summary by Material Report

8.7.3 NC Summary by NC Code Report

The NC Summary by NC Code Report displays the NCs logged for a date range or material by NC codes, as shown in Figure 8.38.

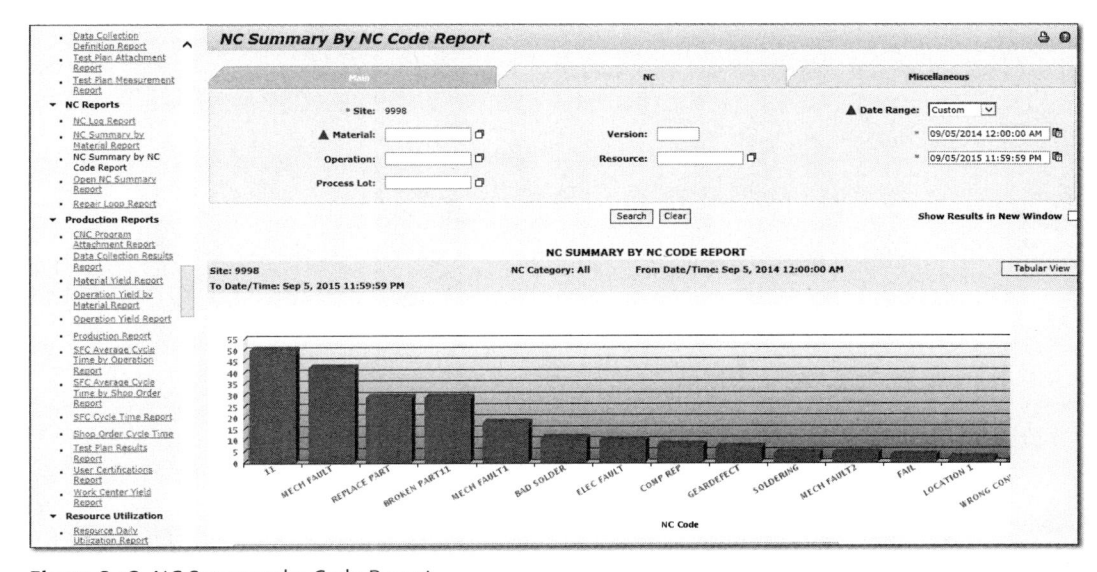

Figure 8.38 NC Summary by Code Report

8 | Nonconformance and Quality Control

8.7.4 Open NC Summary Report

You can use the Open NC Summary Report to view NCs logged for SFCs, as shown in Figure 8.39. In the search parameters, specify SFC and/or SHOP ORDER. You also can filter by NC STATE (OPEN, CLOSED, or ALL). As per your requirements, you can check the SHOW SFCs WITH NC checkbox. Click on the SFC link to display the NCs logged for the SFC and its component SFCs in a tree view. You need to set the rule BOM_LEVEL_CHECK in Activity Maintenance for this report (activity ID: NC760). The default value 0 signifies that only parent SFCs will be checked for NCs, whereas specifying another number will check until the levels of component SFCs of the parent SFC specified in selection have been checked.

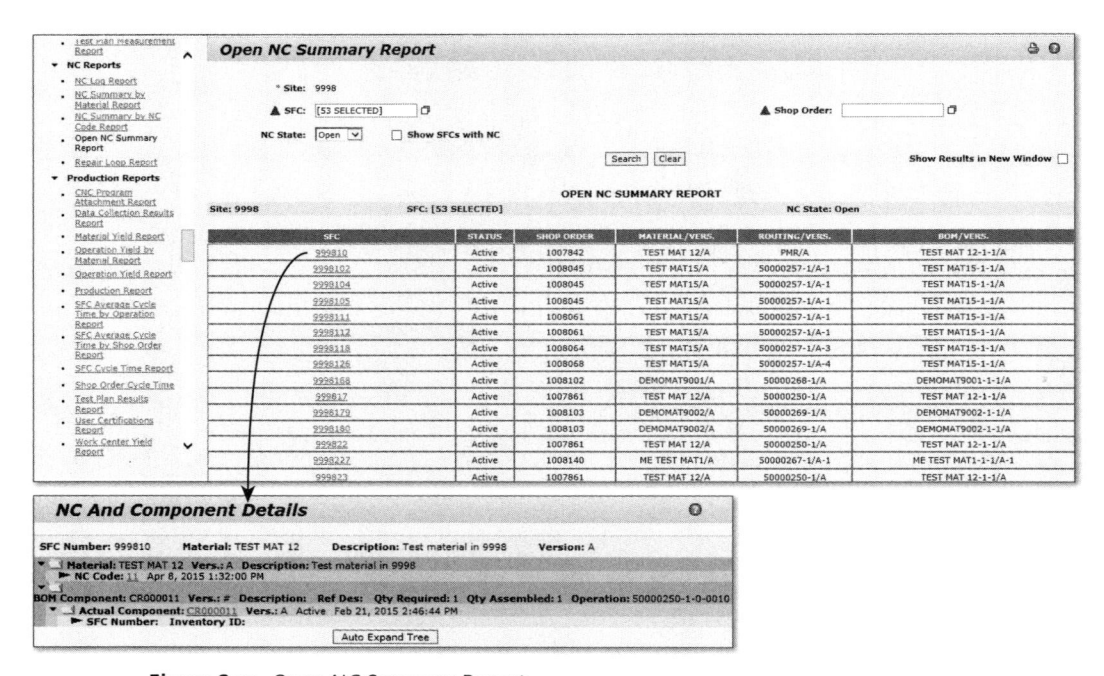

Figure 8.39 Open NC Summary Report

8.7.5 Repair Loop Report

Use the Repair Loop Report to view the NCs logged against a specific SFC for different operations, as shown in Figure 8.40. By clicking on the time event in the DATE/TIME column, you can see the activities performed on that SFC. Click on the NC code in the ACTIVITY CODE column to view the details of the NC logged for the SFC.

262

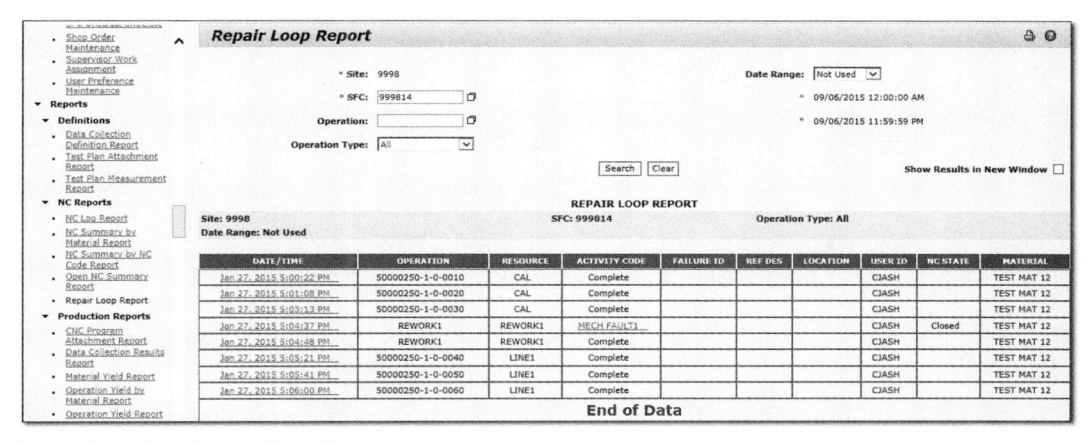

Figure 8.40 Repair Loop Report

8.7.6 DPMO Report

Use the DPMO Report to view the defects and their root causes, as determined during the manufacturing assembly process. You need to enable DPMO for the material (as explained in Chapter 3) and specify the DPMO category in the NC code (as explained in Section 8.1) to use DPMO. Also, you need to define a custom data field type of category NC (explained in Chapter 3) and assign the data fields for DEFECT COUNT and ROOT-CAUSE OPERATION from the Data Field Assignment activity, as shown in Figure 8.41.

Figure 8.41 Data Field Assignment Maintenance for DPMO

When an NC will be logged for the material for a defect, failure, or repair, the field values specified as custom data fields also need to be specified, as shown in Figure 8.42.

8 | Nonconformance and Quality Control

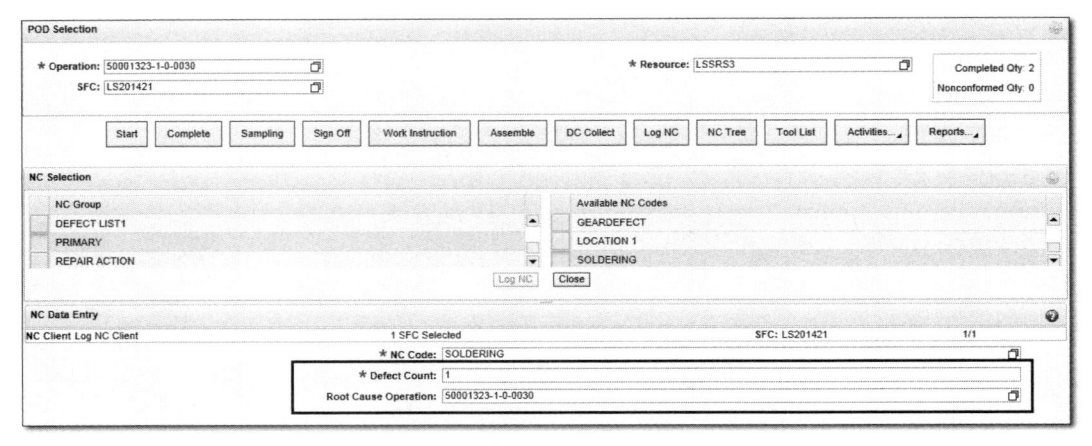

Figure 8.42 DPMO Data Collection for NC Logging

As NCs are logged, the DPMO is calculated by the system. View the DPMO report to see the defect rate, DPMO, and other related information, as shown in Figure 8.43.

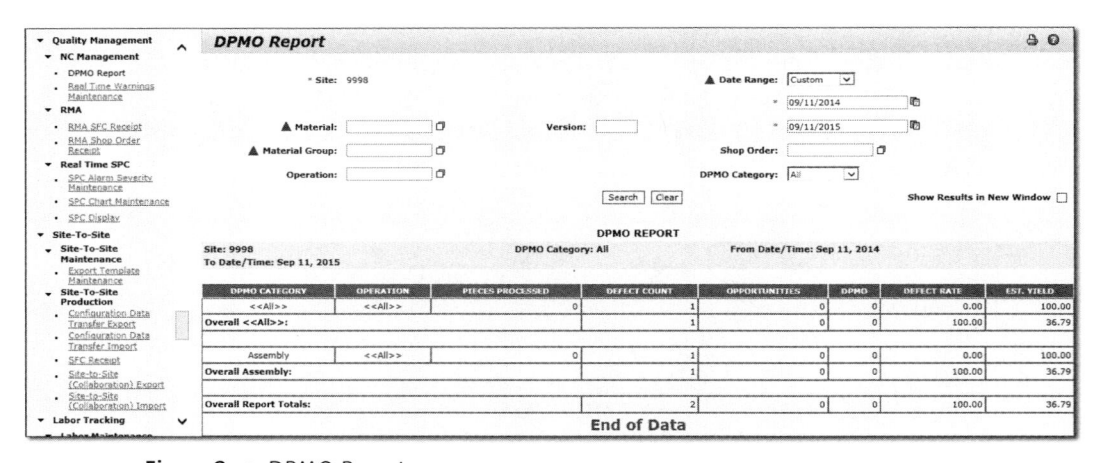

Figure 8.43 DPMO Report

8.8 SPC Analysis and Reporting

The quality inspection results and other data collected during the execution process in DC groups provide important information about the quality of the product and the manufacturing process. It is a common practice in the manufacturing industry to use *statistical process control* (SPC) analysis to measure the variations in a process, analyze process maturity, and prevent defective lots. SAP ME provides SPC analysis for analyzing data collected during the production process in DC groups for materials using SPC charts. There are different types of SPC charts available; the SAP MII SPC engine is used by SAP ME to display the SPC charts. You can also create custom SPC charts in SAP MII, which can be used to display the SPC results in SAP ME SPC charts.

8.8.1 Configuring SPC Charts

To configure and use SPC charts in SAP ME:

1. First, assign the XMII_User action and configure data access for the SAP ME user role to the XML Connector in SAP MII.

2. Log in to SAP User Management Engine (UME), search for the SAP_ME_USER role, and add the XMII_User permission action to it, as shown in Figure 8.44.

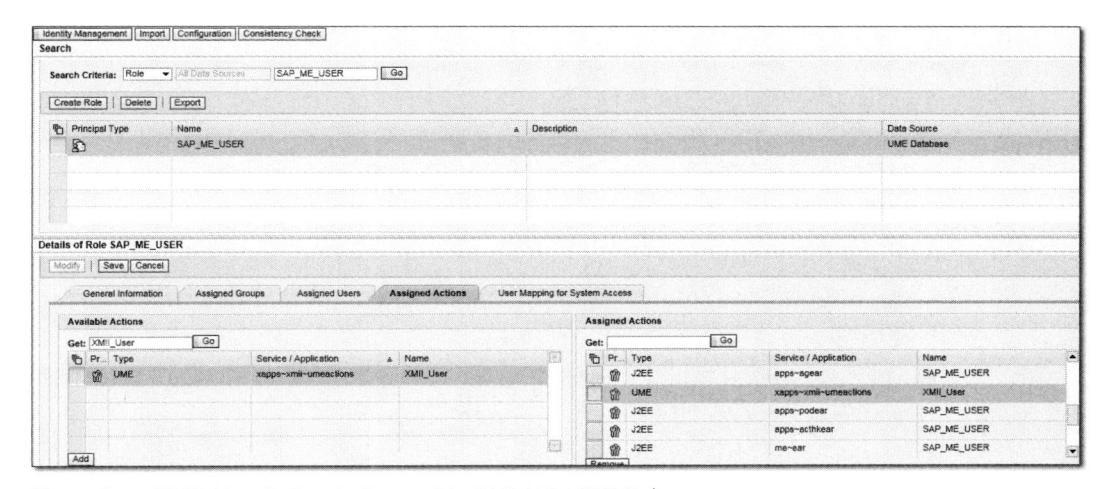

Figure 8.44 XMII_User Action Assignment to SAP_ME_USER Role

3. Log in to the SAP MII instance of SAP ME as an SAP MII administrator user via *http://<host>:<port>/XMII/Menu.jsp*.

4. Open the SECURITY SERVICES • DATA ACCESS menu and assign the SAP_ME_USER role to XMLConnector, as shown in Figure 8.45. This is required for SAP ME to access the SAP MII SPC engine through the XML connector.

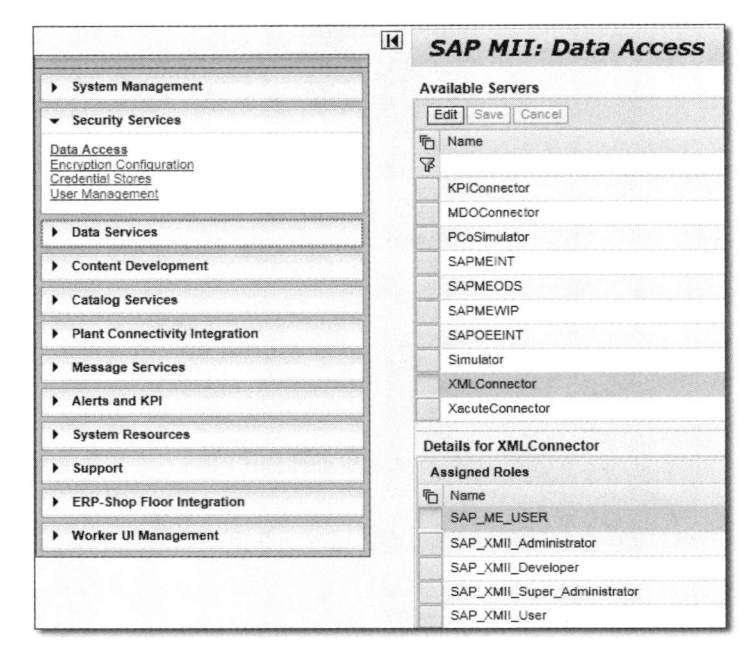

Figure 8.45 SAP ME Role Access to XML Connector in SAP MII

5. Next, log in to SAP NetWeaver Administrator via *http://<host>:<port>/nwa* and navigate to the Configurations • Infrastructure • Destination menu.

6. Create an HTTP destination named `MII_HTTP` with the URL *http://<host>:<port>/XMII/Illuminator*, as shown in Figure 8.46.

7. In the Logon Data configuration tab, specify "MESYS" as the user and enter its password.

8. Create another HTTP destination named `MIICatalog_HTTP` with the URL *http://<host>:<port>/XMII/Catalog*. These destinations are used by SAP ME to access the SAP MII SPC engine.

Once the system configurations are complete, you need to set up the configurations in SAP ME to enable SPC analysis. Create a DC group for SPC data collection, or use an existing DC group that is used for processing data collection, to plot the SPC chart. View the parameter details for the DC group, and on the SPC configuration tab of the details view, check Perform SPC Analysis and the related configurations, as explained in Section 7.1.2 (see Figure 8.47).

8.8 SPC Analysis and Reporting | **8.8**

Figure 8.46 HTTP Destination for SAP MII Illuminator Service

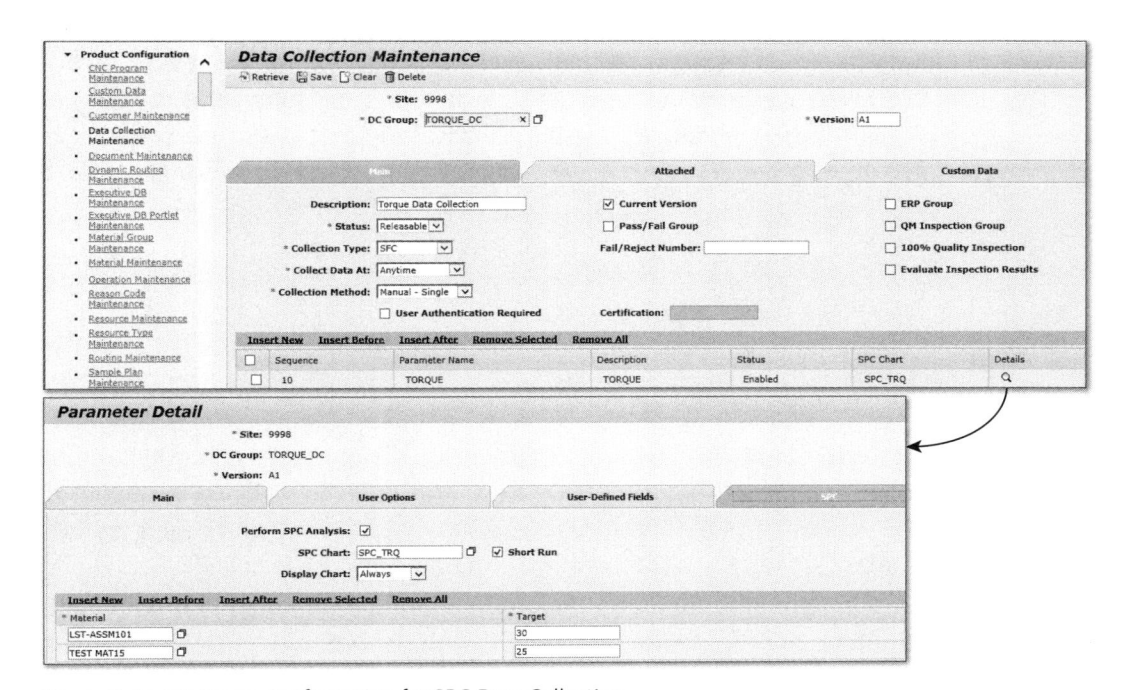

Figure 8.47 DC Group Configuration for SPC Data Collection

267

Open the SPC Chart Maintenance activity and create an SPC chart type, as shown in Figure 8.48. You need to specify a description for the chart and select the chart type you want to plot. Different types of SPC charts are explained in Table 8.1.

You need to specify the SUBGROUP SIZE for the MEDIAN, MOVING AVERAGE, MOVING RANGE, PROCESS CAPABILITY, XBAR & R, and XBAR & S options under CHART TYPES in order to indicate the number of data points to group together for calculating the mean, median, or standard deviation.

> **Note**
>
> For median charts, the subgroup size should be specified as any integer value between 2 and 25; for all other types of charts, the subgroup size should specified as an integer value between 2 and 30.

Enter a number in the MAX PLOT POINTS field to specify the maximum number of points to be displayed in the chart. MAX DATA AGE (DAYS) indicates the maximum allowed age of the data points that are plotted, where the age of the data point is calculated from the date on which it is saved for the first time in the DC group.

You can specify a SPC chart display template configured in the SAP MII workbench in the CHART TEMPLATE field if you want to use a customized template for the SPC chart. You need to create and specify the same subtype of the iSPC or i5SPC chart display template in SAP MII, matching the CHART TYPE specified in this activity. Otherwise, you can leave the CHART TEMPLATE field blank, in which case the standard SPC chart template provided by SAP ME will be used.

> **Note**
>
> SAP MII provides a development platform to create and configure custom charts as display templates as well as logic and query components. The SPC charts are stored in the MII content catalog and can be used in SAP ME.

You can configure alarms for SPC charts, which are triggered when the SPC results follow a certain pattern as defined by each specific rule. To highlight the alarms in the SPC chart, select the PROPAGATE ALARMS checkbox which triggers an SPC alarm message which you can configure in *SPC Severity Maintenance* activity as explained at the end of this section. You can specify SHORT RUN to display short run charts for INDIVIDUALS, INDIVIDUALS & MR, MOVING RANGE, and XBAR & R chart types. When SHORT RUN is selected, the short run displays the difference between the target value and the collected value. The target value is specified in the PRIMARY CHART DETAILS and SECONDARY CHART DETAILS configuration tabs.

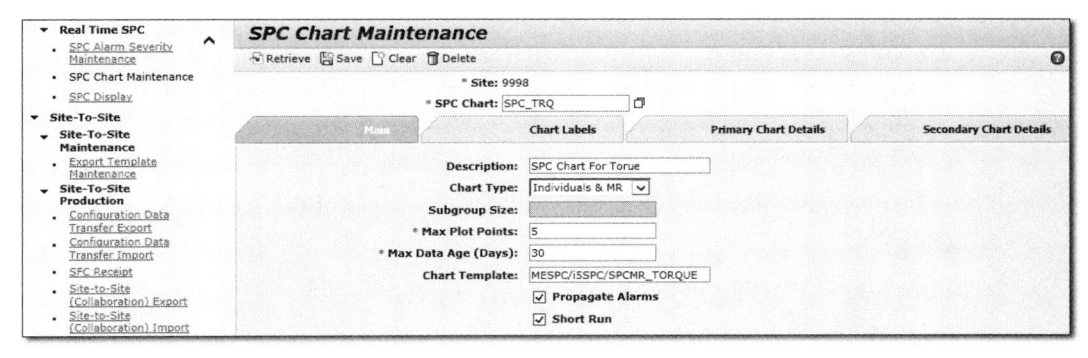

Figure 8.48 SPC Chart Configuration

SPC Chart Types	Description
Individuals	Displays each data value.
Individuals & MR	Displays each data value and moving range—that is, the difference between each data point and its immediately prior one for each data value using two charts.
Median	Calculates and displays the median values for each subgroup of data points. The SUBGROUP SIZE value needs to be specified. Median charts are useful for small subgroup sizes.
Moving Average	Calculates and displays the moving average for each subgroup, specified in SUBGROUP SIZE.
Moving Range	Calculates and displays the moving range for each subgroup, specified in SUBGROUP SIZE.
Process Capability	Calculates and displays a histogram chart with a normal curve. A *histogram* plots the statistical distribution for the set of data by dividing the data points into ranges and then calculating the number of data points in each range to display bars representing the number of data points for each group. You need to specify the UPPER SPEC. LIMIT, LOWER SPEC. LIMIT, and TARGET values in the PRIMARY CHART DETAILS configuration tab.
X-Bar & R	Calculates and displays the mean and range for each subgroup of data points in two charts.
X-Bar & S	Displays the mean and standard deviation for each subgroup of data points in two charts.

Table 8.1 SPC Chart Types

8 | Nonconformance and Quality Control

Configure the various labels and chart titles in the CHART LABELS tab, as shown in Figure 8.49. You can also specify how the X axis will be displayed by choosing one of the following options:

- SEQUENTIAL (1 TO N)
  Displays sequential numbers, starting from 1 and incremented by 1 for each subgroup
- TIME
  Displays the time intervals that represent the time of the data collection
- DATE
  Displays the date intervals that represent the date of the data collection
- DATE/TIME
  Displays the date and time intervals that represent the timestamp of the data collection
- SFC
  Displays the SFC number for which data is collected

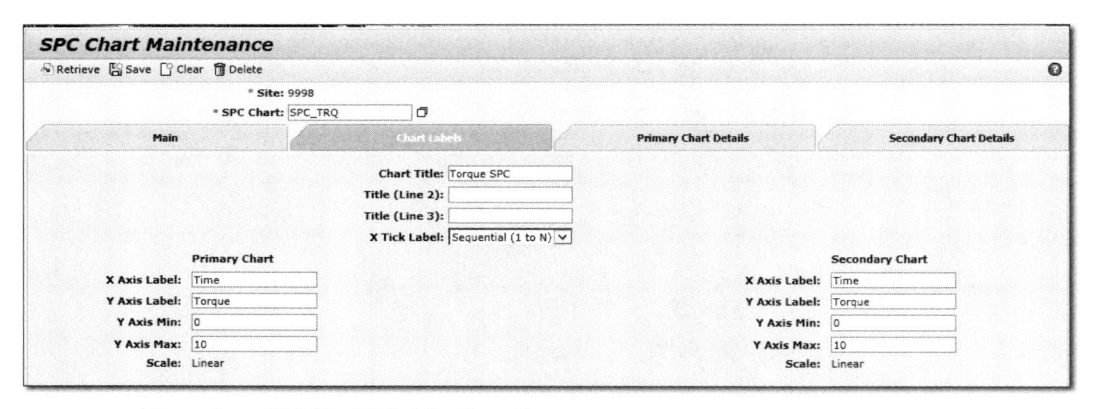

Figure 8.49 SPC Chart Label Configurations

On the PRIMARY CHART DETAILS and SECONDARY CHART DETAILS tabs, you can specify the control limit and specification limits for the SPC charts. The control limit sets the out-of-control deviation levels. If you specify NONE for CONTROL LIMIT OPTION, then the control limit line will not be displayed on the SPC chart. You can also specify fixed control limit values by selecting FIXED for CONTROL LIMIT OPTION. If you select CALCULATED for CONTROL LIMIT OPTION, then you need to specify the Sigma Coefficient value as well, which is a constant used for SPC calculation and based on which the control limits will be calculated automatically. You can also specify the specification limits for the SPC charts on this configuration tab. If you want to determine and display the alarms on the SPC chart, you need to select a Trend Rule from the list available. These are industry-standard SPC trend rules, each of which you can configure from the SPC Alarm Severity Maintenance activity.

You can maintain the same configurations in the Secondary Chart Details tab for chart types that display two charts. See Figure 8.50 and Figure 8.51 for the primary and secondary chart details configurations.

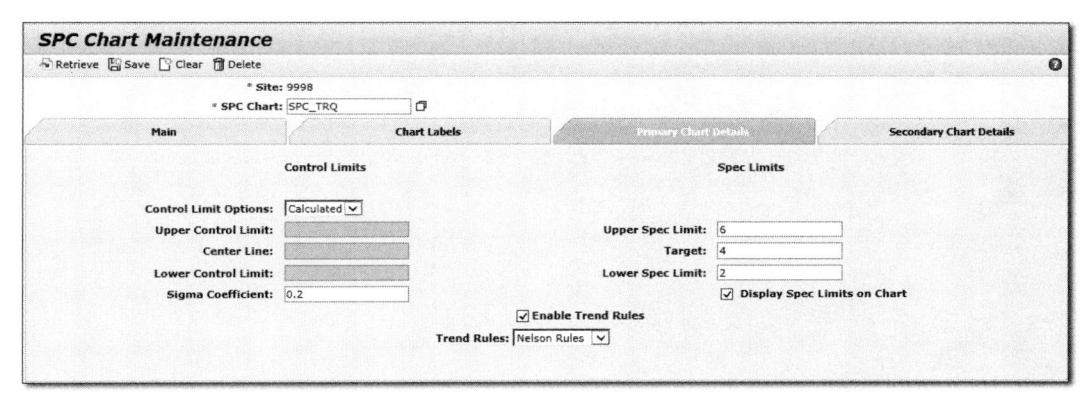

Figure 8.50 SPC Chart: Primary Chart Configurations

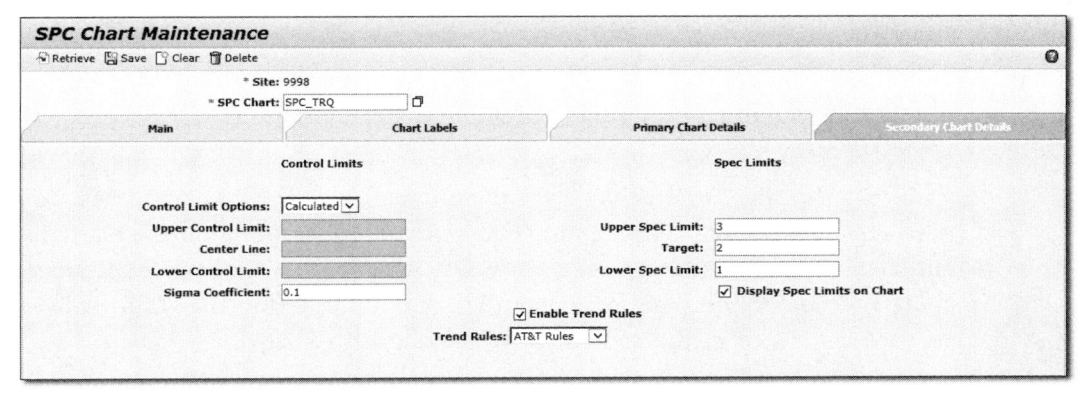

Figure 8.51 SPC Chart: Secondary Chart Configurations

8 | Nonconformance and Quality Control

> **Note**
>
> To use the SAP MII SPC engine, set the STATIT SERVER HOST COMPUTER NAME system rule value as blank in the System Rule Maintenance activity.

Use the SPC Alarm Severity Maintenance activity to assign the message type as warning or error or to just to ignore the alarm for each rule, as shown in Figure 8.52. Warning and error messages are triggered in the Message Board when the corresponding SPC rules are not satisfied. Each rule is defined by specific criteria for certain numbers of the plotted in relation to the control limits and specification limits, which also you can configure here.

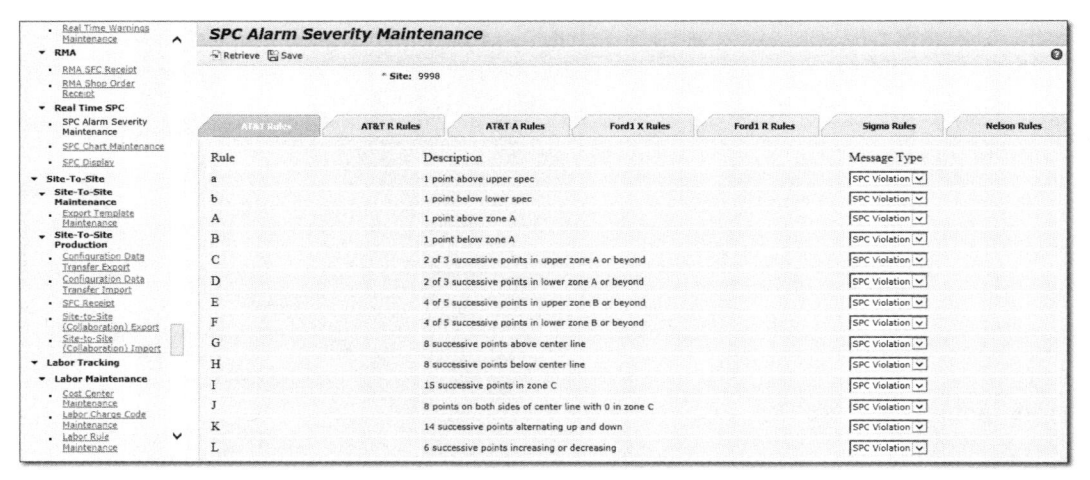

Figure 8.52 SPC Alarm Serverity Maintenance

8.8.2 Displaying SPC Charts

Once you configure the SPC chart, you can use the SPC Display activity in SAP ME to display the SPC charts and analyze them based on SPC rules and alarms. You need to select the SPC CHART configured in the SPC Chart Maintenance activity and the DC GROUP and PARAMETER for which you want to display the SPC chart, along with the time range for which the data points in the DC group will be selected for SPC calculation and display, as shown in Figure 8.53.

Based on the chart type selected, the data points that match the alarms rule selected will be highlighted in red, as shown in Figure 8.54. The last data point on the right of the chart in the example has an alarm and is highlighted.

Figure 8.53 SPC Chart Display Selection

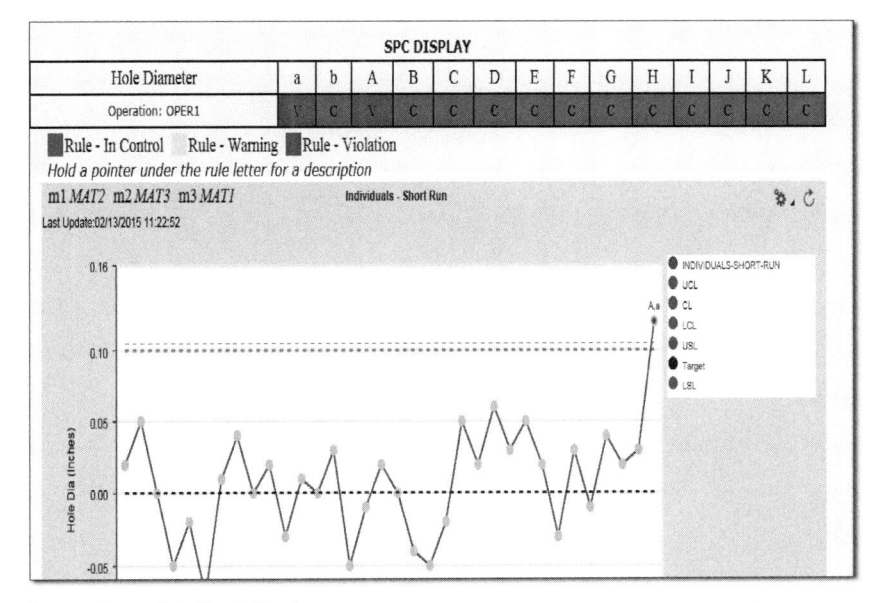

Figure 8.54 SPC Chart Display

8.9 Summary

In this chapter, you learned about the nonconformance management process in SAP ME and about maintaining NC codes, disposition groups, and NC clients for nonconformance logging. You also learned about the sampling process for quality inspection and how to synchronize the inspection lot, inspection results, and quality notification data between SAP ERP and SAP ME. We also discussed the quality reports available in SAP ME and the SPC analyses and configurations.

In the next chapter, you will learn about managing product genealogy and tracking.

This chapter explains discrete and time-based product genealogy and discusses required system settings for discrete and time-based genealogy, Storage Location Maintenance, Floor Stock Receipt, Floor Stock Maintain, and Inventory Transfer. It also describes the Slot Configuration Maintenance and Resource Slot Configuration Setup activities.

9   Product Genealogy and Tracking

In SAP ME, the purpose of product genealogy is to track assembled components into their finished product during the manufacturing process. Product genealogy tracks the components used to assemble the finished product, verifies that all required components are used, places components on hold because of quality issues, loads or replenishes components on resource, and provides vendor information regarding who supplied components. It also provides information about the current status and location of a product, the activities performed for a product, and the shop floor users who are working on a product. Through product genealogy in SAP ME, you can track the complete lifecycle of the product on the shop floor during manufacturing and assembly. Through data collection, SAP ME keeps a record of all activities performed to assemble the product using components and provides reports of historical data that help to trace the root cause of any issue. SAP ME supports discrete and time-based genealogy, defined as follows:

- **Discrete genealogy**
  Discrete genealogy is used to collect, validate, and record assembly data during the product building process. The data can be entered by scanning a barcode or can be entered manually by a shop floor user in assemble component plugin in a SAP ME PODs. Assembly data is recorded for each component used to build the product (each SFC). The assembly data required for a component can be defined through the Material Maintenance or BOM Maintenance activities.

- **Time-based genealogy**
  Time-based genealogy functionality collects, validates, and records assembly data where components are loaded into a slot configuration that is associated to

a resource that produces a product. Time-based genealogy works same way as discrete genealogy, but for a preconfigured resource. For time-based genealogy, component assembly data is stored based upon time slots at the resource level rather than each SFC.

In the next section, you will learn about the required configurations for discrete and time-based genealogy processes.

9.1 Setting Up Discrete and Time-Based Genealogy Processes

To enable product genealogy tracking for discrete and time-based processes, you need to set up SAP ME correctly to perform all activities and collect all required data during the manufacturing processes. Let's first examine the required common setup for both discrete and time-based genealogy and then go over the required settings specifically for time-based genealogy. In the System Rule Maintenance activity, you can revisit the configuration of the COMPONENT TRACEABILITY system rule and change the rule configurations to fit your business requirement, as explained in the following list.

The required settings for both discrete and time-based genealogy are as follows:

- **Allow Assembly Qty as Required**
  If TRUE, SAP ME displays the ASSEMBLY QTY AS REQUIRED checkbox in the COMPONENT DETAILS configuration for the BOM Maintenance activity to allow user to enter the required number of pieces it needed to assemble the component.

- **Allow Non-BOM Components on Add**
  If TRUE, SAP ME allows you to add non-BOM components to the assembly SFC using the As-Built Configuration activity. See Section 9.7 for more information.

- **Allow Ver Change on Purchased Components**
  If TRUE, SAP ME allows you to change the version of a purchased component in the Assemble Component and As-Built Configuration activities.

- **BOM Name Equals Material Name**
  If TRUE, only the routing operation list is shown (which is assigned to a material) in the ASSEMBLY OPERATION or DISASSEMBLY OPERATION browse list in the COMPONENT DETAILS section of the BOM Maintenance activity.

- **Display Auto Fill Components**
  If TRUE, a component that has NONE assigned as the Data Type to collect on assembly will be displayed in the Component List Table plugin in the POD at assembly operations.

- **Enable Pegging on Release**
  If TRUE, a link is created between the subassembly and the top-level shop order during shop order release.

- **Enforce Pegging on Consumption**
  If TRUE, only the associated component subassembly is allowed that was released with the top-level SFC to be assembled during the Assembly Point or As-Built Configuration activities.

- **Max Component Usage Count**
  Using the configured value, you can specify the number of times a shop floor user can add an inventory ID or SFC to an assembly during a discrete assembly operation. You can also override the value in the BOM Component and Material Configuration activities.

- **Max Component Usage Message**
  Specify the message that the system displays when the shop floor user attempts to add an inventory ID/SFC number in Assembly Point that has exceeded the usage count. You need to define the message type in the Message Type Maintenance activity.

- **Ref Des Is Required**
  If YES, SAP ME forces you to enter a reference designator in the COMPONENT DETAILS section of BOM Maintenance.

- **Ref Des Must Be Unique**
  If TRUE, SAP ME prevents entering the same reference designator more than once for the same BOM in the BOM Maintenance activity.

- **Specific BOM Component Version Required**
  If TRUE, you need to enter a version for each BOM component in the VERSION field in the COMPONENT DETAILS section of BOM Maintenance.

- **Validate Component Usage**
  If TRUE, SAP ME prevents adding an inventory ID exceeding the component usage count in the Assembly Point or As-Built Configuration activity.

Figure 9.1 shows the default system rule settings for COMPONENT TRACEABILITY in the System Rule Maintenance activity.

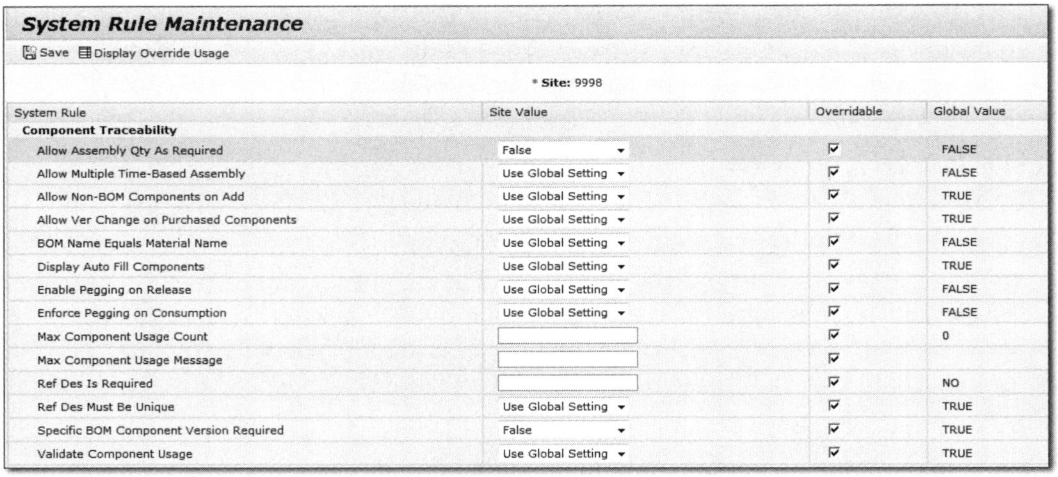

9 | Product Genealogy and Tracking

Figure 9.1 Component Traceability System Rule Maintenance

Additional settings include:

- **Assembly Point Configuration**

    An *assembly point* is the point in an operation at which the shop floor user assembles the components and records the information in the Assemble Component plugin within the POD. Using the Assembly Point (activity ID: CT500) activity, the shop floor user can collect the assembly data for each component. The genealogy record for the product can be found using the assembly data record. The assembly record can be created for each SFC, and you can track component information used to assemble the SFC. The Assembly Point activity also validates location, reservation, and time-sensitive key attributes before consumption of a component during assembly.

    In the BUILD configuration of the Material Maintenance activity, you can assign the data type (the data fields should be configured using the Data Type Definition Maintenance activity and assigned it to the data type assembly category using the Data Field Assignment Maintenance activity) in the DATA TO COLLECT ON ASSEMBLY field, which will be collected during component assembly in the assembly operation. The same material can be used in the BOM Maintenance activity as a component with a specified quantity that will be assembled in the routing operation. You can also check the rules settings for the Assembly Point activity in Activity Maintenance, and you can change the default settings per your requirements. Figure 9.2 shows the default rule settings for the Assembly Point activity in Activity Maintenance.

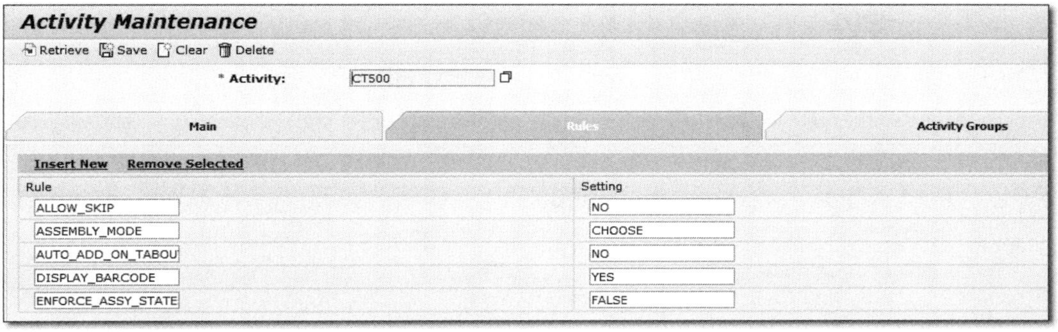

Figure 9.2 Rule Settings for Assembly Point Activity

- **Next Number Maintenance**
  The Next Number Maintenance activity is described in Chapter 2. You can configure next number generation for floor stock receipt using the Next Number Maintenance activity. The purpose of next number generation for floor stock receipt can be found in Section 9.2.1.

- **Vendor Maintenance**
  Using the Vendor Maintenance (PD200) activity, you can define a vendor (supplier) for a particular component and can configure whether components supplied by this vendor can be received into floor stock and consumed in an assembly using the COMPONENTS CAN BE RECEIVED and COMPONENTS CAN BE CONSUMED checkboxes.

The settings that are specific to time-based genealogy are as follows:

- **Time-Based Resource (Genealogy)**
  In System Rule Maintenance, specify TRUE for the TIME-BASED RESOURCE (GENEALOGY) system rule in the PRODUCTION TRACKING activity group. TIME-BASED RESOURCE (GENEALOGY) system rule can also be set in Resource Maintenance activity.

- **Allow Multiple Time-Based Assembly**
  In the COMPONENT TRACEABILITY rule group, set TRUE for the ALLOW MULTIPLE TIME-BASED ASSEMBLY system rule. If set to true, an SFC with time-based components whose entire quantity has been assembled at an assembly operation

9 | Product Genealogy and Tracking

and time-based resource and then removed using As-Built Configuration, can be assembled again when the SFC number is processed at the assembly operation and time-based resource again.

There are additional required configurations for time-based genealogy, such as Slot Configuration, Resource Slot Configuration Setup, and Resource Setup, which are described in Section 9.4, Section 9.5, and Section 9.6.

As an example of discrete genealogy, consider the car assembly scenario, in which a shop floor user assembles multiple components manually and collects and validates the records in SAP ME for traceability purposes. Assembly of multiple components in PCB (printed circuit board) in the electronics industry can be considered an example for time-based genealogy; components are loaded onto a time-based resource using Resource Slot Configuration Setup or Load/Replenish Components, and components are assembled on PCB by a machine automatically. SAP ME records the components and products through resources. In time-based genealogy, records are stored at the resource level.

9.2 Managing Floor Stock

Floor stock management functionality allows you to receive stock, record material traceability data, examine movement of materials from one storage location to another, and reserve materials for a particular shop order, work center, operation, or resource. Through the inventory ID generated for the component stock in SAP ME, a component material can be tracked in the manufacturing process. In this section, we will cover Floor Stock Receipt, Rule Settings for Floor Stock Receipt, Maintain Floor Stock, and SAP ERP integration for Floor Stock Maintenance.

9.2.1 Floor Stock Receipt

In SAP ME, the Floor Stock Receipt (activity ID: IN500) activity is used to record the receipt of materials in the shop floor stock. In the Floor Stock Receipt activity, you can specify the component material and version in the MATERIAL and VERSION fields respectively, as shown in Figure 9.3. In the RECEIVE QTY field, specify the quantity to be received on the shop floor. For a CREATE event, SAP ME will create the line items in the inventory table with auto-generated inventory IDs (if the AUTOMATIC_ID_GENERATION rule for the Floor Stock Receipt activity is set to

TRUE and a numbering pattern is defined in the Next Number Maintenance activity for FLOOR STOCK RECEIPT). The number of line items created for a material quantity depends on the lot size of the material configured in Material Maintenance for the material; the lot size is used in the MATERIAL field in Floor Stock Receipt.

If any data type is defined for the DATA TO COLLECT ON FLOOR STOCK RECEIPT field in Material Maintenance, then the data collection should be performed for the assigned data type during floor stock receipt. The Data Field Definition Maintenance and Data Field Assignment Maintenance activities are described in Chapter 3. You can also define a mask group through the Validation Mask Maintenance activity to use for data field validation. The data type will match the data type offset in the DATA TO COLLECT ON FLOOR STOCK RECEIPT field specified in the Material Maintenance activity. For example, say you have defined a validation mask group and assigned it in the MASK GROUP field for the EXTERNAL_SERIAL data field in the DATA FIELD DEFINITION MAINTENANCE activity. Next, you assign ERP_SERIAL_NUMEBR as the value of the DATA TO COLLECT ON FLOOR STOCK RECEIPT field in Material Maintenance. Because the EXTERNAL_SERIAL data field belongs to ERP_SERIAL_NUMBER, the mask validation will be applied for the EXTERNAL_SERIAL data field in Floor Stock Receipt when you click on the RECEIVE button. Figure 9.3 shows the automatic inventory ID generation in the Floor Stock Receipt activity.

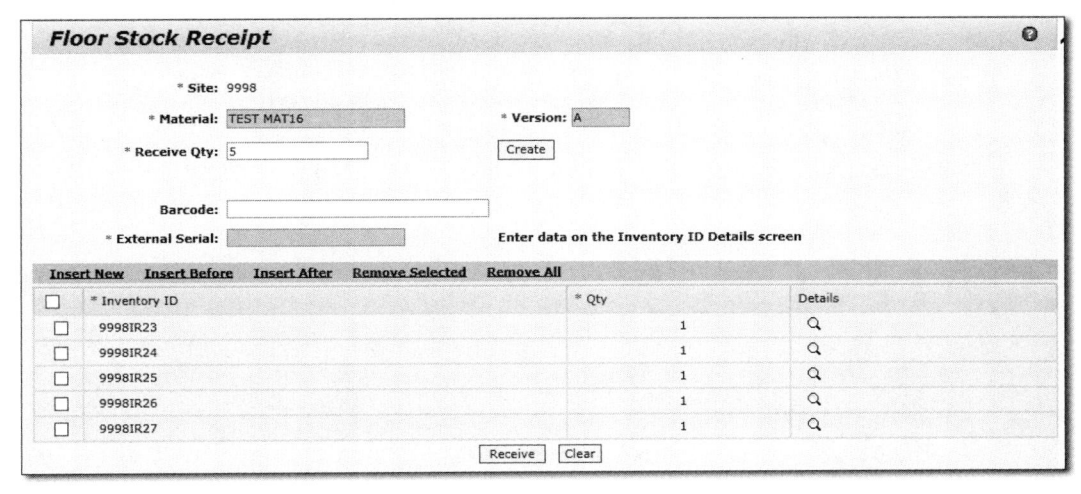

Figure 9.3 Floor Stock Receipt

9.2.2 Rule Settings for Floor Stock Receipt

In Activity Maintenance, you can configure the rules for the Floor Stock Receipt activity, as described in Table 9.1.

Rule	Settings
ALLOW_STORAGE_LOC_MOVE	If the value is set to NO and there is a storage location value assigned in the STORAGE LOCATION field, then the STORAGE LOCATION field becomes read-only and the value is displayed in the STORAGE LOCATION field. For YES, SAP ME allows you to move an inventory ID from one storage location to another, and the STORAGE LOCATION field is enabled for that action.
APPLY_ALL_DATA	If the value is set to NO, then floor stock data fields are disabled in Floor Stock Receipt and you need to enter the data for each inventory ID on the Inventory ID Details screen. For YES, you can specify the values for floor stock data fields, and those values are applied to all inventory IDs created.
AUTOMATIC_ID_GENERATION	If the value is set to NO, then you need to manually enter the inventory ID in Floor Stock Receipt. For YES, inventory IDs are created automatically based on the configuration in the Next Number Maintenance activity for floor stock receipt.
DISPLAY_BARCODE	If the value is set to YES, then SAP ME displays the BARCODE field on the Floor Stock Receipt page. For NO, the BARCODE field is not displayed on the Floor Stock Receipt page.
INVENTORY_LOCATION_REQ	If the value is set to YES, then you need to specify a storage location for each inventory ID; if NO, then it is optional for each inventory ID.

Table 9.1 Activity Rule Configurations for Floor Stock Receipt Activity

9.2.3 Maintain Floor Stock

The Maintain Floor Stock (MAINT_INV) activity is used to edit the existing inventory ID records created either through the Floor Stock Receipt activity in SAP ME or through SAP ERP integration with SAP ME. In the Maintain Floor Stock activity, specify the existing inventory ID in the INVENTORY ID field, and click on the RETRIEVE button to see the details of the existing inventory ID (see Figure 9.4).

After retrieving the existing inventory ID records, you can update the inventory record fields such as STATUS (AVAILABLE, HOLD, and QUARANTINE), MATERIAL, INVENTORY ID SPLIT, and INVENTORY ID LOCATION. To update the existing inventory record, specify a reason code and comments in the REASON CODE and COMMENT fields, respectively.

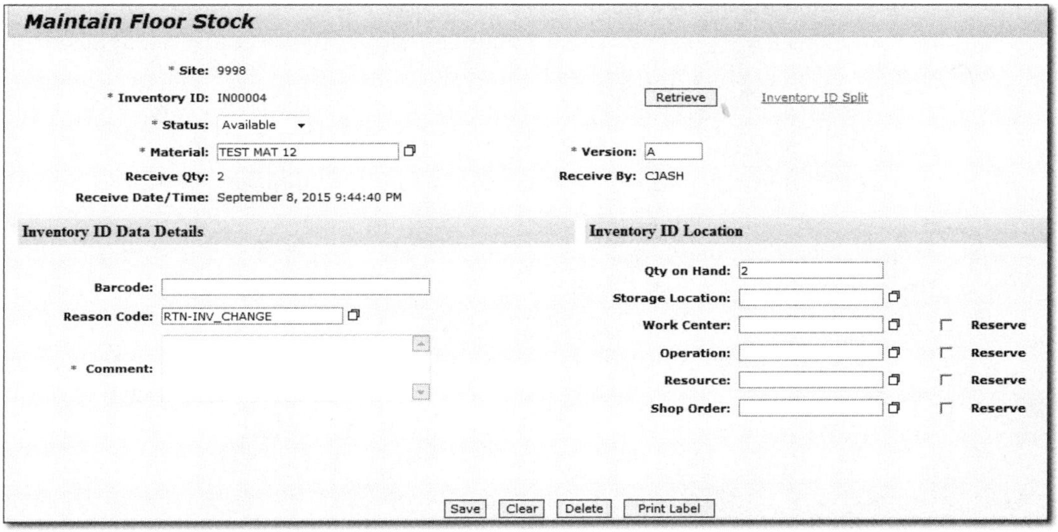

Figure 9.4 Maintain Floor Stock in SAP ME

The STORAGE LOCATION field displays the storage location for the inventory ID if it is specified during the Floor Stock Receipt activity. Alternately, you can browse to the storage location to assign an inventory ID to it. When browsing to a storage location, you can only find a storage location for which a work center is assigned in the Storage Location Maintenance activity. See Section 9.3 for more information about storage locations.

In the WORK CENTER field, specify the value for the work center and select the RESERVE checkbox if desired. If the RESERVE checkbox is selected, then the inventory ID only can be used by SFCs that move through the specified work center. Specify the operation in the OPERATION field, and select the RESERVE checkbox if desired. If the RESERVE checkbox is selected, then the inventory ID can be used only by the SFCs that move through the specified operation. In the RESOURCE field, specify the resource, and reserve it for the inventory ID by selecting the RESERVE checkbox if desired. If the RESERVE checkbox is selected for the OPERA-

TION field, then the inventory ID can be used only by SFCs that move through the specified resource. You can also specify the shop order in the SHOP ORDER field and reserve it for the inventory ID by selecting the RESERVE checkbox.

To perform an inventory ID split, the QTY ON HAND field in Maintain Floor Stock must contain a value greater than 1, and the QTY RESTRICTION field in Material Maintenance must not contain ONLY 1.0 as its value. To split an inventory ID, click the INVENTORY ID SPLIT link in Maintain Floor Stock to open the Split Inventory ID page, as shown in Figure 9.5. There, specify the split quantity in the QTY TO SPLIT field and the number of inventory IDs that will be created through the split in the NUMBER OF INVENTORY IDs field. The split quantity must be greater than zero but less than the QUANTITY ON HAND value, and the inventory ID quantity must be either equal to or less than the quantity to split. After specifying those values, click on the CREATE button. SAP ME will generate the split inventory IDs automatically based on the Next Number Maintenance configuration for Floor Stock Receipt. Through the INVENTORY ID SPLIT button, you can complete the inventory ID split functionality. If you return to Maintain Floor Stock, you will find that the quantity on hand value has decreased by the value used for inventory ID split.

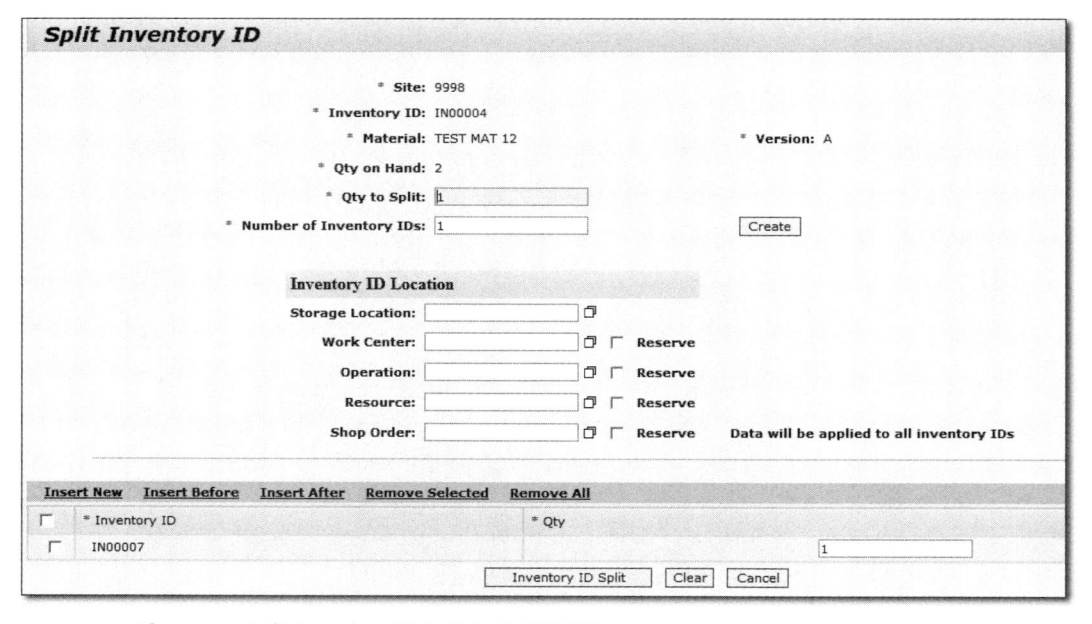

Figure 9.5 Split Inventory ID Activity in SAP ME

In the Maintain Floor Stock activity, configure the rules per your requirements, as shown in Figure 9.6. Here, you can also print a label via the PRINT LABEL button when a new inventory ID is created or an existing one updated. To do so, you must define a document in the Document Maintenance activity and specify the same document name as the value of the LABEL_DOCUMENT rule in Maintain Floor Stock activity.

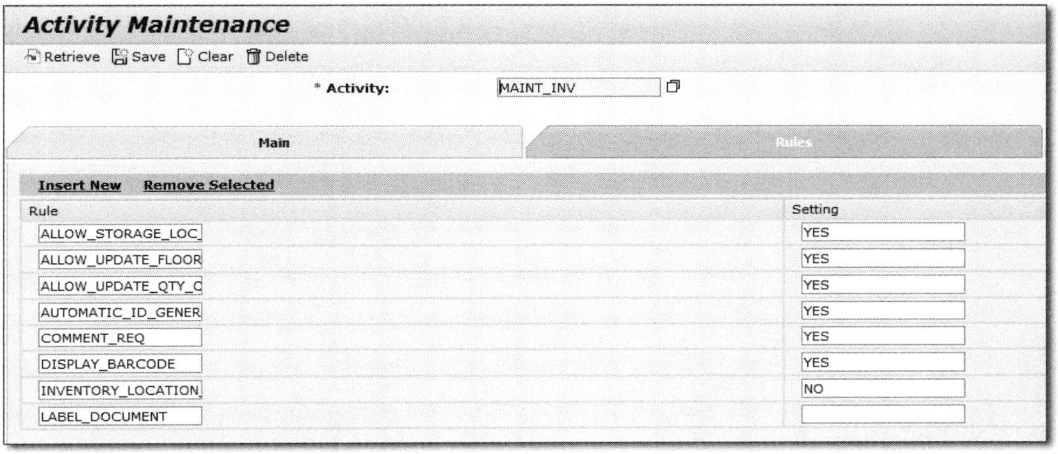

Figure 9.6 Rule Settings for Maintain Floor Stock activity

> **Note: Reason Code for Return and Scrap of Component**
>
> In the Reason Code Maintenance activity, reason codes prefixed with "RTN-" and "SCR-" should be defined to perform the Floor Stock Return and Component Scrap activities. Reason codes prefixed with "RTN-" prefix are used to return to floor stock, and reason codes prefixed with "SCR-" are used to scrap components. The triggering SAP ERP transactions for component return and scrap are described in Table 9.2.

9.2.4 SAP ERP Integration for Floor Stock Maintenance

If SAP ERP integration is enabled, then floor stock data can be received from SAP ERP through the SAPMEINT message type `INVCON02_INV_PEG`. SAP ME can also send notification messages to SAP ERP when floor stock material is returned to inventory or scrapped in SAP ME. Let's discuss scenarios in which notification is sent to SAP ERP due to transfer of inventory ID in the following subsections. The following sub-sections describe inventory transfer to different storage locations and consumption of floor stock in assembly point.

9 | Product Genealogy and Tracking

Transferring Inventory ID to Different Storage Locations in SAP ME

In the Maintain Floor Stock or in Floor Stock Receipt activity, specify a storage location either by entering the storage location value or browsing via the STORAGE LOCATION field. SAP ME validates that the user who is assigned to a work center if the work center is assigned to the specified storage location. You can also split an inventory ID and place the split inventory ID in another storage location. In the System Rule Maintenance activity, if the ERP INTEGRATION ACTIVE system rule is set to TRUE, then SAP ME sends a notification message to SAP ERP through SAPMEINT. Trigger action COLLABORATION_STORAGE_LOC_MOVE and directive ERP_STORAGE_LOC_MOVE are used to send notifications to SAPMEINT, and message type storageLocationMoveRequest is used in SAPMEINT to send the message to SAP ERP (see Figure 9.7).

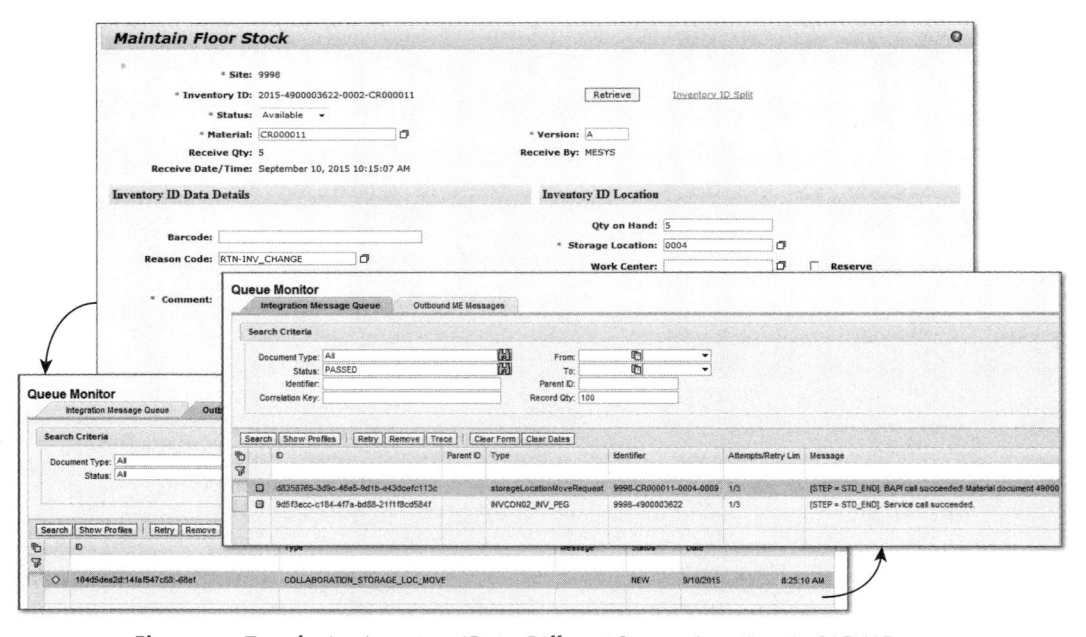

Figure 9.7 Transferring Inventory IDs to Different Storage Locations in SAP ME

Consuming Floor Stock in SAP ME Assembly Point

Floor stock consumption is mostly performed in assembly operations through the Assembly Point (activity ID: CT500) activity. It can also be performed through the

As-Built Configuration (activity ID: CT510) activity (see Section 9.7). Table 9.2 describes floor stock transfer between SAP ERP and SAP ME scenarios and the transactions they trigger in SAP ERP.

Action	SAP ERP Transaction	Direction
Transferring component from to production storage location in SAP ERP	IDoc message type INVCON02 (movement type: 311)	SAP ERP to SAP ME
Return of component to central storage location in SAP ME	Reversal transfer posting (movement type: 312)	SAP ME to SAP ERP
Scrapping component in SAP ME	Scrap movement posting (movement type: 551)	SAP ME to SAP ERP
Issuing component to production order in SAP ERP	IDoc message type INVCON02 (movement type: 261)	SAP ERP to SAP ME
Return of component to central storage location in SAP ME	Goods issue of reserved production order component (movement type: 262)	SAP ME to SAP ERP
Scrapping component to a shop order in SAP ME	First goods issue of reserved production order component (movement type: 262) then scrap movement posting (movement type: 551)	SAP ME to SAP ERP

Table 9.2 Transferring Floor Stock Data, Returns, and Scrap

9.3 Storage Location Maintenance

In SAP ME, the *storage location* is where the floor stock is physically stored within the plant. You must manually create the storage location through the Storage Location Maintenance activity, where the STORAGE LOCATION field contains four characters, as in SAP ERP. You can specify the storage location value and description of the storage location in the STORAGE LOCATION and DESCRIPTION fields, respectively. You can also assign multiple work centers to a storage location by adding work centers from the AVAILABLE WORK CENTERS list to the ASSIGNED WORK CENTERS list, as shown in Figure 9.8. Click on SAVE to save the storage locations in SAP ME.

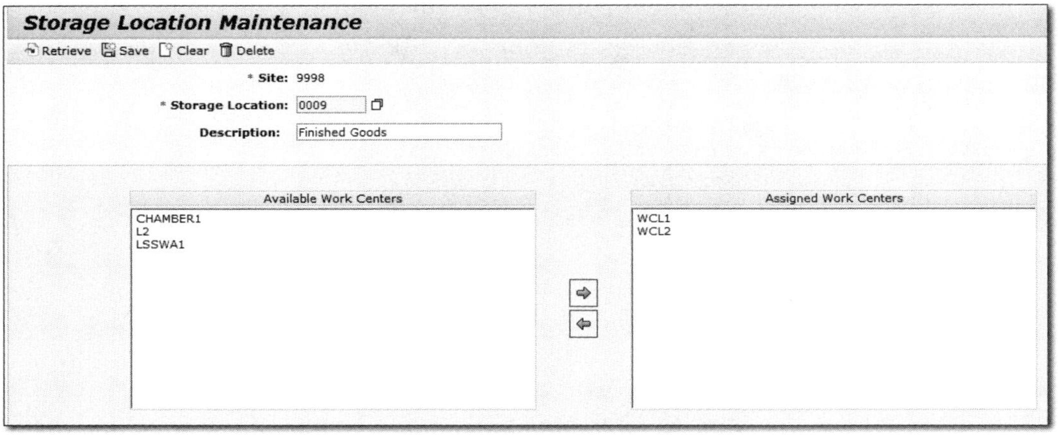

Figure 9.8 Storage Location Maintenance in SAP ME

9.4 Slot Configuration Maintenance

Slot configuration functionality is used for time-based genealogy. It defines which material is loaded in each slot for a time-based resource. In SAP ME, define the slots in the Slot Configuration Maintenance (activity ID: EN040) activity, where you can create a slot configuration number by clicking on the CREATE SLOT CONFIG NUMBER button, as shown in Figure 9.9. SAP ME generates slot configuration numbers based on the pattern defined through the Next Number Maintenance activity for the slot configuration number type. In Slot Configuration Maintenance, the SLOT CONFIG field contains the system-generated number, and you can specify the version in the VERSION field. You can also specify the description in the DESCRIPTION field. The CURRENT VERSION checkbox indicates the version that is active for the slot. Slots can be set to NEW, OBSOLETE, RELEASABLE, FROZEN, and HOLD. You can select one status value from available status list for the STATUS field.

> **Note: Slot Status**
>
> ▶ NEW indicates that slot configuration is new and not ready for production purposes. It also prevents use of that slot configuration when setting up the resource, but it allows you to change the slot configuration record.
> ▶ RELEASABLE lets you use the slot configuration when setting up a resource.

9.4 Slot Configuration Maintenance

- FROZEN lets you use the slot configuration when setting up resource, but with a frozen status, you should not change the slot configuration.
- OBSOLETE prevents you from using the slot configuration when setting up a resource. It indicates that the slot configuration is no longer used.
- HOLD prevents you from using the slot configuration when setting up a resource due to some issue. When the issue is resolved, you can change the status in the slot configuration record.
- HOLD CONSEC NC, HOLD SPC VIOL, HOLD SPC WARN, and HOLD YIELD RATE statuses are not used for slot configurations.

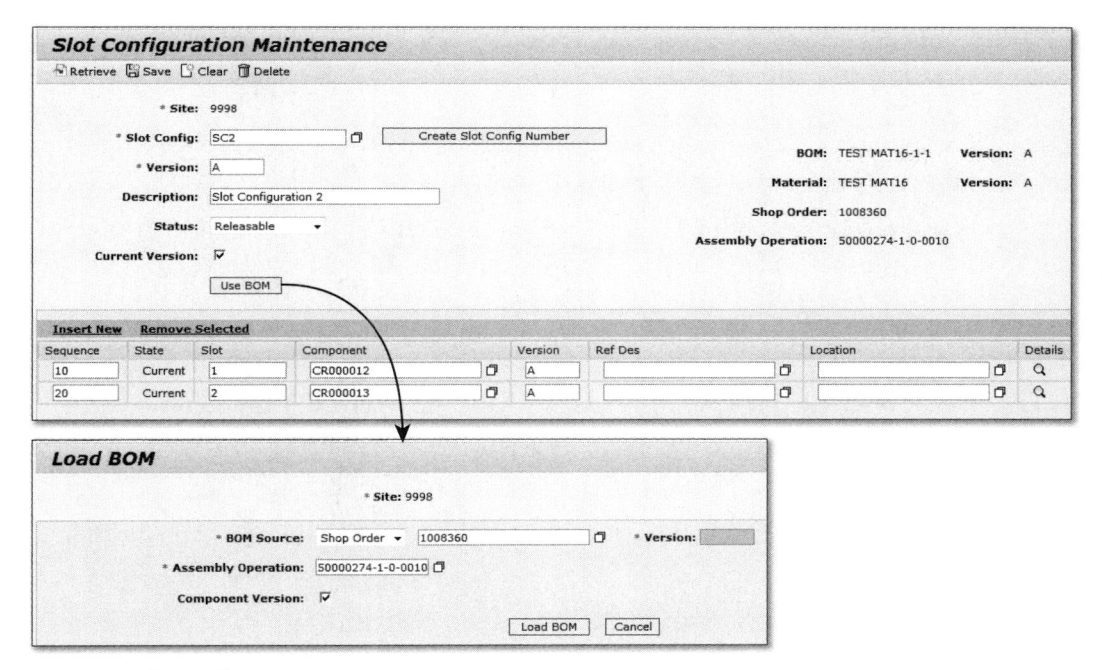

Figure 9.9 Slot Configuration Maintenance in SAP ME

The USE BOM button creates a slot configuration using a BOM. The USE BOM event will open a page called Load BOM, where you can select the BOM source (either MATERIAL or SHOP ORDER) in the BOM SOURCE field, and based on that selection, specify the value in the BROWSE field. In the ASSEMBLY OPERATION field, you can browse for the assembly operation name and specify the operation name. Then, click on LOAD BOM to load the BOM for the slot, and the Load BOM event will return control to the Slot Configuration Maintenance page. On the right-hand side of the top of the Slot Configuration Maintenance page, you can find the BOM, MATERIAL, SHOP ORDER, and ASSEMBLY OPERATION details. At the bottom of the page, you can find the components for the loaded BOMs in a table. Specify the sequence number in the SEQUENCE field for each component in the order in which SAP ME displays the slots.

The STATE column value indicates the state of the each slot, such as NEW (indicates slot is new and not ready for production), CURRENT (indicates slot is the current slot, or this slot matches the BOM for the material), MISSING (indicates slot is missing in Slot Configuration Maintenance, but exists in the BOM), CONFLICT (indicates slot conflicts with the location on a panel associated with the BOM component), and EXCESS (indicates slot exists in Slot Configuration Maintenance, but does not exist in the BOM). The REF DES field indicates the reference designator for where the component is to be placed. Refer back to Chapter 3 for more details about the reference designator. The LOCATION column indicates when on the panel where the component is to be placed.

Clicking on the DETAILS icon of each row of the table will open the Slot Quantity Details page, where you can specify MINIMUM SLOT QTY THRESHOLD, MINIMUM SLOT QTY THRESHOLD MESSAGE TYPE, and ZERO QTY REMAINING MESSAGE TYPE. In the MINIMUM SLOT QTY THRESHOLD field, specify the minimum slot quantity threshold for the selected slot; in the MINIMUM SLOT QTY THRESHOLD MESSAGE TYPE field, specify a message that SAP ME sends when the minimum slot threshold value for the component on the slot is reached; and in the ZERO QTY REMAINING MESSAGE TYPE field, specify a message for when the slot quantity for the component on the slot becomes zero.

9.5 Resource Slot Configuration Setup

In earlier sections, you learned about the slot configuration functionality in SAP ME for time-based genealogy. In this section, you will discover how a slot configuration is assigned to a resource and how to load or replenish a slot configuration for a resource. You can use the Resource Slot Config Setup (activity code: EN530) activity to associate slot configurations with a resource. In Resource Slot Config Setup, browse for or specify a resource in the RESOURCE field, and click on the RETRIEVE button to see the current state of the resource. In the SLOT CONFIG field, browse for a slot, then click on either the PROPOSE button or the VERIFY AND PROPOSE button. SAP ME will load the slot configuration data in a table with SLOT

CONFIG/VERSION, STATE, ASSY DATA, MATERIAL/VERSION, SHOP ORDER, BOM/VERSION, and ASSEMBLY OPERATION columns, as shown in Figure 9.10.

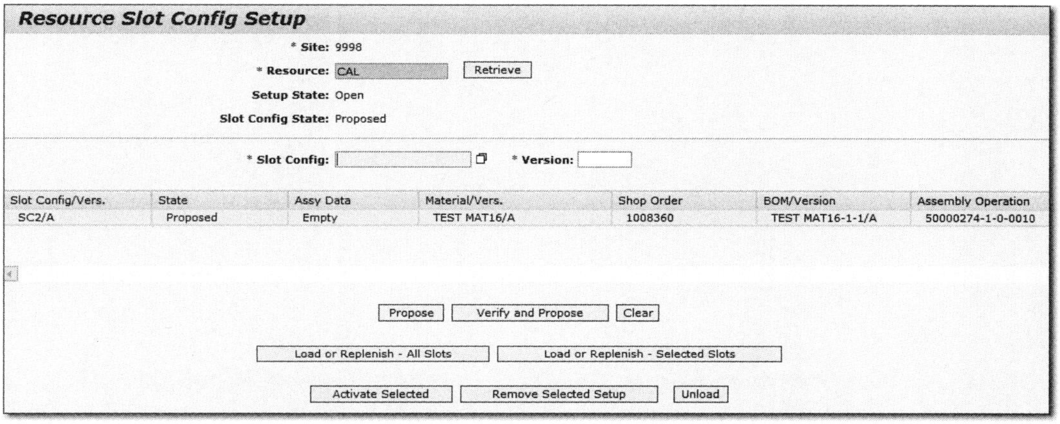

Figure 9.10 Resource Slot Configuration Setup Activity in SAP ME

The different events on the Resource Slot Config Setup page are as follows:

- PROPOSE
  Use PROPOSE to assign a slot configuration (browsed for in the SLOT CONFIG field) to a resource; BOM verification is not performed here. The slot configuration status should be Releasable.

- VERIFY AND PROPOSE
  Use VERIFY AND PROPOSE to assign a slot configuration (browsed for in the SLOT CONFIG field) to a resource with BOM verification. The slot configuration status should be Releasable.

- LOAD OR REPLENISH — ALL SLOTS
  When you click on LOAD OR REPLENISH — ALL SLOTS, it will open the Load or Replenish page to load assembly data for all slots. You can click on the ADD button to load the assembly data. The status of each table row will change to Loaded.

- LOAD OR REPLENISH — SELECTED SLOTS
  If you select a slot in Resource Slot Config Setup and click on the LOAD OR REPLENISH — SELECTED SLOTS button, the LOAD OR REPLENISH page will open to load assembly data for the selected slot, as shown in Figure 9.11. Click on ADD to load the assembly data. The status of each table row will change to Loaded.

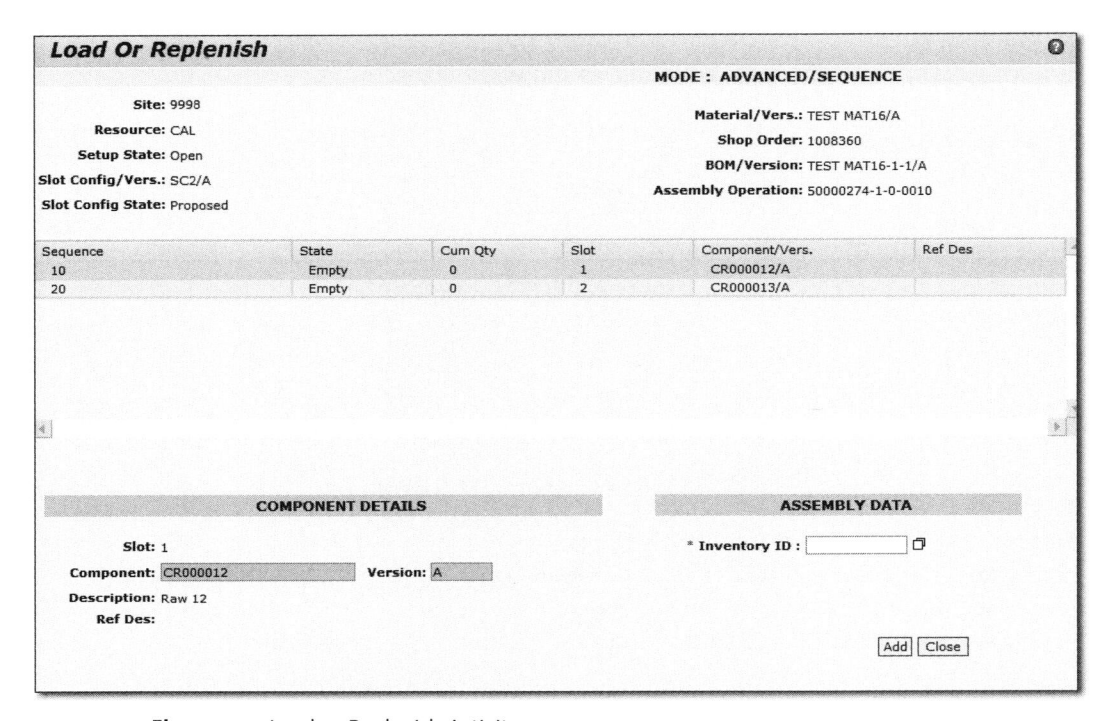

Figure 9.11 Load or Replenish Activity

- ACTIVATED SELECTED
  The ACTIVATED SELECTED event activates a slot configuration; after activation, the slot configuration and resource statuses both update from Proposed to Set Up.

- REMOVE SELECTED SETUP
  To remove a slot configuration from a resource, click on the REMOVE SELECTED SETUP button in Resource Slot Config Setup.

- UNLOAD
  If you want to unload the slot configurations currently loaded for a resource, click on the UNLOAD button in Resource Slot Config Setup. To unload a slot configuration from a resource, it must be in the Set Up state. A confirmation message is displayed upon this action, because all the assembly data loaded for each slot will be unloaded.

The Resource Slot Config Setup activity contains multiple rules and corresponding settings, but you can open the activity using SAP ME Activity Maintenance to change the settings per your requirements. Figure 9.12 shows the available rules and settings for the Resource Slot Config Setup activity.

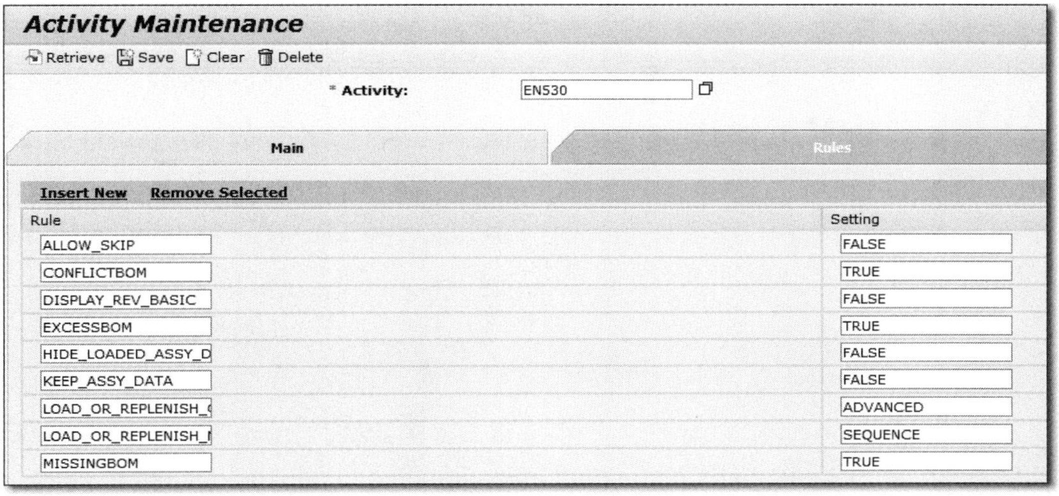
Activity Maintenance
Retrieve
Save
Clear
Delete
* Activity:
EN530
Main
Rules
Insert New
Remove Selected
Rule
Setting
ALLOW_SKIP
FALSE
CONFLICTBOM
TRUE
DISPLAY_REV_BASIC
FALSE
EXCESSBOM
TRUE
HIDE_LOADED_ASSY_D
FALSE
KEEP_ASSY_DATA
FALSE
LOAD_OR_REPLENISH_
ADVANCED
LOAD_OR_REPLENISH_
SEQUENCE
MISSINGBOM
TRUE

Figure 9.12 Rule Setup for Resource Slot Configuration Activity

9.6 Resource Setup

In SAP ME, use the Resource Setup (activity code: EN510) activity to set up the state of a time-based resource and to configure a material, shop order, or tool that will be loaded for the resource. When the material, shop order, or tool is loaded for the resource at the start of the SFC, SAP ME verifies that it matches this setup

In the Resource Setup activity, specify the resource in the RESOURCE field and click on the RETRIEVE button, which will display the current setup state of the resource. The SETUP STATE field can be set to BREAKING DOWN, NOT SET UP, OPEN, SETTING UP, or SET UP. Use the INSERT NEW link to add a row in the table to configure SETUP TYPE and SETUP TYPE VALUE. Select MATERIAL, SHOP ORDER, or TOOL NUMBER for SETUP TYPE, and provide a value in the SETUP TYPE VALUE field for the corresponding type selection. Click on SAVE to save the configuration. Figure 9.13 shows the resource setup for a time-based resource.

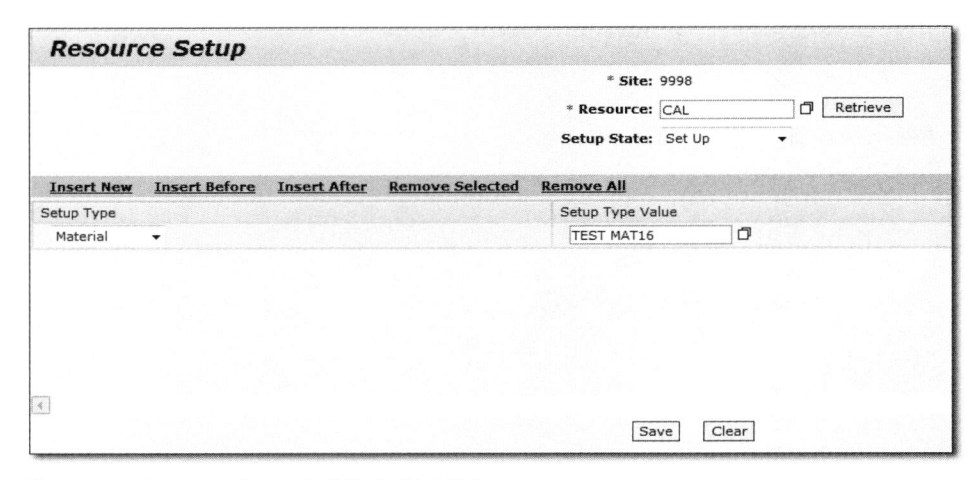

Figure 9.13 Resource Setup Activity in SAP ME

9.7 As-Built Configuration

If you need to add, remove, or replace a component during product assembly, use the As-Built Configuration activity. SAP ME provides the Standalone As-Built Plug-In (activity code: CT511) and As-Built Configuration activities to perform as-built configuration. The As-Built Configuration activity is used within the POD, and the Standalone As-Built Plug-In activity is used as a standalone activity available within the SAP ME activity menu list. Now, let's discuss the available functionalities within the As-Built Configuration activity.

In the As-Built Configuration activity, you can retrieve the as-built configuration records. To perform a search, select a value for the COMPONENT STATE dropdown. The possible values are as follows:

- ALL
  Used retrieve components with any state.

- ASSEMBLED
  Used to retrieve components that are already assembled in an SFC.

- ASSEMBLED AND UNASSEMBLED
  Used to retrieve both components already assembled in an SFC and those that are not assembled in an SFC but are available in a BOM.

▶ AUTO ASSEMBLED
Used to retrieve components that are already assembled in an SFC but that do not contain any assembly data type (i.e., in the Material Maintenance activity, the DATA TO COLLECT ON ASSEMBLY field is set to NONE).

▶ REMOVED
Used to retrieve components that have been removed from an SFC.

▶ UNASSEMBLED
Used to retrieve components of a BOM that have not been used in the assembly of an SFC.

In the SFC field, specify the SFC for which you want to retrieve the as-built component records, and in the FIND COMPONENT field, specify the component name, inventory ID, or SFC. Click on RETRIEVE to see the detailed records of as-built components in an expandable tree structure. At the top-right side of the page, you can find the material (with version), description, routing (with version), BOM (with version), and status details of an SFC, as shown in Figure 9.14. In the expandable tree structure, you can find the BOM component, operation, required quantity, assembled quantity, reference designator, assembly sequence, and component type, and under each BOM component you can find the actual component assembled and its assembly type (auto, manual, time-based, or alternate).

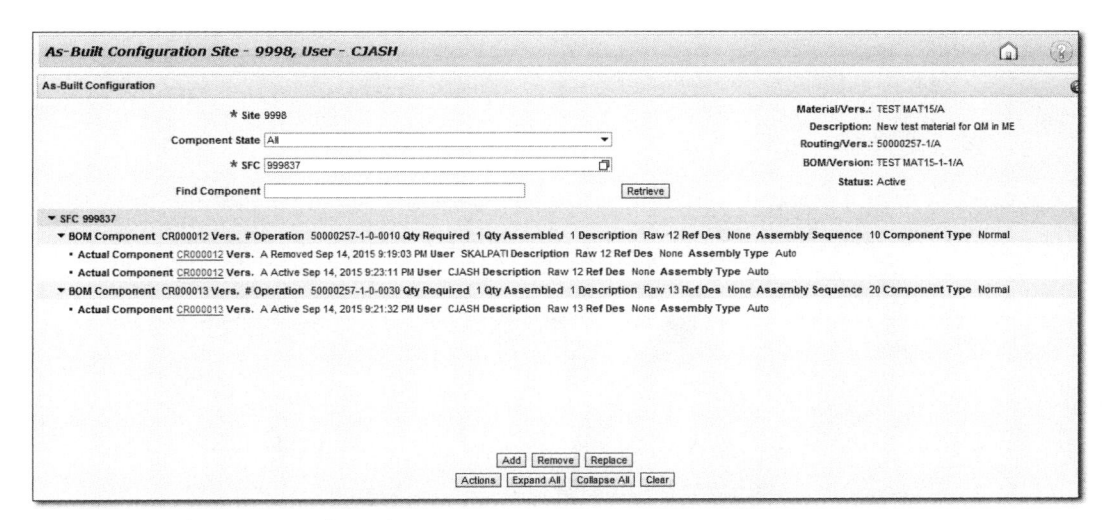

Figure 9.14 Performing As-Built Configuration Activity

9 | Product Genealogy and Tracking

The As-Built Configuration activity lists the following actions, which you can perform per your requirements during product assembly:

▶ ADD
If you want to add a BOM component to an SFC during assembly, select a BOM component from As-Built Configuration and click on ADD. The ADD event will open the ADD COMPONENT popup, which will display the BOM component details selected from As-Built Configuration. Specify operation, resource, and assembly data in the ADD ASSEMBLY DETAILS section, and click on ADD in the ADD COMPONENT pop-up. The BOM component will be added to the SFC, and the added component data will be displayed as an ACTUAL COMPONENT under BOM COMPONENT in As-Built Configuration, as shown in Figure 9.15.

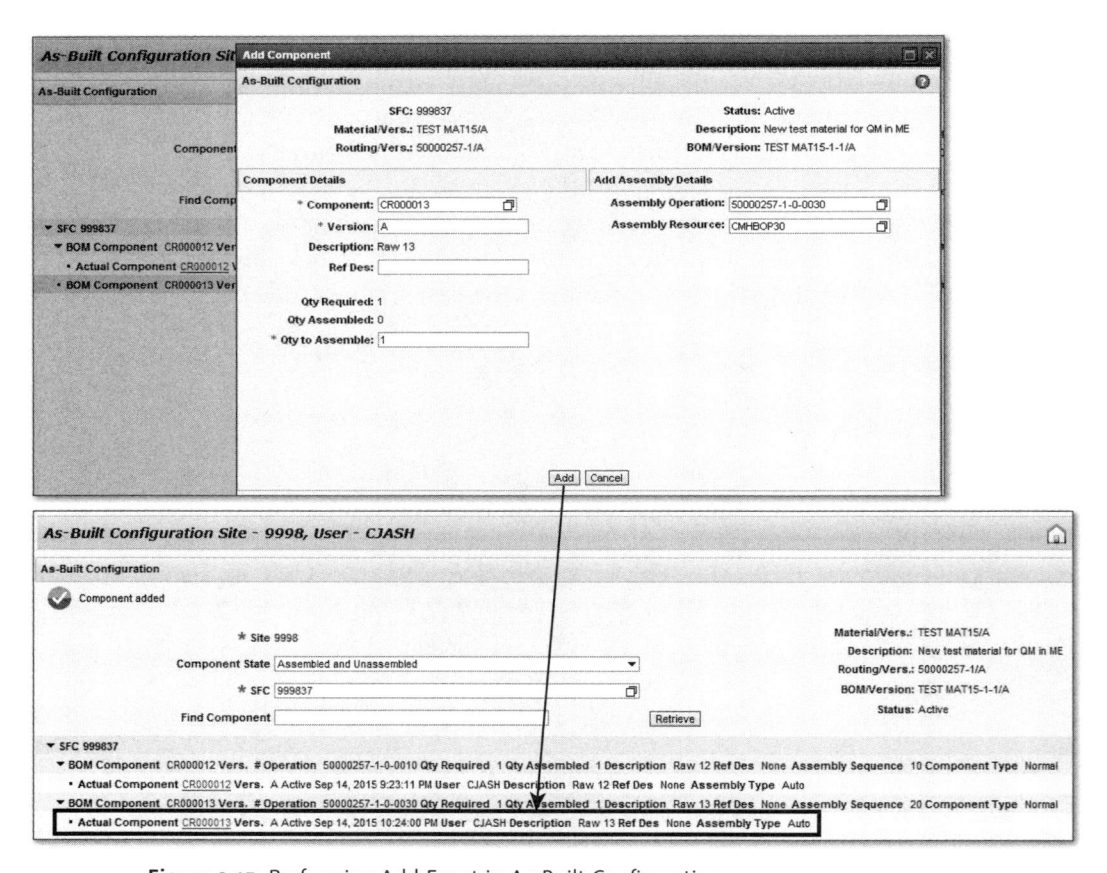

Figure 9.15 Performing Add Event in As-Built Configuration

As-Built Configuration | **9.7**

▶ REMOVE

If you want to remove a component that is assembled in an SFC, select the assembled component in As-Built Configuration and click on REMOVE. The REMOVE event will open a REMOVE COMPONENT pop-up, which will display the component selected from As-Built Configuration. In the REMOVE ASSEMBLY DETAILS section, the QTY TO REMOVE field is mandatory, and you can also specify the remove operation (the operation during which the actual component is removed) and remove resource (the resource at which the actual component is removed) in the REMOVE OPERATION and REMOVE RESOURCE fields, respectively (see Figure 9.16). Four options are available in the REMOVE COMPONENT pop-up: Scrap the component using the SCRAP button, return the component to floor stock (applicable for a component with an inventory ID or SFC) using the RETURN button, send the component to another destination (special or NC routing; also applicable for a component with an Inventory ID or SFC) using the SEND TO ROUTING button, or use the CANCEL button to cancel the REMOVE action.

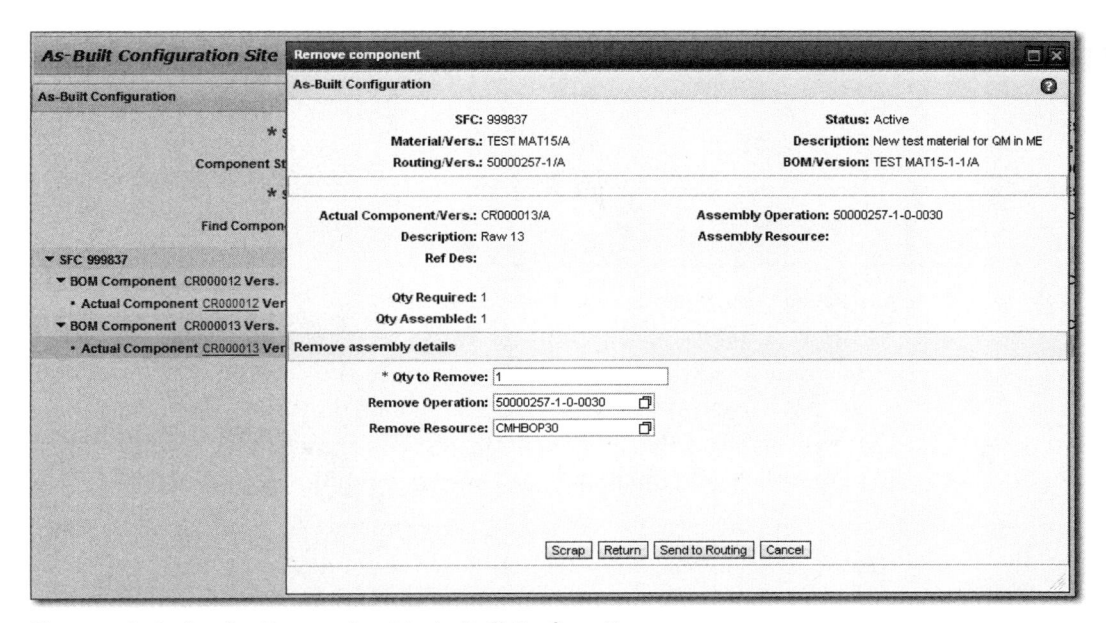

Figure 9.16 Performing Remove Event in As-Built Configuration

- REPLACE

  If you want to replace an assembled component with another componen, select the assembled component in As-Built Configuration and click on REPLACE. The REPLACE event will first open a REMOVE COMPONENT pop-up in which you can remove the component as described for the REMOVE event, then another page will be automatically displayed to add a component, as described for the ADD event.

- ACTIONS

  The ACTIONS button expands to provide ADD NON-BOM COMPONENT, REMOVE ALL ASSEMBLED COMPONENTS, and SHOW SUBASSEMBLY SFC options in a menu list, as shown in Figure 9.17. You would use each option under the following circumstances:

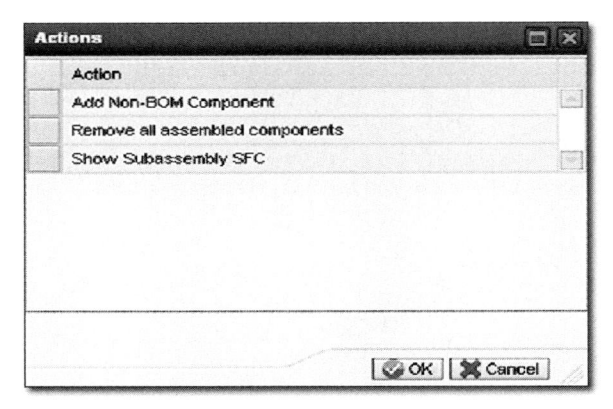

Figure 9.17 Action Event Menu List in As-Built Configuration

- If you want to add a non-BOM component to the current SFC, select ADD NON-BOM COMPONENT and click on OK to open the Add Component screen, where you can specify component details with the assembly quantity; then, click on ADD to add the non-BOM component to the current SFC.

- If you want to remove all assembled components from an SFC, select REMOVE ALL ASSEMBLED COMPONENTS and click on OK.

- If the selected component is another SFC, then clicking on SHOW SUBASSEMBLY SFC will open a new As-Built Configuration activity page where you can click on:

- EXPAND ALL

  If you want to expand all component trees in As-Built Configuration, then click on EXPAND ALL.

- COLLAPSE ALL

  If you want to collapse all component trees in As-Built Configuration, then click on COLLAPSE ALL.

You should now understand the actions that can be performed in As-Built Configuration. Next, you'll learn about the required rule settings for the As-Built Configuration activity, which you can configure using Activity Maintenance in SAP ME. Table 9.3 lists the required rule settings for the As-Built Configuration activity. The activity rules value for activity code CT510 are used by both activity code CT510 and CT511.

Rule	Settings
ALLOW_DONE_SFC	If TRUE, SAP ME allows you to modify the SFCs with Done status.
ALLOW_NEW_SFC	If TRUE, SAP ME allows you to modify the SFCs with New status.
ALLOW_REMOVE_ALL	If TRUE, SAP ME displays the REMOVE ALL ASSEMBLED COMPONENTS action on the ACTIONS button event.
ALLOW_RETURN_COMPONENT	If TRUE, SAP ME displays the RETURN button on the Remove Component page for the REMOVE AND REPLACE event.
ALLOW_SCRAP_COMPONENT	If TRUE, SAP ME displays the SCRAP button when removing or replacing components.
ALLOW_SEND_TO_ROUTER	If TRUE, SAP ME displays the SEND TO ROUTING button to send a component to another routing when removing or replacing components.
COMPONENT_FILTER_REQUIRED	If TRUE, you must enter a value in the FILTER BY COMPONENT field before retrieving component records. When using the filter component option, the component value in this field will result in the display of only those component records that match the value.

Table 9.3 Rule Settings for As-Built Configuration Activity

Rule	Settings
DISPLAY_BARCODE	If TRUE, SAP ME displays the BARCODE field on the Add, Remove, or Replace page.
EXPAND_DATA_UPON_RETRIEVE	If TRUE, SAP ME displays the assembly component (BOM component and actual component) tree with expanded view when you retrieve as-built records.
PLUGIN_URL	Contains the plug-in URL for As-Built Configuration; the specified URL is /COM/SAP/ME/PRODUCTION/CLIENT/ASBUILTCONFIGURATIONPLUGIN.JSP.
USE_COMPONENT_FILTER	If TRUE, SAP ME displays the FILTER BY COMPONENT field on the As-Built Configuration page.

Table 9.3 Rule Settings for As-Built Configuration Activity (Cont.)

> **Note: As-Built Configuration Tabular activity**
>
> The As-Built Configuration Tabular activity is used to view and update actual components in the assembly of a product in the POD (activity id: CT514) or outside of the POD (activity id: CT515). You can remove one or more components from an assembly, or replace components in the assembly by adding and removing them.

9.8 Genealogy Reports

In this section you can find the standard genealogy reports available in SAP ME such as the As-Built Summary Report, BOM Report, Device History Report, Floor Stock Report, and Resource Setup Report.

9.8.1 As-Built Summary Report

To find the genealogy information of an SFC or list of SFCs for a shop order, use the As-Built Summary Report (activity code: CT700) activity in SAP ME. The As-Built Summary report provides the assembly information of an SFC and also its status, material, routing, current operation, BOM, and shop order. In the As-Built Summary Report activity, you can search by SFC or SHOP ORDER and COMPONENT

State (Assembled and Unassembled or All). The search results are displayed in a tabular format for each SFC. To see the As-Built Summary Report Tree View page, click on the SFC hyperlink from a table row. The As-Built Summary Report Tree View page provides SFC assembly information in a tree structure; click on the Auto Expand Tree button to find the tree structure, as shown in Figure 9.18. Access the report print preview via the Print Preview button on the As-Built Summary Report Tree View page.

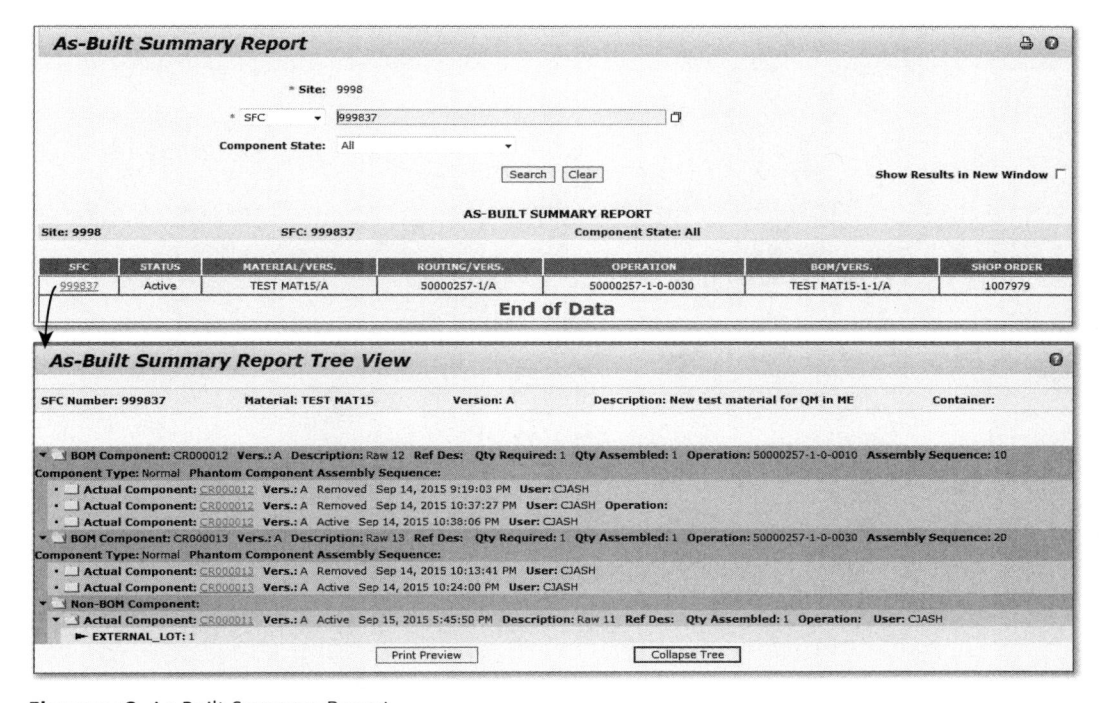

Figure 9.18 As-Built Summary Report

9.8.2 BOM Report

In SAP ME, the BOM Report (activity code: PD100) activity provides the details of all BOM components, including their custom data, assembly operation, required quantities, alternate BOM components, and so on. On the BOM Report page, select Master, Shop Order, or SFC in the BOM Type field. Based on your selection, the screen search fields change. For example, the Master value selection in the BOM TYPE field will change the search criteria to BOM value, SHOP ORDER will change the criteria to shop order number, and SFC will change the criteria to SFC. In the CHOOSE field, select either COMPONENT or REF DES (reference designator). Click RETRIEVE to retrieve the BOM report. The BOM report will be displayed in a tree structure and will provide details of components, alternate components, BOM status assembly data fields, maximum usage as components, max NCs for the BOM components, and so on, as shown in Figure 9.19.

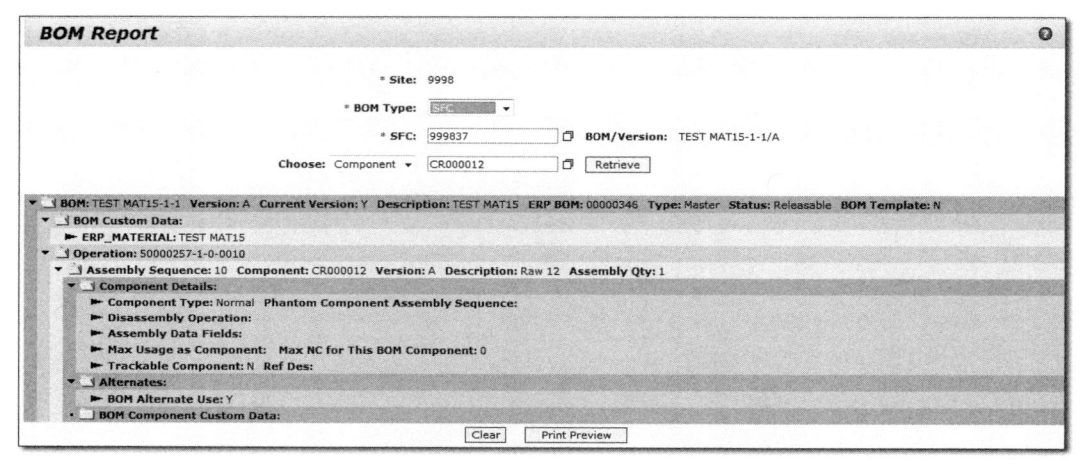

Figure 9.19 BOM Report in SAP ME

9.8.3 Device History Report

If you need to find the history of an SFC in a single view, then use the Device History Report (activity code: PD300) activity in SAP ME. In this activity, you can find the SFC details and activity log in a tree structure. You can expand the tree structure to see the detail-level view. The DETAILS tree structure provides the SFC details, and the ACTIVITY LOG tree structure provides the activities performed on the SFC, as shown in Figure 9.20. From the same DEVICE HISTORY REPORT page, you can access the As-Built Summary report by clicking on the AS-BUILT SUMMARY REPORT button. If the SFC is archived in ODS, then you need to use the ODS As-Built Summary Report (activity code: CT700_ODS) activity.

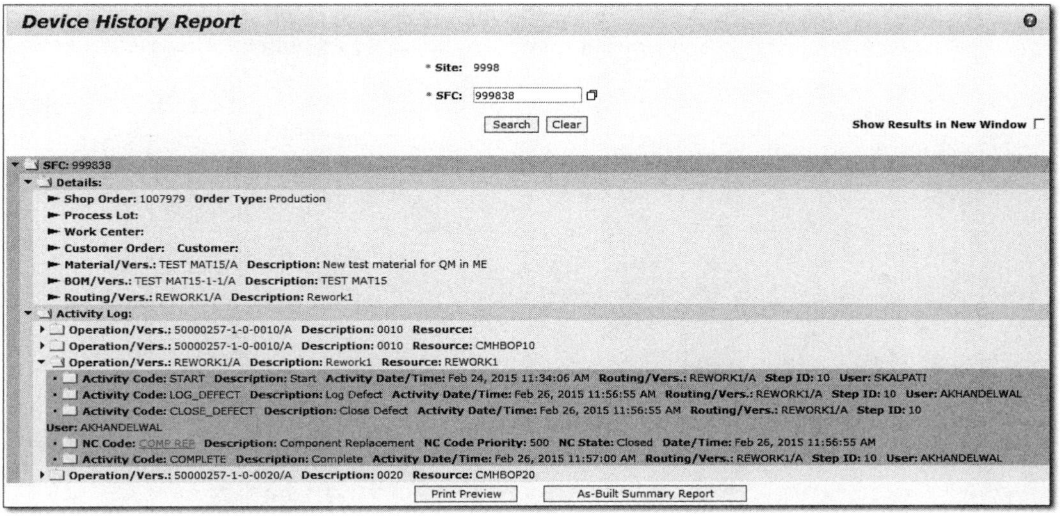

Figure 9.20 Device History Report

9.8.4 Floor Stock Report

Use the SAP ME Floor Stock Report (activity code: IN700) activity to find the quantity of material available as floor stock. Using the Floor Stock Receipt activity, you recorded the receipt of material in stock on the shop floor, and material quantities are consumed for product assembly. In the Floor Stock Report, you can find the details of received quantities and on-hand quantities for the same material along with its inventory ID. From the FLOOR STOCK REPORT page, you can open the Floor Stock Details report and also the Inventory ID Log report. On the Floor Stock Report page, you can search the report using multiple parameters, such as MATERIAL TYPE (INSTALLATION, MANUFACTURED, MANUFACTURED/PURCHASED, PURCHASED, ALL), MATERIAL GROUP, MATERIAL, INVENTORY ID, INVENTORY ID STATUS (ALL, AVAILABLE, HOLD, QUARANTINE), SFC and DATE RANGE, and from the FLOOR STOCK LOCATION tab, you can also specify STORAGE LOCATION, WORK CENTER, OPERATION, RESOURCE, or SHOP ORDER. The search results display the material with version, material type, received quantity, quantity on hand, and information about floor stock detail (as a link) in a tabular format. You can also find the report in a graphical format by clicking on the GRAPHICAL VIEW button. If you click on the FLOOR STOCK DETAIL link, then SAP ME will open Floor Stock Detail Report in a new page, where you can find the list of all inventory IDs with

9 | Product Genealogy and Tracking

status, quantity on hand, and inventory ID log (as a link). By clicking on the Inventory ID Log link for each inventory ID, you can switch to the Inventory ID Log Report page, as shown in Figure 9.21.

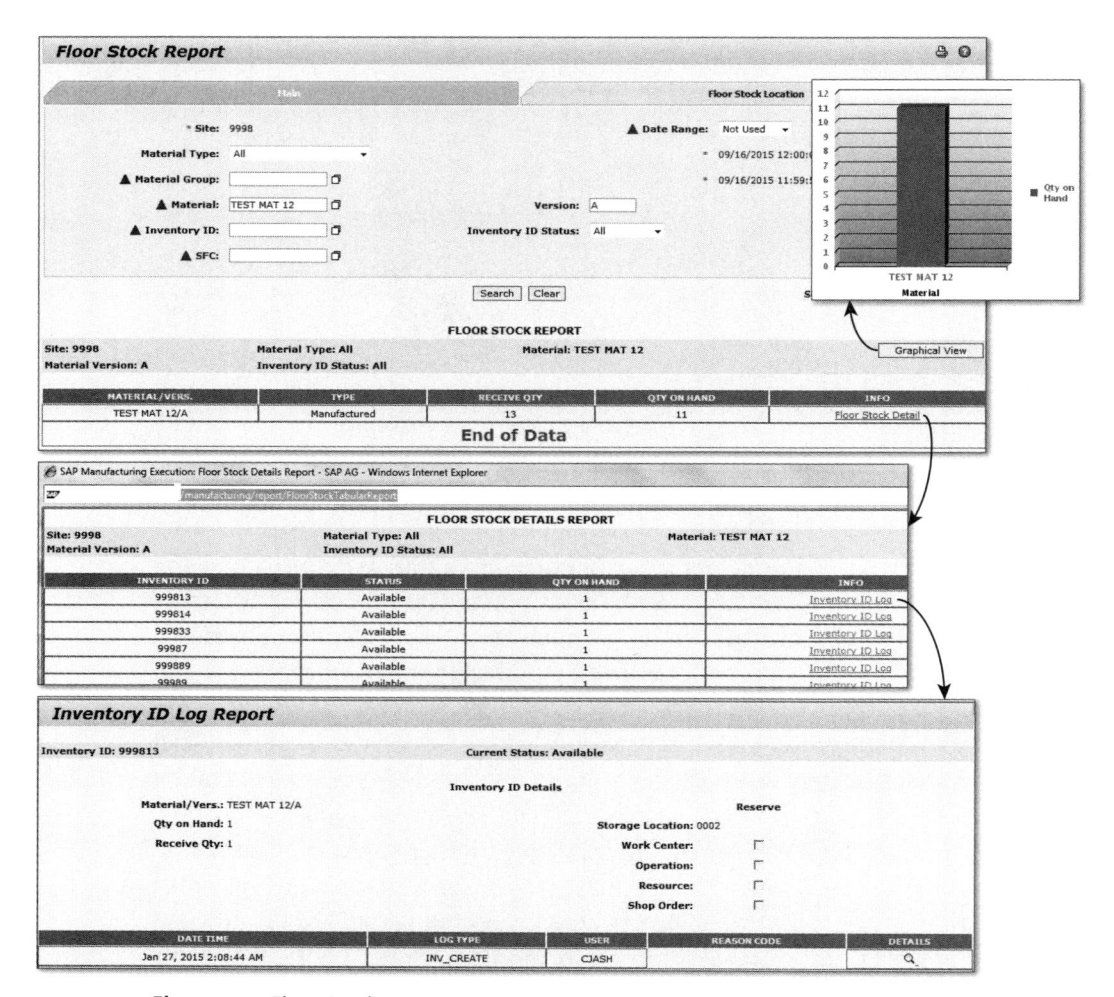

Figure 9.21 Floor Stock Report

9.8.5 Resource Setup Report

If you want to find information about a slot loaded on a resource, use the Resource Setup Report (activity code: CT720) activity in SAP ME. On the Resource Setup Report page, you can specify the resource ID in Resource field and click on

SEARCH. The search event will provide results in a tabular format that includes slots and components loaded on a resource, location information, slot configuration states, and reference designators. In the SLOT column, you can click on a slot (which displays as a link), and the click event will open a new SLOT SETUP DETAIL page which displays resource setup state, slot configuration, slot configuration state, component details, and assembly data details. Figure 9.22 shows the Resource Setup Report details and the slot setup details.

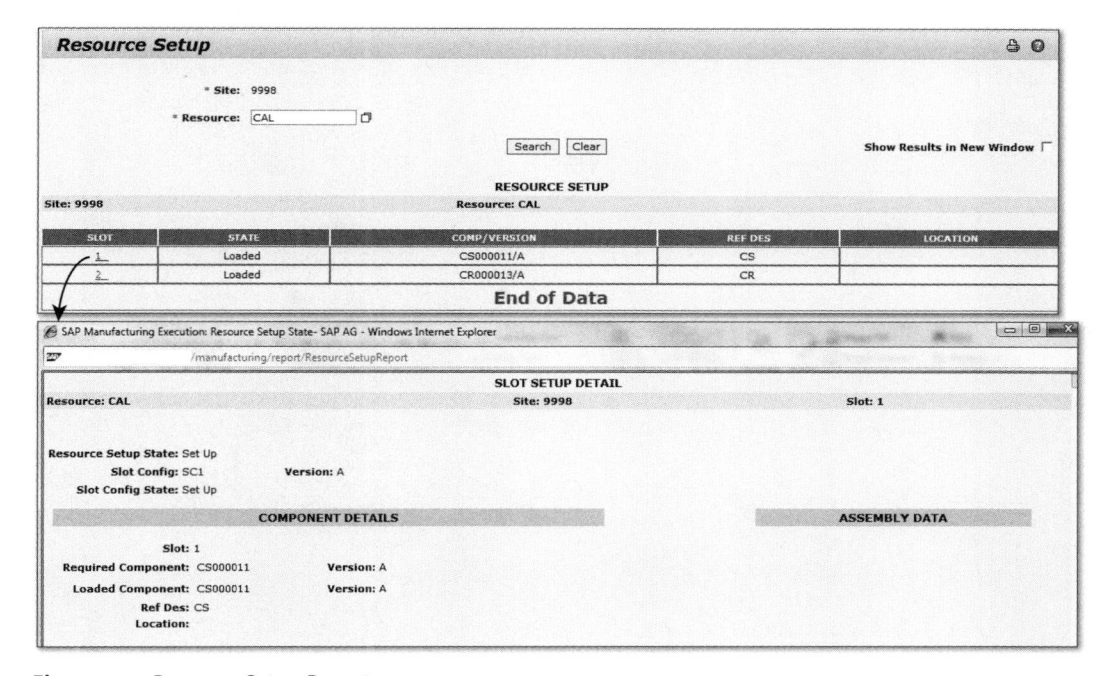

Figure 9.22 Resource Setup Report

9.9 Summary

In this chapter, you learned about discrete and time-based genealogy, the system settings required for both, and when to use each type. You also learned about storage location maintenance, floor stock management in SAP ME using Floor Stock Receipt, rule settings for floor stock receipt, the Floor Stock Maintain activity, and integration of SAP ME with SAP ERP for inventory transfer and floor stock consumption, return, and scrap. This chapter described the required activities for time-based genealogy, such as Slot Configuration Maintenance and Resource Slot Configuration Setup.

You also learned about the As-Built Configuration activity, the different events that you can perform within it, and its required rule settings. We also discussed genealogy reports, such as the As-Built Summary Report, BOM Report, Device History Report, Floor Stock Report, and Resource Setup Report.

In next chapter, you will learn about the Production Operator Dashboard in SAP ME.

This chapter covers the Production Operator Dashboard in SAP ME. It also introduces different types of PODs, details of custom POD design, and execution activities through PODs per business requirements.

10 Production Operator Dashboards

The *Production Operator Dashboard* (POD) is the main user interface for shop floor operators to interact with the SAP ME system during shop floor execution processes. Each step of shop floor execution is recorded in SAP ME by operators through the POD. For example, in a car assembly process, once a shop order is released in SAP ME and all SFCs are placed in queue at the first operation of the routing, the operator working on the first operation can start SFC, perform the required activities, and complete the SFC using the POD through the START and COMPLETE buttons. Then, the same SFC moves to the next operation and is placed in queue at the next operation. Another operator working on next operation can execute the same SFC through start and complete activities using the POD. In the same way, the SFC moves to the last operation of the routing and the shop floor operators perform their tasks (data collection, log NCs, assembly of components, work instruction viewing, etc.), and SAP ME keeps records of all activities performed by operators.

SAP ME provides preconfigured PODs (available as standard activities in SAP ME) that can be used for shop floor execution, or based on your requirements you can copy and modify the PODs. SAP ME also provides the functionality to configure new PODs per shop floor requirement for different data formats and for performing different activities in each individual operations. You will learn about POD configurations in the subsequent sections along with the details of available POD types, list maintenance, POD design, and assigning POD to user groups.

10.1 Types of Available POD

In SAP ME, you can configure different types of PODs using the POD Maintenance activity. In this section, you will learn about the different standard POD types available in SAP ME for operators performing shop floor execution activities.

10.1.1 Operation POD

The operation POD is useful for shop floor execution, where each operator is working on an individual operation of a routing to start and complete the SFC or list of SFCs in queue at that operation. After completion of one operation, the SFC or list of SFCs will move to the next operation per the routing flow. If the resource is configured with operations in Operation Maintenance, then the resource will appear automatically for the selected operation (when you tab out of the selected operation field, then resource is pulled automatically); otherwise, the operator needs to select the resource from the resource list (available resources for the assigned resource type, configured in operation). The main advantage of the operation POD is that the operator can select multiple SFCs (which are in queue at a specific operation) at a time and perform the same activities for all the SFCs. The operation POD also provides the ability to launch other activities such as component assembly, data collection, work instruction viewing, logging NCs, NC trees, and so on.

SAP ME provides a predefined operation POD in which an operator needs to select an operation from the available list, but you can configure the operation POD for each routing operation. In the custom-configured POD, you can set it up so that operators will get specific PODs with predefined operations and resources. Each operator can only select the SFC(s) for that operation and execute that operation. This kind of POD configuration is very useful for discrete industry, where repetitive tasks need to be performed in operations for different SFCs. For example, in a car assembly process, this kind of operation POD will help the operator to minimize the interaction with the SAP ME system, and the operator can use the saved time for car assembling activities. Figure 10.1 shows the standard operation POD provided by SAP ME.

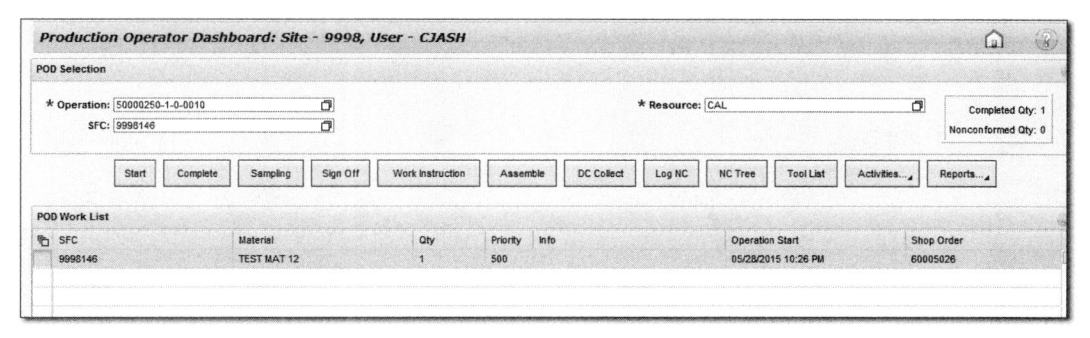

Figure 10.1 Operation POD

SAP ME also provides multiple predefined operation PODs, such as the Operation POD, Integrated POD, Operation Touch POD, and Visual Test and Repair POD. These predefined operation PODs contain different buttons for different activities.

10.1.2 Work Center POD

SAP ME includes another type of POD for complex shop floor assembly processes, called the work center POD. In the work center POD, an operator can search the available SFC list by user, by work center, or by both. The SFC/shop order list appears under the POD WORK LIST area, and by selecting each row an operator can see operation details in the OPERATION LIST area, as shown in Figure 10.2. The work center POD is used when one or more operators are working for a work center for long duration to perform tasks for one or more operations related to the same work center. For example, in heavy engineering assembly processes, more than one operator needs to work on same work center for a long period of time to execute multiple operations.

SAP ME provides a predefined work center POD that can be used for shop floor execution processes, or you can configure your own work center POD by copying the default one (WORK_CENTER_DEF). The default work center POD provides multiple buttons (as plug-ins) perform the shop floor activities, such as data collection, work instruction viewing, component assembly, start and complete operations, tools to be logged, and so on.

Now we can discuss the different type of work center PODs available in SAP ME such as the Supervisor Work Assignment POD, Shop Workbench POD, and Work Center Touch POD.

10 | Production Operator Dashboards

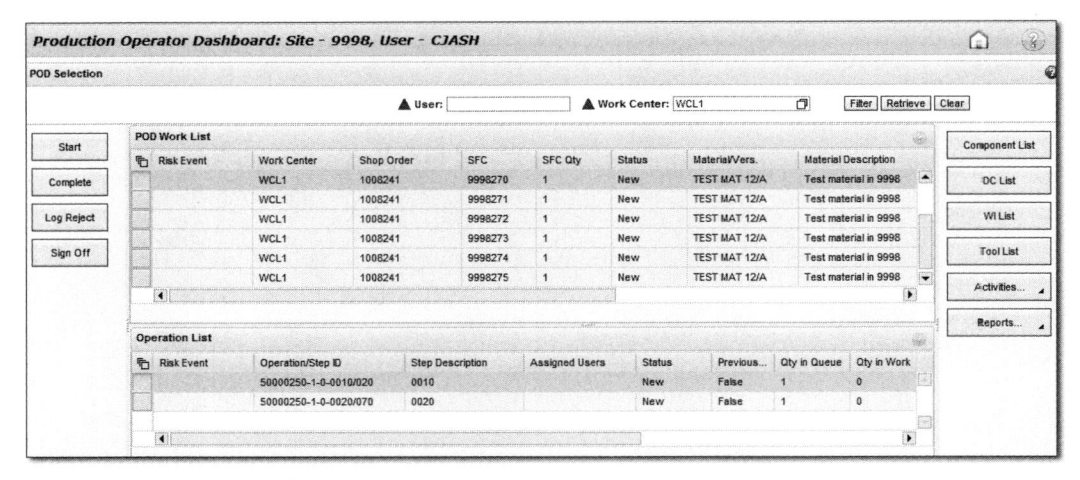

Figure 10.2 Work Center POD

Supervisor Work Assignment POD

The Supervisor Work Assignment POD (`SUPV_WORK_ASSIGN`) is a default predefined work center type of POD provided in SAP ME. Through this POD, a supervisor can assign tasks to one or more users for one or more operations. A supervisor needs to search the work list using the WORK CENTER as input, and the available SFC/shop order list will be displayed in the POD WORK LIST area. Supervisors can select one row from the work list, and associated operation will be displayed in the OPERATION LIST area, as shown in Figure 10.3.

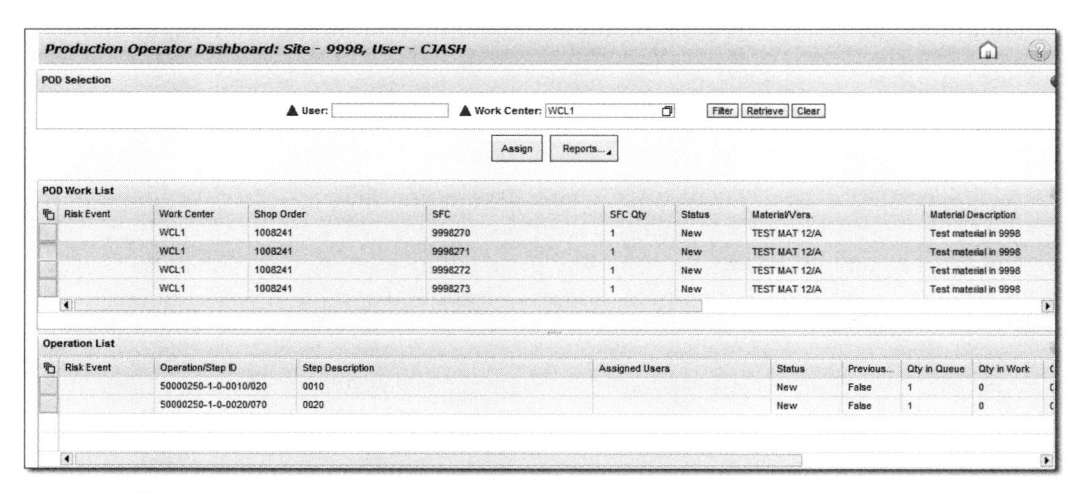

Figure 10.3 Supervisor Work Assignment POD

A supervisor can also select one or more operations from the operation list and assign users for one or more operations through the ASSIGN button. The ASSIGN button opens a pop-up where the supervisor can assign one or more users from the available user list, as shown in Figure 10.4. The user assigned to the specific task can search for the assigned task in the Work Center POD by providing USER as input. The Supervisor Work Assignment POD also provides multiple reports as plug-ins, such as the Activity Log Report, Buyoff Report, Hold Report, NC Log Report, SFC Report, and so on.

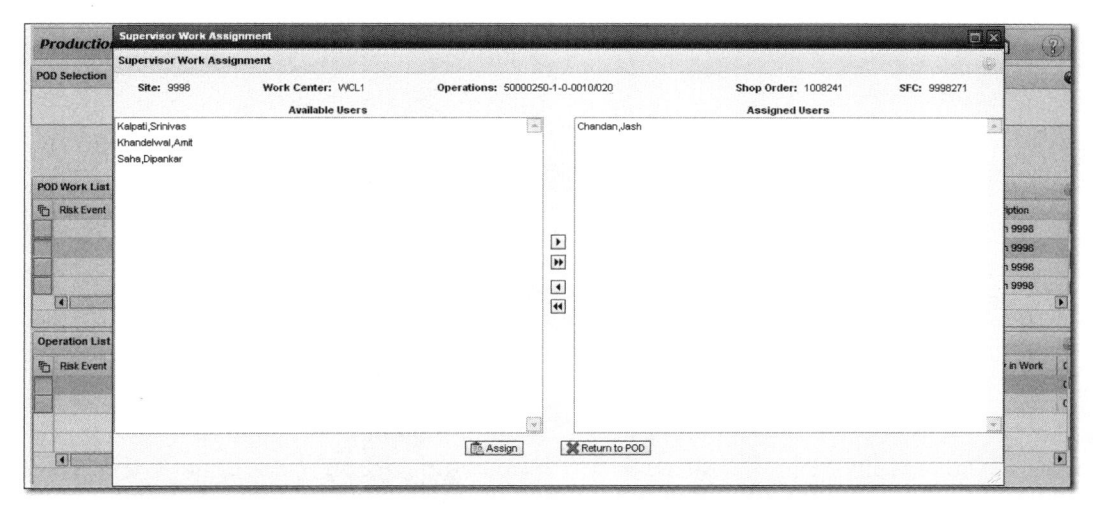

Figure 10.4 Assigning Users to Operations through Supervisor Work Assignment POD

Shop Workbench POD

The Shop Workbench POD (SHOP_WORKBENCH_DEF) is another default, predefined work center type of POD provided by SAP ME. This POD can be used by a production supervisor or shop floor quality inspector or production engineer for quick tracking of shop floor execution processes. The Shop Workbench POD can be used to quickly check the current information of an SFC within a tree-like structure, and it also provides reports related to shop floor production, such as work instruction viewing, data collection, NC log reports, component assembly, and so on. Figure 10.5 shows the predefined Shop Workbench POD used for checking the current SFC information.

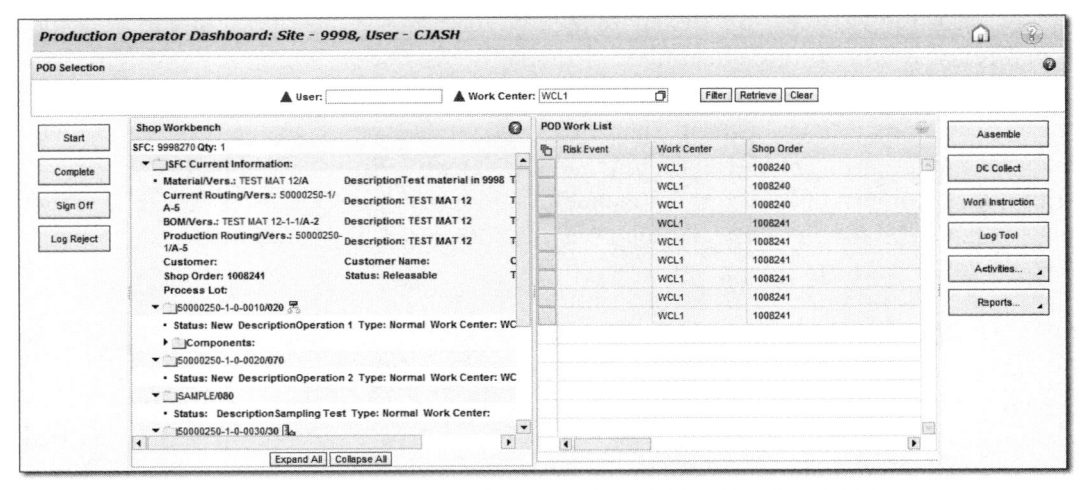

Figure 10.5 Tracking Current SFC Information through Shop Workbench POD

Work Center Touch POD

The Work Center Touch POD (WORK_CENTER_TOUCH) is also a default, predefined Work Center type of POD provided by SAP ME, but it is mainly used for touch-screen devices. Like with the Work Center POD, operators can search the available SFC list by user, work center, or by using both. Available SFCs will appear under the POD WORK LIST area. An operator can access the same functionality from here as in the default Work Center POD. Figure 10.6 shows the default Work Center Touch POD in SAP ME.

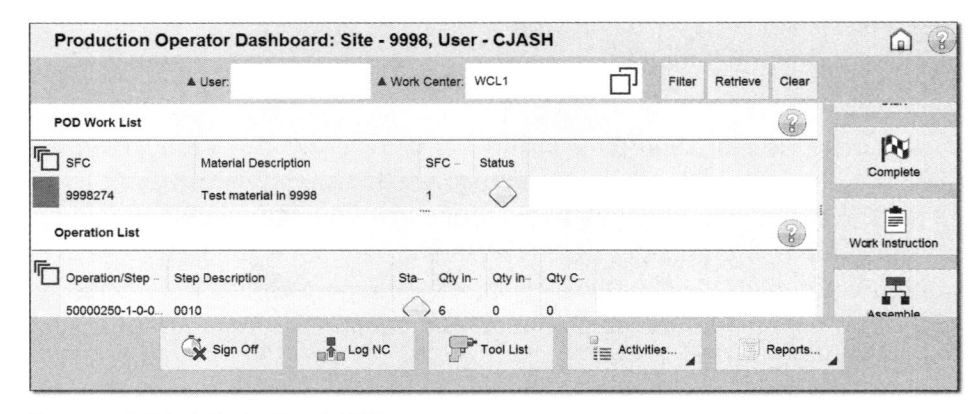

Figure 10.6 Work Center Touch POD

10.1.3 Mobile POD

In recent times, use of mobile devices in shop floor manufacturing has grown. SAP ME now provides a predefined, default Mobile POD (MOBILE_DEVICE). This POD is developed on SAPUI5 technology and can be accessed through a desktop, an Android or iOS tablet, or smartphone devices.

To check the configuration of the default Mobile POD, open the POD Maintenance activity in SAP ME and select MOBILE for TYPE and MOBILE_DEVICE for POD . Then, click on RETRIEVE to display the configuration details of the default Mobile POD, as shown in Figure 10.7.

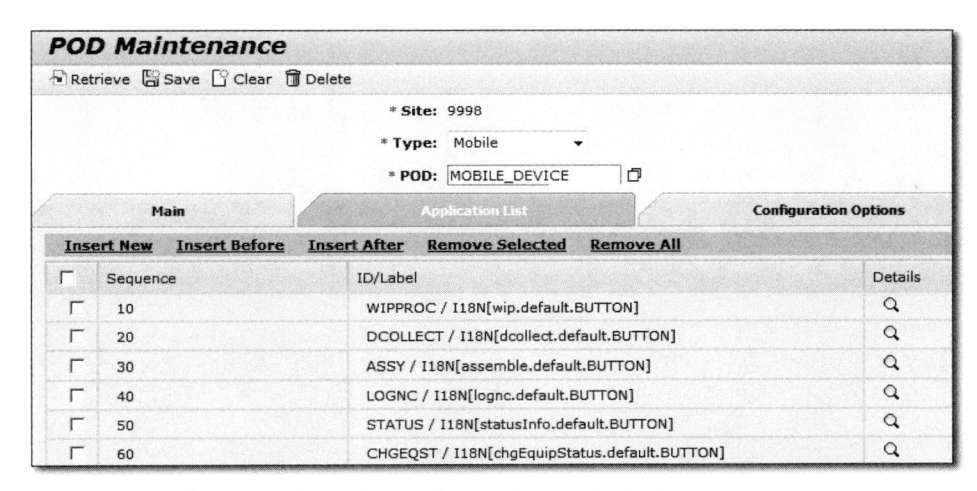

Figure 10.7 Configuration of Default Mobile POD through POD Maintenance

The default Mobile POD contains lists of activities that you can find within the activity list through Activity Maintenance in SAP ME, as shown in Figure 10.8.

Figure 10.8 Activity List Used in Default Mobile POD

You can access the default Mobile POD through the following URL:

http://<Host>:<Port>/manufacturing-mobile/index.jsp?&SITE=<SAP ME Site>& WORKSTATION=MOBILE_DEVICE&sap-ui-theme= sap_bluecrystal

Here, *Host* and *Port* refer to the hostname and port of the SAP ME server.

Figure 10.9 shows the default Mobile POD using the *sap_bluecrystal* theme.

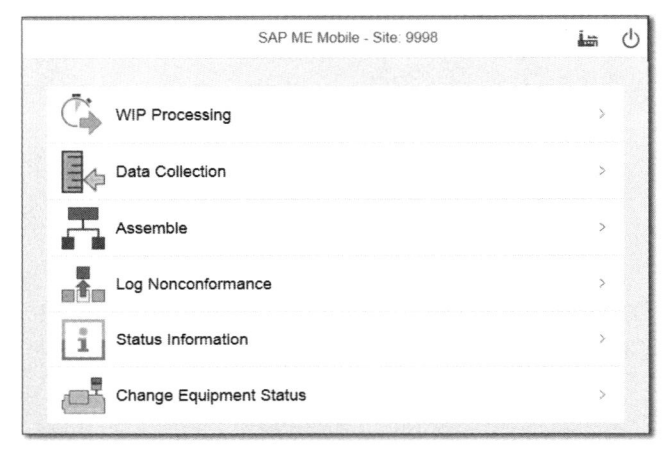

Figure 10.9 Default Mobile POD

10.1.4 Message Board

SAP ME provides another type of POD called the *Message Board*. A predefined default Message Board POD (MESSAGE_BOARD) comes preinstalled with SAP ME. The Message Board POD is used in shop floor manufacturing to search, create, and process real-time manufacturing messages. During the shop floor manufacturing process, SAP ME can generate messages to inform shop floor users that a particular condition has not occurred and requires some action or attention. You will find Message Board setup and execution functionality details in Chapter 11.

10.1.5 Visual Test and Repair POD

Visual Test and Repair (VTR) functionality is used to record defects in the shop floor manufacturing process through NC codes when inspection or repair is performed in an operation for an SFC. The VTR POD allows the operator to view the manufacturing products graphically, and it helps an operator to log appropriate NC codes with correct data for defects. In the graphical model, each model element is associated with an NC code, which helps the operator find the correct NC code for the defective part of the displayed model element, and it also helps to analyze the failure. In the VTR POD, the operator needs to select an operation, resource, and an SFC, then needs to click on MODEL VIEWER to display the graphical model associated with the manufacturing material. When an operator selects a model element from the graphical model, the corresponding NC code for that model element is populated in the NC Data Entry plug-in. Logged NC codes are available in NC Tree plug-in, and by selecting the logged NC code the operator can find the associated model element in the graphical model.

The VTR Model Viewer uses the SAP Visual Enterprise Viewer, which must be installed on the client machine to display the graphical model through the VTR POD. When the operator clicks on MODEL VIEWER in the VTR POD, the Visual Test and Repair plug-in, NC Selection plug-in, and NC Data Entry plug-in open together to enable easy NC logging through the graphical view of the model. From the NC Tree plug-in, an operator can view the logged NC code and perform analysis and repair. The graphical models are actually the input files, which can be stored in a shared folder of same system or web server. The input files can be ECAD models or 3-D models. In System Rule Maintenance, specify the path in the VTR MODEL LOCATION field. SAP ME provides a default Visual Test and Repair (VISUAL_TEST_REPAIR_DEF) POD, which can be used directly on the shop floor (as shown in Figure 10.10), or you can change the configuration per your requirements.

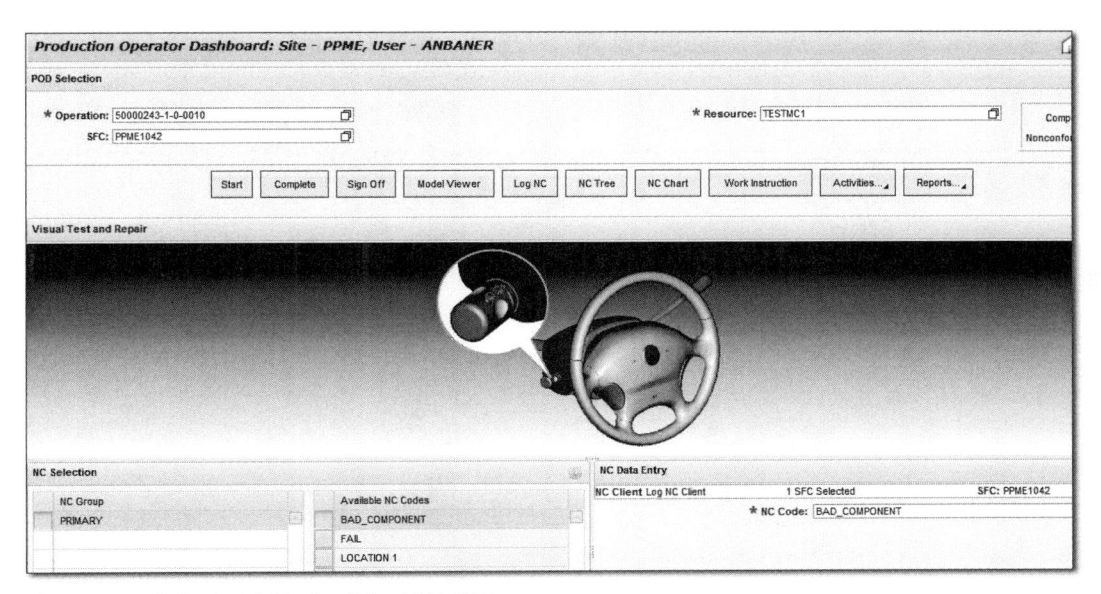

Figure 10.10 3-D Model Display Using VTR POD

The required setup steps for the VTR POD are as follows:

- **Material Maintenance**
  In the Material Maintenance activity, specify file name in the DRAWING NAME field. The file is the graphical model that will be displayed when the operator clicks on MODEL VIEWER from the VTR POD.

- **System Setup**
  In the System Setup activity, configure the `vtr.viewer.me.fields` and `vtr.viewer.vendor.fields` properties. The `vtr.viewer.me.fields` property specifies the ME data fields to which the metadata fields of the model will be mapped. The `vtr.viewer.vendor.fields` property specifies the model metadata fields which can be mapped to ME data fields.

- **Data Field Definition Maintenance**
  The data fields specified in the `vtr.viewer.me.fields` property should be maintained through the Data Field Maintenance activity. SAP ME provides two predefined data fields for VTR—`REF_DES` and `COMPONENT`—which are used in the `vtr.viewer.me.fields` property. You can also define new data fields per your requirements.

- **Data Field Assignment Maintenance**
  To use the data fields in VTR, you need to assign them to an NC data type through the Data Field Assignment Maintenance activity. The `REF_DES` and `COMPONENT` data fields are already assigned with the NC category `COMPONENT` type in SAP ME, as shown in Figure 10.11. Refer back to Chapter 3 for more details about the Data Field Maintenance and Data Field Assignment Maintenance activities.

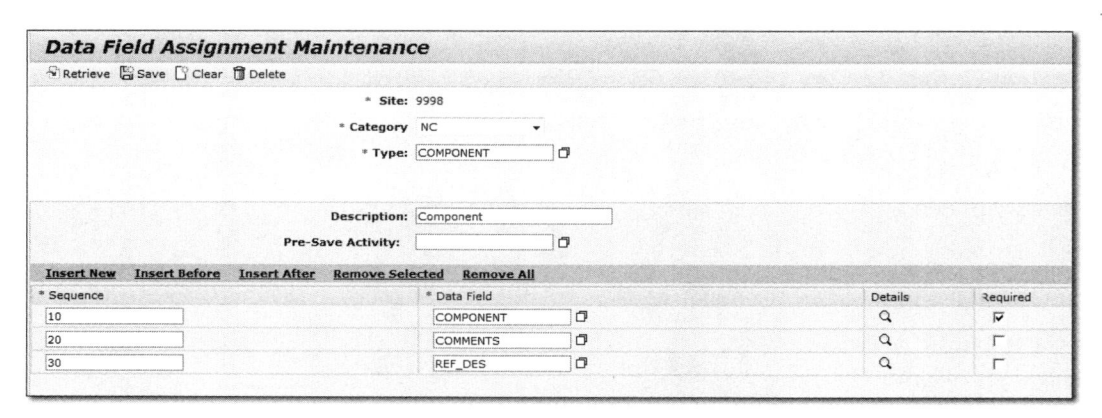

Figure 10.11 Data Field Assignment Maintenance for NC Category

▶ **NC Code Maintenance**
Required NC codes can be defined through NC Code Maintenance, and each NC code must be defined with an SAP ME data type. Refer back to Chapter 8 for more information about the NC Code Maintenance activity.

▶ **NC Client Maintenance**
In the NC Client Maintenance activity, you can find the VTR MODEL LOCATION field, which is used by the VTR Model Viewer. You learned that we need to specify the VTR MODEL LOCATION value in System Rule Maintenance to identify from where the VTR Model viewer will read the file. However, the value can be overridden if you specify a different location in the VTR MODEL LOCATION field of NC Client Maintenance, and the same NC client will be used by VTR, which is configured in POD Maintenance for `VISUAL_TEST_REPAIR_DEF POD`.

▶ **POD Maintenance**
SAP ME provides a default, predefined `VISUAL_TEST_REPAIR_DEF` operation type of POD. In POD Maintenance, retrieve `VISUAL_TEST_REPAIR_DEF` and change the configuration per your requirements.

10.2 List Maintenance

In SAP ME, the List Maintenance activity is used to change the existing list or to define a new list used in PODs. Through List Maintenance, you can define the row sort order and the order sequence of columns that will appear in PODs during the execution process for a particular plug-in. For example, for a data collection plug-in, you can define the order of the columns that will appear when an operator performs a data collection activity on the shop floor. Figure 10.12 shows List Maintenance for data collection.

In the List Maintenance activity, the CATEGORY dropdown provides the predefined categories used in PODs. CATEGORY contains a list of categories, such as ASSEMBLE, DC_COLLECT, DC_ENTRY, MOBILE_STATUS, NC_TREE, OPERATION, TOOL, WORK_INSTRUCTION, and WORKLIST. By selecting each category, you can find the available LIST for that particular category. Select one list for a particular category, and click on RETRIEVE. SAP ME will display the configuration for the selected list. Now, insert a new column or remove an existing column, or you can change the column sequence—that is, the order in which columns will appear in the POD. You can define the maximum number of rows in the MAXIMUM NUMBER OF ROWS field for displaying the list.

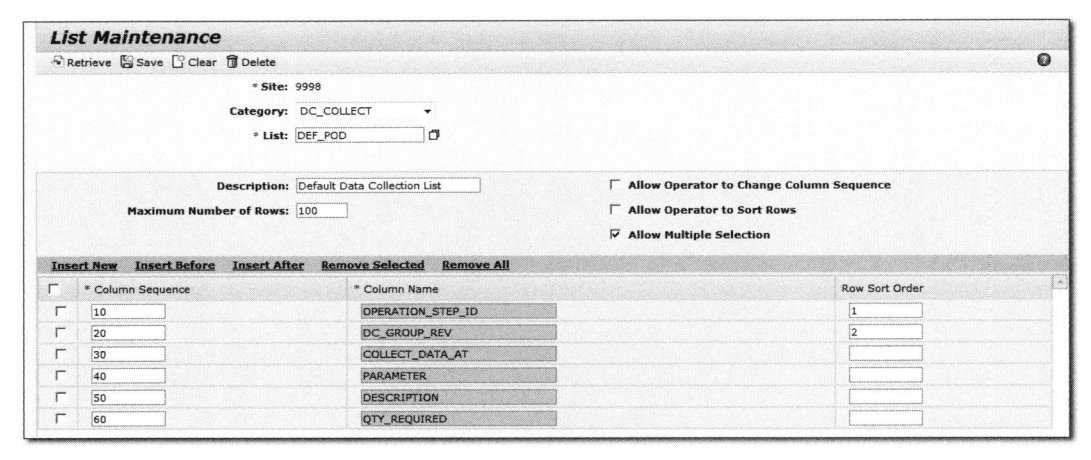

Figure 10.12 Maintaining Lists for DC_COLLECT

Operators can also configure the column sequence if the ALLOW OPERATOR TO CHANGE COLUMN SEQUENCE checkbox is selected, row sorting if the ALLOW OPERATOR TO SORT ROWS checkbox is selected, and can perform multiple row selection if the ALLOW MULTIPLE SELECTION checkbox is selected. Figure 10.13 shows how the configured data collection list (as set in Figure 10.12) appears in the POD.

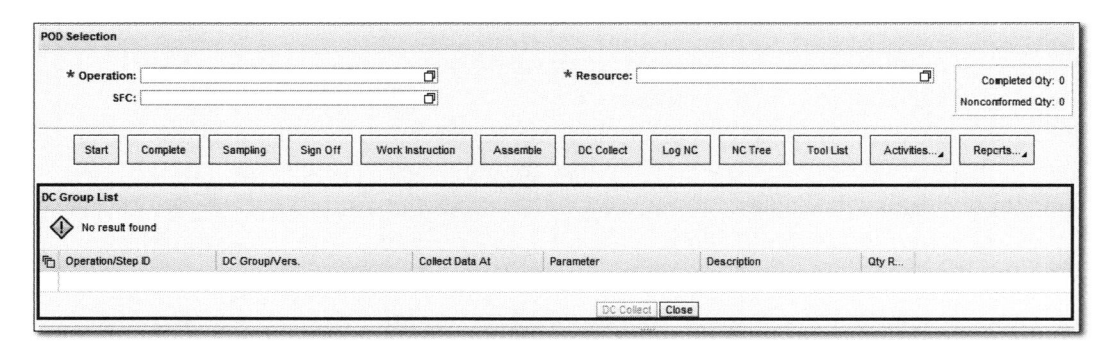

Figure 10.13 Data Collection Column Sequence in POD

10.3 Designing PODs

You've learned about available POD types in SAP ME and also predefined default PODs provided by SAP ME, so now we will discuss how to design a custom POD based on the shop floor execution requirement. We are assuming that we need to design an operation type of POD for shop floor execution that will contain the buttons and related activities shown in Table 10.1 to meet the shop floor manufacturing needs.

Button Sequence	Button ID	Button Label	Activity Sequence	Activity	Clears SFC
10	START_SFC	Start SFC	10	PR500	No
20	COMPLETE_SFC	Complete SFC	10	PR510	Yes
30	DC_COLLECT	Data Collection	10 20	DC_LIST_DISPLAY DC500	No
40	LOG_NC	Log NC	10 20	NC_SELECTION NC_DATA_ENTRY	No
50	WI_VIEW	Work Instruction View	10 20	WI_LIST_DISPLAY WI500	No
60	CHG_EQU_STATUS	Change Equipment Status	10	CHG_EQUIP_STATUS	No
70	HOLD_SFC	Hold SFC	10	SU520	No
80	RELEASE_SFC	Release SFC	10	SU530	No
90	SFC_REPORT	SFC Report	10	DM700	No

Table 10.1 Required Buttons and Assigned Activities for Custom POD Design

To configure the POD, open the POD Maintenance activity in SAP ME from the left navigation panel. Select Operation for Type and enter the POD name as "CUSTOM_OPERATION_POD". In the following sections, we will cover the actions you need to perform on each tab.

10.3.1 Main Tab

In the Main tab Description field, specify Custom ME Operation POD as the POD description. Select Enabled for the Status field value, which will make the POD ready for use. The Display Device field contains two values: Standard and Touch Screen. Standard is used for displaying the POD on normal monitors, and TOUCH SCREEN is used for touch screen monitors. Select STANDARD for the DISPLAY DEVICE field value. The DISPLAY SIZE field includes four options for viewing size of a touch POD. SMALL and MEDIUM are used for tablet devices, and LARGE and EXTRA LARGE are used for touch screens. In this example, select EXTRA LARGE for the value of the DISPLAY SIZE field.

If you want to display shop floor real-time messages, select ICON for the REAL-TIME MESSAGE DISPLAY field; otherwise, select NONE. If you want to display a special instruction (which is configured through the Operation Maintenance activity or Routing Maintenance activity) in the POD, then select INFO MESSAGE or POPUP for the SPECIAL INSTRUCTION DISPLAY field value; otherwise, select NONE. In the NC CLIENT field, enter or lookup the NC client value configured through the NC Client Maintenance activity in SAP ME. In this example, look up and select NC_LOG provided by SAP ME as a default NC client. In the SESSION TIMEOUT (MINS) field, enter the amount of time for which the POD will remain active for shop floor operators without any activity. Figure 10.14 shows the MAIN tab configuration for POD Maintenance.

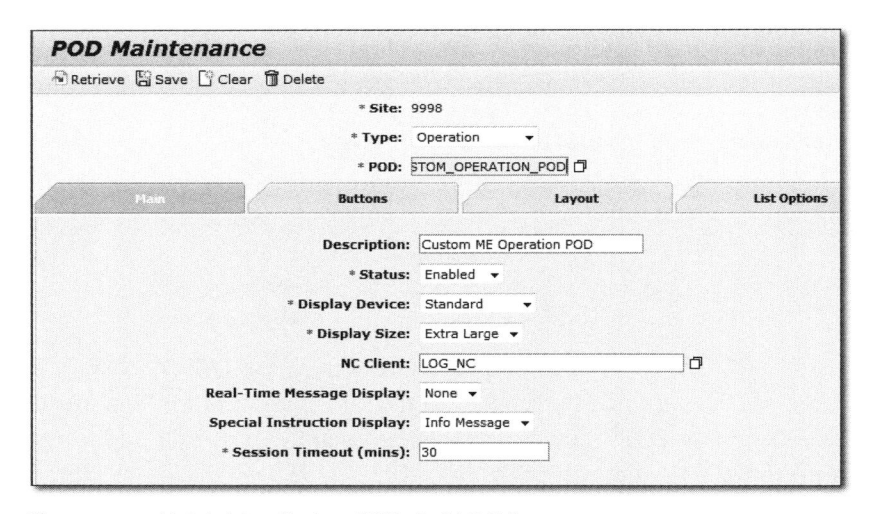

Figure 10.14 Maintaining Custom PODs in SAP ME

10.3.2 Buttons Tab

The BUTTONS tab is used to configure the buttons for the POD and link them to different activities in SAP ME that the operator can perform while using the POD. You can also use button groups to group multiple activities within a single button by providing a label. On the BUTTONS tab, enter the required buttons per Table 10.1. To enter the START SFC button, click on the INSERT NEW link to open the Button Details page, where you can enter "10" in the BUTTON SEQUENCE field. The button sequence maintains the order in which operator will execute the activities on the shop floor.

Next, select a button type in the BUTTON TYPE field. NORMAL is used when you want to execute one or multiple activities for a single button click. GROUP is used when you want to group multiple activities within a single button using a label on the button; after clicking the button, the user needs to choose a particular activity from the list. For this example, select NORMAL.

Now, enter a button ID in the BUTTON ID field. The button ID is a unique ID for the button. As per Table 10.1, enter "START_SFC" in the BUTTON ID field.

The BUTTON LABEL is the label for the button that will be displayed in the POD. Enter "Start SFC" in the BUTTON LABEL field.

> **Note: Button Label**
>
> To make the button label internationalized, enter it using a "I18N[start.default.BUTTON]" format, where *I18N* indicates the internationalization and *[start.default.BUTTON]* is the identification of the button label. The word "internationalization" is abbreviated to i18n which refers to the 18 letters between the letters i and n. Based on the local language settings the button label is displayed in that specific language. For English language the *[start.default.BUTTON]* button label is displayed as "Start".

BUTTON SIZE (%) indicates the size (as a percentage) of the button in the POD. For this example, enter "100" in the BUTTON SIZE (%) field. You can enter any percentage value, but you need to check the fit in the POD.

You can provide an image for the button by entering the image path in the IMAGE ICON field, and also you can provide the hot key for the START SFC button by selecting a value in the HOTKEY field.

BUTTON LOCATION indicates the location of the button in the POD. The button location can be LEFT, RIGHT, ABOVE THE POD SELECTION, BELOW THE POD SELECTION, or PAGE BOTTOM. For the START SFC button, select BELOW THE POD SELECTION for the BUTTON LOCATION field.

The START NEW BUTTON ROW checkbox is enabled only for the BELOW THE POD SELECTION value of the BUTTON LOCATION field. The START NEW BUTTON ROW option is used to place the button in a new row in the POD. For this example, leave the checkbox unchecked.

Now, attach one or more activities to the button by clicking on the INSERT NEW link. For button events, the attached activities will be executed sequentially per the order of insertion. For this example, click on the INSERT NEW link, select the activity PR500 with activity sequence 10, and keep the CLEARS SFC check box unchecked, as shown in Figure 10.15. Click on APPLY to add the START SFC button to the POD.

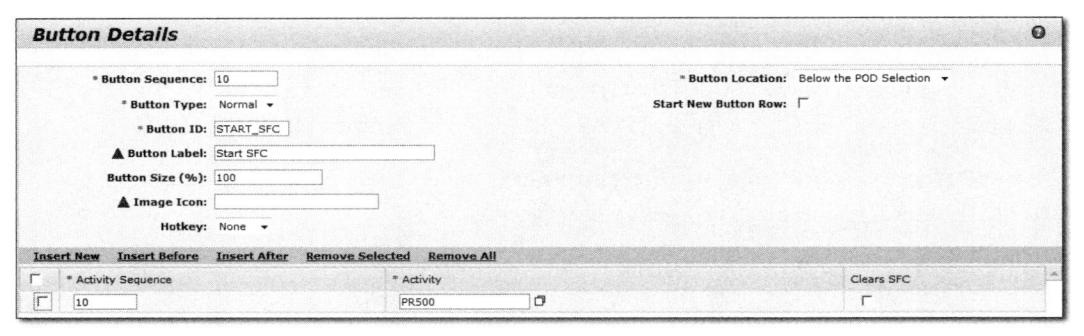

Figure 10.15 Defining Buttons for PODs in Button Details Page

Define other buttons for the POD in the same way and by using the details from Table 10.1. Figure 10.16 shows the list of buttons for the custom POD.

Figure 10.16 Defined Button List for Custom POD

10.3.3 Layout Tab

On the LAYOUT tab, you can define the layout for the POD. SAP ME provides seven layout types under the LAYOUT TYPE dropdown field:

- 1 PANEL HORIZONTAL LAYOUT (WITH POPOVER), one horizontal panel with one popover panel.
- 1 PANEL VERTICAL LAYOUT (WITH POPOVER), one vertical panel with one popover panel.
- 2 PANEL HORIZONTAL LAYOUT (WITH POPOVER), two horizontal panels with one popover panel.
- 3 PANEL HORIZONTAL LAYOUT (WITH POPOVER), three horizontal panels with one popover panel.
- 3 PANEL VERTICAL LAYOUT (WITH POPOVER), three vertical panels with one popover panel.
- 6 PANEL HORIZONTAL LAYOUT, six horizontal panels.
- 6 PANEL VERTICAL LAYOUT, six vertical panels.

Figure 10.17 illustrates the seven layout types available in SAP ME. Each POD layout contains one fixed POD selection panel.

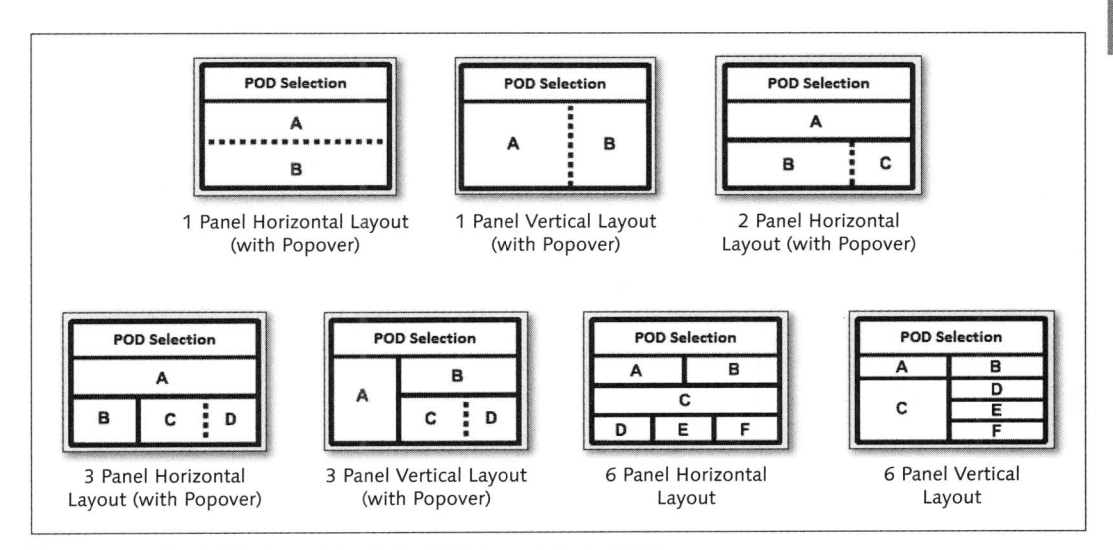

Figure 10.17 Graphical View of Available POD Layouts in SAP ME

On the LAYOUT tab, after selecting the POD layout, you can define plug-ins for different panels. For CUSTOM_OPERATION_POD, choose POD layout type 3 PANEL HORIZONTAL LAYOUT (WITH POPOVER) and define the PS_OPERATION_2ROW plug-in for the POD selection panel in the DEFAULT PLUG-IN field. A default plugin will display upon POD launch and whenever another plugin assigned to that layout area then the default plugin is closed. For panel A, choose the WORKLIST_DISPLAY plug-in in the DEFAULT PLUG-IN field. Panel A will display the POD work list. In OTHER PLUG-INS for panel A, define plug-ins that also will be displayed in the POD WORK LIST area. Click on the OTHER PLUG-INS icon for panel A to define the plug-ins, and the Other Plug-In Details page will open. For CUSTOM_OPERATION_POD, add (by clicking on the INSERT NEW link) three plug-ins, DC_LIST_DISPLAY, NC_SELECTION, and WI_LIST_DISPLAY, with activity sequence 10, 20, and 30 respectively, as shown in Figure 10.18. After adding those plug-ins, click on APPLY.

> **Note: POD Plug-Ins**
>
> In POD configuration, you have assigned different plug-ins and activities for the buttons. The purposes of these plug-ins are as follows:
>
> - WORKLIST_DISPLAY displays the POD work list, which contains the SFC and shop order details.
> - DC_LIST_DISPLAY displays the data collection group list.
> - NC_SELECTION is used to display the NC selection, which contains NC groups and available NC codes.
> - WI_LIST_DISPLAY is used to display the work instruction list within the POD.
> - WI500 is used to view the work instructions. Operators can select the work instructions from the work instruction list (which will be displayed through the WORKLIST_DISPLAY plug-in), and the details of the work instruction will be displayed through the Work Instruction View (WI500) plug-in.
> - DC500 is used to perform the data collection entry. From the DC Group List plug-in, an operator can select the DC group and the value entry for the parameter can be set through the Data Collection Entry (DC500) plug-in.
> - NC_DATA_ENTRY is used to perform the NC logging. The operator needs to select an NC code from the NC_SELECTION plug-in and use that code to enter other details and log NCs through the NC_DATA_ENTRY plug-in.

Designing PODs | 10.3

- CHG_EQUIP_STATUS is used to change the equipment status.
- SU520 is used to put the SFC in hold status.
- SU530 is used to release the SFC from hold status.
- DM700 provides the SFC report.

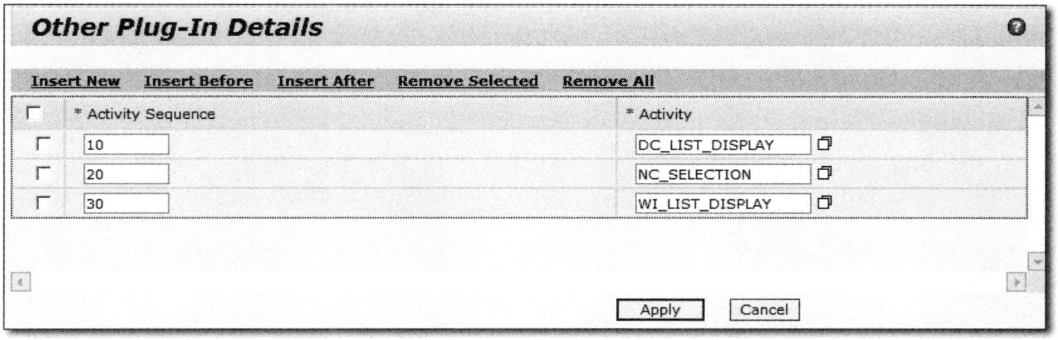

Figure 10.18 Adding Other Plug-Ins for POD Work List

Once you finish adding the activities, click on APPLY, which will take you to LAYOUT tab. There, click on SAVE to save the configuration. Now, click on the OTHER PLUG-INS icon for panel C to open the OTHER PLUG-IN DETAILS page. Insert three rows to add the WI500, DC500, and NC_DATA_ENTRY activities with activity sequences 10, 20, and 30 respectively, and click on APPLY. The purpose of the WI500, DC500, and NC_DATA_ENTRY activities is explained in the earlier note.

Next, configure the layout for Change Equipment Status, Hold SFC, Release SFC, and SFC Report. Suppose you want to display those four plug-ins as pop-ups within the POD. If so, click on the OTHER PLUG-INS icon for the POPUP type to open the Other Plug-In Details page. Insert four rows to add CHG_EQUIP_STATUS, SU520, SU530, and DM700 activities with activity sequences 10, 20, 30, and 40 respectively. After adding those activities, click on APPLY, which will take you again to the LAYOUT tab. Finally, the LAYOUT tab will look like Figure 10.19.

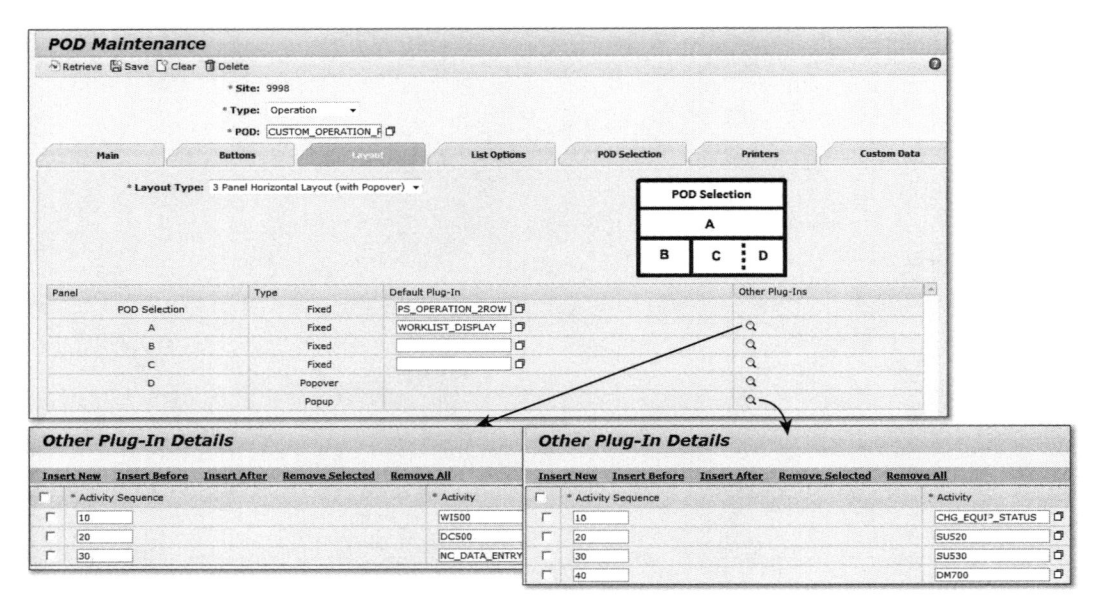

Figure 10.19 Configuring POD Layout

10.3.4 List Options Tab

We talked about List Maintenance in Section 10.2, and now you will learn how the LIST OPTION tab is used to display a particular list within the POD. SAP ME provides seven options on the LIST OPTIONS tab to attach different types of lists:

- BROWSE WORK LIST
  In an operation POD, used to browse SFCs that are in either New or In Queue status. SFC_TASK list (configured in List Maintenance) is assigned to the BROWSE WORK LIST field to browse the SFCs.

- POD WORK LIST
  Displays SFCs in Active, Hold status. The POD WORK LIST field contains the list value SFC_ACTIVE.

- ASSEMBLE LIST
  Contains the list value DEF_POD, which displays the default component list for the SFC.

- DC COLLECT LIST
  Can be mapped with list value DEF_POD to display the default data collection list configured in List Maintenance.

- TOOL LIST
  Can contain default list value TOOL_LIST_ALL to display the tool list per the configuration of TOOL_LIST_ALL in List Maintenance.

- WORK INSTRUCTION LIST
  Can display the default work instruction list WORK_INSTRUCTION_ALL, configured in List Maintenance.

- DC ENTRY LIST
  Contains the list used to display the list for DATA COLLECTION ENTRY. DEF_DATA_ENTRY list is mapped to the DC ENTRY LIST field and displays all the columns as configured in List Maintenance.

Figure 10.20 shows the available lists with configured list values on the LIST OPTION tab.

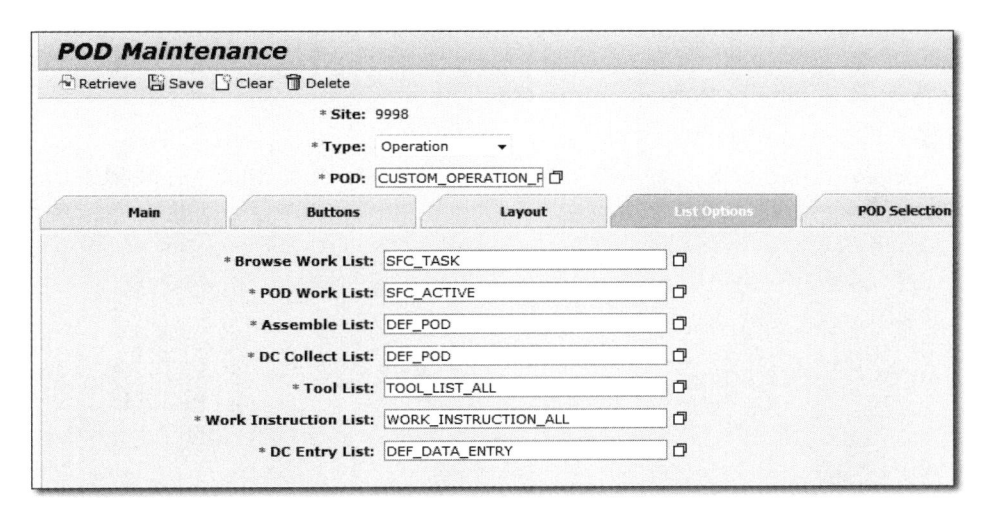

Figure 10.20 Configued List in List Options

For CUSTOM_OPERATION_POD, you can keep the default value setting on the LIST OPTION tab.

10.3.5 POD Selection Tab

The POD SELECTION tab is used to configure the POD selection area of an operation POD. SAP ME provides multiple options for configuring the POD selection area, which we will discuss here:

- MAIN INPUT
  Indicates the label that will be displayed in the POD during execution. By default, it contains the value I18N[SFC.DEFAULT.LABEL] for which the SFC label appears in the operation POD in the POD selection area below the OPERATION field.

- MAIN INPUT HOT KEY
  Select the hot key from the available list, which will be used to place the cursor into the SFC field of the operation POD.

- DEFAULT OPERATION
  Specify an operation that will be displayed in the POD; the operator doesn't need to select the operation from a list.

- DEFAULT RESOURCE
  Specify the resource name that will be fixed for the POD; the operator doesn't need to select the resource from a list.

- SFC QUEUE BUTTON ID
  Specify a button ID. The button ID must be same as is specified on the BUTTONS tab. The activity assigned with the button on the BUTTONS tab will be executed when operator enters an SFC in SFC field in the POD and tabs out of the SFC field when the SFC is in queue at the specified operation in the POD.

- SFC IN WORK BUTTON ID
  Specify a button ID; the button ID must be same as is specified on the BUTTONS tab will be executed when operator enters an SFC in SFC field in the POD and tabs out of the SFC field when the SFC is in work at the specified operation in the POD.

- INFO LINE 1
  The first information message line displayed in the POD during execution.

- INFO LINE 2
  The second information message line displayed in the POD during execution. Both info lines provide lists of values such as NONE, COMPLETED QTY, NONCONFORMED QTY, ACTIVE QTY, IN QUEUE QTY, SHOP ORDER, STATUS (SFC), PROCESS

LOT, COMPLETION DATE, PRIORITY, and MATERIAL. Select a value for the field based on your requirements.

- SHOW OPERATION FIRST
  If selected, then the OPERATION field is displayed first at the top-left side in the operation POD.

- SHOW QUANTITY
  If selected, then the QUANTITY field is displayed in the operation POD in the POD selection area. The operator can enter and process partial SFC quantities.

- OPERATION CAN BE CHANGED
  If selected, then SAP ME allows the operator to change the operation though a fixed operation in configured for the POD.

- RESOURCE CAN BE CHANGED
  If selected, then SAP ME allows the operator to change the resource though a fixed resource in configured for the POD.

For CUSTOM_OPERATION_POD, keep the default setting of the POD SELECTION tab or configure it as needed. Figure 10.21 shows the default configuration of the POD SELECTION tab.

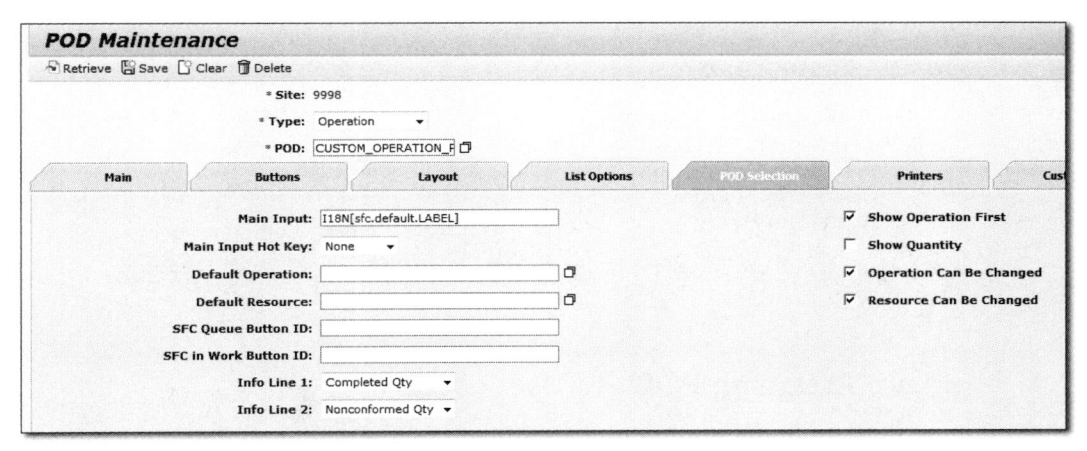

Figure 10.21 Default Configuration of POD Selection Tab for Operation PODs

10.3.6 Printer Tab

On the PRINTER tab, configure the printer for printing from an operation POD. There are three printer configuration options: DOCUMENT PRINTER, LABEL PRINTER, and TRAVELER PRINTER, as shown in Figure 10.22. In the Printer Maintenance activity, you can configure a printer and assign a document type, such as DOCUMENT, LABEL, or TRAVELER. Assign a printer on the PRINTER tab based on the printer type you configured in Printer Maintenance. SAP ME provides two activity hooks for document printing: SY520 (Document Print) and SY521 (ADS Document Print). As per your requirements, choose one or the other as needed. For example, you can use SY520 for one operation and SY521 for another operation if required. To print a document from the POD, specify the printer on the PRINTER tab.

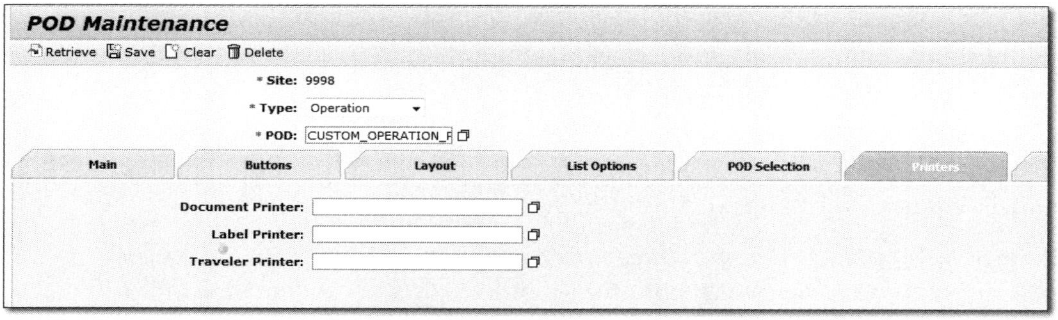

Figure 10.22 Printer Configuration for POD

10.3.7 Custom Tab

Through the Custom Data Maintenance activity, if you define any custom data field for the POD category, then it will appear on the CUSTOM tab of the POD Maintenance activity. For CUSTOM_OPERATION_POD, we have not configured any custom data field.

Now, save the CUSTOM_OPERATION_POD by clicking on the SAVE button.

10.4 Assigning PODs to User Groups

In Section 10.3, you learned how to configure the CUSTOM_OPERATION_POD. Now, in this section, you'll learn how to assign the POD to user groups. Before assigning the POD to a user group, you need to create an activity in SAP ME. Open the Activity Maintenance activity by clicking the link on the left side panel. In Activity Maintenance, enter the name of activity in ACTIVITY field, and on the MAIN tab, enter the description of the activity. For this example, in the ACTIVITY field, enter "CUSTOM_OPER_POD", and in the DESCRIPTION field, enter "POD— Custom Operation".

> **Note: Activity Description**
>
> For making the activity description internationalized, you need to specify the description using the "I18N[DEF_OPER_POD.activity.DESC]" format, where *I18N* indicates the internationalization and *[DEF_OPER_POD.activity.DESC]* is the description of activity.

Select the ENABLED checkbox to enable the activity, and select the VISIBLE IN ACTIVITY MANAGER checkbox to make the activity visible in the Activity Manager list (the name of the activity will appear in the left side panel). In the CLASS/PROGRAM field, specify the URL to access the POD. You need to form the URL using the standard template. For CUSTOM_OPERATION_POD, the URL will be in the following format:

%PROTOCOL%://%SERVER%:%PORT%/manufacturing/com/sap/me/wpmf/client/ template.jsf?WORKSTATION=CUSTOM_OPERATION_POD

You don't need to change *%PROTOCOL%://%SERVER%:%PORT%*. The Web Plugin Management Framework (WPMF) will replace the parameters with correct values when the POD launches from SAP ME using the standard template, and value of *WORKSTATION* is the POD name. You will learn more about WPMF in Chapter 17. You can also select STANDALONE GUI (.JSP) for activity TYPE. The POD will be displayed as a standalone user interface. Figure 10.23 shows the activity creation for CUSTOM_OPERATION_POD.

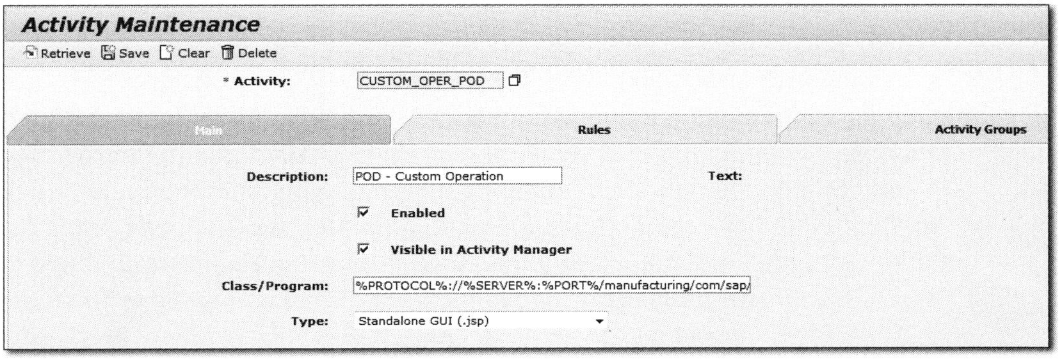

Figure 10.23 Maintaining Activity for Custom POD

Switch to the ACTIVITY GROUPS configuration tab, where you can assign any activity group from AVAILABLE ACTIVITY GROUPS to ASSIGNED ACTIVITY GROUPS including the custom-created activity group created using the SAP ME standard activity Activity Group Maintenance. You created one custom activity group called SHOPFLOOR_OPERATORS (Shop Floor Operators Group) earlier using Activity Group Maintenance, and the same activity group is available in the AVAILABLE ACTIVITY GROUPS area. Now, assign SHOPFLOOR_OPERATORS from the left side, AVAILABLE ACTIVITY GROUPS, to the right side, ASSIGNED ACTIVITY GROUPS, as shown in Figure 10.24 (left side list holds the list of all available activity groups including the custom activity groups and right side list holds the assigned activity groups where the current activity is assigned). Save the activity using the SAVE button.

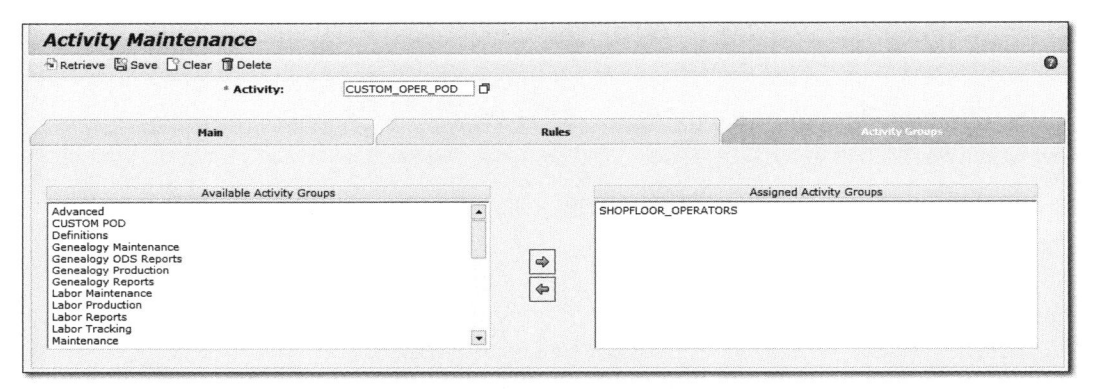

Figure 10.24 Assigning Activity in Activity Group

Now, open the User Group Maintenance activity from the left side panel of the activity list to assign an activity to a particular user group. Suppose you want to assign the CUSTOM_OPERATION_POD to only the OPERATORS group. In User Group Maintenance, you can specify OPERATORS in the USER GROUP field and click on RETRIEVE to retrieve the details of the OPERATORS group. Switch to the USERS tab and assign the users from the available user list that you want to assign in the OPERATORS group. Now, switch to the PERMISSION tab and select the POD—CUSTOM OPERATION activity checkbox, as shown in Figure 10.25; doing so means you are providing permission to the OPERATORS user group to access the POD—Custom Operation activity. Save the OPERATORS user group by clicking on SAVE.

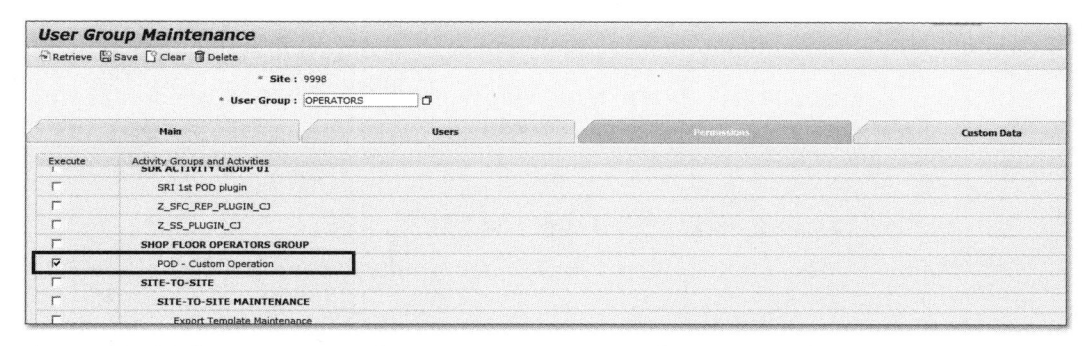

Figure 10.25 Configuring Permission for POD—Custom Operation for OPERATORS User Group

Now, a user who is assigned to the OPERATORS group can log in to SAP ME and see the POD—CUSTOM OPERATION activity link on the left side panel activity list within the activity group SHOP FLOOR OPERATORS GROUP (SHOP FLOOR OPERATORS GROUP is the activity group where the CUSTOM_OPER_POD activity is assigned through Activity Maintenance). By clicking the POD—CUSTOM OPERATION activity link, a user can open the POD, as shown in Figure 10.26.

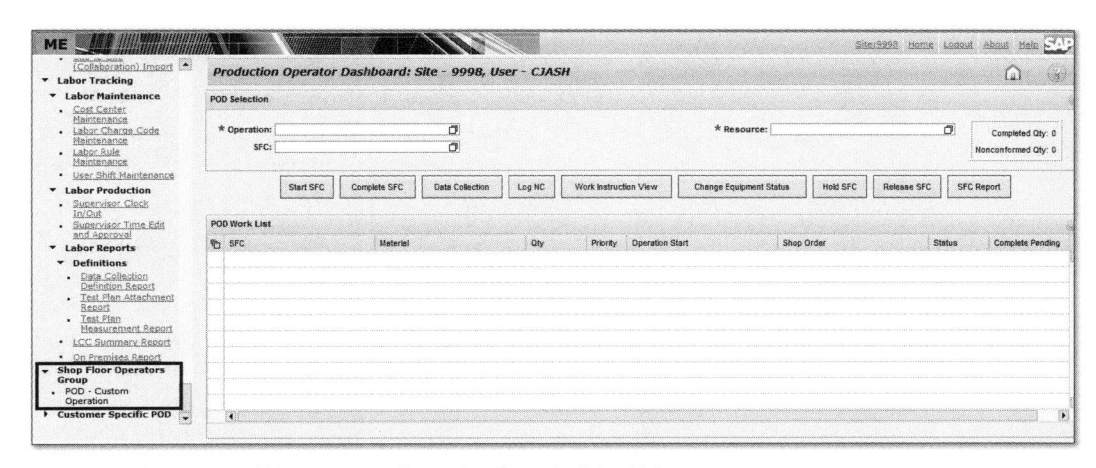

Figure 10.26 Opening POD—Custom Operation from Activity Link

10.5 Executing SFCs in the POD

In previous sections, you designed the POD and assigned it to a user group and individual users. Now, a user has logged in to SAP ME and opened the POD to perform the shop floor execution through the POD. In this section, we will see how this user can perform multiple activities such as Starting and Completing the SFC, Displaying Work Instructions, Performing Data Collection, Performing Nonconformance Logging, and Equipment Status Change using the same POD.

10.5.1 Starting and Completing the SFC

In this section we will discuss how to start and complete the SFC in the POD. Before executing a start activity, we are assuming that you have released a shop order and that SFCs are in queue in the first operation of a routing (a routing used in a shop order). In the POD Selection area, a user can click on the VALUE HELP icon of the OPERATION input field and then select the first operation of the routing. The selected operation will appear in the OPERATION field. If the default resource is configured for the operation, then the resource will appear automatically in the RESOURCE field; otherwise, the user needs to select the resource from the available resource list (the resource list will display the available resources within the resource group you have assigned in the first operation of the routing through the Operation Maintenance activity) by clicking on the VALUE HELP icon of the RESOURCE field.

The user now needs to click on the VALUE HELP icon of the SFC field to open a pop-up with the SFCs in IN_QUEUE status for the operation. The user can select one or multiple SFCs from list, and the selected SFCs will appear in the SFC field. If multiple SFCs are selected, then the number of selected SFCs (for example, [3 SELECTED]) will appear in the SFC field. Next, the user can click on the START SFC button to start the SFCs. SFCs will be displayed in the POD WORK LIST area with status ACTIVE, as shown in Figure 10.27.

To complete the SFCs (the SFCs are already selected in POD WORK LIST), the user clicks on the COMPLETE SFC button. Through the COMPLETE SFC event, SFCs will be completed in the first operation (the selected operation in the POD selection area OPERATION field), and SAP ME will send the SFCs to the next operation of the routing per the routing flow. The same SFCs will be in IN_QUEUE status at the next operation, as shown in Figure 10.28.

Executing SFCs in the POD | **10.5**

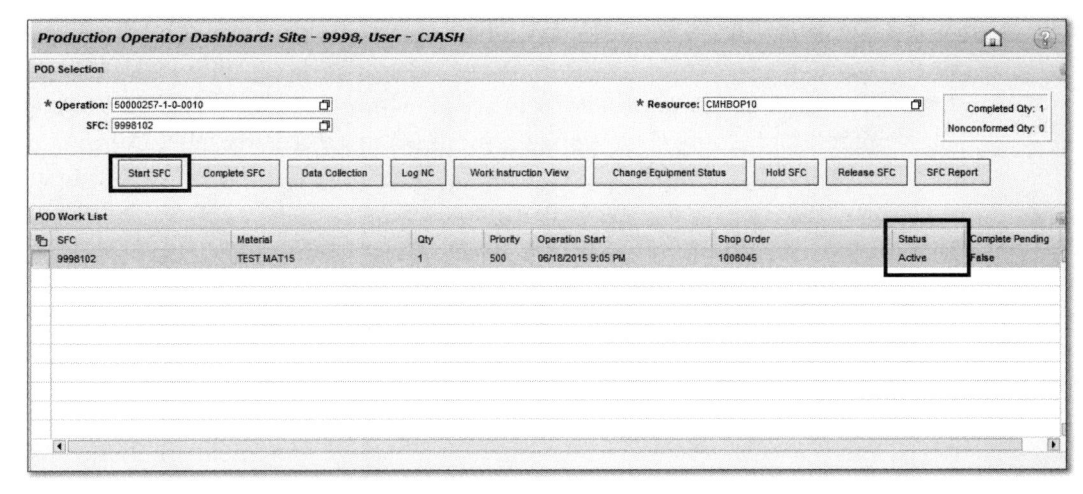

Figure 10.27 Starting SFC through PODs at an Operation

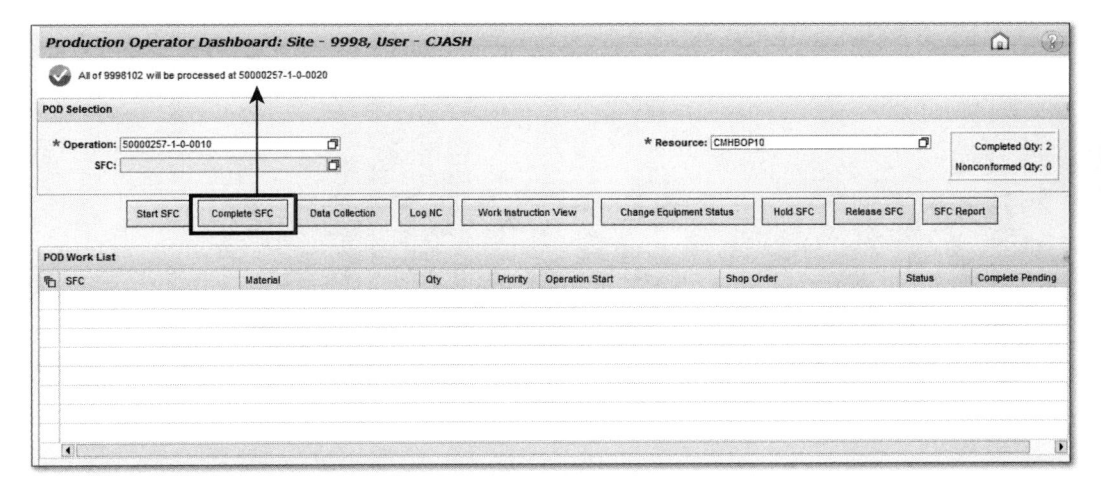

Figure 10.28 Completing SFCs through POD Complete Event

> **Note: SFC Completion at an Operation**
>
> When a shop floor user is completing an SFC at an operation using the POD, a `yield-ConfirmationRequest` message will be triggered from SAP ME to SAP ERP if the operation is an SAP ERP routing operation and the ERP Reporting step is maintained for the operation. The `yieldConfirmationRequest` message will be displayed in SAPMEINT Queue Monitor.

335

10.5.2 Displaying Work Instructions

SAP ME provides a Work Instruction View feature in the POD during the shop floor execution. Work instructions provide instructional information to shop floor operators, helping them perform the tasks in a particular operation easily and accurately. In the POD, say that a shop floor user has started an SFC in an operation and needs to view instructions. The user can click on the WORK INSTRUCTION VIEW button to see the WORK INSTRUCTION LIST. From the WORK INSTRUCTION LIST, the user can select a work instruction (if the list contains multiple work instructions) and click on the VIEW button. The selected work instruction is displayed in the WORK INSTRUCTION VIEWER area, as shown in Figure 10.29.

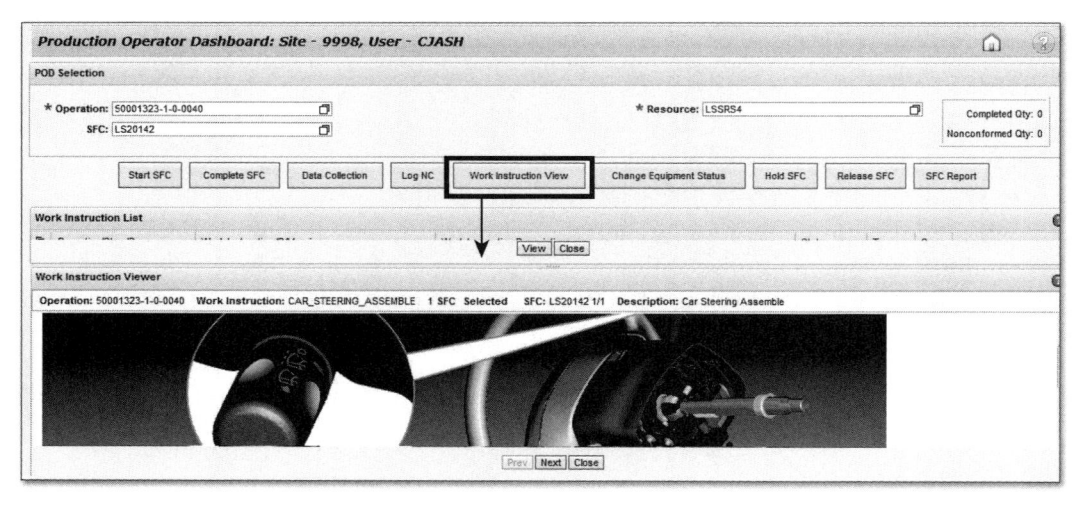

Figure 10.29 Displaying Work Instructions in POD

> **Note: Work Instructions Configuration**
>
> Before viewing the work instructions in the POD for a particular operation, you need to configure the work instruction through the Work Instruction Maintenance activity in SAP ME. To open the work instruction in a new window, you also need to configure that behavior in the Work Instruction Maintenance activity, as explained in Chapter 3, Section 3.1.7.

10.5.3 Performing Data Collection

During shop floor execution, a user can perform data collection from the POD. The user can start an SFC for an operation and then click on the DATA COLLECTION button in the POD. DC groups will be displayed in the DC GROUP LIST area. The user needs to select one DC group from the list if same operation is attached to multiple DC groups through the DC Group Maintenance activity. Next, the user can click on DC COLLECT button to see the data collection parameters in the DATA COLLECTION ENTRY area, where the user can specify the value for data collection and finally click on the SAVE button, as shown in Figure 10.30. After successful data collection, SAP ME will show the successful data collection message in the POD message area.

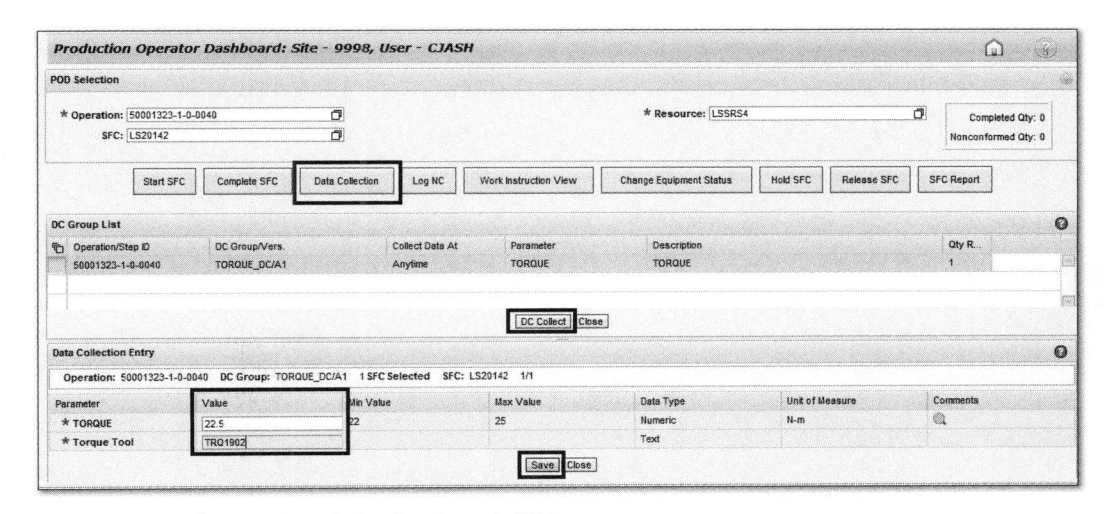

Figure 10.30 Performing Data Collection through POD

10.5.4 Performing Nonconformance Logging

During the shop floor manufacturing process, if any defect is found at any point in time, it can be logged through the Log NC activity available in the POD. Say that a user started an SFC in an operation and found some defect for that SFC. To log the defect, the user clicks on the LOG NC button available in POD – CUSTOM OPERATION to display the NC SELECTION area, which contains NC GROUP and AVAILABLE NC CODES sections corresponding to the NC group. Based on the defect type, the user can select the NC GROUP and NC CODE from the available NC code list. The NC DATA ENTRY area appears below the NC SELECTION area. The selected NC code appears in the NC DATA ENTRY area, where the user can add more information and then save the defect by clicking on the ADD button. Display of additional input fields in the NC DATA ENTRY area depends on NC code configuration and NC data type selection for an NC code in the SAP ME NC Code Maintenance activity. After clicking on ADD, a message will appear based on the NC logged. Figure 10.31 shows NC logging through the POD.

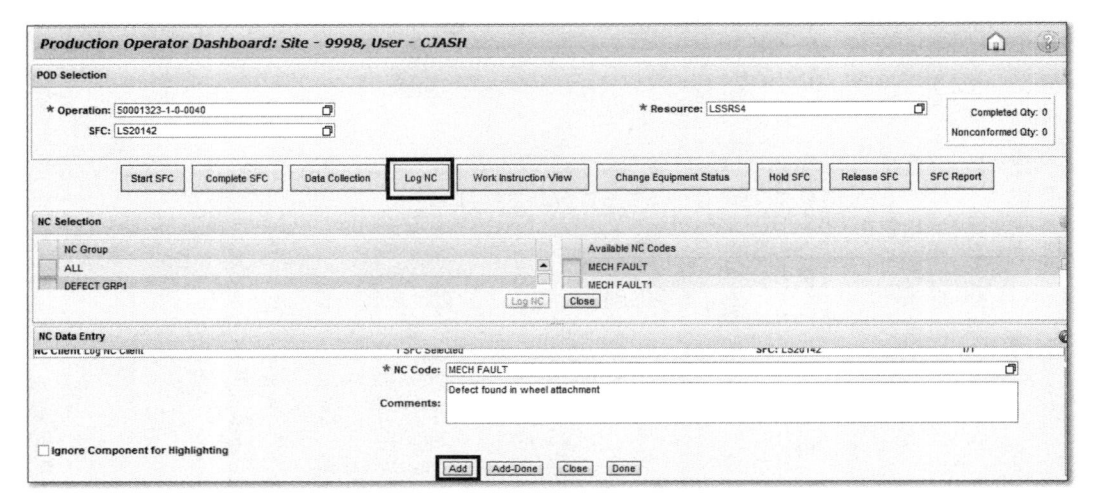

Figure 10.31 Performing NC Logging through POD

> **Note: Log NC**
>
> Before performing NC logging through the POD, configure the NC group and NC code through the NC Group Maintenance and NC Code Maintenance activities, as explained in Chapter 8.
>
> The NC DATA ENTRY area contains four buttons: ADD, ADD-DONE, CLOSE, and DONE. ADD logs the NC for the SFC; ADD-DONE logs the NC and completes the SFC for the current operation, but no yield confirmation will go to the SAP ERP system; CLOSE closes the NC DATA ENTRY area; and DONE completes the SFC for the current operation. At the same time the event dispositions the SFC number if the disposition is set up and clears the screen, but no yield confirmation will move to SAP ERP. Through the NC Client Maintenance activity, you can also hide the ADD-DONE button in the NC DATA ENTRY area of the POD.

10.5.5 Equipment Status Change

In a shop floor manufacturing process, if you want to change the status (for example, Unscheduled Down) of a resource or all resources within a work center or a particular tool or all tools within a group, you can do so through the Equipment Status Change activity. Say that an operator is working in an operation using the POD—CUSTOM OPERATION, and a resource is already selected in the resource field corresponding to that operation. For any shop floor issue, the operator needs to change the resource status to Down until the issue is resolved. In this situation, the operator can click on the CHANGE EQUIPMENT STATUS button in POD—CUSTOM OPERATION. The Change Equipment Status activity page will open in a pop-up with a prefilled operation and resource. The operator must select the status UNSCHEDULED DOWN in the NEW STATUS field and the proper REASON CODE from the value help. The operator can also add comments in the COMMENTS field and click on the CHANGE STATUS button to change the status of resource, as shown in Figure 10.32. The operator clicks on the RETURN TO POD button to return to the POD.

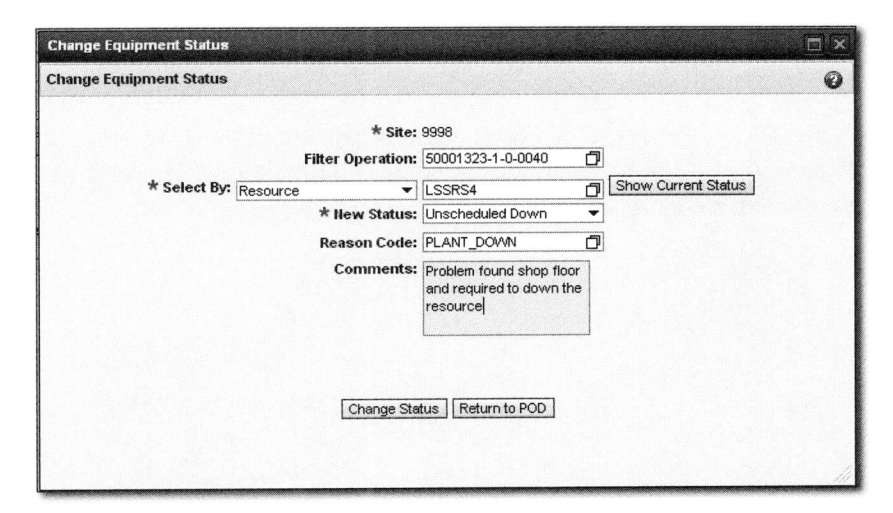

Figure 10.32 Changing Resource Status Using Change Equipment Status Activity

> **Note: Resource Status Change**
>
> If SFCs are active at a resource and the status of resource is changed using the Change Equipment Status activity, the status change will not take effect for that resource until all active SFCs are completed or signed off for the resource. To have an immediate effect, you can make a status change using the Resource Maintenance activity. When the resource

status is changed to Unscheduled Down, the `equipmentStatusChangeRequest_UNSCH_DOWN` message is triggered to SAPMEINT, and the resource status change message is sent to SAP ERP as well.

10.6 Production Reports

In this section, we will discuss the production-related standard reports available in SAP ME such as the Production Report, Operation Yield Report, Operation Yield by Material Report and Material Yield Report.

10.6.1 Production Report

Use the Production Report to find the quantity of SFCs completed at an operation, resource, and work center for a material with date and time. This report also provides the quantity of SFCs that are nonconformed. In the search criteria, you can specify multiple parameters, such as MATERIAL with VERSION, OPERATION, RESOURCE, and DATE RANGE. On the MISCELLANEOUS tab, you can also filter by multiple parameters, such as CUSTOMER ORDER, ORDER TYPE, SHIFT, WORK CENTER CATEGORY, and WORK CENTER. The search results are displayed in a table, as shown in Figure 10.33. This table contains the date and time, material, operation, resource, work center, quantity completed, and quantity nonconformed.

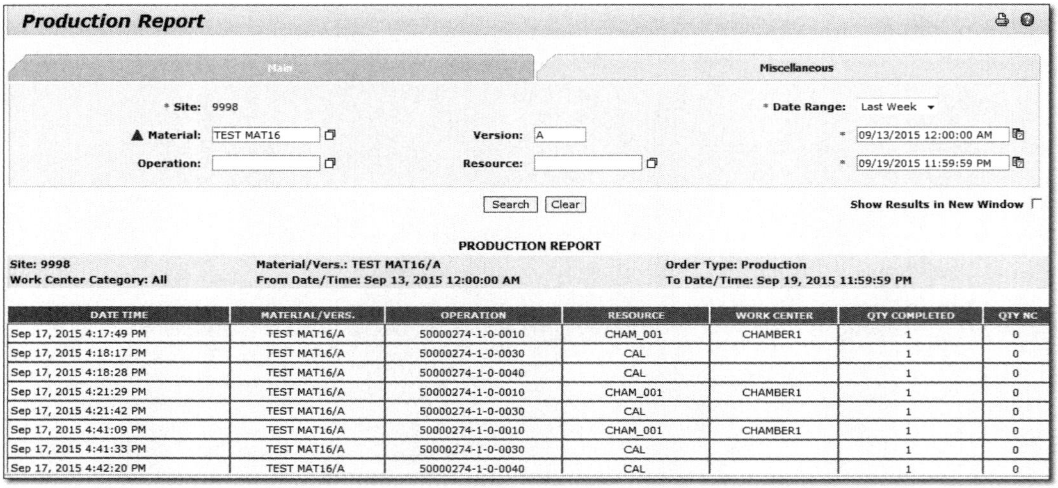
Production Report
Main
Miscellaneous
* Site: 9998
* Date Range: Last Week
Material: TEST MAT16
Version: A
09/13/2015 12:00:00 AM
Operation:
Resource:
09/19/2015 11:59:59 PM
Search
Clear
Show Results in New Window
PRODUCTION REPORT
Site: 9998
Work Center Category: All
Material/Vers.: TEST MAT16/A
From Date/Time: Sep 13, 2015 12:00:00 AM
Order Type: Production
To Date/Time: Sep 19, 2015 11:59:59 PM
DATE TIME | MATERIAL/VERS. | OPERATION | RESOURCE | WORK CENTER | QTY COMPLETED | QTY NC
Sep 17, 2015 4:17:49 PM | TEST MAT16/A | 50000274-1-0-0010 | CHAM_001 | CHAMBER1 | 1 | 0
Sep 17, 2015 4:18:17 PM | TEST MAT16/A | 50000274-1-0-0030 | CAL | | 1 | 0
Sep 17, 2015 4:18:28 PM | TEST MAT16/A | 50000274-1-0-0040 | CAL | | 1 | 0
Sep 17, 2015 4:21:29 PM | TEST MAT16/A | 50000274-1-0-0010 | CHAM_001 | CHAMBER1 | 1 | 0
Sep 17, 2015 4:21:42 PM | TEST MAT16/A | 50000274-1-0-0030 | CAL | | 1 | 0
Sep 17, 2015 4:41:09 PM | TEST MAT16/A | 50000274-1-0-0010 | CHAM_001 | CHAMBER1 | 1 | 0
Sep 17, 2015 4:41:33 PM | TEST MAT16/A | 50000274-1-0-0030 | CAL | | 1 | 0
Sep 17, 2015 4:42:20 PM | TEST MAT16/A | 50000274-1-0-0040 | CAL | | 1 | 0

Figure 10.33 Production Report

10.6.2 Operation Yield Report

Use the Operation Yield Report to gather operation yield details for a particular material or from an operation. The yield from an operation is recorded when the SFC is passed through the operation. SAP ME stores the first-pass yield and retest yield records. For an operation, the first-pass yield is calculated based on the quantity completed on the first pass through the operation divided by the quantity at the start of the operation on the first pass for a specific time. For example, if ten pieces start an operation, seven pieces are completed, and three pieces are nonconformed, then the calculation of the first-pass yield will be (7/10) * 100 = 70%. You can search the report by multiple parameters, such as MATERIAL, OPERATION, WORK CENTER, RESOURCE, OPERATION TYPE, and DATE RANGE. The search results are displayed in a graphical format by default, but you can open a tabular view by clicking on the TABULAR VIEW button. Figure 10.34 shows the Operation Yield Report.

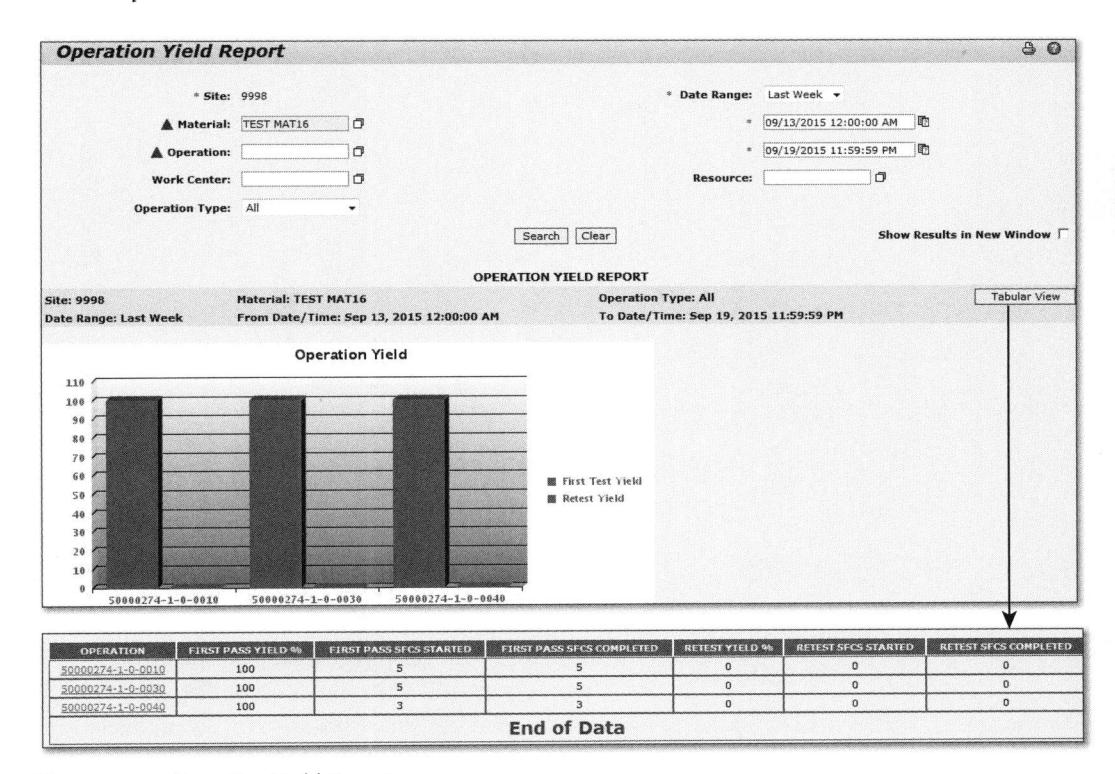

Figure 10.34 Operation Yield Report

10.6.3 Operation Yield by Material Report

Use the Operation Yield by Material Report to see detailed information on operation yield for all materials and operations for a specified date range. The yield for an operation is recorded when SFC is passed through the operation, and SAP ME stores the first-pass yield records and retest yield records. You can search the report by multiple input parameters, such as MATERIAL, OPERATION, WORK CENTER, RESOURCE, OPERATION TYPE, and DATE RANGE. The search results are displayed in a graphical format by default, as shown in Figure 10.35.

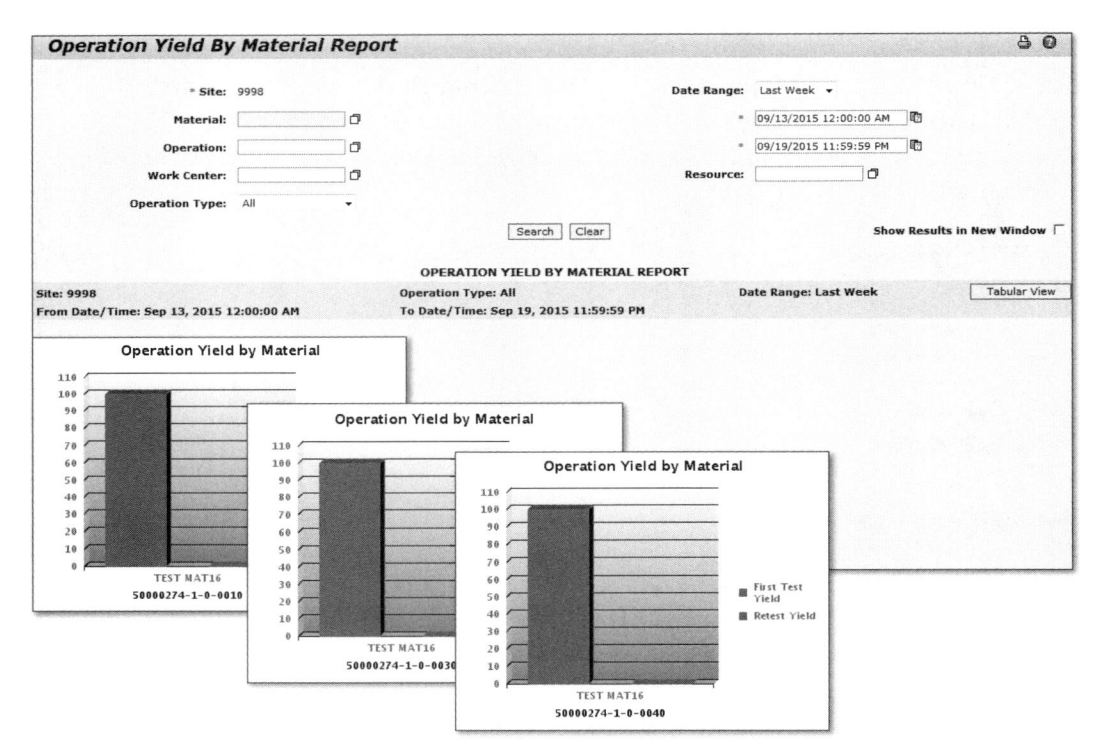

Figure 10.35 Operation Yield by Material Report

10.6.4 Material Yield Report

Use the Material Yield Report to find the production yield for a specific material. SAP ME records yield data for each time an SFC is processed through the operation. SAP ME stores first-pass yield records and retest yield records. You can search the report by MATERIAL, OPERATION, RESOURCE, WORK CENTER, OPERATION

TYPE, or DATE RANGE. The search results are displayed in a graphical view as shown in Figure 10.36. You can also these a tabular view of the same report by clicking on the TABULAR VIEW button on the same page.

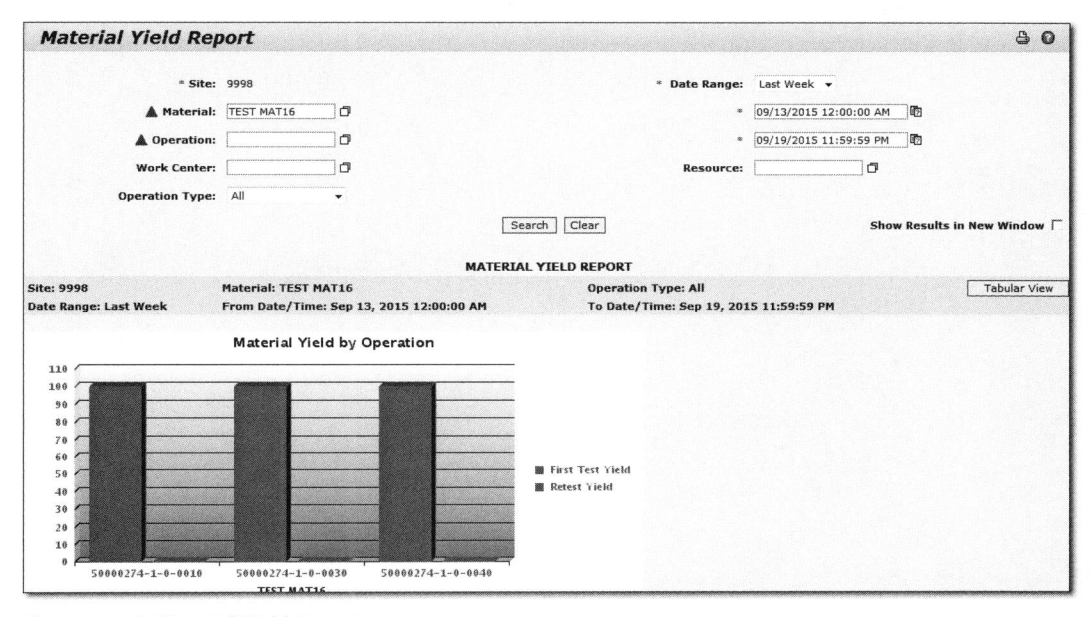

Figure 10.36 Material Yield Report

10.7 WIP Reports

In this section we will discuss three WIP reporting activities available in SAP ME: the WIP by Material Report, the WIP by Operation Report, and the WIP by Work Center Report. The other WIP-related reports were already described in Chapter 5, Section 5.4 and Chapter 6, Section 6.3. These three reports are interlinked and are very useful in the shop floor to track SFCs during the production process.

10.7.1 WIP by Material Report

The WIP by Material Report provides information on materials which are in the queue, being worked on, or have completed status at a specific location. This report is also used to find the quantity of SFCs with different status at a specified location and total quantity of SFCs for a material of a shop order. You search this report with multiple input parameters such as material with specific version, operation, SFC, work center category, work center, shop order, reporting center, RMA number, customer and customer order. You can view the search results in a graphical or tabular view as shown in Figure 10.37. This report shows material (linked to the SFC Report), quantity in queue, quantity in work and quantity total.

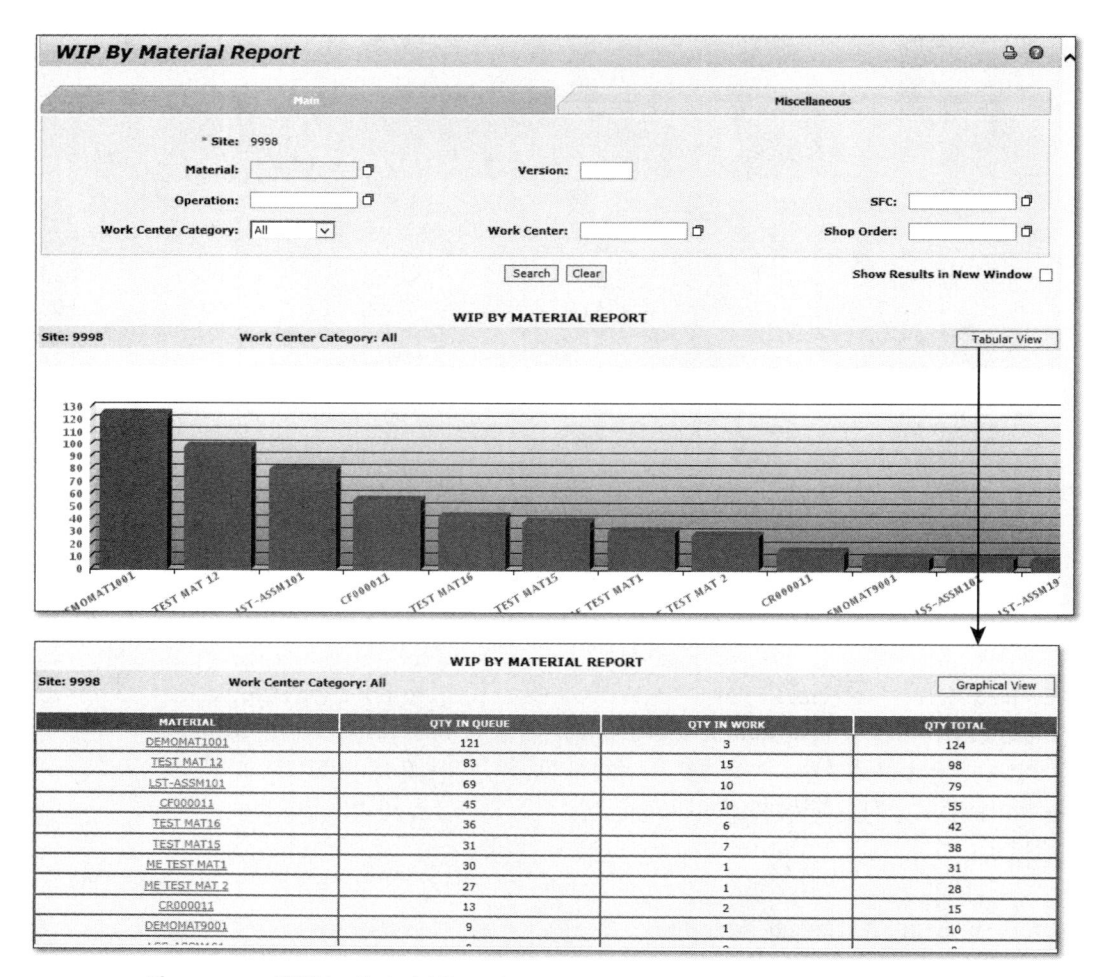

Figure 10.37 WIP by Material Report

10.7.2 WIP by Operation Report

The WIP by Operation Report provides information about quantities accrued by SFCs which are in the queue, being worked on, or have completed status at a specific operation. You search this report with multiple input parameters such as material and its version, operation, SFC, work center category, work center, shop order, reporting center, RMA number, customer and customer order. The search result shows operation (linked to the WIP by Material Report), quantity in queue, quantity in work and quantity total as shown in Figure 10.38.

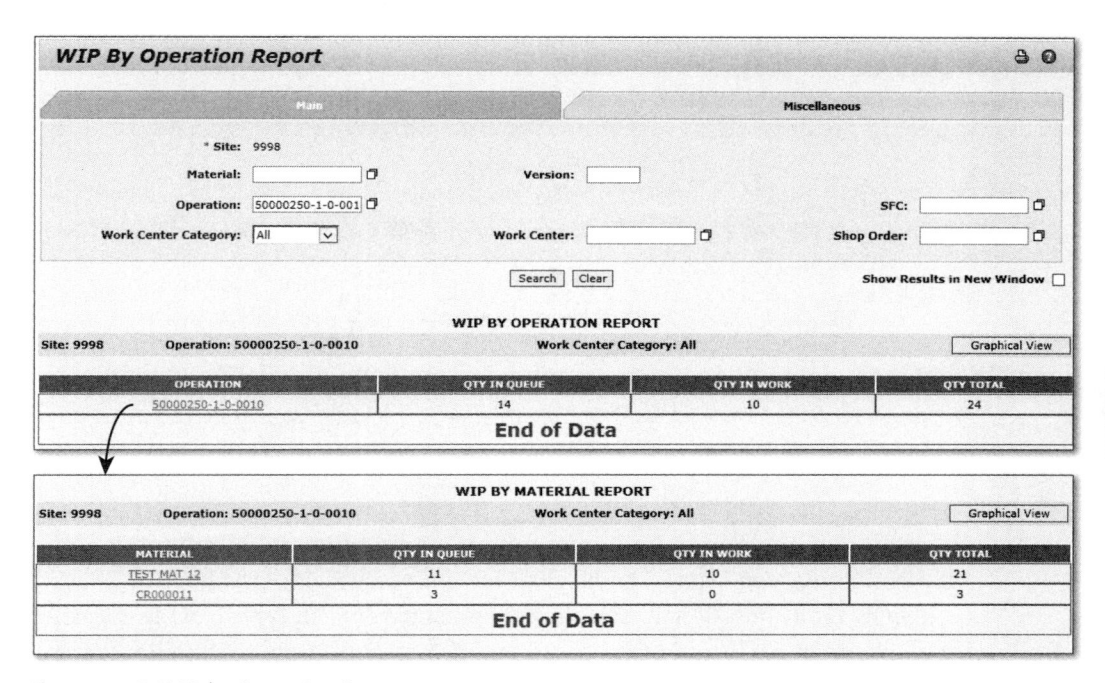

Figure 10.38 WIP by Operation Report

10.7.3 WIP by Work Center Report

WIP by Operation Report provides information regarding the quantities accrued by SFCs which are in the queue or being worked on at a specific work center. Using this report you can find the quantity of materials which are in queue at the particular work center and the quantity of materials that are in work at the particular work center. The search result shows work center (linked to the WIP by Operation Report), quantity in queue, quantity in work and quantity total as shown in Figure 10.39.

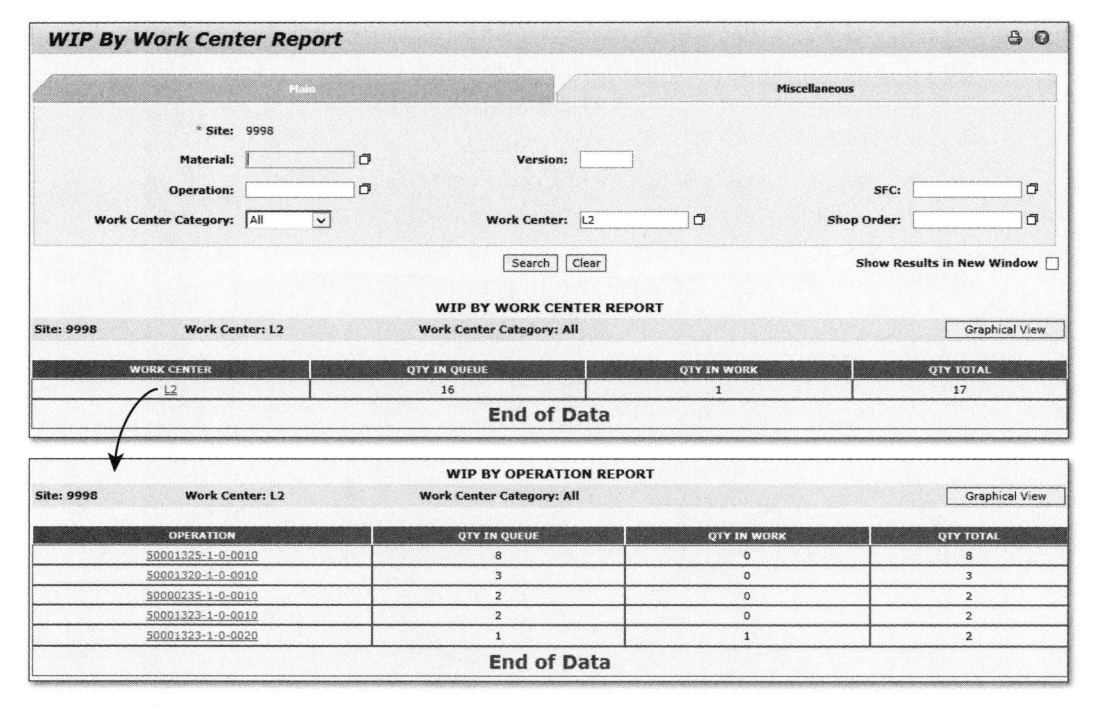

Figure 10.39 WIP by Work Center Report

10.8 Summary

In this chapter, you learned about the Production Operator Dashboard, the available POD types in SAP ME, and the functionality of each type. You also learned how to configure custom PODs based on business requirements and how to execute different shop floor activities through the POD. This chapter also described the List Maintenance activity in SAP ME and the standard production and WIP reports available in SAP ME.

In the next chapter, you will learn about the Message Board service functionality in SAP ME.

This chapter explains the Message Board service in SAP ME. It addresses message type maintenance and process workflow maintenance, which are related to the Message Board service. It also explains how the real-time message display appears on the Production Operator Dashboard.

11   Message Board Service

In manufacturing execution processes, users may need to be notified or alerted by messages for different issues and events that may occur on the shop-floor. SAP ME provides *Message Board* functionality to search and take corrective actions for system-generated or user-generated messages in the manufacturing process. SAP ME provides a list of preconfigured message types, and those message types are invoked and messages are generated based on the production situations that occur. In addition to using system-generated messages, shop floor users can also create new messages through the Message Board; these are called *free-form messages*. These free-form messages can be generated on the fly and sent to shop floor user groups for immediate attention to any production-related issue.

Real-Time Message Display (RTMD) uses the ![icon] icon next to the HELP icon on the POD as the messages are generated. RTMD in the POD communicates the need for immediate attention from a shop floor user. RTMD appears when it is configured to run in a POD and messages are configured as POD NOTIFICATION through the Message Type Maintenance activity. The SEVERITY configuration of a message determines the color of the RTMD icon (see Section 11.2 for more information). System-provided messages are processed through a workflow provided by SAP ME. In Message Type Maintenance, you can find the associated workflow for each message type. As per the assigned process workflow, messages are processed, and they are set to a CLOSED status through appropriate actions.

Another key functionality of the Message Board is sending email notifications. To enable this functionality, configure the E-MAIL SERVER and SOURCE MAIL ADDRESS fields in System Rule Maintenance. When a message is generated for the Message Board, an email is also sent to the designated email address (a single email address or multiple addresses depending on the configuration on the NOTIFICATION tab of Message Type Maintenance). Figure 11.1 shows the SAP ME–provided default Message Board.

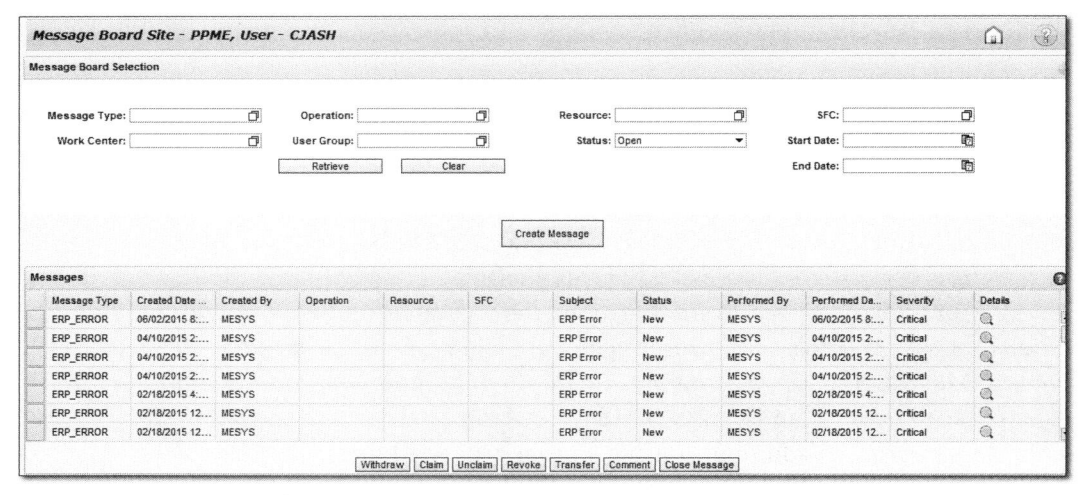

Figure 11.1 Default Message Board in SAP ME

In this chapter, we will discuss the Message Board features and maintaining message type and process workflow to display and process the message in Message Board. Also we will discuss about usages of different message types, creating message and real-time display in Message Board.

11.1 Message Board Features

SAP ME provides a Message Board POD (MESSAGE_BOARD) with a default configuration, which you can find from the POD Maintenance activity. Open the Message Board POD from the SAP ME activity panel list, or from a POD when configured as a POD Plugin from a button or from the Activity List, and search for messages using required filter parameters (such as Message Type, Operation, Resource, SFC, Work Center, User Group, Status, Start Date, and End Date). Next, let's discuss how the Message Board works for shop floor users.

The Message Board POD consists of two sections: MESSAGE BOARD SELECTION and MESSAGE LIST (see Figure 11.1). The MESSAGE BOARD SELECTION area contains multiple input parameters for search functionality. When the Message Board POD loads, it displays all open messages within the MESSAGE LIST area. By specifying filter parameter values, a user can retrieve specific messages. When messages are displayed in the MESSAGES table, a user can click on the DETAILS icon for a message available in the MESSAGES table and view the message details in a new pop-up window. In the Message Board, messages can be processed in several ways, such as by using the action events available in the Message Board POD, action events available in the MESSAGE DETAILS pop-up, and actions based on the process workflow activities associated with a message type. The Message Board POD provides multiple buttons located at the bottom of the MESSAGE LIST area for manual actions by users, such as CREATE MESSAGE, WITHDRAW, CLAIM, UNCLAIM, REVOKE, TRANSFER, COMMENT, and CLOSE MESSAGE. Now, let's explore the purpose of these actions:

- CREATE MESSAGE

    Through this event, a user can create a free-form message that can be sent to the user group per the configuration of the FREE_FORM message type. CREATE MESSAGE opens a pop-up window in which a user can enter the subject of the message in the SUBJECT field and the message content in the MESSAGE BODY field. Clicking on the CREATE button creates the message, as shown in Figure 11.2, and the RETURN TO POD button returns the user to the Message Board POD. You can pre-define the default values for these parameters while configuring the message type as explained in Section 11.2.

> **Note: Opening Create Message dialog from POD**
>
> The Create Message dialog can also be configured as a button on a POD, where a user can create Messages while working in a POD.

- WITHDRAW

    A message can be withdrawn only by its creator. This event is used when the message was created by error and is no longer required. When a user selects a message he or she created from the message list and clicks on the WITHDRAW button, a pop-up dialog appears in which the user can enter a comment and click on the WITHDRAW button to complete the process. Through this event, the message status is changed to WITHDRAWN.

- CLAIM

    A user can lock a message before processing by claiming it so that another user cannot process the same message and they can see that action is already claimed. We recommend locking a message before performing any action on it. After clicking on the CLAIM button from the Message Board POD, a user can enter a comment in the pop-up dialog that appears and click on the CLAIM button within the dialog to claim a message. This event changes the status of the message to CLAIMED.

- UNCLAIM

    This event is used to reverses the CLAIM action for a message. UNCLAIM changes the message status to IN QUEUE so that another user can lock the same message through a CLAIM event.

- REVOKE

    This event changes the status of a message to REVOKE. It is used when no further processing can be performed for the message and the message is no longer needed.

- TRANSFER

    Through this event, a message can be transferred to a different user group. If the message comes to the wrong user group or the current user group can't process the message, then it is sent to another user group for processing. TRANSFER changes the message status to IN QUEUE.

- COMMENT

    This event is used to log comments as additional information against a message; it does not change the status of the message.

- CLOSE MESSAGE

    Through this event, a user can close a message directly from the Message Board POD. It changes the status of the message to CLOSED. This is used primarily for simple message types, when there is no other complex workflow exists against the message.

> **Note: Comment Dialog**
>
> When a user clicks on each action button (available below the MESSAGE LIST area) from the Message Board POD, a comment dialog appears automatically to add comment for the action. After entering a comment, the user can click on the appropriate button to take the action corresponding to the button the user clicked on the Message Board POD.

11.2 Message Type Maintenance

In the previous section, you learned that messages are displayed in the Message Board POD based on message type and that messages can be searched using the MESSAGE TYPE input parameter. The message type can be created, maintained, or managed through the Message Type Maintenance activity in SAP ME. Now, let's discuss how each message type is maintained and its key configurations in Message Type Maintenance. SAP ME provides a list of predefined message types. In Message Type Maintenance, you can select a message type through the value help and then check its details or update its existing configuration, as shown in Figure 11.2.

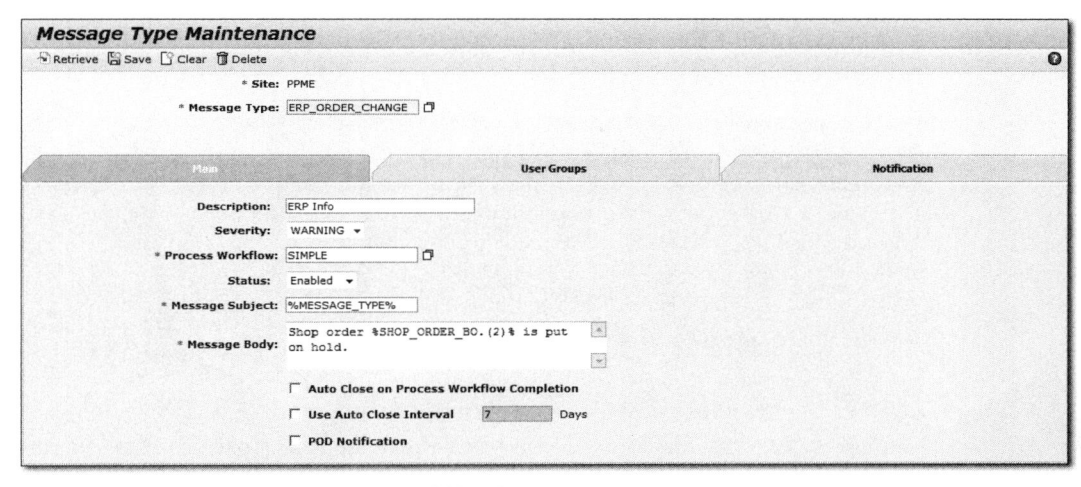

Figure 11.2 Maintaining Message Types in SAP ME

In the Message Type Maintenance activity, you can configure the following options in the Main Tab:

- SEVERITY
  This dropdown sets the message type priority and shows the importance of a message type to a user group. SAP ME provides three values for severity: INFO, WARNING, and CRITICAL. Each severity matches a color code and an icon used in the POD via RTMD functionality.

- PROCESS WORKFLOW
  SAP ME provides a list of predefined process workflows. You can select appropriate process workflow from value help and assign it to a message type. Mes-

sages are processed based on the process workflow selection. See Section 11.3 for more information.

- STATUS
  This field is used to enable or disable the message type. The STATUS dropdown provides ENABLED and DISABLED values.

- MESSAGE SUBJECT
  This field provides the subject of the message; the information is tagged with a message type when it is generated and appears in Message Board. In the MESSAGE SUBJECT field, you can either enter text or replaceable parameters.

- MESSAGE BODY
  This field contains the content of the message. In the MESSAGE BODY field, you can either enter text or replaceable parameters.

> **Note: Replaceable Parameters**
>
> Replaceable parameters are variables that can be used the MESSAGE TYPE or MESSAGE BODY fields. A replacement parameter is an uppercase phrase with percent (%) signs as prefixes and suffixes. When SAP ME reads the percent sign, it replaces the parameter name with the field value. SAP ME provides a list of common replaceable parameters for messages—for example, %.ALL.% to get all available information about a message or %SHOP_ORDER_BO.(2)% to get the shop order number of an SFC.

- AUTO CLOSE ON PROCESS WORKFLOW COMPLETION
  You can select this checkbox if you want the system to close a message automatically when all steps of the assigned process workflow are completed. The user then does not need to manually close the message.

- USE AUTO CLOSE INTERVAL
  You can define the auto close interval of message in days through this checkbox and the DAYS field. After passing the defined time interval, a message will be closed automatically by the background process *Auto Close Message by the System*. To check the Auto Close Message by the System settings, open the Background Processing activity in SAP ME from activity list.

- POD NOTIFICATION
  Select this checkbox if you want to display a message in the POD through the RTMD mechanism. The RTMD message is displayed in the POD when the shop floor user clicks on the RTMD icon, and the system displays the messages in the RTMD list. See Section 11.6 for more details.

On the USER GROUPS tab, you can assign a message type to user groups. Users who are members of the assigned user groups will be able to see messages with this message type on the message list. You also need to assign a user to the appropriate user groups to be able to see and perform activities for a particular message type. There must be at least one user group assigned to a message so it can be processed in Message Board POD.

If you need to send an email notification to a user group for a message type when it is generated, then you can assign an email address on the NOTIFICATION tab. To send the email notification, you need to configure E-MAIL SERVER in System Rule Maintenance.

Now you should have a solid foundation for all message type configurations. You can retrieve existing message types and change configurations per your business requirements. In the next section you will learn how to create a process workflow using the message type to display the messages in the Message Board with user interactions.

11.3 Maintaining Process Workflow

A process workflow processes messages through defined steps and finally completes the message in SAP ME. In SAP ME, process workflows are executed by the workflow engine and are used only for Message Board activity. Process workflows are maintained through the Process Workflow Maintenance activity in SAP ME. SAP ME provides a list of predefined process workflows, such as BUYOFF_WF, OP_RES_HOLD_CONSEC_NC, OP_RES_HOLD_SPC_VIOL, OP_RES_HOLD_SPC_WARN, OP_RES_HOLD_YIELD_RATE, and SIMPLE. Each process workflow consists of a list of activities that are executed per the sequence defined in the process workflow. Activities can be executed manually by shop floor users or automatically by the system. Figure 11.3 shows the configuration of the BUYOFF_WF process workflow.

> **Note**
>
> Each process workflow is specific for the message type for which it is defined and should not be used directly for other message type, unless the implications are understood and reconfigured properly for the new message type.

11 | Message Board Service

Figure 11.3 Configuration of BUYOFF_WF Process Workflow

Now, let's discuss the available process workflows in SAP ME:

- **BUYOFF_WF**
  BUYOFF_WF is used with the BUYOFF_REQUEST message type to complete or reject a generated buyoff request in order to complete work for an SFC. It consists of two activities—ACCEPT_BUYOFF and REJECT_BUYOFF—which are manual activities. Table 11.1 shows its sequence and activities.

Sequence	Activity
10	ACCEPT_BUYOFF
20	REJECT_BUYOFF

Table 11.1 BUYOFF_WF Process Workflow Activity Sequence

In the manufacturing process, a *buyoff* is used when a high-quality tracking standard must be maintained. A buyoff is a paperless, electronic way to approve the completion of an activity in the shop floor manufacturing process. Through a buyoff, validation is performed on the shop floor that the shop floor user has performed a particular task for an operation. The task can be assembly of components, data collection at an operation, completion of an operation, or so on.

To perform a buyoff, you need to maintain it in the Buyoff Maintenance activity, where you can attach the buyoff via any available attachment point, such as Material Group, material, routing, operation, work center, resource, shop order, SFC, and so on. You also need to specify the BUYOFF_REQUEST value for the MESSAGE TYPE field. When a shop floor user works on the POD with the attached operation (assuming that an operation is attached with a buyoff in

Buyoff Maintenance) and performs start and complete of an SFC, the SFC moves to the *Complete Pending* state because of an open buyoff. The assigned user can *accept* or *reject* the BUYOFF_REQUEST message in the Message Board which then automatically completes the SFC from the POD. Using the Buyoff Report, you can find the details of buy-off activities performed by a shop floor user during the manufacturing process.

- **OP_RES_HOLD_CONSEC_NC**

  OP_RES_HOLD_CONSEC_NC is used with the RTW_CONSEC_NC message type, which is triggered when the number of NC logged for an SFC number exceeds the maximum allowed. It consists of five activities: CONSEC_NC_RES_HOLD (Consecutive NC Resource Hold), CONSEC_NC_OP_HOLD (Consecutive NC Operation Hold), LOG_CODES (Log Codes), OP_HOLD_RELEASE (Operation Release Hold), and RES_HOLD_RELEASE (Resource Release Hold). The first two activities place the resource and operation on Hold automatically, while the last two release the hold automatically if the log codes has been successfully completed. LOG_CODES is a manual activity, and a shop floor user needs to perform a manual action. The activities are executed sequentially in message as shown in Table 11.2.

Sequence	Activity
10	CONSEC_NC_RES_HOLD
20	CONSEC_NC_OP_HOLD
30	LOG_CODES
40	OP_HOLD_RELEASE
50	RES_HOLD_RELEASE

Table 11.2 OP_RES_HOLD_CONSEC_NC Process Workflow Activity Sequence

- **OP_RES_HOLD_SPC_VIOL**

  OP_RES_HOLD_SPC_VIOL is used with the SPC_ALARM_VIOLATION message type, which is triggered when an SPC rule violation occurs for an SFC (SPC trend rules are described in the SPC Alarm Severity Maintenance section in Chapter 8). It consists of five activities: SPC_VIOL_RES_HOLD (SPC Violation Resource Hold), SPC_VIOL_OP_HOLD (SPC Violation Operation Hold), LOG_CODES (Log Codes), OP_HOLD_RELEASE (Operation Release Hold), and RES_HOLD_RELEASE (Resource Release Hold). The first two activities place the resource and operation on Hold automatically, while the last two release the hold automatically if the log codes has been successfully completed. The activities are executed sequentially as listed in Table 11.3.

Sequence	Activity
10	SPC_VIOL_RES_HOLD
20	SPC_VIOL_OP_HOLD
30	LOG_CODES
40	OP_HOLD_RELEASE
50	RES_HOLD_RELEASE

Table 11.3 OP_RES_HOLD_SPC_VIOL Process Workflow Activity Sequence

▶ **OP_RES_HOLD_SPC_WARN**
OP_RES_HOLD_SPC_WARN is used with message type SPC_ALARM_WARNING, which is triggered when an SPC warning takes place. It consists of five activities: SPC_WARN_RES_HOLD (SPC Warning Resource Hold), SPC_WARN_OP_HOLD (SPC Warning Operation Hold), LOG_CODES (Log Codes), OP_HOLD_RELEASE (Operation Release Hold), and RES_HOLD_RELEASE (Resource Release Hold). The first two activities place the resource and operation on Hold automatically, while the last two release the hold automatically if the log codes has been successfully completed. The activities are executed sequentially as listed in Table 11.4.

Sequence	Activity
10	SPC_WARN_RES_HOLD
20	SPC_WARN_OP_HOLD
30	LOG_CODES
40	OP_HOLD_RELEASE
50	RES_HOLD_RELEASE

Table 11.4 OP_RES_HOLD_SPC_WARN Process Workflow Activity Sequence

▶ **OP_RES_HOLD_YIELD_RATE**
OP_RES_HOLD_YIELD_RATE is used with message type RTW_YIELD_RATE, which is triggered when a yield rate is not achieved (details of yield rate configuration for Yield Processing are available in the Section 11.4). It consists of five activities: YIELD_RES_HOLD (RTW Yield Rate Resource Hold), YIELD_OP_

HOLD (RTW Yield Rate Operation Hold), LOG_CODES (Log Codes), OP_HOLD_RELEASE (Operation Release Hold), and RES_HOLD_RELEASE (Resource Release Hold). The first two activities place the resource and operation on Hold automatically, while the last two release the hold automatically if the log codes has been successfully completed. The activities are executed sequentially as listed in Table 11.5.

Sequence	Activity
10	YIELD_RES_HOLD
20	YIELD_OP_HOLD
30	LOG_CODES
40	OP_HOLD_RELEASE
50	RES_HOLD_RELEASE

Table 11.5 OP_RES_HOLD_YIELD_RATE Process Workflow Activity Sequence

- **SIMPLE**
  The SIMPLE process workflow is used with FREE_FORM or all other message types and is used for manual messages for which no action is mandatory. No activities are defined in this message flow.

11.4 Use of Different Message Types

In the previous sections, you learned about message types and process workflow configurations. Now, let's discuss how different message types are used in SAP ME to generate messages:

- **Buyoff Maintenance**
  In the Buyoff Maintenance activity, you can specify the BUYOFF_REQUEST message type, which will be triggered when an SFC is started, completed, and moved to the complete pending state because of an open buyoff. The assigned user for the message type will get a notification to accept or reject the message from the Message Board.

- **Real-Time Warnings Maintenance**
  Through the Real-Time Warnings Maintenance activity, you can define yield processing and consecutive identical NCs for an SFC that belongs to a material,

operation, and resource that you need to maintain in input fields. In the YIELD LOWER LIMIT(%) field, specify the lower yield limit. In the MESSAGE TYPE field, specify RTW_YIELD_RATE, which will be triggered when the yield processing rate goes below the specified value in the YIELD LOWER LIMIT(%) field. Figure 11.4 shows the Real-Time Warnings Maintenance activity in SAP ME.

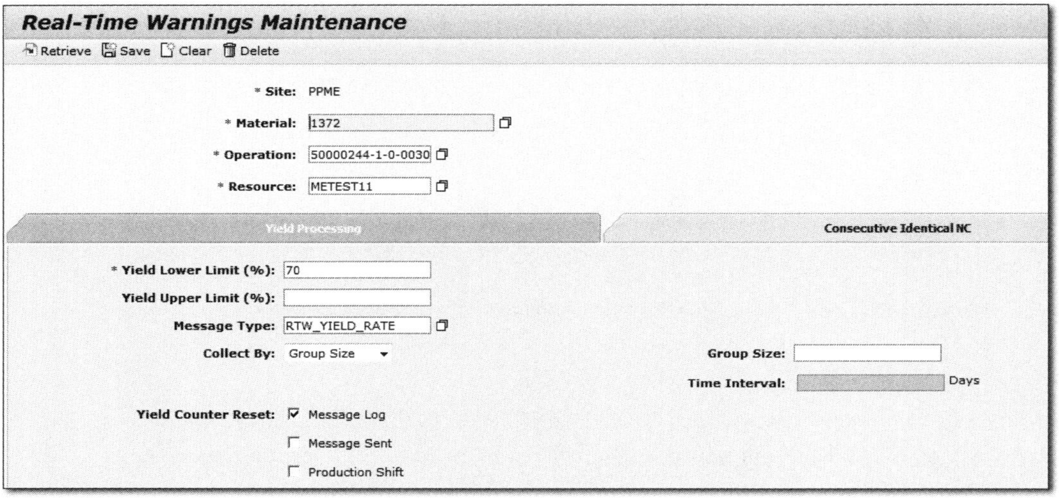

Figure 11.4 Real-Time Warnings Maintenance

On the CONSECUTIVE IDENTICAL NC tab, you can add a new row and specify the NC code or group in the NC COUNT LEVEL column, NONCONFORMANCE based on the NC group or code selection, COUNT, and message type RTW_CONSEC_NC in the MESSAGE TYPE field, as shown in Figure 11.5. Message type RTW_CONSEC_NC is triggered when the consecutive identical NC count reaches or exceeds the specified value in the COUNT field.

▶ **SPC Alarm Severity Maintenance**
In the SPC Alarm Severity Maintenance activity, you can configure SPC Violation (SPC_ALARM_VIOLATION) and SPC Warning (SPC_ALARM_WARNING) message types for SPC trend rule.

▶ **Material Maintenance**
In the Material Maintenance activity, you can configure site-to-site transfer for a material. You can specify the SITE_TO_SITE_MESSAGE message type for sending a message to the users that informs them when an SFC transfer occurs.

▶ **NC Code Maintenance**
In the NC Code Maintenance activity, you specify a message type in the MESSAGE TYPE field for each NC code. The message is triggered when the NC code is logged for an SFC.

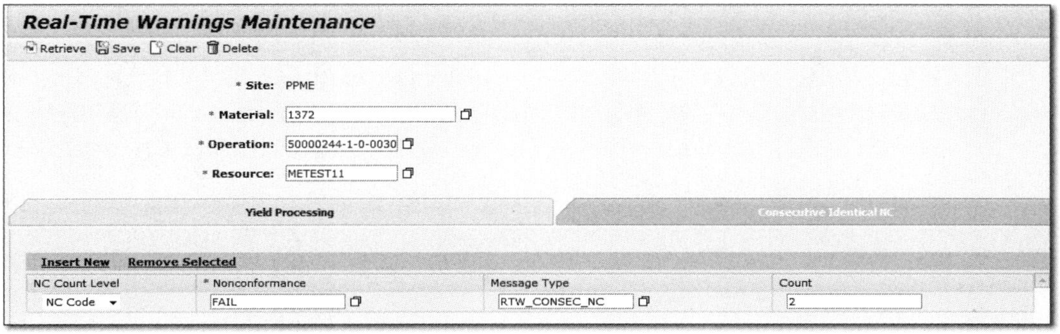

Figure 11.5 Consecutive Identical NC Maintenance

11.5 Creating Message

In the previous section, you learned how and why to use different message types. Now, we will discuss how to create free-form messages with the required configurations. Free-form messages send information from any user to any other users (based on the configured users in a user group in SAP ME) on the fly during the shop floor execution process for additional communication purposes. A shop floor user can create a message from the Message Board or from the POD. The Create Message (CREATE_MESS_PLUGIN) plug-in can be configured in the POD using a button.

To begin, SAP ME provides the SIMPLE process workflow for the FREE_FORM message type; this workflow does not contain any predefined activities. You can use it for your free-form messages, or you can create your own process workflow per your business requirements.

In the Message Type Maintenance activity, you can find the predefined FREE_FORM message type, which you can use for free-form message creation, or you can change the configuration as needed. For example, you can change the message severity based on priority, change the message subject or message body, update the user group list, or add email addresses to send email notifications.

11 | Message Board Service

In the POD Maintenance activity, you can retrieve the MESSAGE_BOARD POD preconfigured by SAP ME. On the BUTTONS tab, you will see that the CREATE_MESSAGE button is already configured, and on the LAYOUT tab, the CREATE_MESS_PLUGIN activity is configured as a pop-up type. Therefore, in the Message Board POD, you will find the CREATE MESSAGE button, and when you click on it, the Create Message plug-in activity opens in a pop-up window.

If you want to add the Create Message plug-in to another POD, add a new button and assign the CREATE_MESS_PLUGIN activity with that button on the BUTTONS tab. On the LAYOUT tab, you can configure the CREATE_MESS_PLUGIN activity as a pop-up, as shown in Figure 11.6.

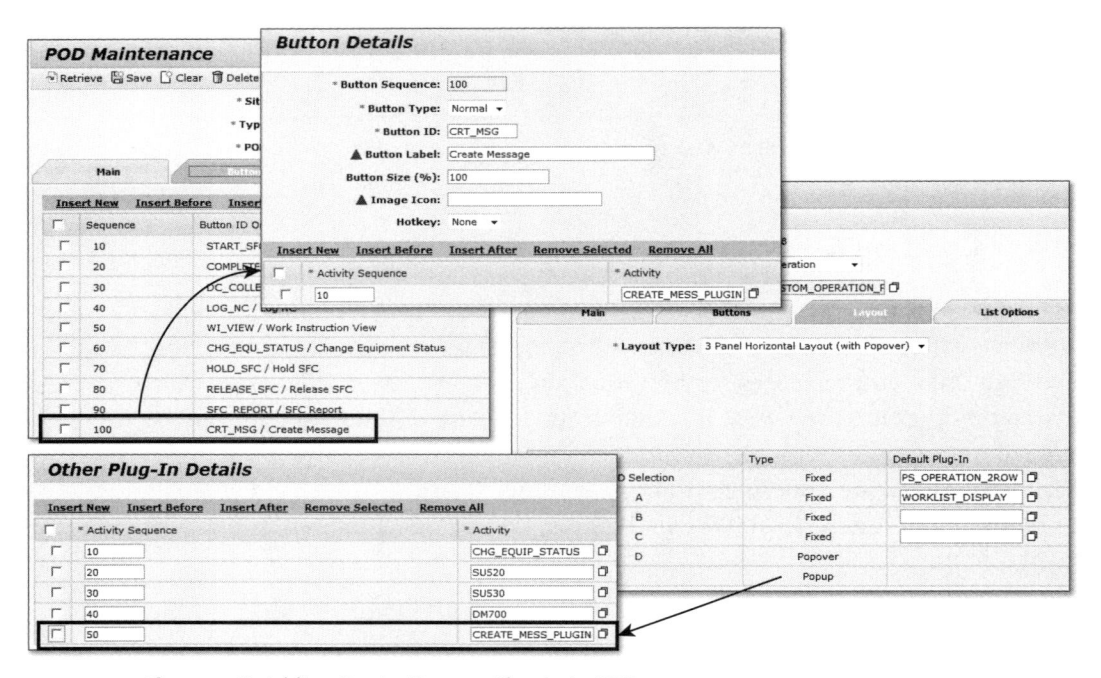

Figure 11.6 Adding Create Message Plug-In in POD

To create a free-form message, a shop floor user can open the Message Board activity from the SAP ME activity menu list and click on the CREATE MESSAGE button. The CREATE MESSAGE pop-up will open, in which the user can find noneditable SEVERITY and USER GROUP fields (which appear based on the message type configuration using the Message Type Maintenance activity) as shown in Figure 11.7. If FREE_FORM is not selected in the MESSAGE TYPE field, then the user can select FREE_FORM as the value for the MESSAGE TYPE field. SUBJECT and MESSAGE BODY also appear, per the configuration, but the user can edit those field values. After specifying the subject and message body, the user clicks on CREATE, the system will create the message, and it will be sent to user groups per the user group configuration of the FREE_FORM message type. Information about the message created will be displayed in the upper part of the CREATE MESSAGE pop-up. If email IDs are configured in the Message Type Maintenance activity for FREE_FORM messages, then email notifications will also be sent. By clicking on the RETURN TO POD button, the user can return to the Message Board. In the Message Board, the user can find the newly created free-form message. Figure 11.7 illustrates the FREE_FORM message creation steps.

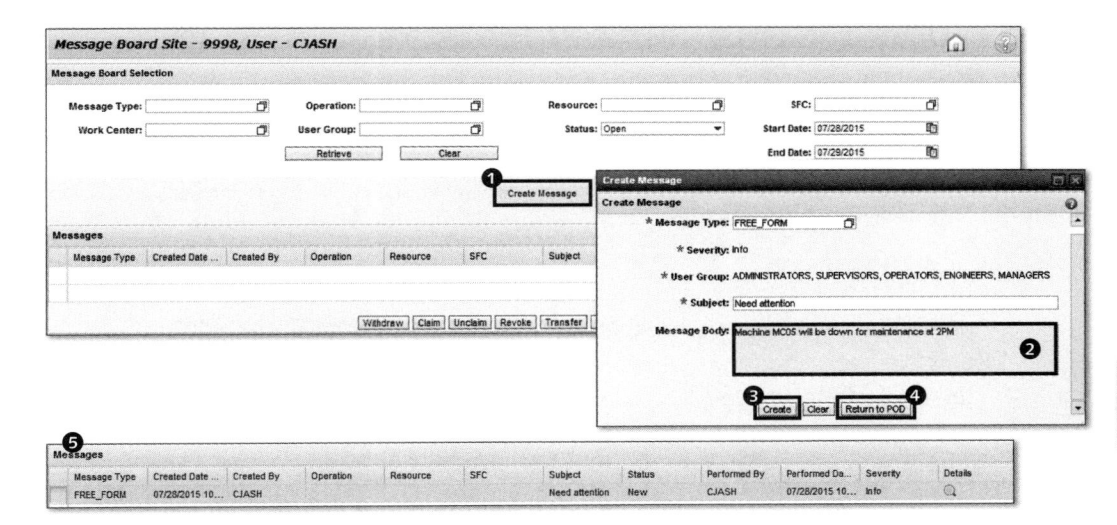

Figure 11.7 Creating FREE_FORM Message from Message Board

> **Note**
>
> The field values of the message that can be configured to be displayed or not depends on the CREATE_MESS_PLUGIN Activity on the Rules tab. Values that can be displayed or not on the Create Message Plugin include:
> - Material
> - Operation
> - Resource
> - SFC
> - Work Center

11.6 Real-Time Message Display

RTMD functionality is used to display the real-time message in the shop floor execution POD for the immediate attention of a shop floor user. RTMD appears in the POD as a colored icon. The color of the icon indicates the severity (INFO, WARNING, or CRITICAL) of the message, which is configured through Message Type Maintenance for each message type. RTMD identifies critically important messages for quick action when the shop floor user is not continuously monitoring the Message Board to find critical messages. To display a message in the POD, select the POD NOTIFICATION checkbox in the Message Type Maintenance activity for a message type. A shop floor user can view the message by clicking on the icon that appears in the POD. Clicking on the icon displays the message list with messages configured for POD notification in order of priority: CRITICAL messages first, then WARNING messages, and finally INFO messages.

> **Note: Icon Color for Severity**
>
> The POD icon color differs depending on message severity. Red indicates CRITICAL, yellow indicates WARNING, and blue indicates INFO.

In the Message Type Maintenance activity, retrieve the message type and select the POD NOTIFICATION checkbox to display the message in the POD. To set the message type priority as critical, select the CRITICAL value in the SEVERITY field of the retrieved message type, as shown in Figure 11.8.

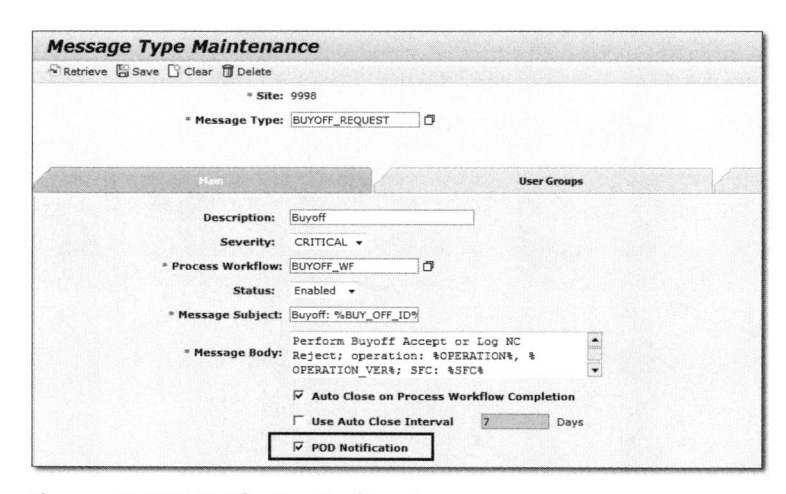

Figure 11.8 POD Notification Configuration

In the POD Maintenance activity, retrieve the POD, and on the MAIN tab, set the value for the REAL-TIME MESSAGE DISPLAY field to ICON, as shown in Figure 11.9. If NONE is selected the Real Time Message will never display.

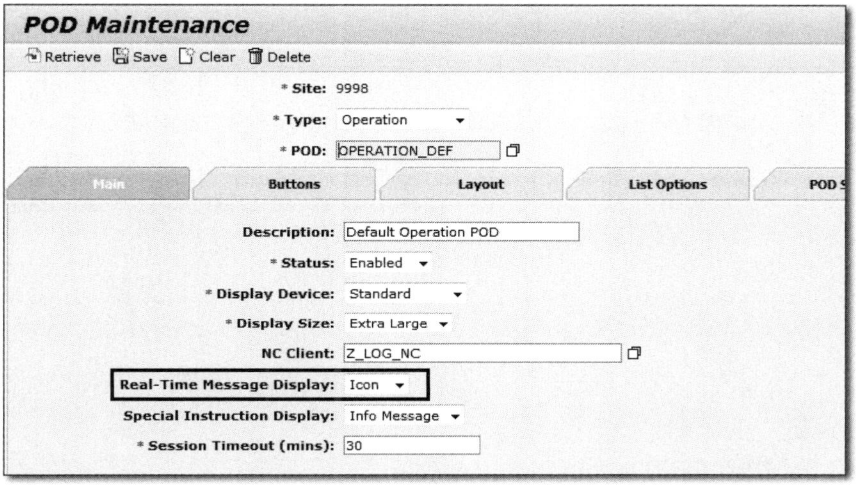

Figure 11.9 Real-Time Message Display Configuration in POD Maintenance

Also assign the MESSAGE_BOARD_LIST activity in the POD layout; switch to the LAYOUT tab, and insert the MESSAGE_BOARD_LIST plug-in as a pop-up.

In the System Setup Maintenance activity, configure the value of the `rted.polling.period.seconds` property (RTMD polling period in seconds) to poll through background processes for messages configured for POD notification; the messages will be displayed in the RTMD list in the POD. Figure 11.10 shows the `rted.polling.period.seconds` parameter value configuration in System Setup Maintenance. This configuration is required only till SAP ME 15.0 release, as from the next release JMS messaging queue is used to provide push notifications.

max.records.for.sfc.browse	Maximum number of records SFC browse can return per request; default is 400	1000
max.upload.filesize	Maximum upload file size is in bytes; default is 1048576	104857600
report.chart.font	Report charts font name; default is Dialog	Dialog
rted.polling.period.seconds	Real-Time Message Display polling period in seconds; default is 5	60
sfc.assignment.timeout	Timeout value for Supervisor Work Assignment in minutes; default is 5	5
sfc.browse.inexact.fast.search.enabled	If true, SFC browse does not use DB full-list ordering of SFC numbers to make search faster; SFC browse returns first several SFC numbers found in database	false

Figure 11.10 rted.polling.period.seconds Property Value Setup

Now, a shop floor user can execute the shop floor manufacturing process, and when a message type is triggered (as configured for POD notification), it will appear in the POD as an icon. Figure 11.11 shows the RTMD icon (upper-right corner) and the message list that appears for the NC log in a quality inspection operation.

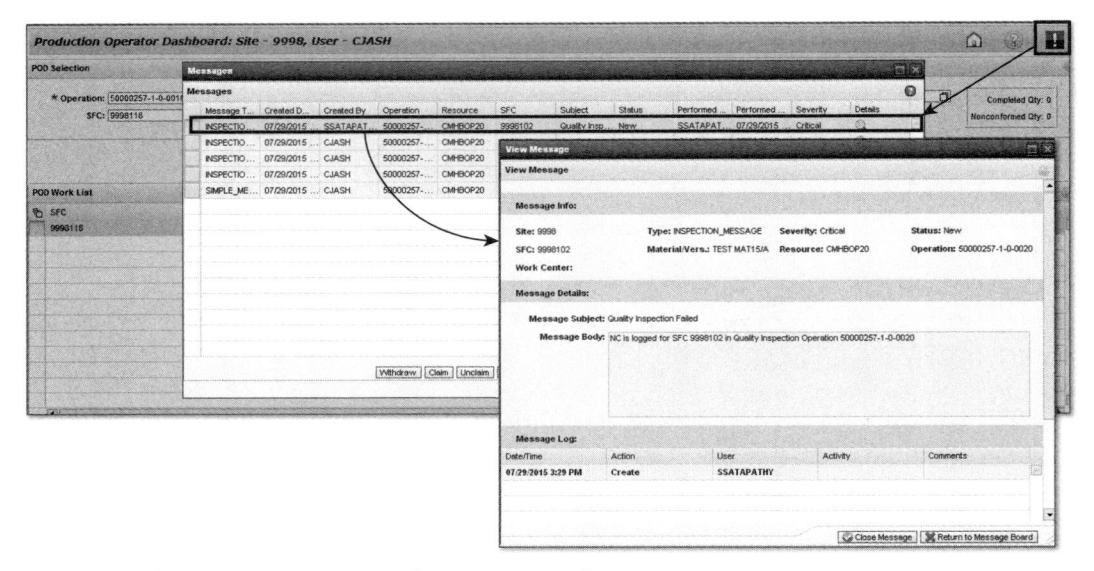

Figure 11.11 RTMD in POD for NC Log in Quality Inspection

11.7 Summary

In this chapter, you learned about the detailed functionality of the Message Board functionality in SAP ME, along with the Message Type Maintenance and Process Workflow Maintenance activities. You also learned about configurations of different process workflows provided by SAP ME and how the process workflows are used for each message type. This chapter also described the use of different message types and how to create free-form messages in SAP ME based on business requirements. We also covered RTMD functionality and required configuration.

In next chapter you will learn about *Labor Tracking* functionality in SAP ME.

This chapter explains labor tracking on the shop floor using SAP ME. It describes how to track time for employee labor and time spent finishing the product on the shop floor along with related activities like labor charge codes, cost centers, configuring shifts, clock in and clock out, and labor rules

12 Labor Tracking

In SAP ME, labor tracking functionality enables tracking time for employee labor and time spent to manufacture a product. Labor tracking is an important activity because employee labor time is related to payroll or billing and because the time spent to manufacture a product is related to the product cost. Through labor tracking, you can capture the attendance of each employee along with direct labor time and indirect labor time. *Direct labor time* means that the operator is performing certain tasks on the shop floor, such as manufacturing a product or restocking, and *indirect labor time* indicates that the operator is not working or the task is not related to production, such as attending training or meetings. Labor tracking time is calculated against the labor charge code (LCC) for a site in SAP ME, and LCC is assigned to a cost center, which is a unit of an organization for which the cost is calculated. Figure 12.1 illustrates the overall functionality of labor tracking in SAP ME.

To set up labor tracking functionality, you need to perform configuration activities in SAP ME, such as maintaining cost centers, LCCs, user shifts, labor rules, the production calendar, and so on. In the following sections, we will discuss different maintenance activities and how labor tracking is performed for the manufacturing process in SAP ME. We will start with an overview of how to maintain production shifts and the production calendar, and then move on to a discussion of maintaining cost centers, LCCs, labor rules, and user shifts. Finally, we will discuss the clock in and clock out functionality for both laborers and supervisors and cover how supervisors can edit and approve records.

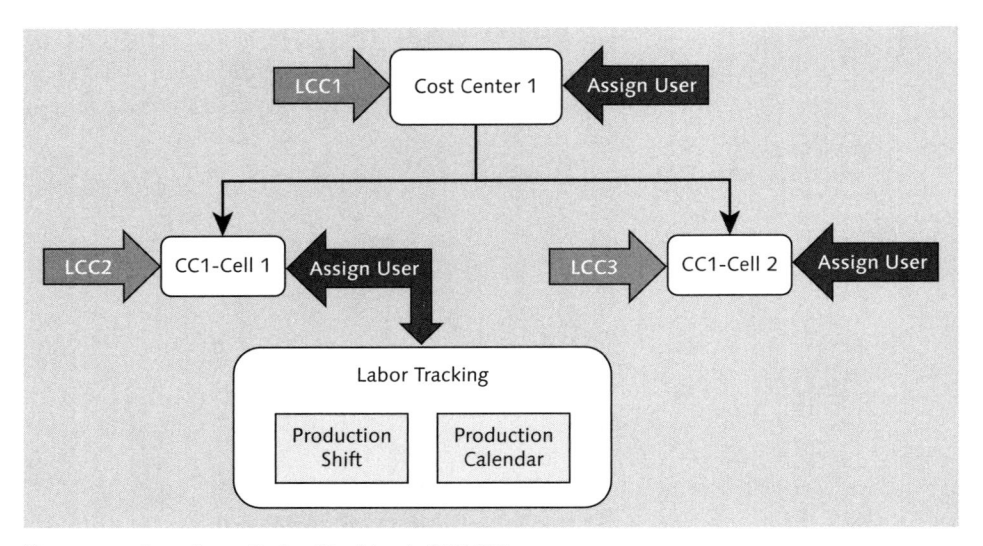

Figure 12.1 Overview of Labor Tracking in SAP ME

12.1 Maintaining Production Shifts and Calendar

In SAP ME, the production calendar is used to define production days, nonproduction days (holidays), and half-production days for a week and for a month for a specific site. To configure the production calendar for a month, you need to define the day type first through the Production Shift Maintenance activity. SAP ME provides a default *day type* called WORKDAY, but you can define other types to meet your business needs. For example, say that for every week you want to define Sunday as a NONPRODUCTION day and Saturday as a HALFPRODUCTION day. To do so, open the Production Shift Maintenance activity and enter the day type and description in DAY TYPE and DESCRIPTION fields, respectively.

For the WORKDAY day type, SAP ME provides preconfigured shifts (such as Shift A, B, and C), as shown in Figure 12.2. To meet your requirements, you can change shift configurations in Production Shift Maintenance for the WORKDAY day type.

Maintaining Production Shifts and Calendar | 12.1

Figure 12.2 Maintaining Production Shifts for WORKDAY

You can create or display a work day type in the DAY TYPE field and specify the production shifts with the corresponding timings for that day type. Day types include the following:

- ACTUAL DAY is the default value for each shift. If you consider each day to have three shifts (24 hours per day, from 00:00 to 23:59), then each shift can be eight hours in duration, and the DAY value can be ACTUAL DAY.

- SHIFT START DAY and SHIFT END DAY are used when a shift crosses midnight. For example, Shift A starts at 06:00 (6 a.m.) and ends at 14:00 (2 p.m.). The first (start)DAY field value for Shift A will be ACTUAL DAY and the second (end) DAY value for shift A will be ACTUAL DAY. Shift B starts at 14:00 (2 p.m.) and ends at 22:00 (10 p.m.). For Shift B, both DAY field values ACTUAL DAY. For Shift C, start time is 22:00 (10 p.m.) and end time is 06:00 (6 a.m.). The first DAY field value for Shift C will be SHIFT START DAY and the second DAY value for Shift C will be SHIFT END DAY, as shown in Figure 12.3.

Figure 12.3 Configuring Actual Day, Shift Start Day, and Shift End Day

> **Note**
>
> You can define different types of production days as well, with different numbers of shifts for different durations. Note that you cannot define a workday more than a maximum duration of 24 hours. It does not necessarily need to start or end at midnight and can span across a calendar day as well.

367

In SAP ME, the production calendar is configured for each month through the Production Calendar Maintenance activity, as shown in Figure 12.4. In this production calendar, two day types are used: *WEEKDAY* and *WEEKEND*. In this example, WEEKDAY consists of three shifts: A (06:00 to 14:00), B (14:00 to 22:00), and C (22:00 to 06:00). WEEKEND contains only one shift: A (08:00 to 16:00). If Sunday is considered a nonproduction day and a holiday every week, then you don't need to define any day type for Sunday.

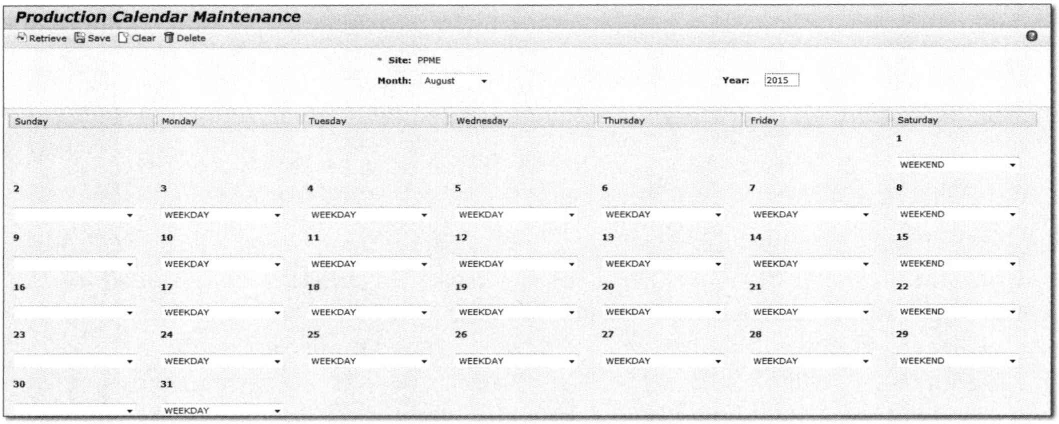

Figure 12.4 Maintaining Production Calendar for a Month

12.2 Maintaining Cost Centers

A cost center is a unit of an organization for which cost is reported. In SAP ME, you can define a cost center in hierarchies and characteristics per the business requirements for a site. To define a cost center, open the Cost Center Maintenance activity and specify the name and description of the cost center in the COST CENTER and DESCRIPTION fields, as shown in Figure 12.5. In the STATUS field, select ENABLED or DISABLED to enable or disable the cost center. Specify the default LCC in the DEFAULT LCC field. The default LCC is used by SAP ME to track the labor time when employees who are assigned in the cost center clock in.

In the User Maintenance activity, you can assign different LCCs for specific users. You will learn more about LCC maintenance in Section 12.3. In the PARENT/ROLLUP CC field, specify the parent or rollup cost center if you have defined a cost center hierarchy for your company. For example, say that an organization has three units: *Production*, *Repair*, and *Quality*. The Repair unit has two child units, *Major Repair* and *Minor Repair*. When you define a Major Repair or Minor Repair cost center in SAP ME, then you can specify Repair as the parent or rollup cost center in the PARENT/ROLLUP CC field. The CUSTOM DATA tab is used to maintain any custom attribute value required for the cost center.

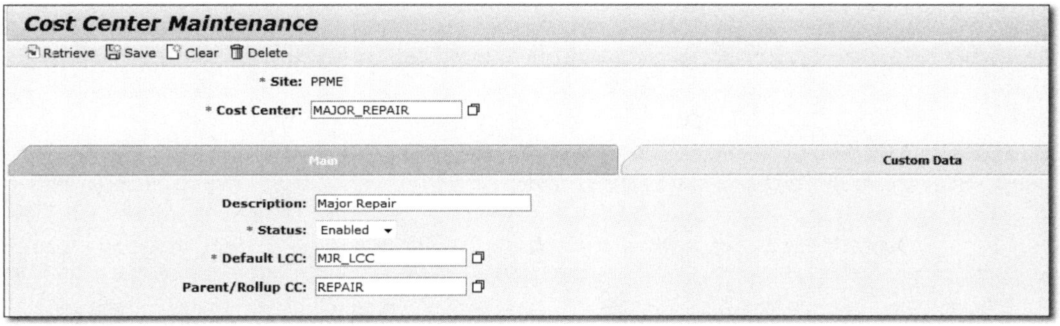

Figure 12.5 Maintaining Cost Center in SAP ME

12.3 Maintaining Labor Charge Codes

In SAP ME, you can define LCCs and characteristics for a site through the Labor Charge Code (LCC) Maintenance activity. The defined LCC is used to track employees' time, and it can be used to track the time spent working on a shop order, which you can assign in the Shop Order Maintenance activity. You can define different LCCs to identify the total labor time taken to perform different types of tasks. In Labor Charge Code (LCC) Maintenance, specify the labor charge code and description in the LABOR CHARGE CODE and DESCRIPTION fields. In the LABOR TYPE field, you can select either DIRECT or INDIRECT, based on whether you want to capture the Direct Labor time (productive) or Indirect Labor time (non-productive). The field value for the LABOR SUBTYPE field depends upon the labor type selection in the LABOR TYPE field. For direct labor, choose from NONE, PRODUCTION, or REWORK; for indirect labor, choose BREAK or IDLE. *Break* indicates break time, and *idle* indicates not on break and not performing any work.

The validity of an LCC is defined through the VALID FROM and VALID TO field values. If the OVERRIDE EXPIRED DATE checkbox is selected, then SAP ME allows you to use the LCC beyond the valid from/to period. Figure 12.6 shows the Labor Charge Code (LCC) Maintenance activity.

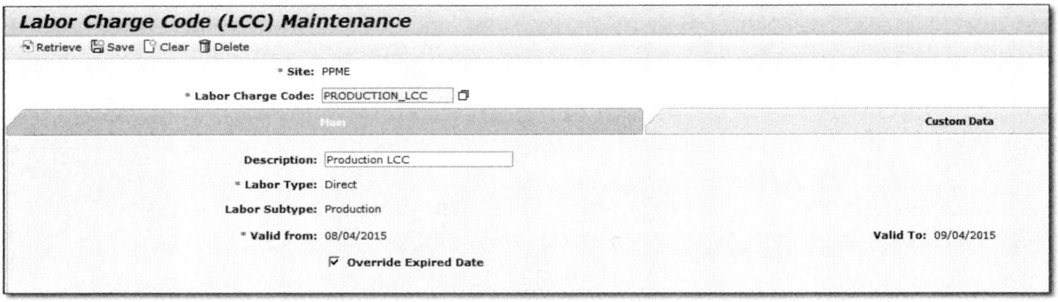

Figure 12.6 Maintaining Labor Charge Codes

> **Note: Labor Charge Code Maintenance**
> Once you define the LCC in SAP ME, the system will not allow you to change the values LABOR TYPE and LABOR SUBTYPE.

12.4 Maintaining Labor Rules

The Labor Rule Maintenance activity allows you to define the labor tracking rules for a site in SAP ME. Through this activity, you can set up rules for Employee Attendance, Default LCC for Shop Orders, and Rollup Processing. In the following subsections, let's discuss how to define each rule in the Labor Rule Maintenance activity.

12.4.1 Attendance Rules

On the ATTENDANCE RULES tab, define rules for user attendance. Select the AUTOMATIC CLOCK-OUT AT SHIFT END checkbox if you want to automatically clock out a user on rollup and assign the normal shift end time for clock out when the user does not clock out at the shift's end.

> **Note: Automatic Clock Out at Shift End**
> If the user is working in the POD at the shift's end, then Automatic Clock-Out at Shift End will not be performed.

If the ALLOW CLOCK-IN ON NON-PRODUCTION DAY checkbox is selected, then SAP ME will allow a user to clock time on a nonproduction day. You learned about the types of days, including nonproduction days, in Section 12.1.

> **Note: Allow Clock In on Nonproduction Day**
> The Supervisor Clock-In/Out activity provides another way for a supervisor to clock a user's time on a nonproduction day.

The CLOCK-IN/OUT RANGE CONTROL field is used to define the control for an employee's clock in and clock out. SAP ME allows three values (ONLY WITHIN INTERVAL, ONLY WITHIN SHIFT AND INTERVAL, and ANYTIME) for the clock in/out range control; select one from the available list. ONLY WITHIN INTERVAL allows you to clock in and clock out during the clock in interval and clock-out interval, respectively. ONLY WITHIN SHIFT AND INTERVAL allows you to clock in during the clock in interval and during the shift and clock out during the clock out interval and during the shift. ANYTIME allows you to clock in and clock out at any time.

The CLOCK-IN CONTROL field is used to define the rule for a user's clock-in time. Clock-in control can be performed three ways: automatic clock in at logon, require clock in before logon, or manual clock in. Select one value from the available list for CLOCK-IN CONTROL field. AUTOMATIC CLOCK-IN AT LOGON will clock in a user automatically when the user logs on. REQUIRE CLOCK-IN BEFORE LOGON will force a user to clock in before logging on in SAP ME. MANUAL CLOCK-IN allows a user to clock in manually in SAP ME.

The ID FOR CLOCK-IN/OUT field is used to define what type of identification will be required to clock in or clock out. The possible field values are BADGE NUMBER, EMPLOYEE NUMBER, and USER ID; select one value from the available list.

The ACTION APPLIED AT CLOCK-OUT TO SFCS IN WORK field is used to define the Clock-Out rule for active SFCs. If you define the value as NONE, then the system leaves the SFC the user is working on at an Active status; if you select SIGNOFF, then the system will sign off the shop floor user's SFC.

The ON PREMISES REPORT RETENTION PERIOD field is used to define the time period in hours for which the On Premises report will show the user's labor time (clock in and clock out) data.

Figure 12.7 shows the ATTENDANCE RULES tab in Labor Rule Maintenance.

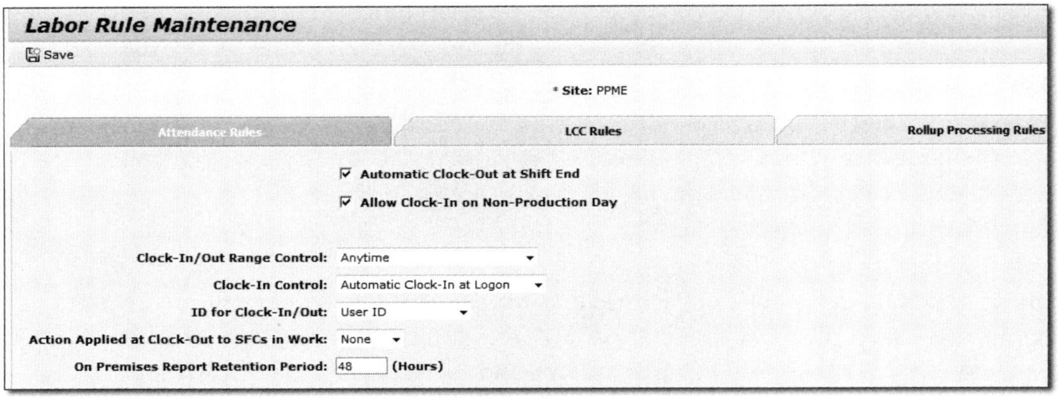

Figure 12.7 Defining Attendence Rules in Labor Rule Maintenance

12.4.2 LCC Rules

On the LCC RULES tab, you can define the rules for SFC LCCs. SFC LCCs are the LCCs that are assigned to the SFCs when they are released. SFC LCCs are used to calculate the total time spent to build each SFC on the shop floor.

In the DEFAULT LCC FOR SHOP ORDERS field, specify the default LCC that will be used by a shop order if the LCC is not specified in the Create and Release SFC, Shop Order Release, or Shop Order Maintenance activities. Also select the USE DEFAULT LCC FOR SHOP ORDERS WHEN LCC NOT PROVIDED checkbox to use the default LCC when an LCC is not provided for a shop order.

12.4.3 Rollup Processing Rules

In SAP ME, rollup functionality is used to get a summary of labor records. Define the rule for summarizing the labor records on the ROLLUP PROCESSING RULES tab.

On the ROLLUP PROCESSING RULES tab, the ENABLE SFC LABOR SUMMARIZATION and ENABLE USER LABOR SUMMARIZATION checkboxes are available to define labor type summarization during rollup. The ENABLE SFC LABOR SUMMARIZATION checkbox allows you to use the summarization records only for SFC labor during rollup, and the ENABLE USER LABOR SUMMARIZATION checkbox allows you to use the summarization only for user labor during rollup. Based on your business requirements, choose either or both checkboxes.

To summarize SFC labor based on a specific object, you can choose single or multiple objects from the available list, such as cost centers, customers, customer orders, materials, operations, reporting centers, resources, routing steps, SFCs, shop orders, and work centers. You can also summarize SFC labor or user labor by specifying custom fields in the SUMMARIZE SFC LABOR BY CUSTOM FIELDS or SUMMARIZE USER LABOR BY CUSTOM FIELDS fields, respectively. The LABOR AGE field is used to define the duration (in days) to keep the SFC labor or user labor records after approval. The IDLE FACTOR FOR LABOR TIME field is used to define how to track the idle time between SFCs. SAP ME provides two options for the IDLE FACTOR FOR LABOR TIME field value: LABOR ON TO LABOR ON and LABOR ON TO LABOR OFF. LABOR ON TO LABOR ON indicates the time between labor on of one SFC to labor on of another SFC. It includes the idle time and SFC labor time previously started by a shop floor user. In this option, you are not capturing the idle time separately and including it with the SFC execution time.

LABOR ON TO LABOR OFF indicates the actual SFC labor time. To find the total idle time, the total SFC labor time can be excluded from the total time between a shop floor user's clock in and clock out. You can use this option to capture the SFC execution and labor times separately.

DISTRIBUTION OF SFC LABOR TIME is used to define the rule when a shop floor user is working on multiple SFCs at a time. Based on the rule settings in the DISTRIBUTION OF SFC LABOR TIME field, the system distributes the time for multiple SFCs. SAP ME provides four options for the value of the DISTRIBUTION OF SFC LABOR TIME field: EQUAL, LCC, ALL, and QUANTITY. EQUAL divides SFC labor time equally among SFCs. LCC divides SFC labor time equally among SFC LCCs. ALL allocates SFC labor time fully to each SFC. QUANTITY divides SFC labor time based on allocated SFC quantity. If the TIME CARD APPROVAL REQUIRED FOR EXPORT checkbox is selected, then the rollup time record can be exported to SAP ERP without preapproval. Figure 12.8 shows the ROLLUP PROCESSING RULES tab in Labor Rules Maintenance.

> **Note: Custom Fields Values**
>
> In SUMMARIZE SFC LABOR BY CUSTOM FIELDS or SUMMARIZE USER LABOR BY CUSTOM FIELDS, you can define the value in the format <Table Name>.<field ID>. To provide multiple custom fields, use commas as delimiters.

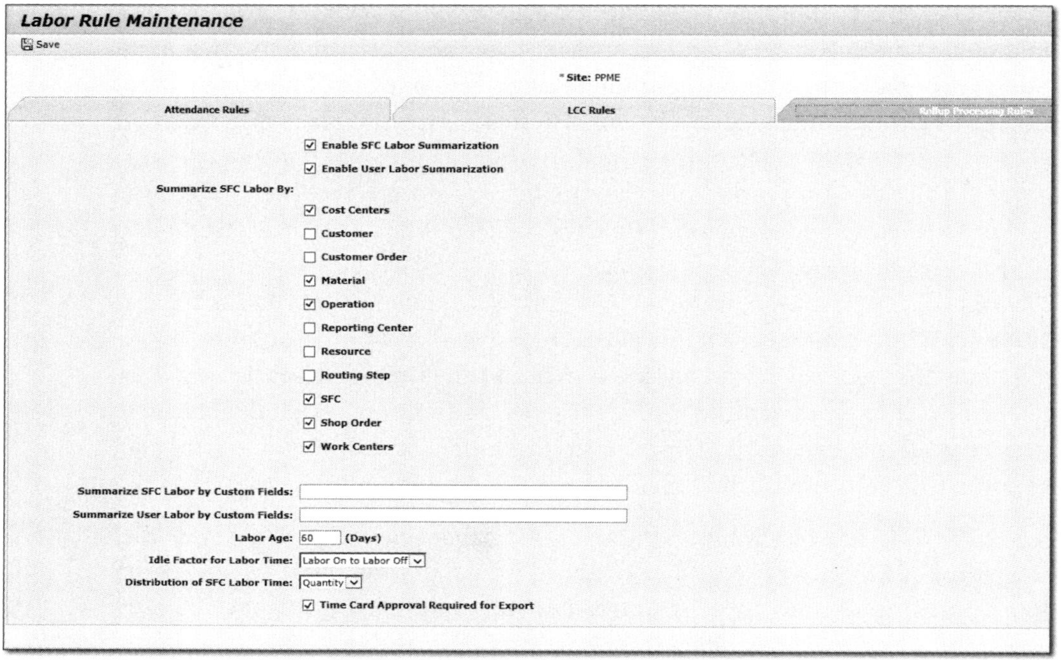

Figure 12.8 Configuring Rollup Processing Rules

12.5 Maintaining User Shifts

In SAP ME, the User Shift Maintenance activity is used to define the characteristics of user shifts. On the MAIN tab of User Shift Maintenance, you can define the validity of shift, begin and end time of shift, start and end time of user clock in and clock out, labor assignment, and break time for a shift, as shown in Figure 12.9. To define the break time for a shift, you need to click on a link in the BREAK column. The *Break Edit* wizard will appear, in which you can specify BREAK START and BREAK END time and also the break type, such as MEAL BREAK or SHORT REST BREAK, for a shift.

> **Note: User Shift Maintenance**
>
> On the MAIN tab of User Shift Maintenance, only one row can be marked as CURRENT. The system will not allow you to use the same VALID FROM date value as an existing row.

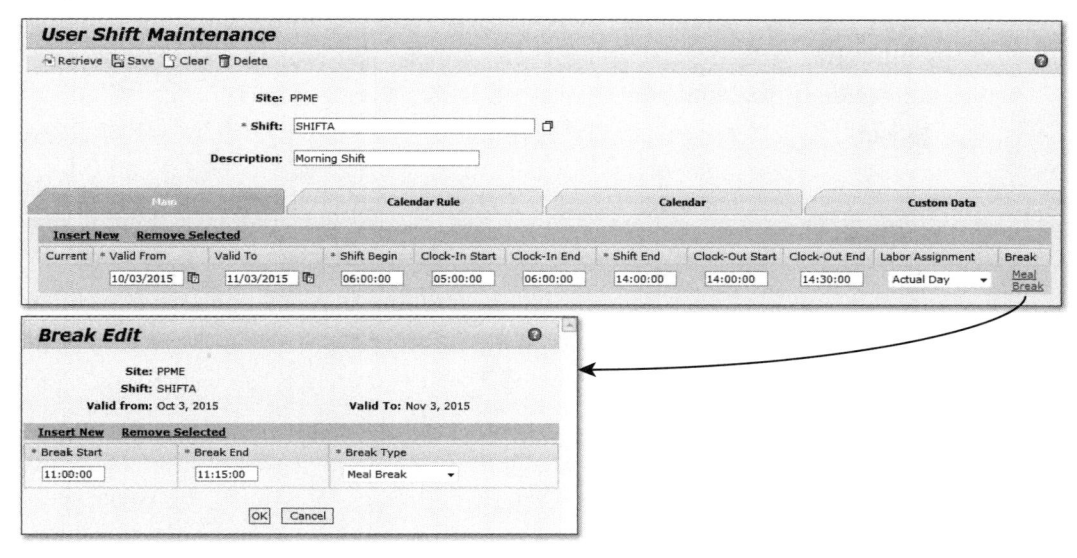

Figure 12.9 Maintaining User Shifts

On the CALENDAR RULE tab, you can define PRODUCTION DAY and DAY CLASS. In the PRODUCTION DAY fields, select PRODUCTION or NON-PRODUCTION for each day of the week. In the DAY CLASS fields, choose NORMAL, HOLIDAY, or WEEKEND, as shown in Figure 12.10.

Figure 12.10 Defining Calendar Rules for User Shifts

On the Calendar tab, click on the Display button to find the calendar for a month of the year. In the calendar, you will see the values of Production Day and Day Class as defined on the Calendar Rule tab page.

12.6 Labor Clock In/Clock Out

You should now understand the functionality of the cost center, LCC, labor rule setup, and user shift maintenance. In this section, you will build on that understanding and learn how those configurations are useful for shop floor users when they execute shop floor manufacturing processes.

You can maintain certain rules in the Labor Rule Maintenance activity to customize the labor clocking. If Automatic Clock-In at Logon in the Clock-In Control field of Labor Rule Maintenance is selected, then the system will allow automatic clock in when user logs on to SAP ME system. If the Manual Clock-In value in the Clock-In Control field of Labor Rule Maintenance is selected, then the user needs to manually clock in. You need to add the Clock In/Out plug-in in the POD for manual user clock in. Now, let's discuss required POD plug-ins related to labor tracking and how they can be used by shop floor users:

The *Labor On* activity is used when a user starts to work on an SFC at an operation through the POD. By default, the AUTH_REQUIRED rules setting for Labor On (activity ID: LT370) is defined as NO, but you can change it per your requirements, especially if another user besides the one currently logged on wants to labor on by entering his/her user name and password.

The system starts to track labor time spent for an SFC execution at an operation when the shop floor user labors on to the SFC. In the POD Maintenance activity you can add the Labor On activity to the Start button with a sequence number. Whenever a shop floor user clicks on the Start button in the POD, Labor On will be activated for the SFC also.

> **Note: System Rule Maintenance**
>
> In System Rule Maintenance, set the Enable Labor Tracking rule to True for a site to enable labor tracking.

The *Labor Off* activity (activity ID: LT380) is used when a shop floor user completes or performs signoff for a task for an SFC at an operation. In the POD Maintenance activity, you can add Labor Off to the COMPLETE AND SIGNOFF button with a sequence number, and on the LAYOUT tab of POD Maintenance, you can add Labor Off as a pop-up.

You can track the time taken by a shop floor user to perform different activities when executing an SFC at an operation through the Labor Off activity. In POD Maintenance, you can add LABOR ON and LABOR OFF as separate buttons if multiple shop floor users work on the same SFC at the same time. Everyone should be able to perform labor on to work on SFCs that were initially started by another user and can perform labor off. In the POD, through the Labor Off plug-in, a shop floor user can collect distributed work time. Through Standard Value Key Maintenance, you can define a standard value key which will be used for collecting distributed work time, as shown in Figure 12.11.

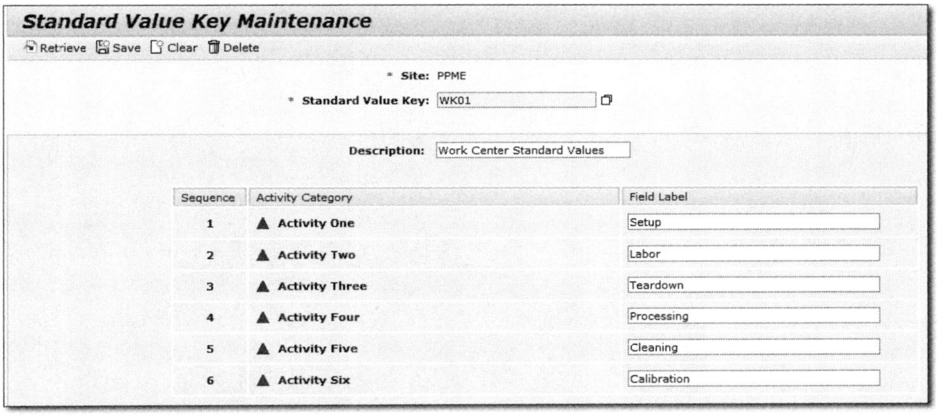

Figure 12.11 Maintaining Standard Value Key

Next, in the Scheduling Standards Maintenance activity, you can assign the standard value key with routing steps in which the shop floor user will collect distributed work time, as shown in Figure 12.12.

From the POD, when a shop floor user works on the operation for which the scheduling standard is maintained and clicks on the LABOR OFF button, then the Collect Work Time plug-in will appear with a standard value key list. The shop floor user can enter the time spent to perform different activities, as shown in Figure 12.13. If the ALLOW_ELAPSED_TIME_EXCESS rule value is set to NO, then the system will not allow you to save entries if the total distributed time is greater than the total elapsed time.

12 | Labor Tracking

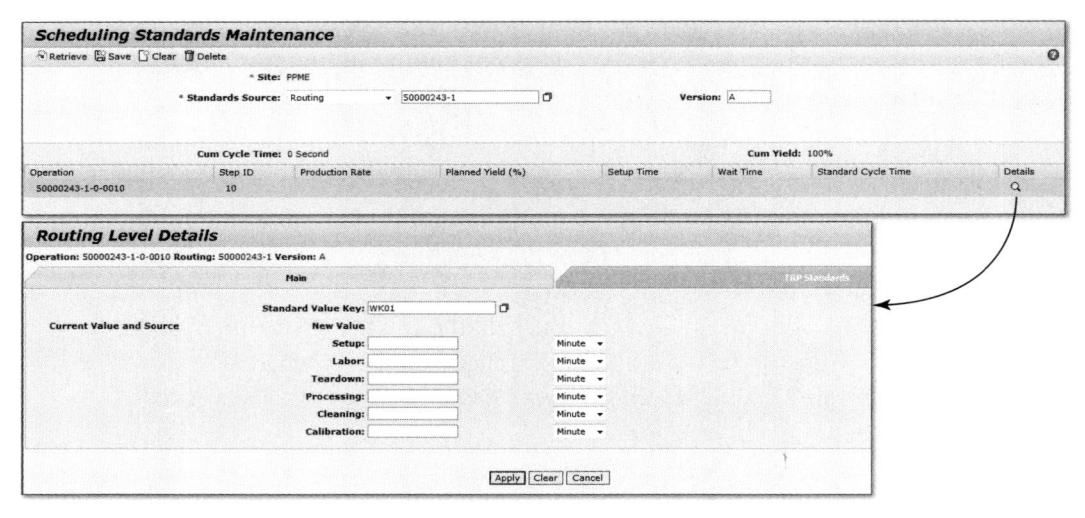

Figure 12.12 Maintaining Scheduling Standards

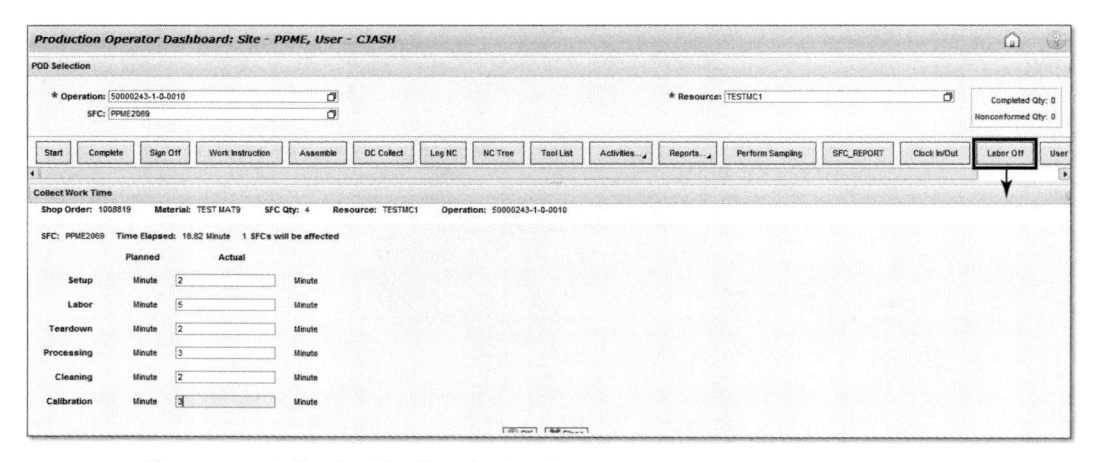

Figure 12.13 Collecting Distributed Labor Time

The *Clock In/Out* activity (activity ID: LT210) allows you to track a user's labor time. Automatic and manual clock in and clock out were discussed at the beginning of this section. In the POD Maintenance activity, you can add a new button for the CLOCK IN/OUT activity to perform manual clock in and clock out for a shop floor user, as shown in Figure 12.14.

Labor Clock In/Clock Out | **12.6**

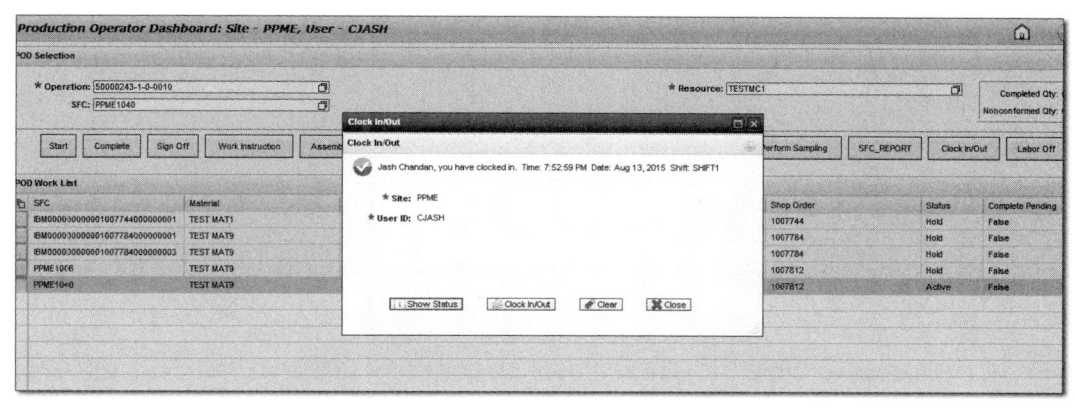

Figure 12.14 Performing Clock In/Out in POD

If the shop floor user is not performing any task in the POD and is working on other tasks, such as moving to a quality area, then the Change User Labor Charge Code activity (activity ID: LT240) is used to change the LCC related to that task. In the POD Maintenance activity, you can add a new button for CHANGE USER LABOR CHARGE CODE. A shop floor user can change an LCC each time a task begins, using an LCC different from the one used for SFC execution, as shown in Figure 12.15.

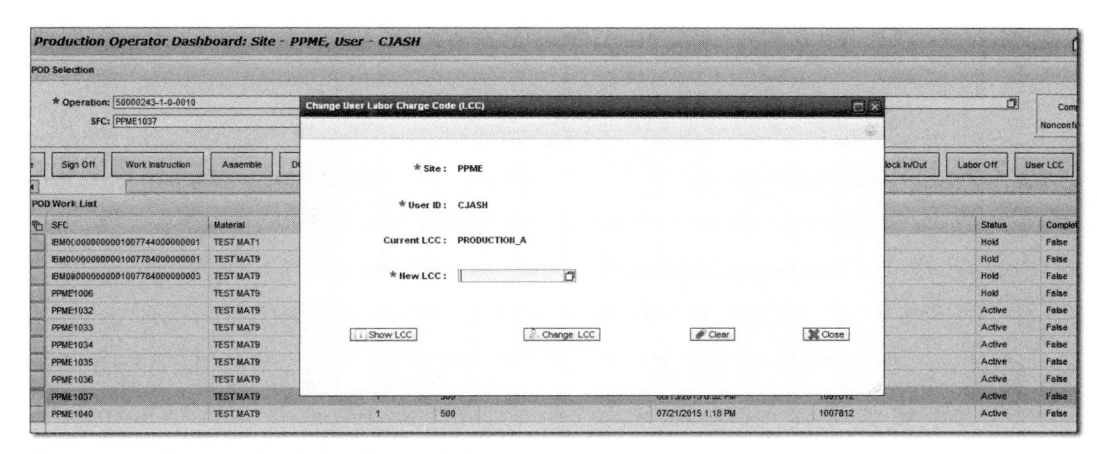

Figure 12.15 Changing User Labor Charge Code

If you want to change the LCC for an SFC after release, use the Change SFC Labor Charge Code activity (activity ID: LT250). In the POD Maintenance activity, you

379

can add a new button for CHANGE SFC LABOR CHARGE CODE. Using this button, a shop floor user can change the LCC for one or multiple SFC numbers from the POD.

12.7 Supervisor Clock In/Out

The Supervisor Clock In/Out activity (activity ID: LT220) is used to clock time for employees that a particular supervisor oversees. For example, say that one employee arrived late to work and cannot clock in, because Labor Rule Maintenance is set up to only allow user clock in within a particular interval. The tardy employee's supervisor can open the Supervisor Clock In/Out activity, enter the employee's user ID in the USER ID field, update the actual time of arrival in the DATE field, enter the reason in COMMENTS field, and click on the CLOCK IN/OUT button to complete the process. The supervisor can also see the clock in/clock out status of an employee by clicking the SHOW STATUS button. Figure 12.16 shows the Supervisor Clock In/Out activity.

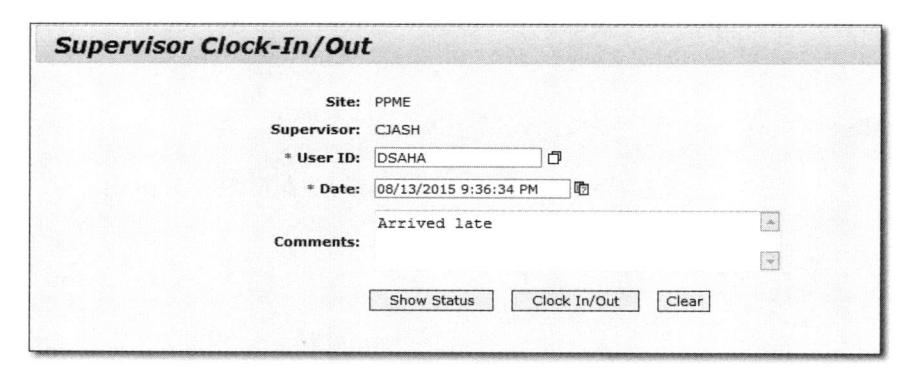

Figure 12.16 Performing Supervisor Clock-In/Out

12.8 Supervisor Time Edit and Approval

Using the Supervisor Time Edit and Approval activity (activity ID: LT260), you can review and edit the summarized labor records for a user for a cost center. This activity uses two modes: supervisor mode and user mode. The mode is defined in rule settings of the Supervisor Time Edit and Approval activity, where you need to set the ACTIVITY_MODE rule value to either SUPERVISOR or USER.

12.8.1 Supervisor Mode

In supervisor mode, a supervisor can review and edit the summarized record of a user. If you are in a supervisor role, then you must be assigned as the supervisor over the cost centers of users on the SUPERVISOR tab of the User Maintenance activity. As a supervisor, you can approve or reject labor records, insert missing days, add/edit/delete labor records, adjust user clock-in and clock-out times, and add/edit distributed labor time. In the Supervisor Time Edit and Approval activity, you can find the supervisor's actions within the MORE list. In supervisor mode, you can search the user records by multiple search parameters, such as COST CENTER, SHIFT, USER ID, LABOR DATE RANGE, and APPROVAL STATE, as shown in Figure 12.17.

> **Note: ODSLaborRollup script execution**
>
> As a prerequisite of Supervisor Time Edit and Approval, you need to run the `ODSLabor-Rollup` database script in SAP ME WIP database to get the labor records.

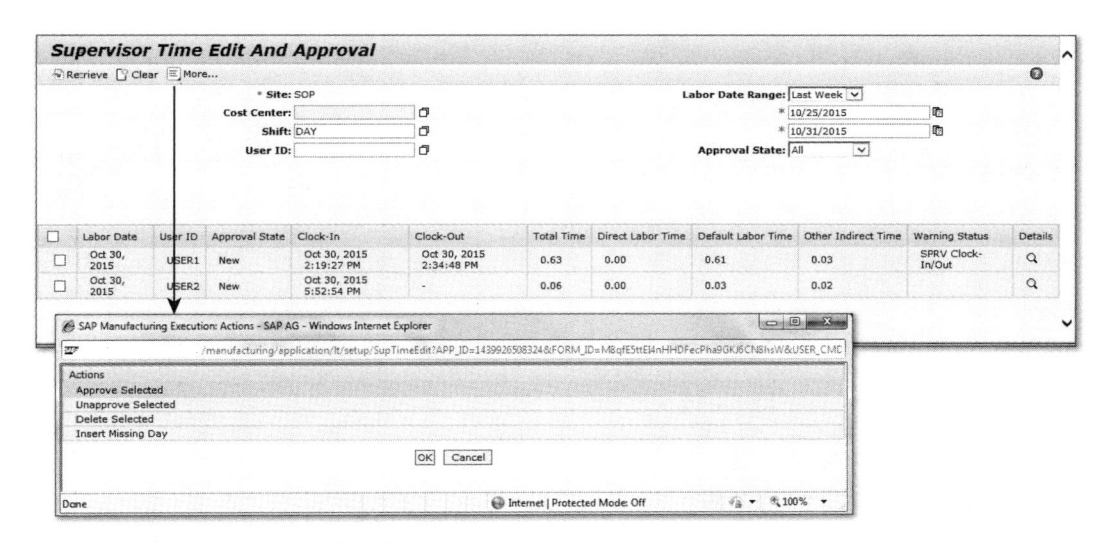

Figure 12.17 Supervisor Time Edit and Approval Layout in Supervisor Mode

12.8.2 User Mode

In user mode, you can retrieve records by APPROVAL STATE (NEW, ALL, ACCEPTED, UNAPPROVED, or APPROVED) or by LABOR DATE RANGE and edit your own summarized record. You can also perform multiple actions, such as inserting and delet-

12 | Labor Tracking

ing existing indirect labor records and accepting or rejecting direct labor records before supervisor approval, as shown in Figure 12.18.

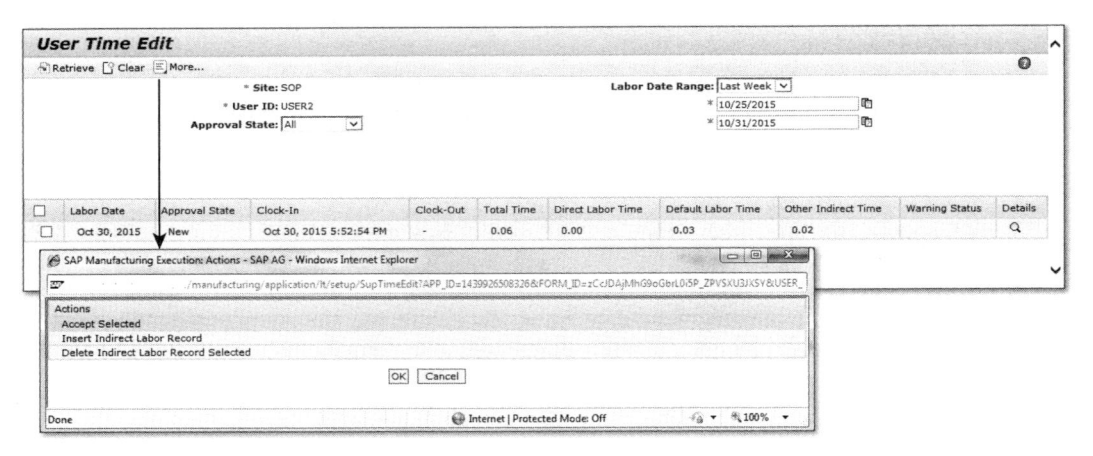

Figure 12.18 Supervisor Time Edit and Approval Layout in User Mode

12.9 Summary

In this chapter, you learned about the labor tracking functionality in SAP ME for user labor and SFC labor time. This chapter described required configuration activities related to labor tracking, such as Cost Center Maintenance, Labor Charge Code Maintenance, Labor Rule Maintenance, User Shift Maintenance, Production Calendar Maintenance, and so on. You also examined the hierarchy of cost centers and how user clock in, clock out, labor on, labor off, and changing user LCCs are performed from the POD by shop floor users. We also discussed the distributed labor time collection using standard value keys for shop floor users.

We also covered the required configurations for labor tracking and the use of the Supervisor Clock In/Out and Supervisor Time Edit and Approval activities to enable supervisors to clock employees in and out and to view summarized labor reports, respectively.

In the next chapter, you will learn about the Packing Service in SAP ME.

This chapter covers the packing service used in SAP ME to track packing of finished products into containers, and unpacking features. It explains the related configurations and document printing during the packing or unpacking process, and the Packing report.

13   Packing Service

In SAP ME, packing and unpacking features are used to track the shop floor packing of manufacturing products into containers or unpacking of the goods from containers. Shop floor users can record which SFCs or containers they pack into or unpack from containers in SAP ME, typically after the production is complete or for transfer to another location. During the packing and unpacking process, you can perform multiple tasks based on business requirements, such the capturing the required data to keep a record of packing or unpacking. Using an SAP ME *Next Number Generation* activity, you can assign the container number and define the container using the Container Maintenance activity, where you can define whether the SFCs will be packed or containers will be packed into the container. You also can define the dimensions of the container, required document printing, and the hook activities that need to be executed during the packing or unpacking process.

In this chapter we will cover the container maintenance activity, the pack and unpack activity, the packing report, and the related activity rules for packing.

13.1   Container Maintenance

The main purpose of Container Maintenance is to define the objects that can be packed or unpacked by shop floor users. In the Container Maintenance activity, you can enter the name and description of a container in the CONTAINER and DESCRIPTION fields. The STATUS field sets the status of container as FROZEN, HOLD, NEW, OBSOLETE, or RELEASABLE. The CONTAINER DATA TYPE field specifies the data type that will be used to collect data for the container during the packing process. The SFC DATA TYPE field specifies the data type that will be used to collect data for the SFC during the packing process. During the Pack/Unpack activity, the system checks the data type to display the fields for data collection that requires a data entry value. You can define the data field and assign it to a Packing Container or Packing SFC data type using Data Field Definition Maintenance and Data Field Assignment Maintenance activities in SAP ME. In the SFC PACK ORDER field, select SFC or FIFO OF PROCESS LOT. SFC indicates that the SFCs in a process lot are packed into container in SFC order, and FIFO OF PROCESS LOT value indicates that the SFCs in a process lot are packed into a container by time stamp on a first-in, first-out basis. The TOTAL MIN QTY field displays the minimum number of SFCs (materials), containers, or process lots that can be packed into a container, and the TOTAL MAX QTY field displays the maximum number of SFCs (materials), containers, or process lots that can be packed into a container.

You can specify what type of object will be packed into a container by clicking on the INSERT NEW link on the MAIN tab of Container Maintenance and adding a new item, as shown in Figure 13.1. SAP ME allows three types of objects to be packed in a container: MATERIAL, CONTAINER, and PROCESS LOT. While adding a new entry, select one of these object types in the PACK LEVEL column. If you select MATERIAL, then you need to specify the material number in the PACK LEVEL VALUE column, and the current material version will appear automatically in the VERSION column based on the material selection using the value help. If you specify the material number manually then you can leave the VERSION field blank to specify the current version. Here, *material* indicates an SFC for a material of type *Manufactured* or *Purchased*, and the SFC will be packed into a container. In the SHOP ORDER column, select the shop order for the SFC that will be packed into the container. In the MIN QTY and MAX QTY columns, specify the minimum and maximum quantity that must be packed into the container.

If you want to pack containers into a parent container, then you need to select CONTAINER in the PACK LEVEL column and specify a container the in PACK LEVEL VALUE column using the value help. The VERSION and SHOP ORDER column values for the container are disabled. You can specify the minimum and maximum quantity to pack into the container in the MIN QTY and MAX QTY columns field, as shown in Figure 13.2.

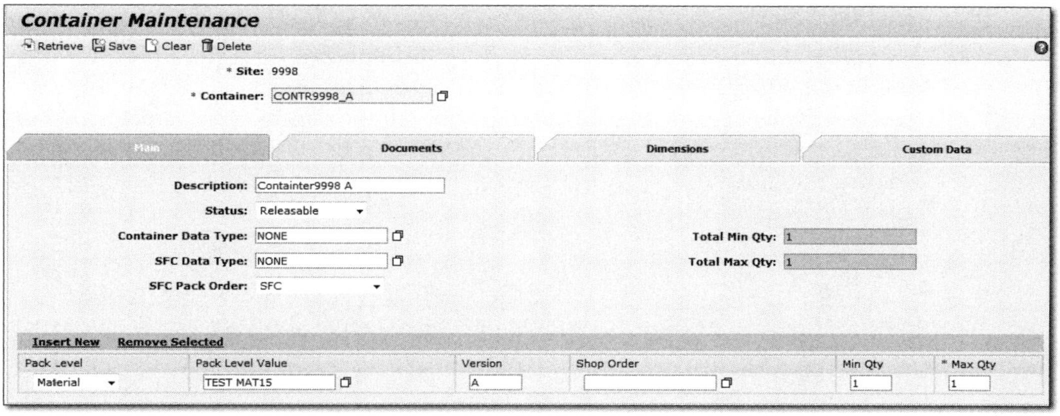

Figure 13.1 Maintaining Container for Material Object

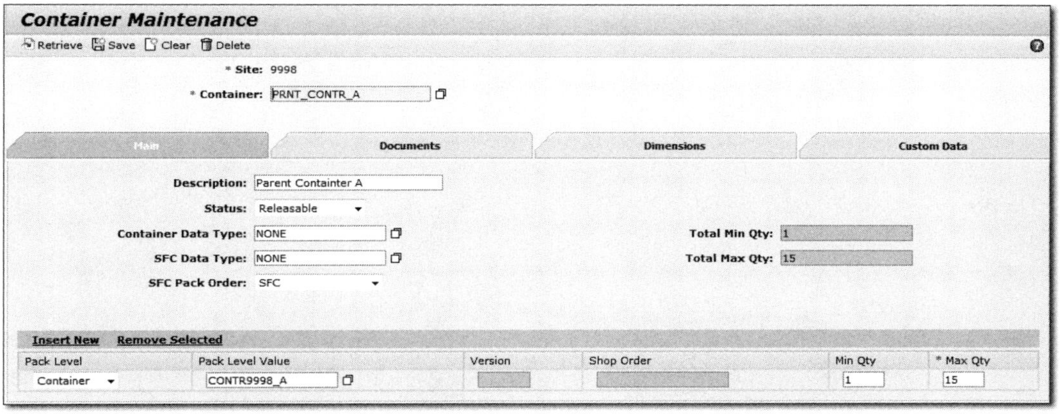

Figure 13.2 Maintaining Container Objects

You can select PROCESS LOT in the PACK LEVEL column and also specify a process lot in the PACK LEVEL VALUE column using the value help. You can also specify the minimum and maximum quantity which must be packed into the container in the MIN QTY and MAX QTY column fields.

> **Note: Container Maintenance**
>
> You can also specify * or a blank value for the PACK LEVEL VALUE column, VERSION column, and SHOP ORDER column. If you don't specify any value in the PACK LEVEL VALUE

column for a material, then the first SFC put into the container specifies the value for MATERIAL, MATERIAL VERSION, and SHOP ORDER for all subsequent SFCs. In the case of a container, the first container put into the container specifies the value of the container for all subsequent containers; the same is true for the process lot. For *, Process Lot can be any value of material, container, or process lot. A blank value in the VERSION column indicates the current version of the material in the inserted row, and * indicates any version of the material.

On the DOCUMENTS tab of Container Maintenance, you can specify the documents that will be printed during the packing or unpacking process. Before specifying the document in Container Maintenance, you need to define the document using the Document Maintenance activity in SAP ME. You can specify the same document on the DOCUMENTS tab using the INSERT NEW link, as shown in Figure 13.3.

Figure 13.3 Specifying Documents in Containter Maintenance

Note: Printing Documents

You can use the Document Print (activity ID: SY520) or ADS Document Print (activity ID: SY521) activity as an activity hook to print information about packed or unpacked containers.

On the DIMENSIONS tab of Container Maintenance, you can define the dimension and weight of a container. Specify the values for HEIGHT, WIDTH, LENGTH, MAX FILL WEIGHT, and CONTAINER WEIGHT.

13.2 Pack and Unpack Activity

Using the *Pack/Unpack* activity (activity ID: PK020), you can pack or unpack an SFC or container. Let's discuss how to pack into a container and unpack from a container.

In the Pack/Unpack activity, you can specify a container (defined in the Container Maintenance activity) in the CONTAINER field and either scan a valid container number or click on the CREATE CONTAINER NUMBER button to enter a system-generated container number in the CONTAINER NUMBER field. To use an existing container number, specify the container and container number in the CONTAINER and CONTAINER NUMBER fields respectively and click on the RETRIEVE button.

> **Note: Container Number Assignment**
>
> Use the Next Number Maintenance activity to maintain the container number pattern. Every time you click on CREATE CONTAINER NUMBER in the Pack/Unpack activity, SAP ME will generate a unique number for the CONTAINER NUMBER field.

To pack an SFC into a container, select SFC in the PACK VALUE dropdown field. Note that if you configured the container for a material object only in Container Maintenance, then SFC will be the only value available in PACK VALUE dropdown field. You also need to specify an SFC number for the PACK VALUE browse field which you want to pack, as shown in Figure 13.4. Click on the ADD button to add the SFC to the RECEIVED table on the right-hand side. At the top-right corner of the page, you will see the MIN QTY, MAX QTY, and CURRENT QTY detail fields for MATERIAL and TOTAL. If you want to stop packing and close the container, click on the DONE AND CLOSE button, or click on the DONE button to save the data without closing the container.

To pack the container into a parent container, specify the parent container (which you configured in the Container Maintenance activity) in the CONTAINER field, then generate a container number by clicking on the CREATE CONTAINER NUMBER button. The system-generated container number will appear in the CONTAINER NUMBER field. Next, select CONTAINER for the PACK VALUE dropdown and specify the container number for the PACK VALUE browse field, as shown in Figure 13.5.

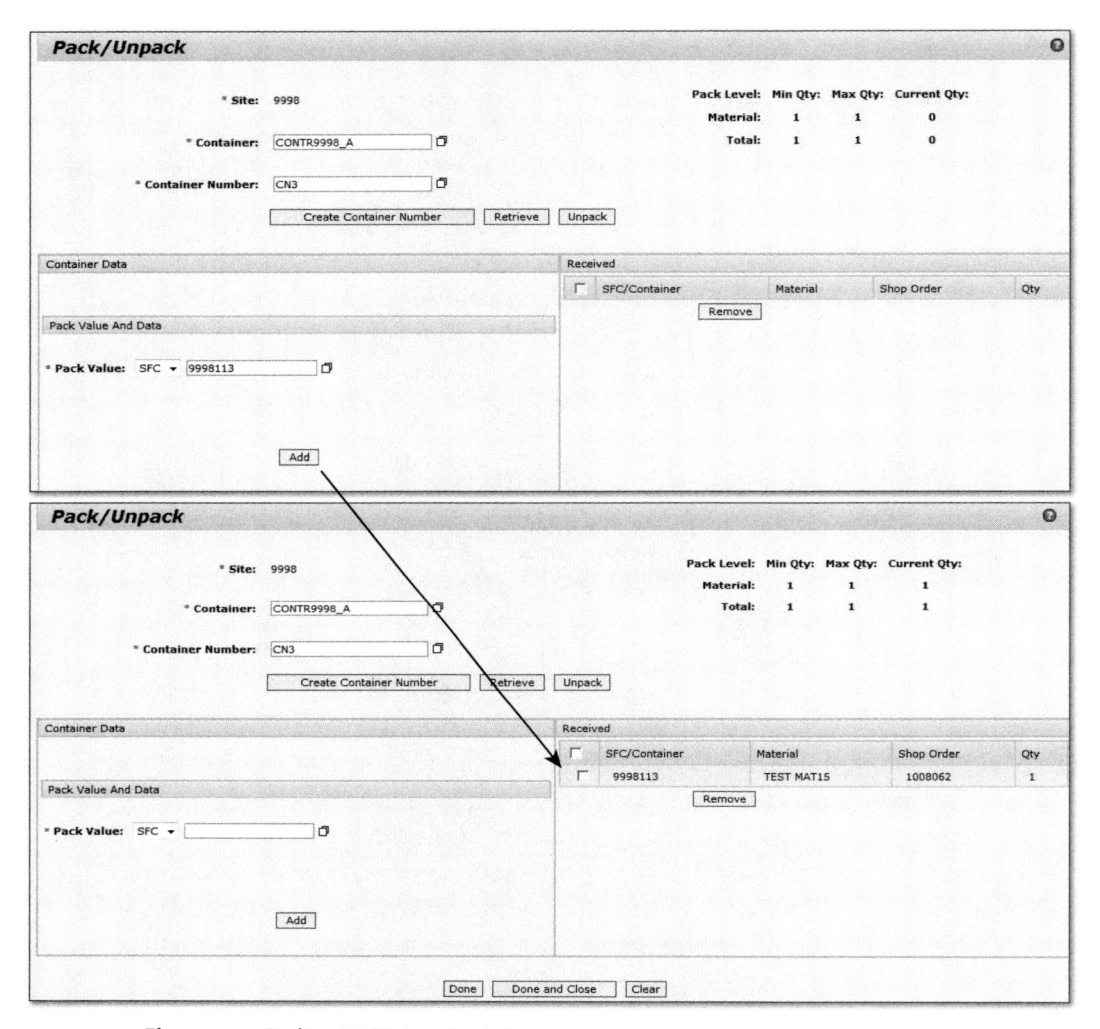

Figure 13.4 Packing SFC into a Container

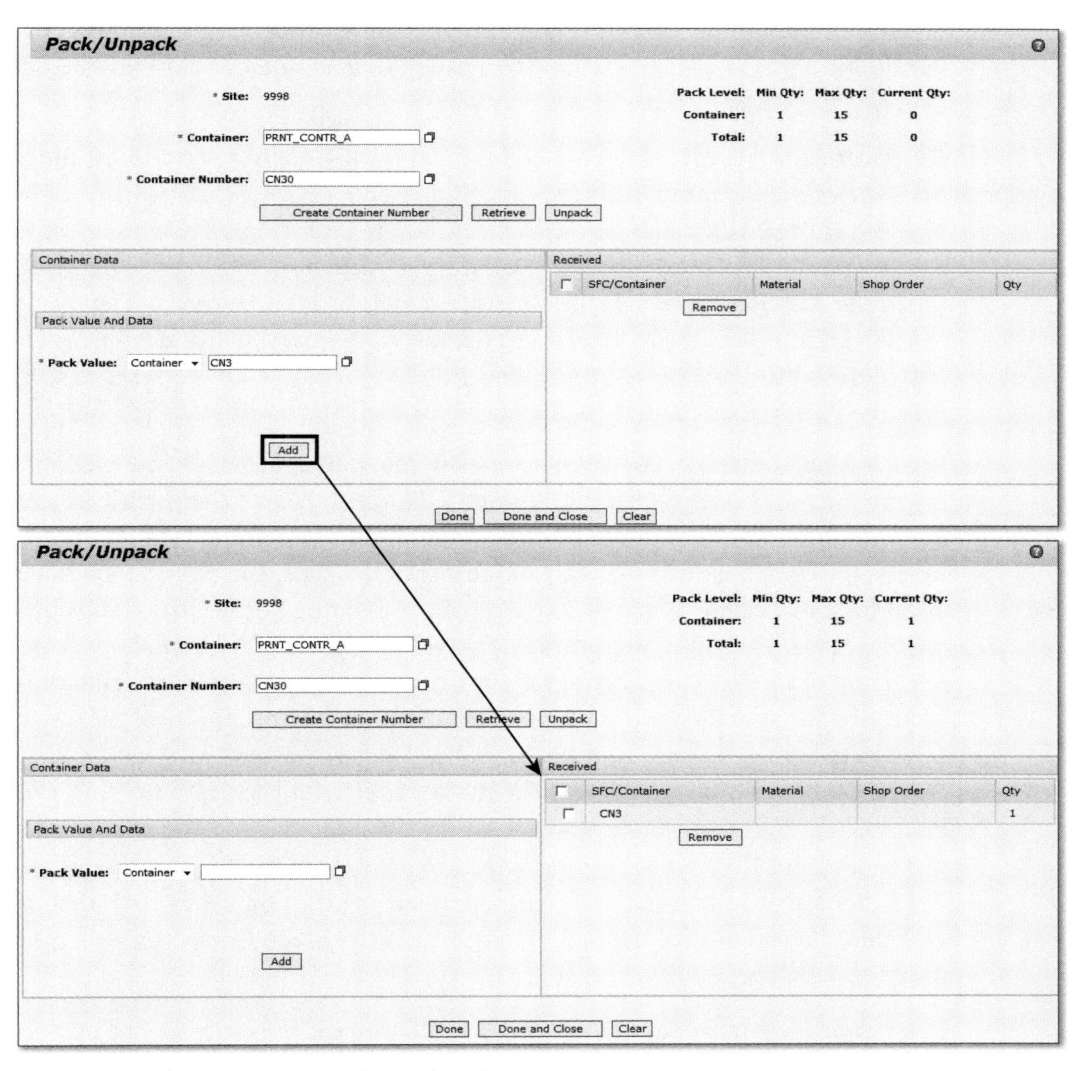

Figure 13.5 Packing Container into Parent Container

If you want to stop packing and close the container, click on the DONE AND CLOSE button, or click on the DONE button to save the data without closing the container.

The Pack/Unpack activity can be used for packing only, for unpacking only, or for both packing and unpacking, based on the rule setup in the Pack/Unpack activity. If the ALLOW_PACK value on the RULE tab of the Pack/Unpack activity is set to NO and ALLOW_UNPACK is set to YES, then the activity will allow only unpacking. If the ALLOW_PACK value in the RULE tab of the Pack/Unpack activity is set to YES and ALLOW_UNPACK is set to NO, then the activity will allow only packing. If the values of ALLOW_PACK and ALLOW_UNPACK are both set to YES, then the Pack/Unpack activity will be used for both.

To unpack a container, you need to specify the container name and container number in the CONTAINER and CONTAINER NUMBER fields. Then, click on the RETRIEVE button to fetch the container details, and click on the OPEN button to reopen the container. In the right-hand corner of the page, you can find the status (REOPEN in this example) of the container along with the current packed quantity and new packed quantity. From the left-hand side of the PACKED table, you can select one or more items packed in the container and click on the UNPACK button to unpack those items from the container. After clicking on the UNPACK button, the selected items will appear in the right-hand side UNPACKED table, as shown in Figure 13.6. You can also click on the REPACK button to pack an unpacked item back into the container. You can also repack a different SFC if it matches the container contents. If you want to stop unpacking and close the container, then you can click on the DONE AND CLOSE button, or you can click on the DONE button to save the data without closing the container. Clicking on the EXIT button will clear the screen without saving the results.

You can also perform unpacking from a Pack/Unpack activity with the activity rule values for ALLOW_PACK and ALLOW_UNPACK set to YES. You can specify the container name and container number in the CONTAINER and CONTAINER NUMBER fields for a closed container and then click on the UNPACK button. This UNPACK event will take you to the usual unpack page. Figure 13.7 shows packing and unpacking from the Pack/Unpack activity.

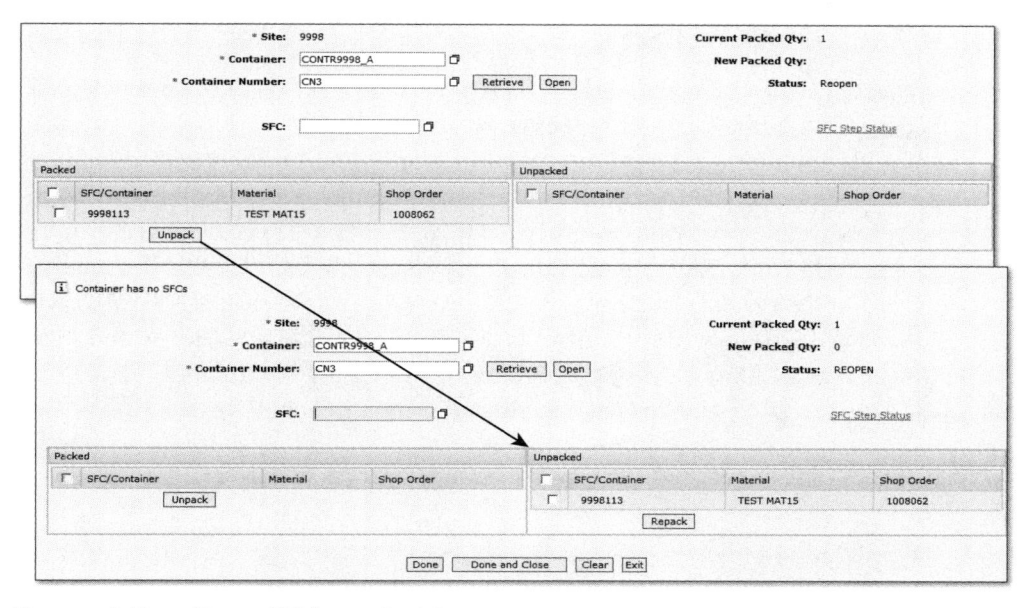

Figure 13.6 Unpacking an SFC from a Container

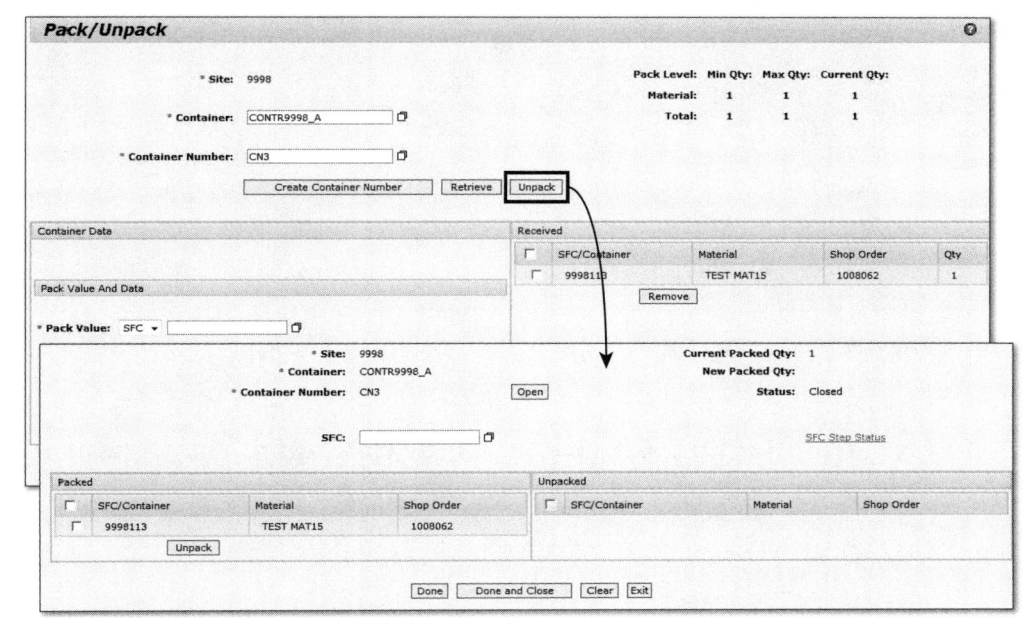

Figure 13.7 Switching to Unpacking Page from Pack/Unpack Activity

13.3 Packing Report

SAP ME provides a Packing Report (activity ID: PK700) to find the packing information for a container number, SFC, or shop order. In Packing Report, select CONTAINER NUMBER, SFC, or SHOP ORDER and specify the corresponding value for the selected item. Then, click on the SEARCH button, and SAP ME will display the packing information for the specified value. If you do not specify any value in the browse field, then SAP ME will display a report for all nonempty containers defined in the system. In the search results, the report shows PARENT CONTAINER, CONTAINER, CONTENTS QTY, CONTAINER NAME/MATERIAL, SHOP ORDER, and MORE INFO in a table. Click on the hyperlink in the MORE INFO column of the table for a particular row to see the Detail Report, as shown in Figure 13.8.

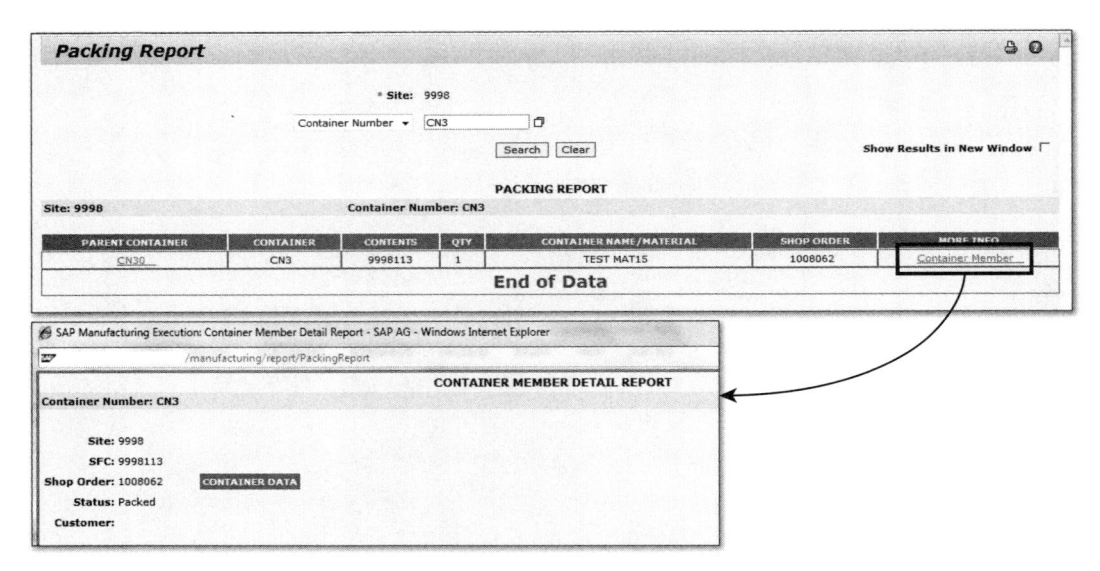

Figure 13.8 Packing Report

13.4 Maintaining Activity Rules for Container Maintenance

For Container Maintenance activity (activity ID: PK010), you can set the activity rules in Activity Maintenance, as described in Table 13.1.

Rule	Settings
MAXIMUM_QTY	If set to YES, a shop floor user needs to enter a value in the MAX QTY field in Container Maintenance. If set to NO, it is not mandatory to enter a value in the MAX QTY field in Container Maintenance.
MINIMUM_QTY	If set to YES, a shop floor user needs to enter a value in the MIN QTY field in Container Maintenance. If set to NO, it is not mandatory to enter a value in the MIN QTY field in Container Maintenance.

Table 13.1 Configuring Rules for Container Maintenance Activity

Before performing the Pack/Unpack activity in SAP ME, you need to configure activity rules in Activity Maintenance for the Pack/Unpack activity (activity ID: PK020), as shown in Table 13.2.

Rule	Settings
ACCESS_CLOSED_CONTAINERS	For YES, SAP ME allows you to retrieve closed containers; for NO, SAP ME prevents retrieving closed containers.
ACCESS_OPEN_CONTAINERS	For YES, SAP ME allows you to retrieve containers; for NO, SAP ME prevents retrieving containers.
ALLOW_ACTIVE_SFC	For YES, SAP ME allows SFCs with ACTIVE status to be packed into a container or unpacked from a container; for NO, SAP ME prevents SFCs with ACTIVE status from being packed into containers or unpacked from containers.
ALLOW_DONE_SFC	For YES, SAP ME allows SFCs with DONE status to be packed into containers or unpacked from containers; for NO, SAP ME prevents SFCs with DONE status from being packed into containers or unpacked from containers.
ALLOW_INQUE_SFC	For YES, SAP ME allows SFCs with INQUEUE or NEW status to be packed into containers or unpacked from containers; for NO, SAP ME prevents SFCs with INQUEUE or NEW status from being packed into containers or unpacked from containers.
ALLOW_PACK	For YES, SAP ME allows you to pack containers; for NO, SAP ME prevents packing containers.
ALLOW_UNPACK	For YES, SAP ME allows you to unpack containers; for NO, SAP ME prevents unpacking containers.

Table 13.2 Configuring Rules for Pack/Unpack Activity

Rule	Settings
AUTO_COMPLETE_SFC	For YES, SAP ME completes the SFC (for an SFC started manually) automatically when the ADD event is performed; for NO, SAP ME does not automatically complete the SFC on the ADD event.
AUTO_START_SFC	For YES, SAP ME starts the SFC automatically when ADD is clicked in the Pack/Unpack activity; for NO value, SAP ME does not start the SFC automatically.
ERP_ITEM_FILTER	SAP ME sends confirmations and corresponding Goods Issued messages to SAP ERP if the SFC that is packed in the container meets one of the filters. Filters are separated by commas (,) and also allow the use of wildcards (*). For a blank value, no message is sent to SAP ERP.
ERP_OPERATION	The operation name in the confirmation message, which is sent to SAP ERP when a container is closed through the DONE AND CLOSE event.
ERP_REPORTING_STEP	The ERP REPORTING STEP field in the confirmation message, which is sent to SAP ERP when a container is closed through DONE AND CLOSE event.
ERP_SEQUENCE	The SEQUENCE field in the confirmation message, which is sent to SAP ERP when a container is closed through the DONE AND CLOSE event.
SFC_MUST_BE_AT_OPERATION	For YES, SAP ME allows you to pack only SFC numbers with INQUEUE or ACTIVE status into the container. For NO, SAP ME allows you to pack SFC numbers with any status into the container at any operation.

Table 13.2 Configuring Rules for Pack/Unpack Activity (Cont.)

13.5 Summary

In this chapter, you learned about the packing and unpacking process in SAP ME along with the purpose of the Container Maintenance and Pack and Unpack activities. You also learned how to view packing information through the Packing Report activity. We also covered the required configurations for the Container Maintenance and Pack and Unpack activities.

In the next chapter, we will discuss available public API web services for SAP ME.

PART III
Advanced Enhancement

This chapter provides an overview of available public API web services for SAP ME and explains how and where to find public API web services, how to test them, and how to consume them from SAP MII to develop custom or extension applications for SAP ME.

14 Custom Enhancements Using Public API Web Services

Now that you've learned about all the features and functionality of SAP ME, you understand that SAP ME is a packaged solution for manufacturing execution in discrete industry and that it comes with a set of functions typically required by users in manufacturing plants. However, you may also need to access certain SAP ME information from an external system or may need to update certain information in SAP ME from an external system. For example, you might need to query SAP ME for SFC information from another shop floor system for a custom report, update equipment status from the corresponding tag values captured in SCADA or Plant Historian, or develop custom PODs using technologies such as SAPUI5 that differ from the standard SAP ME POD maintenance.

SAP ME provides APIs for almost all of its available core functionality as public APIs (PAPIs). These are available as Java APIs as well as with SOAP Web Service and OData services, which can be accessed from any application to perform an activity in SAP ME or query any data if the relevant authorization is available. You can also access the PAPI service from the SAP MII workbench to develop custom applications.

In this chapter you will learn about how you can configure the security and use the PAPI services as well as using the PAPI service action blocks in SAP MII workbench to develop BLS transactions with reference to some business scenarios.

14.1 Finding Required Public API Services

Because all SAP ME PAPI services are documented in Javadoc, provided with SAP ME, you can use Javadoc to search for specific PAPI services. Download the Javadoc for SAP ME PAPI services from SAP Service Marketplace, via the INSTALLATION AND CONFIGURATION GUIDES section. View the service methods from Javadoc for each class, as shown in Figure 14.1. You also can find the parameter details for each method from Javadoc.

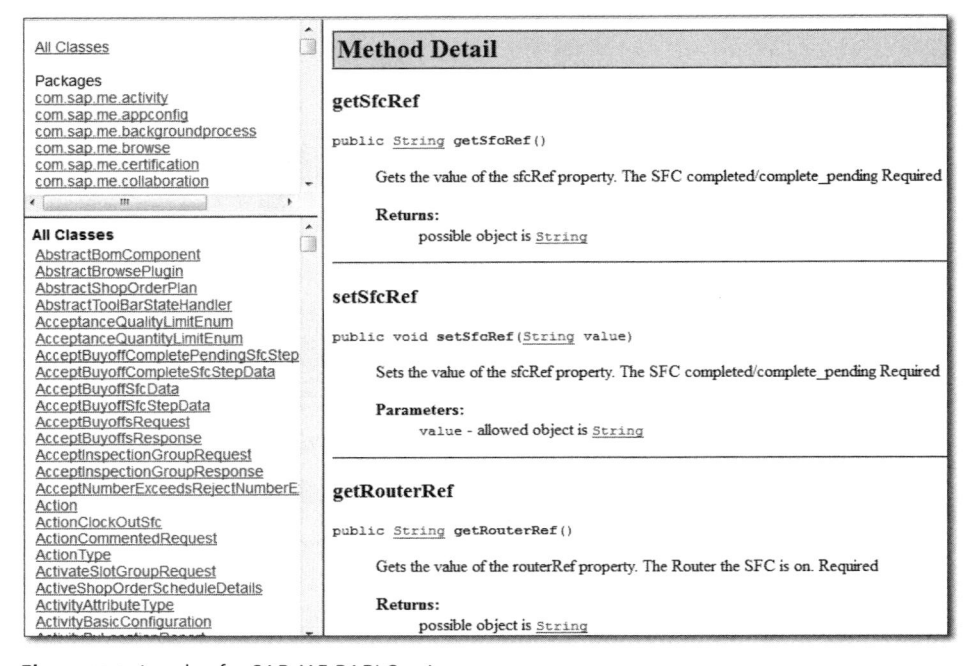

Figure 14.1 Javadoc for SAP ME PAPI Services

> **Note**
>
> You can also create custom SAP ME PAPI services using the SAP ME SDK, which we will discuss in Chapter 17.

14.2 Configuring and Accessing Public API Web Services

You can execute PAPI services with the following methods:

- Using the Java API (i.e., from a Java program running in the SAP ME server)
- Through a SOAP web service call from the same server or an external server

- From an SAP MII BLS transaction in the same server using the PAPI service action

To execute the PAPI service from a Java program, you need to use the SAP ME SDK (see Chapter 17).

To execute the PAPI service as a SOAP web service, you can add a communication profile to specify the authentication method, if not already added, in SAP NetWeaver administrator via the following steps:

1. Log in to SAP NetWeaver Administrator on the server where SAP ME is installed via *http://<host>:<port>/nwa* as an administrator user, and navigate to SOA • TECHNICAL CONFIGURATION • SYSTEM CONNECTIONS.

2. Open the COMMUNICATION PROFILES configuration tab and click on NEW to create a new profile for a PAPI service using basic authentication.

3. Enter the PROFILE NAME as "WS_PAPI_BASIC" and PROFILE DESCRIPTION as "Basis Authentication for PAPI WS", as shown in Figure 14.2.

4. Click on NEXT.

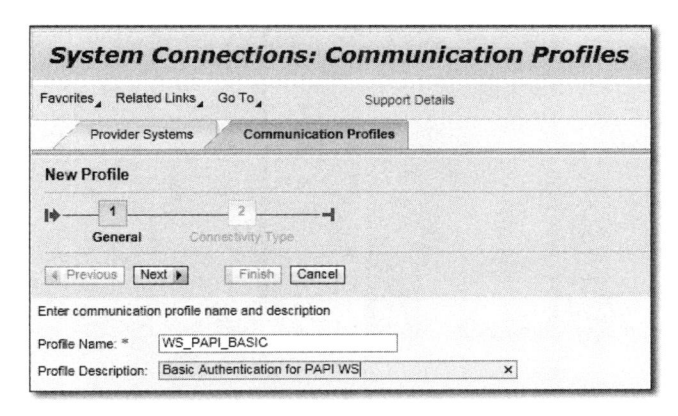

Figure 14.2 Communication Profile for SAP ME PAPI SOAP Service

5. On the next screen, specify the CONNECTIVITY TYPE as WS (web service) and select the AUTHENTICATION METHOD as USER NAME/PASSWORD (BASIC), as shown Figure 14.3.

6. Deselect the NONE checkbox if selected by default.

7. Keep the other configurations as is.

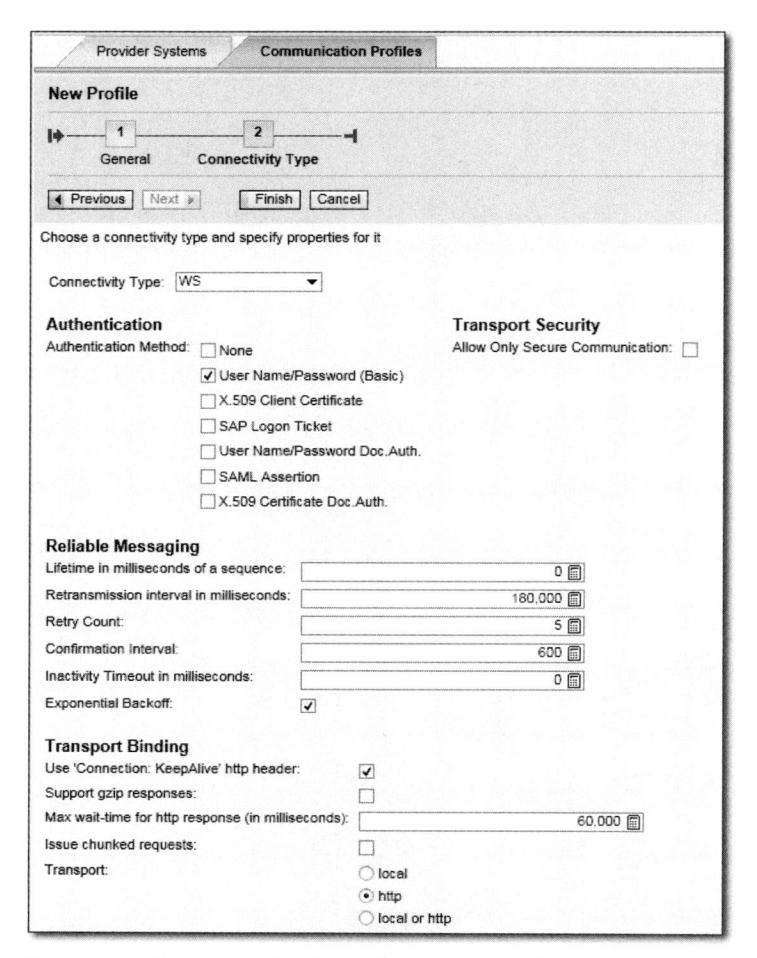

Figure 14.3 Web Service Profile Configuration for SAP ME PAPI Service

8. Navigate to SOA • APPLICATION AND SCENARIO COMMUNICATION • APPLICATION COMMUNICATION.

9. Enter "*papi*" in the SEARCH field and click on GO to display the PAPI services.

10. Select SAP.COM/ME~PAPIWS and select all the corresponding PAPI services from the PROVIDED SERVICES configuration tab shown in Figure 14.4.

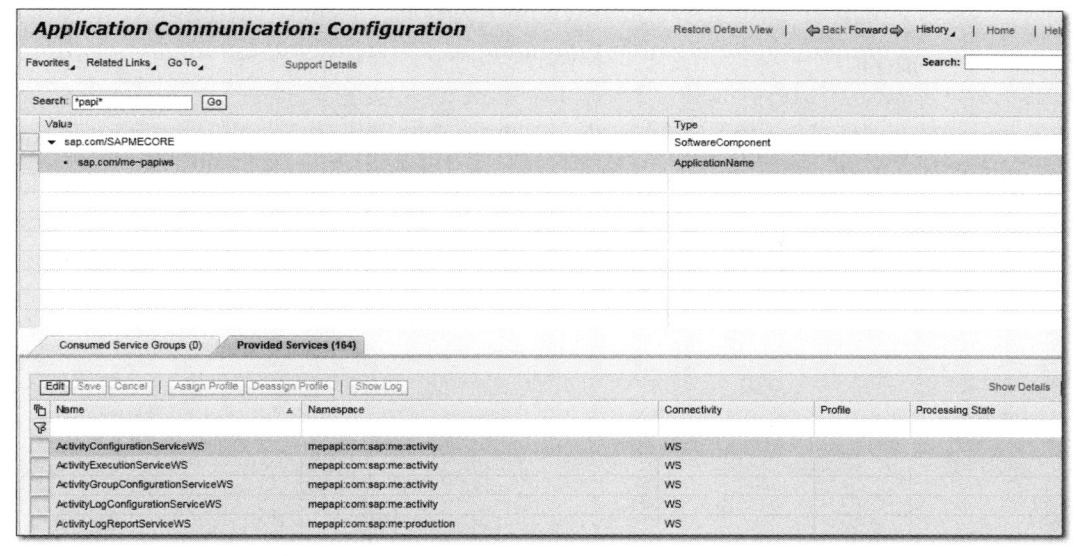

14.2 Configuring and Accessing Public API Web Services

Figure 14.4 PAPI Service Selection

11. Click on EDIT and in the ASSIGN PROFILE pop-up that appears, select the communication profile created in the last step (i.e., WS_PAPI_BASIC) and click on SAVE, as shown in Figure 14.5.

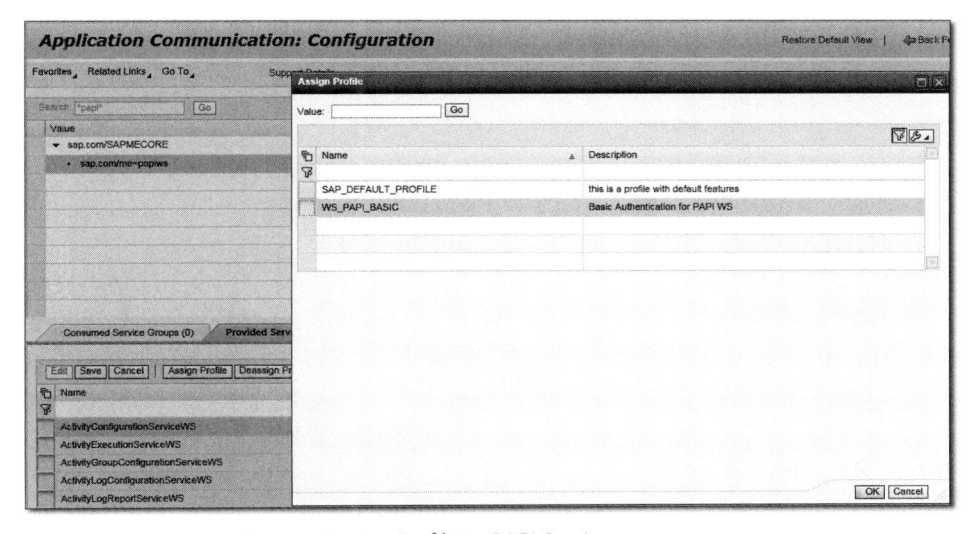

Figure 14.5 Assigning Communication Profile to PAPI Services

14   Custom Enhancements Using Public API Web Services

Now that the service and security configurations are complete, navigate to SOA • APPLICATION AND SCENARIO COMMUNICATION • SINGLE SERVICE ADMINISTRATION. On the SERVICE DEFINITIONS tab, you can either browse the PAPI services or search for a specific service. To search for a service on the SEARCH tab, enter a search string (using wildcard characters as appropriate). All PAPI services matching your search string will appear below the search screen, as shown in Figure 14.6. Select a service and click on the WSDL tab to view the service WSDL URL, through which you can execute the SOAP web service. Select the WSDL URL that includes the communication profile you assigned.

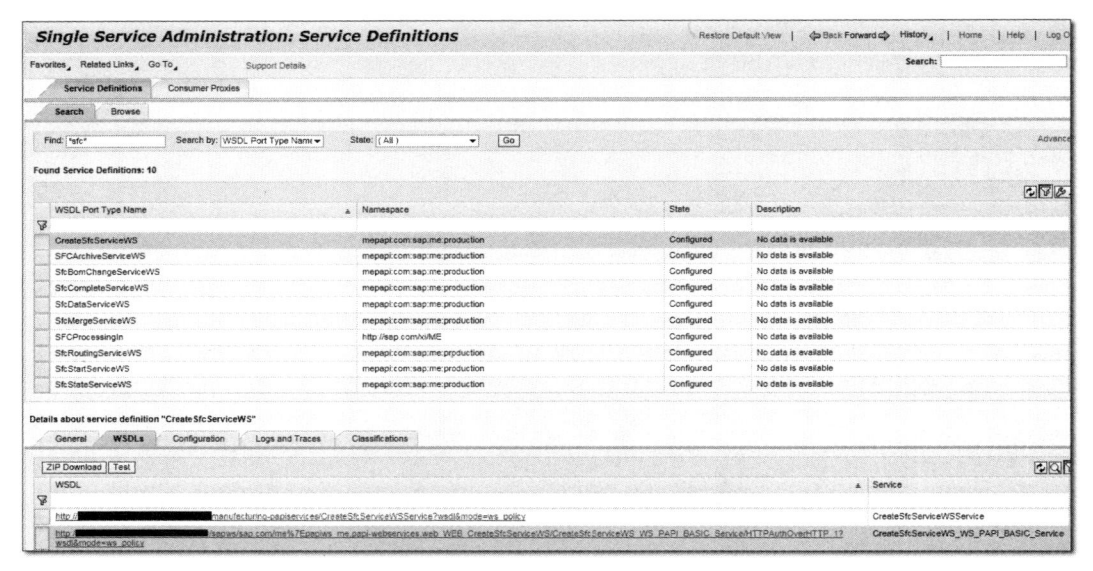

Figure 14.6 Searching PAPI Services

You can also browse PAPI services from the BROWSE tab, and select SOFTWARE-COMPONENTS in the SELECT CLASSIFICATION dropdown, and expand the tree view for SAP.COM/SAPMECORE • SAP.COM/ME~PAPIWS, under which you can find all the SAP ME PAPI services, as shown in Figure 14.7.

Test the PAPI web service from the WSNavigator (*http://<host>:<port>/wsnavigator*) or any external SOAP web service testing tool (such as SOAPUI) using the WSDL of the PAPI web service.

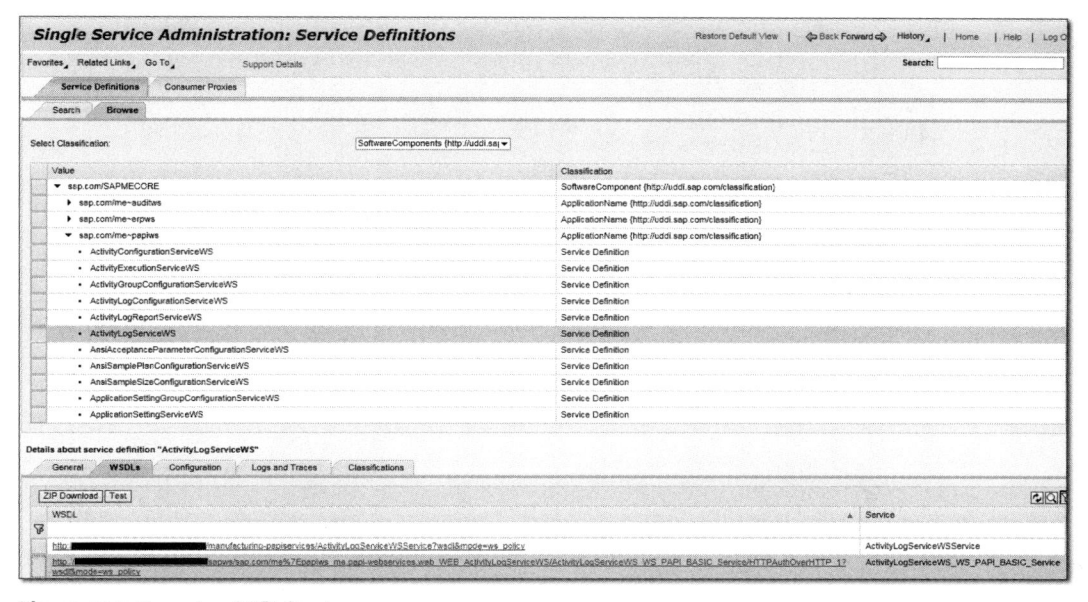

Figure 14.7 Browsing PAPI Services

14.3 Executing PAPI Services from SAP MII Action Blocks

You can also execute PAPI services from the SAP MII instance available on the same SAP ME server by creating a *Business Logic Services* (BLS) transaction in the SAP MII workbench. SAP MII provides a development platform on which you can develop custom business logic by creating BLS transactions, and BLS provides predefined action blocks for various functionalities, using which you can develop almost any custom logic. As explained in Chapter 1, BLS transactions are used to develop services in SAPMEINT as well. For SAP ME, there are some specific action blocks available in SAP MII BLS. You can use the *SAP ME PAPI Interface* action block, which is available under *SAP ME Integration* action categories, to execute any PAPI service in the corresponding SAP ME instance.

As shown in Figure 14.8, you can add the action block in a BLS transaction, search, and select a PAPI service method that you want to execute.

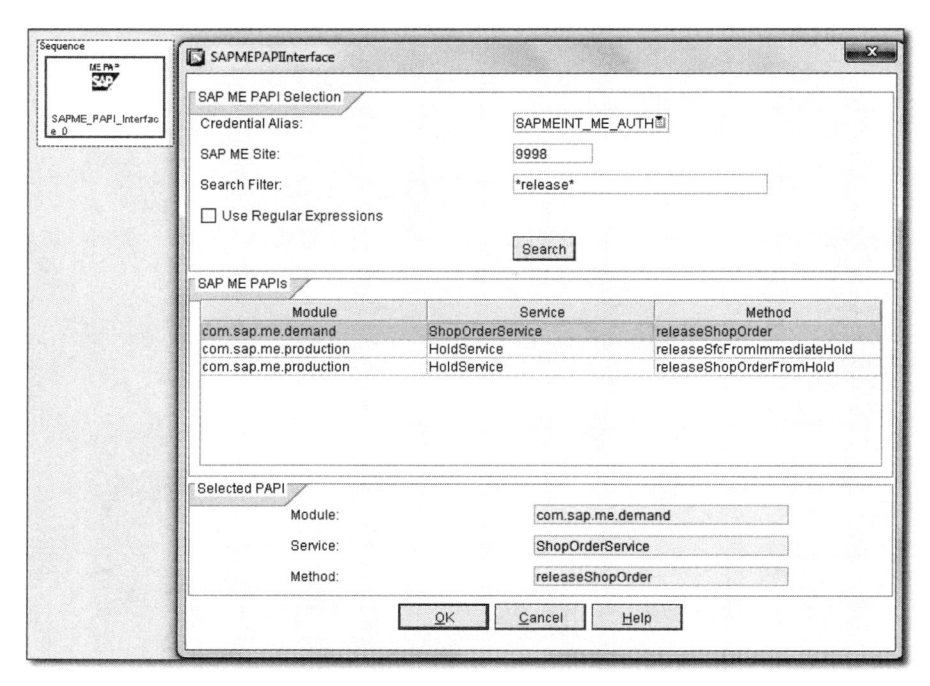

Figure 14.8 SAP ME PAPI Interface Action in SAP MII Business Logic Services

From the link configuration of the action block, specify the input parameters in the request structure required for executing the PAPI service.

14.4 Examples of Enhancements Using PAPI Services

In the same way that you develop different types of custom applications on SAP ME using PAPI web services, you can also use PAPI services from SAP MII business logic and custom user interfaces to develop custom applications. We will discuss these techniques that use BLS transactions in SAP MII in the next sections, using assigning external SFC numbers and developing custom PODs as examples.

14.4.1 Assigning External SFC Numbers

While releasing shop orders in SAP ME, SFCs are generated based on the lot size of the material, and SFC numbers are automatically assigned by SAP ME using the Next Number pattern configured for SFC numbers. In some cases, you may want to assign the SFC number externally instead of using the internally generated SFC number from SAP ME. For example, for a car assembly process, the SFC number must be the engine chassis number, which is generated at the time of production by an external system based on specific business logic. In that case, instead of using an internally generated SFC number, you may want to assign SFC numbers while releasing the shop order in SAP ME. You can create a custom BLS transaction in SAP ME to release the SFCs for a shop order using the corresponding PAPI service and to pass in the external SFC numbers that will be used.

To develop this scenario, create a BLS transaction in SAP MII and the SAP ME PAPI Interface action block, and select the `releaseShopOrder` method of the `ShopOrderService` service, as shown in Figure 14.8.

Define the input parameters of the BLS transaction for `Site`, `ShopOrder`, `Workcenter`, `QuantityToRelease` and the `SFC` (with the custom SFC number). Link the transaction parameters to the PAPI service method request parameters, as shown in Figure 14.9.

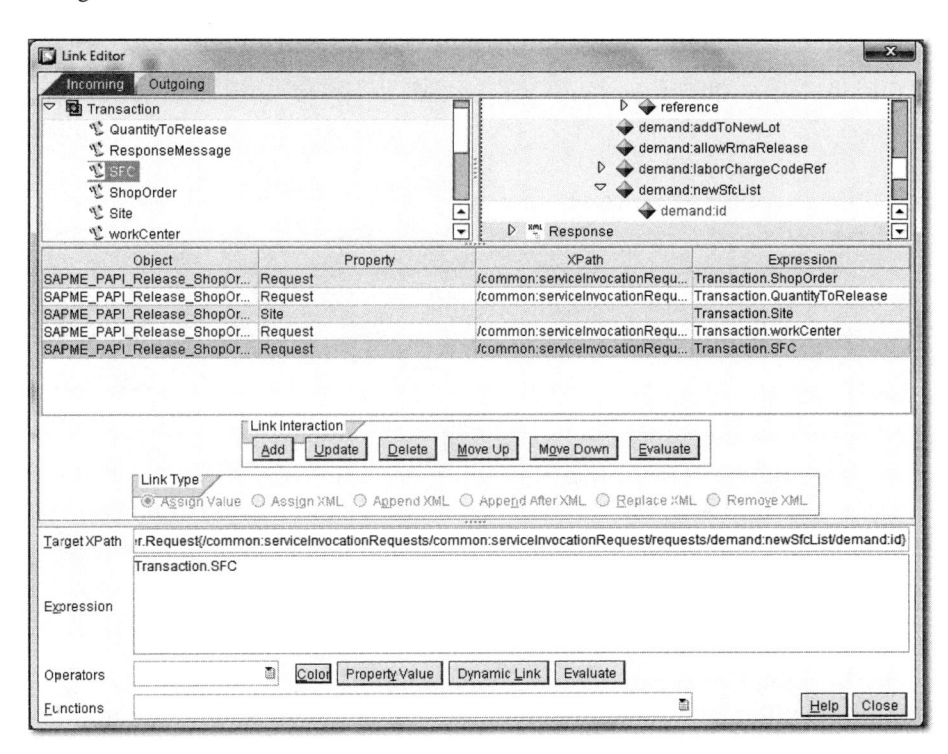

Figure 14.9 Request Link Mapping for releaseShopOrder PAPI Service in SAP MII BLS Transaction

You can generate the SFC numbers by some custom business logic or fetch the numbers from another system or database if required, before executing this action. You can pass the values for the input parameters to the BLS transaction executed from either another BLS transaction or a custom user interface, which executes the PAPI service and releases the shop order with the specified SFC number.

After the PAPI interface action block, you can add an action to check the response XML returned by the PAPI service and provide a user message for success or error accordingly.

14.4.2 Developing Custom PODs

In Chapter 10, you learned how to configure new PODs in the POD Maintenance activity in SAP ME. You can also develop custom PODs by developing the user interface via any UI technology, such as SAPUI5.

You can develop custom PODs using SAPUI5 and BLS transactions in SAP MII, as shown in Figure 14.10. You need to develop BLS transactions in SAP MII to execute the relevant PAPI services and get the data required to be displayed in the POD (e.g., SFC lists, SFC details, operations, NC details, etc.) as well as to update the data in SAP ME from the user interface. You need to develop different BLS transactions for different functionalities and data queries, and update by executing different PAPI services, which you can execute from the user interface via the Xacute Query by HTTP call (using XMLModel from SAPUI5). Finally, add the custom PODs in the SAP MII portal to provide role-based access to the different dashboards to different users. Then, users do not need to log in to SAP ME; you can provide all required user interfaces for users via customized dashboards developed in SAP MII.

One example of a custom POD developed on SAP MII using SAPUI5 as the user interface technology and BLS transactions using PAPI services for the logic and data management is shown in Figure 14.11. Here, a custom user interface has been developed by a third-party JavaScript library to display the routing flow, highlighting the current operation. Also the relevant actions for the operators, such as start and complete operations, data collection, NC logging, and so on, are provided as buttons that execute the corresponding PAPI services of SAP ME as required through SAP MII BLS transactions, which are invoked from the user interface events.

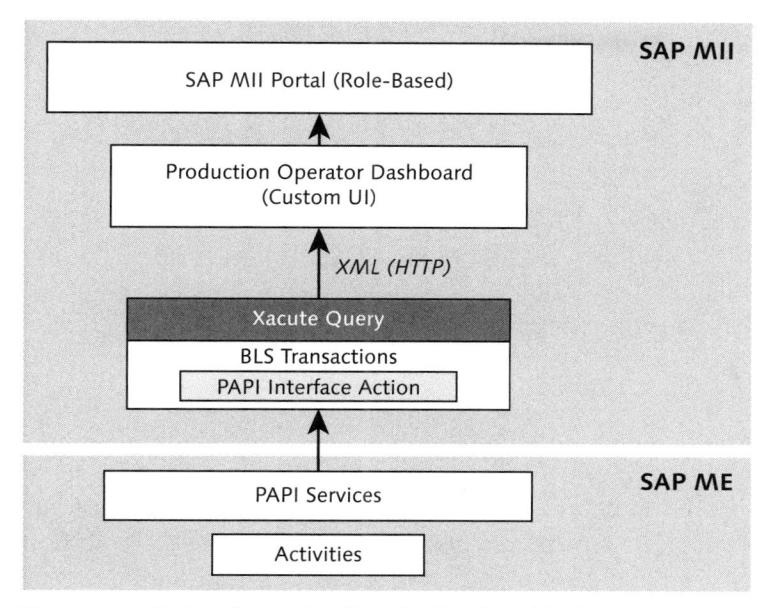

Figure 14.10 Custom Production Operator Dashboard Architecture

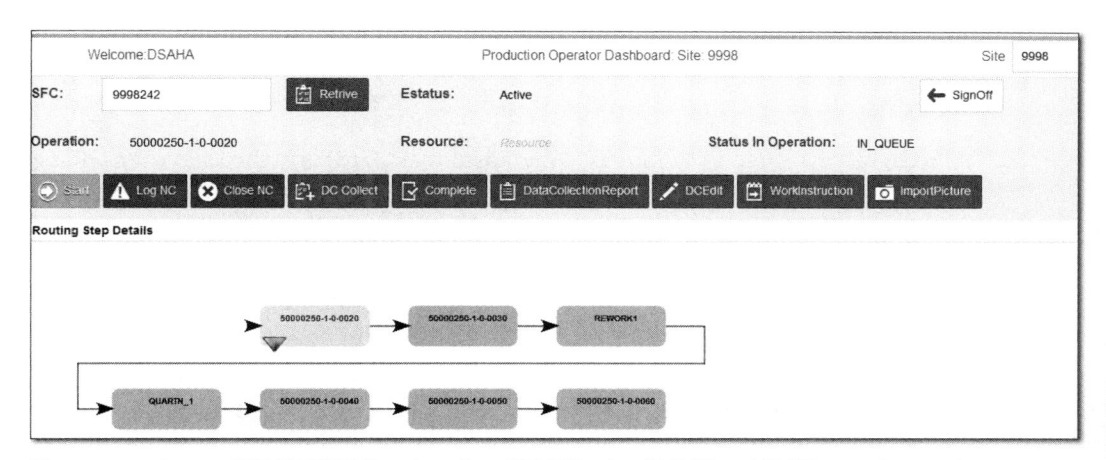

Figure 14.11 Custom SAP ME POD Developed on SAP MII using SAPUI5 and BLS Transactions and PAPI Services

Following this approach, you can develop any custom application on SAP MII using PAPI services. You also can develop custom applications on other platforms, such as Java, Microsoft .Net, or mobile applications.

> **Note**
>
> When you execute the SAP ME PAPI services as SOAP web services from SAP MII or any external program, you need to pass in the field values that end with `Ref` in the following format:
>
> `<Objectname>BO:<Site>,<ItemNo>,<Version>`
>
> For example, if the field name is `ItemRef`, then the value you pass in should be in the following format:
>
> *ItemBO:9998,Mat10,A*
>
> Where `9998` is the site, `Mat10` is the material, and `A` is the version.

14.5 OData Services for SAP ME

SAP ME also provides OData interfaces for all activities, which can be executed by the REST service through HTTP. You can also use the OData services from web user interfaces—for example, custom PODs—by directly consuming the OData services from SAPUI5-based custom web pages, using the OData model feature available in SAPUI5. An advantage of OData-based interfaces is that they can be accessed by simple HTTP calls using the standard HTTP methods `GET`, `POST`, `PUT`, and `DELETE`, which most modern programming languages and UI technologies support.

You can access the OData interface metadata of SAP ME via the following URL:

http://<host>:<port>/manufacturing-odata/<serviceName>/$metadata

Specify the OData service name in the URL to get its corresponding metadata or the service interface structure. Examples of service names include Production.svc, Assembly.svc, and so on; they provide the services for specific activities. You can find the full list of OData services provided by SAP ME in the *SAP ME 15.0 OData Services Guide*, which is available in the SAP Service Marketplace along with the installation and configuration guides for SAP ME.

While executing OData services, you can also pass in specific input parameters based on the service. For example:

http://<host>:<port>/manufacturingodata/Production.svc/ShopOrders('PC_ORDER')/Sfcs?SITE=*

This service retrieves the list of all SFCs available for the shop order ID *PC_ORDER*.

The OData service provides the results in XML format, specifically using the ATOM or JSON formats, which are commonly used by OData services.

14.6 Summary

In this chapter, you learned about SAP ME PAPI services and how to consume them from Java programs and SAP MII BLS transactions. You also discovered some common scenarios in which you can develop custom extensions using PAPI services in SAP MII and OData services provided by SAP ME.

In the next chapter, you will learn how to connect SAP ME with manufacturing automation systems using SAP Plant Connectivity (PCo) and SAP MII.

This chapter provides explains how to use SAP PCo and SAP MII with end-to-end integration scenario for integrating shop-floor automation systems with SAP ME using SAP MII and Plant Connectivity (SAP PCo).

15   Shop Floor Systems Integration Using SAP MII and Plant Connectivity

In earlier chapters, you learned how SAP ME is used to manage the real-time information collected manually by shop floor users from physical machines on the manufacturing shop floor, by resource status, measurement points, parametric data collection for SFCs, and quality inspection results. Most of this machine data is collected by the sensors, and stored in manufacturing automation systems, such as Plant Data Historian, Laboratory Information Systems (LIMS), and so on. Often, you may need to get the data directly from those systems instead of manually entering it in SAP ME (e.g., for automated or semi-automated production lines). You may also need to send some information from SAP ME to these shop floor systems, such as SFC number with status, operation status, or so on. The shop floor automation and control systems provide various connection protocols, such as OPC (OLE for Process Control), Web Services, FTP, JDBC, and so on. Some systems, such as OSIPI Historian, GE Fanuc iHistorian, and others, may need to be connected through proprietary API-based connections. Some common situations in which you may need to connect to automation systems include retrieving the real-time machine status and updating the resource status in SAP ME accordingly, or getting the parametric data or quality inspection results from shop floor systems.

To connect to shop floor automation systems, SAP provides *SAP Plant Connectivity* (PCo), which supports the various connection protocols and easily integrates with SAP MII to query or send the data bi-directionally. In SAP PCo, you can configure query agents or notification agents to query the data from external

15 Shop Floor Systems Integration Using SAP MII and Plant Connectivity

shop floor systems or to get notification messages and send data to SAP MII when the values in the source system change. As you learned in the last chapter, you can develop custom logic in SAP MII to execute SAP ME PAPI services and to update and query data as required. The architecture overview for integrating SAP ME with shop floor automation systems using SAP PCo and SAP MII is shown in Figure 15.1.

In this chapter, we will cover SAP PCo configuration for integration with both OPC and SAP MII, using SAP ME PAPI service for integration with MII and PCo, how SAP ME equipment status is controlled through SAP PCo notifications, and automated shop floor equipment data collection in SAP ME.

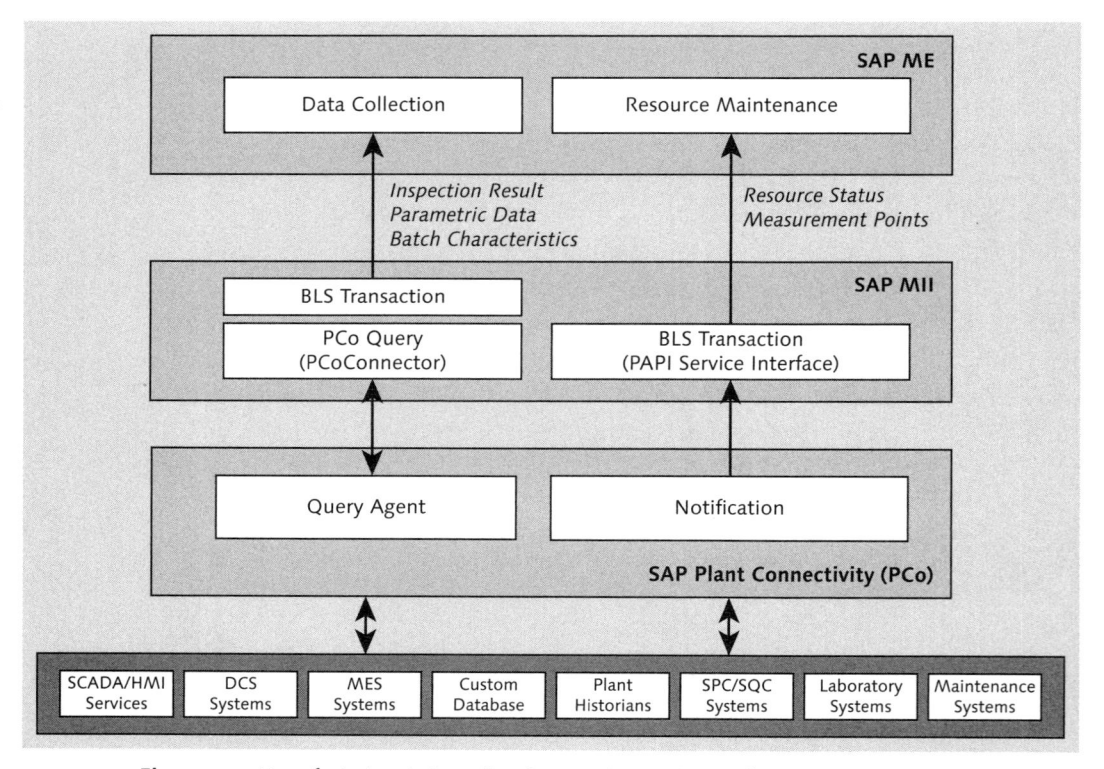

Figure 15.1 Manufacturing Automation Systems Integration with SAP ME via SAP PCo and SAP MII

15.1 End-to-End Integration Scenarios Using SAP PCo, SAP MII, and SAP ME

Let's consider a scenario in which SAP PCo is used to connect to a SCADA system to get the current status of a machine used as the production resource in SAP ME. By querying tag values from the SCADA through SAP PCo and SAP MII, which capture the measuring point data from sensors and PLCs connected to the machine, it indicates the current status of the machine—either down or up for production. Based on the current tag values, the resource status in SAP ME needs to be changed automatically to PRODUCTIVE, UNSCHEDULED DOWN, or so on.

In this scenario, SAP MII will get a notification messages from SAP PCo on change of the tag value in the SCADA or any shop-floor automation system, and based on the notification message, SAP MII can execute the corresponding PAPI services in SAP ME to change the equipment status for which the tag value has changed.

We will also consider another scenario in which the required parametric data collected for an SFC or quality inspection is available in a file generated by an external system (shop floor equipment). The parameter values need to be read from the file when available and need to be updated in a DC group in SAP ME. In this scenario, SAP MII will query the parameter data from the file or any automation system through SAP PCo and update those in SAP ME DC groups as data collection.

15.2 Maintaining Equipment Status through SAP PCo Notification Agent

SAP PCo is an add-on component (developed using Microsoft .Net technology) for SAP MII that is used to connect to shop floor automation systems. It runs on Microsoft Windows and ideally should be installed on the same server where the OPC server or the source system (such as Plant Historian or SCADA) to which it connects is installed. This helps promote easy acquisition of data, minimizing the chance of data loss and eliminate the DCOM security configuration requirements between the source system and SAP PCo.

First, create a source system in SAP PCo, as shown in Figure 15.2. Select the type of source system based on the source system to which you want to connect. In this example, we are connecting with a SCADA system to read tag values, which provides an OPC interface, so the OPC DA AGENT type of source system has been chosen. In the source system details configuration, specify the server details of the source system to which SAP PCo will connect.

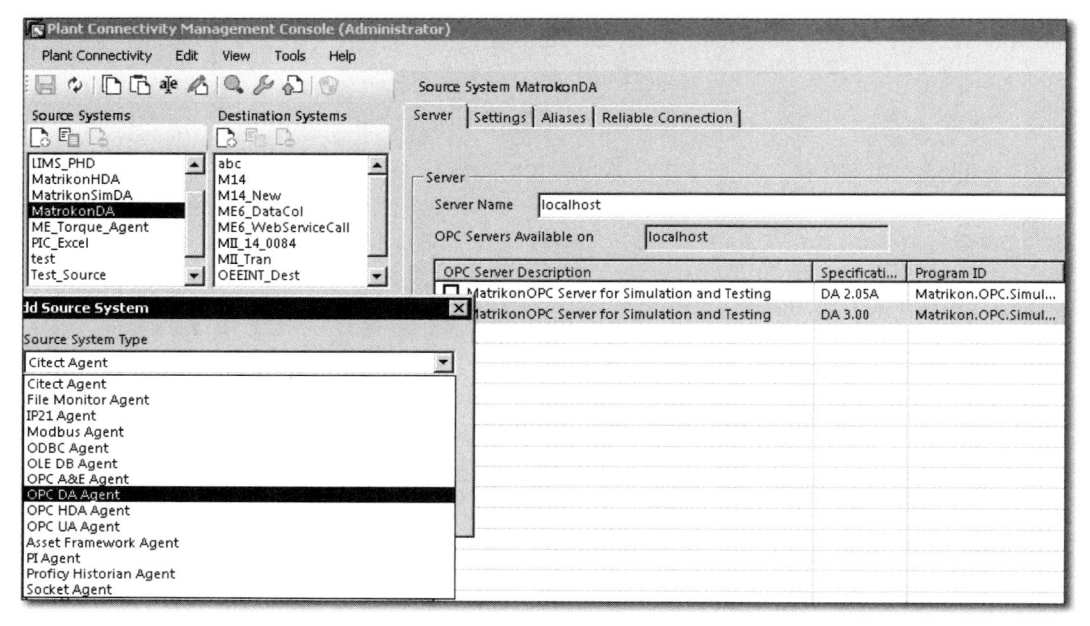

Figure 15.2 Source System in SAP PCo

Also add a destination system to which the information from SAP PCo will be sent on a change of the tag value. For this example, choose type MII Destination. Specify the SAP MII system connection details and authentication details to configure the destination system in SAP PCo, and choose a user with the SAP_XMII_ Administrator role to use to connect to SAP MII from SAP PCo. Please note the SAP MII server configured here is the instance which is running in the SAP ME instance.

Next, create an agent instance of the source system in SAP PCo, and on the SUBSCRIPTION ITEM configuration tab, select the tags from the source system that you want to monitor and for which you want to send a notification when the tag values change, as shown in Figure 15.3.

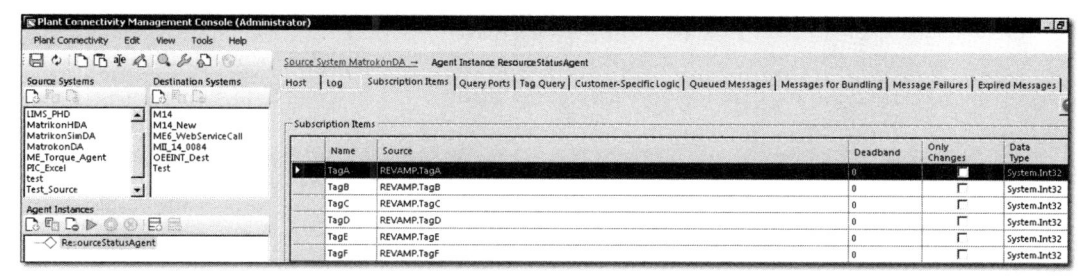

Figure 15.3 Agent Instance Configuration with Subscription Tags

If you want to query the tag values from SAP MII on an ad hoc basis, you also need to specify the port for communicating with SAP MII on the QUERY PORTS configuration tab, as shown in Figure 15.4. This setting is required to configure the *PCoConnector* Data Server in SAP MII in order to create *PCOQueries* to query data from the source system through PCo; here, select the SAP MII type of port for PCOQUERIES and specify an OS port which is not in use by any other application. You can also specify an authentication method if required.

Figure 15.4 Query Port Configuration in SAP PCo Agent

Now, you need to create the notification for the agent that will actually monitor the source system and send the notification message to SAP MII once the data (tag) is changed. Choose ALWAYS for TRIGGER TYPE, as shown in Figure 15.5, which will generate a notification message every time the tag value changes, which are specified in the output. If you want to send the notification only for certain conditions based on the tag values, specify the expression in the expression editor of the TRIGGER CONDITION and set TRIGGER TYPE to TRUE, FALSE, WHILETRUE, or WHILEFALSE. *True* or *False* trigger types trigger the notification when the expression evaluates as true or false. *WhileTrue* and *WhileFalse* trigger the notification as many times as the tag value changes and the condition is sat-

415

isfied, which means that if the trigger type is *WhileTrue* and for five subsequent tag value changes the condition evaluates as true, then five notifications are generated subsequently for the true condition.

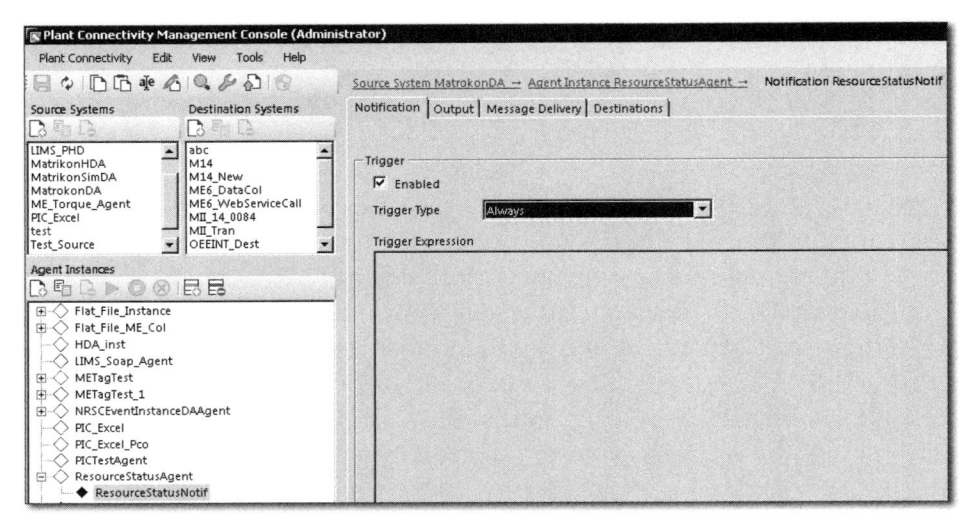

Figure 15.5 SAP PCo Notification Trigger Configuration

Specify the notification message definition in the OUTPUT configuration tab, as shown in Figure 15.6. You can add any element in OUTPUT EXPRESSIONS, which will be added in the XML message of the notification sent to the destination system from SAP PCo. As shown in this example, you can add the relevant information for resource status (e.g., site, tag name, tag value). You also can add a Notif-Status element with the condition for resource downtime—for example, tag value less than 10); when the tag value becomes less than 10, the NotifStatus value is True (signifying a downtime); otherwise, it's False.

Figure 15.6 PCo Notification Output Configuration

You can optionally specify the MESSAGE DELIVERY tab configurations to collect multiple messages based on time or number for the delivery; ignore them if you want to send individual notifications. Finally, you need to complete the DESTINATION tab configuration to specify the BLS transaction in SAP MII that will be executed to send the notification message from SAP PCo. You can create a destination based on any of the destination systems you created earlier, and select a BLS transaction present in your chosen system with an XML input parameter; the custom logic to receive and parse the XML message is implemented there (e.g., execute an SAP ME PAPI service using the notification message XML data that comes from SAP PCo). Figure 15.7 shows a destination configuration example.

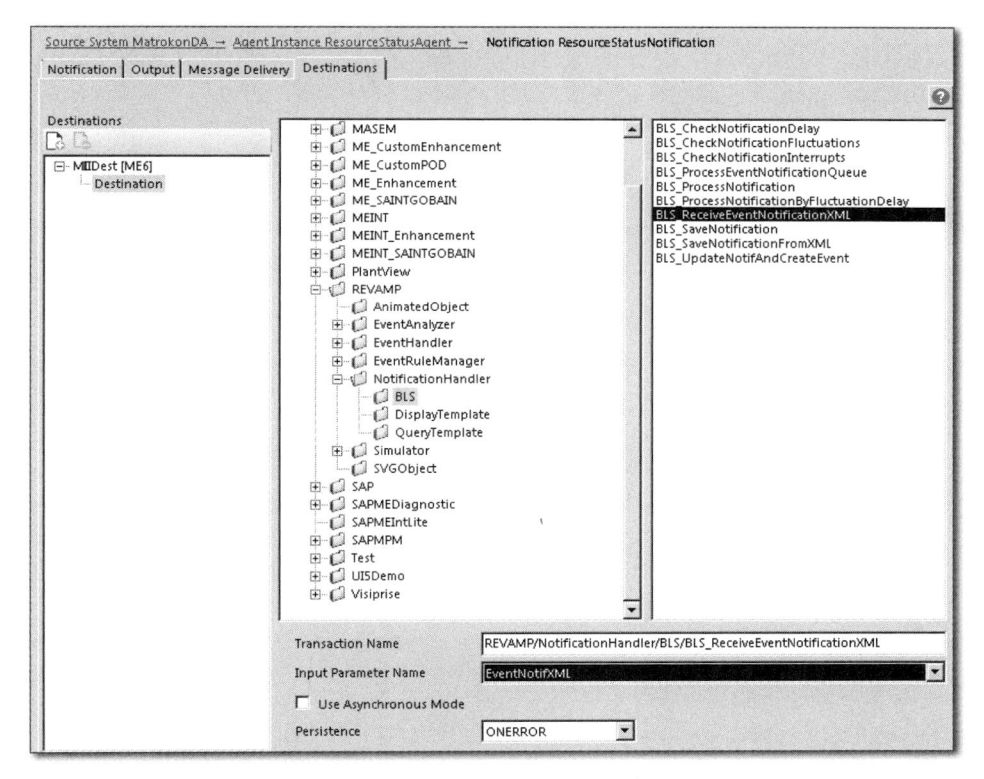

Figure 15.7 Destination BLS Transaction Selection for PCo Notification

Once you complete the configuration, save it, and start the agent instance by selecting it and clicking on the START icon in the AGENT INSTANCES toolbar.

In the BLS transaction developed in SAP MII, you need to add the logic to process the XML sent by SAP PCo. A sample XML message generated by an SAP PCo notification is shown in Figure 15.8. You need to develop the logic in a BLS transaction to process this XML format and extract the site, tag name, and data source information. You can use the *Plant Information Catalog* (PIC) or *Manufacturing Data Objects* (MDO) available in SAP MII or any custom database table to maintain the mappings between the tag name, data source, and resources in SAP ME so that when the notification XML is received in SAP MII, you can query the PIC hierarchy or the database table to find the corresponding resource from the tag name, data source, and plant combination.

```xml
<?xml version="1.0" encoding="UTF-8"?>
<NotificationMessage>
  <Header>
    <Name>ResourceStatusNotification</Name>
    <Description/>
    <Destination>MIIDest</Destination>
    <CreatedDate>2015-09-19T09:27:11</CreatedDate>
    <ID>a06a6eff-5496-4df2-b581-e5db21138c76</ID>
    <Status>Delivered</Status>
  </Header>
  <Body>
    <Values>
      <Site type="xsd:string" timeStamp="0001-01-01T00:00:00.0000000" quality="None">
        <![CDATA[9998]]>
      </Site>
      <TagName type="xsd:string" timeStamp="0001-01-01T00:00:00.0000000" quality="None">
        <![CDATA[TagA]]>
      </TagName>
      <TagValue type="xsd:integer" timeStamp="2015-09-19T09:27:11.3460000Z" quality="Good">
        <![CDATA[8]]>
      </TagValue>
      <NotificationTime type="xsd:dateTime" timeStamp="0001-01-01T00:00:00.0000000" quality="None">
        <![CDATA[2015-09-19T09:27:11]]>
      </NotificationTime>
      <NotifStatus type="xsd:boolean" timeStamp="2015-09-19T09:27:11.3460000Z" quality="Good">
        <![CDATA[1]]>
      </NotifStatus>
      <DataSource type="xsd:string" timeStamp="0001-01-01T00:00:00.0000000" quality="None">
        <![CDATA[SCADA_ABC]]>
      </DataSource>
    </Values>
  </Body>
  <Faults/>
</NotificationMessage>
```

Figure 15.8 Notification XML Message Sent from SAP PCo

Use the PAPI service interface action in SAP MII to execute the ResourceConfigurationService (changeResourecStatus operation), as shown in Figure 15.9. In the LINK configuration of the action block, map the resource name from the PIC or database query and the resource status based on the notification type and tag value along with the reason code (as maintained in SAP ME Reason Code Maintenance activity), comment, and timestamp as required.

When the tag value changes beyond the specific limit, SAP PCo will send a notification message to SAP MII, which in turn will execute the PAPI service to change the resource status in SAP ME.

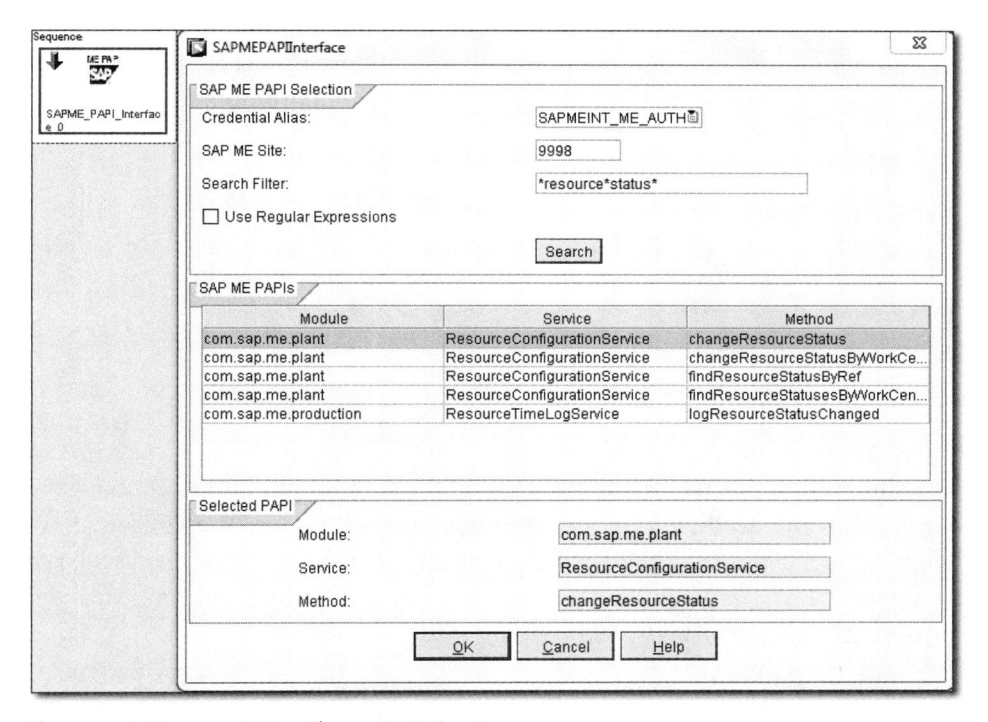

Figure 15.9 Resource Status Change PAPI Service

15.3 Automating Data Collection in SAP ME

You learned how to automate the resource status management by directly integrating with shop-floor automation systems through SAP PCo and SAP MII in the previous example. In a similar way, you can use data collection events to collect parametric data or quality inspection results in DC groups in SAP ME when a tag value change takes place (i.e., a new value is available for the data point either by manual entry in the HMI/SCADA system or by automatic detection of physical parameter changes by PLC and sensors). You can also configure your system to receive the information from a file (which may be generated by the source system periodically) using the FileMonitor source system and agent in SAP PCo. The SAP PCo configuration will remain mostly same as for the previous example, but you may need to modify the output structure of the notification message XML with the file content which provides the parameter information as shown in Figure 15.10.

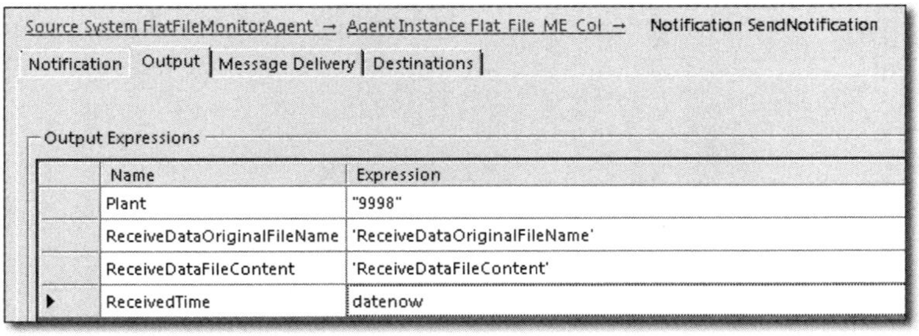

Name	Expression
Plant	"9998"
ReceiveDataOriginalFileName	'ReceiveDataOriginalFileName'
ReceiveDataFileContent	'ReceiveDataFileContent'
ReceivedTime	datenow

Figure 15.10 Output Expression for FileMonitor Notification in SAP PCo

The file content is sent in the XML payload of the notification message sent to SAP MII, which may contain the parameter values as well as the machine name or tag name from which the data is collected. In the receiving BLS transaction for the notification, you need to parse the file content and get the required information. You need to maintain mappings for the tag name, data source, and plant with the parameter names, as maintained in the DC group in SAP ME. In SAP MII, you need to execute the SAP ME PAPI service DataCollectionService (updateParametricData operation) to update the values in a specific DC group or parameter directly in SAP ME.

Also, you can fetch parametric data from the shop floor automation system on an ad hoc basis through SAP MII and SAP PCo using SAP PCo queries developed in SAP MII. The SAP PCo configuration will remain the same as before, and you have to maintain the query port to connect from SAP MII. You do not need to configure notifications for the SAP PCo agent, only for querying through SAP PCo queries.

Create a *data server* in SAP MII of type *PCoConnector* and a PCo query in SAP MII workbench in *TagRetrieveQuery* mode, and add the relevant tags to query. Maintain a mapping between the SAP ME assets (work center, resource) and the corresponding tags in the automation system either by using PIC in SAP MII or through a custom database table. Execute the SAP PCo query from a BLS transaction in SAP MII, which you can add as an activity in SAP ME (see Chapter 17). You can add this activity for a DC COLLECT button in the POD to invoke it and fetch the data in real time from the automation systems through SAP PCo and SAP MII, and update it in the DC group in SAP ME.

15.4 Summary

In this chapter, you learned how to integrate SAP ME with shop floor automation systems or any other external systems through SAP MII and SAP PCo. You learned how to use the notification and query features of SAP PCo to get data from external systems in real time and update it in SAP ME.

In the next chapter, you will learn about SAP ME reports and developing custom reports for SAP ME in MII.

SAP ME offers a list of standard reports, but custom reports can also be developed using SAP MII and other tools as needed. This chapter will explain Executive Dashboard configuration in SAP ME, how to develop custom reports in SAP MII using PAPI services and SQL queries, and how to use the reports delivered in SAP MII.

16   Advanced Reporting in SAP ME

In this chapter we will explain the different reporting options in SAP ME, how to configure Execution Dashboard for reporting, and give an overview of developing custom reports on SAP ME data in SAP MII.

16.1   Reporting Databases and Options in SAP ME

As a manufacturing execution system, reporting WIP information in real time and analysis of trends and activities are important functionalities provided by SAP ME. In SAP ME, all of the configuration data, master data and transactional data used for WIP tracking and recording by the various SAP ME activities is maintained in the WIP database. Because the WIP database grows in size quickly due to frequent transactions, data is archived into the ODS database periodically to keep the WIP database lean, so that the performance of SAP ME activities is not affected due to large database size. The ODS database contains the summarized data from the WIP database in a reporting-friendly structure and acts as an interim data warehouse for production data.

To view and analyze the WIP and production information available in SAP ME, there are several standard reports available for different activities e.g. production reports, SFC reports, nonconformance reports and so on, which were explained in earlier chapters along with their corresponding configuration and data recording options. Apart from the standard WIP reports, there is also a configurable *Executive Dashboard* available in SAP ME through which production supervisors can view consolidated reports from a single dashboard.

There are standard reports available on SAP BusinessObjects Enterprise XI 3.1 (BOBJ) on the ODS database. Fourteen universes are available in ODS for SAP BOBJ reporting, and twenty-five preconfigured standard reports on SAP BOBJ can be downloaded from SAP Service Marketplace and viewed through SAP BOBJ connected to the SAP ME ODS database.

A few standard preconfigured reports also are available on SAP MII (as part of SAPMEINT), developed on the WIP database and SAP ERP. Similarly, any custom report can be also developed on SAP MII using SAPUI5 and queries from the ODS or WIP database.

Typically, the standard WIP reports in SAP ME are suitable for production users, whereas the executive dashboards can be used by production supervisors to monitor and analyze all required information. The SAP BOBJ and custom reports on the ODS database are more suitable for plant managers and planners. The reporting process and options in SAP ME are shown in Figure 16.1.

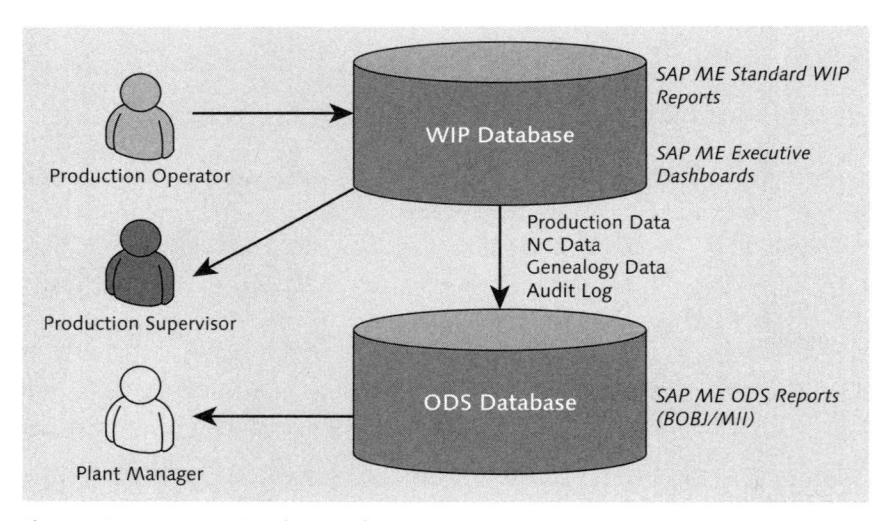

Figure 16.1 Reporting Database and Options in SAP ME

16.2 Executive Dashboards in SAP ME

You can configure the Executive Dashboard in SAP ME to combine multiple reports, which can be useful for production supervisors. To configure the Executive Dashboard in SAP ME, open the EXECUTIVE DASHBOARD MAINTENANCE activity, as shown in Figure 16.2. Here, you can create a new dashboard or configure an existing one. Add dashboard items as portlets by clicking on the INSERT NEW link. Specify a unique sequence number for each portlet, and select the portlet from the available list. SAP ME provides a set of preconfigured portlets that you can use, or you can develop new ones in Java. You also need to specify whether the portlet will be displayed in a new row by selecting the NEW ROW checkbox and selecting the size of the portlet from the SIZE dropdown. The default refresh rate is three hundred seconds, which you can change by entering a value in the REFRESH RATE field. Finally, specify the parameters for each portlet as required. The date range parameter is mandatory for most portlets.

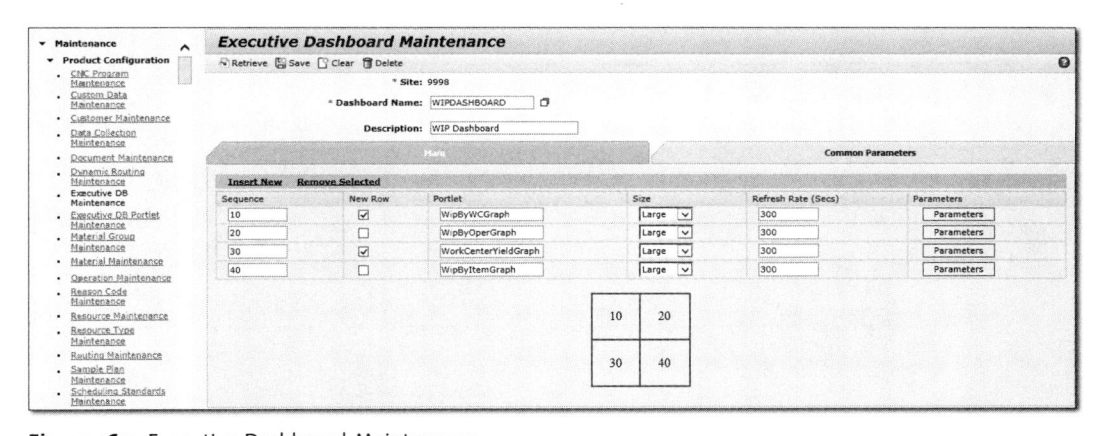

Figure 16.2 Executive Dashboard Maintenance

You can configure or develop a new portlet in Java and deploy it on the SAP ME server, which you can access in the Executive Dashboard. When you develop a new portlet, configure it in the EXECUTIVE DASHBOARD PORTLET MAINTENANCE activity, as shown in Figure 16.3. Specify the class name of the Java program that you deployed on the SAP ME server for the portlet and specify the parameters required for the portlet and its possible sizes.

Once you've configured the Executive Dashboard, view it from the EXECUTIVE DASHBOARD VIEWER activity, as shown in Figure 16.4. Clicking on the link will open the Executive Dashboard in a new browser window.

The executive dashboard displays all the portlets together in a single dashboard per the dashboard configuration, as shown in Figure 16.5. You can open each portlet in a new window or view the parameters passed to it.

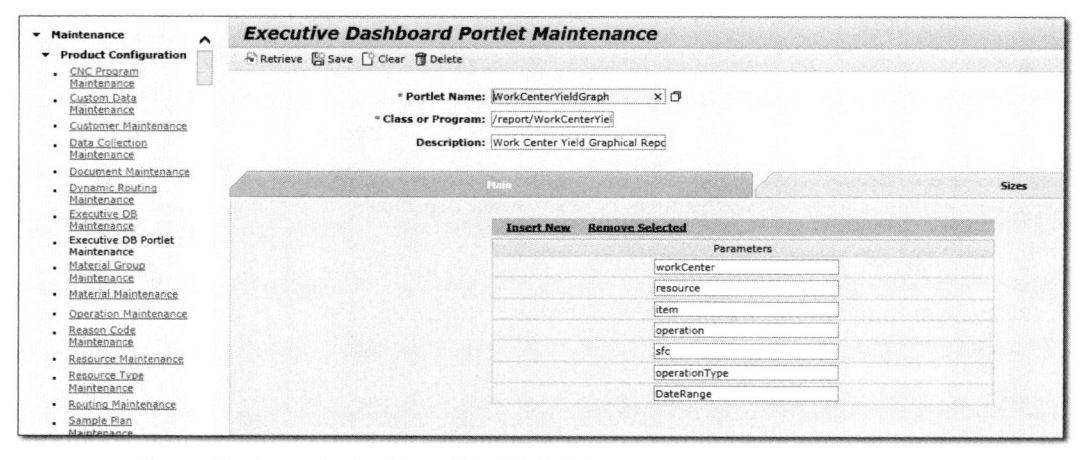

Figure 16.3 Executive Dashboard Portlet Maintenance

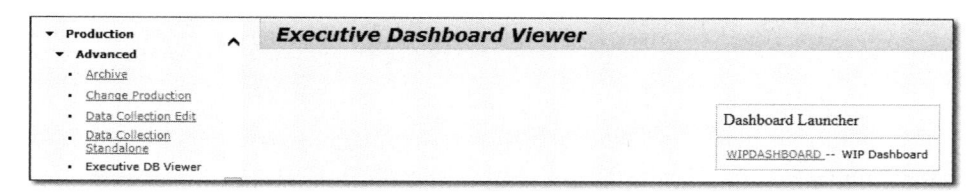

Figure 16.4 Executive Dashboard Viewer

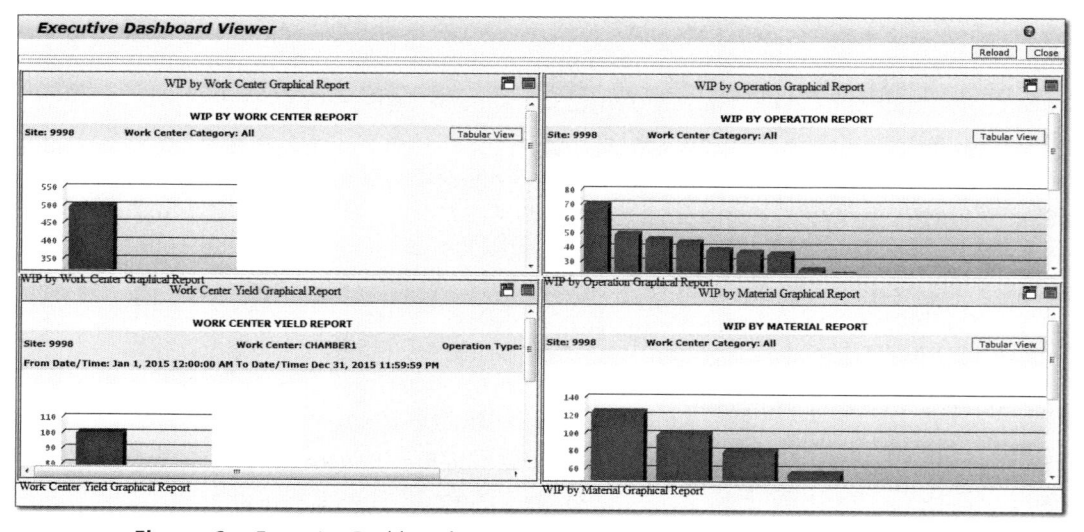

Figure 16.5 Executive Dashboard in SAP ME

16.3 SAP ME Standard Reports in SAP MII

You can use some reports provided in SAPMEINT based on SAP ERP and SAP ME for various purposes. The following reports are available in SAP MII:

- Enhanced Planned Orders
- Batch Traceability Report
- Where Is My Order? Report
- Overall equipment effectiveness (OEE) Report
- WIP Production Monitor

Use the Enhanced Planned Order Report to view the planned orders available in SAP ERP, change the quantities if required, and send them to SAP ME.

Use the Batch Traceability Report to query the SAP ERP production orders for a plant and material and view the goods movement information for the material as recorded in SAP ERP. You can also view the delivery information for the material, the production orders that use the material, and the shop order report from SAP ME for detailed information.

Use the Where Is My Order? Report to view the current status of make-to-order material based on a customer number and purchase order.

The OEE Report provides charts that display the OEE KPI based on the availability, quality, and performance KPIs of the SFC execution recorded in SAP ME. To view the OEE Report, first configure OEE targets for the resources for which you want to view the OEE Report.

16.4 Developing Custom Reports in MII

You can develop custom reports on SAP MII, using the development environment available in SAP MII to develop visualization content for analytics and reporting. SAP MII provides options to develop different types of visualization content for analytics and reporting using SAPUI5-based configurable controls for charts and tabular display and native UI control elements available in SAPUI5.

In the SAP MII Workbench, develop logic components by creating *Business Logic Services* (BLS) from which you can execute PAPI services, as explained in Chapter

14. Alternately, use SQL queries to query the WIP or ODS database from the SAP MII Workbench and use the queries in BLS transactions to develop the logic for analytics.

You can also configure display templates, which can use the Xacute Query created to execute BLS transactions. Also, develop the SAPUI5 user interfaces to embed the display templates with the required UI logic, and develop the reports with the *Self-Service Composition Environment* (SSCE) in SAP MII, using the queries and display templates created in the SAP MII Workbench.

You can also develop user interfaces using SAPUI5 directly by executing the OData interfaces available in SAP ME, as explained in Chapter 14. Use the OData interface to develop simple reports that do not require additional business logic because they're called from the user interface directly. Using SAP MII 15.1 (available with SAP ME 15.1) you can execute OData service from BLS transaction as well using the new OData action block. These reports also can use PAPI interfaces with SAP MII BLS transactions to develop reports with additional or complex logic. The architecture of the solution is shown in Figure 16.6.

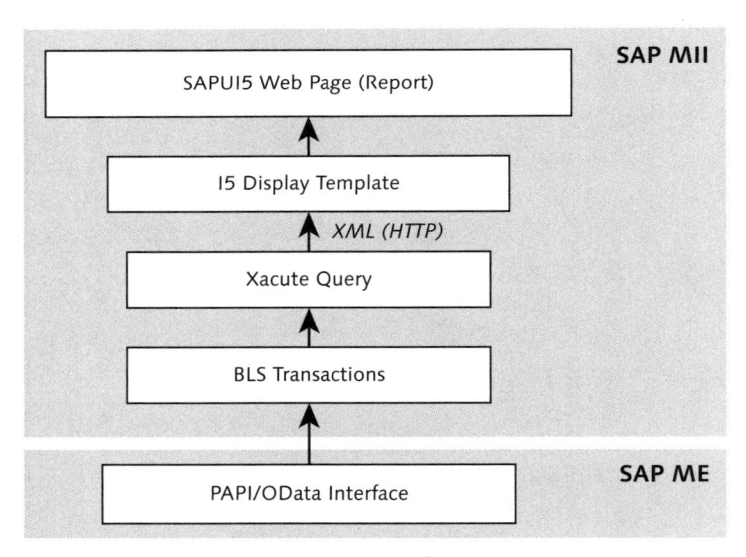

Figure 16.6 Custom SAP ME Report Development on SAP MII

SAP ME provides extended control elements and utility functions in SAPUI5 to develop mobile dashboards, which can be accessed from both desktop and mobile devices. The libraries for these dashboards are available on the server on which SAP ME is installed. Refer to the *SAP Manufacturing Execution Mobile Developers Guide* available in SAP Service Marketplace and to the installation and configuration guides for SAP ME for details about the predefined SAPUI5 libraries available in SAP ME.

Once you create a custom report for SAP ME, you can create an activity for it using the SAP ME Activity Maintenance (type URL activity) and assign a user role to it so that it will appear in the navigation items of SAP ME. Alternately, you can add the report page as a navigation item in SAP MII so that it will appear in the SAP MII Portal navigation.

16.5 Summary

In this chapter, you learned about developing reports for SAP ME using various options—such as Executive Dashboard in SAP ME—custom reports using SAP MII, and the reports available in SAPMEINT.

In the next chapter, you'll learn about the SAP ME SDK and learn how to extend the standard functionalities of SAP ME with custom developments.

This chapter provides an overview of the SAP ME SDK and how to set up an environment for SAP ME SDK–based development. It also explains different enhancement options available in SAP ME via the SDK, how to use the available APIs and Java libraries for the SDK, and how to enhance standard SAP ME functionality through the SDK.

17   Enhancing SAP ME with SDKs

In SAP ME implementation projects, standard SAP ME functionalities may not meet all business requirements, particularly for complex or unique requirements. Sometimes, you need to consider enhancing SAP ME functionality developing a custom application to address additional business requirements. For example, in a manufacturing process, say that you need to create a child shop order with a specific naming convention whenever the parent shop order is released for the first time in SAP ME. You also need to provide validation logic in parent shop order's routing to check whether the SFC from the child shop order is complete before completing the parent shop order's SFC in the first operation of the parent shop order's routing. To achieve those kinds of functionalities, enhance the SAP ME standard functionalities via the SAP ME Software Development Kit (SDK).

In Chapter 14, we discussed SAP ME public APIs, which expose the SAP ME standard functionalities as Java APIs and web services. Using those PAPI services, you can enhance SAPMEINT workflows and develop new custom applications on SAP ME, but to enhance SAP ME core functionalities you need SAP ME SDK–based enhancement. In this chapter, you'll learn about enhancement options in SAP ME via the SDK. In SAP ME, when implementing SDK-based enhancements, you need to perform the environment setup on the server side as well as on the client side, which requires a clear understanding of the Java APIs related to SAP ME. Along with knowledge of the Java API, you should also have strong skillset in Java-based development.

17   Enhancing SAP ME with SDKs

> **Note**
> See *https://www.sap-press.com/3868* to download the custom code that accompanies this chapter.

17.1 Overview of SAP ME SDK

The SAP ME SDK provides a complete toolkit to enhance or develop SAP ME–based applications. The SDK contains SAP ME–specific APIs and Java libraries. The development environment uses SAP NetWeaver Developer Studio (NWDS), which is an Eclipse-based IDE for Java development in SAP NetWeaver, and SAP NetWeaver Development Infrastructure (NWDI) for source control and component build. The SDK supports creation of Java applications, business components such as EJBs and web services, and UI components such as JSP, Servlet, JSF, HTML, and more. Before starting SAP ME SDK–based enhancement, you need to understand the SAP ME core architecture and dependencies between different layers, as shown in Figure 17.1, which will help you make quick design decisions.

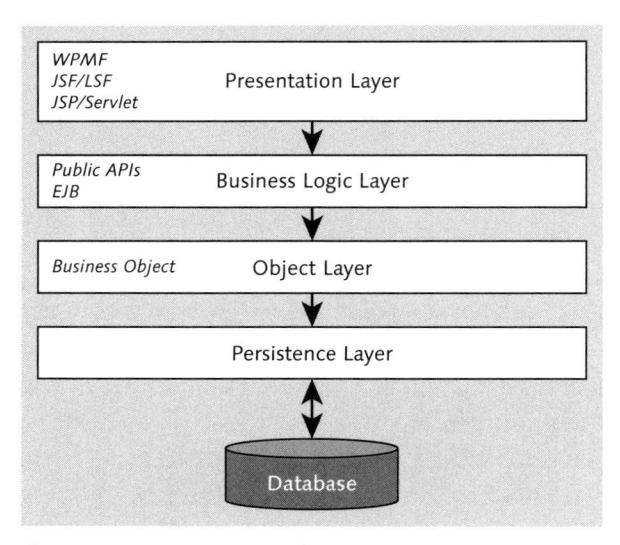

Figure 17.1 SAP ME Core Architecture Overview

Figure 17.1 presents the following layers:

- **Presentation Layer**
  This layer represents user interactions that can be developed using JavaServer Pages (JSP), Servlets, JavaServer Faces (JSF), an SAP provided extension for JSF called LightSpeed Faces (LSF), and the Web Plugin Management Framework (WPMF). Section 17.3 discusses the details of the presentation layer for POD plug-in–related development.

- **Business Logic**
  This layer provides the SAP ME public APIs that are used to enhance or develop the logic components for SAP ME–based applications.

- **Object Layer**
  This layer is also called the *Business Model Layer*. It provides the structure of each business object in SAP ME. Relationships are established between business objects based on business functionalities.

- **Persistence Layer**
  Business objects interact with the SAP ME database (WIP or ODS) through this layer.

In next section, we'll cover setting up the development environment to use the SAP ME SDK.

17.2 Development Environment for SAP ME SDK

Setting up the development environment is an important prerequisite for SAP ME SDK–based development, which relies on SAP NWDI. All required components are stored on a central SAP NetWeaver Application Server Java and multiple developers use the same SAP NWDI services for development locally via SAP NWDS. SAP NWDI installation occurs on the server side and can be accessed by multiple client-side SAP NWDS instances. The environment setup task can be split into two major steps: configuration of SAP NWDI and System Landscape Directory (SLD), and configuration of SAP NWDS in the client system.

In this section, we will walk you through configuration of SAP NWDI and SLD, creation of Software Components, Development Configurations creation, Name

Reservation in SLD, Configuration of SAP NWDS in Client System, Name Servers configuration in SAP NWDS, and Configuration of SAP NetWeaver Application Server (AS) Java in SAP NWDS.

17.2.1 Configuration of SAP NWDI and SLD

SAP NWDI provides the infrastructure for developing Java-based applications and used for versioning of source code, for building, and for lifecycle management of Java-based applications. Because all SAP ME related developments are based on Java, SAP NWDI is used for the entire SAP ME SDK development and for managing the lifecycle of applications. Before configuring SAP NWDI, install SAP NWDI on a separate SAP NetWeaver Application Server (AS) Java or on the same server where SAP ME is installed. We recommend installing SAP NWDI on a separate SAP NetWeaver AS, if the same SAP NWDI setup is used for different types of Java development other than SAP ME. Otherwise NWDI can be installed on the same SAP NetWeaver Java WebAS where SAP ME is installed. The SLD manages information about all available components and systems in the system landscape with the dependency information for software components. In initial SLD configuration, assign SAP_SLD_ADMINISTRATOR, SAP_SLD_CONFIGURATOR, and SAP_SLD_DEVELOPER roles to the Administrator user that will be used for the entire configuration. Next, perform the initial system setup using the Configuration Wizard (CONFIGURATION • SCENARIOS • CONFIGURATION WIZARD), which is available in SAP NWA (*http://<Host>:<Port>/nwa*). Within the Configuration Wizard, click on the FUNCTIONAL UNIT CONFIGURATION UI link to perform the initial technical configuration of functional units, as shown in Figure 17.2.

Click on the ENABLE AUTOMATICALLY button to enable the SYSTEM LANDSCAPE DIRECTORY, NWDI USING CM SERVICES, and CM SERVICES (CHANGE MANAGEMENT SERVICES) functional units one by one. During this process, you need to specify required information such as the administrator password, define a new master password, enable password overwrite for an existing user, and so on. When the three functional units are enabled, open the SAP NWDI home page by going to *http://<Host>:<Port>/devinf/main*, and click on the SLD link.

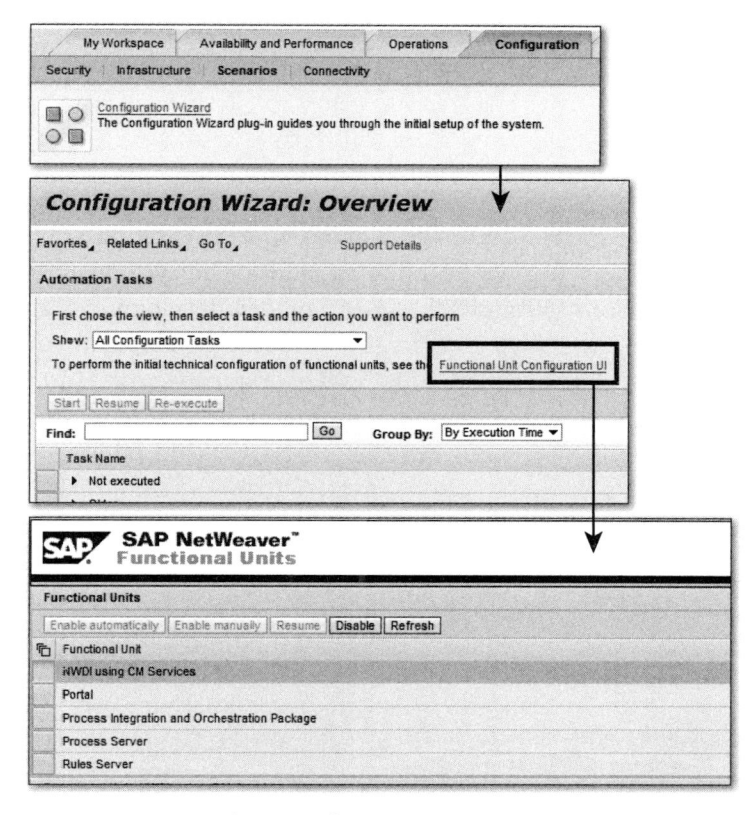

Figure 17.2 Functional Unit Configuration UI

17.2.2 Creating Software Components

Now, you'll learn how to create a *software component* (SC) that will be used for SAP ME related developments inside the SLD. SCs are the delivery units that contain multiple *development components* (DCs). Multiple SCs are grouped together within a *product*. DCs are the actual development units that contain development objects such as classes, interfaces, and so on. To create SCs, click on the SOFTWARE COMPONENTS link from the SLD home page. Click on the NEW button, and on next page select the CREATE NEW SOFTWARE COMPONENT AND VERSION checkbox to create a new SC. On the next page, specify the SC NAME, VERSION, and VENDOR fields, along with PRODUCT NAME, PRODUCT VERSION, PRODUCT INSTANCE, and PRODUCTION STATE, as shown in Figure 17.3. Complete the SC creation by clicking on the FINISH button.

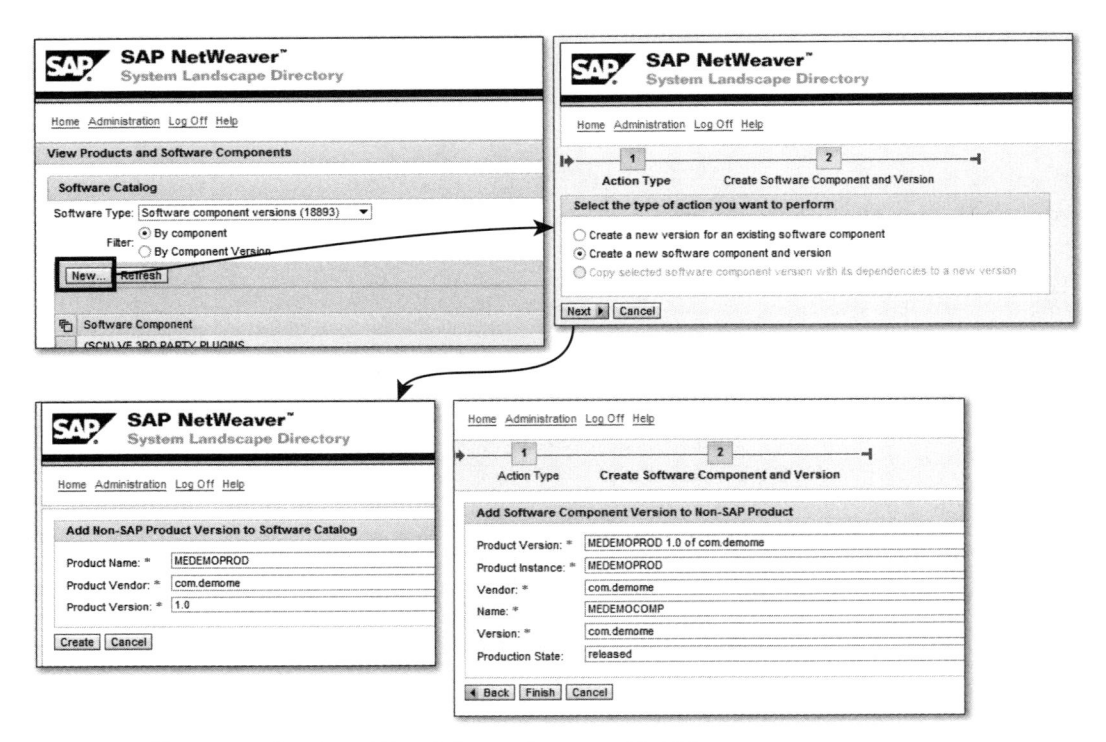

Figure 17.3 Creation of New Software Component in SLD

Next, you need to add the build time dependencies to your newly created SC. On the SOFTWARE COMPONENT page, select the newly created SC, and on the DEPENDENCIES tab, click on the DEFINE AS PREREQUISITE SOFTWARE COMPONENTS button. In the CONTEXT field, specify BUILDTIME. Filter the required software components specified in Table 17.1 by the latest version (you can select the version based on the currently installed SAP NetWeaver version and SAP ME version). Click on the DEFINE AS PREREQUISITE SOFTWARE COMPONENTS button.

Software Component	Name
J2EE ENGINE FAÇADE	ENGFACADE
ENGINEAPI	ENGINEAPI

Table 17.1 Build Time–Dependent Software Components

Software Component	Name
JAVA FRAMEWORK OFFLINE	FRAMEWORK
DI BUILD TOOL	SAP_BUILDT
ESI—WSRM	WSRM
SAP MFG EXECUTION CORE	SAPMECORE
SAP MFG EXECUTION LEGACY	SAPMELEGACY

Table 17.1 Build Time–Dependent Software Components (Cont.)

Prerequisite software components will be added as build time dependencies for your new SC, as shown in Figure 17.4.

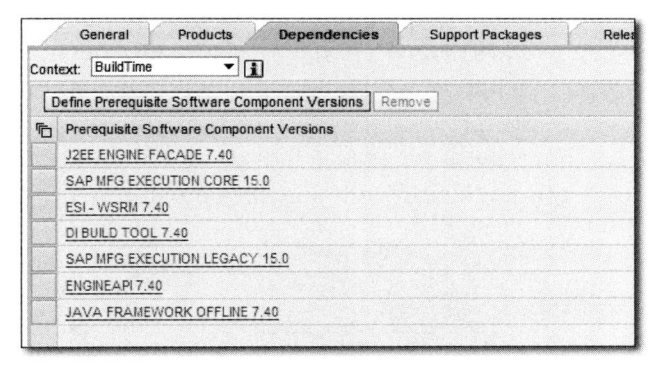

Figure 17.4 Build Time–Dependent Software Components

17.2.3 Creating Development Configurations

To create a development configuration using Development Infrastructure, login to SAP NWA with administrator permissions and go to CONFIGURATION • INFRASTRUCTURE • DEVELOPMENT INFRASTRUCTURE. On the DEVELOPMENT CONFIGURATION MANAGEMENT page, click on the CREATE NEW button to create a new development configuration. Specify a name (maximum of ten characters) and caption in the NAME and CAPTION fields, respectively. Next, configure the SYSTEM LANDSCAPE DIRECTORY, LOCAL SETTINGS, and SOFTWARE COMPONENT DEFINITION in their respective tabs for the same development configuration.

On the SYSTEM LANDSCAPE DIRECTORY tab, view the SLD URL, USER, and CM SERVICES URL. Set the password for the user in the PASSWORD field.

On the Local Settings tab, set the password for the NWDI_CMSADM user, enable Change Outbox Path checkbox and specify the path for export, and enable Change Inbox Path checkbox and specify the path for import.

On the Software Component Definition tab, click on the Add SC button to add your new SC. In the Software Components table, filter by your new SC's name and select it from the results. Next, click on the Add button, and then click on the Close button. The SC will be added to the Software Component Definition tab with its dependencies, which were added as build time dependencies during SC creation.

Now, save the development configuration by clicking on the Save button. Next, import the required Java libraries for the SAP ME SDK into the development configuration. Before importing the libraries, make sure that you have copied the WSRM, FRAMEWORK, SAPBUILDT, ENGINEAPI, ENGFACADE, SAPMECORE, and SAPMELEGACY SCA (Software Component Achieve) files (you can download those SCA files from SAP Service Marketplace) to the inbox path specified on the Local Settings tab. Figure 17.5 shows the required SCA files along with DCs provided by each SC. SAPMECORE and SAPMELEGACY SCA files provide SCs and DCs for SAP ME–related APIs.

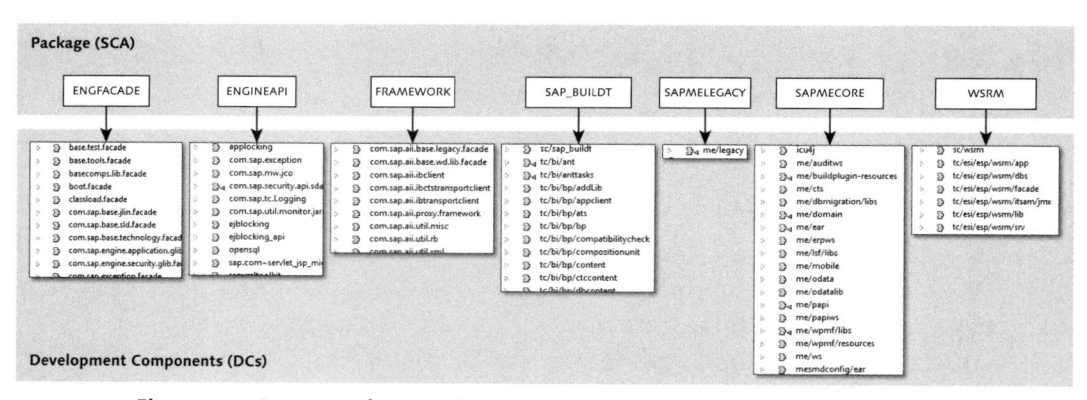

Figure 17.5 Overview of Required SCAs and DCs

On the Development Configuration Management page, select Related Links • Import Service. Next, select your new development configuration from the list and click on the Next button. In the Select Software Components to Be Imported step, you'll see all the SCA files from the inbox path. Click on the Validate button to validate each SCA. From the SCA list, select one SCA at a time and click on the NEXT button. To start the import, click on the IMPORT button; when you're finished, check the import log (Import Log is available at bottom of same page). You must import all SCAs one by one, not all at the same time. For a quick look at imported services, select RELATED LINKS • HISTORY SERVICE from the DEVELOPMENT CONFIGURATION MANAGEMENT page.

17.2.4 Name Reservation in SLD

Namespace prefixes are used when you create a development configuration in SAP NWDS. They ensure that all related development components are under a specific namespace. To setup name prefixes, login to the SLD via *http://<Host>:<Port>/sld* and click on the NAME RESERVATION link. Next, click on the ENABLE THIS SLD AS NAME SERVER FOR NWDI button if not enabled earlier. On the NAME PREFIXES tab, select DEVELOPMENT COMPONENT NAME for the NAME CATEGORY field, then click on the NEW NAME PREFIX... button. Specify the name prefix (for example, *vendorID.com/ apps*) and select the purpose (used everywhere) in the NAME PREFIX field and PURPOSE dropdown field, respectively, and click on the DEFINE button. To apply the name prefix in your development environment, stop and restart SLD.

17.2.5 Configuration of SAP NWDS in Client System

SAP NWDS is an Eclipse-based SAP IDE used to perform Java development on your local client machine. Before configuring SAP NWDS, install the latest version (based on your SAP NetWeaver AS Java version) on your local client machine. At the same time, install Oracle JDK, choosing the version supported by SAP NWDS.

Open SAP NWDS in your local system and import development configuration from SLD. To import a development configuration, select WINDOW • PREFERENCES and then go to DEVELOPMENT INFRASTRUCTURE • SYSTEM LANDSCAPE DIRECTORY. There, specify the SLD URL (*http://<Host>:<Port>/sld*) and click on OK. Then, in SAP NWDS, click on the NEW/IMPORT DEVELOPMENT CONFIGURATION icon, select IMPORT FROM SYSTEM LANDSCAPE DIRECTORY (SLD), and click on NEXT. Now, select the development configuration you created in the CREATING DEVELOPMENT CONFIGURATION section and provide the user and password you have used in DEVELOPMENT CONFIGURATION (e.g., NWDI_CMSADM) to import the development configuration into SAP NWDS. Finally, click on FINISH to complete the import. In the Development Infrastructure perspective, you'll see the development configuration and its SCs, as shown in Figure 17.6 and Figure 17.7.

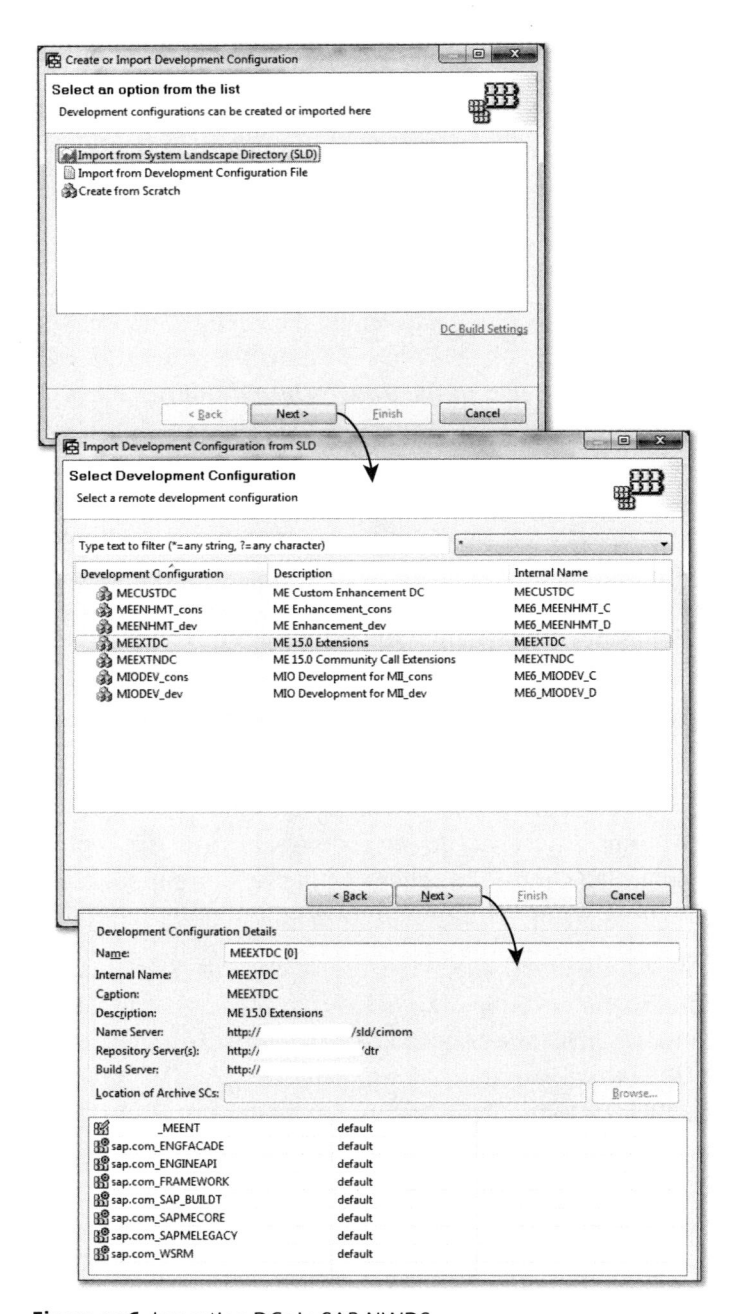

Figure 17.6 Importing DCs in SAP NWDS

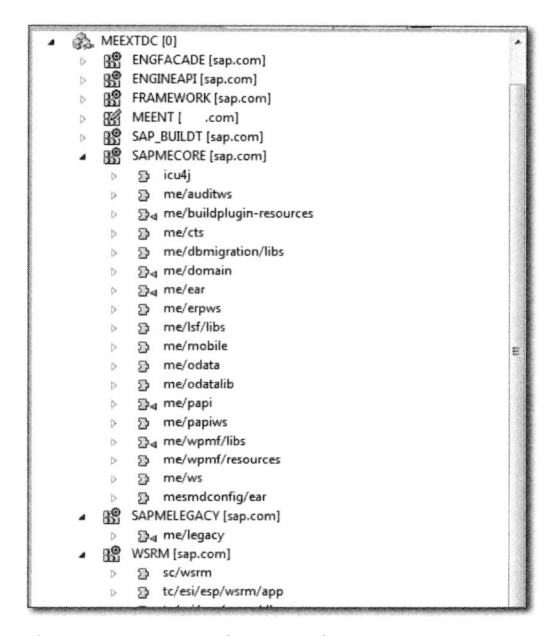

Figure 17.7 Imported SCAs and DCs in SAP NWDS

17.2.6 Configuring Name Servers in SAP NWDS

To configure a *name server* in SAP NWDS, go to the Development Infrastructure perspective and select the development configuration you imported from the COMPONENT BROWSER window. Select the COMPONENT PROPERTIES tab and then the OVERVIEW tab. If the NAME SERVER value is ---, then open the `confdef` file from your local machine workspace and add `name-server-url="http://<nwdihost>:<nwdiport>/sld/cimom"` between the `name` and `sl-location` attributes. To find the confdef file, go to *<NWDS_installed folder>\eclipse\workspace.jdi\0\.confdef*. After making the changes, save the file and reopen SAP NWDS on your local machine.

17.2.7 Configuring SAP NetWeaver Application Server Java in SAP NWDS

To deploy and debug your application, you need to configure SAP NetWeaver AS Java in SAP NWDS. To do so, go to WINDOW • PREFERENCES and select SAP AS JAVA, then click on the ADD button. Specify the INSTANCE HOST NAME and INSTANCE HOST NUMBER for SAP NetWeaver AS Java and click on OK. SAP NetWeaver AS Java will be added in SAP NWDS. Go to WINDOW • SHOW VIEW • OTHER then select SERVER • SERVERS to check the SAP NetWeaver AS Java in SAP NWDS.

17.3 Enhancement Options Using SAP ME SDK

Earlier, you learned about the required environment setup for SAP ME SDK-based development. Now, you'll learn about different enhancement options in SAP ME that use the SAP ME SDK. The development will be performed using the same environment setup. In following subsections we will provide detailed development steps for activity hooks, service extensions, POD plugins, custom webservices, custom PAPI services, and printer plugins.

17.3.1 Activity Hook

Activity hooks enhance the behavior of SAP ME activities. For example, say that you want to create a child shop order with a particular naming convention whenever the parent shop order is released in SAP ME. To do so, you need to develop an activity hook that will be used in the POST_ORDER_RELEASE hook point in Site Maintenance for a specific site in SAP ME. An activity hook is developed using a Java class and it performs custom functionality at the hook point based on the implemented business logic. In Activity Maintenance, you need to configure the custom-developed activity hook, after which you can use it in a hook point.

In SAP ME, hook points are available in different objects, such as Site (Site Maintenance), Operation (Operation Maintenance), NC Code (NC Code Maintenance), Resource (Resource Maintenance), and so on, as explained in Chapter 2. To develop the activity hook using the SAP ME SDK, you need to implement the Java interface `com.visiprise.frame.service.ext.ActivityInterface<T>`. The custom activity hook Java class that implements `ActivityInterface` needs to implement the `execute(<T>)` method, as shown in in Listing 17.1.

```
import java.util.HashMap;
import com.sap.me.extension.Services;
import com.sap.me.production.PostCompleteHookDTO;
import com.visiprise.frame.service.ext.ActivityInterface;
public class CreateOperationHook
implements ActivityInterface<PostCompleteHookDTO> {
    public void execute(PostCompleteHookDTO dto) throws Exception {
        //Business Scenario to be executed at hook point
    }
}
```

Listing 17.1 Method execute(<T>)

The Activity Hook Framework executes the `execute(<T>)` method when a hook point occurs. The `execute(<T>)` method does not return any output, and it takes a parameterized type as its input. The input parameter of the `execute(<T>)` method is a generic type parameter `<T>`. The type is used by the type of the parameter, which is associated with a specific hook point, such as `PostComplete-HookDTO`. The type parameter is passed as input for the execute method when the activity hook is attached to the `POST_COMPLETE` hook point.

> **Note: HookContextSetter Interface**
>
> An activity hook Java class can also implement a `HookContextSetter` interface to get context information, which is optional.

Table 17.2 lists hook points and their associated parameter types.

Hook Point	Parameter Type
PRE_START	com.sap.me.production.StartHookDTO
POST_START	com.sap.me.production.StartHookDTO
PRE_COMPLETE	com.sap.me.production.CompleteHookDTO
POST_COMPLETE	com.sap.me.production.PostCompleteHookDTO
PRE_SIGNOFF	com.sap.me.production.SignoffHookDTO
POST_SIGNOFF	com.sap.me.production.PostSignoffHookDTO
PRE_BATCH_START POST_BATCH_START	com.sap.me.production.StartHookDTO[]
POST_PROD_CHANGE	com.sap.me.production.ChangeItemRouterHookDTO
PRE_BATCH_COMPLETE	com.sap.me.production.CompleteHookDTO[]
POST_ BATCH_COMPLETE	com.sap.me.production.PostCompleteHookDTO[]
POST_ORDER_RELEASE	com.sap.me.demand.ShopOrderReleaseHookDTO
POST_ORDER_CLOSE	com.sap.me.demand.ShopOrderCloseHookDTO
PRE_MARGE POST_MARGE	com.sap.me.production.MergeHookDTO
PRE_SPLIT POST_SPLIT	com.sap.me.production.SplitHookDTO

Table 17.2 Hook Points and Associated Parameter Types

Complete the following steps to develop a custom activity hook using SAP NWDS:

1. Create three DC projects in SAP NWDS: one Java DC project, one Web Module DC project, and one EAR DC project. In the EAR DC project, add the reference of the Web DC project. No coding is required in the Web Module DC project for activity hook development.

    ▸ Java DC: Java DC contains the Java classes where the java codes are written. Java DC does not create a deployable or installable build result. The public parts are defined in Java DC project and added the public parts to EAR DC project as a dependency. The EAR DC is deployed in SAP NetWeaver AS Java.

    ▸ Web Module DC: Web Module DC project is used to create web resources such as JSPs or servlets. The Web Module DC project also contains the deployment descriptors included in the WAR file when the project is built. The reference of Web Module DC project is added in EAR DC project for deployment in SAP NetWeaver AS Java.

    ▸ EAR DC: EAR DC project contains the public part of Java DC project and reference of web module DC project. After building the EAR DC project, the deployable build result is created which can be deployed in SAP NetWeaver AS Java.

2. Within the Java DC project, create a Java class called an activity hook Java class. Implement `ActivityInterface` in the custom activity hook Java class, and write your business logic in the `execute<T>` method.

3. In the Development Infrastructure perspective of SAP NWDS, select your Java DC project and add the required build timedependencies, such as `SAPME-CORE[sap.com]/me/papi public part : "api"`, `SAPMECORE[sap.com]/me/wpmf/libs public part : "api"`, and so on.

4. Within the activity hook Java class, create a *Service Configuration Descriptor*, called *service-config.xml*. Listing 17.2 shows a sample service-config.xml file.

```
<?xml version="1.0" encoding="UTF-8"?>
<!DOCTYPE service-config SYSTEM "http://www.visiprise.com/dtd/
service-config.dtd">
<service-config moduleId="com.<Vendor Id>.sorel.hook">
  <!--If IDAT files are needed for the DC make sure
ConfigDataLoaderParent service is specified-->
  <import moduleId="com.sap.me.plant" service=
"ConfigDataLoaderParent"/>
   <!-- Import required to create a new service extension-->
   <import moduleId="com.sap.me.common" service="Prototype"/>
   <import moduleId="com.sap.me.demand" service="ShopOrderService"/>
   <import moduleId="com.sap.me.customdata" service=
"CustomDataService"/>
```

```xml
    <import moduleId="com.sap.me.productdefinition" service=
"ItemConfigurationService"/>

    <service name="LoaderService" parent="ConfigDataLoaderParent"/>
    <!--
 New service definition. You must declare the service class name. -->
    <service name="CustomReleaseShopOrder" class=
"com.<Vendor Id>.sorel.hook.CustomReleaseShopOrder" parent="Prototype">
      <!--
 Inject a reference to another service by declaring a property and
 using the service-ref attribute to specify the service name. -->
      <property name="shopOrderServiceInterface" service-ref=
"ShopOrderService"/>
      <property name="customDataServiceInterface" service-ref=
"CustomDataService"/>
      <property name="itemConfigurationServiceInterface" service-ref=
"ItemConfigurationService"/>
    </service>
</service-config>
```
Listing 17.2 Service Framework

You should also be aware of the following items related to SAP ME Service Framework:

- **Module ID**
  The module must have a unique name using the `service-config` element's module ID attribute, and the name should not conflict with SAP ME core modules or other custom service module names. The recommended format is `<Vendor Id>.<Java DC Name>`.

- **Service import**
  Services from one module can refer to services from another module if they are imported. Importing a service allows you to use it in the service definition declared within the module. You can import a service in two cases: if you want to use a service as a parent for another service or if you want to declare the service as a property that will be injected into another service.

- **Service properties**
  Service properties allow you to declare custom configuration values supported by a service. Make sure that for each property value, a corresponding Java Setter method is declared. In Listing 17.2, the `setCustomDataServiceInterface`, `setItemConfigurationServiceInterface`, and `setShopOrderServiceInterface` methods are declared within the custom activity hook Java class.

5. Create an Initial Data Load (IDAT) XML file, which is required by the `Config-DataLoaderParent` service (imported in service-config.xml). The IDAT file is packaged into the Java DC project by the package format `<Module Id>.idat`. Create the IDAT XML file with the name ActivityHookIDAT.xml.

```
<?xml version="1.0" encoding="UTF-8"?>
<common:serviceInvocationRequests xmlns:activity="http://www.sap.com/
me/activity" xmlns:common="http://www.sap.com/me/common">
  <common:serviceInvocationRequest>
    <moduleId>com.sap.me.activity</moduleId>
    <serviceName>ActivityConfigurationService</serviceName>
    <methodName>createActivity</methodName>
    <requests xmlns:xsi="http://www.w3.org/2001/XMLSchema-instance"
xsi:type="activity:ActivityConfiguration">
      <common:activity>Z_SOCREATEREL</common:activity>
      <common:description>I18N[Z_SOCREATEREL.activity.DESC]</common:
description>
      <activity:enabled>true</activity:enabled>
      <activity:executionType>SERVICE</activity:executionType>
      <activity:classOrProgram>com.<Vendor Id>.sorel.
hook$CustomReleaseShopOrder</activity:classOrProgram>
      <activity:visible>false</activity:visible>
    </requests>
  </common:serviceInvocationRequest>
</common:serviceInvocationRequests>
```

Listing 17.3 IDAT XML

In the IDAT XML file, specify the activity name and description as in Listing 17.3 (activity name `Z_SOCREATEREL`), and the activity will be created in SAP ME with the same name and description. You'll learn how to specify the description using a localization bundle in Step 8. The `classorProgram` parameter contains the service name for activity hook in the form of `<Module Id>$<Service Name>`.

6. Add a public ASSEMBLY part in DC. Public parts contain the elements of a DC that may be used by other DCs. Two types of public parts are available: ASSEMBLY and COMPILATION. In the Development Infrastructure perspective of SAP NWDS, select the Java DC project, then switch to the PUBLIC PARTS tab to add an ASSEMBLY public part. When you've added the public part on the PUBLIC PARTS tab, you can select the public part, right-click on it, and select MANAGE ENTITIES. Now, select the last folder of your package where the activity hook class belongs and the IDAT from the Java Package Tree, and select CLASS as the SUBTYPE. You also need to select SERVICE-CONFIG.XML in FILE and click on FINISH, as shown in Figure 17.8.

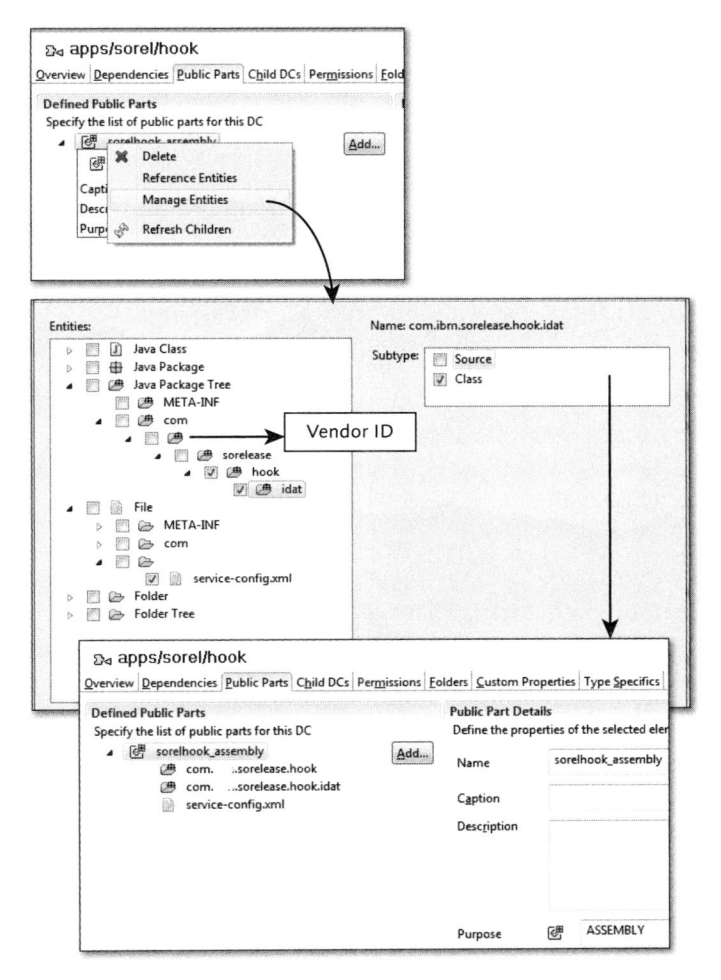

Figure 17.8 Adding Public ASSEMBLY Part in DC

7. Add dependencies to your EAR DC project. In the Development Infrastructure perspective of SAP NWDS, select the EAR DC project and switch to the DEPENDENCIES tab. Add the build time dependencies of the Java DC project to the EAR DC project.

8. Create a Java DC project called *resources* for localization bundles. This Java DC project will be used by all other projects and is a common project for localization purposes. Within the src folder of the resource project, create a package called *com.<Vendor Id>.bundles*. Now, create *LocaleSpecificText.properties* inside

the *com.<Vendor Id>.bundles* package. Within *LocaleSpecificText.properties*, add locale bundles such as *Z_SOCREATEREL.activity.DESC = Activity Hook for Shop Order Release*. Now, create a service-config.xml file in the src folder. The service-config.xml file will contain the code shown in Listing 17.4.

```xml
<?xml version="1.0" encoding="UTF-8"?>
<!DOCTYPE service-config SYSTEM "http://www.visiprise.com/dtd/service-config.dtd">
<service-config moduleId="com.<Vendor Id>.properties">
  <import moduleId="com.sap.me.common" service="Prototype"/>
  <service name="ExtensionTextResourceBundle" parent=
"Prototype" class="com.sap.me.frame.globalization.
LocaleSpecificTextResourcesGlobalizationExtensionService">
    <property name="resourceName" value=
"com.<Vendor Id>.bundles.LocaleSpecificText"/>
  </service>
</service-config>
```

Listing 17.4 service-config.xml

9. Add ASSEMBLY public parts in the resource Java DC project. As in Step 6, add the bundles package in the Java Package Tree with CLASS as SUBTYPE and service-config.xml in FILE from MANAGE ENTITIES. Then, add the build time dependencies of the resources project's public parts to your EAR DC project.

10. Deploy the EAR project to the SAP NetWeaver AS Java configured in SAP NWDS. In the Development Infrastructure perspective of SAP NWDS, select the EAR DC project, right-click it, and select DEPLOY. After successful deployment of the EAR project, log in to SAP ME via *http://<Host>:<Port>/manufacturing*. Open the SITE MAINTENANCE activity and retrieve the current site, then click on the RELOAD INITIAL DATA button. After successful reload of initial data, open the ACTIVITY MAINTENANCE activity and retrieve the Z_SOCREATEREL activity. Attach the activity hook to the appropriate hook point per your requirements.

17.3.2 Service Extension

In SAP ME, a *Service Extension* is a special type of service used to customize the manufacturing business processes. Based on your business requirements, you can create Service Extensions and attach them to service methods to customize the standard functionality. Service Extension is a site-specific task that can be executed synchronously or asynchronously. In synchronous execution, the Service Extension is executed immediately at the execution point; in asynchronous execution, execution is not immediate and will be triggered if the overall transaction is completed successfully. SAP ME provides an activity for Service Extension configuration called SERVICE EXTENSION MAINTENANCE.

The SERVICE EXTENSION MAINTENANCE activity allows you to enable or disable the service extension at the activity level and at the service method level. Service Extension can be executed by a specific condition by using execution filters. You can attach a Service Extension to three execution points: PRE, POST, and EXCEPTION, as shown in Figure 17.9. Service Extensions attached to PRE are executed before the service method, and POST are executed after the service method. Service Extensions attached to EXCEPTION can be used for handling errors.

You can configure Service Extension behavior at runtime by using Service Extension *Options*. In SERVICE EXTENSION MAINTENANCE, you can set parameters for options. Using *Filters*, you can control the extension of Service Extensions by matching service method input values with filter criteria, which ensure that the Service Extension is executed under specific conditions. SAP ME provides the following two standard Service Extension activities if you want to send messages to an external system: `HTTP_TRANSPORTER` and `SAPMEINT_DB_TRANS`.

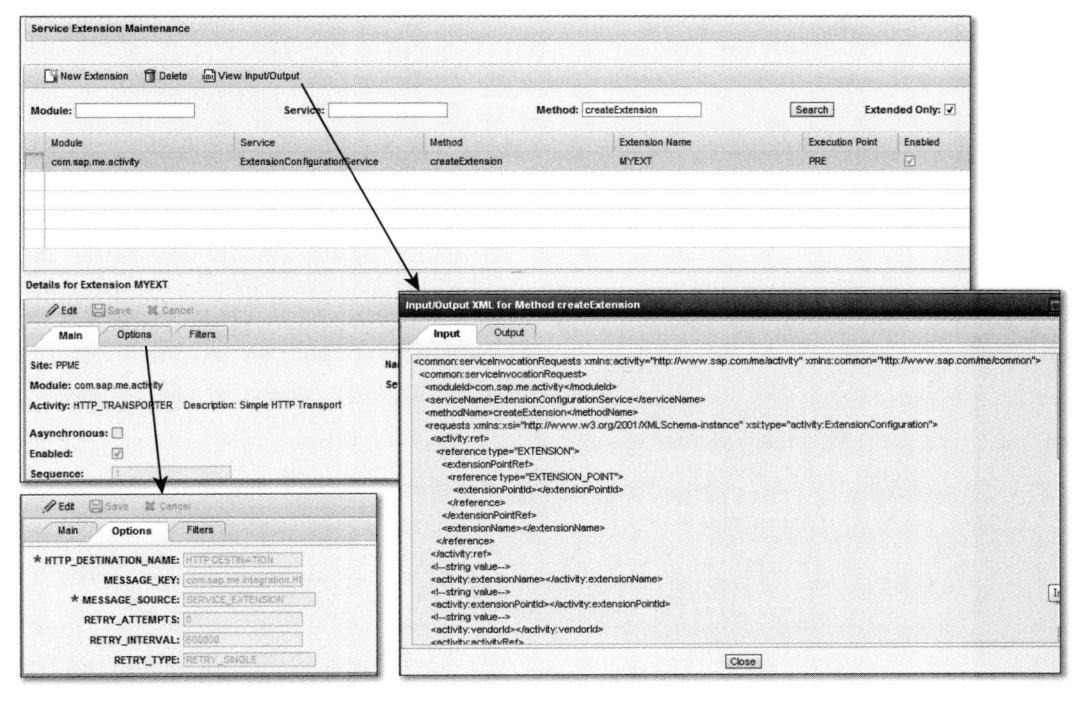

Figure 17.9 Service Extension Maintenance

17 | Enhancing SAP ME with SDKs

In Service Extension development, you need to create a Java class that extends `com.sap.me.activity.ServiceExtension <Object>`. A Service Extension class needs to implement the `execute(Object request)` method. The `execute()` method has no return value and extends functionality of the public API method. Optionally, Service Extensions can implement two interfaces to get more information about context: the `TransactionContextSetter` interface, which provides resource caching during a transaction, and the `InvocationContextSetter` interface, which exposes information about the target method. Listing 17.5 shows sample code for a Service Extension.

```
package com.<vendorID>.service.extension;
//Java imports for Business Logic implementation
import com.visiprise.frame.service.ext.InvocationContext;
import com.visiprise.frame.service.ext.InvocationContextSetter;
import com.visiprise.frame.service.ext.TransactionContextInterface;
import com.visiprise.frame.service.ext.TransactionContextSetter;
public class BusinessServiceExtension extends ServiceExtension<Object>
implements InvocationContextSetter, TransactionContextSetter {
    @Override
    public void execute(Object request) throws Exception {
        if (request instanceof MEStandardRequest) {
            execute((MEStandardRequest) request);
        }
    }
    public void execute(GenerateNextNumberRequest request) {
        //Business Logic
    }
    /*
     * (non-Javadoc)
     *
     * @see com.visiprise.frame.service.ext.InvocationContextSetter#
setInvocationContext(com.visiprise.frame.service.ext.InvocationContext)
     */
    public void setInvocationContext(InvocationContext context) {
        invocationContext = context;
    }
    /*
     * (non-Javadoc)
     *
     * @see com.visiprise.frame.service.ext.TransactionContextSetter#
setTransactionContext(com.visiprise.frame.service.ext.
TransactionContextInterface)
     */
    public void setTransactionContext(TransactionContextInterface
context) {
```

```
            transactionContext = context;
    }
}
```
Listing 17.5 Service Extension Development

Complete the following steps to develop a Service Extension:

1. Create three DC projects in SAP NWDS: one Java DC project, one Web Module DC project, and one EAR DC project. In the EAR DC project, add the reference of the Web Module DC project.

2. Within the Java DC project, create a Java class that extends `com.sap.me.activity.ServiceExtension<Object>`. The Java class optionally can implement the `TransactionContextSetter` or `InvocationContextSetter` interface. Set the execution mode using the `com.sap.me.activity.ExecutionType` annotation, which is optional, and add Service Extension options that you want to support.

3. Write your business logic in the `execute()` method.

4. Create service-config.xml and import the Prototype service. Configure the service in service-config.xml and specify Prototype as parent.

5. Create IDAT XML within a specific folder of the Java DC project, as we covered in Section 17.3.1.

6. Add the Service Extension class, IDAT, and service-config.xml to the Java DC ASSEMBLY public parts.

7. Add the Service Extension DC ASSEMBLY public part to the EAR DC as a build time dependency.

8. For localization purposes, add locale bundles in LocaleSpecificText.properties and use the same resource project. You need to add the DC ASSEMBLY public part of the resource Java DC to the EAR DC as a build time dependency.

9. Build and deploy the EAR DC to the server configured in SAP NWDS.

17.3.3 POD Plugin

In SAP ME, a *POD plugin* is a program that provides certain functionality in the POD. SAP ME provides two types of POD plugins: UI plugins and non-UI plugins, which we will discuss in the following section. As per your business requirements, you can create custom POD plugins that can be run only from custom PODs, which you learned to design in Chapter 10 via the POD MAINTENANCE activity in SAP ME. *UI plugins* consist of a Java plugin class (a *managed bean*) and a JSP view that contains JSF or LSF controls with properties that are bound to the *managed bean. Non-UI plugins* are not directly associated with the UI, but they run in the background to execute the business logic in the SAP ME server.

SAP ME uses the *Web Plugin Management Framework* to manage the POD-related activities and execution of plugins. The WPMF consists of multiple layouts to display plugins in fixed, popover, or popup areas. Learn more about the WPMF at *https://scn.sap.com/docs/DOC-41797*. POD plugins can only be triggered by WPMF-defined events, button clicks, or during POD loading, and plugins cannot run as standalone applications outside of the framework.

Developing UI POD Plugins

To develop custom UI POD plugins, first you need to create a Managed Bean Java class within the Web DC project that extends `com.sap.me.production.podclient.BasePodPlugin` class. All POD plugins running in a POD should be able to interact with a data model that gives information about the various states within the POD during a given session. This model is provided as a session-bound object that implements `com.sap.me.production.podclient.PodSelectionModelInterface` and can be accessed using the following `BasePodPlugin` class method:

`public PodSelectionModelInterface getPodSelectionModel();`

The object represented by the interface provides the appropriate methods for getting and setting of various key states, such as the currently selected Sfc(s), Operation(s), RouterStep(s), Resource, ShopOrder(s), and so on. Any plugin or event handler can update the selection model when required. The base `Plugin` class contains the `fireEvent()` method used to fire an event to other plugins that implement the event listener.

Create the faces-config.xml file within WEBCONTENT • WEB-INF of the Web Module project. Add the Managed Bean plugin in the faces-config.xml file as shown in Listing 17.6.

```
<managed-bean>
    <managed-bean-name>customPodPlugin</managed-bean-name>
    <managed-bean-class>com.<Vendor Id>.CustomPodPlugin</managed-bean-class>
    <managed-bean-scope>session</managed-bean-scope>
    <managed-property>
```

```
            <property-name>tableConfig</property-name>
            <value>#{customPodConfigurator}</value>
        </managed-property>
    </managed-bean>
```
Listing 17.6 faces-config.xml

The faces-config.xml file allows you to reference the plugin by name in JSP pages. Now, create the JSP within WEBCONTENT of the Web Module DC project. Within WEBCONTENT, create the folder structure and create the JSP pages per the UI requirements. Within the JSP page, add the plugin-specific controls, as shown in Listing 17.7.

```
<%@page pageEncoding="UTF-8"%>
<%@ page language="java"%>
<%@ taglib prefix="h" uri="http://java.sap.com/jsf/html"%>
<%@ taglib prefix="f" uri="http://java.sap.com/jsf/core"%>
<%@ taglib prefix="sap" uri="http://java.sap.com/jsf/html/extended"%>
<f:subview id="customPodPluginView">
//Here you can specify plugin controls within <f:subview> tags
</f:subview>
```
Listing 17.7 JSP for UI Requirement

Make sure the Web Module DC project is added as a reference in the EAR DC project and that `webcontext` is defined in the EAR application.xml for the Web Module DC. Then, deploy the EAR to the SAP ME server. After successful deployment, log in to SAP ME and create an activity using ACTIVITY MAINTENANCE. Specify the activity name, description, and class/program (plugin class name with full path), and select JAVA CLASS as the TYPE value. Because the UI plugin contains JSP, you need to select the RULES tab and insert a new rule named called PLUGIN_URL. In the SETTINGS field, enter the fully qualified path (in uppercase characters) of the plugin's JSP, starting with a /. When the activity creation is complete, configure the custom activity in an existing POD using POD MAINTENANCE activity.

Developing Non-UI POD Plugins

WPMF manages the lifecycle of non-UI plugins, and managed beans are not considered. Therefore, you do not need to define a managed bean in faces-config.xml. The non-UI managed bean Java class must extend the `BasePodPlugin` super class. The `execute()` method is the only method that must be implemented for use in WPMF. Once the `execute()` method is finished, the execution process is completed. Non-UI plugins are not directly related to the UI, but they execute the business logic on the server side.

For example, you can create a non-UI plugin that will be executed when you will click a button in the POD, and this plugin can collect some SFC-related data for selected SFCs in the POD and return a Success or Error message to the POD message area.

17.3.4 Developing Custom Web Services

Using the SAP ME SDK, you can develop custom web services if the SAP ME–provided PAPI services cannot meet your business requirements to integrate with other systems. To implement a custom web service using the SAP ME SDK, you need to create a request and response object and a main service implementation class for the web service in SAP NWDS. You can also use an interface from which the service implementation class can implement the J2EE-specific information. The interface declares the methods which are the web service operations and an implementation which defines the methods declared in the interface. To create a web service, follow these steps:

1. In SAP NWDS, select DEVELOPMENT CONFIGURATION from the Development Infrastructure perspective to create a Web Module DC project.

2. Within the JAVA RESOURCES • SOURCE folder of the Web Module DC project, create the package with an appropriate package name—for example, com.<Vendor Id>.ws.meproduction.

3. Within the package, create the WebService endpoint Java class by specifying the class name and add the @WebService annotation to the class. The @WebService annotation marks the class as a web service; it is defined by the javax.jws.WebService interface, as shown in Listing 17.8.

```
import javax.jws.WebService;
@WebService
public class <Class Name> {
}
```

Listing 17.8 Creating WebService Endpoint Class

4. Create WebService methods and annotate with the @WebMethod, as shown in Listing 17.9.

```
import javax.jws.WebMethod;
import javax.jws.WebService;
@WebService
public class <Class Name> {
@WebMethod
public String <Method Name>() { }
}
```

Listing 17.9 Creating WebService Method

5. Next you need to define the `WebService` method parameters by using `@Web-Param` annotation as shown in Listing 17.10.

```
import javax.jws.WebMethod;
import javax.jws.WebService;
import javax.jws.WebParam;
@WebService
public class <Class Name> {
@WebMethod
public String <Method Name>(@WebParam (name=
"<Parameter Name>") <Request Class Name> <Parameter Name>) {
//Write Business Logic
 }
}
```

Listing 17.10 WebService Method Parameters

6. Create two more Java classes for `WebService Request` and `Response`. Also, define the input and output parameters within the request and response call and generate getter and setter methods for each defined parameter, as shown in Listing 17.11 and Listing 17.12.

For the web service request, use the code in Listing 17.11 :

```
import java.util.List;
import javax.xml.bind.annotation.XmlAccessType;
import javax.xml.bind.annotation.XmlAccessorType;
import javax.xml.bind.annotation.XmlElement;
import javax.xml.bind.annotation.XmlRootElement;
import javax.xml.bind.annotation.XmlType;
@XmlRootElement
@XmlAccessorType(XmlAccessType.FIELD)
@XmlType(propOrder = { "site", "name"})
public class WebServiceRequest {
  @XmlElement (required = true, nillable = false)
  private String site;
  @XmlElement (required = true, nillable = false)
```

```
    private String name;
    //Setters & Getters
}
```

Listing 17.11 Request Structure of WebService

For the web service response, use the code in Listing 17.12 :

```
import javax.xml.bind.annotation.XmlAccessType;
import javax.xml.bind.annotation.XmlAccessorType;
import javax.xml.bind.annotation.XmlElement;
import javax.xml.bind.annotation.XmlRootElement;
import javax.xml.bind.annotation.XmlType;
@XmlRootElement
@XmlAccessorType(XmlAccessType.FIELD)
@XmlType(propOrder = { "wbResponse"})
public class WebServiceResponse {
  @XmlElement
  private String wbResponse;
  //Setter & Getter
}
```

Listing 17.12 Response Structure of WebService

7. Add annotation for HTTP or HTTPS basic authentication for security of web service access. In the WebService endpoint Java class, add the annotation for HTTP or HTTPS basic authentication, as shown in Listing 17.13.

```
@AuthenticationDT(authenticationLevel =
AuthenticationEnumsAuthenticationLevel.BASIC)
@AuthenticationRT(AuthenticationMethod = "sapsp:HTTPBasic")
@WebService
public class <Class Name> {
   }
Or
@AuthenticationDT(authenticationLevel =
AuthenticationEnumsAuthenticationLevel.BASIC)
@AuthenticationRT(AuthenticationMethod = "sapsp:HTTPBasic")
@TransportGuaranteeRT(TLSType="sapsp:HTTPS")
@WebService
public class <Class Name> {
   }
```

Listing 17.13 Security Annotations

8. In the Development Infrastructure perspective in SAP NWDS, select the Web Module DC project, and on the DEPENDENCIES tab, add build time dependencies.

9. Create an EAR DC project and add build time dependencies in the EAR DC from the public part *war* of the Web Module DC project.

10. In the Java EE perspective, open application.xml from the EAR DC project and modify `<context-root>` to `<Vendor Id>webservice`, as shown in Listing 17.14.

```
<module>
<web>
<web-uri><<..Keep it as it is..>></web-uri>
<context-root>VendorIDwebservice</context-root>
</web>
</module>
```

Listing 17.14 Updating application.xml from the EAR DC

11. Build and deploy the EAR project on the SAP ME server.

After successful deployment, the custom web service URL (WSDL URL) is available at *http://<Host>:<Port>/nwa* • SOA • APPLICATION AND SCENARIO COMMUNICATION • SINGLE SERVICE ADMINISTRATION. There, select the SERVICE DEFINITIONS tab then the SEARCH tab, specify the service name in the FIND field, and search for the custom web service. Select the service from the results table to see the WSDL URL at the bottom of the table on the WSDL tab.

17.3.5 Developing Custom PAPI Services

In Chapter 14, you learned about SAP ME PAPI services. If your business requirements are not covered by SAP ME–provided standard PAPI services, you can develop custom PAPI services using SAP NWDS, and the services can be deployed to SAP ME server. To develop custom PAPI services, perform the following steps:

1. Create three DC projects in SAP NWDS: one Java DC project, one Web Module DC project, and one EAR DC project. In the EAR DC project, add the reference of the Web DC project.

2. Within the Java DC project, create two Java DTO classes with proper package structures for the request and response structure of the custom PAPI service. You can also define the elements for request and response objects within request and response classes, respectively. Define getter and setter methods for request and response structure elements. Also, create exception classes for all methods.

3. Create a Java service interface and define all methods within the interface. The interface can be created within a separate package of the Java DC project.

4. Create the Java service class that implements the service interface. The Java service class can also be created within a separate package of the Java DC project.

5. Create two more Java classes, called `ObjectFactory.java` and `package-info.java`. Within the `ObjectFactory.java` class, define the request and response structure, as shown in Listing 17.15.

```
import javax.xml.bind.annotation.XmlRegistry;
@XmlRegistry
public class ObjectFactory {
  public ObjectFactory() {
  }
  public CustomRequest createCustomRequest(){
    return new CustomRequest();
  }
  public CustomResponse createCustomResponse(){
    return new CustomResponse();
  }
}
```

Listing 17.15 Creating ObjectFactory Java

6. Within the `package-info.java` class, specify the sample code shown in Listing 17.16.

```
@javax.xml.bind.annotation.XmlSchema(namespace =
"http://www.vendorID.com/services/", elementFormDefault =
javax.xml.bind.annotation.XmlNsForm.QUALIFIED)
package com.<Vendor Id>.service.dto;
```

Listing 17.16 Creating Package-info Java Class

7. Create the service-config.xml file and import the `BusinessServiceParent` service. You also need to configure service in service-config.xml and specify `BusinessServiceParent` as parent.

8. Switch to the Development Infrastructure perspective of SAP NWDS and select the Java DC project. Then, add service interface and DTO classes to the COMPILATION public part and include all service classes and service-config.xml in the ASSEMBLY public part.

9. In the Development Infrastructure perspective, select the Java DC project and add build time dependencies to `SAPMECORE[sap.com]/me/papi` public part "api" and `ENGFACADE[sap.com]/engine.jee5.facade` public parts "api" and "apiwithoutjsf".

10. Add the DC ASSEMBLY public part to the EAR DC as a build time dependency.
11. Build and deploy the EAR to server configured in SAP NWDS.

> **Note: Restarting me~ear**
>
> After successful deployment, open the Deployment perspective from SAP NWDS and stop SAPMECORE • ME~EAR (SAP.COM). When it has fully stopped, restart it. The stop and start of me~ear is required to clear the JAXB cache to make the new custom service available in SAP ME. The *Java Architecture for XML Binding* (JAXB) maps Java classes to XML representations, marshals Java objects into XML, and unmarshals XML into Java objects.

Log in to the SAP ME server via *http://<Host>:<Port>/manufacturing* and open SERVICE EXTENSION MAINTENANCE. Specify a custom service name in the SERVICE field and click on the SEARCH button. The custom service will be displayed in the table. Select the custom service and click on the VIEW INPUT/OUTPUT button to see the input and output of the method in XML format.

17.3.6 Print Plugins

In SAP ME, a *print plugin* is a business extension that allows you to create and transport document content that will be printed. The transported document content can be printed by any third-party printing provider. SAP ME supports three types of print plugins that you can create per your requirements: *Data Acquisition* print plugin, *Formatting* print plugin, and *Transport* print plugin. Print plugins are executed in the sequence *Data Acquisition, Formatting, and Transport.* In SAP ME, DOCUMENT PRINT (activity ID: SY520) is responsible for reading the document configuration as defined in DOCUMENT MAINTENANCE and executing print plugins. The three types of plugins are used as follows:

- **Data Acquisition Print Plugin**

    Used to collect document content data, such as SFC Data, NC Data, Shop Order Header Data, Routing Data, and so on. In DOCUMENT MAINTENANCE, define the Data Acquisition print plugin class based on the document options selected.

    To create a Data Acquisition print plugin, create a Java class within the Java DC project that will implement `PrintingDataAcquisitionServiceInterface` and write the plugin logic in the `acquirePrintingData()` method, which returns `PrintingDataAcquisitionResponse` with collected document contents, as shown in Listing 17.17.

```
public class CustomPrintingDA
implements PrintingDataAcquisitionServiceInterface {

  @Override
  public PrintingDataAcquisitionResponse acquirePrintingData
(PrintingDataAcquisitionRequest request) throws BusinessException {
    //
 get document configuration from Document Maintenance for current
document
  }
}
```
Listing 17.17 Data Acquisition Print Plugin

- **Formatting Print Plugin**
  Used for taking the data created by the Data Acquisition plugin and writing it to a format expected by a printing software vendor. To create a Formatting print plugin, create a Java class within the Java DC project which will implement `PrintingFormatServiceInterface` and write the plugin logic in the `formatPrintingData()` method, which returns `FormatPrintingDataResponse` with collected data formatted to the target format expected by the printing software vendor, as shown in Listing 17.18.

```
public class CustomPrintingFormat
implements PrintingFormatServiceInterface {
  @Override
  public FormatPrintingDataResponse formatPrintingData
(FormatPrintingDataRequest request) throws BusinessException {
//Plugin Logic
  }
}
```
Listing 17.18 Formating Print Plugin

- **Transport Print Plugin**
  Used to physically transfer the document content file to a location from which printing software will read it and print the document. The location of the file is configured in SYSTEM RULE MAINTENANCE • SYSTEM SETUP • DOCUMENT PRINTING TEMPORARY DIRECTORY.

  To create a Transport print plugin, create a Java class within the Java DC project that implements `PrintingTransportServiceInterface` and write the plugin logic in the `transportPrintingData()` method, which returns `TransportPrintingDataResponse`. The `transportPrintingData()` method is responsible for physically transferring the document content file to a location from which printing software can read it. The sample code snippet for the Transport print plugin is shown in Listing 17.19.

```
public class CustomPrintingTransport
implements PrintingTransportServiceInterface {
  @Override
  public TransportPrintingDataResponse transportPrintingData
(TransportPrintingDataRequest request) throws BusinessException {
  }
}
```

Listing 17.19 Transport Print Plugin

To develop custom print plugins using SAP NWDS, perform the following steps:

1. Create three DC projects in SAP NWDS: one Java DC project, one Web Module DC project, and one EAR DC project. In the EAR DC project add the reference of the Web Module project.

2. Within the Java DC project, create a Java class for the Data Acquisition print plugin that implements com.sap.me.document.PrintingDataAcquisitionServiceInterface.

3. Create a Java class for the Formatting print plugin that implements com.sap.me.document.PrintingFormatServiceInterface.

4. Create a Java class for the Transport print plugin that implements com.sap.me.document.PrintingTransportServiceInterface.

5. Create the service-config.xml file and configure services in service-config.xml.

6. Add the classes and service-config.xml to the DC ASSEMBLY public parts and add the print plugins Java DC ASSEMBLY public part to the EAR DC as a build time dependency.

7. Deploy the EAR to SAP ME server.

After successful deployment, log in to SAP ME, open DOCUMENT MAINTENANCE, and create a document with the required configuration as described in Chapter 2, Section 2.2.9. Set up the document options on the DOCUMENT OPTIONS tab per your requirements. On the PRINT INTEGRATION tab of DOCUMENT MAINTENANCE, specify the full call path of the custom print plugin class, as shown in Figure 17.10. You can also select the WRITE ERROR LOG checkbox.

Next, open activity SY520 using ACTIVITY MAINTENANCE and copy it with another name (for example, *MYCUSTOM_ SY520*). On the RULES tab, setup the document you created in Document Maintenance and the printer name in the DOCUMENTS and PRINTER_NAME rules. Open Material Maintenance and retrieve a material for which an SFC is created. On the Documents tab of Material Maintenance, add document from Available Documents to Printing Documents and save the material configuration. Now, you can use the custom document print activity in an operation as a hook point.

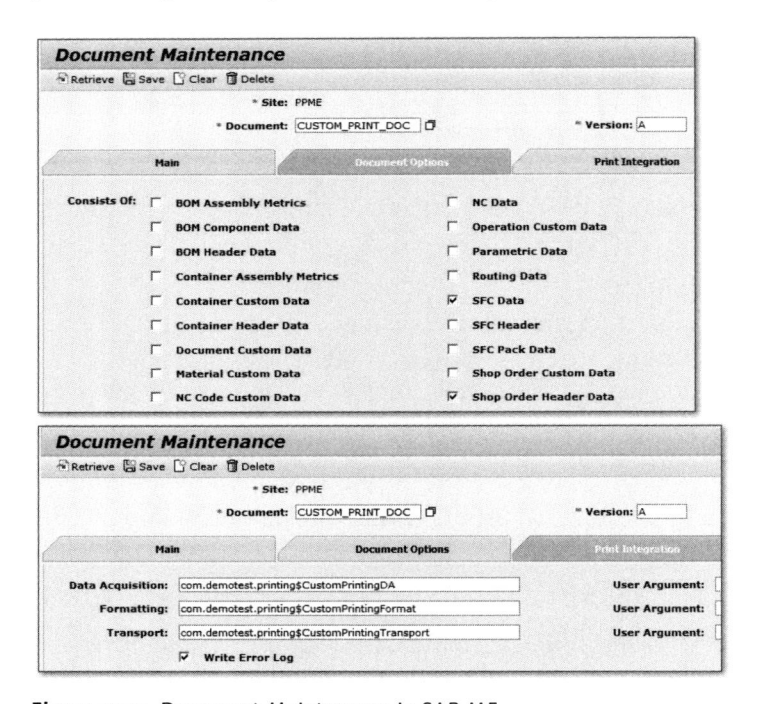

Figure 17.10 Document Maintenance in SAP ME

17.4 SDK APIs and Libraries

Earlier, you learned about the multiple enhancement options for SAP ME, and in this section you will learn about the Java documentation available for SAP ME enhancement using the SAP ME SDK. SAP has exposed all SAP ME APIs as PAPI services with Java documentation that can be downloaded from SAP Service Marketplace (*http://service.sap.com/instguides* and go to SAP Business Suite Applications • SAP Manufacturing • SAP Manufacturing Execution • SAP Manufacturing Execution 15.0 • Javadoc SAP ME 15.0). The APIs are a set of core SAP

ME business services that allow you to access SAP ME business processes and master data. Each API service is grouped according to its functional module. Download the Java document ZIP file in your local system and unzip it. Then, open index.html, which will open in your local browser. On the left-hand side, you'll see the packages. Select a specific package to see the interfaces, classes, exceptions, and so on. Select a specific element to see its details, as shown in Figure 17.11. As per your custom development requirements, you can use the Javadoc to search the API.

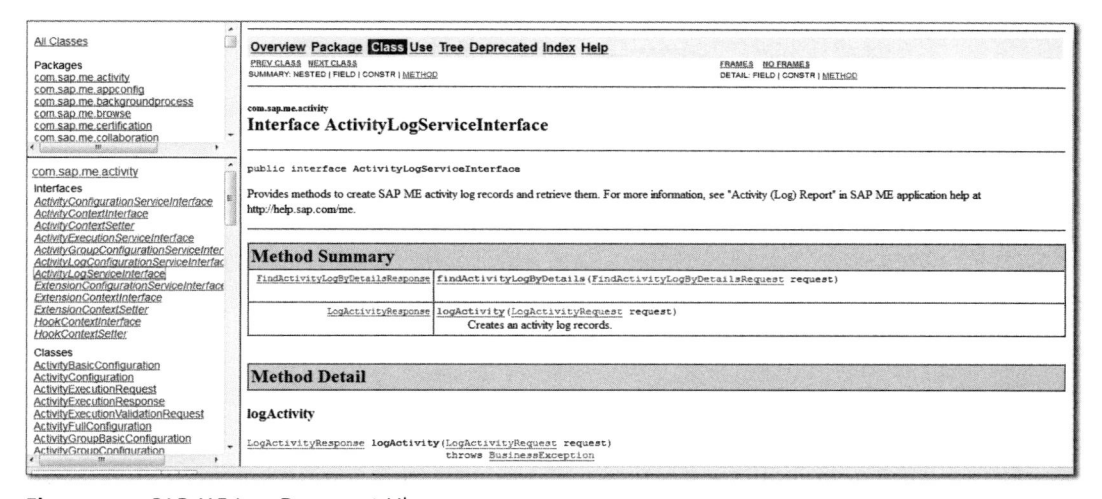

Figure 17.11 SAP ME Java Document Library

In Chapter 14, you learned how to search SAP ME PAPI services and execute those PAPI services from *wsnavigator* or using SOAP UI. Here, we recommend that before using any Java API in a custom development, search for and execute the corresponding PAPI service with test data. After successful execution, you can easily use the Java API in custom code. This process will help you develop projects more quickly and get a clear understanding of request and response structures of services.

17.5 Summary

In this chapter, we covered the SAP ME SDK and its required environment setup for creating enhancements, along with SAP NWDI configuration, SLD setup, and

SAP NWDS configuration in local system. You learned about options to enhance standard SAP ME functionality using the SAP ME SDK such as activity hooks, Service Extensions, POD plugins, custom web service development, custom PAPI service development, and print plugin development. We explained the step-by-step process to use each enhancement option.

Finally, you learned how to find the required Java APIs from SAP ME custom enhancements and the recommended procedure for using those APIs in custom code.

Conclusion

Now that you have completed all the chapters in this book and learned about all the available functionalities and capabilities of SAP ME, you are ready to implement SAP ME for your discrete manufacturing assembly process. As you know, before implementation you need to understand the entire business process for manufacturing execution so that you may create an end-to-end design for the MES solution. For a better understanding of each chapter of this book we have provided you with a car assembly scenario as a real life example.

Once you have your end-to-end design and a plan for your system landscape, you can start your implementation after SAP ERP, SAP ME, SAP MII and SAP PCo are already installed. Before working with SAP ME configurations, you need to prepare the master data setup in SAP ERP such as material, routing, BOM, work center, resource, etc. per your business requirement. Next you need to configure SAPMEINT and download the required master data and transactional data from SAP ERP to SAP ME through the DRF (Data Replication Framework) as explained in Chapter 1. At this point you should have also decided upon any enhancements in SAPMEINT for different message types, if such were required to get the data from SAP ERP to SAP ME, or vice versa.

Next you need to create the SAP ME system configuration as explained in Chapter 2. Once the data is replicated to SAP ME from SAP ERP, you can create new master data as explained in Chapter 3. If you want to add any custom data for any of the data objects in SAP ME, you need to set them up before downloading the messages from SAP ERP, and may also need to create some enhancements in SAPMEINT to populate the custom data from the SAP ERP interfaces. For example, you can use the enhancement of LOIPRO message type in SAPMEINT to get the production version in SAP ME.

One of the most important parts of your implementation is finalizing the routing design in SAP ME. In a car assembly process, the routing design is one of the most complex parts because the assembly process flows differ from one manufacturer to another. Even within the same manufacturer, multiple routings are used based on the model of a car and those cars which are assembled through different production lines. In Chapter 4 you can find the detail description of routing design for a car assembly process. If routing enhancement is required based on the shop floor manufacturing process, then you can complete it first with the help of Chapter 4 and finalize the routing. With the help of Chapter 4 you can also make the decision of whether the routing will be designed in SAP ME and transported to SAP ERP or if the routing can be downloaded from SAP ERP to SAP ME and be enhanced in SAP ME.

When the routing is finalized in SAP ME then you can create and release the production order in SAP ERP and download it in SAP ME through the SAPMEINT message type to generate the shop order in SAP ME as described in Chapter 5.

With the help of Chapter 6 you can release the shop order to generate the SFCs based on the configuration in SAP ME. It can happen that each SFC number of a shop order represents the VIN (Vehicle Identification Number) of each car and each VIN is generated through some custom logic. In this situation you need to integrate and supply the VIN as an SFC number when the shop order is released. To achieve the functionality you need to go with custom development or enhancement of SAP ME standard functionality. In a car assembly process it can be a common requirement to print the VIN every time a shop order is released. Here you need to consider printer integration.

For data collection group and parameter configuration, you can use Chapter 7. Data collection in SAP ME can be done manually or automatically and can be used for quality control or reporting purposes. In a car assembly process, the torque tool is very commonly used to reduce the assemble time, and the requirement can arise to perform automatic torque value collection in SAP ME for each torque tool. The torque can also differ for different models of cars. To perform automatic data collection from shop floor machines you can think of custom development in SAP MII using PAPI service as specified in Chapter 14 and also use SAP PCo to integrate with automated machine or OPC, which is described in Chapter 15. Quality control of finished or semi-finished product is an important obligation of every manufacturing process. Based on business requirements and routing design, quality check can be performed through the operation which is a part of the routing step and is integrated with SAP ERP. Quality records can be tracked through nonconformance in SAP ME and data can be moved bi-directionally between SAP ERP and SAP ME. Chapter 8 describes the nonconformance and quality control related activities in details which can help you to address quality control requirements. In a car assembly routing design, there can be multiple quality check points (operations) and a finished or semi-finished assembled car can be moved from the quality check operation to the rework operation and quarantine based on the NC log. After repairing the defect, the product car can be routed back to quality operation or it can be moved to next operation based on the routing design and NC status.

During the shop floor manufacturing process, tracking of a product's assembly is also a common requirement for every manufacturing scenario. Product genealogy is used to track the components used to assemble the finished product, to verify that all required components are used, place component on hold because of quality issue, load or replenish of components on resource, vendor information maintenance, and for finding genealogy reports to get the details of components used in assembly process. Floor stock management is also an important part of product genealogy to maintain the stock of shop floor components and it can be synced with SAP ERP. All genealogy-related configuration and required standard reports are explained in Chapter 9, which can help you to do product tracking and genealogy management in SAP ME. During a shop floor car assembly you can track each VIN to know the current status and which components are used in different operations in case you need to replace or hold the component because a defective part was supplied by vendor. Genealogy functionality of SAP ME can address these requirements and provides standard reports to track the product.

The Production Operator Dashboard (POD) is the main user interface (UI) for a shop floor user which can be configured per the business requirement and also based on the user role to be performed in shop floor. As per the requirement you need to choose the POD type and configure the POD including required activities and events using the POD Maintenance activity in SAP ME. Chapter 10 describes the detailed functionality of POD design and which activities can be performed through a POD. SAP ME POD can be used through a touch screen or mobile device, either a standard POD or a fully custom developed POD for specific requirement. You can design multiple PODs based on the shop floor user role and separate activities to be performed in each operation of a routing. To determine the POD type to use and design decision you can get help from Chapter 10. In a car assembly process the production line may be very large in size and shop floor users may need to move to different places along the production line, usage of mobile or tablet device can be a valid requirement to make the process faster. You can configure multiple PODs based on the activities to be performed in different operation or you can develop custom POD for tablet device using SAPUI5 technology per your requirements and budgets.

Chapter 11 of this book describes the functionality and usage of the Message Board service in SAP ME. During the manufacturing process, a shop floor user

Conclusion

can take corrective actions based on the system generated or user generated messages in real time manufacturing process. Using the Message Board functionality, one shop floor user can send message immediately to all other shop floor users or trigger a process workflow. For example, during a car assembly process, if it is required to stop the production line's movement immediately due to some critical issue, then the relevant person can trigger a process workflow and send a message to all shop floor users before taking the action.

As per the business requirement it may be required to track time for employee labor and also the time spent to manufacture a product in SAP ME. Both functionalities are available in SAP ME and can be implemented before performing the shop floor manufacturing process as described in Chapter 12. You need to perform all required configuration such as such as Cost Center Maintenance, Labor Charge Code Maintenance, Labor Rule Maintenance, User Shift Maintenance, Production Calendar Maintenance, etc. You can also use the standard activities such as Supervisor Clock in/Clock out and Supervisor Time Edit & Approval activities to get employee's Clock in/Clock out and the summarized labor reports. To know an employee's labor time and the time taken to assemble each car, you need to configure the labor tracking in SAP ME and using the standard reports. This will allow you to calculate the total time, which can be used for planning and utilization reporting purposes.

When you are ready with entire configuration and data setup in SAP ME, you can start the execution of shop floor manufacturing processes using the POD and per the routing design, product will be moved from one operation to next operation till it is reached to final operation of routing and yield confirmation will also be moved to SAP ERP through SAPMEINT. You can monitor the messages in SAPMEINT through queue monitoring page available in SAPMEINT. Shop floor users can record what they pack into or unpack from container in SAP ME, typically after the production is complete. To track the shop floor packing of manufacturing products into a container or unpacking of the goods from a container, you can use packing and unpacking service in SAP ME with the help of Chapter 13. Using the packing feature, each assembled car can be packed to container and moved to different storage location.

For some of the additional functionalities which are not available out of the box in SAP ME you can refer Chapter 14 and 15 to develop custom enhancements in SAP MII using the SAP ME PAPI services and SAP PCo.

Finally you need to setup the Executive Dashboard or develop custom reports on SAP MII, which you can learn in Chapter 16.

If the standard SAP ME functionalities cannot meet your business requirements due to very complex or unique business scenarios, you can go with the enhancement or custom development using SAP ME SDK. To perform SAP ME SDK-based enhancements or custom developments you can use Chapter 17. We cover tracking configuration using NWDI, client environment setup using NWDS, required SCA files, the Java API and library for SDK, and possible enhancement options in SAP ME. You can also perform custom enhancement using SAP ME PAPI service in SAP MII.

In the end, we hope that this book has provided you with a clear understanding of SAP ME functionalities, and that you can use our knowledge and advice to make your SAP ME implementation successful.

The Authors

Chandan Jash is a senior consultant in IBM India and has worked with SAP Manufacturing solutions for more than nine years. He has worked on a number of SAP MII and ME implementation projects, and has helped build SAP ME competency inside IBM. He currently works as an architect and SME for SAP ME implementation projects.

Dipankar Saha is an IT architect and service delivery lead for SAP MII and SAP ME at IBM India who works with clients globally to define SAP ME and MII implementation architectures. He previously worked for SAP Labs India and was involved in the design and development of SAP MII after its acquisition from Lighthammer. He has worked on SAP manufacturing solution development and delivery for more than 10 years.

Index

A

Accept number, 251
Active, 195
Activities, 68, 80
Activity code, 67, 83, 204
    CT510, 299
    CT511, 294
    CT700, 300
    CT720, 304
    DM010, 175
    DM510, 182
    EN510, 293
    EN530, 290
    IN700, 303
    NC540, 248
    PD100, 301
    PD300, 302
    SY520, 330
    SY521, 330
Activity group, 82
Activity hook, 69–70, 142, 442
Activity hooks, 115
Activity Log Report, 204
Activity maintenance, 80
Activity rules, 82
Add component, 296
Adobe Document Services, 91
ALE configuration, 36
ALLOW_PACK, 390
ALLOW_UNPACK, 390
Alternate components, 105
ANSI sampling plan, 249
Any order group, 148, 251
AP ME Activity Maintenance, 292
Archiving, 84
As-Built Configuration, 276, 294
As-Built Summary report, 300
Assembly point, 278
Assembly type, 102
Assigning PODs to user groups, 330
Assigning resource types and resources to an operation, 140
Assignment enforcement, 119

Attachment point, 221
Attendance rules, 370
Audit logging, 89
Auto close, 352
Automatic clock in at logon, 376
Automatic clock out at shift end, 370

B

Background processing, 84
BAPI request, 62
Barcode, 282
Bill of materials, 32, 99, 109, 180
BLS transaction, 63, 417
BOM Maintenance, 278
BOM report, 301
Build quantity, 177
Build time dependency, 437
Business Logic Service (BLS), 47, 56, 427
    transaction, 57
Business model layer, 433
Button label, 321
Buyoff, 354
Buyoff maintenance, 354, 357
BUYOFF_WF, 354
Byproduct components, 110

C

Calendar rule, 375
Certification, 77, 116
Certification assignment in an operation, 143
Certification Expiration Check, 84
Certification type, 77
Change Production, 203
Change request, 96
Check SFCs for Open NCs, 241
Claim, 350
Clock in/out range control, 371
Close message, 350
Collaboration directive, 85
Collaboration link, 86

Index

Collect distributed work time, 377
Collect Work Time plug-in, 377
Collector, 102
Comment dialog, 350
Communication profiles, 399
Complete pending, 194
Complete SFC, 334
Complex assembly, 175
Component traceability, 276
Configuration Diagnostics tool, 64
Configuration of SAP NWDI and SLD, 434
Configuration of SAP NWDS in client system, 439
Configuration Wizard, 434
Configuring name server in SAP NWDS, 441
Configuring SAP NetWeaver Application Server (AS) Java in SAP NWDS, 441
Consuming floor stock, 286
Container number assignment, 387
Context type, 88
Control key maintenance, 164
Control limit, 270
Coproduct component, 110
Correlation key transaction, 53
Correlation workflow, 47, 53
Cost center, 368
Cost center maintenance, 368
Create and release SFC, 189
Create message, 349
Create Subassys on Shop Order Release, 175
Creating Development Configuration, 437
CTC Wizard, 34, 39, 42, 68
Custom data, 32
Custom data field, 127, 263
Custom data maintenance, 127
Custom logic, 46
Custom PODs, 406
Customer order, 189

D

Data Acquisition Plug-In, 86
Data Acquisition print plugin, 459
Data collection, 102, 211, 253, 256
Data collection definition report, 224
Data collection edit, 211, 222

Data collection entry, 337
Data collection limits check, 222
Data collection maintenance, 211
Data collection results report, 226
Data collection scenario, 227
Data collection standalone, 223
Data enhancement, 126
Data field assignment maintenance, 128, 236, 384
Data field definition maintenance, 127, 384
Data Replication Framework (DRF), 33, 179
Data server, 43, 420
Database table, 418
Date range, 204
DC group, 212
DC group list, 337
DC group parameters, 255
DC parameter, 216
Default site, 73
Defect, 234
Defect Transfer Table (DPMO), 97
Deleted, 195
Designing PODs, 318
Develop a custom activity hook, 443
Developing custom PAPI, 457
Developing custom web service, 454
Developing non-UI POD plugins, 453
Developing UI POD plugins, 452
Development Configuration Management, 438
Development environment, 433
Device History report, 302
Discrete genealogy, 275–276
Discrete manufacturing resource, 113
Discriminator transactions, 42
Display routing overview, 167
Disposition function routing, 146
Disposition functions, 243
Disposition group, 238, 243
Disposition Group Maintenance, 238
Disposition routings, 238
Distribution of SFC labor time, 373
Document maintenance, 90
Done, 195
Done (hold), 195
Done and close, 387
DPMO category, 235

DPMO report, 237, 263
Drawing file, 102

E

ELAPSED_TIME_CHECK, 142
Email server, 347
End unit number, 175
Enhanced Planned Order report, 427
Enhancement options using SAP ME SDK, 442
Enqueue, 53
Enterprise Java Beans (EJBs), 80
Equipment number, 114
Equipment status change, 339
equipmentStatusChangeRequest_UNSCH_DOWN, 340
ERP control key, 141
ERP field maintenance, 94
ERP group, 213
ERP order, 172
ERP production storage location, 105
ERP putaway storage location, 105
ERP QN code, 238
ERP_ITEM_FILTER, 394
ERP_OPERATION, 394
ERP_REPORTING_STEP, 394
ERP_SEQUENCE, 394
Error-handling, 32
Executing SFCs, 334
Executing SFCs in POD, 333
Execution Dashboard, 423
Executive Dashboard, 424–425, 429
Exit() method, 150

F

Fail handler transaction, 51
Fail/reject number, 213
Failover support, 22
FileMonitor, 420
Filter priority, 241
First-pass yield, 342
Floor stock receipt, 280
Floor Stock report, 303
Floor stock transfer, 287
Formatting print plugin, 460

Formula, 216
Formula Script window, 216
FREE_FORM message, 359
Function-based disposition, 144

G

Genealogy reports, 300
Generating SFC, 187
Global configuration, 40
Global ODS (GODS), 25
Global site, 68
Golden Unit, 195

H

Histogram, 269
Hold, 195
Hold report, 205
Hook point, 71, 80, 443

I

IDAT, 446
IDoc, 254
IDoc listener, 36
IDoc messages, 33
InboundMessageEnqueuer, 44
Increment ERP batch number, 105
InQueue, 194
Inspection levels, 250
Inspection lot, 253
Inspection procedure, 250
Invalid, 195
Inventory ID, 280
Inventory ID split, 284

J

Java APIs, 431
Java Server Pages (JSP), 80
Javadoc, 397
JAXB cache, 459

L

Labor charge code, 174
Labor clock in/clock out, 376
Labor clocking, 130
Labor rules, 76
Labor time, 76
Labor tracking, 365
Layout type, 323
LCC, 369
LCC maintenance, 370
LCC rules, 372
Lifecycle method, 63
Light Speed Faces (LSF), 80
Link properties, 155
List maintenance, 317, 346
Load or replenish, 291
Log NC, 338
Log Viewer, 64
LOIPRO, 47, 174, 253
LOIWCS interface, 118
Lot size, 101, 182

M

Machine setup time, 131
Machine wait time, 131
Maintain floor stock, 282, 284
Make-to-order (MTO), 23, 179
Make-to-stock (MTS), 23, 179
Managed bean, 452
Managing floor stock, 280
Manual clock in, 376
Manufacturing Data Objects (MDO), 418
Manufacturing execution system (MES), 21
Mapping, 32
Mask, 218
Mask group, 281
Master data, 99
Master data object, 127
Material, 100
Material group, 106
Material maintenance, 165, 358
Material status, 101
Material transfer, 108
Material Yield report, 342
Materials Requirements Planning (MRP), 181

MATMAS IDoc, 100
MATMAS05 IDoc type, 100
Max. floor life, 103
Max. shelf life, 103
Maximum loop count, 141
ME role assignment, 72
Measurement document, 114
Measurement points, 114
Median charts, 268
Merge transaction, 54
Merge validation transaction, 54
Message board, 81, 96, 314, 347
Message Board POD, 348
Message Board selection, 349
Message Board service, 347
Message type, 353
Message type maintenance, 351
MESSAGE_BOARD_LIST, 363
MessageDispatcher, 44
MessageEnqueuer, 44
Milestone operation, 181
Mobile POD, 313
Module ID, 445
MS SQL Server, 25

N

Name reservation in SLD, 439
NC activity hook, 240
NC category, 235
NC client, 244
NC code, 234
NC code maintenance, 70, 235, 359
NC data entry, 338
NC data type, 236
NC disposition routing, 144
NC groups, 240
NC Limit Override, 237
NC logging, 247
NC priority, 237
NC selection, 337
NC Selection POD Plugin, 241
NC trees, 308
Next number, 95
Next Number Maintenance, 173, 279, 387
NO_TRANSFER, 176
Nonconformance (NC), 22, 37, 156, 233–234

Index

Nondestructive testing, 251
Notification message, 417
Notification type, 37

O

Object layer, 433
OData services, 408–409
ODS data, 97
ODS database, 25, 423
ODS rule maintenance, 93
OP_RES_HOLD_CONSEC_NC, 355
OP_RES_HOLD_SPC_VIOL, 355
OP_RES_HOLD_SPC_WARN, 356
OP_RES_HOLD_YIELD_RATE, 356
Open data collections check, 222
Open nonconformance script, 150
Operation flow, 150
Operation Maintenance, 70, 308
Operation POD, 308
Operation type, 139
Operation Yield by Material report, 342
Operation Yield report, 341
Oracle Java Runtime Environment (JRE), 151
Order type, 205
Ordered quantity, 177
Original SFC number, 179
Outbound message, 257
Overall equipment effectiveness (OEE), 427
Override min/max, 216

P

Pack/unpack, 387
Packing service, 383
Panel, 102
PAPI service, 58, 397
Parameter details, 215
Partial quantity, 240
Pass handler transaction, 51
Pass/fail group, 212
PCoConnector, 420
PCOQueries, 415
Performing data collection, 337
Performing nonconformance logging, 337
Permission, 332

Persistence layer, 433
Planned order, 33, 181
Plant code, 42, 68
PluginInterface, 59
POD, 102, 307
 integrated, 309
 maintenance, 308
 Notification, 352
 operation, 309
 operation touch, 309
 plugin, 82, 324, 451
 selection, 328
 types, 308
Portlet, 425
Post-XSLT, 56
Post-XSLT transaction, 51
Presentation layer, 433
Pre-XSLT, 53
Pre-XSLT transaction, 50
Print plugins, 459
Printer maintenance, 92, 330
Printers tab, 329
Printing documents, 386
Process data, 22
Process lot, 385
Process manufacturing resource, 113
Process workflow, 351
Process workflow maintenance, 353
Processing rule, 44
Product genealogy, 275–276
Production calendar, 366
Production calendar maintenance, 368
Production line control, 22
Production order, 32, 181
Production rate, 131
Production report, 340
Production routing, 144
Production shift maintenance, 366
Production site, 68
Production version, 174
Public API (PAPI) services, 26, 211

Q

QM inspection group, 213
Quality control, 22, 233, 466
Quality inspection, 177, 234, 253

Quality inspection results, 256
Quality notification, 258
Quality reports, 260
QUALITY_CHK, 149–150
Quantity multiplier, 101
Quantity restriction, 101
Quantity split, 184
Quarantine task, 238
Queue Monitor, 41, 61
QueueMessageCleaner, 44

R

Real-time message display, 320, 347, 362
Real-time warnings maintenance, 357
Reason code, 96, 285
Reference designator, 111
Reject number, 251
Relaxed Flow Routing, 197
Reload initial data, 69
Remove component, 297
Repack, 390
Repair Loop report, 262
Repetitive manufacturing, 23, 181
Replaceable parameters, 352
Request XSLT address, 51
Required setup for VTR, 316
Required time in process, 142
Resource, 113
Resource maintenance, 70
Resource setup, 293
Resource Setup report, 304
Resource Slot Configuration, 280
Resource Slot Configuration setup, 290
Resource status change, 339
Resource type, 114
Response XSLT address, 51
Retest yield, 342
Return steps, 147
Returned, 195
Revoke, 350
RMA number, 174, 205
RMA SFC data type, 175
RMA SFC receipt, 192
RMA shop order, 179
RMA shop order data type, 175

Rollup processing rules, 372
Root-Cause Operation, 236
Routing, 137, 151, 238
 custom data, 164
 design workbench, 144
 enhancement, 158
 maintenance, 70, 151
 next operation, 149
 operation placement, 203
 status, 146
 type, 144
Routing-based disposition, 144
routingExportRequest, 166

S

Sample plan, 248
Sample Plan Maintenance, 194, 248
Sample routing, 146
Sample size, 253
Sampling process, 251
SAP Business Suite, 462
SAP BusinessObjects Enterprise XI 3.1 (BOBJ), 424
SAP Document Management System (DMS), 124
SAP ERP connection configuration, 43
SAP ERP integration, 285
SAP JCo, 42
SAP JCo connection alias, 37
SAP Manufacturing Execution Mobile Developers Guide, 429
SAP ME Activity Manager, 429
SAP MII Workbench, 428
SAP NetWeaver, 23, 91
SAP NetWeaver Administrator, 34, 43, 399
SAP NetWeaver AS Java, 24, 441
SAP NetWeaver Developer Studio (NWDS), 432, 439
SAP NetWeaver Development Infrastructure (NWDI), 432
SAP OSS Notes, 65
SAP Plant Connectivity (PCo), 23, 211, 411, 417
SAP Service Marketplace, 424
SAP User Management Engine (UME), 72, 265

SAP Visual Enterprise, 23, 125
SAP Visual Enterprise Viewer, 315
SAPMEINT CTC, 34
SAPMEINT database, 53
SAPMEINT message type, 48
SAPMEODS, 43
SAPMEWIP, 43
SAPUI5, 427
Scheduler, 44
Scrap, 33, 102, 147, 195
Scrap confirmation, 86
SDK APIs and libraries, 462
Security configuration, 45
Sequence number, 121
Serial numbers, 178
Service configuration descriptor, 444
Service Extension, 448
Service Extension Maintenance, 449
Service import, 445
Service properties, 445
Service transaction, 51
SFC, 101, 234
SFC Average Cycle Time by Operation Report, 208
SFC Average Cycle Time by Shop Order Report, 209
SFC Cycle Time Report, 185, 210
SFC group, 193
SFC group size, 193, 249
SFC in work button ID, 328
SFC management, 187
SFC merge, 195
SFC numbers, 178
SFC place hold, 197
SFC quantity adjustment, 199
SFC queue button ID, 328
SFC release hold, 198
SFC report, 206
SFC scrap/delete, 200
SFC split, 196
SFC status, 194
SFC unscrap/undelete, 201
SFC_SPAN, 176
Shop Floor Dispatching and Monitoring (SFDM), 174
Shop Floor Dispatching and Monitoring tool, 180

Shop order, 171, 182, 188
 types, 172
Shop Order Cycle Time Report, 185
Shop Order Maintenance, 173
Shop Order Schedule report, 184
Shop workbench POD, 311
Short run analysis, 220
Show operation first, 329
Show quantity, 329
Simultaneous group, 149, 251
Site creation, 68
Site maintenance, 70
Slot configuration maintenance, 288
Slot status, 288
SOAP web service, 399
Software Development Kit (SDK), 431
SPC alarm severity maintenance, 358
SPC analysis, 264, 266
SPC chart, 266, 268
SPC chart types, 269
SPC Severity Maintenance, 268
Special instructions, 142
Split workflow, 47
Standalone NC Logging, 247
Standard cycle time, 131
Standard value key, 130, 132
Standard value key maintenance, 130, 377
Standard workflow, 46
Start SFC, 334
Statistical process control (SPC), 211, 219
Status, 352
Status change, 96
Stock availability, 181
Storage location, 283, 286–287
Storage location maintenance, 287
Store data collection results in ODS, 215
Supervisor clock in/out, 380
Supervisor mode, 381
Supervisor time edit and approval, 380
Supervisor Work Assignment POD, 310
Supported plants, 42
System Landscape Directory (SLD), 433
System rule, 87
System Rule Maintenance, 165, 180, 242
System rules, 117
System setup, 89
System Setup Maintenance, 89

T

TagRetrieveQuery mode, 420
Target system, 53
TCP/IP type, 36
Test components, 110
Time Granularity Assignment Maintenance, 97
Time Granularity Maintenance, 97
Time-based component type, 104
Time-based genealogy, 275–276, 279, 288
Time-sensitive material, 103
Tool group, 120
Tool number, 122
Torque operations, 149
Trackable component, 104
Trackable SFC, 210
Transaction
    CA03, 167
    DRFOUT, 179
    POIT, 179
    QE51N, 257
Transaction Manager, 63
Transactional data, 127
Transfer, 350
Transfer site, 69
Transfer types, 176
Transferring inventory IDs, 286
Transport print plugin, 460

U

Unclaim, 350
Unit of measure, 218
User administration, 72
User certificate assignment, 78
User Certification Report, 79
User Group Maintenance, 74, 332
User groups, 74
User maintenance, 75
User mode, 381
User options, 218
User shift maintenance, 374
User-defined fields, 219

V

Value range, 257
Vendor maintenance, 279
Visiprise, 23, 45, 54
Visual Test & Repair (VTR), 240
Visual Test and Repair (VTR) POD, 309, 314
VTR Model Viewer, 315

W

Web Plugin Management Framework (WPMF), 452
WebService request, 455
WebService response, 456
WIP database, 25, 39, 423
WIP Production Monitor, 427
Withdraw, 349
Work center, 118
Work center category, 205
Work Center POD, 309
Work Center Touch POD, 312
Work instruction, 123, 126, 336
Work instruction configuration, 336
Work instruction list, 336
Work instruction viewer, 336
Workflow configuration, 46

X

XML Style Language Transformation (XSLT), 47
XMLConnector, 265
XPath, 47

Y

Yield, 131, 177
Yield confirmation, 53
yieldConfirmationRequest, 335

Interested in reading more?

Please visit our website for all new
book and e-book releases from SAP PRESS.

www.sap-press.com

SAP PRESS